FORENSIC ACCOUNTING
AND FRAUD EXAMINATION

FORENSIC ACCOUNTING AND FRAUD EXAMINATION

MARY-JO KRANACHER, MBA, CPA, CFE

RICHARD A. (DICK) RILEY, Jr., CPA, PhD, CFE, CFF

JOSEPH T. WELLS, CFE, CPA

WILEY

JOHN WILEY & SONS, INC.

Vice President & Publisher   George Hoffman

Associate Publisher   Chris DeJohn

Project Editor   Ed Brislin

Editorial Assistant   Kara Taylor

Production Manager   Janis Soo

Assistant Production Editor   Yee Lyn Song

Senior Marketing Manager   Julia Flohr

Marketing Assistant   Laura Finley

Executive Media Editor   Allison Morris

Media Editor   Greg Chaput

Cover Designer   RDC Publishing Group Sdn Bhd

Cover Photo Credit   © David Aubrey/CORBIS

This book was set in 10/12 Times Roman by Laserwords Private Limited and printed and bound by Courier Westford. The cover was printed by Courier Westford.

This book is printed on acid free paper. ∞

Library of Congress Cataloging-in-Publication Data
Kranacher, Mary-Jo, 1952-
  Forensic accounting and fraud examination / Mary-Jo Kranacher, Richard A. (Dick) Riley, Jr., Joseph T. Wells.
    p. cm.
  Includes index.
  ISBN 978-0-470-43774-2 (cloth)
  1. Fraud investigation. 2. Forensic accounting. 3. Fraud–Prevention. I. Riley, Richard, 1962 Apr. 18-
    II. Wells, Joseph T. III. Title.
  HV8079.F7K73 2010
  363.25′963–dc22

                                            2010007793

Printed in the United States of America
10 9 8 7 6 5 4 3 2

The text is dedicated

To my mother, Agatha Pirrone (1920–2009),
for her unconditional love and encouragement;
and my husband, Baldur, for his unwavering support
Mary-Jo Kranacher

To my parents Dick Sr. and Betty,
wife Shelley,
and children Connor, Andrew, and Kelsey
Richard A. (Dick) Riley, Jr.

To the 50,000 members of the
Association of Certified Fraud Examiners
in 125 nations;
and to future fraud examiners in this vital profession
Joseph T. Wells

BRIEF CONTENTS

CONTENTS

The year 1492 is remembered for any number of reasons: the construction of the Arboretum Trsteno near Dubrovnik, the ascendancy of Pope Alexander VI, the surrender of the city of Grenada, and, of course, Columbus sailing "the oceans blue." But for some of us, the events of 1492 are surpassed by a singular event two years later. For in the city of Venice in 1494 the book *Summa de arithmetica, geometria, proportioni et proportionalita* by Fra LucaBartolomeo de Pacioli was published. Fra Pacioli, a Franciscan friar, mathematician and buddy of Leonardo da Vinci, included in his *Summa* a detailed treatise of the accounting practices of the Italian merchants of his day. Due to this act of codifying and publishing the accounting practices of contemporary Venetian merchants, Luca Pacioli has earned the title of "Father of Accounting."

Despite the accolades afforded Fra Pacioli, it took almost four centuries before Accounting began to be accepted, and begrudgingly so by many at the time, by American colleges and universities. The first school of commerce in continuing existence in the U.S. was the Wharton School at the University of Pennsylvania, established in 1881, and adding accounting to its curriculum two years later. Contemporaneously, organizations for accountants began to arise. More than mere trade associations, these groups, including predecessor organizations of the AICPA and AAA, sought to establish a self-regulating accounting *profession*: a community of proficient practitioners that advocated formal and continuing education, required members to adhere to a code of ethical conduct, and conferred professional status on only the most capable through a certification process that included experience and examination.

It may have taken almost one hundred years, but by the end of the twentieth century, accounting had found an established place in the academy.

To late twentieth century American academia enters Joseph Wells: CPA, CFE, former FBI Special Agent, white-collar criminologist, and educator. In a 1985 conversation that Wells had with Donald Cressey—the foremost American penologist, sociologist, and criminologist whose innovative contributions to the field include the theory of the "fraud triangle"—Cressey suggested that Wells form an organization for professionals involved in fraud detection and deterrence. Shortly thereafter, the Association of Certified Fraud Examiners was born. With Wells at the helm, the ACFE recognized the multi-disciplinary nature of fraud examination: a profession that included elements of accounting and criminology, law and sociology, among others. And similar to the forefathers of the accounting profession a century earlier, Wells took the tack of establishing the ACFE as much more than a trade organization, but the leading association of the new profession of fraud examination. Under Wells' leadership, fraud examination advanced as a *profession*: a community of practitioners that advocated research and education, that established a multi-disciplinary area of study and body of knowledge that required adherence to a code of conduct, and that certified only those who have proven themselves through examination and experience.

Within 25 years of the founding in 1988 of the Association of Certified Fraud Examiners, the organization had nearly 50,000 members in over 125 countries. The ACFE is recognized as the world's largest anti-fraud organization and the premier provider of anti-fraud training and education.

While Joseph Wells was leading the ACFE in Austin, Texas, another pioneering leader of fraud examination was hard at work in New York City. Mary-Jo Kranacher, CPA, CFE, author, editor, administrator and professor at York College of The City University of New York, was instrumental in establishing fraud examination as an academic area of study; not just at York College, but also at countless colleges and universities across the nation and around the world. One of the first educator members of the ACFE, Kranacher was an early chair of the ACFE's Higher Education Committee, as well as being an elected member of the ACFE Board of Regents.

Meanwhile, in the mountains of Appalachia, Dr. Richard Riley, Jr. combined his education with his years of experience as a CPA, CFE, CFF, and a CFO to lead an effort to build one of the world's top fraud and forensic accounting academic programs at West Virginia University. Riley is also renowned for co-chairing the National Institute of Justice Model Curriculum project: a multi-year undertaking to develop a model educational curriculum in fraud and forensic accounting. Piloting a group of leaders in the field (including both Wells and Kranacher), Riley helped to produce a model curriculum that has proven to

be an invaluable tool for colleges and universities seeking to establish an academic program in forensic accounting and fraud examination.

Now, these three leaders—Wells, Kranacher, and Riley—have authored this breakthrough publication: the first comprehensive textbook covering the entire fraud examination and forensic accounting field of study. Destined to be regarded as a milestone in the rapidly growing academic discipline of fraud examination and forensic accounting, *Forensic Accounting and Fraud Examination* will undoubtedly become both the leading pedagogical resource for academics and the go-to reference book for busy fraud examination and forensic accounting professionals.

But the question must be asked: Will *Forensic Accounting and Fraud Examination* become an honored—and extremely valuable—old tome, similar to Luca Pacioli's *Summa de arithmetica, geometria, proportioni et proportionalita*? Only time will tell. But I do know this: I'm safeguarding a first edition copy *Forensic Accounting and Fraud Examination*, just in case.

William J. Kresse, CPA, CFE, M.S., J.D.
Associate Professor, Graham School of Management
Director, Center for the Study of Fraud and Corruption
Saint Xavier University, Chicago

NOTE TO STUDENTS

This book was created for students by sharing with you the professional expertise that is fraud examination and financial forensics. Your knowledge and skills are developed from the book's best practices in forensic accounting, financial forensics, and the prevention, deterrence, detection, investigation, and remediation of fraud. The book will help you master entry-level skills by thoroughly exploring areas necessary to enter this exciting professional specialization:

- Foundational skills
- Career opportunities
- The psychology of the fraud perpetrator: why people make bad choices
- Complex frauds and financial crimes such as money laundering, organized crime, and cybercrime
- Best practices in detection and investigation
- Effective interviewing and interrogation techniques
- Using information technology for fraud examination and financial forensics engagements
- A detailed review of fraud schemes
  - asset misappropriation
  - corruption
  - financial statement fraud
- A detailed examination of the work of consultants, litigation support professionals and expert witnesses
  - damage claims
  - valuations
  - other civil litigation engagements
- Cleaning up the mess—Remediation and litigation advisory services

As evidenced by the criminal and civil litigation associated with the recent Madoff, Satyam, and alleged Stanford Financial frauds, opportunities and services in this professional space are extensive and growing. Since July 2002, the Department of Justice has obtained nearly 1,300 fraud convictions—some corporate executives are now in jail or repaying their debt to society in other ways. The ACFE's 2008 *Report to the Nation* estimated the annual cost of fraud at almost 1 trillion dollars! But the tragedy associated with fraud goes much further when employees lose jobs, investments are wiped out, and wealth evaporates. In almost every case of criminal charges associated with fraud, civil litigation follows. Beyond fraud, financial forensic professionals support the investigation and remediation of civil litigation arising from damage claims, valuations, personal injury, and wrongful death. This book provides you with the tools required to effectively participate in civil litigation and criminal engagements.

We wish you all the best as you embark on this exciting professional journey,

Mary-Jo Kranacher
Dick Riley
Joseph Wells

PREFACE

The authors of this text had the good fortune to be brought together through the National Institute of Justice's project to develop a model curriculum for the nation in fraud and forensic accounting. Dr. Riley was one of the co-chairs and Professor Kranacher and Joseph Wells were members of the project's Planning Panel. The outcome of the activity was a model curriculum authored by 46 nationally recognized experts, published as the NIJ Research Report, "Education and Training in Fraud and Forensic Accounting: A Guide for Educational Institutions, Stakeholder Organizations, Faculty, and Students," available through the National Criminal Justice Resource System (http://www.ncjrs.gov/pdffiles1/nij/grants/217589.pdf). The document has been well-received by the academic community as demonstrated by the November 2008 edition of *Issues in Accounting Education* which devoted the entire November publication to an in-depth examination of the model curriculum and its adoption by academic institutions.

Upon completion of the NIJ curriculum project, the authors realized that while several excellent textbooks were available in fraud examination or forensic accounting, none adequately explored all of the topical areas addressed by the model curriculum. Consequently, we decided to embark on a project to examine in detail the areas addressed by the model curriculum.

The result is this text: *Forensic Accounting and Fraud Examination*.

IMPORTANT FEATURES

In addition to its grounding in the model educational curriculum, a number of additional features make this book unique:

- The authors maintain the devotion to Joseph Wells' *Fraud Examination* text and the work of the Association of Certified Fraud Examiners to focus not on the accounting numbers but on the individuals and activities behind fraud and civil litigation disputes. People and their choices are at the heart of fraud examination and financial forensic engagements. The book starts, as many others, with a review of the work of Sutherland, Cressey, Hollinger and Clark, and W. Steve Albrecht, but ventures beyond those seminal ideas.

- Some of the concepts examined include:

  - Motivations for nefarious activities beyond money such as ego, ideology, and coercion

  - The modus operandi of predators—individuals who deliberately commit wrongful acts

  - The impact of collusion and management override on preventive and deterrent activities

  - Consideration of ethical decision making

- "The Fraudster's Perspective:" Interviews, thoughts, and contributions by the former CFO of the "Crazy Eddie" fraud, Sam Antar.

- The text embraces contributions by the greater forensic communities including accounting, law, psychology, sociology, criminology, intelligence, information systems, computer forensics, and other forensic science fields.

- The text provides a detailed examination of the investigative process as well as an extensive array of tools and techniques used to investigate fraud and financial forensic issues.

CONTENT

The book has 5 main sections:

I. Introduction to Fraud Examination and Financial Forensics (Ch 1–2)

II. Criminology, Ethics, and the Legal, Regulatory, and Professional Environments (Ch 3–6)

III. Detection and Investigative Tools and Techniques (Ch 7–10)

IV. Fraud Schemes (Ch 11–14)

V. Financial Litigation Advisory Services and Remediation (Ch 15–16)

The book will help students to master the knowledge, skills, and abilities required to enter this emerging and exciting specialization through the following areas:

- Foundational skills
- Career opportunities
- The psychology of the fraud perpetrator: why people make bad choices
- Complex frauds and financial crimes such as money laundering, organized crime, and cybercrime
- Best practices in detection and investigation
- Effective interviewing and interrogation techniques
- Using information technology for fraud examination and financial forensics engagements
- A detailed explanation of fraud schemes
  - asset misappropriation
  - corruption
  - financial statement fraud
- The work of consultants, litigation support professionals, and expert witnesses and their roles with damage claims, valuations, and other engagements
- Cleaning up the mess—Remediation and litigation advisory services

SUPPLEMENTS

The supplements for this text include PowerPoint presentations, instructor's manual, testbank, and solutions manual. The supplements will be available online at *www.wiley.com/college/kranacher.*

Forensic Accounting also includes access to the educational version of IDEA$^{®}$–Data Analysis Software. IDEA is available in 16 languages and used in more than 90 countries by major accounting firms, government, corporations in all industry sectors, and by university internal audit departments and professors as a teaching tool. IDEA can read, display, analyze, manipulate, sample or extract data from data files from almost any source—mainframe to PC, including reports printed to a file such as a PDF. Designed by auditors for auditors, IDEA is both powerful and easy to use.

ACKNOWLEDGMENTS

The authors were able to gather, synthesize, and present this material as a result of their auspicious interactions with the 46 subject matter experts, the work of pioneers in the field, and their contacts with other exceptional professionals at conferences, seminars, and in the classroom. To each of you, we are truly grateful.

Mary-Jo Kranacher
Dick Riley
Joseph Wells
January, 2010

Mary-Jo Kranacher is a CPA and a certified fraud examiner (CFE). She is the ACFE Endowed Professor of Fraud Examination and department chairman for Accounting & Finance in the School of Business & Information Systems at York College of The City University of New York (CUNY). She is also the Editor-in-Chief of *The CPA Journal*, published by the New York State Society of CPAs. Professor Kranacher is a former member of the ACFE Board of Regents and past chair of its Higher Education Committee. She was one of several subject matter experts who developed the model curriculum for fraud and forensic accounting education for the Department of Justice's grant-funded project and was named the 2009 ACFE Educator of the Year. Professor Kranacher has conducted forensic investigations related to asset misappropriation, fraudulent financial statements, expense reimbursement schemes, and others. She writes and speaks extensively on anti-fraud education, forensic accounting, fraud detection and deterrence, professional ethics, and accounting education.

Richard A. (Dick) Riley, Jr. is currently a Louis F. Tanner Distinguished Professor of Public Accounting at West Virginia University, the 2008 Association of Certified Fraud Examiners Educator of the Year, and 2009 American Accounting Association Innovation in Accounting Education Award recipient. Dr. Riley is a CPA, CFE, CFF, forensic accountant, and fraud examiner who has developed and implemented fraud and forensic accounting education programs for the United States National Institute of Justice and the Internal Revenue Service. He is the acting Director of Research for the Institute for Fraud Prevention (IFP). Since 2002, Dr. Riley has performed expert financial analysis and litigation support services, offering deposition and trial testimony. Beyond this text, he co-authored *Financial Statement Fraud: Prevention and Detection* (2nd edition) with Zabihollah Rezaee. Dr. Riley earned an undergraduate degree in accounting from Wheeling Jesuit University, a Masters of Professional Accountancy from West Virginia University, and Doctor of Philosophy Degree from the University of Tennessee.

Joseph T. Wells is founder and Chairman of the Board of the Association of Certified Fraud Examiners, the world's largest anti-fraud organization. After graduating with honors from the University of Oklahoma, Mr. Wells spent two years on the audit staff of Coopers and Lybrand. He then was appointed a Special Agent of the FBI. Over the next ten years, Mr. Wells investigated thousands of fraud cases, ranging from nickel-and-dime con artists to former Attorney John Mitchell for his role in the Watergate case. In 1982, he left the government to form Wells & Associates, a firm of criminologists specializing in fraud detection and deterrence. Since becoming Chairman of the ACFE in 1988, Mr. Wells has lectured to tens of thousands of business professionals, written sixteen books, and authored scores of articles and research projects. His writing has won numerous awards, including the top articles of the year for both *Internal Auditor Magazine* and the *Journal of Accountancy*. Mr. Wells is a former adjunct professor of fraud examination at the University of Texas where his pioneering work has been recognized by the American Accounting Association, which named him Accounting Education Innovator of the Year in 2002. Mr. Wells has served on various senior committees of the American Institute of CPAs and he is a member of the AICPA's Business and Industry Hall of Fame. He has been named to *Accounting Today* magazine's annual list of the "Top 100 Most Influential People" in accounting nine times.

3. Reliance on the false statement by the victim

4. Damages resulting from the victim's reliance on the false statement

In the broadest sense, fraud can encompass any crime for gain that uses deception as its principal technique. This deception is implemented through fraud schemes: specific methodologies used to commit and conceal the fraudulent act. There are three ways to relieve a victim of money illegally: force, trickery, or larceny. Those offenses that employ trickery are frauds.

The legal definition of fraud is the same whether the offense is criminal or civil; the difference is that criminal cases must meet a higher burden of proof. For example, let's assume an employee who worked in the warehouse of a computer manufacturer stole valuable computer chips when no one was looking and resold them to a competitor. This conduct is certainly illegal, but what law has the employee broken? Has he committed fraud? The answer, of course, is that it depends. Let us briefly review the legal ramifications of the theft.

The legal term for stealing is larceny, which is defined as "felonious stealing, taking and carrying, leading, riding, or driving away with another's personal property, with the intent to convert it or to deprive the owner thereof."[2] In order to prove that a person has committed larceny, we would need to prove the following four elements:

1. There was a taking or carrying away

2. of the money or property of another

3. without the consent of the owner and

4. with the intent to deprive the owner of its use or possession.

In our example, the employee definitely carried away his employer's property, and we can safely assume that this was done without the employer's consent. Furthermore, by taking the computer chips from the warehouse and selling them to a third party, the employee clearly demonstrated intent to deprive his employer of the ability to possess and use those chips. Therefore, the employee has committed larceny.

The employee might also be accused of having committed a tort known as conversion.[3] Conversion, in the legal sense, is "an unauthorized assumption and exercise of the right of ownership over goods or personal chattels belonging to another, to the alteration of their condition or the exclusion of the owner's rights."[4] A person commits a conversion when he or she takes possession of property that does not belong to him or her and thereby deprives the true owner of the property for any length of time. The employee in our example took possession of the computer chips when he stole them, and, by selling them, he has deprived his employer of that property. Therefore, the employee has also engaged in conversion of the company's property.

Furthermore, the act of stealing the computer chips also makes the employee an embezzler. "To embezzle means wilfully to take, or convert to one's own use, another's money or property of which the wrongdoer acquired possession lawfully, by reason of some office or employment or position of trust." The key words in that definition are "acquired possession lawfully." In order for an embezzlement to occur, the person who stole the property must have been entitled to possession of the property at the time of the theft. Remember, possession is not the same as ownership. In our example, the employee might be entitled to possess the company's computer chips (to assemble them, pack them, store them, etc.), but clearly the chips belong to the employer, not the employee. When the employee steals the chips, he has committed embezzlement.

We might also observe that some employees have a recognized fiduciary relationship with their employers under the law. The term *fiduciary*, according to *Black's Law Dictionary*, is of Roman origin and means "a person holding a character analogous to a trustee, in respect to the trust and confidence involved in it and the scrupulous good faith and candor which it requires. A person is said to act in a 'fiduciary capacity' when the business which he transacts, or the money or property which he handles, is not for his own benefit, but for another person, as to whom he stands in a relation implying and necessitating great confidence and trust on the one part and a high degree of good faith on the other part."[5] In short, a fiduciary is someone who acts for the benefit of another.

Fiduciaries have a duty to act in the best interests of the person whom they represent. When they violate this duty, they can be liable under the tort of breach of fiduciary duty. The elements of this cause of action vary among jurisdictions, but in general they consist of the following:

1. A fiduciary relationship existed between the plaintiff and the defendant

2. The defendant (fiduciary) breached his or her duty to the plaintiff

3. The breach resulted in either harm to the plaintiff or benefit to the fiduciary

A fiduciary duty is a very high standard of conduct that is not lightly imposed. The duty depends upon the existence of a fiduciary relationship between the two parties. In an employment scenario, a fiduciary relationship is usually found to exist only when the employee is "highly trusted" and enjoys a confidential or special relationship with the employer. Practically speaking, the law generally recognizes a fiduciary duty only for officers and directors of a company, not for ordinary employees. (In some cases a quasi-fiduciary duty may exist for employees who are in possession of trade secrets; they have a duty not to disclose that confidential information.) The upshot is that the employee in our example most likely would not owe a fiduciary duty to his employer, and therefore he would not be liable for breach of fiduciary duty. However, if the example were changed so that an officer of the company stole a trade secret, that tort might apply.

But what about fraud? Recall that fraud always involves some form of deceit. If the employee in question simply walked out of the warehouse with a box of computer chips under his or her coat, this would not be fraud, because there is no deceit involved. (Although many would consider this a deceitful act, what we're really talking about when we say deceit, as reflected in the elements of the offense, is some sort of material false statement that the victim relies upon).

Suppose, however, that before he put the box of computer chips under his coat and walked out of the warehouse, the employee tried to cover his trail by falsifying the company's inventory records. Now the character of the crime has changed. Those records are a statement of the company's inventory levels, and the employee has knowingly falsified them. The records are certainly material, because they are used to track the amount of inventory in the warehouse, and the company relies on them to determine how much inventory it has on hand, when it needs to order new inventory, etc. Furthermore, the company has suffered harm as a result of the falsehood, because it now has an inventory shortage of which it is unaware.

Thus, all four attributes of fraud have now been satisfied: the employee has made a material false statement; the employee had knowledge that the statement was false, the company relied upon the statement, and the company has suffered damages. As a matter of law, the employee in question could be charged with a wide range of criminal and civil conduct: fraud, larceny, embezzlement, or conversion. As a practical matter, he or she will probably only be charged with larceny. The point, however, is that occupational fraud always involves deceit, and acts that look like other forms of misconduct, such as larceny, may indeed involve some sort of fraud. Throughout this book, we study not only schemes that have been labeled fraud by courts and legislatures but any acts of deceit by employees that fit our broader definition of occupational fraud and abuse.

Major Categories of Fraud

Asset misappropriations involve the theft or misuse of an organization's assets. (Common examples include skimming revenues, stealing inventory, and payroll fraud.)

Corruption entails the unlawful or wrongful misuse of influence in a business transaction to procure personal benefit, contrary to an individual's duty to his or her employer or the rights of another. (Common examples include accepting kickbacks and engaging in conflicts of interest.)

Financial statement fraud and other fraudulent statements involve the intentional misrepresentation of financial or nonfinancial information to mislead others who are relying on it to make economic decisions. (Common examples include overstating revenues, understating liabilities or expenses, or making false promises regarding the safety and prospects of an investment.)

Enron founder Ken Lay and former chief executive officer (CEO) Jeff Skilling were convicted in May 2006 for their respective roles in the energy company's collapse in 2001. The guilty verdict against Lay included conspiracy to commit securities and wire fraud, but he never served any prison time because he died of a heart attack two months after his conviction. Skilling, however, was sentenced on October 23, 2006, to twenty-four years for conspiracy, fraud, false statements, and insider trading. In addition, Judge Lake ordered Skilling to pay $45 million into a fund for Enron employees. Former Enron chief financial officer (CFO) Andrew Fastow received a relatively light sentence of six years for his role, after cooperating with prosecutors in the conviction of Lay and Skilling.[6] Enron was a $60 billion victim of accounting maneuvers and shady business deals that also led to thousands of lost jobs and more than $2 billion in employee pension plan losses.

If you were working at Enron and had knowledge of this fraud, what would you do?

On January 14, 2002, a seven-page memo, written by Sherron Watkins, was referred to in a *Houston Chronicle* article. This memo had been sent anonymously to Kenneth Lay and begged the question, "Has Enron Become a Risky Place to Work?" For her role as whistleblower, Sherron Watkins was recognized along with WorldCom's Cynthia Cooper and the FBI's Coleen Rowley as *Time* Magazine's Person of the Year in 2002.

The Association of Certified Fraud Examiners defines financial statement fraud as the intentional, deliberate misstatement or omission of material facts or accounting data that is misleading and, when considered with all the information made available, that would cause the reader to change or alter his or her judgment or decision.[7] In other words, the statement constitutes intentional or reckless conduct, whether by act or omission, that results in material misleading financial statements.[8]

Even though the specific schemes vary, the major areas involved in financial statement fraud include the following:

1. Fictitious revenue (and related assets)
2. Improper timing of revenue and expense recognition
3. Concealed liabilities
4. Inadequate and misleading disclosures
5. Improper asset valuation
6. Improper and inappropriate capitalization of expenses

The essential characteristics of financial statement fraud are (1) the misstatement is material and intentional, and (2) users of the financial statements have been misled.

In recent years, the financial press has had an abundance of examples of fraudulent financial reporting. These include Enron, WorldCom, Adelphia, Tyco, and others. The common theme of all these scandals was a management team that was willing to "work the system" for its own benefit and a wide range of stakeholders—including employees, creditors, investors, and entire communities—that are still reeling from the losses. In response, Congress passed the Sarbanes–Oxley Act (SOX) in 2002. SOX legislation was aimed at auditing firms, corporate governance, executive management (CEOs and CFOs), officers, and directors. The assessment of internal controls, preservation of evidence, whistleblower protection, and increased penalties for securities fraud became a part of the new business landscape.

The ACFE 2008 Report to the Nation noted that financial fraud tends to be the least frequent of all frauds, accounting for only 10.3 percent. However, the median loss for financial statement fraud is approximately $2 million, more than thirteen times larger than the typical asset misappropriation and more than five times larger than the typical corruption scheme. In addition, when financial statement fraud has been identified, in 79 of 99 cases, other types of fraud are also being perpetrated.

The 2003 KPMG Fraud Survey also notes that financial statement fraud and health insurance fraud are the most costly schemes. In addition, the rate of occurrence of financial statement fraud more than doubled since the 2001 survey.

According to the 2005 PricewaterhouseCoopers Global Economic Crime Survey, there has been a 140 percent increase in the number of respondents reporting financial misrepresentation. Furthermore, almost 40 percent of the company respondents report significant collateral damage, such as loss of reputation, decreased staff motivation, and declining business relations. The survey also notes that most frauds involve a lack of internal controls (opportunity), the need to maintain expensive lifestyles (incentive), and the perpetrators' lack of awareness that their actions were wrong (rationalization).

Common Fraud Schemes

Table 1-1 depicts the most common fraud schemes.[9]

Suspected frauds can be categorized by a number of different methods, but they are usually referred to as either internal or external frauds. The latter refers to offenses committed by individuals against other individuals (e.g., con schemes), offenses by individuals against organizations (e.g., insurance fraud), or organizations against individuals (e.g., consumer frauds). Internal fraud refers to occupational fraud committed by one or more employees of an organization; this is the most costly and most common fraud. These crimes are more commonly referred to as occupational fraud and abuse.

TABLE 1-1 Common Fraud Schemes

Fraud Acts

Asset Misappropriation

  Cash

    Larceny (theft)

    Skimming (removal of cash before it hits books): Sales, A/R, Refunds, and Other

    Fraudulent Disbursement

      Billing Schemes - including shell companies, fictitious vendors, personal purchases

      Payroll Schemes - ghost employees, commission schemes, workers compensation, and false hours and wages

      Expense Reimbursement Schemes - including overstated expenses, fictitious expenses, and multiple reimbursements

      Check Tampering

      Register Disbursements including false voids and refunds

  Inventory and Other Assets

    Inappropriate Use

    Larceny (theft)

Corruption

  Conflicts of Interest (unreported or undisclosed)

  Bribery

  Illegal Gratuities

  Economic Extortion

False Statements

  Fraudulent Financial Statements

  False Representations (e.g., employment credentials, contracts, identification)

Specific Fraud Contexts

  Bankruptcy Fraud

  Contract and Procurement Fraud

  Money Laundering

  Tax Fraud

  Investment Scams

  Terrorist Financing

  Consumer Fraud

    Identity Theft

    Check and Credit Card Fraud

    Computer and Internet Fraud

  Divorce Fraud (including hidden assets)

  Intellectual Property

  Business Valuation Fraud

Noteworthy Industry-Specific Fraud

  Financial Institutions

  Insurance Fraud

  Health Care Fraud

  Securities Fraud

  Public Sector Fraud

WHAT IS THE DIFFERENCE BETWEEN FRAUD AND ABUSE?

Obviously, not all misconduct in the workplace amounts to fraud. There is a litany of abusive practices that plague organizations, causing lost dollars or resources, but that do not actually constitute fraud. As any employer knows, it is hardly out of the ordinary for employees to do any of the following:

- Use equipment belonging to the organization
- Surf the Internet while at work
- Attend to personal business during working hours
- Take a long lunch, or a break, without approval

- Come to work late, or leave early
- Use sick leave when not sick
- Do slow or sloppy work
- Use employee discounts to purchase goods for friends and relatives
- Work under the influence of alcohol or drugs

The term *abuse* has taken on a largely amorphous meaning over the years, frequently being used to describe any misconduct that does not fall into a clearly defined category of wrongdoing. Webster's definition of abuse might surprise you. From the Latin word *abusus*, to consume, it means: "1. A deceitful act, deception; 2. A corrupt practice or custom; 3. Improper use or treatment, misuse." To deceive is "to be false; to fail to fulfill; to cheat; to cause to accept as true or valid what is false or invalid."

Given the commonality of the language describing both fraud and abuse, what are the key differences? An example illustrates: suppose that a teller was employed by a bank and stole $100 from her cash drawer. We would define that broadly as fraud. But if she earns $500 a week and falsely calls in sick one day, we might call that abuse—even though each act has the exact same economic impact to the company—in this case, $100.

And, of course, each offense requires a dishonest intent on the part of the employee to victimize the company. Look at the way in which each is typically handled within an organization, however: in the case of the embezzlement, the employee gets fired; there is also a possibility (albeit remote) that she will be prosecuted. But in the case in which the employee misuses her sick time, perhaps she gets reprimanded, or her pay might be docked for the day.

But we can also change the abuse example slightly. Let's say the employee works for a governmental agency instead of in the private sector. Sick leave abuse—in its strictest interpretation—could be a fraud against the government. After all, the employee has made a false statement (about her ability to work) for financial gain (to keep from getting docked). Government agencies can and have prosecuted flagrant instances of sick leave abuse. Misuse of public money in any form can end up being a serious matter, and the prosecutorial thresholds can be surprisingly low.

THE CRAZY EDDIE CASE

Adapted from The White Collar Fraud Web site by Sam E. Antar at http:www.whitecollarfraud.com

Eddie Antar was a retailing revolutionary in his day; he broke the price fixing environment that gripped the consumer electronics industry. To survive in this industry, Eddie circumvented the fair trade laws and discounted the consumer electronics merchandise he was selling. He faced retribution from the manufacturers who stopped shipping merchandise to him. Consequently, he had to purchase his inventory from trans-shippers and grey markets. He built up great customer loyalty in the process and his business volume expanded.

Like numerous other independent small businesses in America, Crazy Eddie paid many of its employees off the books. There was a company culture that believed that nothing should go to the government. Eddie Antar inspired intense loyalty from his employees, most of whom were family. It was us against them—customers, the government, insurance companies, auditors, and anyone else who did not serve the company's interests. The Antar family regularly skimmed profits from the business. If profits couldn't be increased through bait-and-switch tactics, the Antar clan would pocket the sales tax by not reporting cash sales.

The Four Phases of the Crazy Eddie Frauds

- *1969–1979: Skimming to reduce reported taxable income*
- *1979–1983: Gradual reduction of skimming to increase reported income and profit growth in preparation to take the company public*
- *September 13, 1984: Date of Crazy Eddie initial public offering*
- *1985–1986: Increasing Crazy Eddie's reported income to raise stock prices so insiders could sell their stock at inflated values*
- *1987: Crazy Eddie starts losing money. The main purpose of fraud at this stage is to "cover up" prior frauds resulting from the "double down" effect.*

From the Fraudster's Perspective

Sam E. Antar was a CPA and the CFO of the Crazy Eddie electronics chain in the 1980s when that securities fraud scandal hit. The fraud cost investors and creditors hundreds of millions of dollars, and it cost others their careers. In addition to

securities fraud, investigators later learned that the Crazy Eddie business was also involved in various other types of fraud, including skimming, money laundering, fictitious revenue, fraudulent asset valuations, and concealed liabilities and expenses, to name a few. Since then, Sam has shared his views—on white-collar crime, the accounting profession, internal controls, the Sarbanes–Oxley Act, and other related topics—with audiences around the country.

According to Sam, there are two types of white-collar criminal groups: (1) those with common economic interests (e.g., the Enrons and WorldComs) and (2) other cohesive groups (e.g., with family, religious, social, or cultural ties). Fraud is harder to detect in the second category because of behavioral and loyalty issues. Tone at the top is crucial here.

Contrary to the fraud triangle theory—incentive, opportunity, and rationalization—Sam insists that the Crazy Eddie fraud involved no rationalization. "It was pure and simple greed," he says. "The crimes were committed simply because we could. The incentive and opportunity was there, but the morality and excuses were lacking. We never had one conversation about morality during the 18 years that the fraud was going on." He contends that "White-collar criminals consider your humanity as a weakness to be exploited in the execution of their crimes and they measure their effectiveness by the comfort level of their victims." Sam's description of how the Crazy Eddie frauds were successfully concealed from the auditors for so long is a tale of what he refers to as "distraction rather than obstruction." For example, employees of the company wined and dined the auditors to distract them from conducting their planned audit procedures and to eat up the time allotted for the audit. As the end of the time frame approached, the auditors were rushed and didn't have time to complete many of their procedures. Fraudsters use "controlled chaos" to perpetrate their crimes successfully.

The accounting profession doesn't analyze auditor error and therefore learn from it. Sam's advice to the accounting profession, anti-fraud professionals, and Wall Street: "Don't trust, just verify, verify, verify." Audit programs are generic, and auditors have been too process-oriented. Sam recommends that auditors utilize the Internet for searchable items, such as statements to the media and quarterly earnings called *transcriptions*. A pattern of inconsistencies or contradictions found in these sources of information, compared to the financial statements and footnote disclosures, should raise red flags. As an example, Crazy Eddie's auditors never thought to check sales transactions to ensure that the deposits came from actual sales. They never considered that these funds came from previously skimmed money.

Sam believes that white-collar crime can be more brutal than violent crime because white-collar crime imposes a collective harm on society. On using incarceration as a general deterrent, Sam says, "No criminal finds morality and stops committing crime simply because another criminal went to jail."

WHAT IS FINANCIAL FORENSICS?

A call comes in from a nationally known insurance company. Claims Agent Kathleen begins: "I have a problem and you were recommended to me. One of my insureds near your locale submitted an insurance claim related to an accounts receivable rider. The insurance claim totals more than $1 million, and they are claiming that the alleged perpetrator did not take any money and that their investigation to date indicates that no money is missing from the company. Can you assist with an investigation of this claim?"

She asks for your help to do the following:

1. Verify the facts and circumstances surrounding the claim presented by the insured
2. Determine whether accounting records have been physically destroyed
3. To the best of your ability, determine whether this is a misappropriation or theft of funds
4. If this is a theft of funds, attempt to determine by whom

Financial forensics is the application of financial principles and theories to facts or hypotheses at issue in a legal dispute and consists of two primary functions:

1. Litigation advisory services, which recognizes the role of the financial forensic professional as an expert or consultant
2. Investigative services, which makes use of the financial forensic professional's skills and may or may not lead to courtroom testimony

Financial forensics may involve either an attest or consulting engagement.[10] According to the AICPA, Forensic and Litigation Advisory Services (FLAS) professionals provide educational, technical, functional, and industry-specific services that often apply to occupational fraud, corruption, and abuse and to financial statement fraud cases. FLAS professionals may assist attorneys with assembling the financial information necessary either to bolster (if hired by the plaintiff) or to undercut (if hired by the defendant) a case. They can provide varying levels of support—from technical analysis and data mining, to a broader

approach that may include developing litigation strategies, arguments, and testimony in civil and criminal cases. Engagements may be criminal, civil, or administrative cases that involve economic damage claims, workplace or matrimonial disputes, or asset and business valuations.[11]

Forensic and litigation advisory services require interaction with attorneys throughout the engagement. Excellent communication skills are essential for effective mediation, arbitration, negotiations, depositions, and courtroom testimony. These communication skills encompass the use of a variety of means by which to express the facts of the case—oral, written, pictures, and graphs. Like all fraud and forensic accounting work, there is an adversarial nature to the engagements, and professionals can expect that their work will be carefully scrutinized by the opposing side.

THE FINANCIAL FORENSIC PROFESSIONAL'S SKILL SET

Financial forensics is the intersection of financial principles and the law and, therefore, applies the (1) technical skills of accounting, auditing, finance, quantitative methods, and certain areas of the law and research; (2) investigative skills for the collection, analysis, and evaluation of evidential matter; and (3) critical thinking to interpret and communicate the results of an investigation.

Critical thinking, sometimes referred to as lateral thinking or thinking "outside the box," is a disciplined approach to problem solving. It is used as a foundation to guide our thought process and related actions.

CRITICAL THINKING EXERCISE

Everything needed to answer the question "How did they die?" is contained in the following passage.

Anthony and Cleopatra are lying dead on the floor in a villa. Nearby on the floor is a broken bowl. There is no mark on either of their bodies, and they were not poisoned. With this information, determine how they died.[12]

Clue: List all of your assumptions from the preceding passage.

This exercise requires the problem solver to guard against jumping to conclusions. Even though the fraud examiner or forensic accountant needs to think critically, the direction of the investigation is often guided by assumptions. The difficult challenge is not the questioning of assumptions that investigators had identified as assumptions; but the questioning of the assumptions that investigators are making without realizing that they have made them. That is why it is important that investigators continually challenge their investigative approach and outcomes to ensure that the investigation is moving toward a resolution—one that stands up to the scrutiny of others.

THE ROLE OF AUDITING, FRAUD EXAMINATION, AND FINANCIAL FORENSICS

Fraud examination, financial forensics, and traditional auditing are interrelated, yet they have characteristics that are separate and distinct. All require interdisciplinary skills to succeed—professionals in any of these fields must possess a capacity for working with numbers, words, and people.

Financial statement auditing acts to ensure that financial statements are free from material misstatement. Audit procedures, as outlined in PCAOB Auditing Standard No. 5 or AICPA Statement on Auditing Standards (SAS) No. 99, require that the auditor undertake a fraud-risk assessment. However, under generally accepted auditing standards (GAAS) auditors are not currently responsible for planning and performing auditing procedures to detect immaterial misstatements, regardless of whether they are caused by error or fraud. Allegations of financial statement fraud are often resolved through court action, and auditors may be called into court to testify on behalf of a client or to defend their audit work, a point at which auditing, fraud examination, and financial forensics intersect.

However, each discipline also encompasses separate and unique functional aspects. For example, fraud examiners often assist in fraud prevention and deterrence efforts that do not involve the audit of nonpublic companies or the legal system. Financial forensic professionals calculate economic damages, business or asset valuations, and provide litigation advisory services that may not involve allegations of fraud. Finally, most audits are completed without uncovering financial statement fraud or involving

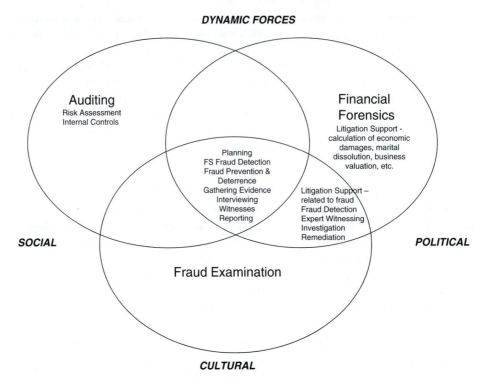

FIGURE 1-1 Auditing, Fraud Examination, and Financial Forensics

the legal system. Thus, as graphically presented in Figure 1-1, auditing, fraud examination, and financial forensics often use the same tools, but they also have responsibilities independent of the other.

The interrelationship among auditing, fraud examination, and financial forensics is dynamic and changes over time because of political, social, and cultural pressure. Because independent auditors operate in an environment impacted by SOX and SAS 99, they are expected to have adequate knowledge and skills in the area of fraud detection and deterrence. In addition, auditing, fraud examination, and financial forensic professionals often have skill sets in multiple areas and are able to leverage their skills and abilities from one area when working in others.[13]

Fraud examination is the discipline of resolving allegations of fraud from tips, complaints, or accounting clues. It involves obtaining documentary evidence, interviewing witnesses and potential suspects, writing investigative reports, testifying to findings, and assisting in the general detection and prevention of fraud. Fraud examination has many similarities to the field of financial forensics. Because the latter uses accounting or financial knowledge, skills, and abilities for courtroom purposes, financial forensics can involve not only the investigation of potential fraud, but a host of other litigation support services.

Similarly, fraud examination and auditing are related. Because most occupational frauds are financial crimes, there is necessarily a certain degree of auditing involved. But a fraud examination encompasses much more than just the review of financial data; it also involves techniques such as interviews, statement analyses, public records searches, and forensic document examination. There are also significant differences between the three disciplines in terms of their scope, objectives, and underlying presumptions. Table 1-2 summarizes the differences between the three disciplines.

Nevertheless, successful auditors, fraud examiners, and financial forensic professionals have several similar attributes; they are all diligent, detail-oriented, and organized critical thinkers, excellent listeners, and communicators.

THE BASICS OF FRAUD

Brian Lee excelled as a top-notch plastic surgeon. Lee practiced out of a large physician-owned clinic of assorted specialties. As its top producer, Lee billed more than $1 million annually and took home $300,000 to $800,000 per year in salary and bonus. During one four-year stretch, Lee also kept his own secret stash of unrecorded revenue—possibly hundreds of thousands of dollars.

TABLE 1-2   Differences between Auditing, Fraud Examination, and Financial Forensics

Issue	Auditing	Fraud Examination	Financial Forensics
Timing	**Recurring** Audits occur on a regular, recurring basis.	**Nonrecurring** Fraud examinations are conducted only with sufficient predication.	**Nonrecurring** Financial forensic engagements are conducted only after allegation of misconduct.
Scope	**General** The examination of financial statements for material misstatements.	**Specific** The purpose of the examination is to resolve specific allegations.	**Specific** The purpose of the examination is to resolve specific allegations.
Objective	**Opinion** An audit is generally conducted for the purpose of expressing an opinion on the financial statements and related information.	**Affix blame** The fraud examination's goal is to determine whether fraud has occurred and who is likely responsible.	**Determine financial impact** The financial forensic professional's goal is to determine whether the allegations are reasonable based on the financial evidence and, if so, the financial impact of the allegations.
Relationship	**Nonadversarial but skeptical** Historically, the audit process was non-adversarial. Since SOX and SAS 99, auditors use professional skepticism as a guide.	**Adversarial** Fraud examinations, because they involve efforts to affix blame, are adversarial in nature.	**Independent** A financial forensic professional calculates financial impact based on formulaic assumptions.
Methodology	**Audit techniques** Audits are conducted primarily by examining financial data using GAAS.	**Fraud examination techniques** Gathering the required financial and nonfinancial evidence to affix culpability.	**Financial forensic techniques** Gathering the required financial and nonfinancial evidence to examine the allegations independently and determine their financial impact.
Presumption	**Professional Skepticism** Auditors are required to approach audits with professional skepticism, as outlined in GAAS.	**Proof** Fraud examiners approach the resolution of a fraud by attempting to gather sufficient evidence to support or refute an allegation of fraud.	**Proof** Financial forensic professionals will attempt to gather sufficient evidence to support or refute the allegation and related damages.

Because plastic surgery is considered by many health insurance plans to be elective surgery, patients were required to pay their portion of the surgery fees in advance. The case that ultimately nailed Brian Lee involved Rita Mae Givens. Givens had elected rhinoplasty, surgery to reshape her nose, and, during her recovery, she reviewed her insurance policy and discovered that this procedure might be covered under her health insurance or, at least, counted toward her yearly deductible. In pursuit of seeking insurance reimbursement for her surgery, Givens decided to file a claim. She called the clinic office to request a copy of her invoice, but the cashier could find no record of her surgical or billing records. Despite the missing records, Givens had her cancelled check, proof that her charges had been paid. An investigator was called in, and Dr. Lee was interviewed several times over the course of the investigation. Eventually, he confessed to stealing payments from the elective surgeries, for which billing records were not required, particularly when payment was made in cash or a check payable to his name. Why would a successful, top-performing surgeon risk it all? Dr. Lee stated that his father and brother were both very successful; wealth was the family's obsession, and one-upmanship was the family's game. This competition drove each of them to see who could amass the most, drive the best cars, live in the nicest homes, and travel to the most exotic vacation spots.

Unfortunately, Lee took the game one step further and was willing to commit grand larceny to win. Luckily for Lee, the other doctors at the clinic decided not to prosecute or terminate their top moneymaker. Lee made full restitution of the money he had stolen, and the clinic instituted new payment procedures. Ironically, Dr. Lee admitted to the investigator that, if given the opportunity, he would probably do it again.[14]

Who Commits Fraud and Why

Fraudsters, by their very nature, are trust violators. They generally have achieved a position of trust within an organization and have chosen to violate that trust. According to the ACFE, owners and executives are involved in only about 23.3 percent of frauds but, when involved, steal approximately $834,000. Managers are the second most frequent perpetrators, committing 37.1 percent of frauds and wreaking $150,000 worth of damage, on average. Finally, line employees are the principle perpetrators in 39.7 percent of schemes, yielding company losses of approximately $70,000. Research suggests that although males are most frequently the perpetrators, in 40.9 percent of fraud cases, a woman is the principle perpetrator. Fraudsters are found in all age categories and educational achievement levels, but victim losses rise with both the age and education of the principle perpetrator. In 63.9 percent of the cases, the perpetrator acted alone; however, when fraudsters collude, the losses to the victim organization increase more than fourfold. The following profile summarizes the characteristics of the typical fraud perpetrator:

Fraud Perpetrator Profile	
Male[15]	Well Educated
Middle-Aged to Retired	Accountant, Upper Management or Executive
With the Company for Five or More Years	Acts Alone
Never Charged or Convicted of a Criminal Offense	

Regardless of whether fraud perpetrators are male or female, they look like average people. Perhaps the most interesting of all the characteristics listed is that fraudsters typically do not have a criminal background.[16] Furthermore, it is not uncommon for a fraud perpetrator to be a well-respected member of the community, attend church services regularly, and have a spouse and children.

Interestingly, in 92.6 percent of the fraud cases examined by the ACFE, the perpetrator had been with the victim organization for more than one year. Dr. W. Steve Albrecht, a pioneer researcher at Brigham Young University, notes: "Just because someone has been honest for 10 years doesn't mean that they will always be honest." Not surprisingly, the longer the tenure is, the larger the average loss is. In only 12.5 percent of the fraud cases examined did the perpetrator have any prior criminal history. In fact, the typical fraudster is not a pathological criminal, but rather a person who has achieved a position of trust. So the critical question remains, what causes good people to go bad?

The Fraud Triangle: Opportunity, Perceived Pressure, and Rationalization

Over the years, a hypothesis developed by Donald R. Cressey (1919–1987), which attempts to explain the conditions that are generally present when fraud occurs, has become better known as the "fraud triangle" (Figure 1-2). One leg of the triangle represents perceived pressure. The second leg is perceived opportunity, and the final leg denotes rationalization.

Perceived Pressure Many people inside any organizational structure have at least some access to cash, checks, or other assets. However, it is a perceived pressure that causes individuals to consider

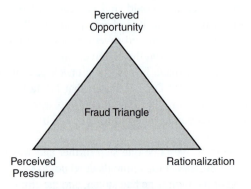

FIGURE 1-2 The Fraud Triangle: Perceived Pressure, Perceived Opportunity, and Rationalization

seriously availing themselves of the opportunity presented by, for example, an internal control weakness. Fraud pressures can arise from financial problems, such as living beyond one's means, greed, high debt, poor credit, family medical bills, investment losses, or children's educational expenses. Pressures may also arise from vices such as gambling, drugs, or an extramarital affair.

Financial statement fraud is often attributed to pressures, such as meeting analysts' expectations, deadlines, and cutoffs, or qualifying for bonuses. Finally, pressure may be the mere challenge of getting away with it or keeping up with family and friends. The word *perceived* is carefully chosen here. Individuals react differently to certain stimuli, and pressures that have no impact on one person's choices may dramatically affect another's. It is important that the fraud examiner or forensic accountant investigating a case recognize this facet of human nature.

Perceived Opportunity Whether the issue is management override, related to a financial statement fraud, or a breakdown in the internal control environment that allows the accounts receivable clerk to abscond with the cash and checks of a business, the perpetrator needs the opportunity to commit a fraud. Furthermore, when it comes to fraud prevention and deterrence, most accountants tend to direct their efforts toward minimizing opportunity through the internal control environment. However, internal controls are just one element of opportunity. Other integral ways to reduce opportunity include providing adequate training and supervision of personnel; effective monitoring of company management by auditors, audit committees, and boards of directors; proactive antifraud programs; a strong ethical culture; anonymous hotlines; and whistleblower protections.

The Perception of Detection Fraud deterrence begins in the employee's mind. Employees who perceive that they will be caught are less likely to engage in fraudulent conduct. The logic is hard to dispute. Exactly how much deterrent effect this concept provides depends on a number of factors, both internal and external. But internal controls can have a deterrent effect only when the employee perceives that such a control exists and is intended for the purpose of uncovering fraud. "Hidden" controls have no deterrent effect. Conversely, controls that are not even in place—but are perceived to be—have the same deterrent value.

Rationalization Finally, according to the fraud triangle hypothesis, the characteristic that puts fraudsters over the top is rationalization. How do perpetrators sleep at night or look at themselves in the mirror? The typical fraud perpetrator has no criminal history and has been with the victim company for some length of time. Because they generally are not habitual criminals and are in a position of trust, they must develop a rationalization for their actions in order to feel justified in what they are doing. Rationalizations may include an employee/manager's feeling of job dissatisfaction, lack of recognition for a job well done, low compensation, an attitude of "they owe me," "I'm only borrowing the money," "nobody is getting hurt," "they would understand if they knew my situation," "it's for a good purpose," or "everyone else is doing it."

The theory of rationalization, however, has its skeptics. Although, it is difficult to know for certain the thought process of a perpetrator, we can consider the following example. Let's say that the speed limit is sixty-five miles per hour, but I put my cruise control on seventy or seventy-five to keep up with the other lawbreakers. Do I consciously think to myself, "I'm breaking the law, so what is my excuse, my rationalization, if I am stopped for speeding by a police officer?" Most people don't think about that until the flashing lights appear in their rear view mirror. Is the thought process of a white-collar criminal really different from that of anyone else?

M.I.C.E

In addition to the fraud triangle, typical motivations of fraud perpetrators may be identified with the acronym M.I.C.E.:

Money

Ideology

Coercion

Ego

Money and ego are the two most commonly observed motivations. Enron, WorldCom, Adelphia, Pharmor, and ZZZ Best provide good examples of cases in which the convicted perpetrators seemed to be motivated by greed (money) and power (ego). Less frequently, individuals may be unwillingly pulled into

a fraud scheme (coercion). These lower-level individuals are often used to provide insight and testimony against the ringleaders and, as such, receive more lenient sentences or no sentence at all. Ideology is probably the least frequent motivation for white-collar crime, but society has seen this occur in the case of terrorism financing. With ideology, the end justifies the means, and perpetrators steal money to achieve some perceived greater good that furthers their cause. Although the M.I.C.E. heuristic oversimplifies fraudulent motivations, and some motivations fit multiple categories, it is easily remembered and provides investigators with a framework to evaluate motive.

Although the fraud triangle was developed to explain fraud, the same motivations can be used to understand financial disputes of all kinds. For example, consider the contract dispute in which company A claims that company B has not fulfilled its contractual obligation. Company B clearly recognizes that company personnel "walked off the job" before meeting the contract specifications. Assuming that companies A and B negotiated a fair, arms-length transaction, something must explain the otherwise unusual action of company B. In contractual disputes, the alleged wrongdoer clearly has the opportunity: that company can simply stop working. Related to pressure and rationalizations, possibly, company B had old equipment, a labor shortage, or a lack of technical expertise to operate under current conditions that have changed over time and is no longer qualified or able to operate profitably. These explanations created pressure on company B to consider not delivering the product to company A. Assume that company A and company B have been working together for many years. How does company B rationalize its behavior? Maybe company B management focuses on contractual ambiguities that were resolved unfavorably from its perspective and then uses that as a basis for the unfulfilled obligation. Consider the divorce situation, where the husband thinks that his former spouse is asking for a more generous settlement than he thinks is appropriate. The fact that his wife is asking for a settlement that is unreasonable (in his mind) may create pressure on him that he is doing the right thing by hiding assets. Furthermore, he may use the size of the settlement request as rationalization for arguing with her over the children. When money is involved, we may see individuals, companies, or organizations behave in ways that are out of character. In those situations, we may often be able to explain their actions in terms of the fraud triangle: pressure, opportunity, and rationalization.

The Cost of Fraud and Other Litigation

The cost of fraud, as estimated by the ACFE, is more than $990 billion annually. Even though this number is staggering in size, it hides the potentially disastrous impact at the organizational level. For example, if a company with a 10 percent net operating margin is a victim of a $500,000 fraud or loses a comparable amount as a result of a lawsuit, that company must generate incremental sales of $5 million to make up the lost dollars. If the selling price of the average product is $1,000 (a computer, for example), the company would need to sell an additional 5,000 units of product.

Organizations incur costs to produce and sell their products or services. These costs run the gamut: labor, taxes, advertising, occupancy, raw materials, research and development—and, yes, fraud and litigation. The cost of fraud and litigation, however, are fundamentally different from the other costs—the true expense of fraud and litigation is hidden, even if a portion of the cost is reflected in the profit and loss figures. Indirect costs of fraud and litigation can have far-reaching impact. For example, employees may lose jobs or be unable to obtain other employment opportunities; the company may have difficulty getting loans, mortgages, and other forms of credit because of the impact of fraud and litigation on the company's finances; the company's reputation in the community may be affected; and the company may become the subject of broader investigations. With regard to either litigation or fraud, prevention and deterrence are the best medicines. By the time a formal investigation is launched and the allegations are addressed within the legal arena, the parties have already incurred substantial cost.

ACFE 2008 Report to the Nation on Occupational Fraud and Abuse

The ACFE began a major study of occupational fraud cases in 1993, with the primary goal of classifying occupational frauds and abuses by the methods used to commit them. There were other objectives, too. One was to get an idea of how antifraud professionals—CFEs—perceive the fraud problems in their own companies.

The ACFE 2008 Report to the Nation on Occupational Fraud and Abuse is a result of what has now become a biannual national fraud survey of those professionals who deal with fraud and abuse on a daily basis.

The Perpetrators of Fraud   Another goal of this research was to gather demographics on the perpetrators: How old are they? How well educated? What percentage of offenders are men? Were there any identifiable correlations with respect to the offenders? Participants in the 2008 National Fraud Survey provided the following information on the perpetrators' position, gender, age, education, tenure, and criminal histories.

The Effect of Position on Median Loss   Fraud losses tended to rise based on the perpetrator's level of authority within an organization. Generally, employees with the highest levels of authority are the highest paid as well. Therefore, it was not a surprise to find a positive correlation between the perpetrators' annual income and the size of fraud losses. As incomes rose, so did fraud losses.

The lowest median loss of $75,000 was found in frauds committed by employees earning less than $50,000 per year. Although the median loss in schemes committed by those earning between $200,000 and $499,999 annually reached $1 million, the median loss skyrocketed to $50 million for executive/owners earning more than $500,000 per year. Approximately 23 percent have the schemes in the executive/owner category also involved financial statement fraud, which might help explain the extraordinarily high median loss. The differences in the loss amounts were likely a result of the degree of financial control exercised at each level: those with the highest positions also have the greatest access to company funds and assets.

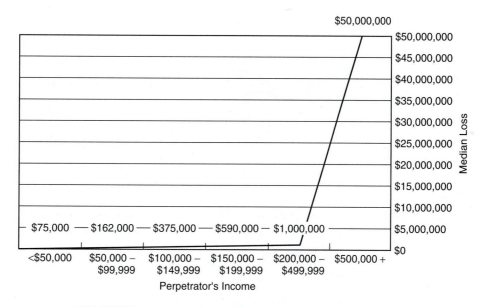

2008 ACFE Report to the Nation: Median Loss vs. Perpetrator's Income

The Effect of Gender on Median Loss   The 2008 ACFE Report to the Nation showed that male employees caused median losses that were more than twice as large as those of female employees; the median loss in a scheme caused by a male employee was $250,000, whereas the median loss caused by a female employee was $110,000. The most logical explanation for this disparity seems to be the "glass ceiling" phenomenon. Generally, in the United States, men occupy higher-paying positions than their female counterparts. And as we have seen, there is a direct correlation between median loss and position. Furthermore, in addition to higher median losses in schemes where males were the principal perpetrators, men accounted for 59.1 percent of the cases, as the following chart shows.

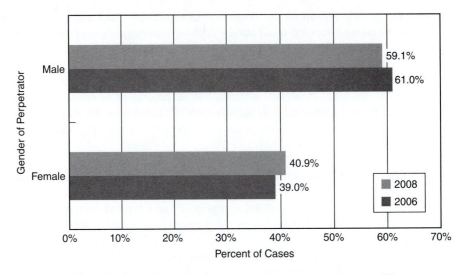

2008 ACFE Report to the Nation: Gender of Perpetrator vs. Percent of Cases

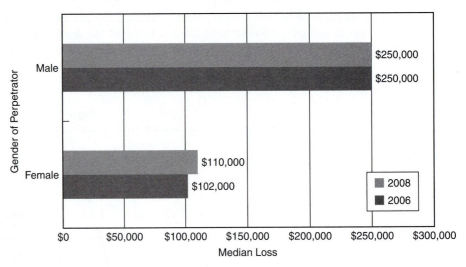

2008 ACFE Report to the Nation: Gender of Perpetrator vs. Median Loss

The Effect of Age on Median Loss   The frauds in the study were committed by persons ranging in age from eighteen to eighty. There was a strong correlation between the age of the perpetrator and the

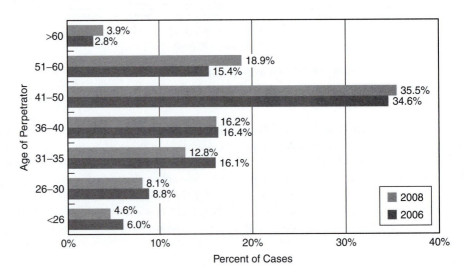

2008 ACFE Report to the Nation: Age of Perpetrator vs. Percent of Cases

size of the median loss, which was consistent with findings from previous reports. Although there were very few cases committed by employees over the age of sixty (3.9 percent), the median loss in those schemes was $435,000. By comparison, the median loss in frauds committed by those twenty-five or younger was $25,000. As with income and gender, age is likely a secondary factor in predicting the loss associated with an occupational fraud, generally reflecting the perpetrator's position and tenure within an organization.

Although frauds committed by those in the highest age groups were the most costly on average, almost two-thirds of the frauds reported were committed by employees in the thirty-one to fifty age group. The median age among perpetrators was forty-five.

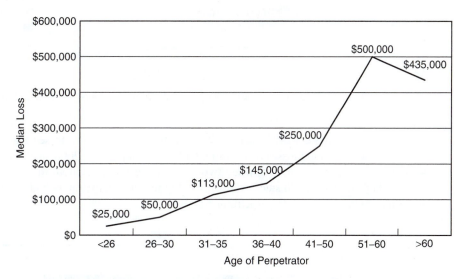

2008 ACFE Report to the Nation: Median Loss vs. Age of Perpetrator

The Effect of Education on Median Loss   As employees' education levels rose, so did the losses from their frauds. The median loss in schemes committed by those with only a high school education was $100,000, whereas the median loss caused by employees with a postgraduate education was $550,000. This trend was to be expected, given that those with higher education levels tend to occupy positions with higher levels of authority.

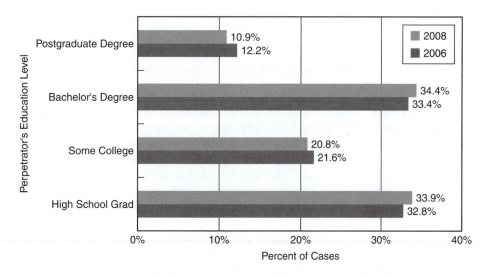

2008 ACFE Report to the Nation: Perpetrator's Education Level vs. Percent of Cases

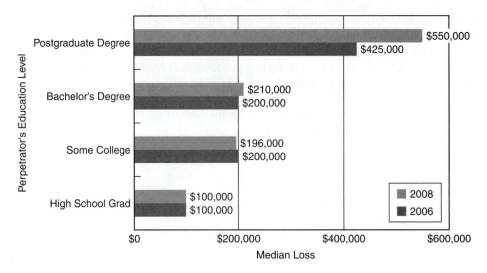

2008 ACFE Report to the Nation: Perpetrator's Education Level vs. Median Loss

The Effect of Collusion on Median Loss　It was not surprising to see that in cases involving more than one perpetrator fraud losses rose substantially. The majority of 2008 survey cases (63.9 percent) only involved a single perpetrator, but, when two or more persons conspired, the median loss was more than four times higher. In the 2006 study, cases involving multiple perpetrators had a median loss that was almost five times higher than single-perpetrator frauds.

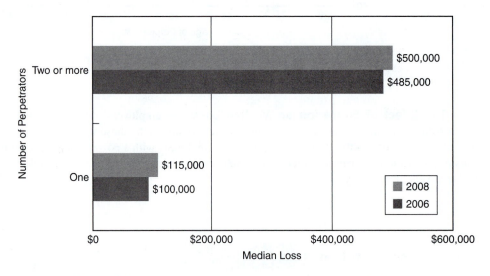

2008 ACFE Report to the Nation: Number of Perpetrators vs. Median Loss

Perpetrators' Tenure with the Victim Organization　There was a direct correlation between the length of time an employee had been employed by a victim organization and the size of the loss in the case. Employees who had been with the victim for more than ten years caused median losses of $250,000, whereas employees who had been with their employers for less than one year caused median losses of $50,000. To some extent, these data may also be linked to the position data shown earlier. The longer that an employee works for an organization, the more likely it is that the employee will advance to increasing levels of authority. However, we believe the critical factors most directly influenced by tenure are trust and opportunity.

It is axiomatic that the more trust an organization places in an employee, in the forms of autonomy and authority, the greater that employee's opportunity to commit fraud becomes. Employees with long tenure, by and large, tend to engender more trust from their employers. They also become more familiar with the organization's operations and controls—including gaps in those controls—which can provide a

greater understanding of how to misappropriate funds without getting caught. This is not to imply that all long-term trusted employees commit fraud; however, in general, those employees are better equipped to commit fraud than their counterparts with less experience. When long-term employees decide to commit fraud, they tend to be more successful.

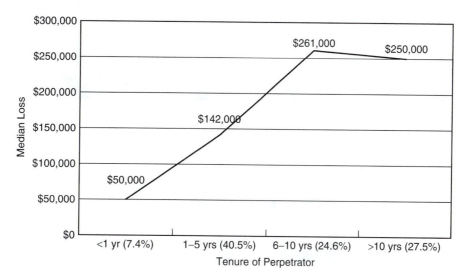

2008 ACFE Report to the Nation: Median Loss vs. Tenure of Perpetrator

Criminal History of the Perpetrators (Figure 1-3)   Less than 7 percent of the perpetrators identified in the 2008 study were known to have been convicted of a previous fraud-related offense. Another 5.7 percent of the perpetrators had previously been charged but never convicted. These figures are consistent with other studies showing that most people who commit occupational fraud are first-time offenders. It is also consistent with Cressey's model, in which occupational offenders do not perceive themselves as lawbreakers.

The Victims   The victims of occupational fraud are organizations that are defrauded by those they employ. The ACFE's 2008 survey asked respondents to provide information on, among other things, the size of organizations that were victimized, as well as the antifraud measures those organizations had in place at the time of the frauds.

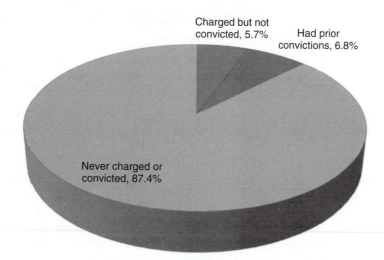

FIGURE 1-3   *2008 ACFE Report to the Nation*: Perpetrator's Criminal History

Median Loss Based on Size of the Organization   Small businesses (those with fewer than 100 employees) can face challenges in deterring and detecting fraud that differ significantly from those of larger organizations. The data show that these small organizations tend to suffer disproportionately large fraud losses, which is similar to the findings in the 2002, 2004, and 2006 reports. The median loss for fraud cases attacking small organizations in our study was $200,000; this exceeded the median loss for cases in any other group. Small organizations were also the most heavily represented group, making up 38.2 percent of all frauds in the study.

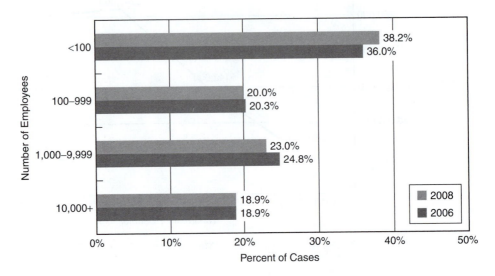

2008 ACFE Report to the Nation: Number of Employees vs. Percent of Cases

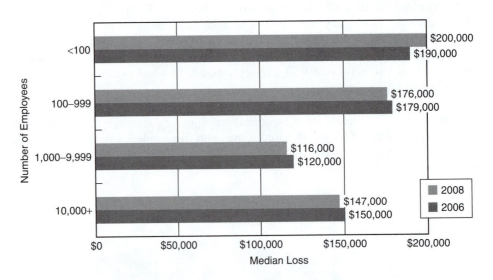

2008 ACFE Report to the Nation: Number of Employees vs. Median Loss

The data for median loss per number of employees confirm what was always suspected. Accountants logically conclude that small organizations are particularly vulnerable to occupational fraud and abuse. The results from the National Fraud Surveys bear this out: losses in the smallest companies were comparable to or larger than those in the organizations with the most employees. It is suspected that this phenomenon exists for two reasons. First, smaller businesses have fewer divisions of responsibility, meaning that fewer people must perform more functions. One of the most common types of fraud encountered in these studies involved small business operations that had a one-person accounting department—that employee writes checks, reconciles the accounts, and posts the books. An entry-level accounting student could spot the internal control deficiencies in that scenario, but apparently many small business owners cannot or do not.

Which brings up the second reason losses are so high in small organizations: There is a greater degree of trust inherent in a situation where everyone knows each other by name. None of us like to think our

TABLE 1-3 *2008 ACFE Report to the Nation*: Median Loss Based on Presence of Anti-Fraud Controls

Control	Percent of Cases Implemented	Yes	No	Percent Reduction
Surprise audits	25.5%	$70,000	$207,000	66.2%
Job rotation/mandatory vacation	12.3%	$64,000	$164,000	61.0%
Hotline	43.5%	$100,000	$250,000	60.0%
Employee support programs	52.9%	$110,000	$250,000	56.0%
Fraud training for managers/execs	41.3%	$100,000	$227,000	55.9%
Internal audit/fraud examination dept	55.8%	$118,000	$250,000	52.8%
Fraud training for employees	38.6%	$100,000	$208,000	51.9%
Anti-fraud policy	36.2%	$100,000	$197,000	49.2%
External audit of ICOFR	53.6%	$121,000	$232,000	47.8%
Code of conduct	61.5%	$126,000	$232,000	45.7%
Mgmt review of internal controls	41.4%	$110,000	$200,000	45.0%
External audit of financial statements	69.6%	$150,000	$250,000	40.0%
Independent audit committee	49.9%	$137,000	$200,000	31.5%
Mgmt certification of financial statements	51.6%	$141,000	$200,000	29.5%
Rewards for whistleblowers	5.4%	$107,000	$150,000	28.7%

co-workers would, or do, commit these offenses. Our defenses are naturally relaxed because we generally trust those we know. There again is the dichotomy of fraud: it cannot occur without trust, but neither can commerce. Trust is an essential ingredient at all levels of business—we can and do make handshake deals every day. Transactions in capitalism simply cannot occur without trust. The key is seeking the right balance between too much and too little trust.

The Impact of Anti-Fraud Measures on Median Loss (Table 1-3) CFEs who participated in the ACFE's National Fraud Surveys were asked to identify which, if any, of several common anti-fraud measures were utilized by the victim organizations at the time the reported frauds occurred. The median loss was determined for schemes depending on whether each anti-fraud measure was in place or not (excluding other factors).

The most common anti-fraud measure was the external audit of financial statements, utilized by approximately 70 percent of the victims, followed by a formal code of conduct, which was implemented by 61.5 percent of victim organizations. Organizations that implemented these controls noted median losses that were 40 percent and 45.7 percent lower, respectively, than those of organizations lacking these controls. Interestingly, the two controls associated with the largest reduction in median losses—surprise audits and job rotation/mandatory vacation policies—were among the least commonly implemented anti-fraud controls.

Case Results A common complaint among those who investigate fraud is that organizations and law enforcement do not do enough to punish fraud and other white-collar offenses. This contributes to high fraud levels—or so the argument goes—because potential offenders are not deterred by the weak or often nonexistent sanctions that are imposed on other fraudsters. Leaving aside the debate as to what factors are effective in deterring fraud, the survey sought to measure how organizations responded to the employees who had defrauded them. One of the criteria for cases in the study was that the CFE had to be reasonably certain that the perpetrator in the case had been identified.

Criminal Prosecutions and Their Outcomes (Figure 1-4) In 69 percent of the cases, the victim organization referred the case to law enforcement authorities. The median loss in those cases was $250,000, whereas the median loss was only $100,000 in cases that were not referred.

For cases that were referred to law enforcement authorities, a large number of those cases were still pending at the time of the survey. However, of the 578 responses for which the outcome was known, 15 percent of the perpetrators were convicted at trial, and another 71.3 percent pled guilty or no contest to their crimes. None of the perpetrators in the cases reported in the 2008 Report were acquitted.

No Legal Action Taken One goal of the ACFE study was to try to determine why organizations decline to take legal action against occupational fraudsters. In cases where no legal action was taken, we

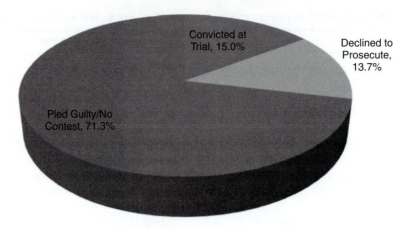

FIGURE 1-4 *2008 ACFE Report to the Nation*: Criminal Prosecutions and Outcomes

provided respondents with a list of commonly cited explanations and asked them to mark any that applied to their case. The following chart summarizes the results. Fear of bad publicity (40.7 percent) was the most commonly cited explanation, followed by a private settlement being reached (31 percent) and the organization considering its internal discipline to be sufficient (30.5 percent).

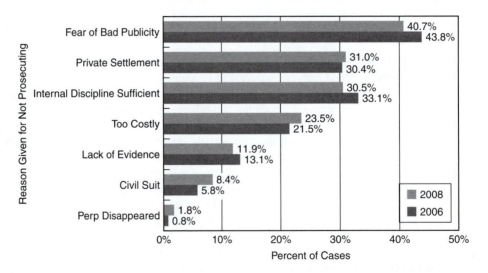

2008 ACFE Report to the Nation: Reasons for Not Prosecuting vs. Percent of Cases

Detecting and Preventing Occupational Fraud The obvious question in a study of occupational fraud is this: What can be done about it? Given that the study was based on actual fraud cases that had been investigated, it would be instructional to ask how these frauds were initially detected by the victim organizations. Perhaps by studying how the victim organizations had uncovered fraud, guidance could be provided to other organizations on how to tailor their fraud prevention and detection efforts. Respondents were given a list of common detection methods and were asked how the frauds they investigated were initially detected. As these results show, the frauds were most commonly detected by tips (46.2 percent). It was also interesting—and a bit disappointing—to note that by accident (20 percent) was the third most common detection method, ranking higher than internal or external audits. This certainly seems to support the contention that organizations need to do a better job of proactively designing controls to prevent fraud and audits to detect them. The most glaring reality in all the statistics in this study is that prevention is the most effective measure to reduce losses from fraud.

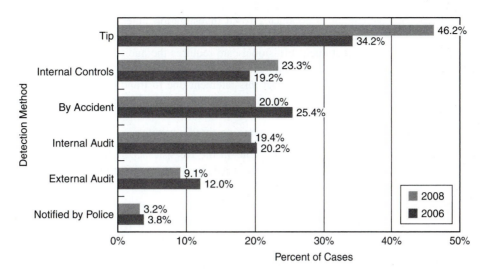

2008 ACFE Report to the Nation: Detection Method vs. Percent of Cases

NON-FRAUD FORENSIC AND LITIGATION ADVISORY ENGAGEMENTS

The forensic accountant can be expected to participate in any legal action that involves money, following the money, performance measurement, valuation of assets, and any other aspect related to a litigant's finances. In some cases, the finances of the plaintiff are at issue; in some cases, the finances of the defendant are at issue; and in some disputes, the finances of both are under scrutiny, and the forensic accountants may be asked to analyze, compare, and contrast both the plaintiff's and defendant's finances and financial condition.

Some of the typical forensic and litigation advisory services are summarized as follows:

Damage claims made by plaintiffs and in countersuits by defendants

Workplace issues, such as lost wages, disability, and wrongful death

Assets and business valuations

Costs and lost profits associated with construction delays

Costs and lost profits resulting from business interruptions

Insurance claims

Divorce and matrimonial issues

Fraud

Anti-trust actions

Intellectual property infringement and other disputes

Environmental issues

Tax disputes

The issues addressed by a forensic accountant during litigation may or may not be central to the allegations made by the plaintiff's or defense attorneys, but they may serve to provide a greater understanding of the motivations of the parties, other than those motivation claims made publicly, in court filings and in case pleadings.

THE INVESTIGATION

The Mindset: Critical Thinking and Professional Skepticism

As previously noted, we observe that individuals who commit fraud look exactly like us, the average Joe or Jane. If typical fraudsters have no distinguishing outward characteristics to identify them as such, how are we to approach an engagement to detect fraud?

It can be challenging to conduct a fraud investigation unless the investigator is prepared to look beyond his or her value system. In short, you need to think like a fraudster to catch one.

SAS No. 1 states that due professional care requires the auditor to exercise professional skepticism. Because of the characteristics of fraud, the auditor should conduct the engagement "with a mindset that recognizes the possibility that a material misstatement due to fraud could be present." It also requires an "ongoing questioning" of whether information the auditor obtains could suggest a material misstatement as a result of fraud.

Professional skepticism can be broken into three attributes:

1. Recognition that fraud may be present. In the forensic accounting arena, it is recognition that the plaintiff and/or the defendant may be masking the true underlying story that requires a thorough analysis of the evidence

2. An attitude that includes a questioning mind and a critical assessment of the evidence

3. A commitment to persuasive evidence. This commitment requires the fraud examiner or forensic accountant to go the extra mile to tie up all loose ends

At a minimum, professional skepticism is a neutral but disciplined approach to detection and investigation. SAS No. 1 suggests that an auditor neither assumes that management is dishonest nor assumes unquestioned honesty. In practice, professional skepticism, particularly recognition, requires that the fraud examiner or forensic accountant "pull on a thread."

Loose threads: When you pull on a loose thread, a knitted blanket may unravel, a shirt may pucker and be ruined, or a sweater may end up with a hole. Red flags are like loose thread: pull and see what happens; you just might unravel a fraud, ruin a fraudster's *modus operandi*, or blow a hole in a fraud scheme. Red flags are like loose thread: left alone, no one may notice, and a fraudster or untruthful litigant can operate unimpeded. A diligent fraud professional or forensic accountant who pulls on a thread may save a company millions.

Fraud Risk Factors and "Red Flags"

What do these loose threads look like in practice? Fraud professionals and forensic accountants refer to loose thread as anomalies, relatively small indicators, facts, figures, relationships, patterns, breaks in patterns, suggesting that something may not be right or that the arguments being made by litigants may not be the full story. These anomalies are often referred to as red flags.

> *Red flags are defined as a warning signal or something that demands attention or provokes an irritated reaction. Although the origins of the term* red flag *are a matter of dispute, it is believed that, in the 1300s, Norman ships would fly red streamers to indicate that they would "take no quarter" in battle. This meaning continued into the seventeenth century, by which time the flag had been adopted by pirates, who would hoist the "Jolly Roger" to intimidate their foes. If the victims chose to fight rather than submit to boarding, the pirates would raise the red flag to indicate that, once the ship had been captured, no man would be spared. Later it came to symbolize a less bloodthirsty message and merely indicated readiness for battle. From the seventeenth century, the red flag became known as the "flag of defiance." It was raised in cities and castles under siege to indicate that there would be "no surrender."*[17]

Fraud professionals and forensic accountants use the term *red flag* synonymously with *symptoms* and *badges* of fraud. Symptoms of fraud may be divided into at least six categories: unexplained accounting anomalies, exploited internal control weaknesses, identified analytical anomalies where nonfinancial data do not correlate with financial data, observed extravagant lifestyles, observed unusual behaviors, and anomalies communicated via tips and complaints.

Although red flags have been traditionally associated with fraudulent situations, forensic accountants are also on the lookout for evidence that is inconsistent with their client's version of what happened. As independent experts, forensic accountants need to look for evidence that runs counters to their client's claims. Opposing council is always looking for weaknesses in your client's case, so whether the professional is investigating fraud or other litigation issues, it is critical that the forensic accountant maintain a sense of professional skepticism, look for red flags, and pull on loose threads.

Fraud risk factors generally fall into three categories:

Motivational: Is management focused on short-term results or personal gain?

Situational: Is there ample opportunity for fraud?

Behavioral: Is there a company culture for a high tolerance of risk?

Evidence-Based Decision Making

Evidence and other legal issues are explored in depth in a later chapter. For now, we'll use the information in *Black's Law Dictionary*, which defines evidence as anything perceivable by the five senses and any proof—such as testimony of witnesses, records, documents, facts, data, or tangible objects—legally presented at trial to prove a contention and induce a belief in the minds of a jury.[18] Following the issues of critical thinking and professional skepticism is that of a commitment to evidence-based decision making. One of the best ways to ruin an investigation, fail to gain a conviction, or lose a civil case is to base investigative conclusions on logic and conjecture. Many people have tried to convict an alleged perpetrator using the "bad person" theory. The investigator concludes that the defendant is a "bad guy" or that he or she will not come off well during trial and thus must be the perpetrator or have done something wrong. Unfortunately, this approach fails to win the hearts and minds of prosecutors, plaintiff and defense lawyers, and juries, and it can result in significant embarrassment for the fraud professional or forensic accountant.

What do we mean by evidence-based decision making? Critical thinking requires the investigator to "connect the dots," taking disparate pieces of financial and nonfinancial data to tell the complete story of who, what, when, where, how, and why (if "why" can be grounded in evidence). Dots can be business and personal addresses from the Secretary of State's office, phone numbers showing up in multiple places, patterns of data, and breaks in patterns of data. These dots helps prosecutors, defense lawyers, and juries understand the full scheme under investigation. However, in order to be convincing, fraud professionals or forensic accountants must ensure that the dots are grounded in evidence that is consistent with the investigators' interpretation of that evidence. The bottom line is this: successful investigators base their conclusions and the results of their investigations on evidence.

The Problem of Intent: Investigations Centered on the Elements of Fraud

Although the fraud triangle provides an effective explanation for the conditions necessary for fraud to occur and is a source of red flags that require investigation, in order to prove fraud, the investigator has to deal with the problem of intent. Intent, like all aspects of the investigation, must be grounded in the evidence. In a fraud case, the challenge is that—short of a confession by a co-conspirator or the perpetrator—evidence of intent tends to be circumstantial. Although less famous than the fraud triangle, the elements of fraud (Figure 1-5) are critical to the investigative process, whether the engagement includes fraud or litigation issues. The elements of fraud include the act (e.g., fraud act, tort, breach of contract), the concealment (hiding the act or masking it to look like something different), and the conversion (the benefit to the perpetrator).

Provided that the investigator has evidence that the alleged perpetrator committed the act, benefited from that act, and concealed his or her activities, it becomes more difficult for accused or litigants to argue that they did not intend to cause harm or injury. Evidence of concealment, in particular, provides some of the best evidence that the act, fraud or otherwise, was intentional. In civil litigation, especially damage claims based on torts and breaches of contract, the elements of fraud remain important: for example, what evidence suggests that a tort occurred (act), how the tortuous actors benefited (convert) from their action, and how the tortuous actors concealed their tortuous activities.[19]

Evidence of the act may include that gathered by surveillance, invigilation, documentation, posting to bank accounting, missing deposits, and other physical evidence. Proof of concealment can be obtained from audits, through document examination, and from computer searches. Further, conversion can be documented using public records searches, the tracing of cash to a perpetrator's bank account, and indirectly using

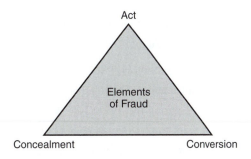

FIGURE 1-5 Elements of Fraud

financial profiling techniques. Finally, interviewing and interrogation are important methods that can be used to supplement other forms of evidence in all three areas: the act, the concealment, and the conversion. There is an ongoing debate in the profession about whether tracing money to a perpetrator's bank account is good enough evidence of conversion or whether the investigator needs to show how the ill-begotten money was used. Although tracing the money into the hands of the perpetrator or his or her bank account is sufficient, showing how the money was used provides a more powerful case and can provide evidence of attributes of the fraud triangle, such as pressure and rationalization, and other motivations included in M.I.C.E. Generally, investigators should take the investigation as far as the evidence leads.

Examples of circumstantial evidence that may indicate the act, concealment, or conversion include the timing of key transactions or activities, altered documents, concealed documents, destroyed evidence, missing documents, false statements, patterns of suspicious activity, and breaks in patterns of expected activity.

The Analysis of Competing Hypotheses (The Hypothesis-Evidence Matrix)

In most occupational fraud cases, it is unlikely that there will be direct evidence of the crime. There are rarely eyewitnesses to a fraud, and, at least at the outset of the investigation, it is unlikely that the perpetrator will come right out and confess. Therefore, a successful fraud examination takes various sources of incomplete circumstantial evidence and assembles them into a solid, coherent structure that either proves or disproves the existence of the fraud. Civil litigation, by its very nature, suggests that there are at least two competing stories, that of the plaintiff and that of the defendant. Thus, in civil litigation, as a starting point, the forensic accountant normally has at least two competing hypotheses. It is inherent in the professional to use the evidence to test each of these hypotheses, as well as others that may arise based on reasonable, objective interpretation of the evidence.

To conclude an investigation without complete evidence is a fact of life for the fraud examiner and forensic accountant. No matter how much evidence is gathered, the fraud and forensic professional would always prefer more. In response, the fraud examiner or forensic accountant must make certain assumptions. This is not unlike the scientist who postulates a theory based on observation and then tests it. When investigating complex frauds, the fraud theory approach is indispensable. Fraud theory begins with an assumption, based on the known facts, of what might have occurred. Then that assumption is tested to determine whether it is provable. The fraud theory approach involves the following steps, in the order of their occurrence:

Analyze available data.

Create hypotheses.

Test the hypotheses.

Refine and amend the hypothesis.

Draw conclusions.

The Hypothesis-Evidence Matrix The analysis of competing hypotheses is captured in a tool called the hypotheses-evidence matrix. This tool provides a means of testing alternative hypotheses in an organized, summary fashion. Consider the following question drawn from the "intelligence community" between the first Gulf War, Desert Storm, and the second Gulf War, Iraqi Freedom: Given Iraq's refusal to meet its United Nations commitments, if the United States bombs Iraqi Intelligence Headquarters, will Iraq retaliate?[20] To answer the question, three hypotheses were developed:

H1   Iraq will not retaliate.

H2   Iraq will sponsor some minor terrorist action.

H3   Iraq will plan and execute a major terrorist attack, perhaps against one or more CIA installations.

The evidence can be summarized as follows:

Saddam's public statements of intent not to retaliate.

Absence of terrorist offensive during the 1991 Gulf War.

Assumption: Iraq does not want to provoke another US war.

Increase in frequency/length of monitoring by Iraqi agents of regional radio and TV broadcasts.

Iraqi embassies instructed to take increased security precautions.

Assumption: Failure to retaliate would be an unacceptable loss of face for Saddam.

Each piece of data needs to be evaluated in terms of each hypothesis as follows:

0 = No diagnostic value for the hypothesis

− = Does not support the hypothesis

+ = Supports the hypothesis

If the United States bombs Iraqi Intelligence Headquarters, will Iraq retaliate?

Hypotheses:

H1 Iraq will not retaliate.	0	No diagnostic value for the hypothesis
H2 Iraq will sponsor some minor terrorist actions.	−	Does not support the hypothesis
H3 Iraq will plan and execute a major terrorist attack, perhaps against one or more CIA installations.	+	Supports the hypothesis

	H1	H2	H3
Saddam Hussein's public statements of intent not to retaliate.	0	0	0
Absence of terrorist offensive during the 1991 Gulf War.	+	0	−
Assumption: Iraq does not want to provoke another US war.	+	+	−
Increase in frequency/length of monitoring by Iraqi agents of regional radio and TV broadcasts.	0	+	+
Iraqi embassies instructed to take increased security precautions.	−	+	+
Assumption: Failure to retaliate would be an unacceptable loss of face for Saddam Hussein.	−	+	+

Based on the evidence evaluated, the only hypothesis without any (−) assessments is H2, with the resulting conclusion that if the United States were to bomb Iraqi Intelligence HQ, the most likely response is that Saddam and Iraq would take some minor terrorist action.

Notice also the direction of the "proof." We can never prove any hypothesis; in contrast, we can have two findings: (1) we have no evidence that directly refutes the most likely hypothesis, and (2) we have evidence that seems to eliminate the alternative hypotheses. As an example, one of the key elements of the fraud triangle is opportunity. By charting the flow of activity and interviewing personnel, it is not that we know that person A took the money but that we eliminate most employees because they had no opportunity to take the money and conceal their actions.

Consider the following scenario:

> You are an auditor for Bailey Books Corporation of St. Augustine, Florida. Bailey Books, with $226 million in annual sales, is one of the country's leading producers of textbooks for the college and university market, as well as technical manuals for the medical and dental professions. On January 28, you receive a telephone call. The caller advises that he does not wish to disclose his identity. However, he claims to be a "long-term" supplier of paper products to Bailey Books. The caller says that since Linda Reed Collins took over as purchasing manager for Bailey Books several years ago, he has been systematically "squeezed out" of doing business with the company. He hinted that he thought Collins was up to something illegal. Although you query the caller for additional information, he hangs up the telephone. What do you do now?

When you received the telephone call from a person purporting to be a vendor, you had no idea whether the information was legitimate. There could be many reasons why a vendor might feel unfairly treated. Perhaps he just lost Bailey's business because another supplier provided inventory at a lower cost. Under the fraud theory approach, you must analyze the available data before developing a preliminary hypothesis as to what may have occurred.

Analyzing the Evidence   If an audit of the entire purchasing function was deemed appropriate, it would be conducted at this time and would specifically focus on the possibility of fraud resulting from the anonymous allegation. A fraud examiner would look, for example, at how contracts are awarded and at the distribution of contracts among Bailey Books' suppliers.

Creating the Hypotheses Based on the caller's accusations, you develop several hypotheses to focus your efforts. The hypotheses range from the null hypothesis that "nothing illegal is occurring" to a "worst-case" scenario—that is, with the limited information you possess, what is the worst possible outcome? In this case, for Bailey Books, it would probably be that its purchasing manager was accepting kickbacks to steer business to a particular vendor. A hypothesis can be created for any specific allegation—i.e., a bribery or kickback scheme, embezzlement, conflict of interest, or financial statement fraud—in which evidence indicates that the hypothesis is a reasonable possibility.

Testing the Hypotheses Once the hypotheses have been developed, each must be tested. This involves developing a "what if" scenario and gathering evidence to support or disprove the proposition. For example, if a purchasing manager such as Linda Reed Collins were being bribed, a fraud examiner likely would find some or all of the following facts:

- A personal relationship between Collins and a vendor
- Ability of Collins to steer business toward a favored vendor
- Higher prices and/or lower quality for the product or service being purchased
- Excessive personal spending by Collins

In the hypothetical case of Linda Reed Collins, you—using Bailey Books' own records—can readily establish whether or not one vendor is receiving a larger proportional share of the business than similar vendors. You could ascertain whether or not Bailey Books was paying too much for a particular product, such as paper, by simply calling other vendors and determining competitive pricing. Purchasing managers don't usually accept offers of kickbacks from total strangers; a personal relationship between a suspected vendor and the buyer could be confirmed by discreet observation or inquiry. Whether or not Collins has the ability to steer business toward a favored vendor could be determined by reviewing the company's internal controls to ascertain who is involved in the decision-making process. The proceeds of illegal income are not normally hoarded; the money is typically spent. Collins's lifestyle and spending habits could be determined through examination of public documents, such as real estate records and automobile liens.

Refining and Amending the Hypotheses In testing the hypotheses, a fraud examiner or forensic accountant might find that all facts do not fit a particular scenario. If such is the case, the hypothesis should be revised and retested. In some cases, hypotheses are discarded entirely. In such cases, the professional should maintain an evidence trail for the discarded hypothesis that demonstrates what evidence was used to suggest that the hypothesis was not supported. Gradually, as the process is repeated and the hypotheses continue to be revised, you work toward what is the most likely and supportable conclusion. The goal is not to "pin" the crime on a particular individual, but rather to determine, through the methodical process of testing and revision, whether a crime has been committed and, if so, how.

Methodologies Used in Fraud and Financial Forensic Engagements

Essentially three tools are available, regardless of the nature of the fraud examination or financial forensic engagement. First, the fraud examiner or financial forensic professional must be skilled in the examination of financial statements, books and records, and supporting documents. In many cases, these provide the indicia of fraud and/or the motivations of the parties under review. Related to such evidence, the fraud examiner must also know the legal ramifications of evidence and how to maintain the chain of custody over documents. For example, if it is determined that Linda Reed Collins was taking payoffs from a supplier, checks and other financial records to prove the case must be lawfully obtained and analyzed, and legally supportable conclusions must be drawn.

The second tool used by fraud examiners or financial forensic professionals is the interview, which is the process of obtaining relevant information about the matter from those with knowledge of it. For example, in developing information about Linda Reed Collins, it might be necessary to interview her co-workers, superiors, and subordinates. In civil litigation, most interview testimony is obtained by counsel during depositions. Despite the fact that financial forensic professionals do not ask the questions, it is common for them to prepare questions for attorneys to ask, attend depositions of key financial personnel and those knowledgeable about the entity's finances, and provide the attorney with feedback and additional questions during the deposition of fact witnesses, who have financial knowledge related to the matters at hand.

FIGURE 1-6   Evidence-Gathering Order in Fraud Examinations

In a fraud examination, evidence is usually gathered in a manner that moves from the general to the specific. That rule applies both to gathering documentary evidence (Figure 1-6) and to taking witness statements (Figure 1-7). Therefore, a fraud examiner most likely starts by interviewing neutral third-party witnesses, persons who may have some knowledge about the fraud but who are not involved in the offense. For example, the fraud examiner may start with a former employee of the company. Next, the fraud examiner interviews corroborative witnesses, those people who are not directly involved in the offense but who may be able to corroborate specific facts related to the offense.

If, after interviewing neutral third-party witnesses and corroborative witnesses, it appears that further investigation is warranted, the fraud examiner proceeds by interviewing suspected co-conspirators in the alleged offense. These people are generally interviewed in order, starting with those thought to be least culpable and proceeding to those thought to be most culpable. Only after suspected co-conspirators have been interviewed is the person suspected of committing the fraud confronted. By arranging interviews in order of probable culpability, the fraud examiner is in a position to have as much information as possible by the time the prime suspect is interviewed. The methodology for conducting interviews is discussed later in the text.

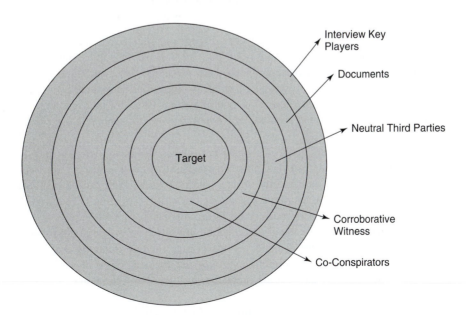

FIGURE 1-7   Fraud Interview Methodologies

Evidence-Gathering Order in Fraudulent Financial Statements and Tax Returns Interestingly, with fraudulent representations, such as materially misstated financial statements and improper tax returns, the investigator starts with the suspected perpetrator. The logic of this is simple: assuming that the person knowingly created false financial statements or tax returns, the act of falsifying is part of the concealment of the act. As such, inherently, the perpetrator has made one of the following assumptions: the auditor or investigator won't find the issue, or, if you identify red flags related to the issue, the auditor or investigator won't be smart enough to unravel the underlying evidence to determine what really happened. Essentially, the alleged perpetrator is betting his or her intellect against that of the auditor or investigator. Thus, by interviewing the suspected perpetrator at the inception of the audit, examination, or investigation, you are documenting his or her claim(s) that the financial statements are not materially misstated or that the tax return properly reflects all items of taxable income. Thus, if auditors find fraudulent financial reporting, they have caught the perpetrators in a lie and have developed further evidence of concealment.

The third tool that must be used in fraud examinations or financial forensic engagements is observation. Fraud examiners or financial forensic professionals are often placed in a position where they must observe behavior, search for displays of wealth, and, in some instances, observe specific offenses. For example, a fraud examiner might recommend a video surveillance if it is discovered that Linda Reed Collins has a meeting scheduled with a person suspected of making payoffs. In forensic litigation, the defendant might argue that the plaintiff had been reassigning his or her employees to another business venture and that action is what caused profits to fall and the business to fail. In that scenario, surveillance of operations and comparison of observation to the payroll records determine whether employees had been inappropriately reassigned. The methodology previously described can be applied to virtually any type of fraud investigation or forensic engagement.

The Importance of Nonfinancial Data

The power of using nonfinancial data to corroborate financial information cannot be overstated. How are nonfinancial data defined? They are data from any source outside of the financial reporting system that can be used to generate an alternative view of the business operation. Consider the following example, in which a husband in a divorce setting argues for a low settlement for his ex-wife:

> A large restaurant sold Southern food and beer, with beer sales being a prominent part of the restaurant. The owner reported only $50,000 of annual income from the business, yet he and his wife drove expensive cars, their children attended private schools, and the husband was buying significant amounts of real estate. Records of the local beer distributors were subpoenaed. Those records detailed exactly how much beer and the types of beer (kegs, bottles, cans, etc.) that were sold to the restaurant during the prior two years. A forensic accountant went to the restaurant and took note of all the beer prices by type. The amount of beer purchased was used to estimate sales by pricing out all of the purchases at retail. Reported sales were found to be approximately $500,000 lower than the calculated amount.[21]

In this case, the nonfinancial data were units of beer purchased and obtained from beer distributors, a source outside the normal accounting reporting function. As examples, similar approaches can be used related to laundromat electricity usage, laundromat wash and dry cycle times, natural gas produced from gas wells, tons of coal mined from underground. Nonfinancial data need not come from sources outside the company; they can be generated from operations and used by management. There has even been a patented data mining technique called NORA (nonobvious relationship analysis) created using nonfinancial data.

Essentially, economists break the world into prices and quantities (p's and q's). Fraud professionals and forensic accountants use this same approach to evaluate expected business relationships. Once critical metrics have been dissected into prices and quantities, each can be evaluated for reasonableness to determine whether the numbers make sense or further investigation is required. Nonfinancial data can then be correlated with numbers represented in the financial accounting system: financial statements and tax returns. Examples of nonfinancial data include employee records and payroll hours, delivery records, shipping records, attorney hours charged, and travel times and destinations. Any data generated outside the normal accounting system can be used to determine the reasonableness of data generated from accounting. Optimally, the nonfinancial data can be reconciled to or at least correlated with the numbers captured in the books and records.

The theory behind the power of nonfinancial data is straightforward. Essentially, managers of operational areas need accurate data to do their jobs. For example, consider managers in a petroleum-refining

business. Petroleum refining is a sophisticated mixture of chemistry and engineering. Without accurate, reliable, and detailed data, managers cannot optimize the refining processes. Although owners and those responsible for the financial data may want to create alternative perceptions of financial performance, they still want the underlying business to maximize profitability. As such, they are not likely to corrupt nonfinancial data. Further, they need to hold operational managers accountable for their performance, and they cannot achieve that goal without accurate nonfinancial data. Finally, even though some executives and financial managers are willing to cook the books, they are not willing to forgo large tax deductions and other benefits from their actions. When nonfinancial data do not reconcile or correlate to financial data, fraud examiners and financial forensic professionals should consider this a red flag. Finally, in most fraud examinations and financial forensic engagements, professionals should seek out nonfinancial data to understand fully the information included in the accounting books and records.

Graphical Tools

As noted in some of the critical thinking analyses, sometimes the only way to figure something out is to use graphical tools—such as who knows who (linkages), who is connected with what business, how the scheme works (flow diagram), who must be involved (links and flows), what the important events are (timelines). During the investigation, these graphical representations, even handwritten ones, can provide important clues and enhance the investigator's understanding of fact and events, interpret evidence, and otherwise draw meaning from seemingly disparate pieces of data. They can also show weaknesses in the case—places where additional evidence is required in order provide a complete evidence trail.

Although completed during the investigation as a work-in-progress tool, the same graphics are often reused during the formal communication process at or near the conclusion of an investigation. Graphical representations can let nonprofessionals and those with less time on the investigation know what happened. Even though catching the bad guy or reconstructing what happened is the primary role of the fraud examiner or financial forensic professional, a successful career requires that the investigators be able to communicate their results in both written and verbal form. The challenge for the typical professional in this field is that they understand and embrace numbers; however, the legal world is one of words. Thus, the successful investigator must move from a world of numbers to the less familiar world of words.

Written format includes meticulously developed work papers and evidence binders, written reports, and written presentation materials. Oral reports include interviewing and interrogation skills, summarizing investigation status and outcomes to attorneys, prosecutors, judges, and juries. Graphical tools, such as link charts, flow charts, commodity and money flow diagrams, timelines, and other graphical representations, are both important investigative tools and excellent communication tools. These tools are examined in more detail in the digital forensic accounting chapter. For now, it is important to note that the investigator needs to ground these graphics in the evidence and needs to maintain backup that indicates where the data came from.

The Importance of the Story Line: Who, What, Where, When, How, and Why

To be successful, the investigator must be able to explain—to prosecutors, attorneys, juries, judges, and other actors in the investigative process—the outcome of the investigation: who, what, when, where, how, and, optimally, why (if the evidence lends itself to explanations of why, such as the perceived pressure, rationalization, and M.I.C.E.). Investigations centered on the elements of fraud (act, concealment, and conversion) that include indications of the fraud triangle, particularly perceived opportunity and M.I.C.E., have the greatest chances of being successful, assuming that these investigative outcomes are grounded in the evidence.

Although fraud examination and financial forensics use evidence-based decision making, critical thinking skills are essential to understanding what the numbers mean. The ability to use nonfinancial information, as well as financial data gathered from the books and records, to tell a compelling story is crucial to success. As fraud examiners or financial forensic professionals move forward in their investigations, they shift from a world grounded in numbers to one where words carry the day. As such, when fraud examiners or forensic accountants reach the point of drawing conclusions, they must be able to tell a complete story that explains who, what, where, when, how, and, possibly, why. Essentially, they need to think like a journalist who is telling a news story.

Teamwork and Leadership

Because thinking like a fraudster is challenging, use of investigative teams can be an effective tool. For example, for larger fraud or financial forensic investigations, one might be part of a team. In those cases, investigators should use other professionals by brainstorming, interpreting the meaning of evidence, helping develop new fraud theories, and working to connect the dots. Even if the fraud examiner or forensic professional is working as the only person "following the money," the broader team might include lawyers, managers, paralegals, and other forensic investigators. All play an integral role as team members and should be consulted regularly.

Being a successful team player requires at least two attributes. First, each team member must be professionally competent at his or her assigned task. In order for your teammates to be able to rely on your work, they must believe that your work will be completed at the highest levels. One of the criteria included in the ACFE code of ethics is that CFEs "at all times, shall exhibit the highest level of integrity in the performance of all professional assignments, and will accept only assignments for which there is reasonable expectation that the assignment will be completed with professional competence." Professional competence is one pillar of successful teamwork. The second major attribute of teamwork is character. Your teammates must be able to count on you as a person. The following gives examples of teamwork attributes that are required for successful completion of fraud and forensic investigations.

Competence

    a. Contributing high-quality ideas

    b. Contributing high-quality written work

    c. Demonstrating a professional level of responsibility to the team: "get it done"

Character

    a. Attending meetings, prepared and on time with something to contribute

    b. Being available to meet with teammates

    c. Completing a fair share of the total workload

    d. Listening to teammates' ideas and valuing everyone's contributions

At a minimum, being a good team participant means being a trusted team member. That allows each teammate to contribute to the overall success of the team. Interestingly, leadership is also important to successful team operations. Leadership not only refers to the person with the assigned role of leader, but to individual team members. Thus, good teammates also demonstrate leadership when their unique abilities are needed by the team.

FRAUD EXAMINATION METHODOLOGY

Fraud examination is a methodology developed by ACFE for resolving fraud allegations from inception to disposition, including obtaining evidence, interviewing, writing reports, and testifying. Fraud examination methodology requires that all fraud allegations be handled in a uniform legal fashion and that they be resolved in a timely manner. Assuming there is sufficient reason (predication) to conduct a fraud examination, specific steps are employed in a logical progression designed to narrow the focus of the inquiry from the general to the specific, eventually centering on a final conclusion. The fraud examiner begins by developing a hypothesis to explain how the alleged fraud was committed and by whom, and then, at each step of the fraud examination process, as more evidence is obtained, that hypothesis is amended and refined. Fraud examiners, as designated by the ACFE, also assist in fraud prevention, deterrence, detection, investigation, and remediation.[22]

Predication

Predication is the totality of circumstances that lead a reasonable, professionally trained, and prudent individual to believe that a fraud has occurred, is occurring, and/or will occur. All fraud examinations must be based on proper predication; without it, a fraud examination should not be commenced. An anonymous tip or complaint, as in the Linda Reed Collins example cited earlier, is a common method for uncovering fraud and is generally considered sufficient predication. Mere suspicion, without any underlying circumstantial evidence, is not a sufficient basis for conducting a fraud examination.

Fraud Prevention and Deterrence

Given the cost of fraud, prevention and deterrence are typically more cost beneficial than attempting to remediate a fraud that has already occurred. Fraud prevention refers to creating and maintaining environments in which the risk of a particular fraudulent activity is minimal and opportunity is eliminated, given the inherent cost-benefit trade-off. When fraud is prevented, potential victims avoid the costs associated with detection and investigation.[23]

Fraud deterrence refers to creating environments in which people are discouraged from committing fraud, although it is still possible. The 2005 *Federal Sentencing Guideline Manual* defines deterrence as a clear message sent to society that repeated criminal behavior will aggravate the need for punishment with each recurrence. Deterrence is usually accomplished through a variety of efforts associated with internal controls and ethics programs that create a workplace of integrity and encourage employees to report potential wrongdoing. Such actions increase the perceived likelihood that an act of fraud will be detected and reported. Fraud deterrence can also be achieved through the use of continuous monitoring/auditing software tools. Fraud deterrence is enhanced when the perception of detection is present and when potential perpetrators recognize that they will be punished when caught.

Fraud Detection and Investigation

Fraud detection refers to the process of discovering the presence or existence of fraud. Fraud detection can be accomplished through the use of well-designed internal controls, supervision, and monitoring and the active search for evidence of potential fraud. Fraud investigation takes place when indicators of fraud, such as missing cash or other evidence, suggest that a fraudulent act has occurred and requires investigation to determine the extent of the losses and the identity of the perpetrator.[24]

Remediation: Criminal and Civil Litigation and Internal Controls

Remediation is a three-pronged process: (1) the recovery of losses through insurance, the legal system, or other means; (2) support for the legal process as it tries to resolve the matter in the legal environment; and (3) the modification of operational processes, procedures, and internal controls to minimize the chances of a similar fraud recurring.

REVIEW QUESTIONS

1-1 Define fraud and identify a potentially fraudulent situation.

1-2 Differentiate between fraud and abuse.

1-3 Describe the services that a forensic accountant might provide related to a marital dispute.

1-4 Explain the differences between an audit, fraud examination, and forensic accounting engagement.

1-5 Explain the theory of the fraud triangle.

1-6 List the legal elements of fraud.

1-7 Identify common fraud schemes.

1-8 Give examples of nonfraud forensic and litigation advisory engagements.

1-9 Describe the fraud examiner/forensic accountant's approach to investigations.

1-10 Explain fraud examination methodology.

ENDNOTES

1. Bandler, James, and Ann Zimmerman, "A Wal-Mart Legend's Trail of Deceit," *Wall Street Journal*, April 8, 2005.
2. Black, Henry Campbell. *Black's Law Dictionary*, 5th ed St. Paul, MN: West Publishing Co., 1979, p. 792.
3. A tort is a civil injury or wrongdoing. Torts are not crimes; they are causes of action brought by private individuals in civil courts. Instead of seeking to have the perpetrator incarcerated or fined, as would happen in a criminal case, the plaintiff in a tort case generally seeks to have the defendant pay monetary damages to repair the harm that he or she has caused.
4. Black, p. 300.
5. *Black's Law Dictionary*, 6th ed., p. 563.
6. Fowler, Tom, "Skilling Gets 24 Years in Prison for Enron Fraud." Chron.com (October 23, 2006).
7. ACFE, "Cooking the Books: What Every Accountant Should Know," Austin, TX, 1993.

8. National Commission on Fraudulent Financial Reporting, "Report to the National Commission on Fraudulent Financial Reporting," NY, 1987.

9. Except from NIJ Special Report: Education and Training in Fraud and Forensic Accounting: A Guide for Educational Institutions, Stakeholder Organizations, Faculty and Students (December 20, 2005).

10. The AICPA Forensic and Litigation Services Committee developed the definition. See also Crumbley, D. Larry, Lester E. Heitger, and G. Stevenson Smith, *Forensic and Investigative Accounting*, 2005.

11. Adapted from Crumbley, D. Larry, Lester E. Heitger, and G. Stevenson Smith, *Forensic and Investigative Accounting*, 2005. See also: AICPA Business Valuation and Forensic & Litigation Services.

12. Source unknown.

13. Adapted from "Education and Training in Fraud and Forensic Accounting: A Guide for Educational Institutions, Stakeholder Organizations, Faculty and Students," a National Institute of Justice project completed at West Virginia University.

14. Adapted from *Occupational Fraud and Abuse*, Joseph T. Wells, Obsidian Publishing Company (1997).

15. According to the ACFE 2008 Report to the Nation, males perpetrate fraud 59.1 percent of the time versus 40.9 percent for females.

16. Some trust violators (fraudsters) are fired with or without paying restitution. Thus, in some cases, the fraud perpetrator is pathological in his or her work, moving from organization to organization. In those cases, some estimates indicate that the fraudster will victimize each new company within twelve to thirty-six months.

17. See http://www.answrs.com/red%20flag.

18. ACFE's Fraud Examiners Manual, Section 2.601.

19. In civil litigation, all the plaintiff has to prove is that the defendant was liable and that the plaintiff suffered damages. Thus, although the elements of fraud are not required, they provide a good framework to investigator allegations in most financial litigation environments.

20. The authors are grateful to West Virginia University Professor Jason Thomas who first shared this example with the forensic accounting and fraud examination students.

21. DiGabriel, James (ed.), *Forensic Accounting in Matrimonial Divorce* (2005), pp. 51–52.

22. Adapted from ACFE *Fraud Examiners Manual*.

23. Albrecht, W. Steve, *Fraud Examination*, 2003.

24. Whether to use the term *fraud investigation* or *fraud examination* is a matter of debate among practitioners. Some, including the ACFE, prefer the term *fraud examination* because it encompasses prevention, deterrence, detection, and remediation elements in addition to investigation. Others prefer *fraud investigation* because the term *examination* has a special meaning for auditors and accountants. The Technical Working Group's position is that either term is acceptable as long as the full term, including the word *fraud* is used: fraud examination or fraud investigation.

CHAPTER 2

CAREERS IN FRAUD EXAMINATION AND FINANCIAL FORENSICS

LEARNING OBJECTIVES

After reading this chapter, you should be able to

2-1 Discuss employment trends in fraud examination and financial forensics and the reasons for these trends.

2-2 Identify employment opportunities for fraud examination and financial forensics specialists and other related professions.

2-3 Define the role of fraud examination and financial forensic skills related to management and those charged with corporate governance responsibilities.

2-4 List professional organizations that support fraud examination and financial forensics professionals and their certifications.

2-5 Discuss international opportunities in fraud examination and financial forensics.

2-6 Describe the role of education in fraud examination and financial forensics.

2-7 Explain the role of research in the fraud examination and financial forensics professions.

CRITICAL THINKING EXERCISE

Why are manhole covers round?[1]

This critical thinking exercise is often supported with visual props such as square and round pieces of plastic containers with lids. Students are encouraged to manipulate the different shaped containers to see if they can determine the answer. This critical thinking activity demonstrates the need to experience your investigative data and evidence using all of your five senses: sight, touch, hearing, taste, and smell. While we don't do much tasting or smelling in forensic accounting, the point is an important one. To be successful, fraud professionals and forensic accountants must immerse themselves in the evidence to answer the essential questions—who, what, where, when, how, and why—of an investigation.

As a result of highly publicized financial scandals and heightened concerns over money laundering associated with terrorism and drug trafficking, the auditor's and accountant's responsibility for detecting fraud within organizations has come to the forefront of the public's awareness. Successful fraud examinations and well-executed forensic investigations may be the difference between whether perpetrators are brought to justice or allowed to remain free. In most cases, success depends upon the knowledge, skills, and abilities of the professionals conducting the work. Consequently, the demand for qualified professionals with education, training, and experience in fraud and financial forensics has increased.

The academic and professional disciplines of fraud examination and financial forensics embraces and creates opportunities in a number of related fields, including accounting, law, psychology, sociology, criminology, intelligence, information systems, computer forensics, and the greater forensic science fields. Each group of these professionals plays an important role in fraud prevention, deterrence, detection, investigation, and remediation.

BACKGROUND

Recent corporate accounting and financial scandals have led to increased legal and regulatory requirements, such as the Sarbanes–Oxley Act of 2002 and the Emergency Economic Stabilization Act of 2008 (EESA). These requirements address internal controls for detecting and deterring fraud, encourage financial statement auditors to be more aggressive in searching for fraud, and have challenged accountants, corporate governance, and other professionals to conduct fraud risk assessments to mitigate its occurrence.

One result has been an increased demand for entry-level and seasoned practitioners. Furthermore, professionals practicing in the traditional areas of tax, audit, management, information systems, government, not-for-profit, external (independent), and internal audit are expected to have a greater understanding of fraud and financial forensics.

The threat of terror activities, public corruption, and organized criminal activities has heightened the need for professionals who are properly trained to investigate and resolve issues and allegations associated with these acts. The emphasis here is on law enforcement and pursuing criminal charges. These engagements are often associated with the Department of Justice, the Department of Homeland Security, the Bureau of Alcohol, Tobacco, Firearms and Explosives, and other federal, state, and local law enforcement agencies. These agencies use legislation, such as the USA PATRIOT (Uniting and Strengthening America by Providing Appropriate Tools Required to Intercept and Obstruct Terrorism) Act, to focus on white-collar crime, money laundering, and terrorist financing.

There is also a growing demand for forensic and litigation advisory services related to damages, divorce, valuations, construction delays, antitrust, lost wages, business interruption, intellectual property infringement, insurance claims, environmental issues, tax evasion, wrongful death, reconstruction, and litigation consulting, to name a few.

Another area is the increasing victimization of individuals targeted in fraud schemes (e.g., identity theft). While the most common victims of such fraud are the fraudster's family and friends, international criminal organizations have developed identity theft and similar frauds into "big business." Raising awareness of fraud prevention techniques and assisting in remediation procedures are crucial to effectively addressing this growing problem in our global society.

The demand for students who have specialized qualifications in fraud and financial forensics has grown significantly and is likely to continue to grow. The increasing demand is creating an unprecedented opportunity for those professionals who develop the knowledge, skills, and abilities associated with fraud examination and financial forensics. For example, *The Wall Street Journal* stated that "forensic accounting is a particularly hot field" (*CPA Recruitment Intensifies as Accounting Rules Evolve*, March 22, 2005).[2] Moreover, each of the Big 4 firms is now recruiting accounting students with some exposure to financial forensics. The need for competent staffing at the SEC, at PCAOB, and in private industry is outpacing the supply. According to author Cecily Kellogg, the anticipated growth in the field is expected to be nearly 25 percent over the next ten years. Kellogg goes on to suggest that it is hard to envision a more stable and in-demand career.[3]

PLACES WHERE FRAUD EXAMINERS AND FINANCIAL FORENSIC SPECIALISTS WORK

Figure 2-1 captures several anticipated career paths for fraud examination and financial forensics.[4] Identified career paths include positions at professional service firms, corporations, and government or regulatory agencies and in law enforcement or legal services. Opportunities for fraud and forensic accounting professionals in professional services firms include external auditing, internal audit outsourcing, and forensic and litigation advisory services.

To become a successful professional requires additional specialized training and continuing professional development. Specialized training for entry-level staff helps them achieve the required level of *competency* within a specific organization. Some of the specialized training may be organization-specific, while other training may be task-specific. Further, experienced staff persons are required to maintain *proficiency* in a dynamic environment through continuing professional education courses.

Professional Services Firms

Fraud examiners and financial forensic specialists work in accounting and professional service firms that provide fraud deterrence, detection, investigation, and remediation services to a variety of organizations. In addition, professional service firms, specialized service, and boutique services firms provide litigation advisory services to individuals, as well as to businesses and other entities.

Public and Private Companies

Internal audit, corporate compliance, security, and internal investigation units all operate within companies and utilize the skills of the fraud examiner and the financial forensic professional.

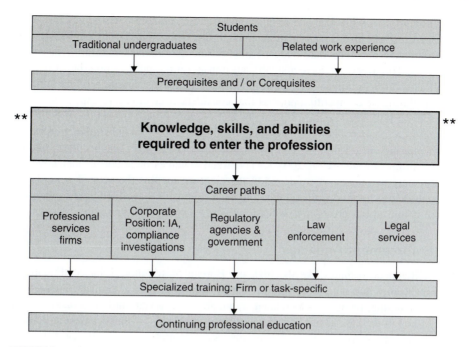

FIGURE 2-1 Career Paths

According to the Association of Certified Fraud Examiners' 2008 "Report to the Nation," internal auditors discover a significantly greater percentage of fraud than external auditors do. Many internal audit departments employ certified fraud examiners (CFE) and financial forensic specialists.

Compliance and risk analysis for SOX, environmental, or health and safety (OSHA) issues are handled by professionals as part of legal and regulatory oversight to prevent misconduct, including fraud. These professionals utilize their skills in terms of compliance and risk assessment as a proactive measure against wrongdoing.

Security, loss prevention, risk management, and investigation professionals with corporations and business entities often have responsibility to protect assets and detect instances of their misuse.

Other business sectors that frequently employ fraud professionals include the insurance, real estate, banking (including investment banking), securities, money management, credit card, health care, construction, and defense contracting industries.

Regulatory Agencies

Regulatory agencies such the Securities and Exchange Commission (SEC), the Public Company Accounting and Oversight Board (PCAOB), and others employ professionals with specialized knowledge, skills, training, education, and experience in fraud examination and financial forensics. Other government organizations, such as the Departments of Defense, Labor, and Homeland Security, may also hire fraud and financial forensic specialists.

Government and Nonprofits

Government accountants and auditors work in the public sector, maintaining and examining the records of government agencies and auditing private businesses and individuals whose activities are subject to government regulations or taxation. Those employed by the federal government may work as Internal Revenue Service agents.

One of the main missions of the Internal Revenue Service (IRS) is to identify unreported or under-reported taxable income and the tax-payment deficiencies related to that income. Penalties and interest levied by the IRS on delinquent tax payments have a deterrent effect on the public. Agents are typically at the front line in detecting fraudulent taxpayer activities, whether in regard to payroll taxes, excise taxes, income taxes, or any other taxes. In recent years, the IRS has devoted increasingly greater resources to develop a workforce skilled in fraud detection and remediation. After IRS agents have sufficiently identified deliberate and egregious instances of tax evasion, the cases are further pursued by IRS professionals in the Criminal Investigation Division (CID), who are more like law enforcement personnel than they are auditors.

Professionals with financial forensic and fraud examination skills may also work at federal government agencies, like the Government Accountability Office (GAO), as well as at the state or local level. They administer and formulate budgets, track costs, and analyze programs for compliance with relevant regulations. This work can have a significant impact on the public good, but it may also be very political, as well as subject to bureaucratic obstruction. Government accounting offers advancement in most organizations through a competitive process that considers education and experience. Places that hire heavily at the federal level include the Department of Defense, the GAO, and the IRS. In addition, offices of the state and local comptrollers hire individuals with accounting knowledge or experience.

Nonprofit entities may include public school systems, charities, hospitals, and other healthcare facilities. According to the ACFE 2008 RTTN, fraud schemes at nonprofit and government agencies lasted approximately two years, as compared to the eighteen months they lasted at public companies. The challenges, related to fraud examination and financial forensics, have bled over to the public sector, and many of these organizations are hiring professionals with expertise in these areas.

Law Enforcement Agencies

Law enforcement agencies like the FBI, the Bureau of Alcohol, Tobacco, Firearms and Explosives, the Postal Inspectors, and others hire forensic accountants and fraud examiners. These professionals investigate money laundering, identity theft–related fraud, arson for profit, and tax evasion.

Although the SEC is not considered to be part of our law enforcement structure because they do not have criminal prosecutorial powers, they develop criminal cases and forward them to the Department of Justice for prosecution.

FROM THE FRAUDSTER'S PERSPECTIVE

Why White-Collar Criminals Do Not Fear Today's FBI

As the heartless, cold-blooded criminal CFO of Crazy Eddie, the Federal Bureau of Investigation was a respected adversary that filled my stomach with butterflies and caused me many sleepless nights as I feared their tenacity to successfully investigate my crimes. Unfortunately, the white-collar criminals of today have much less to fear from the FBI. According to an article in the *New York Times*,

The Federal Bureau of Investigation is struggling to find enough agents and resources to investigate criminal wrongdoing tied to the country's economic crisis, according to current and former bureau officials.

The bureau slashed its criminal investigative work force to expand its national security role after the Sept. 11 attacks, shifting more than 1,800 agents, or nearly one-third of all agents in criminal programs, to

terrorism and intelligence duties. Current and former officials say the cutbacks have left the bureau seriously exposed in investigating areas like white-collar crime, which has taken on urgent importance in recent weeks because of the nation's economic woes.

The pressure on the F.B.I. has recently increased with the disclosure of criminal investigations into some of the largest players in the financial collapse, including Fannie Mae and Freddie Mac. The F.B.I. is planning to double the number of agents working financial crimes by reassigning several hundred agents amid a mood of national alarm. But some people inside and out of the Justice Department wonder where the agents will come from and whether they will be enough.

Even if the FBI doubles the number of agents working financial crimes, it does not solve the main problem of effectively investigating white-collar crime. White-collar crime investigations are often complicated cases that take long periods of time and require enormous resources—and most important, experienced agents.

Top-notch, experienced FBI agents are leaving the bureau for higher-paying private industry jobs as soon as they qualify for retirement, causing a brain drain within the FBI. As white-collar crime becomes increasingly complex, our government must revise employee retention policies to compete with the private sector.

The FBI lacks adequate legal, technological, and personnel resources to meet its responsibilities to investigate white-collar crime. According to the *New York Times* article:

From 2001 to 2007, the F.B.I. sought an increase of more than 1,100 agents for criminal investigations

apart from national security. Instead, it suffered a decrease of 132 agents, according to internal F.B.I. figures obtained by The New York Times. *During these years, the bureau asked for an increase of $800 million, but received only $50 million more. In the 2007 budget cycle, the F.B.I. obtained money for a total of one new agent for criminal investigations.*

Too often, complicated white-collar crime investigations fall apart because the FBI lacks experienced agents with the patience, knowledge, and experience to put together a successful criminal investigation. According to the *New York Times* article:

In some instances, private investigative and accounting firms are now collecting evidence, taking witness statements and even testifying before grand juries, in effect preparing courtroom-ready prosecutions they can take to the F.B.I. or local authorities.

"Anytime you bring to the F.B.I. a case that is thoroughly investigated and reduce the amount of work for investigators, the likelihood is that they will take the case and present it for prosecution," said Alton Sizemore, *a former F.B.I. agent who is a fraud examiner for Forensic Strategic Solutions in Birmingham, Ala.*

In other words, in order for the FBI to give serious consideration to many cases, such cases must be presented to the FBI neatly gift-wrapped and on a silver platter.

The criminals of today are elated by an underresourced and relatively inexperienced FBI. As a result, the cancer of white-collar crime continues to destroy the integrity of our great capitalist economic system.

Sam E. Antar (former Crazy Eddie CFO
and a convicted felon),
Sunday, October 19, 2008.
Adapted from http://whitecollarfraud.blogspot.com.

Law Firms

Law firms often use forensic accountants to help divorcees uncover a spouse's hidden assets and damages associated with contract disputes and tortuous interference. Most of these forensic professionals are employed as consultants and expert witnesses, but some law firms that do a significant amount of work in this area hire professionals to work on their staff. These forensic professionals can complete initial investigations and develop preliminary findings before a firm's clients incur considerable costs associated with hiring outside consultants. Forensic accountants may uncover instances of companies cooking the books to falsely inflate company profits, minimize losses, or divert large amounts of money to company managers.

RELATED PROFESSIONS

Law

The forensic professional needs to know about the law as it relates to mail and wire fraud, violations of the RICO Act (racketeering influence and corrupt organizations), money laundering, false claims, bankruptcy fraud, tax evasion, conspiracy, and obstruction of justice. Individual rights are protected by laws governing investigative techniques and the admissibility of evidence, including the chain of custody, search and seizure, interviewing, and surveillance. These laws require that "probable cause" is established prior to intrusive searches in order to comply with the statutory rules of evidence. Further, fraud examiners and forensic professionals need to be qualified as "experts" to offer evidence at trial.

Psychology

Forensic psychology is the application of the principles of psychology to the criminal justice system. Because fraud requires intent, in some cases it is necessary for forensic psychologists to delve into the psychological motives of white-collar criminals. These professionals must also address the legal issue of competency and whether a defendant was sane at the time the crime occurred.

The knowledge, skills, and abilities of forensic psychologists are used in various circumstances, such as when treating mentally ill offenders, consulting with attorneys (e.g., picking a jury), analyzing a criminal's mind and intent, and practicing within the civil arena. A forensic psychologist may chose to focus her career on researching—to give only two examples—how to improve interrogation methods or how to evaluate eyewitness testimony. Forensic psychologists have also been used to effectively design correctional facilities. With regard to fraud and financial issues, forensic psychology can help us to understand who commits fraud and why.

Sociology

Forensic sociology uses analysis of sociological data for decision making by the courts and other judicial agencies. The forensic sociologist may also serve as an expert witness in a court of law. Functions for these specialists include the profiling of offenders, unlawful discrimination, spousal abuse, pornography, toxic torts, and premises liability. Emphasis is given to the relationship between the standards of validity and reliability in sociology and the rules of evidence. Related to financial crimes, sociology helps us understand the context of these types of crimes. Data provided in the ACFE's biannual "Report to the Nation" helps us put occupational fraud and related crimes into context by addressing such issues as

- Is the incidence of fraud increasing or decreasing?
- What types of fraud are being committed?
- What is the cost of fraud?
- How is fraud committed?
- How is fraud detected?
- What are the victim profiles?
- What are the perpetrator profiles?

Criminology

Criminology is the study of crime and criminals and includes theories of crime causation, crime information sources, and the behavioral aspects of criminals. Beyond examining and attempting to understand human behavior and theories of crime causation, criminology considers the various types of crimes such as white-collar crime, organizational crime, and occupational crime and concerns itself with fraud prevention and deterrence issues. One of the most important contributions of criminology to the study of fraud is criminologist Donald Cressey's fraud triangle. Finally, criminology considers the "punishments" aspects of the remediation process.

Intelligence

When one thinks of business intelligence, developing corporate competitive intelligence systems and counterintelligence programs to prevent industrial espionage normally comes to mind. However, the prevention, deterrence, detection, and investigation of fraud is closely aligned with the skill set used by the intelligence community. Fraud examiners and forensic accountants take disparate pieces of information and pull them together into a coherent case that tells the story of who, what, when, where, how, and why. In addition, these professionals need to identify potential sources of evidence and then methodically collect that evidence for use in the case. Sources might include documents, interviews, surveillance tapes, public records, and data obtained from the Internet.

Information Systems and Computer Forensics

The impact of information systems in the areas of fraud examination and financial forensics is enormous. Information technology (IT) reaches every aspect of our lives today, and the digital environment plays a crucial role in fraud-related crimes and investigations due to the following factors:

- Increased use of information technology in business
- Large businesses centered on technology, such as Dell, IBM, Google, eBay, and Microsoft
- Increased data use by independent auditors, fraud examiners, and forensic accountants
- Increased exploitation of information technology by fraudsters and cybercriminals

IT professionals, including those with fraud and forensic accounting expertise, need to ensure that the organization's digital environment is adequately protected.

Electronic information feeding the financial reporting process needs to be timely and accurate, and reasonable controls should be in place to support organizational viability in a digital world and its associated threats and opportunities.

Information Systems Governance and Controls Information systems governance and controls are concerned with the prevention, deterrence, and detection of fraud in a digital environment. An organization's information technology group must adhere to best practices consistent with those of the organization as a whole. Information Systems Audit and Control Association (ISACA) is a global organization for information governance, control, security, and audit whose information systems auditing and control standards are followed by practitioners worldwide. ISACA defines IT governance as a set of principles to assist enterprise leaders in their responsibility to ensure that (1) the organization's information technology needs are aligned with the business's goals and deliver value, (2) the organization's performance is measured, (3) the organization's resources are properly allocated, and (4) the organization's risks are mitigated. Best practices associated with IT governance should include preventive countermeasures against fraud and cybercrime, such as continuous auditing and proactive fraud auditing.

Risk assessment is a critical aspect of good corporate governance and the same concept is applicable in an information technology environment. An IT risk assessment should identify risks associated with the digital environment. That assessment requires that IT leadership know and understand how IT prevents and detects internal and external attacks, including those associated with the commission of frauds, computer crimes, and cybercrimes. As part of that risk assessment, IT professionals need to identify and understand the ways in which IT systems are typically exploited during fraud and cybercrime, how IT systems are used to facilitate fraud concealment, and how IT security is commonly breached or circumvented.

Cyberforensics The increased role of information technology in fraud and cybercrime results in a corresponding increase in the need for organizational professionals with digital knowledge, skills, and abilities—in operations systems, but also in fraud, computer crime, and cybercrime. Evidence about who, what, where, when, and how often exists in digital form—in some cases, exclusively. Furthermore, most state-of-the-art digital forensics tools and techniques have come into existence in the last ten to twenty years. The pervasiveness of digital media and information in virtually every aspect of an organization's life illustrates the increased need for cyberforensic specialists. Cyberforensics involves capture, preservation, identification, extraction, analysis, documentation, and case preparation related to digital data and events.

Digital Evidence Capturing electronic information is the first step in the investigation of digital evidence. Because it is possible to hinder a successful legal outcome if the legal requirements associated with digital capture are not followed, a successful cyberforensics investigation requires a professional who has the required technical background in computer technology and systems and who is also familiar with the relevant rules of the legal system and investigations. For example, turning on a confiscated computer can make all the evidence on that computer inadmissible in a courtroom, because this simple act alters the hard drive, thus breaking the chain of custody. Only those persons with specialized training, experience, and appropriate professional certifications should initially capture digital evidence.

The sources of digital evidence are evolving and expanding but include cell phones, personal digital assistants (PDAs), Blackberrys and similar phones, trinkets with digital storage (watches, USB pens, digital cameras, etc.), jump drives, media cards, e-mail, voicemail, CDs, DVDs, printer memory, RAM, slack space, removable drives, iPods/MP3 players, and XM/Sirius radio players. There are also such conventional sources as laptops, office computers, home computers and external drives, servers on the Internet that store e-mail messages, and the entity's own servers. Special software and hardware tools are available to capture digital evidence, such as SF-5000, RoadMASSter, and write blockers.

Electronic Detection and Investigation Notwithstanding the utilization of traditional detection and investigation techniques applied in a digital environment, some additional tools and techniques are also important. Those tools and techniques include data mining software useful for data extraction and analysis and continuous monitoring and auditing software. Most data extraction and analysis tools can retrieve, filter, extract, sort, and analyze data from accounting databases as well as identify gaps, duplicates, missing information, and statistical anomalies.

Cybercrime The Department of Justice defines cybercrime as any violation of criminal law that involves knowledge of computer technology for its perpetration, investigation, or prosecution. Cybercrime knowledge, skills, and abilities include a basic understanding of the types of crimes, as well as of special laws and relevant criminal code. Some typical cybercrimes include unauthorized computer intrusion, hacking, infrastructure attacks, digital credit card theft, online/e-mail extortion, viruses, worms, identity theft, online gambling, theft of computers, online narcotic sales, cyberterrorism, and telecommunications fraud.

Other Forensic Science Fields

Fraud examination and forensic accounting also utilize knowledge, skills, and abilities from other forensic sciences such as crime scene investigation, forensic chemistry, and biology. For example, in crime scene investigation, the investigator has three primary goals: protection of evidence (e.g., crime scene tape), preservation of evidence, and collection of evidence. Although an accounting department and the IT systems cannot be "roped off" with crime scene tape, it is important for the fraud examiner or forensic accountant to be thinking about three concepts: (1) protecting the evidence by using backup tapes of the computer system collected and protected in such a way as to be admissible in court, (2) preserving the evidence by preventing physical and electronic corruption and destruction, and (3) collecting the evidence in sufficient amounts and in a manner that protects the chain of custody. These types of lessons are routinely available from our colleagues in other forensic fields.

Related Career Titles In short, forensic accountants and fraud examiners have opportunities in a number of fields and under a number of titles wherein they combine their forensic and investigative training with other forms of expertise:

Actuary	FBI Agent	Administrator
Internal Auditor	CIA Agent	Business Teacher
Auditor	Financial Analyst	Contract Administrator
Consumer Credit Officer	Methods/Procedures Specialist	Financial Investment Analyst
Bank Examiner	Claims Adjuster	EDP Auditor
Controller	Collection Agent	Insurance Investigator
Benefits/Compensation	Governmental Accountant	Inventory Control Specialist
IRS Investigator	Personal Financial Planner	IRS Investigator
Budgetary Control Analyst	Commercial Banker	Property Accountant
Credit and Collection	Industrial Accountant	Systems Analyst
Loan Administrator	Plant Accountant	Tax Compliance Specialist
Entrepreneur	Professor	Treasurer
Loan/Consumer Credit	Systems Analyst	Treasury Management Specialist
Management Consultant	Systems Accountant	Tax Supervisor/Auditor
Chief Financial Officer	Budget Accountant	Treasury Management
Accountant, Public Practice	Claim Adjuster/Examiner	

BUSINESS ADMINISTRATION, MANAGEMENT, AND CORPORATE GOVERNANCE

FROM THE FRAUDSTER'S PERSPECTIVE

Advice to President-Elect Barack Obama from a Convicted Felon about Combating White-Collar Crime

To President-Elect Barack Obama:
While our capital markets require reform, no amount of regulation or oversight can be effective unless those persons charged with carrying it out have the proper amount of experience, knowledge, competence, and professional skepticism to successfully perform their respective jobs and responsibilities. As the cold-blooded and heartless criminal CFO of Crazy Eddie, I had no fear of oversight from outside or independent board members and our external auditors. I took advantage of their lack of requisite skills, knowledge, and experience to effectively carry out my crimes. If you want to see capitalism succeed as an engine for our future economic

prosperity, I respectfully ask you to first consider the issue of competence before looking at the issue of regulation and oversight.

Window Dressing Boards of Directors

We need better standards of qualification for public company board members. Too often, company boards are packed with people with great résumés, but such persons have no specialized experience and training to effectively carry out their functions, or boards are packed with cronies of company management. Instead, we must require that board members have the proper amount of specialized education, background, and experience necessary to perform their duties effectively. We do not need well-meaning, intelligent people serving in

positions they are not well suited for, since in many cases they make ineffective board members. The time for "window dressing" must end.

Today, too many board members are appointed for window dressing purposes only, rather than because of their specific competence to carry out their duties. Michelle Leder's blog, Footnoted.org, once noted:

> So where do former members of the House and Senate, not to mention Governors and former Cabinet members go when they exit from the political stage? Many of them wind up filling seats on boards of directors.

For example, your new Chief of Staff Rahm Emanuel was appointed by President Bill Clinton to serve on Freddie Mac's (NYSE: FRE) board of directors after serving in Clinton's administration. I am assuming that Mr. Emanuel took the job and served on Freddie Mac's board from 2000 to 2001 with the best of intentions. However, like many other well-meaning but gullible board members, he found himself in the wrong place at the wrong time, in the hands of an unscrupulous management team.

According to the SEC complaint filed against Freddie Mac:

> Freddie Mac misreported its net income in 2000, 2001 and 2002 by 30.5 percent, 23.9 percent and 42.9 percent, respectively. Furthermore, Freddie Mac's senior management exerted consistent pressure to have the company report smooth and dependable earnings growth in order to present investors with the image of a company that would continue to generate predictable and growing earnings.

> "As has been seen in so many cases, Freddie Mac's departure from proper accounting practices was the result of a corporate culture that sought stable earnings growth at any cost," said Linda Chatman Thomsen, the SEC's Director of Enforcement. "Investors do not benefit when good corporate governance takes a back seat to a single-minded drive to achieve earnings targets."

Rahm Emanuel was not named in the SEC's complaint against Freddie Mac. However, in a statement before the Senate Committee on Banking, Housing, and Urban Affairs, Acting Director of the Office of Federal Housing Enterprise Oversight, James B. Lockhart III noted:

> For the most part, the same long-tenured shareholder-elected Directors oversaw the same CEO, COO, and General Counsel of Freddie Mac from 1990 to 2003. The non-executive Directors allowed the past performance of those officers to color their oversight. Directors should have asked more questions, pressed harder for resolution of issues, and not automatically accepted the rationale of management for the length of time needed to address identified weaknesses and problems. The oversight exercised by the Board might have been more vigorous if there had been a regular turnover of shareholder-elected Directors or if Directors had not expected to continue to serve on the Board until the mandatory retirement age. Conversely, the terms of the presidentially appointed Directors are far too

> short, averaging just over 14 months, for them to play a meaningful role on the Board. The position is an anachronism that should be repealed so shareholders can elect all Directors. The Board of Directors was apprised of control weaknesses, the efforts of management to shift income into future periods and other issues that led to the restatement, but did not recognize red flags, failed to make reasonable inquiries of management, or otherwise failed in its duty to follow up on matters brought to its attention.

The problem is that intelligent and well-meaning boards of directors are often duped by unscrupulous company management teams who take advantage of their lack of requisite skills and professional cynicism.

Prospective qualified board members must know how to make effective inquiries and spot red flags. They must know how to ask questions, whom to direct their questions to, and how to handle false and misleading answers by management with effective follow-up questions. Such skills only come from adequately qualified board members who have proper training, education, and experience *before* they join company boards.

Lack of Truly Independent and Properly Qualified Audit Committee Members

So-called independent audit committee members of boards of directors are *less* independent and *less* competent than the external auditors whom they oversee. Too many audit committee members have no formal educational background in accounting and auditing, and no specialized training in fraud detection.

Many "independent" board members own stock and receive stock options in their respective companies, while independent external auditors *cannot* own stock or receive stock-based compensation from their audit clients. Owning company stock and receiving stock-based compensation provides a disincentive to effective independent audit committee oversight of financial reporting and can adversely affect an audit committee member's professional skepticism. Audit committee members cannot be considered truly independent if they own company stock or receive stock-based compensation. I suggest that our securities laws be amended to require truly independent and adequately qualified audit committees.

Lack of Properly Trained Auditors

External auditors receive too little or no training in forensic accounting, fraud detection, or criminology. Most CPAs never take a single college-level course devoted exclusively to issues of white-collar crime or internal controls, and many important subjects covered in the CPA licensing exam are learned *after* graduation, in a cram CPA exam review course.

College-level accounting education needs to be reformed to teach future CPAs the necessary tools to do battle in audits against corporate crooks who take advantage of their lack of skills. We should mandate that a larger proportion of the continuing professional education required by CPAs to maintain their licenses be devoted to issues of white-collar crime and fraud detection.

Not Enough Law Enforcement Resources Devoted to White-Collar Crime

While I never feared Crazy Eddie's board of directors and auditors, I did fear the Securities and Exchange Commission and the Federal Bureau of Investigation. However, I doubt that many criminals have such fear for the SEC and FBI today.

Both the SEC and FBI are underresourced and overwhelmed, and as a result, they are unable to successfully investigate very many complicated white-collar crime cases unless such cases are handed to them on a silver platter by others. The most experienced SEC and FBI personnel are leaving government work for better-paying private sector jobs. Therefore, if you really want criminals to think twice before executing their crimes, I suggest that you beef up our nation's investigative and law enforcement resources.

Our capital markets depend on the integrity of financial information that is supposed to be insured by external auditors, audit committees, and consistently effective law enforcement. Inadequately trained independent external auditors, the first line of defense for ensuring the integrity of financial reporting, are supervised by even less competent and less independent audit committees. On top of that, our regulators and law enforcement agencies lack the required resources to effectively prosecute many crimes enabled by the lack of effective audits and company oversight by boards of directors. Therefore, we face a perfect storm for disaster, as the cancer of white-collar crime destroys our economic fabric and inflicts a collective harm on our great society.

If you want capitalism to succeed as an engine of prosperity for our great nation, I ask you to heed my advice based on my experience as a cold-blooded convicted felon.

Respectfully:

Sam E. Antar (former Crazy Eddie CFO and a convicted felon)

PS: While Rahm Emanuel may not have been an effective board member of Freddie Mac, he can provide valuable insight to you about the perils of lack of effective oversight by boards of directors. After all, the wisest people are those that learn from past mistakes.

In addition, I will continue to provide you with more unsolicited advice from time to time. You can learn a lot from a convicted felon who scammed the system and took advantage of gullible human beings in ways your advisors never dreamed of.

Sunday, November 16, 2008. http://whitecollarfraud.blogspot.com/2008/11/advise-to-president-elect-barack-obama.html

In recent years, corporate governance, including boards of directors, audit committees, executive management, internal audit, external audit, the government, and regulators have been intensely scrutinized by those concerned with the public's interests. Corporate governance simply means the way a corporation is governed through proper accountability for managerial and financial performance. The integrity and quality of the capital market primarily depends on the reliability, vigilance, and objectivity of corporate governance. Particularly, with respect to financial statement fraud, there has been a great deal of concern about the issue of corporate governance and accountability of publicly traded companies. The corporate governance concept has advanced from the debates on its relevance to how best to protect investor interests and effectively discharge oversight responsibility over the financial reporting process. High-profile financial statement frauds allegedly committed by major corporations such as Waste Management, Phar-Mor, ZZZZ Best, Crazy Eddie, Sunbeam, Enron, WorldCom, Adelphia, HealthSouth, Lucent, Xerox, MicroStrategy, Cendant, Rite Aid, and KnowledgeWare have renewed the interest and increasing sense of urgency about more responsible corporate governance and more reliable financial statements.

There has also been a growing awareness that corporate governance can play an important role in preventing and detecting financial statement and other types of fraud and corporate malfeasance. Management's ethical behavior and operating style can have a significant impact on the effectiveness of corporate governance. An operating style that shows excessive risk-taking, for example, is generally a red flag for fraud.

The following outlines the basics of fraud risk management for those charged with corporate governance: the board of directors, the audit committee, management, internal auditors, and external auditors. "Managing the Business Risk of Fraud: A Practical Guide," developed by the IIA, AICPA, and ACFE, suggests that with regard to corporate malfeasance, fraud risk management needs to include five key features:[5]

1. A written policy that outlines the fraud risk management program

2. (Targeted) fraud risk assessment of the exposure of the organization to potential schemes that need mitigation.

3. Prevention techniques

4. Detection techniques:

   - In place in case preventative measures fail
   - In place to address unmitigated risks (where the cost of mitigation exceeds the benefits)
   - In place to address concerns over collusion and management override

5. A reporting process

Boards of Directors

One of the primary roles of the board of directors in corporate America is to create a system of checks and balances in an organization through its authority to hire and monitor management and evaluate their plans and decisions and the outcomes of their actions. The separation of ownership and control in corporations requires the board of directors to (1) safeguard assets and invested capital, (2) review and approve important management decisions, (3) assess managerial performance, and (4) allocate rewards in ways that encourage shareholder value creation.

The board of directors, as an important internal component of corporate governance, receives its authority from shareholders who use their voting rights to elect board members. The board of directors' primary responsibility is one of gatekeeper, an ultimate internal control mechanism to protect the interests of shareholders, creditors, and other stakeholders. Therefore, one goal is to minimize the ability of management to expropriate shareholder value through financial statement and other forms of fraud and financial malfeasance.

Audit Committees

The audit committee is a subcommittee of the board of directors and has the primary responsibility of monitoring the financial reporting and auditing processes. Thus, reviewing the effectiveness of internal controls to ensure the reliability of financial reports is an essential part of the audit committee's role. The audit committee oversees the adequacy and effectiveness of the company's internal control structure to ensure

1. The efficiency and effectiveness of operations
2. The reliability of financial reporting
3. Compliance with applicable laws and regulations

Additionally, the audit committee is charged with addressing the risk of collusion and management override of internal controls. In February 2005, the American Institute of Certified Public Accountants (AICPA) issued a report titled "Management Override of Internal Controls: The Achilles' Heel of Fraud Prevention." It notes that management may override internal controls and engage in financial statement fraud by (1) recording fictitious business transactions and events or altering the timing of recognition of legitimate transactions, (2) recording and reversing biased reserves through unjustifiable estimates and judgments, and (3) changing the records and terms of significant or unusual transactions.

To be proactive, the audit committee should ensure that

- Audit committee members have knowledge, education, awareness, and sophistication concerning the various fraudulent management override and collusive schemes that may be perpetrated by management
- Both the internal and external audit groups have knowledge, education, awareness, and sophistication concerning the various fraudulent management override and collusive schemes that may be perpetrated by management
- The audit committee has reviewed the comprehensive fraud risk assessment provided by management and also considers how collusive fraud and management override schemes are mitigated and detected
- The audit committee periodically participates in continuing education programs that can prepare its members to appraise management's fraud risk assessment
- The audit committee identifies who has the specific responsibility for the collusive and management override fraud risk assessment process: its members, the internal audit group, or the independent audit group?
- The audit committee is interacting with personnel beyond executive management and asking the tough questions of knowledgeable employees, financial managers, internal auditors, and external auditors
- The audit committee has a protocol for acting on allegations of unethical and potentially fraudulent conduct

Senior/Executive Management

Management is primarily responsible for the quality, integrity, and reliability of the financial reporting process, as well as the fair presentation of financial statements in conformity with generally accepted accounting principles (GAAP). Management is also accountable to users of financial statements, particularly investors and creditors, to ensure that published financial statements are not misleading and are free of material errors, irregularities, and fraud.

To effectively discharge its financial reporting responsibility, management should (1) identify and assess the circumstances, conditions, and factors that can lead to fraud, (2) assess and manage the risk of fraud associated with the identified circumstances, conditions, and factors, and (3) design and implement an adequate and effective internal control process for prevention and detection of fraud.

Internal Audit

Internal auditors are an important part of corporate governance and, if assigned, can be tasked and positioned to help ensure a reliable financial reporting process. Internal auditors' day-to-day involvement with both operational and financial reporting systems and the internal control structure provides them with the opportunity to perform a thorough and timely assessment of high-risk aspects of the internal control environment and financial reporting process. However, the effectiveness of internal auditors to prevent and detect fraud depends largely on their organizational status and reporting relationships. Financial statement fraud is normally perpetrated by the top management team. As such, internal audit standards issued by the Institute of Internal Auditors (IIA) require that internal auditors be alert to the possibility of intentional wrongdoing, errors, irregularities, fraud, inefficiency, conflicts of interest, waste, and ineffectiveness in the normal course of conducting an audit. These professionals are also required to inform the appropriate authorities within the organization of any suspected wrongdoing and follow-up to ensure that proper actions are taken to correct the problem.

External (Independent) Audit

Financial statement fraud has been, and continues to be, the focus of the auditing profession. During the early 1900s, external auditors viewed the detection of fraud, particularly financial statement fraud, as the primary purpose of their financial audit. During the twentieth century, the auditing profession moved from acceptance of fraud detection as their primary responsibility to the mere expression of an opinion on the fair presentation of the financial statements. Recently, the accounting profession directly addressed the external auditor's responsibility to detect financial statement fraud in its Statement on Auditing Standards (SAS) No. 99, titled "Consideration of Fraud in a Financial Statement Audit." SAS No. 99 requires independent auditors to obtain information to identify financial statement fraud risks, assess those risks while taking into account the entity's programs and controls, and respond to the results of this assessment by modifying their audit plans and programs.

Auditors in identifying and assessing the risks of material financial statement fraud should (1) make inquiries of the audit committee or other comparable committee of the board of directors, senior executives, legal counsel, chief internal auditors, and others charged with government governance within the client organization to gather sufficient information about the risk of the fraud, (2) communicate with the audit committee, management, and legal counsel about the allegations of fraud and how they are addressed, (3) consider all evidence gathered through analytical procedures that is considered unusual, unexpected, or even suspiciously normal based on the financial condition and results of the business, and (4) consider evidence gathered through the audit of internal control of financial reporting that may suggest the existence of one or more fraud risk factors, and that adequate and effective internal controls did not address and account for the detected risk. Auditors should inquire of the audit committee, management, and others charged with government governance about the entity's antifraud policies and procedures and whether they are in writing, updated on a timely basis, implemented effectively, and enforced consistently.

Regulators and Governing Bodies

Regulatory reforms in the United States are aimed at improving the integrity, safety, and efficiency of the capital markets while maintaining their global competitiveness. Regulations should be perceived as being fair and in balance in order to inspire investor confidence. Regulations, including SOX, are aimed at protecting investors. The provisions of SOX- and SEC-related rules include strengthening the corporate

board and external auditor independence, instituting executive certifications of both financial statements and internal controls, and creating the PCAOB to oversee the accounting profession. These provisions helped to rebuild investor confidence in public financial information.

The various corporate governance participants are being held to greater levels of accountability to create an environment where the risk of fraud is mitigated, at least to levels below the materiality threshold. As such, individuals with knowledge, skills, and abilities in these areas are in demand, which has created employment opportunities for those professionals who have developed this type of expertise.

PROFESSIONAL ORGANIZATIONS AND THEIR RELATED CERTIFICATIONS

Association of Certified Fraud Examiners (ACFE)

The ACFE is the world's premier provider of antifraud training and education. Together with its nearly 50,000 members, the ACFE is reducing business fraud worldwide and inspiring public confidence in the integrity and objectivity within the profession. The mission of the Association of Certified Fraud Examiners is to reduce the incidence of fraud and white-collar crime and to assist the membership in fraud detection and deterrence. To accomplish its mission, the ACFE

- Provides bona fide qualifications for certified fraud examiners through administration of the CFE Examination
- Sets high standards for admission, including demonstrated competence through mandatory continuing professional education
- Requires certified fraud examiners to adhere to a strict code of professional conduct and ethics
- Serves as the international representative for certified fraud examiners to business, government, and academic institutions
- Provides leadership to inspire public confidence in the integrity, objectivity, and professionalism of certified fraud examiners

Certified Fraud Examiner (CFE) The ACFE established and administers the Certified Fraud Examiner (CFE) credential. The CFE credential denotes expertise in fraud prevention, detection, and deterrence. There are currently more than 20,000 CFEs worldwide. As experts in the major areas of fraud, CFEs are trained to identify the warning signs and red flags that indicate evidence of fraud and fraud risk. To become a CFE, one must pass a rigorous examination administered by the ACFE, meet specific education and professional requirements, exemplify the highest moral and ethical standards, and agree to abide by the CFE Code of Professional Ethics. A certified fraud examiner also must maintain annual CPE requirements and remain an ACFE member in good standing. The FBI officially recognizes the CFE credential as a critical skill set for its diversified hiring program, and the U.S. Department of Defense officially recognizes the CFE credential as career advancement criteria. the Forensic Audits and Special Investigations Unit (FSI) of the Government Accountability Office announced that all professionals in the FSI unit must obtain CFE credentials.

American Institute of Certified Public Accountants (AICPA)

The AICPA is the national professional organization for all certified public accountants. Its mission is to provide members with the resources, information, and leadership to enable them to provide valuable services in the highest professional manner to benefit the public as well as employers and clients. In fulfilling its mission, the AICPA works with state Certified Public Accountant (CPA) organizations and gives priority to those areas where public reliance on CPA skills is most significant. The CPA is still one of the most recognized and valued professional certifications of any profession and is the standard bearer for accountants working in the United States.

Furthermore, the Forensic and Valuation Services (FVS) Center of the AICPA is designed to provide CPAs with a vast array of resources, tools, and information about forensic and valuation services. The center has information and resources for the following issues:

- Analytical guidance
- Family law

- Antifraud/forensic accounting
- Laws, rules, standards, and other guidance
- Bankruptcy
- Litigation services
- Business valuation
- Practice aids and special reports
- Document retention and electronic discovery
- Practice management
- Economic damages
- Fair value for financial reporting

Accredited in Business Valuation (ABV) The mission of the ABV credential program is to provide a community of business valuation experts with specialized access to information, education, tools, and support that enhance their ability to make a genuine difference for their clients and employers. The ABV credential program allows credentialholders to brand or position themselves as CPAs who are premier business valuation service providers. ABV credentialholders differentiate themselves by going beyond the core service of reaching a conclusion of value to also create value for clients through the strategic application of this analysis. The ABV credential program is designed to

- Increase public awareness of the CPA as the preferred business valuation professional
- Increase exposure for CPAs who have obtained the ABV credential
- Enhance the quality of the business valuation services that members provide
- Ensure the continued competitiveness of CPAs versus other valuation services providers through continuous access to a comprehensive community of resources and support
- Increase the confidence in the quality and accuracy of business valuation services received from CPA/ABV providers

Certified Information Technology Professional (CITP) A Certified Information Technology Professional (CITP) is a certified public accountant recognized for technology expertise and a unique ability to bridge the gap between business and technology. The CITP credential recognizes technical expertise across a wide range of business and technology practice areas. The CITP credential is predicated on the facts that in today's complex business environment, technology plays an ever-growing role in how organizations meet their business obligations, and that no single professional has a more comprehensive understanding of those obligations than a certified public accountant. An increasingly competitive global marketplace has organizations clamoring for new technologies and the capacities, efficiencies, and advantages they afford. While IT professionals have the technical expertise necessary to ensure that technology solutions are properly deployed, they lack the CPA's perspective and ability to understand the complicated business implications associated with technology. The CITP credential encourages and recognizes excellence in the delivery of technology-related services by CPA professionals and provides tools, training, and support to help CPAs expand their IT-related services and provide greater benefit to the business and academic communities they serve.

Certified in Financial Forensics (CFF) In May 2008, the AICPA's governing council authorized the creation of a new CPA specialty credential in forensic accounting. The Certified in Financial Forensics (CFF) credential combines specialized forensic accounting expertise with the core knowledge and skills that make CPAs among the most trusted business advisers. The CFF encompasses fundamental and specialized forensic accounting skills that CPA practitioners apply in a variety of service areas, including bankruptcy and insolvency, computer forensics, economic damages, family law, fraud investigations, litigation support, stakeholder disputes, and valuations. To qualify, a CPA must be an AICPA member in good standing, have at least five years' experience practicing accounting, and meet minimum requirements in relevant business experience and continuing professional education. The objectives of the CFF credential program are to

- Achieve public recognition of the CFF as the preferred forensic accounting professional
- Enhance the quality of forensic services that CFFs provide
- Increase practice development and career opportunities for CFFs
- Promote members' services through the Forensic and Valuation Services (FVS) Web site

Forensic CPA Society (FCPAS)

The Forensic CPA Society was founded July 15, 2005. The purpose of the society is to promote excellence in the forensic accounting profession. One of the ways the society has chosen to use to accomplish this is the Forensic Certified Public Accountant (FCPA) certification. The use of this designation tells the public and the business community that the holder has met certain testing and experience guidelines and has been certified not only as a CPA, but also as a forensic accountant.

Forensic Certified Public Accountant (FCPA). An individual must be a licensed CPA, CA (Chartered Accountant) or another country's CPA equivalent to be eligible to take the five-part certification test and receive the FCPA designation. If an individual is a licensed CPA and a CFE, Cr.FA, or CFF, he or she is exempt from taking the certification exam and can automatically receive the FCPA. Once an individual has earned his or her FCPA, he or she must take twenty forensic accounting– or fraud-related hours of continuing professional education (CPE) each year to keep his or her membership current.

Information Systems Audit and Control Association (ISACA)

Since its inception, ISACA has become a pace-setting global organization for information governance, control, security, and audit professionals. Its IS auditing and IS control standards are followed by practitioners worldwide. Its research pinpoints professional issues challenging its constituents, and its Certified Information Systems Auditor (CISA) certification is recognized globally and has been earned by more than 60,000 professionals since inception. The Certified Information Security Manager (CISM) certification uniquely targets the information security management audience and has been earned by more than 9,000 professionals. The Certified in the Governance of Enterprise IT (CGEIT) designation promotes the advancement of professionals who wish to be recognized for their IT governance–related experience and knowledge and has been earned by more than 200 professionals. It publishes a leading technical journal in the information control field (the *Information Systems Control Journal*) and hosts a series of international conferences focusing on both technical and managerial topics pertinent to the IS assurance, control, security, and IT governance professions. Together, ISACA and its affiliated IT Governance Institute lead the information technology control community and serve its practitioners by providing the elements needed by IT professionals in an ever-changing worldwide environment.

Certified Information Systems Analyst (CISA) The technical skills and practices that CISA promotes and evaluates are the building blocks of success in the field. Possessing the CISA designation demonstrates proficiency and is the basis for measurement in the profession. With a growing demand for professionals possessing IS audit, control, and security skills, CISA has become a preferred certification program by individuals and organizations around the world. CISA certification signifies commitment to serving an organization and the IS audit, control, and security industry with distinction.

Certified Information Security Manager (CISM). The Certified Information Security Manager (CISM) certification program is developed specifically for experienced information security managers and those who have information security management responsibilities. CISM is unique in the information security credential marketplace because it is designed specifically and exclusively for individuals who have experience managing an information security program. The CISM certification measures an individual's management experience in information security situations, not general practitioner skills. A growing number of organizations are requiring or recommending that employees become certified. For example, the U.S. Department of Defense (DoD) mandates that information assurance personnel be certified with a commercial accreditation approved by the DoD. CISM is an approved accreditation, signifying the DoD's confidence in the credential. To help ensure success in the global marketplace, it is vital to select a certification program based on universally accepted information security management practices. CISM delivers such a program.

Institute of Internal Auditors (IIA)

Established in 1941, the Institute of Internal Auditors (IIA) is an international professional association of more than 150,000 members with global headquarters in Altamonte Springs, Florida. Worldwide, the IIA is recognized as the internal audit profession's leader in certification, education, research, and technical guidance. The IIA is the internal audit profession's global voice, recognized authority, acknowledged leader, chief advocate, and principal educator. Members work in internal auditing, risk management, governance,

internal control, information technology audit, education, and security. The mission of the IIA is to provide dynamic leadership for the global profession of internal auditing. Although the institute does not have a designation directly associated with fraud examination and forensic accounting, its dedication to this area is demonstrated in its training programs, its work with the Institute for Fraud Prevention, and its leadership in developing (along with the ACFE and AICPA) "Managing the Risk of Fraud: A Practical Guide."

Certified Internal Auditor. The Certified Internal Auditor (CIA) designation is the only globally accepted certification for internal auditors and remains the standard by which individuals demonstrate their competency and professionalism in the internal auditing field. Candidates leave the program with educational experience, information, and business tools that can be applied immediately in any organization or business environment.

National Association of Certified Valuation Analysts (NACVA)

NACVA's Financial Forensics Institute (FFI) was established in partnership with some of the nation's top authorities in forensic accounting, law, economics, valuation theory, expert witnessing, and support fundamentals to offer practitioners comprehensive training in all facets of forensic financial consulting. The Certified Forensic Financial Analyst (CFFA) designation offers five different pathways to acquire the specialized training.

Financial Litigation Path. The Financial Litigation specialty program requires the five-day Litigation Bootcamp for Financial Experts training, designed to provide participants with a foundation in the role of a financial expert. Among other requirements, applicants must have been involved in eight different litigation matters, for three of which the applicant gave deposition or expert testimony. (This experience requirement can be met by attending the three-day Financial Forensics Institute-sponsored course Expert Witness Bootcamp.)

Forensic Accounting Path. The Forensic Accounting specialty program requires attendance at the five-day Forensic Accounting Academy, plus the three-day litigation workshop Forensics Workshop for Financial Professionals. Among other requirements, applicants must have also been involved in ten engagements or have 1,000 hours of experience in the applicable field.

Business and Intellectual Property Damages Path. The Business and Intellectual Property Damages specialty program requires attendance at the five-day Business and Intellectual Property Damages Workshop (BIPD), plus the three-day Forensics Workshop for Financial Professionals. Among other requirements, applicants must have also been involved in ten engagements or have 1,000 hours of experience in the applicable field.

Business Fraud—Deterrence, Detection, and Investigation Path. The Business Fraud Deterrence, Detection, and Investigation specialty program requires attendance at the five-day Business Fraud—Deterrence, Detection, and Investigation Training Center (FDDI), plus the three-day Forensics Workshop for Financial Professionals.

Matrimonial Litigation Support Path. The Matrimonial Litigation Support specialty program requires attendance at the five-day Matrimonial Litigation Support Workshop, plus the three-day Forensics Workshop for Financial Professionals. Among other requirements, applicants must have also been involved in ten engagements in the applicable field or have 1,000 hours of experience providing valuation services, 200 hours of which were in the applicable field.

NACVA also has four certifications: Accredited Valuation Analyst (AVA), Certified Forensic Financial Analyst (CFFA), Certified in Fraud Deterrence (CFD), and Certified Valuation Analyst (CVA).

Society of Financial Examiners (SOFE)

The Society of Financial Examiners is a professional society for examiners of insurance companies, banks, savings and loans, and credit unions. The organization has a membership of over 1,600 representing the fifty states, the District of Columbia, Canada, Aruba, and the Netherlands Antilles. SOFE is the one organization in which financial examiners of insurance companies, banks, savings and loans, and credit unions come together for training and to share and exchange information on a formal and informal level. The society was established in 1973 to establish a strict code of professional standards for members engaged in the examination of financial institutions, to promote uniform ethical standards to engender employer and public confidence to the degree that those interested can identify professionally qualified practitioners, and to promote and enforce minimum requirements of conduct, training, and expertise for members engaged in financial examination. SOFE offers three professional designations, which may be earned by completing

extensive requirements including the successful completion of a series of examinations administered by the society. The designations are Accredited Financial Examiner, Certified Financial Examiner, and Automated Examiner Specialist.

INTERNATIONAL FRAUD EXAMINATION AND FINANCIAL FORENSICS

Chartered Accountant (CA), one equivalent of the CPA around the globe, is the title used by members of certain professional accountancy associations in the British Commonwealth nations and Ireland. The term "chartered" comes from the Royal Charter granted to the world's first professional body of accountants upon their establishment in 1854.

The Association of Certified Fraud Examiners, which administers the certified fraud examiner (CFE) credential, has international activities in more than 120 countries around the world. Other international certifications related to the fraud examination and forensic accounting specializations include the following:

- AAFM: The American Academy of Financial Management offers sixteen separate financial certifications recognized worldwide
- MFP: Master Financial Professional
- CWM: Chartered Wealth Manager
- CTEP: Chartered Trust and Estate Planner
- CAM: Chartered Asset Manager
- RFS: Registered Financial Specialist in Financial Planning
- CPM: Chartered Portfolio Manager
- RBA: Registered Business Analyst
- MFM: Master Financial Manager
- CMA: Chartered Market Analyst
- FAD: Financial Analyst Designate
- CRA: Certified Risk Analyst
- CRM: Certified in Risk Management
- CVM: Certified Valuation Manager
- CCC: Certified Cost Controller (offered in the Middle East, Europe, Asia, and Africa)
- CCA: Certified Credit Analyst (offered in Asia, the Middle East, and Africa)
- CCA: Chartered Compliance Analyst
- CITA: Certified International Tax Analyst (for lawyers or LLM holders)
- CAMC: Certified Anti-Money Laundering Consultant (for lawyers or LLM holders)
- Ch.E.: Chartered Economist (for PhDs and double master's degree holders)
- CAPA: Certified Asset Protection Analyst

EDUCATION: BUILDING KNOWLEDGE, SKILLS, AND ABILITIES IN FRAUD EXAMINATION AND FINANCIAL FORENSICS

The progression of knowledge, skills, and abilities for fraud and forensic accounting for entry-level professionals is presented in Figure 2 (found in the DOJ's National Institute of Justice model curriculum project "Education and Training in Fraud and Forensic Accounting: A Guide for Educational Institutions, Stakeholder Organizations, Faculty and Students"; available at www.ncjrs.gov/pdffiles1/nij/grants/217589.pdf). This section and Figure 2 (NCJRS) were developed with the extensive use of the DOJ's project. This project was also highlighted in the November 2008 volume of *Issues in Accounting Education*.

As noted above, fraud examination and financial forensics embraces many more disciplines than accounting. Those disciplines and professionals include the law, psychology, sociology, criminology, intelligence, information systems, computer forensics, and the greater forensic science fields. One of the

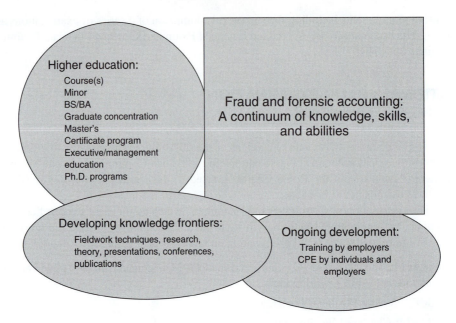

FIGURE 2-2 Fraud Examination and Forensic Accounting: A Continuum of Knowledge, Skills, and Abilities

challenges for individuals with these backgrounds is that most fraud and financial forensics engagements require at least some knowledge of accounting, finance, and economics because of the nature of the work. Thus, the first two columns in Figure 2 (NCJRS) address prerequisite accounting, auditing, and business law knowledge that is considered necessary for the fraud and financial forensics curriculum. Students with an accounting degree will have met these prerequisites as part of their degree requirements. Students who do not have an accounting degree will need to obtain the prerequisite knowledge and skills before embarking on the fraud examination and financial forensics curriculum. That prerequisite knowledge, skills, and abilities can be developed through experience, and many educational programs recognize past professional accomplishments.

Figure 2-2 depicts the continuum of knowledge development, transfer (education), and use in practice.

Prerequisite Knowledge and Skills

The knowledge and skills students should obtain when they study fraud and financial forensics include the following:[6]

Basic Accounting Concepts

- Key concepts of accounting such as the definitions of assets, liabilities, stockholders' equity, revenue and expenses, revenue recognition, expense measurement, reliability, objectivity, verifiability, materiality, accruals, deferrals, etc.
- Basic financial statement presentation and appropriate disclosure
- The effects of debits and credits on account balances. This understanding is essential in identifying fraud schemes and financial statement manipulation. Students need to be able to analyze accounts (i.e., recognize a normal balance for each type of account and ascertain how a given transaction would affect each account balance) and determine whether each component has been examined directly or indirectly for under- and overstatement
- Account balance analysis for both over- and understatement
- Basic ratio analysis—students need to be able to calculate ratios and interpret the results, such as identifying trends across time and unusual variances in comparison to key industry ratios and other benchmarks (skills normally covered in entry-level accounting courses)

Basic Auditing Concepts

- The basic elements of auditing, including professional skepticism in evaluating statements or representations made

- Different types and quality of audit evidentiary matter and how to evaluate types of evidence (definitive, circumstantial, direct, corroborative, and conflicting)
- Relevant current accounting and auditing standards and the roles and responsibilities of standard-setting, professional, and regulatory bodies
- Organization and development of working papers

Transaction Processing Cycles and Control Environment

- Internal control concepts and an ability to recognize potential weaknesses in a company's internal control structure
- Corporate governance and culture (e.g., tone at the top), including ethics and entity-level controls
- Operational processes and transaction flows within an organization, and tracing transactions (cash and noncash) from source documents to initial entry in the accounting system through the various subledgers and ledgers to reported financial statements. The documentation of processes and transaction flows includes both manual activities and those that incorporate automated information systems

Basic Finance and Economics

- The time value of money
- Net present value concept
- Basic working of markets
- An understanding of opportunity costs
- Valuation techniques

Business Law Concepts

- The fundamental legal principles associated with contracts, civil and criminal matters, social goals associated with the legal system, and the role of the justice system
- Securities and other laws that demonstrate how fraud and fraudulent financial reporting violate the law and how the regulatory, professional, civil, and law enforcement systems operate to prevent, detect, and deter violations
- Ethical duties and legal responsibilities associated with confidentiality

General Business Communications Skills and Business Ethics

- Communications: The second column in Figure 2 (NCJRS) identifies two courses that are often included as business core or business electives: general communications and business ethics. These courses are not listed as prerequisites, but are highly recommended. Fraud and forensics professionals must have strong written and oral presentation skills. Therefore, a general communications course is extremely beneficial. Students without formal training in oral and written communication may wish to complete such a course before entering a fraud and forensics program
- Ethics: Many states specify a business ethics course as a requirement to sit for the CPA exam. Business majors are likely to have completed a business ethics course as part of their degree requirements. Because ethics is such an important part of the fraud and financial forensics curriculum, students who have the opportunity to take a business ethics course are advised to do so

Basic Computer Skills

- Familiarity with computers, computer operations, and general business software packages such as Word, WordPerfect, Excel, Quattro, and PowerPoint. Enhanced computer skills associated with Visio, IDEA, ACL, and Analysts Notebook's I-2 are also beneficial

Exposure Material/Course

Column 3 of Figure 2 (NCJRS) shows the exposure to fraud and forensic accounting topics that may be covered in an undergraduate or graduate accounting curriculum. Colleges, universities, and other curriculum providers may use this outline of topical areas as a guide to provide exposure to students by incorporating coverage in current offerings or may add a single course/training module. Some of these topics are covered

briefly—for example, as one chapter in the auditing text or one chapter in the accounting systems text. Because the coverage of these topics in traditional texts is relatively minimal, they should be reinforced and explored in greater depth as part of the fraud and forensic accounting curriculum.

In-Depth Course Material

Columns 4 and 5 of Figure 2 (NCJRS) provide an overview of the model curriculum areas required for in-depth study. Entry-level fraud and forensic accounting professionals should possess knowledge, skills, and abilities in the following areas:

1. Criminology
2. The legal, regulatory, and professional environment
3. Ethics
4. Fraud and financial forensics:

   - Asset misappropriation, corruption, false representations, and other frauds
   - Financial statement fraud
   - Fraud and forensic accounting in a digital environment

5. Forensic and litigation advisory services

THE ROLE OF RESEARCH IN A PROFESSION

The long-term success of any professional endeavor is derived from three sources: research, practice, and education. Research drives professional innovation. Practitioners in the field implement the products of research (concepts, ideas, theories, and evidence) by applying, testing, and refining theory and research findings in the "real world." Finally, educators create learning frameworks through which students benefit from the combined efforts of practice and research. For fraud examination and forensic accounting to be a viable specialization over the long term, research opportunities and recognition are required to take the profession to the highest levels possible. To date, auditing and behavioral research focusing on fraud and forensic accounting issues has been published in many journals. In other related business disciplines such as economics and finance, forensically grounded research has also been completed and published.

Descriptive research, such as the ACFE's biannual "Report to the Nation," has been funded and completed by such organizations as the ACFE, the AICPA, the large accounting firms, the U.S Department of Treasury, the IRS, the ATF, the Secret Service, the U.S. Postal Service, and others. Topics have typically answered questions such as

- Is the incidence of fraud increasing, or decreasing?
- What types of fraud are being committed?
- What is the cost of fraud?
- How is fraud committed?
- How is fraud detected?
- What are the victim profiles?
- What are the perpetrator profiles?

The Institute for Fraud Prevention (IFP)

The Institute for Fraud Prevention (IFP) is a voluntary association of organizations and researchers dedicated to fraud prevention and orientated toward research and education as a basis for developing antifraud best practices.

As documented by the ACFE's 2008 "Report to the Nation," despite the tremendous impact fraud and corruption have on our economy, there is relatively little research available on the costs of fraud and how and why fraud occurs. Similarly, there exists no repository for gathering, storing, and disseminating fraud-related research findings and descriptive statistics. The primary goal of the IFP is to develop our

understanding of the causes and effects of fraud by serving as a catalyst for the exchange of ideas among top antifraud practitioners, government officials, and academics.

The IFP fulfills its mission in two ways. First, member organizations support research by selecting projects and providing funding, guidance, and data that will help us better understand fraud with a long-term goal of reducing its incidence and effects. Second, the IFP's mission is to provide independent, nonpartisan expertise on antifraud policies, procedures, and best practices. The IFP was founded by the ACFE and the AICPA. A select group of intellectual partners, including the FBI, the GAO, the U.S. Postal Inspectors, the National White-Collar Crime Center (NW3C), and the Council of Better Business Bureaus, have provided guidance to the IFP.

The IFP identifies potentially fruitful research projects in the disciplines of accounting, law, psychology, sociology, criminology, intelligence, information systems, computer forensics, and the greater forensic science fields related to issues specific and unique to white-collar crime, fraud examination, and forensic accounting with a focus on antifraud efforts and best practices.

Where Are the Knowledge Frontiers?

In summer 2008, the IFP solicited white papers in several key areas in an attempt to identify the current body of knowledge:

- Financial Statement Fraud: Joseph Carcello (University of Tennessee) and Dana Hermanson (Kennesaw State University)
- The Legal Environment and White Collar Crime/Forensic Accounting: John Gill (Director of Research at the ACFE)
- White Collar Crime and Psychology, Sociology and Criminology: Sri Ramamoorti (Grant Thornton), Daven Morrison (board of the Chicago-based Information Integrity Coalition (IIC)), and Joseph Koltar (noted author)
- Fraud and Forensic Accounting in a Digital Environment: Conan Albrecht (Brigham Young University)
- Asset Misappropriation: Ethical and International Perspectives: Chad Albrecht (Utah State University), Mary-Jo Kranacher (Editor-in-Chief, CPA Journal and York College), and Steve Albrecht (Brigham Young University)

Each white paper includes a brief overview of past research (descriptive and investigative) at the beginning of the article and answers the following questions:

- What do we currently know about the topical area?
- What research has been done?
- What are the lessons that we have learned?
- What don't we know, and what are we missing?
- What additional resources are needed to do research on the topical area (additional theory, data, subjects, research methodology, etc.)?

Each white paper also has underpinnings with practice and bridges the gap between the research findings and its implications to practitioners. These papers will help members, intellectual partners, and academics understand the knowledge frontiers as they exist. The IFP Web site, www.theifp.org, includes recent IFP studies and research, best practices, and antifraud resources for practicing professionals.

REVIEW QUESTIONS

2-1 According to this chapter, what employment trends are expected for professionals in the fields of fraud examination and financial forensics? Why?

2-2 What employment opportunities currently exist for fraud examiners and financial forensics specialists?

2-3 What role do fraud examination and financial forensic skills have in the corporate governance area?

2-4 Which professional organizations support fraud examination and financial forensics professionals? What certifications do they offer?

2-5 What international opportunities exist in fraud examination and financial forensics?

2-6 Other than accounting, which disciplines do fraud examination and financial forensics encompass?

2-7 What is the role of research in the fraud examination and financial forensics professions?

ENDNOTES

1. Source unknown.
2. See also Mark Anderson, "Accountants Rock," *Sacramento Business Journal* (July 29, 2005), www.sacramento.bizjournals.com/sacramento/stories/2005/08/01/focus1.html.
   Kate Berry, "Business Booming for Forensic Accountants," *Los Angeles Business Journal* (June 6, 2005), http://www.thefreelibrary.com/Business+booming+for+forensic+accountants.-a0133465662.
   Neil A. Martin, "Super Sleuths," *Barron's Online* (February 28, 2005).
3. Cecily Kellogg, "Accounting CSI: The World of Forensic Accounting," http://ezinearticles.com/?Accounting-CSI—The-World-of-Forensic-Accounting&id=817884.
4. Figure 2-1 was developed as part of the DOJ's National Institute of Justice model curriculum project "Education and Training in Fraud and Forensic Accounting: A Guide for Educational Institutions, Stakeholder Organizations, Faculty and Students," www.ncjrs.gov/pdffiles1/nij/grants/217589.pdf.
5. "Managing the Business Risk of Fraud: A Practical Guide," The Institute of Internal Auditors (IIA), American Institute of Certified Public Accountants (AICPA), and Association of Certified Fraud Examiners (ACFE), 2008, http://www.acfe.com/documents/managingbusinessrisk.pdf.
6. University students who develop an early interest in fraud and forensic accounting may also want to take criminology and risk management courses to the extent that such courses are available and fit into their course of study.

CRIMINOLOGY, ETHICS, AND THE LEGAL, REGULATORY, AND PROFESSIONAL ENVIRONMENTS

CHAPTER 3

WHO COMMITS FRAUD AND WHY: CRIMINOLOGY AND ETHICS

LEARNING OBJECTIVES

After reading this chapter, you should be able to:

3-1 Describe occupational fraud and abuse.

3-2 Compare and contrast theories of crime causation.

3-3 Identify the six situational categories that cause nonshareable problems from Cressey's research.

3-4 Discuss the essence of organizational crime.

3-5 Give examples of behavioral or other environmental indications of fraud.

3-6 Explain the relationship between an employee's position and the level of theft (according to Hollinger and Clark's research).

3-7 Analyze the role of corporate governance mechanisms in fraud prevention.

3-8 Describe corporate governance breakdowns in the facilitation of historical fraudulent acts.

3-9 Identify ethical issues, conflicts of interest, and noncompliance with corporate policies and procedures in the context of a specific case.

3-10 Discuss alternative courses of action in a given scenario within the framework of appropriate ethical conduct.

CRITICAL THINKING EXERCISE

The Killer Apartment[1]

Colin McFee had a Manhattan apartment to die for, an enormously spacious duplex that looked down on Park Avenue from the 18th and 19th floors. He also had a fortune worth killing for. So it wasn't too surprising when the old man was found to be a victim of foul play. The day of the murder began innocently enough. McFee's two nephews and his niece were all visiting him from Duluth, and the old millionaire had been so captivated by the charming trio that he impulsively decided to change his will.

The generous millionaire spent the morning signing the new document, which left his entire estate divided equally among the three vacationing relatives. McFee's faithful maid witnessed the document, ushered the lawyer out, and, with an uneasy glance at the shiny-eyed heirs, retreated to her room.

Nothing happened until shortly after noon. The maid was in her upper floor bedroom watching TV when she heard McFee's unmistakable voice screaming out in pain. For a few seconds, she was in shock, wondering what her employer's voice was doing on an old Columbo episode. And then she realized it wasn't the TV.

The maid went out into the hall and found Nick, the older nephew, standing at the top of a rarely used back staircase. "It came from downstairs," Nick stammered.

Pushing past Nick, the maid led the way down the narrow stairs. "Mr. McFee!" she shouted, and a moment later caught a spider web across the face. The back staircase went directly down to the east library. The dim, wood-paneled room was empty, except for the corpse on the floor by the bookshelves. Colin McFee, it seemed, had been hacked to death, although there was no weapon in sight.

The three McFee heirs sat with the maid in the center of the lower level, by the main staircase, awaiting the police and rehearsing their stories. "I was in my second floor bedroom," Nick said, "watching an old murder mystery show. When Uncle Colin screamed, I didn't do anything for a minute. Then I went out into the hall. That's where I met up with you." Nick smiled at the maid, his alibi.

"I was upstairs in the west dining room," Nora volunteered, "examining the old dumbwaiter. Even though the scream came from downstairs and on the far side of the apartment, I still heard it. I thought it must be robbers, so, I barricaded the dining room door and didn't come out until I heard you all calling my name."

Astor McFee, the younger nephew, claimed to have been asleep. "I was reading a magazine right here in this chair and I nodded off. The scream woke me. It took a few seconds to realize that something was wrong. When I heard people talking in the library, I went off in that direction. That's when I ran into you," he said, nodding toward Nick and the maid.

When the police arrived, they took everyone's statement, and then went to the main floor kitchen in search of the murder weapon. They found it in a utensil drawer, a huge butcher knife that had been wiped clean of blood, the same blood type as the victim's."This tells us everything we need to know," the homicide chief said with a grin.

Who killed Colin McFee?

This critical thinking exercise emphasizes the importance of drawing a picture. Without visually representing the crime scene, very different conclusions are reached about who committed this crime. Upon drawing out the crime scene, however, and placing the suspects in their various locales, it becomes clear who killed Colin McFee, or at least who was involved.

CRIMINOLOGY

Bethany holds the position of office manager at a small commercial real estate company. Jackson Stetson, the owner, conducts numerous entertainment events each month to interact with and locate new clientele. In addition, Mr. Stetson prides himself on his support of charitable organizations. In his capacity as a leader, organizer, and board member of several high-profile charities, Jackson has additional charity events each month. In her position, Bethany is a trusted assistant to Mr. Stetson, runs many aspects of the company, and organizes and hosts many of the social events for Mr. Stetson. Bethany has been with the company for many years, and has a company credit card to pay for social events and incidentals associated with the events. The company pays the monthly credit card balance, although Bethany is supposed to save receipts and match those receipts to her company credit cards before seeking Mr. Stetson's approval for company payment.

Initially, Bethany lost a few receipts, and Mr. Stetson waived the requirement that she provide all receipts. As the business grew, Bethany's schedule became even crazier, and she had less time for administrative bureaucracy. Mr. Stetson was so happy with her work on his beloved social events that he was willing to overlook her lack of attention to administrative details. The problem was that, over time, Bethany started charging personal expenses on the company-paid credit card. Not only was the company paying Bethany a salary, they paid her grocery bills and household expenses to retailers where she would shop for social event incidentals. Over a twenty-four month-period, Bethany was able to double her $40,000 take-home pay, and the additional income was tax-free!

Criminology is the sociological study of crime and criminals. Understanding the nature, dynamics, and scope of fraud and financial crimes is an important aspect of an entry-level professional's knowledge base. As noted in Chapter 1, fraudsters often look exactly like us, and most are first-time offenders. As such, to understand the causes of white-collar crime our research needs to focus on perpetrators of fraud, not street crime.[2]

Before talking about crime, it is prudent to consider why the vast majority of people do not commit crime. A number of theories have been put forth but essentially, people obey laws for the following reasons:

1. fear of punishment

2. desire for rewards

3. to act in a just and moral manner according to society's standards.

Most civilized societies are dependent upon people doing the right thing. Despite rewards, punishment, and deterrence, the resources required to fully enforce all the laws would be astronomical. Even deterrence is costly to implement and does not guarantee an adequate level of compliance. The bottom line is that a person's normative values of right and wrong dictate their behavior and determine compliance or noncompliance with the law.[3]

Occupational Fraud and Abuse

Occupational fraud and abuse is defined as "the use of one's occupation for personal enrichment through the deliberate misuse or misapplication of the employing organization's resources or assets."[4] By the breadth of this definition, occupational fraud and abuse involves a wide variety of conduct by executives, employees, managers, and principals of organizations, ranging from sophisticated investment swindles to petty theft. Common violations include asset misappropriation, fraudulent statements, corruption, pilferage, petty theft, false overtime, using company property for personal benefit, fictitious payroll, and sick time abuses.

Four common elements to these schemes were first identified by the Association of Certified Fraud Examiners in its 1996 *Report to the Nation on Occupational Fraud and Abuse* (Section 3, p. 3), which stated: "The key is that the activity (1) is clandestine, (2) violates the employee's fiduciary duties to the organization, (3) is committed for the purpose of direct or indirect financial benefit to the employee, and (4) costs the employing organization assets, revenues, or reserves."

Employee in the context of this definition is any person who receives regular and periodic compensation from an organization for his or her labor. The employee moniker is not restricted to the rank and file, but specifically includes corporate executives, company presidents, top and middle managers, and other workers.

White-Collar Crime

The term *white-collar crime* was a designation coined by Edwin H. Sutherland in 1939, when he provided the following definition: crime in the upper, white-collar class, which is composed of respectable, or at least respected, business and professional men. White-collar crime is often used interchangeably with occupational fraud and economic crime. While white-collar crime is consistent with the notion of trust violator and is typically associated with an abuse of power, one difficulty with relying on white-collar crime as a moniker for financial and economic crimes is that many criminal acts such as murder, drug trafficking, burglary, and theft are motivated by money. Furthermore, the definition, though broad, leaves out the possibility of the perpetrator being an organization where the victim is often the government and society (e.g., tax evasion and fixed contract bidding). Nevertheless, the term *white-collar crime* captures the essence of the type of perpetrator that one finds at the heart of occupational fraud and abuse.

Organizational Crime

Organizational crimes occur when entities, companies, corporations, not-for-profits, nonprofits, and government bodies, otherwise legitimate and law-abiding organizations, are involved in a criminal offense. In addition, individual organizations can be trust violators when the illegal activities of the organization are reviewed and approved by persons with high standing in an organization such as board members, executives, and managers. Federal law allows organizations to be prosecuted in a manner similar to individuals.[5] For example, although the Arthur Andersen conviction was later overturned by the U.S. Supreme Court, the organization was convicted of obstruction of justice, a felony offense that prevented them from auditing public companies. Corporate violations may include administrative breaches, such as noncompliance with agency, regulatory, and court requirements; environmental infringements; fraud and financial crimes, such as bribery and illegal kickbacks; labor abuses; manufacturing infractions related to public safety and health; and unfair trade practices.

Organizational crime is more of a problem internationally and often consists of unfair pricing, unfair business practices, and tax evasion. Organizations are governed by a complex set of interactions among boards of directors, audit committees, executives, and managers. In addition, the actions of external stakeholders such as auditors and regulators also impact the governance of organizations. As such, it is often difficult to distinguish between those individuals with responsibility for compliance with particular laws and regulations, and those infractions committed by the organization. In addition, when considerable financial harm has been inflicted on society as a result of corporate wrongdoing, the organization is often an attractive target because of its deep pockets with which to pay fines and restitution.

It is more common for corporations to become embroiled in legal battles that wind up in civil court. Such litigation runs the gamut of forensic litigation advisory services, including damage claims made by plaintiffs and defendants; workplace issues such as lost wages, disability, and wrongful death; assets and business valuations; costs and lost profits associated with construction delays or business interruptions; insurance claims; fraud; anti-trust actions, intellectual property infringement; environmental issues; tax claims; or other disputes. If you open any 10-K or annual report, you will likely find mention of a pending lawsuit in the notes to the financial statements. Furthermore, these filings include only those lawsuits deemed to be "material" as defined by accounting standards. Most corporations are involved in numerous lawsuits considered to be below the auditor's materiality threshold.

Organized Crime

These crimes are often complex, involving many individuals, organizations, and shell companies, and often cross jurisdictional borders. In this context, fraud examiners and financial forensic professionals often think of terrorist financing, the mob, and drug trafficking. Some of the crimes typically associated with organized crime include money laundering, mail and wire fraud, conspiracy, and racketeering. Money laundering addresses the means by which organized criminals take money from illegal sources and process it so that it looks like it came from legitimate business sources. Conspiracy is a means of prosecuting the individuals involved in the illegal organized activity. RICO (Racketeering Influence and Corrupt Organizations Act) addresses organizations involved in criminal activity. For example, portions of the RICO Act:

- outlaw investing illegal funds in another business
- outlaw acquisition of a business through illegal acts
- outlaw the conduct of business affairs with funds derived from illegal acts.

Torts, Breach of Duty, and Civil Litigation

Black's Law Dictionary defines "tort" as "a private or civil wrong or injury, other than breach of contract, for which the law will provide a remedy in the form of an action for damages." When a tort is committed, the party who was injured is entitled to collect compensation for damages from the wrongdoer for that private wrong.[6] The tort of contract interference or tortuous interference with contracts occurs when parties are not allowed the freedom to contract without interference from third parties. While the elements of tortuous interference are complex, a basic definition is that the law affords a remedy when someone intentionally persuades another to break a contract already in existence with a third party.[7]

Another tort—negligence—applies when the conduct of one party did not live up to minimal standards of care. Each person has a duty to act in a reasonable and prudent manner. When individuals or entities fail to live up to this standard, they are considered "negligent." The legal standard for negligence has five elements:[8]

a. Duty—a duty to act exists between the parties

b. Breach—a determination that the defendant failed to use ordinary or reasonable care in the exercise of that duty

c. Cause In Fact—an actual connection between the defendant's breach of duty and the plaintiff's harm can be established

d. Proximate Cause—the defendant must have been the proximate cause or contributed to the injury to the plaintiff

e. Damages—the plaintiff must establish that damages resulted from the defendant's breach of duty.

In order to win an award for damages, the injured party must generally prove two points:

1. liability—that the other party was liable for all or part of the damages claimed, and

2. damages—that the injured party suffered damages as the results of the actions or lack of actions of the offending party.

Furthermore, the amount of damages must be proven with a reasonable degree of certainty as to the amount claimed, and that the defendant could reasonably foresee the likelihood of damages if they failed to meet their obligations. Thus, generally speaking, the threshold for suing another person in civil court for a tort, breach of contract, or negligence is fairly low. While judges have the ability to issue summary

judgments and dismiss frivolous lawsuits, most judges are more apt to let the parties negotiate a settlement or let the jury decide the case based on the merits of the arguments put forth by the plaintiff and defense.

RESEARCH IN OCCUPATIONAL FRAUD AND ABUSE

Edwin H. Sutherland

Considering its enormous impact, relatively little research has been done on the subject of occupational fraud and abuse. Much of the current literature is based upon the early works of Edwin H. Sutherland (1883–1950), a criminologist at Indiana University. Sutherland was particularly interested in fraud committed by the elite upper-world business executive, either against shareholders or the public. As Gilbert Geis noted, Sutherland said, "General Motors does not have an inferiority complex, United States Steel does not suffer from an unresolved Oedipus problem, and the DuPonts do not desire to return to the womb. The assumption that an offender may have such pathological distortion of the intellect or the emotions seems to me absurd, and if it is absurd regarding the crimes of businessmen, it is equally absurd regarding the crimes of persons in the economic lower classes."[9]

For the uninitiated, Sutherland is to the world of white-collar criminality what Freud is to psychology. Indeed, it was Sutherland who coined the term *white-collar crime* in 1939. He intended the definition to mean criminal acts of corporations and individuals acting in their corporate capacity. Since that time, however, the term has come to mean almost any financial or economic crime, from the mailroom to the boardroom.

Many criminologists believe that Sutherland's most important contribution to criminal literature was elsewhere. Later in his career, he developed the theory of differential association, which is now the most widely accepted theory of criminal behavior in the twentieth century. Until Sutherland's landmark work in the 1930s, most criminologists and sociologists held the view that crime was genetically based, that criminals beget criminal offspring.

While this argument may seem naive today, it was based largely on the observation of non–white-collar offenders—the murderers, rapists, sadists, and hooligans who plagued society. Numerous subsequent studies have indeed established a genetic base for "street" crime, which must be tempered by environmental considerations. (For a thorough explanation of the genetic base for criminality, see *Crime and Punishment* by Wilson and Herrnstein.) Sutherland was able to explain crime's environmental considerations through the theory of differential association. The theory's basic tenet is that crime is learned, much like we learn math, English, or guitar playing.[10]

Sutherland believed this learning of criminal behavior occurred with other persons in a process of communication. Therefore, he reasoned, criminality cannot occur without the assistance of other people. Sutherland further theorized that the learning of criminal activity usually occurred within intimate personal groups. This explains, in his view, how a dysfunctional parent is more likely to produce dysfunctional offspring. Sutherland believed that the learning process involved two specific areas: the techniques to commit the crime; and the attitudes, drives, rationalizations, and motives of the criminal mind. You can see how Sutherland's differential association theory fits with occupational offenders. Organizations that have dishonest employees will eventually infect a portion of honest ones. It also goes the other way: honest employees will eventually have an influence on some of those who are dishonest.

Donald R. Cressey

One of Sutherland's brightest students at Indiana University during the 1940s was Donald R. Cressey (1919–1987). Although much of Sutherland's research concentrated on upper-world criminality, Cressey took his own studies in a different direction. Working on his Ph.D. in criminology, he decided his dissertation would concentrate on embezzlers. To serve as a basis for his research, Cressey interviewed about 200 incarcerated inmates at prisons in the Midwest.

Cressey's Hypothesis   Embezzlers, whom he called "trust violators," intrigued Cressey. He was especially interested in the circumstances that led them to be overcome by temptation. For that reason, he excluded from his research those employees who took their jobs for the purpose of stealing—a relatively minor number of offenders at that time. Upon completion of his interviews, he developed what still remains as the classic model for the occupational offender. His research was published in *Other People's Money: A Study in the Social Psychology of Embezzlement*.

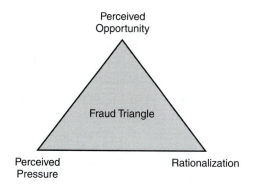

FIGURE 3-1 Fraud Triangle

Cressey's final hypothesis read as follows:

> *Trusted persons become trust violators when they conceive of themselves as having a financial problem that is nonshareable, are aware this problem can be secretly resolved by violation of the position of financial trust, and are able to apply to their own conduct in that situation verbalizations which enable them to adjust their conceptions of themselves as trusted persons with their conceptions of themselves as users of the entrusted funds or property.*[11]

Over the years, the hypothesis became known as the *fraud triangle* (Figure 3-1). One leg of the triangle represents a *perceived pressure (or nonshareable financial need)*. The second leg represents *perceived opportunity*, and the final leg denotes *rationalization*.

Nonshareable Financial Pressures The role of perceived nonshareable financial pressures is important. Cressey said, when the trust violators were asked to explain why they refrained from violation of other positions of trust they might have held at previous times, or why they had not violated the subject position at an earlier time, those who had an opinion expressed the equivalent of one or more of the following quotations: (a) "There was no need for it like there was this time." (b) "The idea never entered my head." (c) "I thought it was dishonest then, but this time it did not seem dishonest at first."[12] "In all cases of trust violation encountered, the violator considered that a financial problem which confronted him could not be shared with persons who, from a more objective point of view, probably could have aided in the solution of the problem."[13]

What is considered nonshareable is, of course, wholly in the eyes of the potential occupational offender, as Cressey noted:

> *Thus a man could lose considerable money at the racetrack daily, but the loss, even if it construed a problem for the individual, might not constitute a nonshareable problem for him. Another man might define the problem as one that must be kept secret and private. Similarly, a failing bank or business might be considered by one person as presenting problems which must be shared with business associates and members of the community, while another person might conceive these problems as nonshareable.*[14]

In addition to being nonshareable, the problem that drives the fraudster is described as "financial" because these are the types of problems that can generally be solved by the theft of cash or other assets. A person with large gambling debts, for instance, would need cash to pay those debts. Cressey noted, however, that there are some nonfinancial problems that could be solved by misappropriating funds through a violation of trust. For example, a person who embezzles in order to get revenge on her employer for perceived "unfair" treatment uses financial means to solve what is essentially a nonfinancial problem.[15]

Through his research, Cressey also found that the nonshareable problems encountered by the people he interviewed arose from situations that could be divided into six basic categories:

- violation of ascribed obligations
- problems resulting from personal failure
- business reversals
- physical isolation
- status gaining
- employer-employee relations

All of these situations dealt in some way with status-seeking or status-maintaining activities by the subjects.[16] In other words, the nonshareable problems threatened the status of the subjects, or threatened to prevent them from achieving a higher status than the one they occupied at the time of their violation.

Violations of Ascribed Obligations Violation of ascribed obligations has historically proved to be a strong motivator of financial crimes. Cressy explains in this way:

> *Financial problems incurred through nonfinancial violations of positions of trust often are considered as nonshareable by trusted persons since they represent a threat to the status which holding the position entails. Most individuals in positions of financial trust, and most employers of such individuals, consider that incumbency in such a position necessarily implies that, in addition to being honest, they should behave in certain ways and should refrain from participation in some other kinds of behavior.[17]*

In other words, the mere fact that a person has a trusted position carries with it the implied duty to act in a manner becoming his status. Persons in trusted positions may feel they are expected to avoid conduct such as gambling, drinking, drug use, or other activities that are considered seamy and undignified.

When these persons then fall into debt or incur large financial obligations as a result of conduct that is "beneath" them, they feel unable to share the problem with their peers because this would require admitting that they have engaged in the dishonorable conduct that lies at the heart of their financial difficulties. Basically, by admitting that they had lost money through some disreputable act, they would be admitting—at least in their own minds—that they are unworthy to hold their trusted positions.

Problems Resulting from Personal Failure Problems resulting from personal failures, Cressey writes, are those that the trusted person feels he caused through bad judgment and therefore feels personally responsible for. Cressey cites one case in which an attorney lost his life's savings in a secret business venture. The business had been set up to compete with some of the attorney's clients, and though he thought his clients probably would have offered him help if they had known what dire straits he was in, he could not bring himself to tell them that he had secretly tried to compete with them. He also was unable to tell his wife that he'd squandered their savings. Instead, he sought to alleviate the problem by embezzling funds to cover his losses.[18]

> *While some pressing financial problems may be considered as having resulted from "economic conditions," "fate," or some other impersonal force, others are considered to have been created by the misguided or poorly planned activities of the individual trusted person. Because he fears a loss of status, the individual is afraid to admit to anyone who could alleviate the situation the fact that he has a problem which is a consequence of his "own bad judgment" or "own fault" or "own stupidity."[19] In short*, pride goeth before the fall.[20] *If the potential offender has a choice between covering his poor investment choices through a violation of trust and admitting that he is an unsophisticated investor, it is easy to see how some prideful people's judgment could be clouded.*

Business Reversals Business reversals were the third type of situation Cressey identified as leading to the perception of nonshareable financial problems. This category differs from the class of "personal failures" described above because here the trust violators tend to see their problems as arising from conditions beyond their control: inflation, high interest rates, economic downturns, etc. In other words, these problems are not caused by the subject's own failings, but instead by outside forces.

Cressey quoted the remarks of one businessman who borrowed money from a bank using fictitious collateral:

> *Case 36. There are very few people who are able to walk away from a failing business. When the bridge is falling, almost everyone will run for a piece of timber. In business there is this eternal optimism that things will get better tomorrow. We get to working on the business, keeping it going, and we get almost mesmerized by it . . . Most of us don't know when to quit, when to say, 'This one has me licked. Here's one for the opposition.'[21]*

It is interesting to note that even in situations where the problem is perceived to be out of the trusted person's control, the issue of status still plays a big role in that person's decision to keep the problem a secret. The subject of Case 36 continued, "If I'd have walked away and let them all say, 'Well, he wasn't a success as a manager, he was a failure,' and took a job as a bookkeeper, or gone on the farm, I would have been all right. But I didn't want to do that."[22] The desire to maintain the appearance of success was a common theme in the cases involving business reversals.

Physical Isolation   The fourth category Cressey identified consisted of problems resulting from physical isolation. In these situations, the trusted person simply has no one to turn to. It's not that he is afraid to share his problem; it's that he has no one to share the problem with. He is in a situation where he does not have access to trusted friends or associates who would otherwise be able to help him. Cressey cited the subject of Case 106 in his study, a man who found himself in financial trouble after his wife had died. In her absence, he had no one to go to for help and he wound up trying to solve his problem through an embezzlement scheme.[23]

Status Gaining   The fifth category involves problems relating to status gaining, which is a sort of extreme example of "keeping up with the Joneses" syndrome. In the categories that have been discussed previously, the offenders were generally concerned with maintaining their status (i.e., not admitting to failure, keeping up appearance of trustworthiness), but here the offenders are motivated by a desire to *improve* their status. The motive for this type of conduct is often referred to as "living beyond one's means" or "lavish spending," but Cressey felt that these explanations did not get to the heart of the matter. The question was, what made the desire to improve one's status nonshareable? He noted,

> *The structuring of status ambitions as being nonshareable is not uncommon in our culture, and it again must be emphasized that the structuring of a situation as nonshareable is not alone the cause of trust violation. More specifically, in this type of case a problem appears when the individual realizes that he does not have the financial means necessary for continued association with persons on a desired status level, and this problem becomes nonshareable when he feels that he can neither renounce his aspirations for membership in the desired group nor obtain prestige symbols necessary to such membership.[24]*

In other words, it is not the desire for a better lifestyle that creates the nonshareable problem (we all want a better lifestyle), rather it is the inability to obtain the finer things through legitimate means, and at the same time, an unwillingness to settle for a lower status that creates the motivation for trust violation.

Employer-Employee Relations   Finally, Cressey described problems resulting from employer-employee relationships. The most common, he stated, was an employed person who resents his status within the organization in which he is trusted and at the same time feels he has no choice but to continue working for the organization. The resentment can come from perceived economic inequities, such as pay, or from the feeling of being overworked or underappreciated. Cressey said this problem becomes nonshareable when the individual believes that making suggestions to alleviate his perceived maltreatment will possibly threaten his status in the organization.[25] There is also a strong motivator for the perceived employee to want to "get even" when he feels ill-treated.

The Importance of Solving the Problem in Secret   Given that Cressey's study was done in the early 1950s, the workforce was obviously different from today. But the employee faced with an immediate, nonshareable financial need hasn't changed much over the years. That employee is still placed in the position of having to find a way to relieve the pressure that bears down upon him. Simply stealing money, however, is not enough; Cressey found it was crucial that the employee be able to resolve the financial problem in *secret*. As we have seen, the nonshareable financial problems identified by Cressey all dealt in some way with questions of status; the trust violators were afraid of losing the approval of those around them and so were unable to tell others about the financial problems they encountered. If they could not share the fact that they were under financial pressure, it follows that they would not be able to share the fact that they were resorting to illegal means to relieve that pressure. To do so would be to admit the problems existed in the first place.

The interesting thing to note is that it is not the embezzlement itself that creates the need for secrecy in the perpetrator's mind; it is the circumstances that led to the embezzlement (e.g., a violation of ascribed obligation, a business reversal, etc.). Cressey pointed out,

> *In all cases [in the study] there was a distinct feeling that,* because of activity prior to the defalcation, *the approval of groups important to the trusted person had been lost, or a distinct feeling that present group approval would be lost if certain activity were revealed [the nonshareable financial problem], with the result that the trusted person was effectively isolated from persons who could assist him in solving problems arising from that activity*[26] (emphasis added).

Perceived Opportunity   According to the fraud triangle model, the presence of a nonshareable financial problem by itself will not lead an employee to commit fraud. The key to understanding Cressey's theory

is to remember that all three elements must be present for a trust violation to occur. The nonshareable financial problem creates the motive for the crime to be committed, but the employee must also perceive that he has an opportunity to commit the crime without being caught. This *perceived opportunity* constitutes the second element.

In Cressey's view, there were two components of the perceived opportunity to commit a trust violation: general information and technical skill. *General information* is simply the knowledge that the employee's position of trust could be violated. This knowledge might come from hearing of other embezzlements, from seeing dishonest behavior by other employees, or just from generally being aware of the fact that the employee is in a position where he could take advantage of his employer's faith in him. *Technical skill* refers to the abilities needed to commit the violation. These are usually the same abilities that the employee needs to have to obtain and keep his position in the first place. Cressey noted that most embezzlers adhere to their occupational routines (and their job skills) in order to perpetrate their crimes.[27] In essence, the perpetrator's job will tend to define the type of fraud he will commit. "Accountants use checks which they have been entrusted to dispose of, sales clerks withhold receipts, bankers manipulate seldom-used accounts or withhold deposits, real estate men use deposits entrusted to them, and so on."[28]

Obviously, the general information and technical skill that Cressey identified are not unique to occupational offenders; most, if not all, employees have these same characteristics. But because trusted persons possess this information and skill, when they face a nonshareable financial problem they see it as something that they have the power to correct. They apply their understanding of the *possibility* for trust violation to the specific crises they are faced with. Cressey observed, "It is the next step which is significant to violation: the application of the general information to the specific situation, and conjointly, the perception of the fact that in addition to having general possibilities for violation, a specific position of trust can be used for the specific purpose of solving a nonshareable problem"[29]

Rationalizations

The third and final factor in the fraud triangle is the *rationalization*. Cressey pointed out that the rationalization is not an *ex post facto* means of justifying a theft that has already occurred. Significantly, the rationalization is a necessary component of the crime *before* it takes place; in fact, it is a part of the motivation for the crime. Because the embezzler does not view himself as a criminal, he must justify his misdeeds before he ever commits them. The rationalization is necessary so that the perpetrator can make his illegal behavior intelligible to him and maintain his concept of himself as a trusted person.[30]

After the criminal act has taken place, the rationalization will often be abandoned. This reflects the nature of us all: the first time we do something contrary to our morals, it bothers us. As we repeat the act, it becomes easier. One hallmark of occupational fraud and abuse offenders is that once the line is crossed, the illegal acts become more or less continuous. So an occupational fraudster might begin stealing with the thought that "I'll pay the money back," but after the initial theft is successful, she will usually continue to steal past the point where there is any realistic possibility of repaying the stolen funds.

Cressey found that the embezzlers he studied generally rationalized their crimes by viewing them: (1) as essentially noncriminal, (2) as justified, or (3) as part of a general irresponsibility for which they were not completely accountable.[31] He also found that the rationalizations used by trust violators tended to be linked to their positions and to the manner in which they committed their violations. He examined this by dividing the subjects of his study into three categories: *independent businessmen, long-term violators*, and *absconders*. He discovered that each group had its own types of rationalizations.

Independent Businessmen

The *independent businessmen* in Cressey's study were persons who were in business for themselves and who converted deposits that had been entrusted to them.[32] Perpetrators in this category tended to use one of two common excuses: (1) they were "borrowing" the money they converted, or (2) the funds entrusted to them were really theirs—you can't steal from yourself. Cressey found the "borrowing" rationalization was the most frequently used. These perpetrators also tended to espouse the idea that "everyone" in business misdirects deposits in some way, which therefore made their own misconduct less wrong than stealing.[33] Also, the independent businessmen almost universally felt their illegal actions were predicated by an "unusual situation," which Cressey perceived to be in reality a nonshareable financial problem.

Long-Term Violators

Cressey defined long-term violators as individuals who converted their employer's funds, or funds belonging to their employer's clients, by taking relatively small amounts over a period of time.[34] Similar to independent businessmen, the long-term violators also generally preferred the "borrowing" rationalization. Other rationalizations of long-term violators were noted, too, but they

almost always were used in connection with the "borrowing" theme: (1) they were embezzling to keep their families from shame, disgrace, or poverty; (2) theirs was a case of "necessity;" their employers were cheating them financially; or (3) their employers were dishonest towards others and deserved to be fleeced. Some even pointed out that it was more difficult to return the funds than to steal them in the first place, and claimed they did not pay back their "borrowings" because they feared that would lead to detection of their thefts. A few in the study actually kept track of their thefts but most only did so at first. Later, as the embezzlements escalated, it is assumed that the offender would rather not know the extent of his "borrowings."

All of the long-term violators in the study expressed a feeling that they would like to eventually "clean the slate" and repay their debt. This feeling usually arose even before the perpetrators perceived that they might be caught. Cressey pointed out that at this point, whatever fear the perpetrators felt in relation to their crimes was related to losing their social position by the exposure of their nonshareable *problem*, not the exposure of the theft itself or the possibility of punishment or imprisonment. This is because their rationalizations still prevented them from perceiving their misconduct as criminal. "The trust violator cannot fear the treatment usually accorded criminals until he comes to look upon himself as a criminal."[35]

Eventually, most of the long-term violators finally realized they were "in too deep." It is at this point that the embezzler faces a crisis. While maintaining the borrowing rationalization (or other rationalizations, for that matter), the trust violator is able to maintain his self-image as a law-abiding citizen; but when the level of theft escalates to a certain point, the perpetrator is confronted with the idea that he is behaving in a criminal manner. This is contrary to his personal values and the values of the social groups to which he belongs. This conflict creates a great deal of anxiety for the perpetrator. A number of offenders described themselves as extremely nervous and upset, tense, and unhappy.[36]

Without the rationalization that they are borrowing, long-term offenders in the study found it difficult to reconcile converting money, while at the same time seeing themselves as honest and trustworthy. In this situation, they have two options: (1) they can readopt the attitudes of the (law-abiding) social group that they identified with before the thefts began; or (2) they can adopt the attitudes of the new category of persons (criminals) with whom they now identify.[37] From his study, Cressey was able to cite examples of each type of behavior. Those who sought to readopt the attitudes of their law-abiding social groups "may report their behavior to the police or to their employer, quit taking funds or resolve to quit taking funds, speculate or gamble wildly in order to regain the amounts taken, or "leave the field' by absconding or committing suicide."[38] On the other hand, those who adopt the attitudes of the group of criminals to which they now belong "may become reckless in their defalcations, taking larger amounts than formerly with fewer attempts to avoid detection and with no notion of repayment."[39]

Absconders   The third group of offenders Cressey discussed was *absconders*—people who take the money and run. Cressey found that the nonshareable problems for absconders usually resulted from physical isolation. He observed that these people, "usually are unmarried or separated from their spouses, live in hotels or rooming houses, have few primary group associations of any sort, and own little property. Only one of the absconders interviewed had held a higher status position of trust, such as an accountant, business executive, or bookkeeper."[40] Cressey also found that the absconders tended to have lower occupational and socioeconomic status than the members of the other two categories.

Because absconders tended to lack strong social ties, Cressey found that almost any financial problem could be defined as nonshareable for these persons, and also that rationalizations were easily adopted because the persons only had to sever a minimum of social ties when they absconded.[41] The absconders rationalized their conduct by noting that their attempts to live honest lives had been futile (hence their low status). They also adopted an attitude of not caring what happened to themselves, and a belief that they could not help themselves because they were predisposed to criminal behavior. The latter two rationalizations, which were adopted by absconders in Cressey's study, allowed them to remove almost all personal accountability from their conduct.[42]

In the 1950s, when Cressey gathered this data, embezzlers were considered persons of higher socioeconomic status who took funds over a limited period of time because of some personal problem such as drinking or gambling, while "thieves" were considered persons of lower status who took whatever funds were at hand. Cressey noted,

> *Since most absconders identify with the lower status group, they look upon themselves as belonging to a special class of thieves rather than trust violators. Just as long-term violators and independent businessmen*

do not at first consider the possibility of absconding with the funds, absconders do not consider the possibility of taking relatively small amounts of money over a period of time.[43]

Conjuncture of Events   One of the most fundamental observations of the Cressey study was that it took all three elements—perceived nonshareable financial problem, perceived opportunity, and the ability to rationalize—for the trust violation to occur. If any of the three elements were missing, trust violation did not occur.

> *[a] trust violation takes place when the position of trust is viewed by the trusted person according to culturally provided knowledge about and rationalizations for using the entrusted funds for solving a nonshareable problem, and that the absence of any of these events will preclude violation. The three events make up the conditions under which trust violation occurs and the term "cause" may be applied to their conjecture since trust violation is dependent on that conjuncture. Whenever the conjuncture of events occurs, trust violation results, and if the conjuncture does not take place there is no trust violation.*[44]

Cressey's Conclusion   Cressey's classic fraud triangle helps explain the nature of many—but not all—occupational offenders. For example, although academicians have tested his model, it has still not fully found its way into practice in terms of developing fraud prevention programs. Our sense tells us that one model—even Cressey's—will not fit all situations. Plus, the study is nearly half a century old. There has been considerable social change in the interim. And now, many antifraud professionals believe there is a new breed of occupational offender—those who simply lack a conscience sufficient to overcome temptation. Even Cressey saw the trend later in his life.

After doing this landmark study in embezzlement, Cressey went on to a distinguished academic career, eventually authoring thirteen books and nearly 300 articles on criminology. He rose to the position of Professor Emeritus in Criminology at the University of California, Santa Barbara.

Joe Wells Remembers Donald Cressey

It was my honor to know Cressey personally. Indeed, he and I collaborated extensively before he died in 1987, and his influence on my own antifraud theories has been significant. Our families are acquainted; we stayed in each other's homes; we traveled together; he was my friend. In a way, we made the odd couple—he, the academic, and me, the businessman; he, the theoretical, and me, the practical.

I met him as the result of an assignment in about 1983. A Fortune 500 company hired me on an investigative and consulting matter. They had a rather messy case of a high-level vice president who was put in charge of a large construction project for a new company plant. The $75 million budget for which he was responsible proved to be too much of a temptation. Construction companies wined and dined the vice president, eventually providing him with tempting and illegal bait: drugs and women. He bit.

From there, the vice president succumbed to full kickbacks. By the time the dust settled, he had secretly pocketed about $3.5 million. After completing the internal investigation for the company, assembling the documentation and interviews, I worked with prosecutors at the company's request to put the perpetrator in prison. Then the company came to me with a very simple question: "Why did he do it?" As a former FBI Agent with hundreds of fraud cases under my belt, I must admit I had not thought much about the motives of occupational offenders. To me, they committed these crimes because they were crooks. But the company—certainly progressive on the antifraud front at the time—wanted me to invest the resources to find out why and how employees go bad, so they could possibly do something to prevent it. This quest took me to the vast libraries of The University of Texas at Austin, which led me to Cressey's early research. After reading his book, I realized that Cressey had described the embezzlers I had encountered to a "T." I wanted to meet him.

Finding Cressey was easy enough. I made two phone calls and found that he was still alive, well, and teaching in Santa Barbara. He was in the telephone book, and I called him. Immediately, he agreed to meet me the next time I came to California. That began what became a very close relationship between us that lasted until his untimely death in 1987. It was he who recognized the real value of combining the theorist with the practitioner. Cressey used to proclaim that he learned as much from me as I from him. But then, in addition to his brilliance, he was one of the most gracious people I have ever met. Although we were only together professionally for four years, we covered a lot of ground. Cressey was convinced there was a need for an organization devoted exclusively to fraud detection and deterrence. The Association of Certified Fraud Examiners, started about a year after his death, is in existence in large measure because of Cressey's vision. Moreover, although Cressey didn't know it at the time, he created the concept of what eventually became the certified fraud examiner. Cressey theorized that it was time for

a new type of corporate cop—one trained in detecting and deterring the crime of fraud. Cressey pointed out that the traditional policeman was ill equipped to deal with sophisticated financial crimes, as were traditional accountants. A hybrid professional was needed; someone trained not only in accounting, but also in investigation methods, someone as comfortable interviewing a suspect as reading a balance sheet. Thus, the certified fraud examiner was born.

Dr. Steve Albrecht

Another pioneer researcher in occupational fraud and abuse—and another person instrumental in the creation of the certified fraud examiner program—was Dr. Steve Albrecht of Brigham Young University. Unlike Cressey, Albrecht was educated as an accountant. Albrecht agreed with Cressey's vision—traditional accountants, he said, were poorly equipped to deal with complex financial crimes.

Albrecht's research contributions in fraud have been enormous. He and two of his colleagues, Keith Howe and Marshall Romney, conducted an analysis of 212 frauds in the early 1980s under a grant from the Institute of Internal Auditors Research Foundation, leading to their book entitled *Deterring Fraud: The Internal Auditor's Perspective*.[45] The study's methodology involved obtaining demographics and background information on the frauds through the use of extensive questionnaires. The participants in the survey were internal auditors of companies that had experienced frauds.

Albrecht and his colleagues believed that, taken as a group, occupational fraud perpetrators are hard to profile and that fraud is difficult to predict. His research included an examination of comprehensive data sources to assemble a complete list of pressure, opportunity, and integrity variables, resulting in a list of fifty possible red flags or indicators of occupational fraud and abuse. These variables fell into two principal categories: perpetrator characteristics and organizational environment. The purpose of the study was to determine which of the red flags were most important to the commission (and therefore to the detection and prevention) of fraud. The red flags ranged from unusually high personal debts, to belief that one's job is in jeopardy; from no separation of asset custodial procedures, to not adequately checking the potential employee's background.[46] Table 3-1 shows the complete list of occupational fraud red flags that Albrecht identified.[47]

The researchers gave participants both sets of twenty-five motivating factors and asked which factors were present in the frauds they had dealt with. Participants were asked to rank these factors on a seven-point scale indicating the degree to which each factor existed in their specific frauds. The ten most highly ranked factors from the list of personal characteristics, based on this study, were:[48]

1. Living beyond their means
2. An overwhelming desire for personal gain
3. High personal debt
4. A close association with customers
5. Feeling pay was not commensurate with responsibility
6. A wheeler-dealer attitude
7. Strong challenge to beat the system
8. Excessive gambling habits
9. Undue family or peer pressure
10. No recognition for job performance

As you can see from the list, these motivators are very similar to the nonshareable financial problems Cressey identified.

The ten most highly ranked factors from the list dealing with organizational environment were:[49]

1. Placing too much trust in key employees
2. Lack of proper procedures for authorization of transactions
3. Inadequate disclosures of personal investments and incomes
4. No separation of authorization of transactions from the custody of related assets
5. Lack of independent checks on performance
6. Inadequate attention to details
7. No separation of custody of assets from the accounting for those assets

TABLE 3-1 Occupational Fraud Red Flags

Personal Characteristics	Organizational Environment
1. Unusually high personal debts.	26. A department that lacks competent personnel.
2. Severe personal financial losses.	27. A department that does not enforce clear lines of authority and responsibility.
3. Living beyond one's means.	28. A department that does not enforce proper procedures for authorization of transactions.
4. Extensive involvement in speculative investments.	29. A department that lacks adequate documents and records.
5. Excessive gambling habits.	30. A department that is not frequently reviewed by internal auditors.
6. Alcohol problems.	31. Lack of independent checks (other than internal auditor).
7. Drug problems.	32. No separation of custody of assets from the accounting for those assets.
8. Undue family or peer pressure to succeed.	33. No separation of authorization of transactions from the custody of related assets.
9. Feeling of being underpaid.	34. No separation of duties between accounting functions.
10. Dissatisfaction or frustration with job.	35. Inadequate physical security in the employee's department such as locks, safes, fences, gates, guards, etc.
11. Feeling of insufficient recognition for job performance.	36. No explicit and uniform personnel policies.
12. Continuous threats to quit.	37. Failure to maintain accurate personnel records of disciplinary actions.
13. Overwhelming desire for personal gain.	38. Inadequate disclosures of personal investments and incomes.
14. Belief that job is in jeopardy.	39. Operating on a crisis basis.
15. Close associations with suppliers.	40. Inadequate attention to details.
16. Close associations with customers.	41. Not operating under a budget.
17. Poor credit rating.	42. Lack of budget review or justification.
18. Consistent rationalization of poor performance.	43. Placing too much trust in key employees.
19. Wheeler-dealer attitude.	44. Unrealistic productivity expectations.
20. Lack of personal stability such as frequent job changes, changes in residence, etc.	45. Pay levels not commensurate with the level of responsibility assigned.
21. Intellectual challenge to "beat the system."	46. Inadequate staffing.
22. Unreliable communications and reports.	47. Failure to discipline violators of company policy.
23. Criminal record.	48. Not adequately informing employees about rules of discipline or codes of conduct within the firm.
24. Defendant in a civil suit (other than divorce).	49. Not requiring employees to complete conflict-of-interest questionnaires.
25. Not taking vacations of more than two or three days.	50. Not adequately checking background before employment.

8. No separation of duties between accounting functions

9. Lack of clear lines of authority and responsibility

10. Department that is not frequently reviewed by internal auditors

All of the factors on this list affect employees' opportunity to commit fraud without being caught. Opportunity, as you will recall, was the second factor identified in Cressey's fraud triangle. In many ways, the study by Albrecht et al. supported Cressey's model. Like Cressey's study, the Albrecht study suggests there are three factors involved in occupational frauds:

> ... it appears that three elements must be present for a fraud to be committed: a situational pressure (nonshareable financial pressure), a perceived opportunity to commit and conceal the dishonest act (a way to secretly resolve the dishonest act or the lack of deterrence by management), and some way to rationalize (verbalize) the act as either being inconsistent with one's personal level of integrity or justifiable.[50]

The Fraud Scale (Figure 3-2) To illustrate the concept, Albrecht developed the "Fraud Scale," which included the components of: *situational pressures, perceived opportunities*, and *personal integrity*.[51] When situational pressures and perceived opportunities are high and personal integrity is low, occupational fraud is much more likely to occur than when the opposite is true.[52]

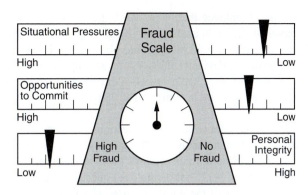

FIGURE 3-2 The Fraud Scale

Albrecht described situational pressures as "the immediate problems individuals experience within their environments, the most overwhelming of which are probably high personal debts or financial losses."[53] Opportunities to commit fraud, Albrecht says, may be created by individuals, or by deficient or missing internal controls. Personal integrity "refers to the personal code of ethical behavior each person adopts. While this factor appears to be a straightforward determination of whether the person is honest or dishonest, moral development research indicates that the issue is more complex."[54]

In addition to its findings on motivating factors of occupational fraud, the Albrecht study also disclosed several interesting relationships between the perpetrators and the frauds they committed. For example, perpetrators of large frauds used the proceeds to purchase new homes and expensive automobiles, recreation property, and expensive vacations, support extramarital relationships, and make speculative investments. Those committing small frauds did not.[55]

There were other observations: perpetrators who were interested primarily in "beating the system" committed larger frauds. However, perpetrators who believed their pay was not adequate committed primarily small frauds. Lack of segregation of responsibilities, placing undeserved trust in key employees, imposing unrealistic goals, and operating on a crisis basis were all pressures or weaknesses associated with large frauds. College graduates were less likely to spend the proceeds of their loot to take extravagant vacations, purchase recreational property, support extramarital relationships, and buy expensive automobiles. Finally, those with lower salaries were more likely to have a prior criminal record.[56]

Richard C. Hollinger and John P. Clark

In 1983, Richard C. Hollinger of Purdue University and John P. Clark of the University of Minnesota published federally funded research involving surveys of nearly 10,000 American workers. In their book, *Theft by Employees*, the two researchers reached a different conclusion than Cressey. They found that employees steal primarily as a result of workplace conditions. They also concluded that the true costs of employee theft are vastly understated: "In sum, when we take into consideration the incalculable social costs . . . the grand total paid for theft in the workplace is no doubt grossly underestimated by the available financial estimates."[57]

Hypotheses of Employee Theft In reviewing the literature on employee theft, Hollinger and Clark noted that experts had developed five separate but interrelated sets of hypotheses to explain employee theft. The first was that external economic pressures, such as the "nonshareable financial problem" that Cressey described, motivated theft. The second hypothesis was that contemporary employees, specifically young ones, are not as hardworking and honest as those in past generations. The third theory, advocated primarily by those with years of experience in the security and investigative industry, was that every employee could be tempted to steal from his employer. The theory basically assumes that people are greedy and dishonest by nature. The fourth theory was that job dissatisfaction is the primary cause of employee theft, and the fifth was that theft occurs because of the broadly shared formal and informal structure of organizations. That is, over time, the group norms—good or bad—become the standard of conduct. The sum of their research led Hollinger and Clark to conclude that the fourth hypothesis was correct, that employee deviance is primarily caused by job dissatisfaction.

Employee Deviance Employee theft is at one extreme of employee deviance, which can be defined as conduct detrimental to the organization and to the employee. At the other extreme is counterproductive employee behavior such as goldbricking and abuse of sick leave. Hollinger and Clark defined two basic categories of employee deviant behavior: (1) acts by employees against property, and (2) violations of the norms regulating acceptable levels of production. The former includes misuse and theft of company property such as cash or inventory. The latter involves acts of employee deviance that affect productivity.

Hollinger and Clark developed a written questionnaire that was sent to employees in three different sectors: retail, hospital, and manufacturing. The employees were presented with lists of category 1 and category 2 offenses and were asked which offenses they had been involved in, and with what frequency. The researchers eventually received 9,175 valid employee questionnaires, representing about 54 percent of those sampled. Below are the results of the questionnaires. The first table represents category 1 offenses—acts against property.[58] Hollinger and Clark found that approximately one-third of employees in each sector admitted to committing some form of property deviance.

Combined Phase I and Phase II Property-Deviance Items and Percentage of Reported Involvement, by Sector

Items	Involvement				
	Almost daily	About once a week	Four to twelve times a year	One to three times a year	Total
Retail Sector (N = 3, 567)					
Misuse the discount privilege	0.6	2.4	11	14.9	28.9
Take store merchandise	0.2	0.5	1.3	4.6	6.6
Get paid for more hours than were worked	0.2	0.4	1.2	4	5.8
Purposely underring a purchase	0.1	0.3	1.1	1.7	3.2
Borrow or take money from employer without approval	0.1	0.1	0.5	2	2.7
Be reimbursed for more money than spent on business expenses	0.1	0.2	0.5	1.3	2.1
Damage merchandise to buy it on discount	0	0.1	0.2	1	1.3
Total involved in property deviance					35.1
Hospital Sector (N = 4, 111)					
Take hospital supplies (e.g., linens, bandages)	0.2	0.8	8.4	17.9	27.3
Take or use medication intended for patients	0.1	0.3	1.9	5.5	7.8
Get paid for more hours than were worked	0.2	0.5	1.6	3.8	6.1
Take hospital equipment or tools	0.1	0.1	0.4	4.1	4.7
Be reimbursed for more money than spent on business expenses	0.1	0	0.2	0.8	1.1
Total involved in property deviance					33.3
Manufacturing Sector (N = 1, 497)					
Take raw materials used in production	0.1	0.3	3.5	10.4	14.3
Get paid for more hours than were worked	0.2	0.5	2.9	5.6	9.2
Take company tools or equipment	0	0.1	1.1	7.5	8.7
Be reimbursed for more money than spent on business expenses	0.1	0.6	1.4	5.6	7.7
Take finished products	0	0	0.4	2.7	3.1
Take precious metals (e.g., platinum, gold)	0.1	0.1	0.5	1.1	1.8
Total involved in property deviance					28.4

Adapted from Richard C. Hollinger, John P. Clark, *Theft by Employees*. Lexington: Lexington Books, 1983, p. 42.

Following is a summary of the Hollinger and Clark research with respect to production deviance. Not surprisingly, they found that this form of employee misconduct was two to three times more common than property violations.[59]

Combined Phase I and Phase II Production-Deviance Items and Percentage of Reported Involvement, by Sector

Items	Almost daily	About once a week	Four to twelve times a a year	One to three times a year	Total
Retail Sector (N = 3, 567)					
Take a long lunch or break without approval	6.9	13.3	15.5	20.3	56
Come to work late or leave early	0.9	3.4	10.8	17.2	32.3
Use sick leave when not sick	0.1	0.1	3.5	13.4	17.1
Do slow or sloppy work	0.3	1.5	4.1	9.8	15.7
Work under the influence of alcohol or drugs	0.5	0.8	1.6	4.6	7.5
Total involved in production deviance					65.4
Hospital Sector (N = 4, 111)					
Take a long lunch or break without approval	8.5	13.5	17.4	17.8	57.2
Come to work late or leave early	1	3.5	9.6	14.9	29
Use sick leave when not sick	0	0.2	5.7	26.9	32.8
Do slow or sloppy work	0.2	0.8	4.1	5.9	11
Work under the influence of alcohol or drugs	0.1	0.3	0.6	2.2	3.2
Total involved in production deviance					69.2
Manufacturing Sector (N = 1, 497)					
Take a long lunch or break without approval	18	23.5	22	8.5	72
Come to work late or leave early	1.9	9	19.4	13.8	44.1
Use sick leave when not sick	0	0.2	9.6	28.6	38.4
Do slow or sloppy work	0.5	1.3	5.7	5	12.5
Work under the influence of alcohol or drugs	1.1	1.3	3.1	7.3	12.8
Total involved in production deviance					82.2

Adapted from Richard C. Hollinger, John P. Clark, *Theft by Employees*. Lexington: Lexington Books, 1983, p. 45.

Income and Theft   In order to empirically test whether economics had an effect on the level of theft, the researchers sorted their data by household income under the theory that lower levels of income might produce higher levels of theft. However, they were unable to confirm such a statistical relationship. This would tend to indicate—at least in this study—that absolute income is not a predictor of employee theft.

Despite this finding, Hollinger and Clark were able to identify a statistical relationship between employees' *concern* over their financial situation and the level of theft. They presented the employees with a list of eight major concerns, ranging from personal health to education issues to financial problems. They noted the following:

> Being concerned about finances and being under financial pressure are not necessarily the same. However, if a respondent considered his or her finances as one of the most important issues, that concern could be partially due to "nonshareable (sic) economic problems," or it could also be that current realities are not matching one's financial aspirations regardless of the income presently being realized.[60]

The researchers concluded "in each industry, the results are significant, with higher theft individuals more likely to be concerned about their finances, particularly those who ranked finances as the first or second most important issue."[61]

Age and Theft   Hollinger and Clark found in their research a direct correlation between age and the level of theft. "Few other variables... have exhibited such a strong relationship to theft as the age of the employee."[62] The reason, they concluded, was that the younger employee generally has less tenure with his organization and therefore has a lower level of commitment to it than the typical older employee. In addition, there is a long history of connection between youth and many forms of crime. Sociologists have suggested that the central process of control is determined by a person's "commitment to conformity." Under this model—assuming employees are all subject to the same deviant motives and opportunities—the probability of deviant involvement depends on the stakes that one has in conformity. Since younger

employees tend to be less committed to the idea of conforming to established social rules and structures, it follows that they would be more likely to engage in illegal conduct that runs contrary to organizational and societal expectations.

The researchers suggested that the policy implications from the commitment to conformity theory are that rather than subjecting employees to draconian security measures,

> *companies should afford younger workers many of the same rights, fringes, and privileges of the tenured, older employees. In fact, by signaling to the younger employee that he or she is temporary or expendable, the organization inadvertently may be encouraging its own victimization by the very group of employees that is already least committed to the expressed goals and objectives of the owners and managers.*[63]

Although this may indeed affect the level of employee dissatisfaction, its policy implications may not be practical for non–fraud-related reasons.

Position and Theft   Hollinger and Clark were able to confirm a direct relationship between an employee's position and the level of the theft, with thefts being highest in jobs with greater access to the things of value in the organization. Although they found obvious connections between opportunity and theft (for example, retail cashiers with daily access to cash had the highest incidence), the researchers believed opportunity to be "… only a secondary factor that constrains the manner in which the deviance is manifested."[64] Their research indicated that job satisfaction was the primary motivator of employee theft; the employee's position only affects the method and amount of the theft *after* the decision to steal has already been made.

Job Satisfaction and Deviance   The research of Hollinger and Clark strongly suggests that employees who are dissatisfied with their jobs—across all age groups, but especially younger workers—are the most likely to seek redress through counterproductive or illegal behavior in order to right the perceived inequity. Other writers, notably anthropologist Gerald Mars and researcher David Altheide, have commented on this connection. Mars observed that among both hotel dining room employees and dock workers it was believed that pilferage was not theft, but was "seen as a morally justified addition to wages; indeed, as an entitlement due from exploiting employers."[65] Altheide also documented that theft is often perceived by employees as a "way of getting back at the boss or supervisor."[66] Jason Ditton documented a pattern in U.S. industries called "wages in kind," in which employees "situated in structurally disadvantaged parts [of the organization] receive large segments of their wages invisibly."[67]

Organizational Controls and Deviance   Hollinger and Clark were unable to document a strong relationship between control and deviance in their research. They examined five different control mechanisms: company policy, selection of personnel, inventory control, security, and punishment.

Company policy can be an effective control. Hollinger and Clark pointed out that companies with a strong policy against absenteeism have less of a problem with it. As a result, they would expect policies governing employee theft to have the same impact. Similarly, they believed employee education as an organizational policy has a deterrent effect. Hiring persons who will conform to organizational expectations exerts control through selection of personnel. Inventory control is required not only for theft, but for procedures to detect errors, avoid waste, and ensure a proper amount of inventory is maintained. Security controls involve proactive and reactive measures, surveillance, internal investigations, and others. Control through punishment is designed to deter the specific individual, plus those who might be tempted to act illegally.

Hollinger and Clark interviewed numerous employees in an attempt to determine their attitudes toward control. With respect to policy, they concluded, "the issue of theft by employees is a sensitive one in organizations and must be handled with some discretion. A concern for theft must be expressed without creating an atmosphere of distrust and paranoia. If an organization places too much stress on the topic, honest employees may feel unfairly suspected, resulting in lowered morale and higher turnover."[68]

Employees in the study also perceived, in general, that computerized inventory records added security and made theft more difficult. With respect to security control, the researchers discovered that the employees regarded the purpose of a security division as taking care of outside—rather than inside—security. Few of the employees were aware that security departments investigate employee theft, and most such departments had a poor image among the workers. With respect to punishment, the employees interviewed felt theft would result in job termination in a worst-case scenario. They perceived that minor thefts would be handled by reprimands only.

Hollinger and Clark concluded that formal organizational controls provide both good and bad news. "The good news is that employee theft does seem to be susceptible to control efforts.... Our data also indicate, however, that the impact of organizational controls is neither uniform nor very strong. In sum, formal organizational controls do negatively influence theft prevalence, but these effects must be understood in combination with the other factors influencing this phenomenon."[69]

Employee Perception of Control

Employee Perception of Control   The researchers also examined the perception—not necessarily the reality—of employees believing they would be caught if they committed theft. "We find that perceived certainty of detection is inversely related to employee theft for respondents in all three industry sectors—that is, the stronger the perception that theft would be detected, the less the likelihood that the employee would engage in deviant behavior."[70]

This finding is significant and consistent with other research. It suggests that increasing the perception of detection may be the best way to deter employee theft while increasing the sanctions that are imposed on occupational fraudsters will have a limited effect. Recall that under Cressey's model, embezzlers are motivated to commit illegal acts because they face some financial problem that they cannot share with others because it would threaten their status. It follows that the greatest threat to the perpetrator would be that he might be caught in the act of stealing because that would bring his nonshareable problem out into the open. The possibility of sanctions is only a secondary concern. The perpetrator engages in the illegal conduct only because he perceives there is an opportunity to fix his financial problem *without getting caught*. Therefore, if an organization can increase in its employees' minds the perception that illegal acts will be detected, it can significantly deter occupational fraud. Put simply, occupational fraudsters are not deterred by the threat of sanctions because they do not plan on getting caught.

Control in the workplace, according to Hollinger and Clark, consists of both formal and informal social controls. Formal controls can be described as external pressures that are applied through both positive and negative sanctions; informal controls consist of the internalization by the employee of the group norms of the organization. These researchers, along with a host of others, have concluded that—as a general proposition—informal social controls provide the best deterrent. "These data clearly indicate that the loss of respect among one's acquaintances was the single most effective variable in predicting future deviant involvement." Furthermore, "in general, the probability of suffering informal sanction is far more important than fear of formal sanctions in deterring deviant activity."[71] Again, this supports the notion that the greatest deterrent to the fraudster is the idea that he will be caught, not the threat of punishment by his employer.

Other Hollinger and Clark Conclusions

Other Hollinger and Clark Conclusions   Hollinger and Clark reached several other conclusions based on their work. First, they found that "substantially increasing the internal security presence does not seem to be appropriate, given the prevalence of the problem. In fact, doing so may make things worse."[72]

Second, they concluded that the same kinds of employees who engage in other workplace deviance are also principally the ones who engage in employee theft. They found persuasive evidence that slow or sloppy workmanship, sick-leave abuses, long coffee breaks, alcohol and drug use at work, coming in late and/or leaving early were more likely to be present in the employee-thief.

Third, the researchers hypothesized that if efforts are made to reduce employee theft without reducing its underlying causes (e.g., employee dissatisfaction, lack of ethics), the result could create a "hydraulic effect." Therefore, tightening controls over property deviance may create more detrimental acts affecting the productivity of the organization—that is, if we push down employee theft, we may push up goldbricking as a result.

Fourth, they asserted that increased management sensitivity to its employees would reduce all forms of workplace deviance.

Fifth, they concluded special attention should be afforded young employees, as these are the ones statistically the most likely to steal. However, it must be pointed out that although the incidence of theft is higher among younger employees, the losses associated with those thefts are typically lower than losses caused by more senior employees who have greater financial authority.

Hollinger and Clark asserted that management must pay attention to four aspects of policy development: (1) a clear understanding regarding theft behavior, (2) continuous dissemination of positive information reflective of the company's policies, (3) enforcement of sanctions, and (4) publicizing the sanctions.

The researchers summed up their observations by saying,

perhaps the most important overall policy implication that can be drawn . . . is that theft and workplace deviance are in large part a reflection of how management at all levels of the organization is perceived by the employee. Specifically, if the employee is permitted to conclude that his or her contribution to the workplace is not appreciated or that the organization does not seem to care about the theft of its property, we expect to find greater involvement. In conclusion, a lowered prevalence of employee theft may be one valuable consequence of a management team that is responsive to the current perceptions and attitudes of its workforce.[73]

ETHICS[74]

Oreo Linderhoof, Loss Prevention Manager, takes a videotape labeled *Store 522 Backroom Surveillance*, and carefully places the videotape on top of his desk near the guest chairs. Jim Thomas, Store Manager for retail location 522, arrives for his interview with Oreo. When Jim arrives, Oreo escorts Jim to his office and almost immediately is interrupted by a call. He asks Jim to please excuse the interruption and heads out of the office. Oreo returns fifteen minutes later and Jim "spills his guts." He confesses to the theft of inventory, signs a written statement and is taken from headquarters in handcuffs by the local police.

The rest of the story . . .

Oreo knows that Jim Thomas is stealing high value inventory from the store but he doesn't know how. Based on examination of daily inventory counts correlated with scheduling over weeks, Oreo has concluded that Jim is the only person with the opportunity to have committed the theft. Despite surprise inventory counts, store surveillance and other loss prevention techniques, Oreo cannot figure out how Jim is perpetrating the theft. Surveillance suggests that the inventory is not leaving through the front door and that Jim does not have an accomplice. Cash register analysis suggests that Jim is not taking cash through voids and refunds, a method that would also leave the inventory short.

Oreo hatches a scheme to catch Jim . . .

Oreo calls Jim at the store and schedules an interview at corporate headquarters. Store employees being called to corporate headquarters is never a good sign, and Oreo is hoping that this visit will make Jim nervous. In advance, Oreo instructs the receptionist to call him as soon as he and Jim are in his office. After excusing himself, Oreo goes to the break room, gets a cup of coffee, and then visits with several fellow employees. Essentially, he wants Jim to see the videotape labeled *Store 522 Backroom Surveillance*, and as noted above, his scheme works. As soon as Jim sees the videotape, he believes that he has been caught "red-handed." The issue: the videotape was blank; there was no backroom video surveillance. Oreo, being one of the best professionals in his field, caught his man.

Question: Was Oreo's scheme to obtain Jim's confession ethical?

Ethics, trust, and responsibility are at the heart of fraud examination and financial forensics, and the above scenario highlights some of the dilemmas faced by professionals confronting persons perpetrating financial crimes. Ethics is defined as the branch of philosophy dealing with values relating to human conduct, with respect to rightness and wrongness of actions and the goodness and badness of motives and ends.[75] The definition of ethics has certain key elements:

1. Ethics involves questions requiring reflective choice and their consequences to the individual and others (decision problems).

2. Ethics considers the rules and regulations that are in place to guide behavior as well as the consequences for breaking those rules and regulations.

3. Ethics often relies on moral principles to guide choices of right and wrong. (These ethical frameworks are discussed in more detail below).

4. Ethics is concerned with outcomes, the assigned impact associated with making a decision where the impact reflects the underlying values of individuals and organizations.

A discussion of ethics goes hand-in-hand with that of criminology because fraudsters often make poor ethical decisions prior to committing criminal acts. Consider, for example, financial statement fraud: perpetrators frequently find themselves on an ethical slippery slope, using an accounting choice as a tool for earnings management to maximize bonuses and influence the financial markets. When earnings management isn't enough, the individual finds himself at a point of no return, moving from the slippery slope of earnings

management to fraudulent financial statements. When does the fraud examiner or forensic accountant face an ethical dilemma? Whenever there are several choices, all outcomes have somewhat negative effects, and the correct choice is not obvious. Such dilemmas arise when many people could be harmed and some may benefit while others will not.

Consider another scenario: is it ethical for a fraud examiner or forensic accountant to lie to a perpetrator during an interview to elicit a confession? Most people agree that lying is wrong. Most also agree that an embezzler should not get away with their crime. If lying is the only way to get a white-collar criminal to confess, is lying ok? The answer isn't obvious because both choices are imperfect: (1) not lying, but the perpetrator gets away; (2) lying and the perpetrator confesses. In either case, the fraud examiner or forensic professional must choose from a flawed set of options. Closely associated with ethics is the concept of values. Values are the personal and social criteria that influence choice: family, friends, peer groups, nationality, culture, and economic and social classes. Values are learned beginning in childhood and are the conventions upon which choices are evaluated.

Approaches to Ethical Problem Solving

Is it Legal, or Does the Conduct Violate Known Rules? The law and rules is one approach to resolving an ethical dilemma. Most codes of conduct and professional associations, for example, require that professions avoid breaking the law. This is a practical approach and a starting point for determining if certain conduct should be avoided. The law, however, is the lowest threshold for ethical decision making.

It may happen that a law might permit an action that is prohibited by a profession's code of ethics. As an example, for years the American Institute of Certified Public Accountants (AICPA) had rules of ethics that prohibited advertising by its members. The profession believed that dignity and objectivity were enhanced by keeping practitioners out of this aspect of the commercial world. The U.S. Federal Trade Commission and the U.S. Department of Justice, however, disagreed. They decided that the prohibitions against advertising violated the laws barring restraint of trade. The government forced the profession to eliminate its rules against advertising. This example illustrates the triumph of one set of values (the government's belief that competition through advertising would benefit consumers) over another set (the profession's belief that dignity should be preserved).

The Means Versus the Ends A second approach to ethics suggests that it is ok to "fight fire with fire." As Sean Connery's character, Malone, asks Elliott Ness (Kevin Costner) in *The Untouchables*, "What are you prepared to do?... You wanna know how to get Capone? They pull a knife, you pull a gun. He sends one of yours to the hospital; you send one of his to the morgue." Essentially, this is an outcome-based ethical framework. This has the purpose of justifying actions that otherwise could be considered immoral, unethical, or illegal. The problem with means-ends analyses is that they are often superficial, ending with the needed justification but failing to consider other aspects and consequences of the actions.[76]

Ethical Principles

The Imperative Principle Ethical principles, on the other hand, refer to the process upon which an ethical decision is analyzed or evaluated. Inherently, values are incorporated into the principles that help guide choice. The imperative principle is one of three ethical principles that provide a framework for ethical decision making, and is based on the work of philosopher Immanuel Kant. Although the following characterization is overly simplistic, Kantian philosophy tends to ignore outcomes by providing directives and rules without exception that are in the best interest of society as a whole. For example, under Kantian imperatives, "lying is always wrong." A society cannot exist if it is based on lies. Furthermore, society should value telling the truth over lying because society cannot exist if everyone is told to lie all the time (the alternative imperative to never tell a lie).

This unconditional obligation assumes that all people are aware of the rule and all agree to follow the rule. The Kantian imperative is very strict but provides an easy to understand framework for ethical decision making. However, Kant himself recognizes that at times, all general rules must have exceptions. While the Kantian imperative is almost impossible to follow all of the time, in practice, when a person is faced with violating an imperative, it alerts persons that they are faced with an ethical problem. Once the dilemma is identified, then the fraud examiner or forensic accountants can seek out additional consideration for weighing the consequences.

The Utilitarian Principle The utilitarian principle, championed by John Stuart Mills, suggests that ethical problems should be solved by weighing the good consequences and the bad consequences. The correct course of action is that which provides the most good or minimizes the bad. Like Kantian imperatives, the consequences to society generally are more important than those to individuals. Mills identifies two forms of utilitarianism, "act" and "rule." Act utilitarianism suggests that it is the consequences of the act that matter. For example, "honesty (an action) is the policy," subject to the evaluation of the specific circumstances that might suggest that an alternative action, lying, provides better consequences in this particular situation. The individual making the decision has the power to decide, so their value system drives the evaluation process of possible outcomes (consequences) and the final decision.

In contrast, rule utilitarianism emphasizes the benefits to society of general rules (similar to a Kantian imperative) and suggests that the decision to break a rule is one that requires very careful consideration. Rule utilitarianism requires that society as a whole be able to determine which rules are important and ought to be followed. Rules then are also influenced by history, nationality, culture, social goals, and at some level economics.

The difficulty with utilitarianism is the variation in outcomes. In any situation, almost any act can be justified and the choice is always a product of from where a person (act) or society (rule) came: family, friends, peer groups, nationality, ethnic background, and economic and social classes. Furthermore, it is difficult for everyone to agree on universal principles.

The Generalization Principle The generalization principle is an attempt to marry Kantian imperatives with utilitarianism, and was proposed by Marcus G. Singer. The generalization argument is as follows:

> *If all relevantly similar persons acting under relevantly similar circumstances were to act a certain way and the consequences would be undesirable, then no one ought to act in that way without a reason.*

More simplistically, the generalization argument poses the following questions as a first assessment:

> *What if everyone acted that way?*

If the outcome is considered undesirable, then that conduct ought to be avoided unless the person has a very good reason. Generalization provides the flexibility needed to address the shortcomings of Kant and the specific direction that seems to be missing from utilitarianism. Of course, the success of the generalization argument is dependent on the specific value assessments of the individual decision makers. Furthermore, generalization is invalid when an argument is either invertible or reiterable. Invertibility occurs when both doing something and not doing something leads to bad consequences. In such a circumstance, no generalization argument can be formulated. Reiterability occurs when arbitrary times, places, persons, or other factors can be inserted into a generalization in such a way as to make the generalization outcome to be nonsensical.

Ethics, Trust, and Responsibility

Although the preceding principles provide a framework for ethical decision making, alternative decisions may result in variations of good and bad consequences. Therefore, the task is a difficult one and the choice must be left to individuals. It is impossible to provide a blueprint for every situation with laws, rules, and exceptions. The bottom line is that civilized societies are based on trust with underlying values and implicit codes of conduct that guide our behavior. The decision process is difficult, and the range of possible outcomes suggests that the right choice is not always obvious. Though doing the right thing can be difficult, as members of society, we have a responsibility to reach for that goal every day, without exception.

ETHICS IN PRACTICE

Ethics and Values as Drivers of Personal Behavior

To be successful, professionals in the specialized field of fraud examination and financial forensics must have an ethical framework for appropriate decision making. Although the preceding material has suggested approaches to solving ethical problems, the fraud and forensic professional needs to strive for the highest degree of ethics. This perspective requires that the individual think about possible difficult situations and develop their own framework for decision making and, to the extent possible, in advance. Next, the

individual needs to make the commitment required to follow their ethical values in all cases except those that have extreme consequences.

In practice, fraud and forensic professionals can start with rules, laws, and Kantian imperatives to identify ethical situations (ethical dilemmas) that require more in-depth evaluation. Once the ethical problems have been identified, the evaluation process begins and professionals can use their own framework for ethical problem solving, including using personal rules and processes for decision making. The fraud and forensic professional is not alone and should solicit the input and opinions of other practicing professionals. In some cases, guidance and advice from professional organizations and associations can assist the individual in making the best decision. After careful consideration of the alternative outcomes and the decision is made, the professional can then move forward to implement that decision. This process will help to ensure that the anticipated goals are realized while also attempting to mitigate any negative consequences.

Students who are considering entering the field of fraud examination and financial forensics must consider decisions that they made in the past. For example, some may have past criminal convictions that might exclude them from entry into the profession. While most offenses should not prevent a prospective student from exploring their options, they should be aware that honesty is the best policy. Get caught in a lie, and your career could be over. Tell the truth and explain the facts and circumstances of a less than perfect past, and at least the individual (applicant) will have created a foundation of trust to repair the damage caused by prior conduct.

Professional Conduct

Professions are set apart by five characteristics:[77]

1. A specialized body of knowledge.
2. Admission governed by standards and qualifications.
3. Recognition and acceptance by society (a characteristic that inflicts social responsibility back on the profession).
4. Standards of conduct for dealing with the public, other professionals, and clients.
5. An organizational body devoted to the advancement and responsibilities of the profession.

These characteristics inflict responsibility on both the profession and the individual professionals. Normally, such responsibilities are captured in the profession's code of conduct. For example, Certified Fraud Examiners (CFE), as designated by the Association of Certified Fraud Examiners (ACFE), have the following code of ethics:[78]

1. A Certified Fraud Examiner shall at all times demonstrate a commitment to professionalism and diligence in the performance of his or her duties.
2. A Certified Fraud Examiner shall not engage in any illegal or unethical conduct, or any activity which would constitute a conflict of interest. (Note that the Certified Fraud Examiner has no exception for cases where they may be unaware that a particular law exists.)
3. A Certified Fraud Examiner shall, at all times, exhibit the highest level of integrity in the performance of all professional assignments, and will accept only assignments for which there is reasonable expectation that the assignment will be completed with professional competence.
4. A Certified Fraud Examiner will comply with lawful orders of the courts, and will testify to matters truthfully and without bias or prejudice.
5. A Certified Fraud Examiner, in conducting examinations, will obtain evidence or other documentation to establish a reasonable basis for any opinion rendered. No opinion shall be expressed regarding the guilt or innocence of any person or party.
6. A Certified Fraud Examiner shall not reveal any confidential information obtained during a professional engagement without proper authorization.
7. A Certified Fraud Examiner shall reveal all material matters discovered during the course of an examination, which, if omitted, could cause a distortion of the facts.
8. A Certified Fraud Examiner shall continually strive to increase the competence and effectiveness of professional services performed under his or her direction.

Ethics at Client Entities: The Foundation for Fraud Prevention and Deterrence

Whereas the prior sections dealt with ethics at the individual and professional level, ethics are an important part of organizational behavior. In fact, ethics is the foundation for fraud prevention both by individuals within an organization and the organization itself.

Tone at the Top and a Culture of Ethical Behavior   Ethics at the organizational level starts with corporate governance. The Board of Directors, the Audit Committee, executives, managers, clerical support, and line personnel are the living, breathing embodiment of ethics within the organization. The Board of Directors, Audit Committee, and corporate officers set the "tone at the top." Tone at the top refers to a culture that is open, honest, and communicates the values of the organization to persons at all levels, both internal and external to the organization. The first step in developing an ethical culture is a code of ethics signed by all personnel. In addition, the company's position on ethics should be posted in visible places, such as lunchrooms, and communicated across the organization. Employee awareness programs such as periodic ethics training are effective tools, and, of course, leaders lead by example. Employees will take their cues from their managers, managers from executives, and executives from their interaction with board members, audit committee members, and auditors. It is important that individuals in leadership positions not only communicate the value of ethical actions, they must also practice what they preach. In addition, important financial, operational, and compliance information should be disseminated to individuals who need it and can act on it. Furthermore, individuals at the top must be willing to listen to those operating at lower levels of the organization.

Second, the organization should be committed to hiring honest executives, managers, and staff. While most organizations attempt to contact prior employers and resume references, many organizations provide only minimal information about former employees and are remiss to provide any negative feedback for fear of legal retribution. References provided by prospective employees are typically friends and professional acquaintances; so prospective employers should seek out prior supervisors. While costly, organizations should consider background checks on prospective employees. Due to cost constraints, organizations may want to restrict the positions for which background checks are completed. To avoid charges of discrimination, prospective employers need to complete such checks in a consistent manner and in compliance with corporate policy.

Once individuals are hired, they need to be properly supervised. The most common excuse by managers for inadequate supervision is time constraints. While "too much to do, in too little time" is a common complaint in today's business environment, proper supervision is essential to maintaining good internal controls.

Training is another area that needs adequate attention. Many companies spend a considerable amount of time and resources developing their employees' technical abilities, but little time or resources are generally spent developing supervisory skills.

Maintain an Environment Dedicated to Fraud Prevention and Deterrence   Once an organization has created the infrastructure to minimize fraud opportunities, the system has to be maintained. Supporting the anti-fraud environment requires continuing education of fraud awareness. The fraud triangle indicates that one of the factors necessary for fraud to occur is rationalization. Failing to maintain a work environment that discourages fraud may enable an employee to justify unethical or illegal actions. Such rationalizations may include the following: an employer's failure to recognize a job well done, an employee's overall job dissatisfaction, an employee's perception that they are inadequately compensated for their work, an employee's perception that the company owes them, and the misperception that no one is being hurt by their actions.

Another part of a good anti-fraud maintenance program is to provide assistance for employees with problems. In smaller companies, the human resources department may serve this function. In larger companies, there may be specific personnel devoted to assisting employees in exploring their options to solve a problem. This gives the employee the comfort to know that they are not alone, that their problem is "shareable."

Part of maintaining a strong anti-fraud environment includes appropriate disciplinary procedures, such as prosecuting fraudsters where evidence suggests that such action is warranted. Effective discipline requires a well-defined set of sanctions for inappropriate behavior and strict adherence to those sanctions in order to avoid claims of discriminatory conduct.

One of the most effective anti-fraud deterrents is a hotline to receive anonymous tips from employees, customers, suppliers, vendors, contractors, and others. According to the 2006 ACFE Report to the Nation, tips and accidental discovery (candidates for tip reporting) account for almost 60 percent of fraud detection. Thus, anonymous tip hotlines are a tool that should be in place at all organizations of any size.

In cases where tips are made by employees, especially lower-level employees who report wrongdoing by their supervisors, whistleblower protections should be in place. Unfortunately, even those whistleblower protections that are established by law may not protect employees from subtle, informal retribution, such as exclusion from meetings or not being given important information pertinent to doing their job.

Creating an anti-fraud environment also means minimizing opportunities for fraud. To accomplish this goal, companies need to establish and maintain a good internal control environment; discourage collusion and monitor employee relationships for collusion opportunities; alert vendors and contractors to company policies; monitor employees and, as noted above, create tip hotlines; create expectations that fraudsters will get caught and will be punished; and proactively audit for fraud.[79] Best practices to deter fraud include job rotation, surprise audits and reviews, open-door policies by upper-level management, and periodic testing of internal controls. Actively creating an anti-fraud environment means considering the following questions before fraud occurs:

What?

What could go wrong?

What assets are most susceptible?

Who?

Who has the opportunity to commit fraud?

Who has partial opportunity and who might they collude with to commit fraud?

How?

How could fraud be committed—asset misappropriation and financial statement fraud?

How effective is the internal control environment—policies and procedures?

How susceptible is the company to management override?

When (timing)?

When is fraud most likely to occur?

Where?

Where would the fraud occur?

Where would red flags (symptoms) manifest themselves?

Why?

Why might fraud occur? i.e., pressures (nonshareable problems) created internally such as performance bonus plans

Why might certain employees be driven to commit fraud? i.e., pressures (nonshareable problems) observed in certain employees (e.g., gambling problems, debt, drug or alcohol abuse, or marital issues)

The *who, what, where, when, how*, and *why* are questions fraud examiners and forensic professionals often investigate once fraud is discovered. Those same attributes need to be considered, proactively, as companies develop their anti-fraud environment.

React to Early Warning Signs   The last aspect of a good antifraud environment requires that the organization react appropriately to symptoms of fraud, red flags, badges of fraud, and other early warning signals. Dr. Steve Albrecht references six types of anomalies that should be investigated at the earliest point of recognition: accounting anomalies, weak internal controls, analytical anomalies, lifestyles symptoms, behavior symptoms, and tips from potential informants. These issues will be more formally explored in later chapters, but some of these anomalies are listed below.

Accounting Anomalies

Irregular, unusual, and missing source documents

Excessive voids and refunds

Faulty journal entries and journal entries with missing documentation

Missing cash or assets (with coincidental reduction in the G/L with a credit)

Unusual account debits that are frequently used to conceal at fraud

Inaccuracies in ledgers

Underlying account detail does not equal balance

Underlying account detail does not reconcile to the general ledger

Subsidiary ledgers with missing support

Two sets of books and records

False ledger entries or alterations

Back-dated and post-dated documents and transactions

False invoices

False applications

False financial statements elements

Invoice numbers that do not make sense

Failure to keep and maintain records

Concealment of records

Refusal to make records available

Unexplained variances between tax returns and underlying books and records

False interview statements

Interference with an audit, examination, and investigation

Failure to follow advice of attorneys and accountants

Less than full disclosure (e.g., masking the true financial impact)

Taxpayer knowledge

Testimony of employees and other witnesses

Destruction of books and records

Inappropriate transfer of assets

Patterns inconsistent over time

Attempts to bribe the auditor, examiner, or investigator

Weak Internal Controls

Lack of segregation of duties

Lack of physical safeguards for valuable assets (e.g., intellectual property)

Lack of independent checks and balances

Lack of proper authorization

Lack of proper supervision

Lack of proper documents and records (e.g., missing originals)

Observations of management overriding existing controls

Inadequate accounting and information systems

Related parties transactions

Analytical Anomalies

Unexplained inventory and cash shortages

Deviations from quality specifications (e.g., warranty liability down)

Excess scrap

Excess voids

Excess purchases compared to revenue levels

Ratios that don't make sense

Nonfinancial numbers that do not correlate with account balances and other numbers presented in the financial statements

Excessive late charges in accounts payable, notes payable, and company credit cards

Strange financial relationships

e.g., Revenues up; inventory down; A/R up; cash flows down

e.g., Increased inventory; A/P down

e.g., Increased volume; increased costs per unit

e.g., Increased inventory; decreased inventory holding costs

e.g., A/R up; bad debts down

Lifestyles Symptoms

New luxury cars

Pricey clothes

New or high-priced house

Expensive jewelry

High-end recreational toys, such as boats, vacation homes, motor homes

Behavior Symptoms

Can't look people in the eye

Embarrassment with friends, family

Irritable and suspicious

Defensive

Argumentative

Unusually belligerent in stating opinions

Needs to see a counselor, psychiatrist, etc.

Complains of being unable to sleep

Drinks too much

Using illegal, illicit drugs

Can't relax

Potential Informants

Employees

Customers

Suppliers

Family

Friends

Five-Step Approach to Fraud Prevention, Deterrence, and Detection

1. Know the exposures (brainstorming, risk assessment, audit planning)
2. Translate exposure into likely symptoms
3. Always be on the lookout for symptoms
4. Build audit and data-mining programs to look for symptoms
5. Pursue these issues to their logical conclusion and ground decisions in the evidence (evidence-based decision-making)

REVIEW QUESTIONS

3-1 Describe occupational fraud and abuse.

3-2 Compare and contrast Cressey's and Albrecht's theories of crime causation.

3-3 Identify from Cressey's research the six situational categories that cause nonshareable problems.

3-4 Discuss the essence of organizational crime.

3-5 Give examples of behavioral indications of fraud.

3-6 Explain the relationship between an employee's position and the level of theft (according to Hollinger and Clark's research).

3-7 Analyze the role of corporate governance mechanisms in fraud prevention.

3-8 Describe corporate governance breakdowns in the facilitation of Enron's fraudulent acts.

3-9 Identify ethical issues, conflicts of interest, and noncompliance with corporate policies and procedures in the Enron case.

3-10 Discuss alternative courses of action in the Enron case within the framework of appropriate ethical conduct.

ENDNOTES

1. Source unknown
2. See Albrecht's Fraud Examination and the ACFE's *Fraud Examiners Manual*. Fraud statistics can be found in the ACFE's 2004 *Report to the Nation*.
3. Adapted from the ACFE's *Fraud Examiners Manual*, Section 1.21.
4. The Association of Certified Fraud Examiners, *The Report to the Nation on Occupational Fraud and Abuse* (Austin: ACFE, 2008).
5. "Thompson Memo," U.S. Department of Justice Memorandum, January 20, 2003: "Principles of Federal Prosecution of Business Organizations."
6. Jennings, Marriance M., *Business: Its Legal, Ethical and Global Environment* (Thompson-West 2006), 367.
7. Ibid., 377.
8. Ibid., 383.
9. Gilbert Geis, *On White Collar Crime* (Lexington: Lexington Books, 1982).
10. Larry J. Siegel, *Criminology*, 3rd Edition (New York: West Publishing Company, 1989), 193.
11. Donald R. Cressey, *Other People's Money* (Montclair: Patterson Smith, 1973), 30.
12. Ibid., 33.
13. Ibid., 34.
14. Ibid., 34.
15. Ibid., 35.
16. Ibid., 36.
17. Ibid., 36.
18. Ibid., 42.
19. Ibid., 42.
20. Proverbs 16:18.
21. Cressey, 47.
22. Ibid., 48.
23. Ibid., 52–53.
24. Ibid., 54.
25. Ibid., 57.
26. Ibid., 66.
27. Ibid., 84.
28. Ibid., 84.
29. Ibid., 85.
30. Ibid., 94–95.
31. Ibid., 93.
32. Ibid., 101–102.
33. Ibid., 102.
34. Ibid., 102.
35. Ibid., 120–121.
36. Ibid., 121.
37. Ibid., 122.
38. Ibid., 121.
39. Ibid., 122.
40. Ibid., 128.
41. Ibid., 129.
42. Ibid., 128–129.
43. Ibid., 133.
44. Ibid., 139.
45. W. Steve Albrecht, Keith R. Howe, and Marshall B. Romney, *Deterring Fraud: The Internal Auditor's Perspective* (Altamonte Springs: The Institute of Internal Auditor's Research Foundation, 1984).
46. Although such red flags may be present in many occupational fraud cases, one must reemphasize Albrecht's caution that the perpetrators are hard to profile, and fraud is difficult to predict. To underscore this point, Albrecht's research does not address—and no current research has been done to determine—whether nonoffenders have many of the same characteristics. If so, then the list may not be discriminating enough to be useful. In short, although one should be mindful of potential red flags, they should not receive undue attention absent other compelling circumstances.
47. Ibid., 13–14.
48. Ibid., 32.
49. Ibid., 39
50. Ibid., 5.
51. Ibid., 6.
52. Ibid., 5.
53. Ibid., 5.
54. Ibid., 6.
55. Ibid., 42.
56. Ibid., 15.
57. Richard C. Hollinger and John P. Clark, *Theft by Employees* (Lexington: Lexington Books, 1983), 6.
58. Ibid., 42.
59. Hollinger and Clark, p. 57.
60. Ibid., 57.
61. Ibid., 57.

62. Ibid., 63.

63. Ibid., 68.

64. Ibid., 77.

65. Ibid., 86.

66. Ibid.

67. Ibid.

68. Ibid., 106.

69. Ibid., 117.

70. Ibid., 120.

71. Ibid., 121.

72. Ibid., 144.

73. Ibid., 146.

74. Ethics should be considered pervasive, a common thread, and included in all aspects of the fraud and forensic accounting curricula.

75. Random House Webster's *College Dictionary* (1991).

76. Association of Certified Fraud Examiners, *ACFE Fraud Examiners' Manual* (2006).

77. Association of Certified Fraud Examiners, *Fraud Examiners Manual* (2005), 4.902.

78. Ibid., 4.901.

79. W. Steve Albrecht, Conan C. Albrecht, and Chad O. Albrecht, *Fraud Examination*, South-Western, 2002, p. 90–96.

CHAPTER 4

COMPLEX FRAUDS AND FINANCIAL CRIMES

LEARNING OBJECTIVES

After completing this chapter, you should be able to:

4-1 Differentiate between a predator and an "accidental fraudster."

4-2 Explain why collusion poses unique prevention and detection challenges.

4-3 Describe how the concept of an "organization" is involved in mixing illegal activities with legitimate ones.

4-4 Discuss why financial statement fraud is often considered a complex fraud.

4-5 List different types of schemes associated with complex frauds.

4-6 Contrast the objectives of terrorists and organized criminals.

4-7 Identify and describe the different types of banks.

4-8 Explain the difference between tax avoidance and tax evasion.

4-9 List and discuss some of the more common securities fraud schemes.

CRITICAL THINKING EXERCISE

A woman came home with a bag of groceries, got the mail, and walked into the house. On the way to the kitchen, she walked through the living room. In the living room, she glanced in her husband's direction. Sadly, her husband had blown his brains out. She then continued to the kitchen, put away the groceries and made dinner.
  What might explain this behavior?

"PREDATORS" VERSUS THE "ACCIDENTAL FRAUDSTER"

The common fraudster is usually depicted with the following characteristics: first-time offender, middle-aged, male, well educated, married with children, trusted employee, in a position of responsibility, and possibly considered a "good citizen" through works in the community or through a church organization. This individual is often described as having some nonsharable problem, typically financial in nature or that the problem can only be solved with money, which creates the perceived pressure. When aligned with opportunity and the ability to rationalize his or her actions, the otherwise good citizen succumbs to pressure, develops one or more fraud schemes and misappropriates assets or commits an act involving some form of corruption. This person might be characterized as the "accidental fraudster."

Not withstanding the fraud act, the accidental fraudster is considered a good, law-abiding person, who under normal circumstances would never consider theft, breaking important laws, or harming others. When discovered, family members, fellow employees, and other persons in the community are often surprised or even shocked by the alleged behavior of the perpetrator. Because many of these perpetrators are in positions of trust (which creates opportunity), well educated, and have leadership-level employment, Edwin H. Sutherland, in 1939 described them as "white-collar criminals."

White-collar crime, as designated by Sutherland, is crime in the upper, white-collar class, which is composed of respectable or respected business and professional men (and now, almost as often as not, women). White-collar crime is also referred to as occupational fraud or economic crime. The white-collar criminal's actions are consistent with the notion of a trust violator, and the crime is typically associated with an abuse of power. Despite some shortcomings with this type of descriptive terminology, white-collar

crime captures the essence of the type of perpetrator that one often finds at the heart of occupational fraud and abuse.

The fraud triangle was created with the accidental fraudster in mind. The fraud triangle helps investigators to understand who might commit fraud and why. The notion of perceived pressure and opportunity and the development of a rationalization for the crime provides a profile, not only to help understand the typical accidental fraudster, but also to help identify meaningful, nonfinancial, sociological, and psychological red flags that can be used as part of the investigatory process to determine who perpetrated the identified occupational fraud or abuse.

On the other hand, what if the person has committed an act of fraud at a prior organization? Franco Frande, ATF Financial Investigations Chief, often tells the story of ten-year-old Christopher Woods. Christopher Woods was killed by his father for life insurance money. His father strangled the boy and tossed him onto the side of the road near a lake. The father then started a fire in his home, but when inquiries were made by investigators and the TV news media, he blamed Christopher for accidentally starting the fire. He stated that his son had run away after starting the fire and Mr. Woods tearfully pleaded to the TV newscaster for his son's safe return home. At the time, no one except the father knew that Christopher Woods was dead. The father had set up the crime by talking with others about the "problem" he was having with his son's playing with matches. He also placed matches under the couch seat cushion where Christopher's mother would discover them during routine cleaning. The fire allowed the husband to collect additional insurance proceeds related to the home structure and contents. All of this was to repay his most recent former employer as restitution for a fraud that he had been perpetrating.

Mr. Woods' most recent employer had agreed to desist from filing charges against him or making any public disclosures of the fraud incident provided that Mr. Woods reimburse the company for the missing funds. What the employer did not know is that the current incident was the fourth time that Mr. Woods had perpetrated a fraud. In the prior three incidents, upon discovery, the previous employer had quietly terminated Mr. Woods. It's possible that Christopher Woods might be alive today if any of the prior employers had prosecuted Mr. Woods. The choice made by each of his former employers allowed him to quietly move on to his next victim.

Mr. Woods is not an accidental fraudster; he is a predator. The predator seeks out organizations where he or she can start to scheme almost immediately upon being hired. At some point, many accidental fraudsters, if not caught early on, move from behavior characterized by the description of an accidental fraudster to that of a predator. Financial statement fraud perpetrators often appear to start as accidental fraudsters or even as managers of earnings and, sooner or later, become predators.

Beyond the predator-type person who seeks to deliberately defraud organizations with seemingly little remorse, we also find individuals and organizations that have operational modus operandi where a complex fraud or financial crime is inherently part of their goals and objectives. Organizational crimes occur when public and private companies, nonprofits, and government entities, otherwise legitimate and law-abiding organizations, are involved in a pattern of criminal activity. Corporate violations include administrative violations that involve noncompliance with agency, regulatory, and legal requirements. In other cases, organizations are deliberately established with at least some nefarious purposes in mind. We often think about organized crime, drug trafficking, and terrorism financing for the more complex frauds and financial crimes involving organizations. Organized criminal activities often involve many individuals, organizations, shell companies, and cross-jurisdictional borders. Some of the crimes that are typically observed include conspiracy and RICO (Racketeer Influenced and Corrupt Organizations) Act violations, money laundering, and mail and wire fraud. With terrorism financing, illegal acts derived from the USA Patriot Act come into play.

The important point is that predators and organizations focused on criminal activities exist and that reference to these types of entities as predators helps us to better understand their activities and motives in order to better investigate allegations of fraud and financial crimes. Typically, these types of entities are involved in complex frauds, corruption schemes, and financial crimes. Because their activities are far more deliberate from the outset than those of the accidental fraudster, they are better organized, have better concealment schemes, and are better prepared to deal with auditors and other oversight mechanisms. The concern is that in many cases the fraud triangle may not apply to the predator. Nevertheless, the primary investigative approach that focuses on the elements of fraud and adheres to evidence-based decision making holds quite well. Investigations centered on the act (the complex fraud or financial crime), the concealment of the crime, and the conversion (the personal benefit derived by the perpetrator from his actions) will lead to the development of a solid case from which the judicial community may determine the best course of remediation. Complex fraud and financial crime schemes include the following: money laundering

associated with organized criminal activities, terrorism financing, money flows associated with drug trafficking, tax evasion, deliberate misrepresentation of an entity's financial performance, and deliberate bankruptcy misreporting. Violations arising from these schemes may include money laundering, corruption, tax fraud, financial statement fraud, conspiracy, and mail and wire fraud.

COLLUSION: MULTIPLE INDIVIDUALS, ORGANIZATIONS, AND JURISDICTIONS

One of the central elements to complex frauds and financial crimes is that of collusion. Collusion may be among individuals within an organization, individuals across organizations, and multiple organizations. Collusion often spans multiple jurisdictions, including local, state, federal, and international boundaries and related laws. ACFE's report to the nation indicates that when collusion is involved, dollar amounts associated with fraud losses increase dramatically. The losses caused by individual predators can be substantial, but when those individuals work in concert with others, the damage can be devastating and far more pervasive.

The primary concern when collusion is involved is that internal controls are generally ineffective in preventing fraud and other financial crimes. The primary internal control of segregation of duties helps to ensure that no individual controls every aspect of a transaction and separates the custody, accounting, and approval functions. Internal controls also include independent checks on performance and assurance of compliance with applicable laws and regulations. While internal controls cannot prevent collusive fraud and financial crimes, they may assist in the detection of such activities. In particular, independent monitoring may reveal that internal controls have been circumvented through collusion.

If the predators are organized around criminal activities, however, it is unlikely that monitoring will have any impact because part of the goals and objectives of an illicit organization is to disguise the nature of its real operations from outsiders, including auditors, regulators, and law enforcement. Persons inside the organization, across organizations, and across jurisdictions act in such a manner so that the true underlying nature of the organization and its activities cannot be discovered.

LEGITIMATE ACTIVITIES MIXED WITH ILLEGAL ACTIVITIES AND THE NEED TO ISOLATE ILLEGAL ACTIVITIES

Another element of complex frauds and financial crimes is that the perpetrators often mix legitimate business activities with their unlawful transactions. Money laundering provides an excellent example of a complex financial crime that is designed to mix monies from some legitimate and legal activity with proceeds obtained through some illegal activity. Understanding the essence of complex frauds and financial crimes requires attention to the definition of "the organization." Using the crime of money laundering as an example, assume that a local neighborhood tavern is used as a conduit for this activity. The operations of the tavern may be completely legitimate, except for the money laundering activity. The tavern is also part of a greater organization in which other persons and/or entities are transacting illegal business activities that generate illicit cash proceeds. This cash needs to be "laundered" to appear legitimate.

To understand the motivation of the tavern's owner, we refer to the M.I.C.E acronym: the motivation could be **m**oney, **i**deology, **c**oercion, or **e**go. While it is unlikely that the tavern owner would get involved in an illegal money laundering operation to satiate his ego, they may be willing to play a role to obtain a "piece of the action" (money), to further a cause in which they believe (e.g., to fund terror operations) or because they are being threatened (coerced). Examples of coercion could be threats of physical harm to the owner, patrons of the tavern, the owner's family, or the physical premises of the tavern. Investigators must also have some sense of the entire story: who, what, when, where, how, and why (if known). To attempt to prosecute the tavern owner without a sense of the greater story will be far more difficult because the investigator will be unable to communicate that understanding to prosecutors, defense attorneys, judges, and jurors. To tell a more complete story, fraud and forensic accounting professionals must know the greater "organization," even if the organization is not recognized as a legal entity.

Inherently, most complex fraud and financial crime schemes include a mixture of legitimate and illicit activities. One of the main challenges for investigators is to isolate the illicit from the legitimate activities. This is an essential element for successful remediation of the crime and can be accomplished by using the investigative tools and techniques highlighted in this textbook.

DISMANTLING ORGANIZATIONS: ASSET FORFEITURE AND SEIZURE

Asset forfeiture or seizure is an important part of the process of dismantling an organization, particularly with complex frauds or financial crimes. As discussed above, the nature of the activities is such that collusion is likely involved. In more serious cases, the underlying design, goals, and objectives constitute illegal activities. By seizing assets, the perpetrators are being punished and the organization is dismantled to make it more difficult for another person in the chain of command to take over the remaining operations.

First, money and other assets must be identified during the investigative process. The investigation needs to show that the perpetrator(s) or the organization(s) involved received assets and what happened to those assets. This requires that all records—banking, public, business, personal, financial, and nonfinancial—are searched to identify assets available for seizure, and to help separate those related to illegal activities from those generated from legitimate sources. This is accomplished through a process of "following" or "tracing" the money. Chapter 16 discusses this process in detail.

Dismantling the organization by seizing operational assets, confiscating cash, and freezing funds is an effective tool for forensic professionals in the pursuit of their responsibilities. Criminal organizations, drug traffickers, and terrorists need money to achieve their goals because they must cover operating costs, including paying employees, investing in infrastructure, paying legal fees, and covering other costs comparable to those of a legitimate business enterprise. While criminal organizations cannot declare bankruptcy, the seizure of assets can have the effect of putting them out of business, at least for the short term.

SCHEMES AND ILLEGAL ACTS ASSOCIATED WITH COMPLEX FRAUDS AND FINANCIAL CRIMES

As noted above, the profile of perpetrators of complex frauds and financial crimes tends to align more with those of predators rather than the accidental fraudster. Their motivation and intent is generally more nefarious and deliberate, and their mode of operation more sophisticated. Furthermore, the perpetrators of complex frauds and financial crimes often collude with others who can provide additional resources or legitimacy for their activities.

Financial statement fraud is more often than not a complex fraud. It almost always involves the chief financial officer, controller, or some other sophisticated participant within the financial reporting structure. It also often involves top leadership in the organization such as the chief executive officer, chief operating officer, president, or others with significant levels of authority. While not always predatory, at least at the time of inception, it is almost always collusive. Executive-level individuals work in concert (collusively) to override the system of internal controls through the sophisticated use of journal entries, significant estimates, and other financial reporting choices, and through material, unusual, one-time transactions. Due to the unique nature of financial statement fraud, the large dollars involved, its impact on stakeholders, and its connection with the audit profession, it is addressed separately in Chapter 14.

Similarly, corruption schemes are addressed in Chapter 13. Corruption includes bribery, illegal gratuities, economic extortion, and conflicts of interest. Corruption is collusive by its very nature and tends to be predatory. At least one party, and possibly all parties, to the corruption scheme set out to achieve certain goals as a result of their activities. While illegal gratuities and conflicts of interest may fall close to being ethically questionable, specific laws make such activities illegal.

When one thinks of organized criminals, drug traffickers, and terrorists and their financiers, one typically thinks of strong organizations and carefully planned operational activities. These types of organizations are sophisticated and tend to be very disciplined. Furthermore, they tend to make extensive use of technology. The advent of disposable cell phones, Internet money transfers, money transfers via beaming (infrared) cell phone technology, the easy movement of money around the world, and banking and legal jurisdictions committed to secrecy and privacy have made tracking these types of criminals and their activities (financial and nonfinancial) challenging for those saddled with the responsibility of policing them and stopping such activities.

Organized Crime

The definition of organized crime is a hotly debated subject. The Organized Crime Control Act of 1970 defines the activity as "The unlawful activities of … a highly organized, disciplined association." The traditional understanding is that organized crime or criminal organizations are entities controlled and

operated by criminals for the common purpose of generating positive cash flows from illegal acts. The term "organized" is central to the definition. Many of these organizations are professionally run as if they were a traditional for-profit business. Their operations include hiring (firing), training, mentoring, information systems, a hierarchical structure, and other attributes associated with effective and efficient business entities. As such, the organizations are opportunistic, diversified, and require political support (legal or otherwise) and capital investment. Racketeering is the act of engaging in criminal activity as a structured group, and organized criminal organizations are often prosecuted under RICO.

Most people think of the Italian Mafia (as portrayed in the film *The Godfather*), Al Capone, and similar images when organized crime is mentioned. Organized crime, however, is far more global and complex than these traditional images suggest. Organized crime can be found in even the tiniest and most remote regions of the world. Some of the more recognized organized crime activities in recent times include the rise of the Russian mob in the wake of the collapse of the Soviet Union, organized criminals from Africa who specialize in narcotics and financial scams, Asian crime organizations grounded in secret societies, and crime groups located in former Eastern Bloc countries. The FBI estimates the annual impact of organized crime profits to be approximately $1 trillion. Organized crime, when the opportunity presents itself, will manipulate and monopolize financial markets, particularly those in less developed areas; infiltrate labor unions; align itself with traditional businesses, such as construction and trash hauling; engage in the purchase of political support through bribery, extortion, blackmail, intimidation, and murder; as well as organize and carry out various financial frauds.

The more famous criminal enterprises are those associated with the Italian Mafia. Italian organized crime consists primarily of four major groups, estimated to have 25,000 members and more than 250,000 affiliates worldwide. In recent years, the Italian mob has collaborated with other criminal organizations. The Italian groups have been involved in heroin smuggling for decades, as well as money laundering activities. In addition to narcotics, the Italian mob, earning as much as $100 million annually, has been involved in bombings, counterfeiting, fraud, illegal gambling, kidnapping, murder, political corruption, and the infiltration of legitimate business. The four major organizations that make up the Italian mob consist of the Sicilian Mafia, the Camorra or Neapolitan Mafia, the Ndrangheta or Calabrian Mafia, and the Sacra Corona Unita or United Sacred Crown.

In the United States, the FBI is most concerned about La Cosa Nostra (LCN). The literal translation of La Cosa Nostra is "this thing of ours." LCN consists of several aligned family organizations and cooperates with the four groups identified above who operate out of Italy. LCN is involved in a multitude of criminal acts including corruption, drug trafficking, illegal gambling, infiltration of legitimate business, labor racketeering, loan sharking, murder, stock manipulation, and tax fraud. Labor racketeering has been a significant source of LCNs national profit, power, and influence.

Balkan organized criminal enterprises are associated with Albania, Bosnia-Herzegovina, Croatia, Kosovo, Macedonia, Serbia, Montenegro, Bulgaria, Greece, and Romania. The groups from these areas arose from their traditional protection and support needs that were provided for by various clans. Over time, these clans morphed into organizations entrenched in organized crime. Many of these countries were under the control of the Soviet Union until its collapse. At that time, these groups, which had been working in the black market, infiltrated and exploited the new democratic governing bodies. These groups are not as well organized as others, still holding to their clan roots, but are involved in fraud, gambling, money laundering, drug trafficking, human smuggling, robbery, murder, and other violence.

Asian crime groups grew out of triads, tongs, and street gangs. These groups arise from, and operate in, Asian countries such as China, Japan, Korea, Thailand, the Philippines, Cambodia, Laos, and Vietnam. The groups from China predominantly arose from triads or underground societies. In contrast, the organizational structure of the groups from the remaining countries were influenced by tongs, triad affiliates, and street gangs. These groups tend to commingle legal and illegal activities. The illegal activities often include extortion, murder, kidnapping, illegal gambling, prostitution, loan sharking, human trafficking, drug trafficking, theft of intellectual property, counterfeit computer, textile, and other products, money laundering, and financial fraud.

Eurasian criminal enterprises grew out of the Soviet prison system, emigrated to the West, and proliferated in the former Soviet Union after its collapse. Eurasians specialize in sophisticated fraud schemes, tax evasion, and public corruption. The activities of the Eurasian groups have destabilized the governments of the former Soviet Union. A major concern is the access of these groups to leftover Soviet nuclear weapons. Some of the fraud schemes include those associated with healthcare, auto insurance, securities and investment fraud, money laundering, human smuggling, prostitution, drug trafficking, auto theft, and the transportation of stolen goods.

African organized crime is most known for its efforts with illegal drug trafficking and online financial frauds. Nigeria is known as one of the hubs for organized crime enterprises in Africa. Other locales for organized criminals include Ghana and Liberia. Nigerian organized crime is famous for its financial frauds, which the FBI estimates cost Americans $1 billion to $2 billion annually. Some of the criminal activities include auto insurance fraud, healthcare billing fraud, life insurance scams, bank, check, and credit card fraud, as well as other sophisticated fraud schemes.

Middle Eastern crime groups are engaged in a variety of criminal acts including money laundering, cigarette smuggling, and identity theft. Generally, these groups are for-profit enterprises and are not overtly affiliated with terrorist groups such as Al Qaeda. Like the Balkan groups, these organized criminal groups are less well organized, and their affiliations tend to be based on tribal and family associations. These groups are known to be involved in auto theft, financial fraud, interstate transportation of stolen items, drug trafficking, document fraud, healthcare fraud, identity theft, cigarette smuggling, and the theft of baby formula for the purposes of cutting drugs.

Organized crime, including drug trafficking as discussed below, is investigated using traditional techniques such as undercover operations, surveillance, wire tapping, confidential informants, victim interviews and testimony, document review and analysis, examination of public records, and following the money (direct, indirect, and ad hoc financial analyses). With the exception of terrorists, the primary motivation of organized criminals is the ability to make more money through collaboration than when working alone or in smaller, less organized, and less disciplined groups. The flow of money, along with an understanding of the rest of the story line (how, what, when, where, how, and why), provides a solid investigative approach for case development.

Drug Trafficking

Drug trafficking is a specific example of an organized criminal organization. The primary difference is that these organizations specialize in trafficking narcotics for illegal sale in countries all over the world. Mexican drug traffickers have a significant market share of illegal drugs transported into the United States, including cocaine, marijuana, heroin, and methamphetamine. In recent years, the Mexican traffickers have become more professional and violent. Due to the significant profits associated with illegal drugs, drug producers, traffickers, and distributors are more likely to collaborate. Around the world, the United States and other nations forge partnerships to address the various problems associated with illegal drugs.

According to Drug-Free America, illegal drug trafficking costs the United States $70 billion annually. Mexican transporters exploit the 2,000-mile shared border between the United States and Mexico as the entry point for the majority of illegal drugs into America. During 2000, 89 million automobiles, 4.5 million trucks, and 293 million people entered the United States from Mexico.[1] In addition to border crossings, drug traffickers also utilize airplanes, high-speed boats, and cargo ships entering and exiting U.S. waters. The Drug Enforcement Agency (DEA) estimated in 2000 that 50 percent of the cocaine entering the United States, and 85 percent of methamphetamines, entered from Mexico.

Mexican traffickers are organized, have the skills necessary to be effective, and demonstrate high levels of professionalism. Some of the Mexican trafficking organizations include the Juarez Cartel, Arellano-Felix Brothers' organization, the Caro-Qunitero organization, and the Amezcua-Contreras organization, all of which control the Tijuana and Ciudad Juarez areas around the Gulf of Mexico. These groups have loosely organized themselves as the Federation. The partnership provides greater security and profitability to the membership. These groups are estimated to earn tens of billions of dollars annually.[2] The Mexican organizations appear to be more specialized (drug manufacturing and transportation, related money laundering, and unrelated robbery) than most organized criminal groups, which tend to be more opportunistic and engage in broader ranges of illegal activity.

Although the groups are not known for their violence within the borders of the United States, outside of the United States they have been known for corrupting and killing law enforcement and public officials who threaten their livelihood. Within the United States, their efforts are more directed to corruption, including massive bribes. These bribes, for example $50,000 for allowing one vehicle to cross the border unimpeded, are concentrated at the point of entry because once in the United States, the probabilities of being detected drop considerably until the illegal drugs are sold to end users. These groups are considered to be professionally operated with centralized decision making. While these groups are known for trafficking, they do not distribute the narcotics once the drugs are inside the United States. Most of that part of the operation is handled by organized criminal organizations rooted in Dominica and Columbia.

These groups are considered highly professional. The narcotics transfers from the traffickers to the distributors are carefully orchestrated and often include surveillance of local law enforcement anti-drug units to ensure that the transfers will not be disrupted. Like the bootleggers of Al Capone's time, the traffickers will also partner with legitimate cargo carriers and conceal the narcotics among legal goods. Traffickers also exploit the advances in technology by communicating over the Internet, using various forms of encryption as well as more traditional communications via fax, phone, and pagers. The sophisticated groups also employ accountants, lawyers, and other professionals that are necessary to conduct their operations. Mexican criminal organizations are not alone in the global efforts to supply drugs. Almost all organized crime groups from around the world including those from Asia, Eurasia, the Balkans, Africa, the Middle East, and the former Soviet Union are participants in drug manufacture, transportation, and distribution to some degree.

Recommendations for effectively attacking the drug trafficking problem in the United States include the following:

- Improving coordination among U.S. drug fighting agencies
- Strengthening the legal institutions in Mexico and other countries where drugs are produced and transported, including the development of effective and respected law enforcement, prosecution, and judicial systems that address both the illegal acts and the associated corruption
- Improving multilateral coordination between the United States and other nations involved in counter-narcotics efforts
- Continuing and expanding programs that emphasize demand reduction in the United States and other countries with large numbers of narcotics users

In short, bilateral and multilateral counter-narcotics efforts are the key effective responses to fighting drug trafficking. Only with coordinated and sustained efforts, including those centered on information and intelligence sharing, will law enforcement worldwide be able to successfully combat illegal drugs.

Terrorism Financing

Even before September 11, 2001, the United States faced unprecedented challenges in this area. Terrorists, determined to undermine our way of life, made security a primary concern for government entities such as the CIA and Department of Defense. Because terror organizations need funds to operate and purchase guns, explosives, and other supplies; require training; and often function loosely or efficiently as organizations; fraud professionals and forensic accountants are integral to following and tracing their funding sources. The goal of fraud examiners and financial forensic professionals is to deny terrorist groups access to the international banking system. This has the affect of impairing their ability to raise funds, thus exposing, isolating, and incapacitating their financial networks.

Terrorism, as its main objective, is designed to intimidate a population or to compel a government to do or abstain from doing any act. Terrorists attempt to intimidate or coerce persons, governments, and civilian populations through the use of force or violence, real or threatened, to achieve political or social objectives. While drug traffickers and organized criminals are organized around deriving financial gain from their activities, terror groups' objectives are publicity, legitimacy, and influence. Like all entities, however, terrorist groups must build and maintain infrastructure and operations to achieve their objectives. Money is required to attract and retain personnel, to support their activities, and to pay for training facilities, firearms, explosives, media campaigns, political influence, and even to support social projects such as schools and hospitals in order to further their ideological objectives. Terrorists often live modestly, a characteristic in contrast with that of drug traffickers and organized criminals. Although the international banking system is required for successful terrorist activities, funding requirements for the organization may be relatively small by comparison. The small nature of the transactions makes the investigation similar to looking for a needle in a haystack.

Two primary sources of terrorist financing are state sponsorship and revenue generating from legitimate and illegitimate activities. Iran, North Korea, Syria, and others are often denoted as state sponsors of terrorism. Each of these countries, for differing reasons, awards resources to active terrorist organizations. Due to bank secrecy laws and other impediments to transparent financial transactions, the Cook Islands, Dominica, Egypt, Grenada, Guatemala, Hungary, Indonesia, Israel, Lebanon, the Marshall Islands, Myanmar, Nauru, Nigeria, Niue, Philippines, Russia, St. Kitts and Nevis, St. Vincent, the Grenadines, and the Ukraine are considered places where terrorists may find some safety. In a post-9/11 world, these countries

appear to have improved their efforts to assist international law enforcement in tracking and prosecuting criminals. Nevertheless, their laws do not afford the reporting requirements and financial reporting transparency commonly found within the United States.

Osama bin Laden, leader of the al-Qaeda terrorist network, is one of fifty-three children of a Saudi construction magnate. He inherited the foundations for his fortune, which is estimated at $5 billion. Beyond his inheritance, Osama bin Laden has invested in legitimate companies including a bakery, a furniture company, and a cattle-breeding operation. Osama Bin Laden is an example of an individual sponsor of terror, whereas his legitimate business operations are organizational examples.

Charities may be an additional source of terrorist funding. Examples include the Holy Land Foundation in Texas (now disbanded), and the Al-Aqsa Foundation in Germany. Each of these has been investigated for funneling donations to terrorists. In many cases, the donors to these "charities" do not know that they are funding terrorist activity.

Terrorists also obtain funds from both legitimate and illegitimate revenue generating activities; by mixing funding from legal business activities and unlawful acts, terrorist organizations appear similar to other criminal organizations. Related to criminal behavior, terror organizations support themselves with kidnapping, extortion, and protection money. For example, terrorist organizations such as FARC (Revolutionary Armed Forces of Columbia) and the AUC (United Self-Defense Forces of Columbia) in Columbia, are characterized by the kidnapping of both governmental and nongovernmental persons for ransom. FARC and AUC also enforce the payment of "taxes" on cocaine production. Criminal activities by terror organizations have been observed in the United States and include large-scale identity theft, smuggling, fraud, theft, robbery, and narcotics trafficking. Consistent with other criminal organizations, funds from legitimate sources are commingled with those from illegitimate sources. Legitimate sources of income may include donations, membership dues, sale of publications, cultural and social events, and solicitations and appeals to wealthy individuals with similar ideological beliefs.

When a criminal activity generates income, like other criminal organizations, terror groups must find a way to position the money for its intended use without attracting attention to the terrorist organization, the persons involved, or the underlying unlawful behaviors. Criminals do this by money laundering: disguising the sources, changing the form, and moving the funds to places where they are less likely to attract attention. In addition, terrorist groups have been known to utilize less restrictive overseas banks, to use informal banking systems such as Hawala, to smuggle cash, to structure banking transactions to sufficiently small amounts, and to use travelers' checks and money orders.

Countries like the United States attempt to monitor and track terrorists and their supporting organizations on several fronts, including the monitoring of financial transactions. Similar to the fraud triangle for the accidental fraudster, the "terrorism triangle" is necessary as a precursor set of conditions for terrorism activities to exist. Terrorists and their related activities exist only under the conditions of opportunity, ideological motivation (versus pressure), and ideological rationalization. Inherently, terrorists have the ideological motivation to inflict terror; similarly, most terrorists show little remorse and rationalize their activities based on their ideological beliefs. This observation is true not only for al-Qaeda, but also for Timothy McVeigh and Ted Kaczynski, the Unabomber. Opportunity may be the most important attribute for investigators because without the opportunity to generate, move, and control cash flows, the financing of terror cannot occur.

The elements of fraud provide a solid structure to investigate attempts at terror financing and to identify illegal financial activities associated with terror: the act, the concealment, and the conversion. First, the terrorist financier must commit an illegal financial or fraud act, for example, identity theft. Knowing that an illegal act has taken place and tracing the funds associated with the act back to the perpetrator is a traditional investigative tactic. Secondly, terrorists and their sponsoring organizations must conceal their illegal activities so that no one knows the act has taken place, or if the act is discovered, the act cannot be traced to terror. Finally, the perpetrator needs to obtain benefit (conversion) from committing the act. In the case of the terrorists, the funds must become available for unrestricted use to attract and retain the knowledge, skills, and abilities required to carry out terror acts. Like traditional fraud detection activities, fraud professionals and forensic accountants need to be observant, searching for accounting anomalies, internal control weaknesses, and lifestyle symptoms such as:

1. Movement of funds through the Cook Islands, Dominica, Egypt, Grenada, Guatemala, Hungary, Indonesia, Israel, Lebanon, Marshall Islands, Myanmar, Nauru, Nigeria, Niue, Philippines, Russia, St. Kitts and Nevis, St. Vincent and the Grenadines, and Ukraine.

2. Money flowing to foreign beneficiaries located in Persian Gulf States, particularly those known for state-sponsored terrorism.

3. The use of wire transfers for business activities that would not normally generate the wire transfer activity.

4. Financial activities inconsistent with the stated purpose of the business.

5. Financial activities not commensurate with the stated occupation of the individual.

6. The use of multiple accounts at a single bank with no apparent legitimate purpose.

7. Use of high-dollar currency and travelers' checks not commensurate with the business's purpose, or the individual's lifestyle or occupation.

8. The structuring of deposits at multiple branches of the same bank to avoid CTR (currency transaction reporting) requirements.

9. The use of false identities, documents, or "straw men."

10. Exploiting the privacy and secrecy benefits of sympathetic international jurisdictions.

Money Laundering

Money laundering is the disguising of the existence, nature, source, ownership, location, and/or the disposition of assets derived from criminal activity. More simply, money laundering is a **PROCESS** to make dirty money appear clean. The world is a smaller place due to technology and travel options. People and assets can move all over the world at almost any time with minimal legal restrictions, moving by air, land, and sea. Money, communications, and information can move even easier by traveling inside small fiber optic cables as pulses of electricity.

Fundamental to understanding money laundering is the need to define money. Money is "anything of value" that can be easily transferred from person to person and is such that most persons would accept it as an item of value or as a form of payment for goods, services, and debts owed. Money, or at least the concept of money as it applies to money laundering, can be currency, diamonds, gold, credit cards, money orders, stocks, bonds, cashier's checks, rare coins, wire transfers, gift cards, prepaid phone cards, debit cards, prepaid credit cards, etc. As long as it has value, is considered an acceptable form of payment, and is transferable among participants for a transaction it can be characterized as money.

The process of money laundering relies upon movement and takes place in three distinct stages:

Placement: The initial stage of money laundering involves placing it into the financial system. This stage requires some mechanism or vehicle for getting the money into the financial system without being noticed. At least three general methods are available for placement:

1. A cash-based or cash-heavy business can be integral to the placement stage of money laundering. Banks and other financial institutions are used to receiving large sums of cash from cash-based businesses. Restaurants, bars, laundromats, nightclubs, vending machine businesses, and check cashing businesses, as examples, operate with large amounts of cash and can be used as a means to place cash into the financial system through periodic deposits.

2. Structuring of cash deposits to fall under federal reporting guidelines can be a means of placing cash into the financial systems. Federal standards require that any cash deposit in excess of $10,000 to a financial institution be reported through a CTR. Furthermore, any cash payment to any business in excess of $10,000 must be reported to the federal government on a Form 8300. By structuring deposit transactions to be below the federal reporting guidelines, cash can be placed into the financial system.

3. Carrying the money offshore to a country with bank secrecy and privacy laws can be used to place the money into the worldwide financial system.

Once in the financial system, a paper trail (actually, an electronic trail) of the money and its movement begins. Most money laundering schemes are most vulnerable to detection at or before the placement stage.

Layering: Layering is the second stage and is used to hide or disguise the source of the money. An inherent goal of layering is concealment of the true source and business to business, account to account, etc. in an attempt to disguise the money source and confuse investigators because the amounts are no longer equal to those originally received. Furthermore, the transactions may have seemingly legitimate

business reasons and may even have paper documentation that lends seeming legitimacy to the nature of the transaction. Layering may involve foreign countries, especially those countries where bank secrecy and privacy laws make it difficult, if not impossible, for investigators to continue to follow the money trail. Once in a foreign locale with a strong commitment to bank secrecy, the money can be moved to another bank account, possibly in another country that also has strong bank secrecy laws, with complete anonymity. By this time, the funds are ready for the last stage of money laundering (integration). By using currency and offshore bank accounts, a perpetrator can make it almost impossible to follow any sort of money trail.

Integration: Integration, the third and final stage, is the attempt to convert the placed and layered money back into the hands of the perpetrator in a form that the perpetrator can use without risk of prosecution for being associated with dirty money. As examples, integration can take the form of payment for consulting services to a business or individual to which the perpetrator appears to have no association. Integration may take the form of a loan for which the repayment terms may range from legitimate to non-existent. Recall that even if the perpetrator repays the loan, he or she is only repaying the proceeds to their own business or bank account. From the perpetrator's perspective, the main issue with integration is ensuring that the source of the money and the transaction itself appears to be legitimate.

The good news for investigators is that perpetrators have two choices: spend money that they cannot show came from legitimate sources or launder the ill-gotten proceeds so that it appears that the sources of their money are legitimate. If necessary, some perpetrators may even pay taxes on laundered funds to further the appearance of legitimacy and make it appear that the perpetrator is a normal, tax-paying citizen. One nice attribute of money laundering is that ultimately the money must start and end at the same spot. Thus, if the investigator identifies the ultimate beneficiary, he or she knows that the same person is controlling the activity on the front end. Likewise, if the investigator identifies the source of the laundered funds, he or she knows who ultimately must benefit from the money laundering activity.

While the Bank Secrecy Act of 1970 improved the financial reporting and record keeping associated with cash transactions, the Money Laundering Control Act (MLCA) of 1986 was the first time that money laundering itself was considered a prosecutable offense. The MLCA has been amended over the years to strengthen the laws and eliminate various loopholes as follows:

- 1988—Anti-Drug Abuse Act
- 1992—Annunzio-Wylie Anti-Money Laundering Act
- 1994—Money Laundering Suppression Act
- 1996—Terrorism Prevention Act
- 1996—Health Insurance Portability and Accountability Act
- 2001—USA Patriot Act

In order to prove money laundering, the government must demonstrate (1) that a financial transaction was either attempted or conducted, (2) that the defendant knew that the proceeds derived from some unlawful act, (3) the property derived from a specified unlawful act, and (4) that the defendant attempted to accomplish one of the following objectives:

1. Promote a specified unlawful act (SUA).
2. Conceal the nature, source, location, ownership, or control the proceeds of a SUA.
3. Attempted to avoid federal reporting requirements (e.g., $10,000 for a CTR).
4. Attempted to evade taxes.

Furthermore, if the money laundering activity involves the international movement of money, the perpetrator can be charged with violation of international money laundering sections of the federal statutes.

One of the principal goals behind money laundering laws and regulations is that of seizure. The principle is consistent with that described earlier: to deprive the criminal of the use of their ill-gotten gains. The legal basis of the forfeiture is that the claim is made not against the alleged criminal, but against the property itself. Forfeiture requires probable cause that connects the property to an illegal act. The civil litigation threshold is a direct association between the criminal act and the property subject to seizure. In the criminal realm, courts will allow substitute property to be seized. Civil forfeiture funds are used to supplement the budgets of law enforcement agencies and are usually shared among the law enforcement agencies that participate in the investigation (providing an incentive to participate in a meaningful way).

Under federal law, all property involved in money laundering, as well as violations of the Bank Secrecy Act involving currency reporting, are forfeitable. To seize the funds of a money launderer, the federal government must be able to prove the elements of the money laundering offense. If money from a specifically unlawful act (SUA) is commingled with funds generated from legitimate sources, all of the funds are subject to confiscation. If the laundered money is then converted into other assets (e.g., stocks, bonds, homes, cars, etc.), the other assets are subject to forfeiture. Furthermore, if the other assets are in the names of persons other than those involved in the money laundering or criminal activity, the assets would still be subject to forfeiture. Criminal, civil, and administrative seizures are facilitated with a seizure warrant. In some cases where the property or its value may be at risk, a temporary restraining order may be obtained to prevent the transfer of title to the property or encumbering the property in some other manner.

Internationally, foreign countries have not always been as willing or able to attack money laundering in the manner in which it has been in the United States. In a post-9/11 world, more countries have started to cooperate in identifying and investigating money laundering activities. Some of the international commitment to anti-money laundering is demonstrated through such entities as the International Criminal Police Organization (INTERPOL) headquartered in France, the United Nations' Narcotics and Vienna Conventions, the British Commonwealth, which includes countries beyond Great Britain, a number of whom have been known as bank secrecy and tax havens, and the Organization of American States (OAS). In addition, the Financial Action Task Force (FATF), formed in July 1989 by the G7 (Britain, Canada, France, Germany, Italy, Japan, and the U.S.), the European community, and eight other nations analyzes international money laundering and makes recommendations for changes in banking and criminal laws. In recent years, the FATF also has started to investigate terrorism financing. The FATF has identified three times when money laundering is ripe for detection:

- Domestic entry into the financial system (placement)
- Transfers of fund abroad for the purposes of integration (layering)
- Transfers back to the originating country for repatriation (integration)

The Egmont Group is an association of financial intelligence units from around the world that share financial intelligence. Overall, it is now easier to obtain information from the international financial community than ever before. In addition, the United States is often able to gain or coerce assistance in the retrieval of moneys located in foreign lands. The mechanism for information sharing and money retrieval is the MLAT system or Mutual Legal Assistance Treaty.

Racketeering Influence and Corrupt Organizations Act (RICO)

Criminal organizations need a process to clean up their money. They also need an "organization" and bank accounts for money to enter the financial system and from which to initiate the money laundering placement stage. While money laundering is about the process used to make dirty money appear legitimate, RICO addresses the *ORGANIZATIONS* involved. Thus, RICO, enacted in 1970, the same year as the Bank Secrecy Act, is closely aligned to money laundering laws and regulations. While the original goal was to allow investigators to go after businesses and other entities involved in organized crime, it has been used to prosecute a wide variety of organizations including those associated with corrupt public officials, drug dealers, gangs, labor unions, and others.

Portions of the RICO Act outlaw:

- Investing illegal funds in another business
- The acquisition of a business through illegal acts
- The conduct of business affairs with illegal acts

Essentially, it is illegal for any person who has received funds that derived directly or indirectly from a pattern of racketeering to invest or acquire any other business that is involved in interstate or foreign commerce. It is also unlawful for persons involved in a racketeering activity to acquire or maintain any interest or control of any entity where the entity is involved in interstate or foreign commerce using illegal means such as fraud, extortion, bribery, or money laundering. Finally, a person employed by or associated with an entity involved in interstate or foreign commerce may not be involved in the operations of an enterprise's affairs in a pattern consistent with racketeering or the collection of unlawful debt.

RICO provides for criminal penalties up to $25,000 and twenty years in prison. Like the money laundering statutes, RICO also provides for the forfeiture of assets used in racketeering crimes and permits

treble damages in civil cases. Individuals, corporations, and loosely organized "entities" may be prosecuted civilly and criminally under the RICO statutes. Racketeering acts include:

- Violent crimes such as kidnapping, murder, arson, and robbery
- Other felonies such as unlawful gambling, bribery, extortion, the distribution of obscene material, and controlled substance trafficking
- Violations of money laundering laws
- Violations of the Bank Secrecy Act
- Mail and wire fraud
- Labor offenses
- Securities fraud

RICO and the money laundering statutes are somewhat circular in that money laundering laws and regulation identify RICO violations as a SUA and RICO specifically names money laundering as a RICO offense.

Conspiracy

As noted above, criminals in complex crimes, frauds, and financial activities require a process, money laundering, to clean up their funds and require entities as a means of accomplishing their operational goals, laundering money, and as an integration option. The organizations and the money laundering process also require individual participants. Whereas money laundering statutes go after the process and RICO goes after the organizations, conspiracy targets the individuals involved in the illegal activity. Thus, conspiracy deals with the *PEOPLE*.

A conspiracy involves three elements:

1. The coconspirators must have an agreement (actus reus) between them
2. The coconspirators must act or demonstrate an inclination to commit a crime
3. The participants must mentally commit to the act through their state of mind (mens rea or intent)

From a practical perspective, prosecutors need to prove:

1. The existence of a conspiracy
2. Willing participation in the conspiracy
3. The defendant's knowledge of the conspiracy
4. At least one overt act was completed in carrying out the conspiracy

Independent acts toward common criminal purpose may be linked together as a single conspiracy. Related to money laundering, conspiracy may be involved assuming that the coconspirator knew that the funds were coming from at least one specified unlawful activity. Conspiracy is also a specifically prohibited conduct under RICO.

The acts and statements of one coconspirator may be admissible against others involved in the conspiracy. Thus, lawyers and prosecutors will use conspiracy as a means of linking persons together and obtaining convictions of each of the coconspirators related to the underlying offense. The overt act required to prosecute conspiracy need not be illegal itself and may seem innocuous, such as sending an email or making a phone call, as long as the act is integral to the conspiratorial activity. While conspiracy charges have far-reaching implications, an entity and its employee cannot be coconspirators because they are legally viewed as one. However, an entity may conspire with another entity or with independent, third-party individuals.

USA Patriot Act

The USA Patriot Act is formally known as the Uniting and Strengthening America by Providing Appropriate Tools Required to Intercept and Obstruct Terrorism Act. Terrorism, like many crimes, is rooted in money. Money provides control, operating funds, and the means to acquire and maintain infrastructure. It is not coincidental that the 9/11 attacks chose to target Washington, D.C., the political hub of the United States and also to target New York, the U.S. financial center. At least one of the goals for targeting New York was to disrupt the international financial markets and wreak havoc on the American and Western economies worldwide.

Title III of the USA Patriot Act is the International Money Laundering Abatement and Anti-Terrorist Financing Act of 2001. Overall, the Patriot Act identified new types of money laundering crimes and increased the penalties associated with them. Specifically, the Patriot Act outlaws money laundering as follows:

- Funds generated from foreign crimes of violence or political corruption
- Funds generated from cybercrime
- Funds generated from offenses related to supporting terrorist organizations
- Funds related to bulk cash smuggling

In addition, the Patriot Act sets out the procedure for the forfeiture of bulk cash that had been smuggled. The felony penalty for bulk cash smuggling is five years. The anti-money laundering provisions of the Patriot Act supplement those discussed above. The Act also eliminated a prior requirement that the defendant knew that the proceeds being laundered had been generated from illegal business operations. Furthermore, the attempted transport of more than $10,000 in currency or monetary instruments into or out of the country is illegal if the funds are concealed and the transporter was attempting to avoid the U.S. federal reporting requirements.

The Patriot Act is particularly aggressive on the forfeiture of assets related to terrorism. The Act permits the confiscation of all property of an individual or entity who participates in the planning of a terrorist attack. Furthermore, any proceeds used to facilitate an act of terrorism or derived from a terrorist act are subject to forfeiture. If an individual or entity has assets in a foreign country and U.S. officials are unable to obtain those funds, the Patriot Act allows the seizure of funds from any correspondent banks where the terror organization has correspondent bank accounts. These provisions provide a significant incentive for financial institutions to avoid transactions associated with terrorists.

One of the techniques of terrorists and others interested in money laundering is to utilize shell banks, or banks that have no physical presence in any jurisdiction. The USA Patriot Act prohibits U.S. financial institutions from allowing correspondent account transactions with shell banks. The USA Patriot Act also increased the availability of banking records to investigators, increased due diligence requirements for banks, and established standards for customer identity verification. U.S. financial institutions are also required to have anti-money laundering programs in place. The U.S. Department of Justice has reported a number of successes as a result of the money laundering regulations that were improved by the USA Patriot Act, and these successes go beyond terrorism and terrorism financing to include the capture of fugitives, the prosecution of child pornography, the dismantling of complex cybercrime schemes, and the prosecution of drug and illegal weapons traffickers.

The Bank Secrecy Act

Like RICO, the Bank Secrecy Act (BSA) was passed in 1970 to assist in the investigation of illegal acts associated with drug trafficking and tax evasion. The BSA requires that financial institutions maintain adequate records and that financial institutions report certain types of transactions to the federal government. Any currency transaction in excess of $10,000 must be reported to the Department of the Treasury on IRS Form 4789, or the Currency Transaction Report (CTR). In addition, financial institutions may also report other transactions when the nature of the financial transactions or the activities of the persons involved appears to be suspicious. Such transactions or activities are reported on the Suspicious Activity Report (SAR). Because the CTR reporting requirements are more specific, the number of submissions tends to far exceed those of the SAR. In addition to financial institutions, businesses whose customers initiate transactions with more than $10,000 in currency and coin are required to file an IRS Form 8300. This form was originally designed to identify potential tax evaders and thus, the information was maintained within and only utilized by the IRS. Subsequent to 9/11, however, the information disclosed on Form 8300 has been made more widely available to law enforcement. The data from these submissions is collected and disseminated by the Financial Crimes Enforcement Network, otherwise known as FinCen.

Beyond the CTRs, SARs, and Form 8300s, the BSA has the following additional reporting requirements:

- The movement of more than $10,000 into or out of the United States must be filed on FinCen Form 105, Report of International Transportation of Currency or Monetary Instruments. Monetary instruments include negotiable checks, travelers' checks, and bearer money equivalents

- The CTRC must be filed by casinos (the "C" tacked on to the end of CTR) when a person conducts a transaction in more than $10,000 in currency. Casinos are known for their elaborate and sophisticated surveillance methods and have the ability to track suspicious transactions
- The FBAR requires that each U.S. person who has a foreign bank account report its existence on Treasury Form 90-22.1, or Foreign Bank Account Report
- Any person who owns or controls a money transmitting business must register that business within 180 days of its creation. These businesses are required to maintain records and obtain customer identification for transactions in excess of $3,000, including the person's name, address, passport number or taxpayer identification number, transaction date, amount, currency names, country, and total amount of each type of currency

The BSA attacks the placement stage of the money laundering process. It is at this stage where the money launderer is most vulnerable because they have control over funds from unexplained sources. Once the money launderer starts layering and integrating the proceeds, money laundering is difficult to identify because the true source of the funds has been concealed.

Mail Fraud

Mail fraud statutes may be invoked any time that a scheme to defraud someone has been devised by false or fraudulent pretenses, representations, or promises and such fraud takes place in any U.S. Post Office, U.S. mail depository, or through transport by the U.S. Postal Service. The person needs only to cause the mail service to be used to facilitate the fraud act, and the item sent or delivered may be transported by private or commercial carrier in furtherance of the fraud act. The violation is punishable by not more than a fine of $1,000,000 and imprisonment of up to thirty years. Thus, any time that the mail is used to facilitate a fraud, no matter how large or small a part the mail aspect may be, mail fraud may have been committed. Mail fraud is one of the workhorses of federal white-collar prosecutions and is available among other offenses to investigate and prosecute complex frauds and financial crimes. As an example, a person who mails a fraudulent tax return to the Internal Revenue Service has not only committed tax fraud but also committed a mail fraud offense. The mailing itself does not need to contain any fraudulent representation but must be integral to the overall fraud scheme. The scheme does not need to succeed or the intended victim suffer any loss for the mail fraud statute to be applicable.

Wire Fraud

While mail fraud occurs when a fraudster or other criminal utilizes the various mail services to facilitate a fraud, the use of wire, radio, or television to communicate false or fraudulent pretenses, representations, or promises is a violation called wire fraud. Unlike mail fraud, the electronic transmission must be associated with interstate or foreign commerce for wire fraud statutes to apply. The electronic communications may be writings, signs, signals, pictures, or sounds used to further the fraud scheme. Like mail fraud, a wire fraud violation is punishable by not more than a fine of $1,000,000 and up to thirty years of imprisonment.

THE U.S. BANKING SYSTEM

The banking system in the United States provides a number of services including mortgages, secured property loans (e.g., cars, recreational vehicles, trucks, boats, etc.), secured cash loans, credit cards, personal lines of credit, business loans, business lines of credit, letters of credit for overseas transactions, student loans, overdraft protection options, home equity loans, demand deposit accounts, time deposits, check writing and cashing services, periodic account statements, cashiers' checks, certified checks, money orders, bank drafts, travelers' checks, and exchanges documents. Banks also facilitate currency exchanges, have trust department services, and provide personal banking services for high net worth individuals.

The benefit of the U.S. banking system is that everything is written down and most transactions and their backup documentation are captured on microfiche or some form of electronic imaging. Loan applications are the initiating point for bank loans. The bank then evaluates the applicant's ability to repay the loan (debt capacity), the person's willingness to repay the loan (character), the collateral offered by the borrower (if any), and other conditions such as the borrower's employment history, prior loan experience with the type of loan sought, the overall economy, and any other conditions that might be applicable. As part of evaluating capacity to repay, the lending institution will obtain a credit report on the prospective borrower, prior tax returns, borrower W-2s and pay stubs, borrower investment statements, and other

borrower financial records. As such, the loan application file has a wealth of financial information included. Once the loan is approved, the loan documents are signed, and funds are transferred, the financial institution maintains meticulous records concerning repayment. If an investigator is able to obtain a subpoena for the loan records, these should be reviewed carefully not only for the financial information but also for leads to other individuals, accounts, businesses, etc.

Banking records for regular checking accounts owned by individuals and entities also contain a wealth of information. The signature card contains the names, Social Security numbers, and signatures of all persons able to withdrawal funds from the account. The initial deposit may be an employment check or a check drawn on another account. In either case, this information can be quite valuable. Once the account is opened, the detailed activity can be analyzed from the monthly statement and supporting documentation that accompanies that statement to develop patterns of spending habits, a profile on the account holder, the financial condition of the account holder, changes in activity patterns, and the timing of those changes. All of this information can be useful during an investigation. The depository activity should also be analyzed. Deposits may come from employers, in the form of cash, from investment accounts, friends, businesses, business associates, ATM deposits, wire transfers, mail, and other sources within the bank. While each of these may hold important clues and linkages to businesses, people, and places, wire transfers, particularly those into and out of the country, should warrant special attention.The check itself may contain valuable information.

In the example in Figure 4-1, the 0905 is the check number that also appears on the bottom line. The 48–567 over the 1234 is a code that identifies the issuing bank. The numbers above the line, 48–567 are the ABA (American Bankers Association) transit number: the first number, 48, represents the state where the bank is located and the second, 567, is a code that ties to the issuing bank's name. The number below the line with the numbers 1234 is the Federal Reserve Routing Code: the first two digits represent the Federal Reserve District, the third number identifies the District Office, and last digit indicates when the cash proceeds should be made available, assuming that the issuing account has sufficient funds. The payee is Innovative Learning Place. The amount or face value of the instrument is $53.21. The paying bank is First Huntington Commerce Bank. The following string of numbers are magnetic ink character recognition or MICR numbers:

12345678910 002398765410 905 2125 : 0000053.21

12345678910 is a combination check routing number (1234), and ABA transit number (567 plus 8910). The numbers 002398765410 represent the checking account number of Jimmy–Jo Venture Capital. The number 905 is the check number in MICR format. The number 2125 is the process code and the number 0000053.21 represents the check amount or face value.

Check 21, Check Clearing for the 21st Century Act, went into effect on October 28, 2004. This Act effectively allows the first bank to touch a check to image the front and bank of the check and then shred the original. Investigators will have access to the electronic images that can serve as evidence. The check is then processed almost instantly. With the advent of efficient and effective EFT (electronic funds transfer), electronic payment via the Internet, and debit cards, the paper check will become scarce over time. Although the backs of checks will change, the front of paper checks will contain the same information under Check 21 as they have in the past. The items reviewed above may provide valuable clues such as connections between individuals, businesses, and physical locations as well as other clues. This information should be carefully evaluated to further the investigation.

Cashiers' checks, money orders, and travelers' checks are favorites of money launderers. Once purchased, these monetary instruments facilitate the easy movement of large sums of money. Cashiers' checks,

0905 48-567/1234

Jimmy-Jo Venture Capital
A West Virginia Corporation
1 (800) Got-CASH

November 26 2008

Pay to the order of Innovative Learning Place $ 53.21

FIFTY THREE AND 21/100 Dollars

First Huntington Commerce Bank

Memo Booklets _signed / John Q Public

12345678910 002398765410 905 2125:0000053.21

FIGURE 4-1 Sample Check

money orders, and travelers' checks are very transportable and are accepted by most financial institutions. The primary drawback is that the initial transaction has a significant amount of documentation with it.

Cashiers' checks are often used as a down payment for big–ticket items such as homes, cars, boats, etc. Despite the amount of documentation available, because the check is tied to a bank's checking account instead of that of an individual, the tracing of these instruments can be complicated. Cashiers' checks come with three copies, the original check (top copy), a copy for the bank's records, and a copy for the customer. In addition, the bank teller logs the check in a ledger. If the acquisition involves cash greater than $3,000, that fact will be noted in the log. Cash in excess of $10,000 generates a CTR. If the proceeds are generated from the customer's bank account, tracing the check becomes a little easier. If the goal of the investigator is to identify all checks with the customer's name associated with it, the bank will usually require the branch name and the approximate date as a starting point. Because the only record is the log or ledger, tracing cashiers' checks can be difficult.

Money orders typically have limited dollar amounts. For example, at the U.S. Post Office the largest money order is $700. Travelers' checks can be traced only by serial number, so the investigator needs a starting point there as well. Otherwise, tracing travelers' checks can be very difficult. Bank customers may also rent a safe deposit box. Banks have no means of knowing the contents of these boxes, and access is strictly limited. An investigator cannot gain access without the use of a search warrant. The safe deposit box records include a rental application, and the bank keeps detailed record of access to the box including the date, time in, time out, and the person signing in.

Investigators may run across a number of different types of banks. Commercial banks are those most persons are familiar with. Other persons have accounts at federal savings banks (also known as savings and loan banks). Savings and loans got into significant financial trouble in the 1970s and 80s by speculating in commercial real estate. Since that time, regulation of these banks has been changed to avoid a similar crisis.

Offshore banks exist in foreign countries. It is not uncommon for high net worth U.S. citizens to bank internationally to take advantage of the various banking and tax laws. Criminal types, however, often attempt to exploit the secrecy laws of other countries' banking systems to hide their own nefarious activities, including money laundering. An investment bank underwrites the securities of companies issuing stocks and bonds to investors. The investment banker buys the securities and then resells them to the investing public at a preordained date.

Private banks are established by individuals and businesses to facilitate transactions. Many U.S. banks offer private banking to high net worth individuals. Private banking arrangements often come with various privileges and services not provided to regular clientele.

Central banks, such as the U.S. Federal Reserve, are responsible for maintaining and protecting the country's currency. Correspondent banks provide banking services for another bank's customers where the other bank does not have a local branch operation or other physical presence. Cyber banks are available on the Internet. Other banking arrangements include credit unions, auto finance companies, bank holding companies, and securities brokerages.

Businesses competing internationally will usually require international banking services as well as those located domestically. Typically, international banking customers do so for privacy reasons, to enhance security (especially true for unstable countries and their local banking options), convenience, and financial benefits such as tax breaks, better interest rates, longer float, etc.

MOVING MONEY INTERNATIONALLY

In order to transact business internationally, most companies also need to issue forms of payment that complement normal check disbursements through the domestic checking account. Some businesses located in foreign locales require cash payments in advance. This cash flow timing is advantageous for the provider of goods and services but has the potential to put the buyer in a cash flow crunch. As a substitute for cash in advance, some providers of goods and services accept documentary letters of credit. This is a common form of international payment because both the buyer and seller are afforded some protection.

The bank operates as the honest third-party broker. The bank essentially guarantees the provider of goods and services payment, assuming contractual performance as soon as the buyer confirms that the terms and conditions have been met. In advance of the transaction, the buyer specifies the documentation required in order for the seller to be paid. Such details may be the subject of negotiation between seller and buyer. Once the goods and services have been provided, the seller provides the required documentation to

the bank, including the sign-off of third-party shippers and other agents to the transaction. Upon receipt of the documentation, funds are transferred from the buyer to the seller as agreed upon in the contract. The documentation typically includes a bill of lading issued by the transporter, a certificate of inspection by an agent of the buyer, certificate of manufacture by the seller, certificate of origin, commercial invoice, the draft bill of exchange, a copy of the export license of the seller, the buyer's import license, and any insurance documents required as part of the transaction.

Documentary collection, a third form of international payment, is similar to domestic cash on demand (C.O.D.). Essentially, title for goods purchased is held until payment is made. Upon payment to the seller, the intermediary bank provides the documentation to the buyer. Because this is a documents-only transaction, the buyer has little protection against poor quality. Open account is the fourth international payment method and is virtually the opposite of cash in advance; under this arrangement, the seller is at risk until the buyer pays.

Trillions of dollars move around the world every day. The knowledge of how much money flows also indicates the difficulty that persons engaged in anti–money laundering activities face. Most of the trillions of dollars in money movement are legitimate. The number of transactions and relative dollars that are associated with money laundering are relatively few in number and small in amount (estimated to be 1 percent or less of all international movements). This money moves around the world electronically, in the form of electronic funds transfer (EFT). Cyber banking, smart cards, prepaid phone, debit, credit, and gifts cards and other similar methods for the movement of money will only ensure that the amount of money moving around the world increases as time goes by. As examples, electronic money flows are engaged by banks, businesses, credit card companies, money transmitters, governments, investment brokerages, stock exchanges, and commodity dealers.

Any electronic transmitter of money located in the United States must register with FinCen as a money services business (MSB). Money transmitters can be large, such as American Express, CitiBank, Bank of America, or can be relatively small businesses. Transmitters use a messaging system. The message communicates that money has been received on one end of a transaction and is available at some other place around the world for pickup. Typically, the person picking up the money must identify himself by name or some other security measure. The transmitters who facilitate the transaction for their customers collect a fee for their service. Federal law requires identification by the customer if the transfer involves cash in excess of $3,000. A CTR is required for cash transfers in excess of $10,000. Because of the ease and speed of movement and relative anonymity, electronic funds transfer around the world is a favorite tool for use by money launderers.

In addition to relatively small money transmitters, three systems exist for major money movement. First, Fedwire is the primary mechanism for domestic wire transfers in the United States and connects all of the twelve Federal Reserve Banks in the United States and approximately 12,000 domestic financial institutions. Fedwire may process 300,000 transactions a day, encompassing hundreds of billions of dollars. The second system involved in electronic funds transfer is the Clearing House Interbank Payments System (CHIPS). CHIPS serves as the main EFT system for processing international electronic transfers of money. CHIPS handles almost a trillion dollars a day in transfers among over 130 banks in more than thirty countries. CHIPS fund transfers are supported by the Society for Worldwide Interbank Financial Telecommunications (SWIFT). SWIFT is the messaging system that handles the communications by banks that accompany most CHIPS transactions. SWIFT is analogous to an email system. The messages over SWIFT initiate most of the transfers made with the CHIPS system. Telex provides a similar system to SWIFT to which businesses can subscribe.

Numerous records are generated with an electronic funds transfer. First, the person requesting the transfer must complete a transfer request. At the completion of the transactions, a confirmation is generated. In addition, debit and credit memos and various other documents, logs, and ledger transactions are created during the transaction.

In addition to the formal bank systems, domestic and international, informal arrangements exist as well. Hawala is an informal banking system originally created to support immigrants located around the world. Hawala (meaning "trust") allows transfers of money between individuals with no record of the transaction. This money transmittal system is international, informal, and unregulated. A person that wants to move money goes to his local contact and gives the money to the person, as well as instructions concerning who will collect the funds at the destination. The local Hawala representative then makes a call to his contact at the destination and communicates the instructions for collection. The Hawala representative at the destination then provides the funds to the recipient. Of course, the Hawala representatives collect fees for their services. The Hawala system is based on trust and is fast, efficient, unregulated, and maintains

almost no paperwork so the transactions are made in a relative vacuum. The value of such a system to money launderers cannot be overemphasized.

To investigate money movement through wire transfer, the investigator generally needs a lead and a customer bank account. Thus, the focus is on the beginning point of the wire transfer. From there, the investigator can obtain a subpoena and visit local branches to determine whether such movement has taken place. The data gathered, if found, should include the name and address of the originator, the amount, date, remittance instructions, the beneficiary, the recipient bank, and any other pertinent information captured during the transaction.

OTHER COMPLEX FRAUDS AND FINANCIAL CRIMES

Tax Evasion and Fraud

The Internal Revenue Service (IRS) is responsible for determining, assessing, and collecting taxes imposed by Congress. The IRS is divided into four major divisions:

- Wages and Investment
- Small Business/Self-Employed, including Excise Taxes
- Large and Mid-size Business Division (in excess of $10 million in assets)
- Tax-exempt and Governmental Entities

The IRS also has smaller divisions that deal with appeals, communications, and liaisons and criminal investigations. The Criminal Investigations Division (CID) is the law enforcement arm of the IRS. The IRS has responsibility for a number of taxes imposed by Congress including personal income taxes, corporate income taxes, employment taxes, including FICA (Social Security), Medicare, and federal unemployment tax (FUTA), excise taxes, and estate and gift taxes. In addition to federal income taxes, states, counties, cities, and other municipalities also assess and collect taxes including personal income taxes, corporate income taxes, state unemployment taxes, personal property taxes, sales and use taxes, and other taxes as required by those jurisdictions.

The primary distinction in whether an individual or entity has committed tax fraud or simply committed an error is the intent of the individual. The intent of the party to the tax return will determine the difference between tax errors and tax evasion. Tax avoidance consists of using legal means and methodology to minimize taxes within the existing framework of tax rules and regulations. Tax evasion is the intentional wrongdoing to evade taxes believed to be owed. Tax evasion is fraud and implies bad faith, intentional wrongdoing, and a sinister motive.[3] One defense against tax fraud is an objectively reasonable "good faith" misunderstanding of the law. The belief that taxes are unconstitutional is not considered objectively reasonable. Thus, tax evasion (fraud) requires an intentional wrongful doing with the specific purpose of evading a tax known or believed to be owed. Furthermore, tax fraud requires that the defendant have taxes owing, and evasion requires at least one "affirmative act" to demonstrate intent. Affirmative Acts are compelling and are actions that establish intent (deliberate action), often focusing on concealment. Common tax evasion schemes include:

- Deliberate understatement of taxes owed
- The omission of taxable transactions and activities
- Fictitious events and activities
- Hidden events and activities
- False statements made to tax agents
- False documentation to support fraudulent tax filings
  Examples of affirmative acts include the following:[4]
- Deceit—Lying when giving statements
- Subterfuge—An artifice to hide an act (evade a rule)
- Camouflage—To hide
- Concealment—To hide
- Coloring events to making them appear different
- Obscuring events to making them appear different

In contrast to affirmative acts, affirmative indicators are not deemed compelling in and of themselves, but are considered badges of fraud, red flags, symptoms, or signs of potential fraudulent conduct. Badges of fraud arise in a number of areas:

- Actions of the Taxpayer:[5]
  - Previous tax filings but the taxpayer stops without reasonable cause
  - The taxpayer correctly classifies transactions for some suppliers/vendors but not for others (e.g., unusual source)
  - Taxes have been passed on to customer but not reported or paid
  - The taxpayer handles identical products but considers one to be taxable and the other nontaxable
- The Treatment of Income:[6]
  - Omissions of specific revenue sources
  - Omission of revenues from specific products
  - Omission of revenues from product lines
  - Omissions of entire sources of revenue
  - Unexplained failure to report revenue
- The Treatment of the Books and Records:[7]
  - Two sets of books and records
  - False entries or alterations
  - Backdated or postdated documents and transactions
  - False invoices
  - False applications
  - False financial statements
  - Invoice numbers that do not make sense
  - Failure to keep and maintain records
  - Concealment of records
  - Refusal to make records available
  - Unexplained variances between returns and the underlying books and records
- Related Parties[8]
- Conduct of Taxpayer:[9]
  - False statements
  - Interference with tax agent's examination
  - Failure to follow the advice of attorneys/accountants
  - Less than full disclosure
  - Taxpayer knowledge (e.g., taxpayer has an accounting degree)
  - Testimony of employees or other unrelated third-party individuals
  - Destruction of books and records
  - Transfer of assets to conceal their true nature or their ownership
  - Patterns inconsistent over time
  - Attempts to bribe the examiner

The process of investigating tax fraud starts with first indications (badges of fraud) and concludes with either a finding of no fraud or a finding of tax evasion due to the presence of affirmative act(s). Consistent with other fraud examinations, when attempting to prove intent, investigators may find it helpful to consider the following:

- Present evidence in chronological order, particularly examining the timing of key transactions
- Identify altered, concealed, or destroyed documents or evidence (e.g., deliberate backdating)
- Carefully record false statements by the taxpayers

- Look for pattern or repetition of suspicious behavior
- Obtain the testimony of coconspirator
- Obtain a confession from the taxpayer

If predication exists that tax fraud may be present, the following is a seven-step process to convincingly resolve any badges of fraud.[10]

Step 1—Consider the risk of fraud by brainstorming, considering how and where tax return information might be susceptible to fraud, how and where tax return fraud might be hidden, and exercising professional skepticism.

Step 2—Obtain information needed to identify the risk of fraud by interviewing owners, management, internal auditors, and clerks, and carefully documenting their statements, considering the results of analytical and preliminary examination procedures and any other observed badges of fraud.

Step 3—Consider policies, procedures, and controls in place to prevent fraud by understanding the internal control environment; evaluating whether policies, programs, and controls are operational; evaluating whether policies, programs, and controls address the identified risks of fraud; and drawing conclusions about the risk of fraud.

Step 4—Respond to the results of the risk assessment steps. Specifically, as the risk of fraud increases, the agent or criminal investigator should respond with more creative procedures and investigative techniques, utilize more nonfinancial performance metrics, consider the need to gather additional evidence, and consider altering the nature and extent of examination procedures.

Step 5—Evaluate the evidence by continually assessing the risk of fraud throughout the examination, evaluating results of analytical and examination procedures performed, and reevaluate the risk of fraud near completion of fieldwork.

Step 6—Draw conclusions by obtaining taxpayer explanations for errors, misstatements, omissions, and other irregularities, corroborating explanations, and making any necessary judgments. Step 6 may need to be completed in concert with the investigator's manager or one of the IRS's Fraud Technical Advisors.

Step 7—Communicate about the tax evasion (fraud) by making sure that all aspects of the investigation have been properly documented, and write the required reports. After consultation with a Fraud Technical Advisor, the investigator prepares an IRS Form 2797 (Referral Report of Potential Criminal Fraud Cases) that includes a detailed factual presentation including:

- Affirmative acts
- Taxpayer's explanation
- Estimated criminal tax liability
- Method of proof used to determine taxes owed

When an examiner discovers failure to file, he or she must document the affected taxable periods, the explanations of the taxpayer, and determine if badges of fraud exist. Investigators should be careful about accepting the taxpayer's assertions or explanations without grounding the statements in the evidence.

Like other frauds, the burden of proof falls on the investigating agent. Tax-evading persons can be pursued civilly or criminally. The primary determinant is what the investigating agent and their supervisors and managers believe that they can prove. Civil cases never rise to the level of overtly deliberate acts to evade taxes, and criminal cases involve behavior deemed too deliberate to be dealt with civilly. For example, the failure to cooperate or the maintenance of two sets of books and records might be considered so egregious that criminal pursuit is the only proper disposition.

Taxpayers have several defenses that should be evaluated as the investigator winds up his or her investigation. First, the taxpayer may argue that no taxes are due. Second, the taxpayer may claim that their scheme was set up to avoid rather than evade taxes owed. Third, the taxpayer may claim that the unpaid taxes were based on an objectively reasonable position based on a reasonable evaluation of the tax law, regulations, and prior court findings. Fourth, related to taxable revenues, the taxpayer may claim that they did not have unrestricted access or rights to the funds. Other defenses that may be presented and need to be evaluated include the mental competence and capacity of the taxpayer, the competence of paid bookkeeping services, ignorance of a complicated tax law, the innocent spouse defense, and reliance on an accountant or attorney. The innocent spouse defense is particularly applicable now that returns can be filed electronically without the signature of all parties to the return.

Bankruptcy Fraud

All bankruptcy cases are filed in federal court at the local district of the U.S. Bankruptcy Court. The Office of the Trustee, within the Department of Justice, is responsible for administering bankruptcy cases including appointing trustees, examiners, Chapter 11 committees, overseeing and monitoring trustees, reviewing employment and fee applications, and appearing in court on matters of interest to the estate and creditors. Within the Office of the Trustee, special investigative units investigate criminal referrals and complaints in bankruptcy cases. These units sometimes work with the Internal Revenue Service and FBI when the circumstances warrant cooperation as well as when jurisdictional issues arise.

Examiners are sometimes appointed in reorganization (Chapter 11) bankruptcy cases, particularly when assertions of fraud and misconduct by the debtor in possession have been alleged. In reorganization, the debtor in possession's primary goal is to preserve and protect the assets and operations while the plan of reorganization is developed and subsequently confirmed by the bankruptcy judge. Secured and unsecured creditors hold claims against the bankrupt entity. Secured creditors hold some claim of collateral, which acts to protect the value of their claim against the bankrupt entity. Because security claims are typically filed at the state level (e.g., UCC (uniform commercial code) filing), the bankruptcy court must examine and rely on state law to determine the validity of secured claims against collateral. At the time of the bankruptcy filing, an automatic stay precludes any creditor, secured or otherwise, from taking any action detrimental to the health and well–being of the bankrupt entity. When the bankrupt estate is settled, secured creditors' claims have priority over those of the unsecured creditors.

The bankruptcy code of the United States has several chapters:

- Chapter 1 contains general provisions
- Chapter 3 provides guidelines for bankruptcy case administration
- Chapter 5 establishes the rights and obligations of the creditors, debtors, and the estate
- Chapter 7 deals with the liquidation of the debtor's assets, including individuals and businesses
- Chapter 9 applies to municipalities
- Chapter 11 contains provisions for those debtors hoping to reorganize and emerge from bankruptcy
- Chapter 12 is designed to address the needs of farmers and fishermen
- Chapter 13 contains reorganization bankruptcy provisions for high net worth individuals who cannot qualify for Chapter 7 liquidation

The bankruptcy court has the right to appoint a trustee in cases where there are claims of fraud, dishonesty, incompetence, or gross mismanagement if such appointment is in the best interest of the creditors, equity holders, and others with an interest in the estate. When a trustee is appointed, allegations of fraud and gross misconduct often underlie the appointment. In Chapter 7 cases, the trustee must investigate the affairs of the debtor. In Chapter 11, the duties and responsibilities are more far-reaching and include taking control of the business and making operational decisions.

One of the roles of the trustee is to attempt to identify missing assets and locate them, if possible. To do so, the trustee normally has access to the bankrupt entity's attorneys as well as the accountants and their work papers, tax returns, and client books and records. To fulfill their fiduciary responsibilities, the trustee may need to gather information, not only from the bankrupt entity's books and records, but also from banks, customers, related parties, suppliers, employees, pension funds, and others as needed. Once gathered, the trustee may consider the following investigative procedures:[11]

- Reconstruct cash receipts and disbursements journals and general ledgers
- Identify new bank accounts, related party transactions, and hidden or concealed assets
- Take depositions of uncooperative witnesses
- Take depositions of third-party witnesses and others who can authenticate and corroborate documents, records, transactions, and other information
- Take declaration testimony from cooperative witnesses
- Interview witnesses
- Prepare an investigative report
- Submit a copy of the report to the U.S. Attorney's Office if allegations of fraud appear justified

Bankruptcy crimes are investigated by the FBI and prosecuted by the U.S. Attorney's Office, if warranted. The penalty for each bankruptcy offense is a fine of up to $500,000 and imprisonment for up to 5 years, or both. Title 18 of the U.S. code identifies nine offenses:

Paragraph 1—Knowingly and fraudulently concealing property from a custodian, trustee, marshal, or other officer of the court. Property is defined not only as assets, but also as books, records, and anything of value.

Paragraph 2—Knowingly and fraudulently giving false oath or account, including oral testimony during depositions, hearings, and trials.

Paragraph 3—Knowingly and fraudulently giving false declarations, certifications, verifications, or statements, including written documents such as the debtor's petition, bankruptcy schedules, statement of affairs, interim statements, operating reports, and declarations in court such as court filings and motions.

Paragraph 4—Knowingly and fraudulently giving false proof of claims against the bankruptcy estate by creditors, agents, attorneys, or others on behalf of a claimant.

Paragraph 5—Knowingly and fraudulently receiving any material amount of property from the bankruptcy estate, including creditors or any other person.

Paragraph 6—Knowingly and fraudulently giving, offering, receiving, or attempting to obtain money, property, remuneration, compensation, reward, advantage, or promises for acting or agreeing not to act, including the bribery or attempted bribery of a court official.

Paragraph 7—Knowingly and fraudulently transferring or concealing any property in contemplation of a bankruptcy filing (i.e., pre-bankruptcy actions).

Paragraph 8—Knowingly and fraudulently destroying and altering documents during or in contemplation of a bankruptcy filing, including concealing, mutilating, falsifying, or making false entries in the books, records, documents, or papers relating to the bankrupt estate's property or financial affairs.

Paragraph 9—Knowingly and fraudulently withholding books, records, documents, or papers relating to the bankrupt estate's property or financial affairs from a custodian, trustee, marshal, or other officer of the court.

Title 18 also outlaws embezzlement against the estate. Bankruptcy fraud includes schemes to file a false bankruptcy petition, file documents during a proceeding, or make false or fraudulent statements, representations, claims, or promises before or after the filing of a bankruptcy petition. This applies not only to the actions of debtors and claimants during a legitimate bankruptcy, but also to the efforts of perpetrators to use bankruptcy as part of a scheme to defraud others, such as a bust-out scheme. Common bankruptcy schemes include concealing assets (most common), the planned bust-out, multiple voluntary bankruptcy filings, the credit card bust-out, forged filings, and filings by petition mills on behalf of unsuspecting clients. The planned bust-out includes the setting up of a seemingly legitimate business, buying goods on credit, selling those goods, closing the business, and disappearing while leaving the creditors unpaid. The credit card version is similar except the fraud beneficiary is the individual cardholder instead of the business.

FROM THE FRAUDSTER'S PERSPECTIVE

Adapted from the whitecollarfraud.com blog by Sam E. Antar Tuesday, October 16, 2007

A Warning to Wall Street Analysts from a Convicted Felon

To Wall Street Analysts:

During my years at Crazy Eddie, I found that securities analysts often did not know how to ask intelligent questions. When they asked intelligent questions, they did not know how to formulate the proper followup questions to our deceptive answers. Most Wall Street analysts were too trusting of the answers that they received from us.

Good questioning will often result in irritable behavior from company management. However, you are not doing your job to be in management's good graces. Your job is to obtain not readily apparent facts, analyze them properly, and communicate them accurately and effectively to your readers. Top-notch financial journalist Herb Greenberg advises that you consider "what many companies don't say as they spin the story their way."

For example, be careful of corporate managements that

- accentuate positive information and spin and deflect negative information
- blame others for their company's problems
- attempt to intimidate you

Beware of companies that exclude critics and provide "selective" access to management. Too often, Wall Street

analysts in their quest to gain access to management end up corrupting their required professional skepticism and cynicism. I played this game very well with Wall Street analysts, as the CFO of Crazy Eddie.

It's not about gaining access at the cost of your professional integrity. It's about understanding what is really happening and communicating it accurately and effectively to your readers.

I played you analysts very well by rewarding you with selective access as the CFO of Crazy Eddie. I had you eating out of my hand with "selective" disclosures and "favored" access. While you craved for access and wrote your glowing reports in gratitude for your coveted access, you unwittingly helped make the frauds that we perpetrated at Crazy Eddie easier.

If you had any backbone, you would all boycott any presentation that excludes the more skeptical professionals among you. Frankly, after reading many transcripts lately, you guys look like amateurs with your lack of questioning skills, your inability to ask proper follow-through questions, and obtain straight, clear, unambiguous, and honest answers.

You seem like hand-picked patsies as I read your unchallenging questions and the lame answers that management gives you without any challenge or follow up. You never seem to learn as you compete with one another for the affections of management and let access to them rule your work at almost any cost.

Eventually you will run into a guy like I was. You will wish you asked the proper questions and follow-up questions too. You will wish that your other peers attended the meetings and asked questions you would not ask or could not ask. The questions that will never be asked by you and others will cause you to miss detecting the lies and deceit being spun upon you.

When the "earnings surprises" eventually come out, your previous work will be considered negligent and amateurish. Your future work will always be under a cloud of suspicion. You will be remembered for the glowing reports you made as management ran circles around you. Do you want people to think you are fools?

The managements that spread deceit and lies to the selective few who gain coveted access are not your friends. They are using your humanity against you as a weakness to be exploited in furtherance of their crimes. They know about how your efforts at coveted access end up corrupting your professionalism. They don't care about what happens to you as a result of their actions. As a criminal, I never cared about you, too.

You have been warned.

Respectfully,

Sam E. Antar (former Crazy Eddie CFO & convicted felon)

P.S. I see that nothing much has changed since my time. Keep it up. When a company that you wrote a glowing report on ends up a train wreck, will these same managements rescue you?

Securities Fraud

The Securities Act of 1933 is otherwise known as the "truth in securities act." This Act deals primarily with the initial issuance of securities including stocks, bonds, treasury stock, debentures, investment contracts, puts, calls, straddles, options, some oil and gas investments, and other investment vehicles known as securities, focusing on full and fair disclosure. The Securities Exchange Act of 1934 focuses on the regulation of investment securities after their initial offering to the public. The 1934 Act contains a full range of anti-fraud measures. The 1933 and 1934 Acts were followed by the Investment Advisor Act of 1940, the Investment Company Act of 1940, and the Sarbanes–Oxley Act of 2002. The following outlines some of the more common securities fraud schemes.

Pyramid Schemes. In a pyramid scheme, fees or dues are paid by new members to join the organization. The new member, upon joining, is expected to attract and sign up new members and collect their membership fees on behalf of the organization. The organization generates cash flow, not by selling goods and services to clientele but by the collection of membership fees from new members. The membership fees are then distributed in part to the old members as a form of return on investment (e.g., dividend) to keep the old members attracting new members and to keep the scheme from collapsing. The scheme is dependent not only on the distribution of cash to old members, but also on the solicitation of new members and the collection of their membership fees as a source of funding distributions to old members. If the old members either fail to see returns on investment or fail to solicit and sign up new members, the scheme collapses, as they all invariably do.

"Prime Bank" Fraud. Though this fraud scheme, like most others, has various derivations, usually, investors are promised high rates of return with little inherent risk by investing in "prime bank" notes. The underlying methodology is supposed to be an offshore trading program that yields extremely high rates of return. The investment prospectus is usually confusing and makes reference to legitimate banks and recognized financial institutions from around the world. The prospective investor is usually required to sign a nondisclosure agreement. Of course, the entire investment is a sham and the investor will lose all of their money in the process.

Churning. Churning is the excessive sale of securities by a broker for the purposes of generating commissions. To prove churning, the alleged victim must prove that the broker controlled the trading in the account, the volume of activity was excessively high when compared to the investor's trading objectives, and the broker acted with intent to defraud or with reckless disregard for the investor's interests. According to the ACFE Fraud Examiners Manual, the best method for evaluating a claim of churning is to calculate the percentage of monthly commissions generated from the average account balance. Given this calculation by month, the investigator can look for signs of churning such as these:

- The percentage of commission increases during periods of less market volatility
- The percentage of commission increases over time but not in relation to the average account balance (which presumably stays the same)
- The gross commissions for some months are substantially higher than other months, and the underlying rationale for the trades is questionable
- The average gross commissions exceed 5 percent of the average monthly account balance
- The trades generated gross commissions but generated little or no realized investment gains
- The pattern of price changes in the securities sold, subsequent to the sale of the securities, is inconsistent with a need to sell the securities

And the investigator can ask these questions:

- Was the broker acting alone or as a result of investment recommendations and appropriate analysis?
- Did the broker make unauthorized trades?

Unsuitable Recommendations. Securities professionals are supposed to understand their customer's investing objectives, their customer's financial profile, and the customer's level of sophistication. Placing customers in inappropriate investment vehicles is prohibited, and brokerages are supposed to have due diligence procedures in place to ensure that brokers are not abusing their trading responsibilities.

Parking. Parking is a technique used by an investor to avoid ownership reporting requirements and net capital rules. The parking investor sells the security to another individual with the intent and ability to repurchase the security at a later date with the intent of avoiding ownership reporting requirements and net capital rules.

Front Running. Front running is a derivation of insider trading. The perpetrator, possibly a back office clerk or exchange floor order filler, becomes aware of a large buy or sell order, a trade large enough to move the market. In advance of executing the large order, the perpetrator makes a trade in his or her account so as to benefit from the large order trade and the subsequent movement in the market.

Bucket Shops. Bucket shops act as a normal licensed brokerage business, but neither the enterprise nor its employees are registered or licensed. Such operations are illegal and usually created with the intent to defraud prospective clientele.

Misuse or Misappropriation of a Customer's Securities. This scheme involves the theft of investment securities from a client's account or the use of those securities as collateral for other transactions such as loans or margin trading. Periodically, such abuses are observed in trust accounts where few persons are monitoring the investments or the account activity.

Market Manipulations. Market manipulations usually occur in penny or micro-cap stocks, those with very small market capitalization. The manipulation occurs when trading activity is designed to artificially move the security price in one direction or another to give the appearance of activity and momentum to entice others to buy or sell.

Insider Trading. The use of nonpublic information by insiders with fiduciary responsibilities to their company and its shareholders in order to profit from the purchase and sale of securities is illegal.

REVIEW QUESTIONS

4-1 What is the difference between a predator and an "accidental fraudster?"

4-2 Why does collusion pose unique prevention and detection challenges?

4-3 How is the concept of an "organization" involved in mixing illegal activities with legitimate ones?

4-4 Why is financial statement fraud often considered a complex fraud?

4-5 What are the different types of schemes associated with complex frauds?

4-6 How are the objectives of terrorists and organized criminals different?

4-7 What are the different types of banks in the U.S. banking system? How are they different?

4-8 What is the difference between tax avoidance and tax evasion?

4-9 How have some of the more common securities fraud schemes been perpetrated?

ENDNOTES

1. James O. Finckenauer, Joseph R. Fuentes, and George L. Ward, "Mexico and the United States of America: Neighbors Confront Drug Trafficking," *Forum on Crime and Society* 1, no. 2 (2001) http://www.ncjrs.gov/pdffiles1/nij/218561.pdf

2. Ibid., 4

3. ACFE *Fraud Examiners Manual*, 1.1401 (2005)

4. *Internal Revenue Manual*, 25.1.1.2.4

5. *Internal Revenue Manual*, 4.24.8.3

6. *Internal Revenue Manual*, 25.1.2.2

7. *Internal Revenue Manual*, 25.1.2.2

8. *Internal Revenue Manual*, 25.1.2.2

9. *Internal Revenue Manual*, 25.1.2.2

10. Modified and adapted from SAS No. 99

11. 2005 ACFE *Fraud Examiners Manual*, section 1.309

CHAPTER 5

CYBERCRIME: COMPUTER AND INTERNET FRAUD

LEARNING OBJECTIVES

After completing this chapter, you should be able to:

5-1 Discuss the role of the computer in cybercrime.

5-2 Differentiate between computer fraud and computer crime.

5-3 Identify the types of economic damages related to computer crimes.

5-4 Describe the methods and indications of insider computer fraud.

5-5 Explain what is meant by "hacking."

5-6 Discuss various ways that a hacker may access and manipulate a computer for illegal purposes.

5-7 Explain how computer viruses work.

5-8 List and describe various types of computer viruses.

5-9 List some common virus carriers.

5-10 Identify some indicators that a computer has been infected.

5-11 Explain why today's viruses are more difficult to detect.

5-12 Discuss why Internet fraud is particularly difficult to investigate.

5-13 Identify the federal law enforcement agencies that investigate domestic Internet crimes.

CRITICAL THINKING EXERCISE[1]

There are five different colored houses, occupied by people of five different nationalities, who smoke five different cigar brands, drink five different types of alcohol, and have five different pets. The houses are lined up in a row.

1. The Brit lives in the red house.
2. The Swede keeps dogs as pets.
3. The Dane drinks tea.
4. The green house is on the left of the white house.
5. The green house's owner drinks coffee.
6. The person who smokes Pall Mall rears birds.
7. The owner of the yellow house smokes Dunhill.
8. The man living in the center house drinks milk.
9. The Norwegian lives in the first house.
10. The man who smokes Blends lives next to the one who keeps cats.
11. The man who keeps the horse lives next to the man who smokes Dunhill.
12. The owner who smokes Bluemasters drinks beer.
13. The German smokes Prince.
14. The Norwegian lives next to the blue house.
15. The man who smokes Blends has a neighbor who drinks water.

Question: Who owns the fish?

OVERVIEW OF CYBERCRIME

Nick Tranto, Headquarters Excise Tax Policy Manager for the Internal Revenue Service (retired), describes three eras of fraudulent activities. He refers to the first era as the "Paleolithic Era." In this era, fraudulent criminal activity centered on cash, laundering cash, and evading taxes. Organized criminal activities and creative fraud schemes also usually involved other illegal activities, such as alcohol, gambling, prostitution, guns, and drugs. These activities became large scale in the 1920s and 1930s due to prohibition of the distribution and sale of alcoholic beverages. Many were orchestrated by individuals ranging from small-time thugs to "the mob," and call to mind images of Al Capone and Hollywood movies such as *The Godfather*. The primary problem was the need to handle large amounts of cash generated from the illicit and illegal activities, as well as bribes and kickbacks to keep elected officials and law enforcement from scrutinizing the activities too carefully. Some of the early and more creative money laundering schemes were developed during this time and a fundamental goal was also to evade taxes.

The second major era started in the 1960s and can be described as the "Neolithic Era" of organized criminal operations and the sophisticated predator fraudster. At this point in time, the bad guys discovered that "an accountant with a sharp pencil could steal more than twenty criminals armed with guns." Many of the perpetrators were first-generation college graduates and sons of mobsters (SMOB). Tax evasion and money laundering continued to be the major focus of the organized criminal activities. The structure, however, included more traditional organizational forms such as legitimate casino businesses, other cash-heavy businesses, and the interaction between legitimate and illegitimate business activities. The proceeds from these activities could be concealed and then made available for the perpetrators to use openly because of seemingly legitimate business fronts. This arrangement was, to some degree, a reaction by the bad guys to more sophisticated law enforcement investigation methods, improvements in the judicial system, and a greater intolerance by society for blatant deviant behavior. These changes put pressure on individuals with bad intentions to better conceal their illegal activities so they could fit into society as "upstanding citizens."

Mr. Tranto describes the third period as the "Geek-olithic Era." In the third era, cash and cash generated from illegal activities still is a primary problem. But in the Geek-olithic era, smart individuals with questionable ethics became significant fraud perpetrators. The bad actors now included computer specialists, attorneys, MBAs, Wall Street professionals, and others who now used tools and techniques such as offshore bank accounts, Internet servers, jurisdictional differences around the world, and technology to move and hide billions of dollars of cash. Once money appeared to be legitimate (laundered), it was then able to be moved and used as if it came from legitimate sources. In addition, more creative fraud schemes were created and the use of technology often became integral to the act, the concealment, and the conversion. In the Geek-olithic era, investigators need to use digital tools and techniques for data extraction and analysis to catch the crooks. The complexity of the schemes often demands the ability to connect seemingly disparate activities and financial transactions to businesses and organizations located around the world. Without computer resources, the effectiveness of the investigator can be greatly diminished. In short, because the bad guys have made computers integral to the act, the concealment, and conversion, investigators need to arm themselves with the same tools in order to level the playing field.

For example, a current scheme in the Philippines involves the electronic transfer of funds via cell phone. Assume, for example, that a drug dealer on the neighborhood street corner hands over drugs to a customer and the customer pays for the contraband by "zapping" money from his Internet-connected cell phone to the dealer's cell phone. The police observe the transaction and approach the dealer. The dealer, perceiving the approach of the police, ejects a memory card from his phone and drops the useless cell phone in the closest sewer, tucking the tiny memory card into his pocket. By the time the police grab the suspect, all evidence is gone except for a tiny memory stick that the police have confiscated but have no idea what it contains. The Geek-olithic perpetrator, from the small-time but electronically savvy hood to the well-organized, international Internet scammer, presents new and challenging problems for law enforcement and other investigators. In our tech-savvy world, data exists in many forms and places but it requires a targeted approach and an embrace of technologically-based investigative solutions.

Cybercrime, in the "Geek-olithic Era," usually describes criminal activities in which a computer or network of computers is an integral part of the crime. Examples include spamming, theft of electronic intellectual property, unauthorized access (e.g., defeating access controls), malicious code (e.g., computer viruses), denial-of-service attacks, theft of service (e.g., telecom fraud), and computer-based investment and other financial frauds. Some cybercrime, such as the Nigerian cash transfer emails and other email scams,

are grounded in the gullibility (social engineering) and greed of the victim. Other cybercrimes include hacking, "phishing," identity theft, child pornography, online gambling, securities fraud, cyberstalking, theft of trade secrets, and industrial or economic espionage. Some cybercrimes, such as "information warfare," have national security implications. Thus, cybercrime includes a blend of traditional crimes and newer derivations in which computers or networks are used to facilitate, conceal, and generate benefits to the perpetrator for the illicit activity.

As an example of the use of cyberspace to advance nefarious activities, according to *Gangbangers Invade Cyberspace*, by Steve Macko, ENN Editor, cyberspace is now

> *a place for gang members to exchange ideas on how to improve drug sales, what's the best gun to use to shoot your business rivals and what are the best drugs to use in your spare time? ... all of that and more can be found on the Glock3 Web site. This site is said to link members of street gangs from around the world, from 'Lil Shorty's Click in London to the Gangster Disciples in Chicago to the West Side Crips in Phoenix. Experts say that the site provides a virtual how-to-be a street gang member.*

Another way to describe cybercrime is criminal activity involving information technology infrastructure including unauthorized asset destruction, file and software deletion, service attacks that result in deterioration, alteration, or suppression of computer data, and unauthorized use of devices. Personal computers, computer systems and digital devices that capture and process electronic data are powerful, small, inexpensive, and user friendly. As computers and digital technology have advanced, electronic devices have proliferated in society, businesses, and in our everyday lives. Modern business, government, and other organizations including criminal enterprises depend on computer systems to support their operations.

Initially, transactions captured and processed by computer systems had hard copy supporting documentation. In the absence or destruction of computer storage where data was damaged, transactions could be reconstructed from manual forms and documents. In today's environment, the computer is integrally embedded in most business and government processes and less hard copy backup exists. Computers have invaded almost every aspect of our lives including tax return processing, electronic calendars and contact lists, cooking recipes, robotics, budgeting, automobile operations, weapons systems, law enforcement systems, and automated teller machines (ATM). More and more people around the globe rely on computers and digital devices in their everyday lives. As businesses, government agencies, and individuals become increasingly dependent on computers, so do those with criminal intentions. Individual criminals and criminal enterprises use computers to support their illegal operations for everything from facilitating the movement of cash around the world to real-time communications through email, text messaging, and disposable cell phones. Cybercrime and computer and Internet frauds are increasing in frequency and size, and this trend is likely to continue. More computers, and thus criminals, are networked internationally, giving global access to cybercriminals.

The following results were derived from the 2006 Computer Crime and Security Survey, conducted by the Computer Security Institute in conjunction with the San Francisco Federal Bureau of Investigation's (FBI) Computer Intrusion Squad:[2]

- According to the organizations surveyed, the top four categories of computer-based losses were viruses, unauthorized access, financial losses related to laptops (or mobile hardware), and theft of proprietary information

- 52 percent of organizations had unauthorized use of computer systems within the last year, down from 56 percent in 2005

- 38 percent of organizations stated that there was no unauthorized use of their computer systems; this number is up from 31 percent in 2005

- 10 percent said that they did not know if such unauthorized use occurred; this number is down from 12 percent the previous year

- The types of attacks or misuse detected in the past twelve months included the following:

  - Virus contamination—65 percent

  - Laptop/Mobile theft—47 percent

  - Insider abuse of Internet access—42 percent

  - Unauthorized access to information—32 percent

  - Denial of service attacks—25 percent

  - Computer system penetration—15 percent

- Abuse of wireless network—14 percent
- Theft of proprietary information—9 percent
- Financial fraud—9 percent
- Telecom fraud—8 percent
- Misuse of public web application—6 percent
- Website defacement—6 percent
- Sabotage—3 percent

This survey also asked respondents to estimate attacks coming from inside an organization versus those from the outside with the following results:

- 32 percent of respondents believe that insider threats account for none of their organization's cyber losses
- 29 percent attributed a percentage of losses greater than zero but less than 20 percent to actions of insiders
- The remaining 39 percent of respondents attribute a percentage of their organization's losses greater than 20 percent to insiders. In fact, 7 percent thought that insiders account for more than 80 percent of their organization's losses
- 59 percent of organizations experienced ten or more website security incidents, 2 percent experienced between six and ten incidents, 3 percent reported between one and five incidents, and 36 percent of respondents were unable to specify the number of attacks
- 48 percent of those acknowledging cybersecurity attacks reported one to five incidents, 15 percent of those acknowledging attacks reported six to ten incidents, and 9 percent acknowledged more than ten incidents
- 70 percent of respondents indicated that their organization shared information about a security breach, while 30 percent did not report their security breaches
- 25 percent of the responding organizations had reported serious incidents to law enforcement in the last year; 15 percent reported incidents to legal counsel, and 30 percent did not report the incident at all. Of those who did not report the incident:
  - 48 percent did not report for fear that negative publicity would hurt the organization's stock or image
  - 36 percent did not report for fear that competitors would use it to their advantage
  - 27 percent did not report because they felt a civil remedy seemed the best course
  - 22 percent were unaware of law enforcement interest
- 82 percent of organizations use security audits conducted by their internal staff, making security audits the most popular technique in the evaluation of the effectiveness of information security
- Total losses for 2006 were $52,494,290 for the 313 respondents that were willing and able to estimate losses, down from the $130,104,542 losses for the 639 respondents that were willing and able to estimate losses in 2005

Unlike traditional fraud cases, computer fraud can be difficult for the fraud examiner or forensic professional because it:

- Lacks a traditional paper audit trail
- Requires an understanding of the technology used to commit the crime
- Usually requires an understanding of the technology of the victim computer
- Very often requires the use of one or more specialists to assist the fraud examiner or financial forensics expert, even when the professional is computer literate

The Role of the Computer in Cybercrime

Computer crime is a crime that is committed where the computer or electronic data device is integral to the criminal act. The computer, however, has several roles in high-tech crime, both as tool and target. According to Donn B. Parker, a cybercrime authority and author, the function of the computer in crime is fourfold, as an object, a subject, a tool, and a symbol.

- The Computer as an Object—Computers and network systems are themselves often objects or targets of crime, subject to physical sabotage, theft, or destruction of information
- The Computer as a Subject—Computers can be the direct subjects of crime when technologists use the computer to commit a crime. This category includes virus attacks, illegal access, etc.
- The Computer as a Tool—Computers can be integral to the act, the concealment, and the conversion associated with a fraud or financial crime when the electronic device is used to commit crime, whether embezzlement, theft of proprietary information, or hacking
- The Computer as a Symbol—Computers lend fraudsters an air of credibility and are often used to deceive victims into investment, pyramid, and other "traditional" fraud schemes that have been adapted to the digital environment

Some common examples of computer crimes include the following:

- Data alteration
- Unauthorized access and entry to systems and information
- Reading another's e-mail without permission
- Data destruction and sabotage
- Internet consumer fraud
- Sale of proprietary data
- Desktop counterfeiting
- Data extortion
- Disclosure of confidential data
- Identity theft
- Electronic letter bombing
- Software piracy
- PBX fraud
- Voice mail fraud
- Cellular telephone fraud
- Stolen long-distance calling cards

Computer Fraud versus Computer Crime

Two terms that are commonly used interchangeably are computer fraud (and financial crimes) and computer crime, yet substantial differences exist between them. First, computer-based fraud and financial crimes are any defalcation, fraud, or financial crime accomplished by tampering with computer programs, data files, operations, equipment, or media, and resulting in losses sustained by the organization whose computer system was compromised. One of the distinguishing characteristics of computer-based fraud is that access occurs with the intent to execute a fraudulent scheme or financial criminal act.

Historically, in the early 1980s law enforcement agencies faced the dawn of the computer age with growing concern about the lack of criminal laws available to fight emerging computer crimes. Although wire and mail fraud provisions of the federal criminal code were capable of addressing some aspects of computer-related criminal activity, neither entirely addressed the new computer-based crimes. In response, Congress included provisions in the Comprehensive Crime Control Act of 1984 to address unauthorized access and use of computers and computer networks.[3] The Act made it a felony to access classified information in a computer without authorization and a misdemeanor to access financial records or credit histories stored in a financial institution or to trespass into a government computer. The 1984 Act was updated and improved in 1986 when Congress enacted the Computer Fraud and Abuse Act (CFAA). In the CFAA, Congress limited federal jurisdiction to cases with a compelling federal interest—i.e., where computers of the federal government or certain financial institutions were involved or where the crime itself is interstate in nature. Some of the other provisions included those:

- To penalize the theft of property via computer that occurs as a part of a scheme to defraud
- To penalize those who intentionally alter, damage, or destroy data belonging to others
- To criminalize the trafficking of passwords and similar electronic access items

These Acts have been regularly updated into the 2000s to ensure that the statutes continue to respond to current trends and techniques of computer-based criminal acts and give law enforcement the tools necessary to fight computer-based crimes, fraud, and financial crimes.[4] Computer-based fraud statutes and laws have established two very important principles:

1. Most statutes explicitly define computer-based terminology that is to be used in a legal context when enforcing the statute. These statutes allow the prosecutor to avoid having to explain to the jury technical "computer jargon" and its inexact fit with common law enforcement terminology.

2. Most statutes create the illegal offense grounded in the proof of access associated with a particular intent to commit an illegal act. Thus, success in carrying out the act (e.g., stealing property (money) through a fraud act) does not have to be proven. For example, tracing cash flows (proceeds) can be difficult without paper records and unauthorized (illegal) computer access may be the only provable event.

In short, most jurisdictions have defined computer-fraud as an "attempt crime." By viewing the computer as a protected asset, the protection is independent of the actual loss to the owner as a result of the intrusion.

In contrast to computer fraud, computer crime is defined as an act where the computer hardware, software, or data is altered, destroyed, manipulated, or compromised due to acts that are not intended. Generally, computer crime differs from computer fraud in at least three major ways:

1. Employees who, as a part of their assigned duties and responsibilities, have access to the computer systems are deemed to have authorized access. As a result, those with authorized access cannot fall under statutes that address computer fraud (outlawing unauthorized access), even if their actions subsequent to access are judged illegal. Individuals with some authorized access but who exceeded that authorization can be prosecuted under computer-based fraud statutes. Thus, "without authorization" generally refers to intrusions by outsiders or those with no access, but some courts have also applied the term to intrusions by insiders who access computers other than the computer they are authorized to use, intrusions by insiders acting as agents for outsiders, and intrusions by insiders who violate clearly defined access policies.

2. The manipulation, alteration, or destruction of data (including computer software) is considered independent of computer-based fraudulent schemes.

3. Because data are intangible, the destruction or compromising of the integrity of computer data does not fall under vandalism statutes.

As a result of the preceding discussion, computer-based fraud and financial crimes are technically not "computer crimes" but often involve the use of computers as a means to break the law. In some cases, traditionally illegal acts can yield more ill-gotten gains by utilizing the speed, power, and global access of computers, other digital devices, and their users. A more apt term may be computer-assisted crimes. In such cases where traditional frauds and financial crimes are facilitated through the incorporation of electronic devices, existing criminal laws can be applied to the acts. The main benefit of the computer fraud and computer crime statutes, however, is derived when proving traditional crimes is difficult because the evidence of such acts have been destroyed electronically. In such cases, computer fraud and computer crime laws are invaluable as an alternative method of prosecution.

Losses or Other Damages Related to Computer Crimes

The most common types of losses associated with computer crimes are economic. Economic losses may include:

- Cost to respond to the damage caused by the perpetrator
- Damage assessments
- Restoration of data or programs
- Wages of employees for these tasks
- Lost sales from websites
- Lost advertising revenue from websites
- Harm to reputation or goodwill
- Other reasonable costs associated with the act

Nevertheless, the economic losses generally do not include costs associated with assisting law enforcement. Of the various losses, the most common definition of economic loss is "any reasonable cost to any victim, including the cost of responding to the illegal act, conducting a damage assessment, and restoring data, programs, systems, or information to its original condition and any revenue lost, incremental costs incurred, or other consequential damages incurred."

Costs to make a system better or more secure than it was prior to the intrusion may not qualify as "reasonable" in many cases. In general, the cost of installing completely new security measures "unrelated to preventing further damage resulting from [the offender's] conduct" should not be included in the loss total. Thus, the types of losses considered by the courts "have generally been limited to those costs necessary to assess the damage caused to the plaintiff's computer system or to restore the system. Losses also include lost advertising revenue or lost sales due to a website outage and the salaries of company employees who are unable to work due to a computer shutdown. Fraud and forensic accounting professionals need to think critically and creatively about what types of harm in a particular situation meet this standard, and work with victims to measure and document the losses. At least one court has held that damage to a company's reputation and goodwill as a consequence of an intrusion might properly be considered a loss for purposes of alleging harm.

In addition, federal statutes also address four cases of "special losses":

1. An actual or potential effect on medical care
2. Physical injury to a person
3. Threat to public health or safety
4. Damage to a computer related to the administration of justice, national defense, or national security

The first special loss is related to the "modification or impairment, or potential modification or impairment, of the medical examination, diagnosis, treatment or care of one or more individuals."[5] This provision provides strong protection to the computer networks of hospitals, clinics, and other medical facilities because of the importance of those systems and the sensitive data that they contain. This type of special harm does not require the victim to show any financial loss. The evidence only has to show that at least one patient's medical care was at least potentially affected as a consequence of the intrusion.

The second special loss occurs when the damage to a computer causes "physical injury to any person."[6] Computer networks control many vital systems in our society. Examples include traffic signals, air traffic control, and 911 emergency telephone services. The disruption of these computers could directly result in physical injury. Generally, so long as there is a reasonable connection between the damaged computer and the physical injury, the perpetrator can be held accountable for those physical injuries that result from their illegal actions associated with computer access or other computer crime.

The third special loss includes threats to public health or safety, a concept that closely aligns to physical harm discussed above. The key word is "threat" to public health or safety. In these cases, the prosecution is not required to demonstrate actual physical harm, only the threat to a person or persons. This aspect of loss addresses a wider array of government-type services such as electricity transmission, gas distribution, water purification, nuclear power, and transportation systems. Damage to the computers that operate and control these systems and associated safety mechanisms can create a threat to the safety of many persons. Such statutes have broad implications for perpetrators who disrupt services to the general public.

The final special loss category addresses computer compromises that affect "a computer system used by or for a government entity in furtherance of the administration of justice, national defense, or national security."[7] The "administration of justice" aspect includes courthouse computers and systems operated by federal, state, and local law enforcement, prosecutors, and probation offices. Similarly, computers used "in furtherance of national defense or national security" are generally operated by the armed services and the Department of Defense. Normally, the statute is broad enough so that computers owned and operated by a defense contractor, for example, could arguably involve national security implications.

International Aspects of Computer Crime

With the explosive growth of computer use around the globe and more people gaining access to and using the World Wide Web, computer-based frauds and financial crimes are increasingly likely to have international dimensions. In most cases, the legal environment for computer-based crimes is different in every country. Consequently, identifying, locating, and extraditing suspects from another country poses

additional challenges. Finally, due to differing privacy rights of individuals in the various jurisdictions of the world, securing electronic evidence of computer-based frauds, financial crimes, and other criminal acts is very difficult. Essentially, jurisdictional complexities arise at every step in the process: prevention, deterrence, detection, and investigation. In the United States, the Department of Justice and the Federal Bureau of Investigation work with foreign governments through many channels to address global threats related to computer-based crimes. The FBI's approach reflects the increase in cybercrime worldwide as well as the networking of local criminals with those located around the globe. In 2006, complaints to the FBI's Internet Crime Complaint Center declined 10 percent to 207,492; however, losses associated with those crimes increased by 8 percent to $198.4 million.

Perhaps more importantly, criminals are following principles outlined in Freidman's book, *The World is Flat*. Increasingly, cybercriminals are organized and span the globe. Members of cyberfraud networks share profits and carry out crimes utilizing the various specialties of the participants. For example, one member of a criminal consortium may send out millions of spam e-mails. The e-mail responses may be handled by another member, or even another criminal organization that specializes in electronically harvesting and exploiting credit card numbers. The proceeds from the crime may then be laundered by a third individual or organization that then distributes the "profits" according to previously outlines agreements. The perpetrators may never meet, physically see one another, or even speak on the phone. Despite the physical distance between them, the groups are highly organized and effective. In response to threats to U.S. citizens within its borders and territories, the FBI has agents in sixty countries investigating cybercrimes.

On November 23, 2001, in Budapest, Hungary, the United States and twenty-nine other countries signed the Council of Europe Cybercrime Convention. The Cybercrime Convention is the first multilateral instrument designed to begin to address the problems posed by the spread of criminal activity on dispersed computer networks around the globe. The Conventions require the parties to establish laws against cybercrime, to ensure that law enforcement officials have procedural authority to investigate and prosecute cybercrime offenses, and to provide international cooperation to other signatories in the their fights against computer-based criminals. On August 3, 2006, the United States Senate voted to ratify the Cybercrime Convention and on September 22, 2006, the president signed the United States instrument of ratification for the Council of Europe Convention on Cybercrime.

FRAUDS AND OTHER THREATS IN THE DIGITAL WORLD OF COMPUTERS

Insider Threats

One of the greatest threats to information systems in terms of computer crime comes from employees inside an organization. It is not uncommon for operators, media librarians, hardware technicians, and other staff members to find themselves in positions of high levels of access privilege in relation to the key functions and assets of their organizations. A consequence of this situation is the probability that such individuals have the opportunity to commit fraud, one of the three elements of the fraud triangle. When combined with pressure such as a nonsharable financial need and the ability to rationalize their actions, such opportunity can be costly for an organization. As such, computer operations should have, at a minimum and where appropriate, an effective separation of duties. Even separation of duties, however, will not prevent all computer-based frauds and crimes perpetrated from within. To address the possibility of collusive frauds, detection controls need to support and supplement prevention controls. In addition, an environment where deterrence is also emphasized (e.g., high ethical standards, an organizational commitment to prosecution of fraudsters) also helps to minimize the risk of collusive fraud.

A further complication is the tendency on the part of management to tolerate less stringent supervisory controls over information system personnel. The premise is that the work is not only highly technical and specialized, but difficult to understand and control. As an example, systems software support is often entrusted to a single programmer who generates the version of the operating system in use, establishes password or other control lists, and determines the logging and accounting features to be used. In addition, such personnel are often permitted, and sometimes encouraged, to perform these duties during nonprime shift periods, when demands on computer time are light. As a result, many of the most critical software development and maintenance functions are performed in an unsupervised environment. It is also clear that operators, software librarians, and information system technicians often enjoy a degree of freedom quite different from that which would be considered normal in a more traditional employment area.

Insiders are typically aware of the "holes" in the system of internal controls in the digital environment and often exploit weaknesses "just to see if they can get away with it." The most prevalent method of committing computer fraud is alteration or falsification of input transactions (and/or documents), including:

- Alteration of input
- Alteration of output
- Data file manipulation
- Communications systems disruptions
- Operating systems modifications
- Computer operations policy violations

The characteristics of the insider computer fraudster are very similar to those of the traditional fraudster: intelligent, hard working, minimal absences (the appearance of dedication), bored with "the routine," confident, and egotistical. Computer fraudsters often demonstrate greater loyalty to technology than to their employer. This technology loyalty can create an attitude that any behavior is acceptable if it is in the name of technology.

The following are indicators of insider computer fraud that suggest increased risk and require additional scrutiny:

- Access privileges beyond those required to perform assigned job functions
- Exception reports not reviewed and resolved
- Access logs not reviewed
- Production programs run at unusual hours
- Lack of separation of duties in the data center

Computer Hacking

Although the term "hacker" was originally used to describe a computer enthusiast, the term has now grown to mean someone seeking unauthorized access to computer systems and the information contained therein. Hackers can include employees, individuals operating alone, hacker gangs, and entrepreneurial hackers who seek financial reward for their illegal acts. Motives vary according to the targeted system, information desired, and the perpetrator. While hacking was once commonly thought of as a precocious teenager's hobby, it has changed dramatically in the last twenty years to encompass a large and diverse group.

Hacking entails breaking into computer systems by determining the vulnerabilities of the hardware and software components. Then the hacker uses technology to systematically "guess" the authorized user's access codes.

Hackers generally use various "rogue" software applications to penetrate a system. Sometimes they surreptitiously incorporate unsuspecting computer owners into their schemes by installing programs that are downloaded via an e-mail or by visiting a website. These programs operate in the background of the infected computer and can disable security settings and capture information that is then sent back to the hacker.

The most direct way of gaining access to a computer is to use someone else's user identification and password, or generate (without authorization) a system-acceptable user name and password. The user name and password combination is designed to keep computers safe from unauthorized use. Without inputting this security information, the device won't operate. Most users choose passwords that follow predictable patterns. Computer users often choose user names and passwords that are familiar and easy to recall. For example, a deep-sea fisherman might choose the word "marlin" as a password, or the man's secretary, who received a mug about "soaring with the eagles and working with turkeys" from her boss last Christmas, might use "turkey" as her password.

If the hacker knows or can develop a profile about a target, his or her ability to crack a user name/password combination may be enhanced. Information about the target's family, children's names and birthdays, parents' names, maiden names, anniversaries, and similar data are often used as passwords. User names are often some derivation or abbreviation of a person's name or email address. A simple lesson here: real-word passwords, even in variation, are not secure. The safest passwords are more than eight characters and combine letters, numbers, and nonalphanumeric characters such as punctuation.

Social Engineering Another means of gaining access to information or a computer system involves simple deception. The hacker uses some known information, his or her alleged authority, and verbal skills to deceive victims into disclosing information they ought not to divulge or to commit acts that facilitate the hacker's scheme. The victim believes that sharing the information or following the bad guy's instructions is the "right thing" to do. Social engineers have been known to pose as an employee or someone hired by the organization. Based on their alleged purpose and authority, the hacker easily deceives real employees into revealing private, trusted, and confidential information.

The hacker may assume a number of different disguises to accomplish this deception. He or she may pose as a new or temporary worker and ask information systems employees for a password so that he or she can begin work. He or she may pose as someone in a position of authority and intimidate employees into revealing confidential information. Sometimes overt deception is not required. In large corporations, hackers can take advantage of the anonymity among employees. By donning office attire, they can blend into the crowd and thus peruse the premises, perhaps gaining a password written down at an employee's desk in the process.

In order to improve his or her chances of compelling the victim to assist the perpetrator, he or she may retrieve documents from the company dumpster, such as internal telephone directories and correspondence. Such knowledge provides an illusion of being on the inside, being on the team, being one of the good guys who plans to make life better for the victim, other employees, and the organization.

Hacker Computer Manipulations Hackers may use a variety of methods to invade computer systems including those described below.

Trojan Horse Virus. A Trojan horse is the covert placement of instructions in a program that causes the computer to perform unauthorized functions but usually still allows the program to perform its normal functions. This method is one of the most commonly used techniques in computer-based frauds and sabotage.

Trap Doors. When developing large programs, programmers insert instructions for additional code and intermediate output capabilities. The design of computer operating systems attempts to prevent this from happening. Therefore, programmers insert instructions that allow them to circumvent these controls. When located, hackers take advantage of these trap doors.

Salami Techniques. Salami techniques involve the execution of unauthorized programs used to steal small amounts of assets from a large number of transactions without noticeably reducing the whole. For example, in a banking system, the amount of interest to be credited to an account is typically rounded off. A fraudster might set up the system so that the rounded-off portion of the number is credited to a special account owned by the perpetrator.

Logic Bombs. A logic bomb is a computer program executed at a specific time period or when a specific event occurs. For example, a programmer can write a program to instruct the computer to delete all personnel and payroll files if his access (user name) were ever to be removed from the file.

Data Diddling. Data diddling is the changing of data before or during entry into the computer system. Examples include forging or counterfeiting documents used for data entry and replacing valid disks and tapes with modified replacements.

Scavenging and Dumpster Diving. Scavenging is obtaining information left around a computer system, in the computer room trashcans, etc. Dumpster diving refers to gleaning sensitive information from an organization's trash receptacles and dumpsters. Such techniques can be used to obtain user names and passwords to gain access to computer systems.

Data Leakage. Data leakage is the removing of information by smuggling it out of an organization as part of a printed document, disguising, or hiding the information and removing it from the facility.

Piggybacking/Impersonation. Piggybacking and impersonation are frequently used to gain access to restricted areas. Examples include following someone with a badge reader in through a door, using an authorized user's identification and password to gain computer access, and tapping into the terminal link of a user to cause the computer to believe that both terminals are the same person.

Simulation and Modeling. Simulation and modeling is a computer manipulation technique using the computer as a tool or instrument to plan or control a criminal act.

Wire Tapping. Wire tapping into a computer's communications links is another technique used by hackers. This method enables perpetrators to read the information being transmitted between computers

or between computers and terminals. Properly designed and implemented encryption techniques can be used to minimize the risk that any intercepted data can be used for nefarious purposes.

Network Weaving. This technique, also known as "looping," involves using numerous networks in an attempt to avoid detection. For example, a hacker might dial into Company A's PBX system to obtain an outside line that can be used to dial into Company B's network. If Company B can track the origin of the hacker's call, it will lead them to Company A, not to the hacker. Hackers have been known to "loop" through fifteen or twenty different networks before arriving at their final destination.

Altering Password Generation. Some user names and passwords are generated by a computer system's "randomizer" function. For example, some Internet-based retailers (ISPs) give first-time users a randomly generated password (and sometimes a random user name as well), which allows the person online access. Subsequent to the first visit, the user may change the log on information to his or her preference. By learning how a system's randomizer works, the hacker can imitate the generation of user names, passwords, or even alter how the system operates.

Buffer Overflow Exploits. Buffer overflow exploits are a significant problem in computer security. In application programs, buffer storage areas temporarily hold data. These buffers have a fixed size. A hacker can execute a data "overflow" program and then initiate a data overload; he or she overflows a program and then siphons off data generated by the system that cannot be stored in the buffer storage. The buffer overflow program may execute any number of tasks, from sending captured passwords to Russia, to altering system files, installing backdoors, etc., depending on what instructions the attacker sent to the buffer.

Privilege Escalation Exploits. Privilege escalation exploits grant administrator or root-level access to users who are not authorized such access.

Backdoors. Backdoors allow attackers to remotely access systems at any point in the future, where computer operators do not know such access exists.

HTTP Exploits. HTTP exploits involve using web server applications to perform malicious activities. These attacks are very common and are growing in popularity because firewalls typically block most traffic from the Internet to keep it away from corporate servers. HTTP traffic used for web browsing, however, is almost always allowed to pass through firewalls unhindered.

Anti-Hacker Measures. Because hackers require remote access (e.g., dial-in capability), the best prevention strategy is to eliminate as many remote access options as possible. Given the popularity of the Internet and the productivity gains from allowing customers, vendors, and suppliers direct access to company servers, however, the trend is to install more, not fewer, remote access capabilities.

Adequate hacker detection programs contain three primary components:

- Almost all communication systems maintain log files that record all successful and unsuccessful system access attempts. Log files should be printed and regularly reviewed by the data security officer. Special reports related to unsuccessful access attempts should also be created. Controls should be instituted that prevent hackers from altering log files. Otherwise a hacker can complete their work and then alter the log file so that evidence of their unauthorized access and activities are erased

- The data security function should have sufficient resources and staff to administer passwords, maintain security software, review system activity reports, and follow up on potential security violations

- Periodic reviews of telecommunications security should be performed by internal or external auditors or other professionals

Computer Viruses

Viruses are hidden computer programs that use computer resources or other computer activities in such a way as to shut down the system or slow it down significantly. Computer viruses typically use the infected computer's resources to replicate itself and spread the infection to other computer systems on a network or through the Internet via e-mail, text messages, or other electronic medium. Computer viruses range from those that are relatively harmless (displaying a message or greeting) to those that shut down entire computer networks for extended periods, ruin data, or destroy the ability of the computer to function properly.

A computer virus attacks software. Many computer viruses can replicate themselves on other computers. This replication ability can affect large networks. In recent years, viruses have cost millions of dollars in staff and machine hours to remove these viruses and restore normal operations.

Viruses have also garnered significant media attention in recent years. The fear of being infected with a virus has even resulted in virus "scares" that are nothing more than hoaxes. Although it is fortunate that the threat is not real, these phony warnings cause harm of their own. They slow down transmission of information and have been known to cause overloads of organizational e-mail networks. Some of these fraudulent warnings urge recipients to "forward this to everyone you know." Before forwarding a questionable warning, it is wise to consult a few of the authorities that track viruses. The following sites can be accessed to confirm or debunk virus notifications:

- www.symantec.com/avcenter/hoax.html
- www.vmyths.com
- www.fsecure.com/virus-info/hoax/

Types of Computer Viruses *Macro Virus.* A macro is an instruction that automatically carries out program commands. Many common applications (e.g., word processing, spreadsheet, and slide presentation applications) make use of macros. Macro viruses are macros that self-execute and replicate. If a user accesses a document containing a viral macro and unwittingly executes this macro virus by a command as simple as "open," it can then copy itself into that application's startup files. The computer is now infected—a copy of the macro virus resides on the machine.

Any document on that machine that uses the same application can then become infected. If the infected computer is on a network, the infection is likely to spread to other machines on the network. Moreover, if a copy of an infected file is passed to anyone else (for example, by e-mail or disk), the virus can spread to that recipient's computer as well; from there, the recipient computer will be used as a staging point for the virus to replicate itself on that computer's network, and so on, and so on. This process of infection will end only when the virus is noticed and all viral macros are eradicated.

Macro viruses are the most common type of viruses. Macro viruses can be written with very little specialist knowledge, and these viruses can spread to any platform on which the application is running. However, the main reason for their success is that documents are exchanged far more frequently than executable files or physical storage devices such as disks, a direct result of e-mail's popularity and web use. The ease of use and convenience of "stick" or "thumb" drives may cause such media to be used more regularly in the future.

The "I Love You" (also known as LoveLetter) virus is a type of macro virus. LoveLetter is a Win32-based e-mail worm. It overwrites certain files on hard drives and then sends itself out to everyone in the e-mail address book. LoveLetter arrives as an e-mail attachment named LOVE-LETTER-FOR-YOU.TXT.VBS, though new variants have different names including Very Funny.vbs, virus_warning.jpg.vbs, and protect.vbs. The subject of the message containing the infected attachment varies as well. Opening the attachment infects your machine. This attachment will most likely come from someone you know. As a rule of thumb, do not open any attachment unless you are certain that it is virus free. If you're unsure, ask for the sender to confirm that the attachment was intended for you.

Boot Sector Viruses. The boot sector is the first logical sector of a hard disk or floppy disk. A large majority of viruses have been boot sector viruses. These viruses use system BIOS, replace the boot sector, or move the boot sector to another location. It then writes a copy of its own program code, which will run every time the system is booted or when programs are run. A boot sector cannot infect a computer if it is introduced after the machine is running the operating system. An example of a boot sector virus is Parity Boot. This virus's payload displays the message Parity Check and freezes the operating system, rendering the computer useless. This virus message is taken from an actual error message that is displayed to users when a computer's memory is faulty. As a result, a user whose computer is infected with the Parity Boot virus is led to believe that the machine has a memory fault rather than a disruptive virus infection.

Parasitic Viruses. Parasitic viruses attach themselves to programs, also known as executable files. When a user launches a program that has a parasitic virus, the virus is surreptitiously launched first. To cloak its presence from the user, the virus then triggers the original program to open. The parasitic virus, because the operating system understands it to be part of the program, is given the same rights as the program to which the virus is attached. These rights allow the virus to replicate, install itself into memory, or release its payload. In the absence of antivirus software, only the payload might raise the normal user's

suspicions. A famous parasitic virus called Jerusalem has a payload of slowing down the system and eventually deleting every program the user launches.

TSRAM Viruses. Terminate and Stay Resident (TSR) viruses usually hide in memory and cause system crashes, depending on their memory location. The TSR takes control of the operating system by passing its request to DOS each time DOS is executed. The virus Cascade B is a TSR virus that sometimes causes the system to crash. It also causes characters to fall down the screen.

Application Software Viruses. These types of viruses copy their virus code to a program file and modify the program so the virus code gets executed first. It does this by writing over the existing code or attaching itself to the program file. The more sophisticated types replicate themselves with a ".COM" extension each time the user accesses an executable program file. The virus Vienna is a type of application virus. Vienna increases infected files by 648 bytes and destroys the system by making it reboot when running certain programs.

Multi-Partite Viruses. Multi-partite viruses share some of the characteristics of boot sector viruses and file viruses, which increases their ability to spread. They can infect .COM and .EXE files, and the boot sector of the computer's hard drive. On a computer booted up with an infected diskette, a typical multi-partite virus will first reside in memory and then infect the boot sector of the hard drive. From there the virus can infect a PC's entire environment. This type of virus accounts for a large number of infections.

The Tequila virus is a type of multi-partite virus. Tequila is a memory resident master boot sector (partition table) and .EXE file infector. It uses a complex encryption method and garbling to avoid detection. When a program infected with Tequila is executed, the virus will modify the hard disk master boot sector, if it is not already infected. The virus also copies itself to the last six sectors of the system hard disk. When the workstation is later rebooted from the system hard disk, Tequila will become memory resident. Once Tequila is memory resident, it infects .EXE files when they are executed.

Polymorphic Viruses. Polymorphic viruses create varied (though fully functional) copies of themselves as a way to avoid detection from antivirus software. Some polymorphic viruses use different encryption schemes and require different decryption routines. Thus, the same virus may look completely different on different systems or even within different files. Other polymorphic viruses vary instruction sequences and use false commands in the attempt to thwart antivirus software. One of the most advanced polymorphic viruses uses a mutation engine and random number generators to change the virus code and its decryption routine. The Spanska.4250 is a type of polymorphic virus. This virus infects program files (files with .EXE and .COM extensions).

Stealth Viruses. The stealth viruses are the more sophisticated viruses. They constantly change their patterns in an effort to blend into the system like a chameleon. They attempt to avoid detection by bypassing DOS interrupt calls when they are installed, and remove their code from the infected files before the file is accessed by the requesting program.

The 4096 virus is a type of stealth virus. It increases the file size by 4096 bytes and decreases the memory by approximately 6 kb. The message "FRODO LIVES" might appear in the middle of the screen. If the infected file is run on September 21, it causes the system to crash.

Mutation Engine Viruses. This "modern day" virus uses a special language-driven algorithm generator that enables it to create an infinite variety of original encryption algorithms. It avoids the checksum detection method like the stealth viruses by not changing the infected file size. Each time they replicate, they produce a new and different code. The Pogue virus is a type of mutation virus. It only infects .COM files less than 61,439 bytes. If activated on May 1 or before 9 a.m. on any other day, it will make a variety of musical sounds. It contains the strings "TNX2DAV" (Thanks to Dark Avenger) and "Pogue Mahone" in its code.

Network Viruses. It was just a matter of time before network-specific viruses were developed to attack the increased number of Local Area Networks (LANs) and other types of networks coming online. These viruses generally are developed to attack the file servers. The boot sector and partition table viruses infect the boot operation of the file server. This virus does not spread from the workstation to the file server. If you are using NetWare, however, it can cause the software to lose the location of its partition table on the file server if the file server is booted with infected boot code. Viruses that infect programs seem to be limited to infecting files on the server. Because the files are continuously being accessed by workstations, this type of virus is difficult to contain.

At least two NetWare-specific viruses have been discovered in Europe. One is the GP1 (Get Password 1) virus. It was allegedly created to penetrate Novell security features and then spread throughout the network. The second was CZ2986 virus, developed in Czechoslovakia. This virus places itself in memory

and intercepts NetWare function calls when the workstations log into the server. After it collects fifteen user name/password combinations, it saves them in an infected file and uses them to gain access to the network.

Worms. A worm is a self-replicating program that resides as a file on a system, executes an autonomous process, and deliberately moves from system to system. It looks for other nodes on the networks, copies itself to them, and causes the self-copy to execute on other nodes. These programs find network utilities showing node names, monitor network traffic, randomly select network identification codes as well as other mischief.

An example of a worm is the SQL Slammer, which raced across the globe and wreaked havoc on the Internet in January 2003. This worm doubled the number of computers it infected every 8.5 seconds in the first minute of its appearance. The worm, which exploited a flaw in Microsoft Corporation's SQL Server database software, caused damage by rapidly replicating itself and clogging the pipelines of the global data network. The worm did not erase or cause damage to desktop computers, but was designed to replicate itself so quickly and so effectively that no other traffic could get through networks.

Virus Carriers and Indicators   Viruses can infect computer systems from many sources. Some of the more common virus carriers are:

- Unknown or unchecked application software
- Software or media brought in by employees
- Programs downloaded from modem bulletin boards
- Unsolicited e-mails
- Vendors and suppliers with infected software
- Uncontrolled and shared program applications
- Demonstration software
- Freeware and Shareware

The following are some of the indicators that a computer might be infected:

- A sudden and sometimes dramatic decrease of free space on your media
- The system suddenly and for no apparent reason slows down its response time to commands
- An increase in the size of some files
- A change in the length of executable files, a change in their content, or a change in their file date/time stamp
- An unexpected number of disk accesses, especially to particular file(s)
- An operating system and/or other program that suddenly begins behaving in unpredictable ways. Sometimes disk files that should be there cannot be accessed or are erased with no warning
- Unusual messages and graphics
- An inability to boot the system
- An inability to access files
- Unexplained and repeated maintenance repairs
- System or data files disappear or become fragmented
- Unexplained changes in memory
- Unexplained changes in program sizes
- Display messages that indicate that a virus has been encountered. Note that until the source of the virus has been identified and removed from the system, antiviral systems might continually inform the operator that a virus is being encountered and removed

Hardware, Software, and Data Security

Effective computer security ensures the availability of accurate and timely data provided at a cost, including security that meets traditional cost-benefit considerations. Such a position suggests that all threats are not eliminated, but that threats are managed in such a way that the hardware, software, and data have

reasonable protection given the threats and costs associated with addressing those threats. In general, technology security includes protecting data and programs from unauthorized or accidental alteration or destruction. Furthermore, the data must be protected so as to maintain confidentiality, integrity, and availability. Hardware, software, and data must be secure from physical threats such as water, storm, and fire damage. Information technology departments must also have the ability to restore data center operations in the event that a disaster causes complete destruction.

The most effective components of internal security are education, reporting facilities, and vigorous disciplinary action against offenders, including prosecution of illegal acts. An enterprise-wide employee awareness program should be combined with formal training in the area of information security. For employees to fulfill their security responsibilities they should know what information needs to be kept confidential, how to recognize threats to security, and how to use backups and other aids for their desktop machines.

Passwords are the predominant form of authenticating valid users. Effective password administration is essential for maintaining security. Passwords should be of sufficient length (usually a minimum of eight characters) and a combination of letters, numbers, and other characters such as punctuation marks to avoid vulnerability to guessing. Group passwords and sharing of passwords should be prohibited in order to maintain individual accountability. Passwords of all terminated employees should be revoked immediately. Security administration often coordinates the notification of terminated employees with the personnel function. Employees who have changed job functions or transferred should have their old password canceled and a new one issued, if appropriate.

Securing a computer network by means of logical controls is a difficult but necessary requirement for ensuring the safety of a computer system from attacks by outsiders. Logical controls include management security policies, user authentication systems, data access controls, network firewalls, security awareness training, encryption algorithms, penetration testing, intrusion detection software, and incident response plans.

Network security also can be provided by a combination of design, hardware devices, and software. Data encryption is carried out by a combination of hardware and software. Encrypted data is scrambled by a formula using a unique key and can only be unscrambled with the same formula and key at the receiving end. The decision to use encryption should be made in light of the risks and after a cost-benefit analysis. Drawbacks to encryption are the cost of the hardware and software, the cost of the administration, and the inherent delays incurred by the extra steps required for processing.

Digital signatures are becoming more common, in part because Congress and many states have passed legislation to legitimize the electronic "signing" of documents. On October 1, 2000, the Electronic Signatures in Global and National Commerce Act (E-SIGN Act) became effective. This federal statute basically provides a mechanism whereby any document that is required to be signed, can be signed "electronically." The E-SIGN Act does not require a party to use or accept electronic signatures, electronic contracts, or electronic records, but rather seeks to facilitate the use of electronic signatures and documents by upholding their legality regardless of the type or method of execution selected by the parties. The E-SIGN Act is also technology-neutral and does not require a specific type or method that businesses and consumers must use or accept in order to conduct electronic transactions. The Act regulates any transactions involving interstate or foreign commerce. Many states, however, have enacted their own digital signature laws, which regulate purely intrastate transactions. Additionally, many state and federal agencies, including the Internal Revenue Service and the Securities and Exchange Commission, are encouraging the use of electronic filing and digital signatures as a means to speed up the collection and processing of information. Biological access verification, also known as biometrics, is now available. This verification technique includes fingerprints, palm prints, voice prints, signatures, retina scans, and facial recognition.

Profiling software authenticates users by monitoring their statistical characteristics, such as typing speed and keystroke touch. Smartcard access devices are similar to an ATM card; like ATM cards, they are susceptible to loss and forgery.

Protecting the network from external threats requires some additional considerations. The less an external perpetrator knows about the technology environment (for example, type of hardware and software packages used), the harder it is to obtain fraudulent access. Part of the security policy should address how much and what kind of information regarding the technology of an organization should be made public.

Organizations should guard against providing too much access to third parties. There is pressure to establish connectivity by marketing, purchasing, research, and other branches. Connectivity should be granted only after it has been established that the benefits outweigh the risks and costs.

Computer users should take measures to protect their computers against viruses. Some of the steps that can be taken are:

- Do not use a diskette to boot your system
- If you must boot your system from a diskette, make sure it is properly labeled, and continuously protected
- Do not install Shareware or other untested programs on your systems, but if you do, do not put them in the root directory
- In a network environment, do not place untested programs on the server
- If you are sharing information on diskettes, ensure they only contain information and no executable files
- Use current antivirus software to detect potential viruses
- Backup all programs and files
- Write virus-free warranties and indemnities into your purchase orders and contracts
- Always write-protect your systems and program disks
- Teach computer users about computer viruses so that they can recognize them
- Always use caution when opening e-mail attachments

Antivirus Software   There are several techniques that may be used by antivirus software to help detect computer viruses and other malware. In some cases, more than one method may be used.

Traditional Scanners. This is the most commonly used method. These programs work by looking for known viruses by checking for recognizable patterns and specific "strings" or virus "signatures." Its usefulness is limited in that it can only identify known viruses.

Heuristic Scanners. These scanners inspect executable files for code using algorithms to identify operations that would indicate an unknown virus. They might also examine macros to detect virus-like behavior.

Behavior Blocking Scanners. These applications run continuously, looking for behavior that might indicate virus activity (for example, instructions to format a hard drive). Unlike the traditional signature-based approach, this method can detect new and previously unknown viruses. Nevertheless, it is not foolproof and has a tendency to give false positives.

Change Detection Scanners. Change detection scanners generate a database of characteristics for executable files and check for changes to these files that might signify a virus attack.

The effectiveness of antivirus software has decreased over the years, primarily because of the intent of the virus authors. Years ago, it was much more immediately apparent when a computer had been infected. Today's viruses are often well hidden and used to steal information without the user's knowledge.

Investigating Virus Infections   Virus infections can be investigated by taking the following action:

- Isolate the system and all media
- Run antivirus software
- Document findings
- Interview the system custodian and all users, and determine:
  - Symptoms
  - Damage
  - Prior clean-up conducted
  - Access controls in place and working
  - System malfunction
  - Personal media used
  - Unauthorized media used
  - Virus identification
- Follow the audit trail of the infection
- Determine the source of the virus—person, system, and media

- Make users aware of protection policies and procedures
- Ensure countermeasures are in place and working
- Track the costs/damages related to virus problems

INTERNET FRAUD

A booming segment of computer fraud, Internet fraud has become a growing concern to the law enforcement community. This type of fraud has proliferated and will continue to grow because of the ripe conditions that exist on the World Wide Web for fraudulent activities. The Internet is still a developing technology for much of international business and thus has not been subjected to much litigation or policing. Laws that currently apply to the Internet are difficult to enforce, because the Internet crosses international borders. The lack of a common set of international laws and the difficulty related to enforcing existing laws gives Internet fraudsters a better-than-average chance of avoiding capture and punishment.

The Internet has also risen to become a major means of conducting business globally. As of June 2006, there were over 1 billion users, or 16 percent of the world's population, on the Internet. In the United States alone, 69 percent of the population was online, which equated to approximately 227 million users. Internationally, the Internet saw a growth increase of 189 percent between 2000 and 2005.

In order that consumers retain their confidence in Internet transactions, the perception that the Internet is a safe way to shop and do business must be fostered. Consumer awareness to online fraud must be raised without causing a loss of consumer confidence. This difficult endeavor may require an unprecedented effort by the private sector in conjunction with law enforcement. In this new era, private investigative resources may be called upon in greater numbers than ever, given law enforcement's deficiencies in the area of computer fraud.

According to the National Consumers League's Internet Fraud Watch, the top ten Internet schemes, as of December 2005, are as follows:

Internet Scheme	Percentage of Complaints
Online auctions	42%
General merchandise sales	30%
Nigerian money offers	8%
False checks	6%
Lotteries/Lottery clubs	4%
Phishing	2%
Advance fee loans	1%
Information/Adult services	1%
Work-at-home plans	1%
Internet Access Services	1%

"More people are on-line and more people are getting scammed," according to Susan Grant, Director of the Internet Fraud Watch (IFW). "Consumers need to remember that con artists are everywhere, even in cyberspace." Grant says the safest way of paying for goods and services online is with a credit card: if there are problems with billing, the charges can be disputed. Businesses that ask for cash or money orders should be avoided, according to Internet Fraud Watch. "Requesting cash is a clear sign of fraud," says Grant. For those businesses that are not equipped to take credit card payments, IFW recommends escrow services.

According to the 2006 Identity Fraud Survey Report conducted by the Council of Better Business Bureaus and Javelin Strategy and Research, identity fraud in the United States decreased slightly from 4.7 percent to 4 percent of the adult population. But while the number of victims marginally decreased from 10.1 million people to 8.9 million people, the average fraud loss per case increased from $5,249 to $6,383. As a result, the total one-year cost of identity fraud in the United States between 2003 and 2006 increased from $53.2 billion to $56.6 billion. Some of the key findings of the survey were the following:

- The vast majority of identity fraud victims (68 percent) incur no out-of-pocket expenses. This demonstrates that businesses are victims of fraud as well
- Victims are spending more time to resolve identity fraud cases, which has increased from 33 hours in 2003 to 40 hours in 2006

- Most data compromise—90 percent—takes place through traditional offline channels and not via the Internet, where the victim can identify the source of data compromise*
- Lost or stolen wallets, checkbooks, or credit cards continue to be the primary source of personal information theft when the victim can identify the source of data compromise (30 percent)*
- Almost half (47 percent) of all identity theft is perpetrated by friends, neighbors, in-home employees, family members, or relatives—someone known—when the victim can identify the perpetrator of data compromise**
- Nearly 70 percent of consumers are shredding documents, so that trash as a source of data compromise is now less than 1 percent
- The "65 + " demographic age group has the smallest rate of identity fraud victims (2.3 percent)
- The 35–44 demographic age group has the highest average fraud amount ($9,435)

* 47 percent of victims could identify the source of the data compromise

** 36 percent of victims could identify the person who misused their information

Electronic Commerce (E-Commerce)

E-commerce is generally thought to describe retailing, marketing, advertising, and interpersonal communications taking place on the semi-autonomous Internet. Such electronic activity generally includes authentication for participant identification and some form of "electronic signature" to ensure that participants initiating transactions cannot deny that the transaction occurred. Efforts to secure e-commerce transactions are described below.

Encryption. From an e-commerce security perspective, the solutions offered by conventional and public-key encryption technologies are usually adequate to ensure that e-commerce transactions are as secure as the value of transactions requires. The vast majority of transmissions over the Internet and the World Wide Web, however, are not encrypted. If there is no need to hide the contents of a message or communication, there is little need to expend resources on the encryption of such traffic and the decryption at the other end. Encryption can be an expensive solution, whether in terms of actual monetary cost or the cost in increased computational load on the user's machines. The needs of the organization to keep confidential transmissions secret should be weighed against the effort and cost of encryption.

Smart Cards. A smart card is a credit card–sized plastic card embedded with an integrated circuit chip that makes it "smart." This marriage between a convenient plastic card and a microprocessor allows an immense amount of information to be stored, accessed, and processed either online or offline. Smart cards can store several hundred times more data than a conventional card with a magnetic stripe. The information stored in the IC chip is transferred through an electronic module that interconnects with a terminal or a card reader. A contactless smart card has an antenna coil that communicates with a receiving antenna to transfer information. Depending on the type of embedded chip, smart cards can be either memory cards or processor cards.

Memory Cards. Any plastic card is made "smart" by including an IC chip. But the chip may simply be a memory storage device. Memory cards can hold information thousands of times greater in amount than a magnetic stripe card. Nevertheless, their functions are limited to basic applications.

Processor Cards. Smart cards with a full-fledged microprocessor on board can function as a processor device that offers multiple functions such as encryption, advanced security mechanisms, local data processing, complex calculation, and other interactive processes. Most stored-value cards integrated with identification, security, and information purposes are processor cards. Only processor cards are truly smart enough to offer the flexibility and multifunctionality desired in e-commerce.

Typical Internet Schemes

Earlier in the decade, the media often cautioned about the dangers of sending credit card numbers through the Internet. For good reason, many businesses and individuals have apprehensions concerning Internet commerce; the Internet is an impersonal form of communication. While much has been done to create and maintain trust, some precautions are appropriate before purchasing online items. As a result, conducting

financial transactions on the Internet is usually as safe as making an order from a legitimate company for legitimate products and service via the telephone. Nevertheless, the careless and unsuspecting can become victims. In addition, scams and schemes similar to the conventional frauds have found new and lucrative homes on the Internet, while new scams, such as modem hijacking, are of an entirely new breed.

Old Frauds Adapted for the Computer and Internet   Just about every traditional scam can be facilitated or perpetrated with the use of computers or over the Internet. Clever, technologically savvy fraudsters can be quick to take old fraud schemes and adapt them to a digital environment. Computer users and those who rely on digital devices such as cell phones, personal digital assistances, MP3 players, iPods, and other digital devices with memory and processing capacity can be used in fraud acts and the related concealment and conversion.

Get Rich Quick. Entering the phrase "get-rich-quick" in an Internet search results in sites with names like $50,000 First Ten Months, Secrets of the Millionaires, and Best Business Resource Center. These types of sites hawk everything from home businesses to investment opportunities. The common denominator in these schemes is that "wannabe entrepreneurs" who throw their money away on such schemes find themselves with worthless materials and information. As with all get-rich-quick schemes, victims are pulled in by their desire to make easy money.

Pyramid Schemes. The tried and true pyramid has a high tech home on the Internet. Consistent with most pyramid schemes, the initial participants of the scheme are rewarded handsomely, while later participants are bilked out of their investment money. Pyramid schemes are also referred to as franchise fraud or chain referral schemes. Generally, the alleged opportunity is a marketing or investment fraud in which an individual is offered a distributorship or franchise to market a particular product. The real profit is earned not by the sale of the product, but by the sale of new distributorships. Emphasis on selling franchises rather than the product eventually leads to a point where the supply of potential investors is exhausted and the pyramid collapses.

Foreign Trusts. Schemers in this fraud cater to those who desire a "taxless" life. For a fee, the company purports to be able to create a foreign trust to which taxpayers can transfer their assets. Since the trust is not within the taxpayer's country, the logic goes, the assets are not subject to taxation. Naturally, the logic is faulty. First, if the taxpayer derives use from the funds in the trust, according to law those funds are considered taxable income. Thus, consumers who fall for this scam subject themselves to prosecution for tax evasion. That is, of course, only if the trust is set up at all. Some of the operators of this scheme simply take the consumer's money and disappear. Some who have fallen for this pitch find that they have transferred all of their assets to a trust of which they are not the beneficiaries; their assets legally belong to another entity and getting them transferred back to their control is virtually impossible.

Prime Bank Note. International fraud artists have invented an investment scheme that offers extremely high yields in a relatively short period of time. In this scheme, they purport to have access to "bank guarantees" which they can buy at a discount and sell at a premium. By reselling the "bank guarantees" several times, they claim to be able to produce exceptional returns on investment. For example, if $10 million worth of "bank guarantees" can be sold at a two percent profit on ten separate occasions, or "traunches," the seller would receive a twenty percent profit. Such a scheme is often referred to as a "roll program." To make their schemes more enticing, con artists often refer to the "guarantees" as being issued by the world's "Prime Banks." Other official sounding terms are also used such as "Prime Bank Notes" and "Prime Bank Debentures." Legal documents associated with such schemes often require the victim to enter into nondisclosure and noncircumvention agreements, offer returns on investment in "a year and a day," and claim to use forms required by the International Chamber of Commerce (ICC). In fact, the ICC has issued a warning to all potential investors that no such investments exist. The purpose of these frauds is generally to encourage the victim to send money to a foreign bank where it is eventually transferred to an offshore account that is in the control of the fraudster.

Chain Letters. This fraud has once again become popular due to the Internet's e-mail capabilities. The letter sent to unsuspecting targets generally forewarns of the grave dangers that await the target should he or she not reply to the letter. The letter asks for a small cash donation in exchange for the target's piece of mind that no bad tidings will be spread, providing examples of some of the unfortunates who did not heed the letter. The money should be sent to a P.O. box, the e-mail often instructs.

Investment and Securities Fraud. Numerous websites offer investment or securities advice. Many of these sites are reputable but some are not. A fraudulent website will claim to have superior information or information sources about the value of a given stock, suggesting that something unexpected will

soon happen to that company. When the unknowing stock investor takes the advice of the supposedly knowledgeable investment advisor, the "advisor" manipulates the stock price to his advantage.

"Ponzi" Scheme. A Ponzi scheme is essentially an investment fraud where the operator promises high financial returns or dividends that are not available through traditional investments. Instead of investing victims' funds, the operator pays "dividends" to initial investors using the amounts "invested" by subsequent victims. The scheme generally falls apart when the operator flees with all of the proceeds, or when a sufficient number of new investors cannot be found to allow the continued payment of "dividends."

New Threats for the Computer and Internet   *Modem Hijacking.* While Internet users are online, their computer Internet connections are secretly disconnected from their ISP and reconnected to the Internet, only this time through an expensive international line. Once activated, hijacking software continues the disconnection and reconnection process. Long-distance charges accrue until victims shut down their computers.

Spamming. Spamming involves sending e-mail to subscribers whose names appear on electronic versions of the phone list and posting ads to the plethora of discussion and chat groups using the Internet. These postings are often disguised to look like tips from individual citizens who are supposedly engaged in a lawful enterprise when in fact they are part of an Internet boiler room.

Counterfeit Check Scams. This scam has several variations but usually starts with the victim offering something for sale on the Internet. Usually it is a big ticket item. Somehow the fraudster has obtained a legitimate check from a person or company, scanned it, and altered it to support the scheme. The fraudster then contracts with the victim to buy the item but must supply a down payment first. The check is delivered by a highly recognized international carrier such as FedEx, further adding to the false impression that this is a legitimate deal. The victim deposits the check, but before it clears, the fraudster requests a refund and backs out of the deal offering to let the victim keep a portion of the funds for his trouble. The victim forwards part of the money back. The victim later learns that his bank has reversed the deposit amount because the check was bad.

Phishing. "Phishing" is a scheme that involves tricking businesses or individuals into providing passwords, account numbers, or other sensitive data by claiming to be from an actual company the victim does business with. A solicitation for information appears to come from a legitimate business and can occur over the phone (e.g., a call from the victim's "bank" saying their account has been compromised and requesting PIN numbers, account numbers, or passwords), or via e-mail (which is the most common technique). An individual receives an e-mail that appears to come from eBay, PayPal, or a financial institution. The e-mail states that the customer must immediately log into his account in order to update his information. The link directs the individual to a fake site that captures his identifying information such as Social Security and PIN numbers, mother's maiden name, and financial account numbers. Phishing occurs mostly by e-mail. Internet users should never respond to these e-mails. Legitimate banks, government agencies, and retailers do not e-mail you for your password of other identifying information.

Spear Phishing. Spear phishing is a targeted attack generally focused on a corporate entity. The ruse is meant to fool the corporate employee into believing that the phishing e-mail originated not from a bank or financial institution but from their own IT or HR department. The goal is to obtain employees user names and passwords to access the corporate network.

Pharming. Pharming is an attack in which a user is fooled into entering sensitive data (such as a password or credit card number) into a malicious website that impersonates a legitimate website. It is different from phishing in that the attacker does not have to rely on having the user click on a link in the e-mail to direct him or her to the fake website. Pharming actually exploits vulnerabilities in the DNS server software that allow hackers to acquire the domain name for a site and redirect the website traffic from a legitimate site to a false one. So even though a user may type the correct website address, the pharming program sends the user to an illegitimate site that looks like the real thing. Unknowingly, the user is then providing passwords and information directly to the hacker.

Internet Auction Fraud. According to the Internet Crime Complaint Center (IC3), Internet auction fraud was by far the most reported offense, comprising 44.9 percent of referred complaints. Nondelivered merchandise and/or payment accounted for 19.0 percent of complaints. Check fraud made up 4.9 percent of complaints. Credit/debit card fraud, computer fraud, confidence fraud, and financial institutions fraud round out the top seven categories of complaints referred to law enforcement.

Combating Internet Fraud

Conducting business on the Internet is generally a safe proposition for legitimate persons doing business with legitimate product and service providers. Nevertheless, safety precautions are prudent:

1. Confidential information of any type (e.g., credit card numbers, Social Security numbers, etc.) should be encrypted. Most simplistically, encryption scrambles an outgoing electronic transmission and the recipient's system provides inverse decryption, which restores the transmission to its original state. Encryption hardware and software utilize complex mathematical formulas. Encryption is used to prevent people who intercept data from harvesting valuable and confidential information.

2. The Internet is anonymous, with user names and passwords being the only identifiers. Internet websites set up for commerce install customer validation protocols. The validation is usually a user name or customer code combined with a password that becomes the customer's identity for transaction authorization. A downside to this type of protocol is that most users develop such a large number of user names and passwords that most are written down and kept in easily accessible places such as a desk drawer or under the keyboard. In such cases, the benefits of the validation process have been eliminated.

3. Financial information, customer data, and other valuable databases should be stored in places other than a web server. Internet websites can be hacked, and volumes of personal and financial data are often primary targets. Financial and other valuable information should be maintained on an internal system with processing interaction restrictions in place. The process protection should have additional safeguards to minimize the risk that a hacker who penetrates a website can harvest vast amounts of financial and customer information from internal systems.

4. Firewalls are software programs that attempt to prevent unauthorized access to an Internet site or e-mail transmission. Firewalls are designed to control interactions between network servers and the Internet. This technology monitors Internet traffic, inbound and outbound, with a goal of preventing questionable transmissions from accessing sensitive information databases. Firewalls do not offer "silver bullet" protection but they provide a layer of protection against Internet attacks or other types of security breaches.

COMPLEX FRAUDS AND FINANCIAL CRIMES IN CYBERSPACE

In the late twentieth century, the emergence of transnational criminal organizations introduced a significant challenge for law enforcement worldwide. The challenges arose from many sources, including the anonymity of technology, the speed of information and money movement worldwide, jurisdictional issues, the challenges of effective and efficient law enforcement communication, as well as others. Complex criminal organizational structure offers the ability to utilize a large labor force, synchronize the labor force, and carry out large-scale criminal operations and have multiple criminal enterprises. Such structures are also amenable to cyberspace. Essentially, organized cybercriminal organizations blend combinations of the tools and techniques discussed above with traditional fraud schemes and financial crimes in a large-scale, organized fashion. The organized cybercriminal is interested in operating in cyberspace the way traditional organized criminals, drug traffickers, and terrorists operate in the physical world. Large-scale, business-like applications of fraud and financial schemes in cyberspace yield large sums of cash to those who control the organized cybercriminal organization.

Organized cybercriminal enterprises profit from exploiting computer vulnerabilities. Hackers, who previously wreaked havoc for the fun of it or as a means of making political statements, are now organized, professional, and cash flow oriented, and some are associated with traditional organized crime groups. Cybercriminals include skilled programmers who design and operationalize sophisticated phishing attacks and other techniques to harvest consumer personal, financial, and log in information. As an example, cybercriminals have used "malware" to steal millions of credit and debit card numbers, Social Security numbers, and financial account user IDs and passwords; once this data is harvested it can be used to commit identity theft and online fraud. Another example of potential damage by hackers occurs when distribution systems are compromised and freight deliveries are redirected to criminal-controlled warehouses. Organized cybercriminals have management structure, functional responsibility, and a support labor force that enables them to traffic in stolen information using many of the same business practices employed by corporate America.

Organized cybercriminal enterprises have created "botnets," collections of tens of thousands of computers to launch Distributed Denial of Service (DDoS) attacks on enterprise websites, DNS servers, email systems, and VoIP services. Botnets can be used to extort companies, especially those dependent on e-commerce. Even if a legitimate business does not become a blackmail victim, it's possible that if left unprotected, many of its own computers can become part of a botnet. Cybercriminals use the botnets to distribute spam, child pornography, and malware in mass quantity to accomplish their nefarious goals.

In a 2005 article called *Shadowcrew: Web Mobs*, Deborah Gage, the author, described the activities of Andrew Mantovani, David Appleyard, Brandon Monchamp, and more than a dozen other members of the Shadowcrew. The group auctions off stolen and counterfeit credit and identification cards, and according to Gage, business was booming. Shadowcrew has more than 4,000 members, and according to the U.S. Secret Service, ran a worldwide marketplace in which 1.5 million credit card numbers, 18 million e-mail accounts, and scores of identification documents (e.g., passports, driver's licenses, student IDs, etc.) were offered to the highest bidder.

According to the article, many of the credit card numbers sold on the site were subsequently used by Shadowcrew's customers, who had no intent of paying for what they bought. The result was more than $4 million in losses suffered by card issuers and banks, says the Secret Service, which is charged by the U.S. government to investigate counterfeiting, credit card fraud, and some computer crimes.

Gage goes on to state that Shadowcrew is a web mob: a highly organized group of criminals. Unlike the American Mafia or the Russian syndicates, however, these web mobs work solely in the online world. Members know each other only by computer aliases, interact with each other through the Internet, and commit their crimes in the darkness of cyberspace. The electronic marketplaces they establish to trade their illicit wares can be set up and later disbanded with little more than keystrokes. "They basically can pop up anytime and anywhere," says Secret Service Special Agent Larry Johnson. The Secret Service says they operate under names such as Carderplanet, Stealthdivision, and Darkprofits.

These cybermobs are designed to foster more crime and criminals on the Web. Much like La Cosa Nostra, members of web mobs don't have to break into a bank to rob it. Instead, they provide a framework and services for criminals to trade in their chosen stock—stolen credit cards and identity documents. And their efforts, including the "commerce" sites where they trade in stolen merchandise, will only accelerate what is already a thriving trade in numbers that are regarded on the Web as currency.

Several attributes of the Internet make it an attractive operational location for criminal enterprises. First, individuals and businesses have come to realize that information is power. Likewise, criminals have determined that they can profit by stealing and selling information. Others can then exploit the value of that private information for their own profit.

Second, cyberspace gives the criminal a worldwide reach. In the old days, organized crime might be restricted to a few city blocks, a city, a geographical region, etc. With the World Wide Web, criminals can be located anywhere and can exploit victims located anywhere in the world, provided that they are using the Internet and demonstrate the vulnerabilities exploited by these criminal groups. Thus, criminals with the proper skill set may be located in the former Soviet Union, Eastern Europe, South America, or other distant countries, and target victims through fraudulent or illegal Internet commerce in relatively wealthy countries in Europe, Canada, and the United States with little fear of retaliation by law enforcement.

Third, the World Wide Web is relatively anonymous. Persons online have no face; their existence is only a user name and password that may have no logical, physical, or legal connection to the digital identity. In addition, a cybercriminal can create any number of identities on the Web, none of which may be tied together or tied to the person's real identity. Members of organized crime groups communicate using their various digital identities. They are also computer savvy enough to know to encrypt their digital transmissions and transactions, and often float their communications through networks of servers and anonymous "re-mailers" that conceal the IP address of their computers. They can also route traffic through proxy servers, making it almost impossible to trace electronic transmission to their source.

Fourth, beyond the difficulty of catching cybercriminals is successfully prosecuting them. Determining the proper jurisdiction is often a difficult task. Once jurisdictional issues are resolved, applying traditional laws to online activity presents further challenges. More problematic is the location of many cybercriminals. Many of these individuals locate in countries that do not cooperate with law enforcement officials in nations seeking extradition; the choice of locale by the cybercriminal is deliberate. Organized crime groups operating in places such as countries formerly part of the Soviet Union, Eastern Europe, South America, and Russia are virtually immune from prosecution.

Money Laundering in Cyberspace

Gains from criminal activity can be readily laundered through money transfers using a series of Internet bank accounts, wagering on Internet gaming sites, artificial purchases on auction sites, and the traditional organized crime practice of using legitimate businesses to hide illegal transactions. Since the beginning of criminal enterprise, the bad guys have used banks as a means to launder money gained through illegal activities. However, the creation of Internet banking makes following the money more difficult than ever.

The following example illustrates the practice of money laundering in cyberspace.

> *Alexandra is the head of an international identity theft operation, specializing in the mass sale of stolen Social Security numbers, with matching names and dates of birth. Having the big three pieces of identifying data makes her a triple threat.*

Alexandra is known around the underworld as a ruthless and vicious operator and yet, she has a problem: she has tons of currency, the profits from her illegal activities that she cannot spend without attracting the attention of law enforcement. More problematic is that if the identity theft ring is busted and prosecuted, without some sort of money laundering operation, the funds can be tied directly to her. She has the ability to pay her employees, contractors, suppliers, and vendors through the organization's bank accounts, but not herself.

> *Alexandra needs to get this currency from her organization's offshore bank account into the legitimate U.S. economy so that she can safely draw on these ill-gotten gains without attracting attention. Alexandra is a true patriot—she has even gone so far as to faithfully and completely pay her U.S. income taxes. Maybe she's not such a patriot—if she is ever caught, she can avoid being prosecuted for tax evasion.*

To gain anonymity, Alexandra uses her money to buy e-currency, a relatively anonymous and unregulated currency she then moves in varying amounts, small and large, across a series of e-currency accounts and ultimately transfers the money into her own bank.[8] From there she loans money to herself in the United States and pays a consulting fee to an international company (controlled by her) for services rendered to her U.S. real estate company, where she receives cash distributions both as an employee and as an owner. Now she is free to use that money for loans, salary, and dividends as she chooses with little risk to her freedom.

Money laundering, which involves disguising the origins of illegally generated cash flow to give it the appearance of legitimate income, is enhanced on the Internet due to the near anonymity that can be achieved. Furthermore, Internet banks provide access to accounts anywhere in the world from anywhere. As a result, it is often not clear whether an account is accessed from a country other than the one where the money is held. In addition, monitoring the activity of individual account holders is nearly impossible.

In addition to financial institutions, other businesses, such as Internet-based gambling operations, can also be hijacked for money laundering purposes. Online casino operations further complicate the identification of transactions that might be illegal because the entire operation, including all gambling records, are housed in electronic formats and located offshore in jurisdictions where access is extremely limited. Criminals can facilitate money laundering by "gambling" dirty money at the cybercasinos, converting winnings into cybercash and then requesting the remittance of seemingly clean money through various cyberpayment and other fund transfer systems. Transactions are quick and may be completed from a computer located anywhere—from the privacy of their own home to the local public library or cybercafé. The borderless nature of the Internet makes it possible for users to play at any casino around the world, often in jurisdictions with minimal or unenforced money laundering laws. Work completed by Forrester Research suggests that there are more than 1,400 Internet gambling sites, most of which are based outside of the United States.[9]

According to a 1996 study, global Internet money laundering accounted for about $500 billion annually.[10] Given the exponential growth of the Internet, that number is likely far greater today. The working paper by Kellerman suggests four models for payment in cyberspace:[11]

1. The Merchant Issuer Model—In this case, both the smart card issuer and the seller of goods are the same person or entity. An example of this model would be the Creative Star fare card used by riders of the Hong Kong transit system.

2. The Bank Issuer Model—The merchant and the smart card issuer are separate entities. Financial transactions are cleared through traditional financial systems such as the Banksys' Proton card in Belgium.

3. Nonbank Issuer Model—Users buy electronic cash from issuers using traditional money and then spend their e-cash at participating merchants. The merchant then redeems cash from the issuer. An example of this is Cybercash's electronic coin product.

4. Peer-to-Peer Model—Bank– or nonbank–issued electronic cash is transferable between users. The only point of contact between traditional payment systems and initial e-cash is the initial purchase of e-cash from the issuer and the redemption of electronic cash from individuals or merchants. An example would be the Mondex stored value card.

E-gold is an electronic currency issued by e-gold Ltd., a Nevis corporation, and is 100 percent backed at all times by gold bullion in allocated storage. E-gold claims to be a global currency. As such, a Canadian business can pay a German or Japanese supplier the correct weight of gold (e-gold) for goods and services as easily as if the price had been quoted in his own national currency. E-gold is borderless, quick, possibly cost effective, and touts all the benefits of a traditional currency. E-gold can be used in a myriad of transactions:

- E-commerce
- Business-to-business payments
- Point of service sales
- Person-to-person payments
- Payroll
- Bill payments
- Charitable donations[12]

E-gold can also be used for money laundering purposes because it is anonymous and unregulated. In addition, the following attributes provide extensive opportunities for bad actors to disguise their actions and eliminate trails that connect them to illegal activities:

- No CTRs are completed for transactions exceeding $10,000
- No records are verified or stored
- "Know your customers" requirement is not followed
- The service provides the ability to circumvent regulated financial institutions and their corresponding oversight/regulatory mechanisms
- Intangible services like consulting are common facades for the disbursement of funds between organized criminal syndicates

E-gold is just one such service. Others include e-currency, Digital Currency, Digital Gold Currency, WebMoney, and the list goes on.

In response, worldwide efforts, often led by U.S. law enforcement, The International Monetary Fund (IMF), and the World Bank, have tried multiple approaches to combat money laundering in cyberspace, including those described below.[13]

Identify and Reduce the Ability to Make Anonymous Financial Transactions. Financial Sector Assessment Program (FSAP) is a joint IMF and World Bank effort introduced in May 1999 to increase efforts to promote the soundness of financial systems in member countries. Supported by experts from a range of national agencies and standard-setting bodies, FSAP seeks to identify the strengths and vulnerabilities of a country's financial system, to determine how key sources of risk are managed, to ascertain developmental and technical assistance needs, and to help prioritize policy responses. Related specifically to cyberbased money laundering, FSAP provides assistance and training on how to identify and reduce new means of money laundering, cybercrime, and terrorist financing using transactions such as the Nonbank Issuer Model and the Peer-to Peer Model.

Map Global Payment Systems. The goal of the "Global Payments Systems Mapping Project" is to develop a better understanding of the flow of money, which can, in turn, be converted into knowledge for helping nations craft monetary policies and financial risk assessment models.

Facilitate International Information Sharing. Using the U.S. Financial Services Information Sharing and Analysis Center (ISAC) as a model, the goal is to provide real-time information sharing, alerts, notifications, web-based education, and training on e-money laundering and other cybercrimes. In addition, the data could be used to operate a cyberthreat analysis center.

Require All Financial Transactions to Include "Know your Customers" Policies and Procedures. To increase transparency, authentication solutions, including the use of biometric and public key infrastructure (PKI), can be implemented for users who initiate large value transfers. Two-factor authentication could also be required for all financial transactions.

Harmonize and Coordinate International Money Movement Regulations. The standardization of laws and regulations of money movement for all entities would mitigate the threat of nonregistered and informal money transmitters (e.g., e-gold) that are used to facilitate money laundering activities by organized criminal syndicates in cyberspace. Greater entry barriers, such as licensing and registration for all money movement entities, will hinder the effectiveness of money laundering techniques in cyberspace.

REPORTING CYBERCRIME: COMPUTER AND INTERNET CRIME

The primary federal law enforcement agencies that investigate domestic crime on the Internet include the Federal Bureau of Investigation (FBI), the United States Secret Service, the United States Immigration and Customs Enforcement (ICE), the United States Postal Inspection Service, and the Bureau of Alcohol, Tobacco, Firearms and Explosives (ATF).

In addition, the Internet Crime Complaint Center (IC3) was established as a partnership between the Federal Bureau of Investigation (FBI) and the NW3C (formerly the National White Collar Crime Center) to serve as a means to receive Internet-related criminal complaints and to further research, develop, and refer criminal complaints to federal, state, local, or international law enforcement and/or regulatory agencies. The IC3 emphasizes serving the broader law enforcement community to include federal, state, local, and international agencies that are combating Internet crime and, in many cases, participating in the Cyber Crime Task Forces around the world. Since its inception, the IC3 has received complaints across the spectrum of cybercrime, including online fraud in its many forms, such as computer intrusions (hacking), economic espionage, identity theft, intellectual property rights violations, international money laundering, online extortion, theft of trade secrets, as well as Internet-facilitated crimes.

IC3 serves as a repository organization to receive, develop, and refer criminal complaints regarding cybercrime. The IC3 provides a convenient and easy-to-use reporting mechanism for victims. Based on the data provided by victims, the IC3 alerts authorities to suspected criminal or civil violations. For law enforcement and regulatory agencies at the federal, state, local, and international level, IC3 provides a central referral mechanism for complaints involving Internet-related crimes. In addition to partnering with law enforcement and regulatory agencies, IC3 also works to establish effective alliances with industry. Such alliances enable the IC3 and their law enforcement partners to leverage intelligence and subject matter expertise of their industry partners. The goal is to be proactive and aggressive as well as responsive to cybercrime.

REVIEW QUESTIONS

5-1 How are computers used in cybercrime?

5-2 What is the difference between computer fraud and computer crime?

5-3 Which types of economic damages are related to computer crimes?

5-4 What methods are used by insiders to commit computer fraud? What red flags might indicate that insider computer fraud is occurring?

5-5 What is meant by "hacking?"

5-6 How might a hacker access and manipulate a computer for illegal purposes?

5-7 How do computer viruses work?

5-8 List and describe various types of computer viruses.

5-9 What are some common virus carriers?

5-10 What are some indicators that a computer has been infected?

5-11 Why are today's viruses more difficult to detect?

5-12 Why is Internet fraud particularly difficult to police?

5-13 Which federal law enforcement agencies investigate domestic Internet crimes?

ENDNOTES

1. Source unknown
2. ACFE *Fraud Examiners Manual*, 1.18
3. Computer Fraud and Abuse Act: United States Department of Justice, Computer Crime & Intellectual Property Section.

4. Individual states also have their own computer-based criminal acts. In fact, Congress deliberately tried to design federal laws to ensure that the federal government had a compelling, constitutionally-based interest in the actions of the bad actors. Fraud examiners and forensic

accountants will need to work closely with federal, state, and local law enforcement to determine the subtleties and nuances of the various applicable laws and statutes.

5. Computer Fraud and Abuse Act: United States Department of Justice, Computer Crime & Intellectual Property Section.

6. Ibid.

7. Ibid.

8. According to http://www.offshoresimple.com/offshore _banks.htm, "we can establish, create or sell a bank in many jurisdictions. We do all the work and can establish a bank in 2–6 months." The Web site offers banks in St. Vincent, Belize, and Dominica.

9. For further information see: http://www.ecommercetimes .com/story/31962.html.

10. "Money Laundering in Cyberspace," a World Bank Financial Sector working paper by Tom Kellerman (November 15, 2004).

11. Ibid.

12. www.e-gold.com.

13. "Money Laundering in Cyberspace," a World Bank Financial Sector working paper by Tom Kellerman (November 15, 2004).

CHAPTER 6

LEGAL, REGULATORY, AND PROFESSIONAL ENVIRONMENT

LEARNING OBJECTIVES

After completing this chapter, you should be able to

6-1 Compare and contrast the remedies available in the civil and criminal justice systems.

6-2 Identify the circumstances that require a Miranda warning.

6-3 Explain what constitutes "good cause" in the discharge of an employee.

6-4 Discuss the different approaches used by investigators to obtain documents.

6-5 Describe what is meant by demonstrative evidence and give examples.

6-6 Discuss the difference between probation and parole.

6-7 Describe the factors that affect the decision to prosecute an entity.

6-8 Explain the discovery process.

6-9 Differentiate between the three major types of negotiated remedies.

6-10 Discuss the primary purpose of the Sarbanes–Oxley Act of 2002.

CRITICAL THINKING EXERCISE

A scientist has two buckets, one holds four gallons and the other holds five gallons. In addition, the scientist also has an unlimited water supply. By using nothing but the buckets and water, how can the scientist accurately measure three gallons of water?

INTRODUCTION

Fraud may be prosecuted criminally or civilly. Almost any dispute between entities (individuals, businesses, organizations, government entities, etc.) can be prosecuted in civil court. Any time the legal issue at hand involves money an opportunity arises for forensic accountant involvement. Similarly, any time the legal issue involves claims of fraudulent activity, fraud examiners and forensic accountants can play an important role in investigating and resolving the issue. In either case the process begins when one or more parties make a claim against another.

In the criminal justice system, a person from the private sector may report a crime. Individuals, families, neighbors, businesses, not-for-profits, nonprofits, associations, industry, newspapers, TV, radio, and the Internet are some of the sources where a legal issue may come to light. These same organizations are part of the crime prevention fabric as well. One of the major crime prevention tools is the fear of getting caught. In fact, it is generally accepted that this fear is a greater deterrent than the fear of punishment. Most people think of law enforcement when they consider the legal environment, but other entities often play a part as well, such as public health departments, educational institutions, welfare and social justice organizations, public works departments, and public housing. The watchful eye of those members of the greater community is critical to the success of both the criminal and civil justice systems.

Furthermore, members of the community directly participate in the civil and criminal systems. They report crimes and civil actions; they serve as witnesses, jurors, and other officers of the court. One of the most important aspects of the American and Western judicial systems is the willingness to accept

the outcomes of the legal process. Both sides to an issue are committed to their position; that is why they are in the civil or criminal justice system to begin with. Both sides commit considerable time and economic resources to pursuing their goals and positions. Yet despite the battles waged inside our courtrooms everyday—from local magistrates to the U.S. Supreme Court—when the final verdict is announced, generally the participants and society at large accept the outcomes. Another interesting aspect of our legal system is that most people are law-abiding citizens. If desired, many could get away with relatively minor crimes periodically and possibly even major crimes. But the vast majority of Americans and citizens of Western society agree to "play by the rules" because they believe that while some legal outcomes may be less than perfect, generally the system works, and our society is better off if everyone follows the rules.

Criminal cases are brought forth by the government through the criminal justice system. The government apprehends, tries, and punishes convicted individuals for criminal behavior. The foundation for this approach is that criminal behavior is considered a "crime against the state" as well as against individual victims. If the victims or others with a stake in the outcome are not satisfied with the results of the criminal justice system, they may pursue their claim through the civil justice system. Cases may also be pursued criminally and civilly at the same time. The primary difference between the criminal and civil systems is the potential remedy for the victim: the primary allowable remedy in the civil process is monetary damages, whereas the criminal justice system may result in fines, community service, probation, incarceration, censure, and even capital punishment. In the United States, however, there are no fraud crimes that carry the death penalty.

Most criminal cases never end up in the criminal justice system. This is known as the *criminal justice funnel*. The funnel analogy is derived from the fact that while many crimes go in the top at the wide part of the funnel, few come out at the bottom in the form of convictions and incarcerations. In fact, most crimes are not discovered, and many that are discovered are not reported. Reports from victims, other citizens, law enforcement personnel, informants, investigators, and intelligence activities may result in the observation of criminal behavior. Nevertheless, there is a tremendous amount of discretion inherent in the American and Western criminal justice systems. Just because a criminal or civil offense is observed does not mean that it will be reported or pursued. Even if an actual crime in observed, before the criminal justice system can pursue the matter, the suspect must be identified and apprehended.

In addition to the criminal and civil justice systems, regulatory agencies also play an important role in monitoring illegal activities and pursuing those responsible. The U.S. Securities and Exchange Commission (SEC) regulates securities exchanges, securities brokers and dealers, investment advisors, and mutual funds. The SEC may bring civil or administrative actions to seek remedies for violations of law or the Commission's rules, and works closely with law enforcement agencies to bring criminal cases, when appropriate. The Public Company Accounting Oversight Board (PCAOB) was created by the Sarbanes–Oxley Act of 2002 to oversee the auditing firms of public companies. Its main purpose is to protect investors by promoting fair and informative financial reports. The board members are appointed by the SEC.

Governmental agencies regulate activities involving utilities, communications, and air transportation, to name a few. Taxpayer money provides the resources needed for government operations, and the Internal Revenue Service (IRS) is charged with collecting those taxes and enforcing the tax laws under the Internal Revenue Code. The IRS can also bring actions against taxpayers in civil and/or criminal court for noncompliance with the tax code.

THE RIGHTS OF INDIVIDUALS

When persons consider individual rights, most of those rights are associated with formal actions in the criminal and civil justice environments. Generally individuals have far fewer rights as employees than as citizens. Most fundamentally, individual rights are grounded in four amendments to the U.S. Constitution associated with due process:

- The Fourth Amendment prohibits unreasonable searches and seizures
- The Fifth Amendment provides that a person cannot be compelled to provide incriminating information against himself in a criminal case
- The Sixth Amendment provides that an individual has the right to an attorney to defend himself and the right to confront witnesses against him
- The Fourteenth Amendment entitles a person to due process of law and equal protections under the law

As employees, individuals have an obligation to cooperate with their employer or be subject to dismissal. Other rights may be granted to employees as set out in employment contracts and collective bargaining agreements. Federal law and many state laws protect employees who report improper or illegal acts of their employer. Such laws normally protect the employee against overt retaliatory or punitive action by the employer, although as a practical matter, subtle forms of discrimination are hard to combat.

Interviews

An employee's or individual suspect's right to avoid self-incrimination applies to employers, investigators, and law enforcement personnel. An employee who refuses to cooperate during an interview while invoking the Fifth Amendment, however, may be subject to termination. In custodial settings by law enforcement, and in those settings where the suspected perpetrator has been taken into custody and denied freedom presumably against their will, federal law may require that a Miranda warning be read to the suspect. Because employers do not have the right to place employees in a custodial setting, an employee has limited Fifth Amendment rights. Public employers, however, are held to a higher standard, and their employees can invoke their Fifth Amendment protections without fear of reprisal.

The Miranda warnings consist of the following:

- The interviewee has a right to remain silent
- The interviewee's answers may be used against him
- The interviewee has a right to an attorney
- If the interviewee cannot afford an attorney, one will be provided at no cost
- The interviewee can decide at any time to invoke these rights

A second issue arises with interviewees with regard to the Sixth Amendment, by which employees are entitled to legal counsel. As long as a nonpublic entity is conducting the interview, an employee does not have the right to have a lawyer present nor does the employee have the right to consult their attorney prior to an interview. The employee maintains the right to consult an attorney if they request one, however. With regard to the Fourteenth Amendment, private employers do not have to offer employees due process of law. In contrast, law enforcement and public entities have such an obligation under this amendment. For example, federal employees may have a right of notice of charges and may have the right to rebut any charges put forward.

The Fourth, Fifth, Sixth, and Fourteenth Amendments are all federal rights. In many cases, other federal and state laws regulate the rights of individuals. While such statutes and laws cannot have the impact of limiting federal constitutional rights, those rights may be expanded. Some of the common means by which federal rights are altered are via employment contracts, collective bargaining and other union agreements, various nondiscrimination statutes, and the Fair Labor Standards Act.

In addition, individuals may be entitled to various common law protections with regard to interviews. These include:[1]

- Minimization of invasion of the employee's privacy
- Limitations on interview content to employee job duties and responsibilities
- Limitations on public disclosure of the employee's private facts
- Limitations on intentional infliction of emotional distress on the employee
- Limitations on defamation—unfounded facts and accusations made by the interviewer
- A duty to deal fairly and in good faith
- No false imprisonment—false imprisonment may be inferred based on the size, nature, and lighting of the room, the amount of force involved, any violent behavior by the interviewer, limitations of ability to leave the interview room, and number of persons involved

While interviews may be conducted subject to the rules, laws, and other issues cited above, confessions resulting from interviews and interrogations create additional challenges. First, in order for confessions to be valid, they must be deemed voluntary. Confessions cannot be obtained as a result of coercion or under threats of violence. Furthermore, promises by the interviewer of leniency can nullify a confession. Promises to recommend a lighter sentence or to report cooperation by the subject, however, are generally not thought to be coercive in nature. Courts have weighed the "substantial risk" of a false

confession when determining whether a confession has been coerced.[2] Small deceptions are generally permitted and will not risk the validity of the confession. With regard to deceptions, a simple rule is to ask yourself, "Is what I am about to say apt to make an innocent person as well as a guilty person confess?" If the answer is "yes," the statement should not be made.[3]

Searches

The Fourth Amendment protects individuals against unreasonable searches and seizures. First, unreasonable searches and seizures are forbidden. All warrants for searches and arrest must be supported by probable cause, and all warrants must be reasonably specific as to persons, places, and things.[4] The overriding rule is that individuals have a "reasonable expectation of privacy." Whether a search or surveillance is reasonable is generally based on the totality of the circumstances. A search warrant based on probable cause has the effect of being reasonable. A major exception to the need for a warrant is in instances where law enforcement has reason to believe that a crime has been committed (or is about to be committed) and an immediate search is required.

Fourth Amendment protections are further refined in specific circumstances as follows.[5] First, public employers, e.g., government, are not required to obtain a search warrant when they conduct workplace searches for investigations of workplace misconduct. The issue is that workplace investigations are substantially different from those conducted by law enforcement because the goal is not law enforcement but rather efficient office operations, a premise upheld by the U.S. Supreme Court. Furthermore, while individuals have a reasonable expectation of privacy in many places, such as homes and automobiles, such an expectation does not apply in the workplace. For example, items of a personal nature may be left at home and need not be stored in the confines of an office, desk, or filing cabinet.

A workplace search is considered reasonable under two circumstances:

1. The search must be justified at its inception because it is likely to reveal evidence of work-related misconduct. The requirement implies that a clear suspicion exists based on a preliminary review of the evidence.

2. The search is necessary to further the investigation. An example of this concept is that the investigator is able to obtain files that are a required part of the investigation. The requirement implies that the search is likely to reveal pertinent information.

Assuming that the search is reasonable based on these criteria, the scope of the search must be no broader than is necessary to serve the organization's legitimate, work-related purpose. The investigator may, in fact, have no search limitations if the employee has no reasonable expectation of privacy in the place to be searched. For example, a general filing cabinet with travel reimbursement forms has no reasonable expectation of privacy whereas the individual's desk is much more likely to yield items of a personal nature. Thus many workplace areas have no reasonable expectation of privacy for any employee. The key factor is *exclusive control*. If the individual has exclusive control over a particular area, a reasonable expectation of privacy is more likely to become an issue. As noted above, even with exclusive control, the only standard that an employer must meet is that the search is reasonable based on the above guidelines.

A second area of special consideration for the Fourteenth Amendment is searches incidental to arrest. First, an arrest can be made only based on probable cause. (A citizen may make an arrest only for a crime committed in his or her presence.) As such, law enforcement officers may search an area within his or her immediate control at the time of the arrest without a warrant for the purposes of self-protection and to prevent the destruction of evidence. If the arrest is later invalidated, however, the search is also invalidated. This potential suppression of evidence can be very frustrating to law enforcement investigators. Of course, no warrant is required for evidence that is in plain view. Furthermore, borders and customs agents are provided an exception for searches without warrants.

Search of motor vehicles, including cars, truck, watercraft, and airplanes, may be conducted without a warrant if the law enforcement personnel believe that contraband is present or the vehicle contains other evidence of a crime. The risk of flight with regard to motorized vehicles makes them inherently more risky. Once moved, evidence may be removed or destroyed and such a risk necessitates prompt action. In addition, unlike a home where expectation of privacy is paramount, motorized vehicles are subject to a much lower expectation. The motorized vehicle may be moved to a police facility and inventoried prior to search, and law enforcement may proceed with the search without a warrant. The ability to search vehicles also applies to the contents of the vehicle (e.g., luggage) but does not extend to passengers. Passengers may not be searched without a prior arrest or warrant.

Individuals may waive their Fourth Amendment rights that prevent certain types of searches. Consent by an individual eliminates the need for a search warrant by law enforcement. Like confessions, the waiver of this right will be scrutinized to ensure that it was not coerced in any way. Thus, law enforcement personnel must be able to defend the waiver against claims of false imprisonment, force, violence, and limitations of ability to leave the area, as well as accusations of deceit, bribery, or misrepresentation. Unlike the Miranda warning related to statements, no warning must be made regarding an individual's right to refuse a search. Illegally obtained evidence may not be introduced in court. Furthermore, any information derived from illegal evidence cannot be introduced. This is known as "fruit from the forbidden tree."

Surveillance

Surveillance can be more complex than interviews and searches. Although the rules of conduct for interviews and searches have been defined through federal and state laws and interpretations by the U.S. Supreme Court, the conduct of surveillance has many more issues to consider. As such, counsel should be consulted when surveillance is contemplated. Such techniques include electronic surveillance, including audio and video monitoring and recording. Generally these techniques are not conducted by fraud examiners and forensic accountants because these professionals do not have the required training and skill set. Furthermore, such operations are more common when the suspected activity is complicated and involves multiple individuals, organizations, and jurisdictions. Many of these types of investigative operations are conducted by private investigators or law enforcement officers who have the necessary training and experience.

Several types of surveillance are possible:

- Fixed-point surveillance (e.g., stakeout) involves observing activity from a stationary, discreet location
- Mobile surveillance
- Videography (If audio is also captured during the surveillance, different laws, rules, and regulations are in effect, because audio surveillance has much more stringent requirements)
- Audio or electronic surveillance (e.g., wiretapping)

Surveillance is generally legal. Once the investigator enters the realm of electronic (audio) surveillance, the laws and requirements become more complicated. Generally, federal law prevents the *interception and/or recording* of wire, oral, or electronic communications except by the following:[6]

- Law enforcement officers with a warrant
- Operator of a switchboard or common carrier providing services carrying out job duties and responsibilities
- An employee of the FCC carrying out job duties and responsibilities
- A party to a communication who has given prior consent to the interception (one-party consent)
- A person acting under the Foreign Intelligence Act of 1978

The warrant requirement is the most complicated issue faced by forensic accountants and fraud examiners. With the exception of thirteen states, any party to a conversation may record their own conversation. Although the interception and recording of live communication is generally forbidden by federal law without a warrant, stored communication (including voicemail and e-mail) is not nearly as well protected. For example, an employer can access stored voicemail and e-mail on their own servers but cannot access the same communications stored by an outside provider (e.g., messages stored on Sprint voicemail). More interestingly, any party to the communication may provide the necessary permission and access to persons not party to the communication.

Generally, video surveillance is permissible as long as it does not violate a person's reasonable expectation of privacy. Anyone in a public park, parking lot, or mall may be videotaped without violating any laws as long as no audio of the target is recorded. Where individuals have a reasonable expectation of privacy, however, such as in their own home, employee restrooms, employee locker rooms, or employee changing areas, video surveillance is not permitted without the existence of extenuating circumstances and a warrant.

Generally, a private employer is prohibited from conducting polygraph examinations (lie-detector tests) unless the employer has suffered economic loss and has reasonable suspicion that the particular employee was involved in the issue under investigation. Like other aspects of the investigation, reasonable

suspicion is an evidence-based decision. Under no circumstances, however, can a nongovernment employer use a polygraph examination to screen applicants.

Discharging a Suspected Wrongdoer from Employment

Assuming that an internal, private investigation by an employer results in the conclusion that a particular individual committed a fraud act, can the employer dismiss that employee? Perhaps more intriguing, what if the suspected employee refuses to cooperate and that investigation cannot continue? What then? While public employers are governed by a stricter standard, employer rights are dictated by the jurisdiction in which they operate. Generally, employment is considered *at will*. This characteristic allows either the employee or employer to sever the relationship at any time for almost any reason. Employees may have some protections against dismissal for improper reasons, however, even in at will states.

As such, it is advisable that employers document *good cause* for any termination in the employee's personnel file. Good cause might include the following:

- The employee's conduct was against written policy
- The employee's conduct made for unsafe or inefficient business operations
- The company completed a reasonable investigation to ensure that any such questionable act was committed by the employee and has evidence to support such a claim
- The investigation was fair, objective, and evidence suggested the elimination of alternative suspects
- The termination was nondiscriminatory, meaning that all persons committing such an act were or would be terminated
- The punishment fits the crime, meaning that the punishment is reasonable given the nature of the offense

Such incidents and punitive actions by the company should be carefully considered and well documented. Nothing prevents an employee from suing a former employer in civil court, even if the termination is arguably a reasonable response to the alleged offense.

Privileges

Legal privileges are protections against certain types of testimony. With the exception of the privilege against compelled self-incrimination, most of the following privileges are not constitutionally based:

- Attorney–client privilege
- Attorney work-product privilege
- Physician–patient privilege
- Marital privileges
- Miscellaneous privileges

Attorney–Client Privilege   The attorney–client privilege is the right to not disclose any confidential communication relating to the professional relationship, where the client can be an individual or a corporation. Interestingly, the privilege belongs to the client and the client has the right to compel nondisclosure by the attorney, whereas the attorney may only assert the privilege if acting on behalf of the client. The attorney–client privilege applies only to communications that are intended to be confidential. This privilege does not permit an attorney to conceal physical evidence or documents and does not apply to future acts of a crime or fraud.

Attorney Work-Product Privilege   Attorneys have a work-product privilege. The privilege protects all materials prepared by an attorney in anticipation of litigation and is designed to preserve the adversarial trial process by shielding materials that would disclose the attorney's theory of the case or trial strategy. Attorney work-product is defined as any written materials, charts, notes of conversations and investigations, and other materials directed toward preparation of a case. To preserve this privilege, the material must be prepared in anticipation of litigation or the factual context must make it probable that litigation will arise.

Physician–Patient Privilege In most states, confidential communications made to a physician, as well as psychiatrists, psychotherapists, and psychologists, for the purpose of obtaining treatment or diagnosis are privileged. Consultations that take place with regard to litigation, however, are not covered (e.g., examinations by court-appointed physicians or expert witnesses). Furthermore, when patients are involved in litigation and put their medical condition at issue, they are deemed to have waived this privilege.

Marital Privileges In some cases, marital privileges exist. The first is spousal immunity and protects a person from having to testify against his or her spouse—although such testimony is permitted, and cannot be stopped by the spouse. At the state level, a slight majority of states give the privilege to the spousal defendant, which protects them from adverse testimony. This privilege is usually allowed in both civil and criminal cases and covers statements made during the marriage and applies even if the parties are no longer married at the time of trial. Neither privilege applies to crimes or torts within a family.

Miscellaneous Privileges Nearly all states recognize a privilege for confidential communications made to members of the clergy in their professional capacity as spiritual advisors. The government also has a variety of privileges that protect the disclosure of sensitive information in its possession. Finally, some courts recognize qualified privileges for trade secrets for businesses. Contrary to popular belief, there is no legal privilege for accountant–client relationships.

PROBABLE CAUSE

Underlying any arrest or warrant is probable cause. Probable cause is the standard by which law enforcement may make an arrest, conduct a personal or property search, or obtain a warrant. The term also refers to the standard used by grand juries when they believe that a crime has been committed. One of the first issues associated with probable cause is to define the players. A witness is a person who is not suspected of the crime at issue. As one moves to the top of the culpability scale, a target is believed to stand a better than fifty percent probability of being criminally charged with a crime. Somewhere between witnesses and targets are subjects. Subjects may have committed unethical conduct and may be involved in suspicious activity but they have not crossed the line to the point where their behavior is considered likely to be judged criminal (based on the current state of the investigation and the evidence). As evidence is developed and the investigation proceeds, players' roles may change. For example, subjects may become targets or subjects may be relegated to witnesses.

The origins of probable cause rest with the Fourth Amendment to the U.S. Constitution, which states, "The right of the people to be secure in their persons, houses, papers, and effects, against unreasonable searches and seizures, shall not be violated, and no warrants shall issue, but upon probable cause, supported by oath or affirmation, and particularly describing the place to be searched, and the persons or things to be seized." Despite this phraseology, the threshold for probable cause is not as high as one might expect.

In *Terry v. Ohio* (1968), the U.S. Supreme Court established that some brief seizures may be made without probable cause. Known as the *Terry Stop*, the court ruled that if a police officer has reasonable suspicion (not probable cause) that a crime has been committed or will soon be committed, that officer may briefly detain an individual, search him or her for weapons, and question the person.

In 1974, in *The United States v. Matlock*, the U.S. Supreme Court ruled that the cooccupant of a residence may permit a search in the absence of any other cooccupant. This rule is known as the *cooccupant consent rule* and established that an officer who makes a search with a reasonable belief that the search was consented to (i.e., voluntary) by a resident does not need to have probable cause for the search.

Finally, in *Illinois v. Gates* (1983) the U.S. Supreme Court lowered the threshold for probable cause by ruling that a "substantial chance" or "fair probability" of criminal activity could establish probable cause and that a better-than-even chance of criminal behavior is not required.

Related more specifically to fraud, financial crimes, and white-collar crime, in recent times, law enforcement and other investigators have resorted to more sophisticated methods for identifying and investigating fraud. They have, therefore, turned to tools traditionally set aside for organized crime, drug trafficking, and similar investigations such as wiretaps, video surveillance, undercover operations, seizure of records, and allowing less culpable individuals to plead guilty to lesser charges for their testimony against decision makers and those considered more culpable. In addition to these investigative techniques, alleged perpetrators also are pursued in both the civil and criminal justice systems. These tools and techniques allow investigators and prosecutors to gain leverage over the defendant, maximize pressure on

alleged perpetrators, and achieve as much cooperation as possible. Charges of mail fraud, wire fraud, money laundering, racketeering, or conspiracy typically come from these investigations.

Not surprisingly, most frauds and financial crimes are solved using documentary evidence. Such evidence is typically the key to, or the basis for, most white-collar crime cases. The challenge, and where probable cause comes into play, is the issue of how to obtain the necessary documents (i.e., physical documentary evidence). Generally, investigators can obtain documents using three approaches:

- Voluntary consent
- Subpoena
- Search warrant

Subpoenas are issued by grand juries and used to compel witnesses to testify. They may also be used to compel people to turn documents over to the authorities (known as a *subpoena duces tecum*). While grand juries have great leeway related to issuing subpoenas, the Fourth Amendment requires reasonableness. To meet the reasonableness standard, the subpoena must be likely to generate evidence that is (a) relevant to the issue under consideration, (b) be particular and reasonably specific, and (c) be limited to a reasonable time frame. One of the shortcomings of the subpoena approach to obtaining documents is that the investigator is relying on the subpoena recipient to determine what documents fall under the subpoena's particular details. An investigator reviewing the records may come to a different conclusion than a suspect or a suspect's lawyer. Even assuming good faith on the part of the subpoena recipient, the person may not provide all the necessary or required documents and the investigators would have no way of knowing what documents were missed. Given the above, subpoenas are best used for witnesses and subjects who are less likely to be adversarial to the receipt of the document and information request.

An issue arises concerning the choice of voluntary production of documents and physical evidence or grand jury subpoenas, especially when the subject offers to voluntarily supply evidence. Voluntary consent gives the defense lawyer and/or their client time to gather and review relevant documents, negotiate limitations on irrelevant material, copy documents that are essential to the operations of the client's business, and schedule document production that does not disrupt day-to-day business operations. One of the shortcomings of the subpoena is that its use may prevent criminal investigators from sharing the documentary evidence with other government agencies that may be conducting parallel inquiries. One should note that the discovery process used to gather documents in civil actions is almost always through subpoena, and generally, each side is at the mercy of the other in the sense that they must trust that the other side has provided all available documents that meet the criteria set out in the subpoena.

Beyond subpoenas, search warrants may be used to obtain documents and other physical evidence. Search warrants are issued by a judge based on probable cause and put the investigator in charge of the evidentiary search. As noted in the review of the three important court cases above, the threshold for probable cause is not that high: there must be some evidence (probable cause) that a crime has been committed and some belief (probable cause) that the search warrant will yield evidentiary support from the person or place that is the subject of the warrant that will help solve the crime. The limitations of the search warrant are in the details included in the warrant itself. It must include details of the place to be searched, the people involved, and types of evidence likely to be seized. As such, a search warrant requires a reasonable level of specificity. Assuming these items are covered by the warrant, the types of records seized include:

- Any property that constitutes evidence of the commission of a criminal offense
- Contraband, the fruits of crime, or things otherwise criminally possessed
- Property designed or intended for use, or that are or have been used, as a means of committing a criminal offense

What is the threshold of probable cause in order to obtain a judge's signature on a warrant? Generally, probable cause made through an affidavit is sufficient. Furthermore, a judge considering the warrant application may find probable cause based entirely on hearsay evidence. Finally, in extraordinary circumstances, warrants may even be issued based on an oral application. These are typically reserved for emergencies.

The warrant has several advantages over a subpoena. First, a warrant allows the holder of the warrant, not the target or the defense counsel, to decide which documents are relevant and must be produced. Second, a warrant avoids, but does not eliminate, the possibility of the destruction of evidence. An interesting attribute of a warrant is that while the search is being conducted, it gives the investigator the ability to interview key witnesses. If handled properly, those key witnesses will not have had the

opportunity to consult with counsel or prepare for the interview. In law enforcement investigations where the target is operating an illegal enterprise or has an organization tied up in unlawful activities, the warrant permitting the seizure of documents provides tremendous advantages. By seizing documents and computers, as a practical matter, they take away an entity's ability to continue their activities as a going concern. Regarding the seized items, all that is required is that the person holding the warrant provides the target with a written inventory of any property taken. The main disadvantage of the warrant is that this document can later be challenged because it lacks specificity.

RULES OF EVIDENCE

Without evidence there is no proof; without proof there are no convictions or civil verdicts. As the Bible says, "the truth shall set you free." In the world of fraud and forensic accounting, truth needs to be grounded in evidence. One of the surest ways to lose a conviction is to base a case on the "bad person" theory and not conduct a thorough and complete investigation. Conclusions must be grounded in the evidence.

Evidence is anything legally presented at trial to prove a contention and convince a jury. Generally, evidence is admissible in court if it is relevant, its probative value outweighs any prejudicial effects, and it is trustworthy, meaning that it is subject to examination and cross-examination. The definition and types of evidence will be further explored in the following chapter. For the purposes of exploring the rules of evidence, evidence may be testimonial, real (e.g., documents) or demonstrative, or circumstantial or direct (e.g., testimony of an eye witness). At the federal level, rules of evidence apply in both civil and criminal courts. Most states have their own rules of evidence but those rules are generally modeled after the federal rules of evidence.

At trial, attorneys attempt to prove *facts at issue*. These facts at issue are not evidence, but facts supported by evidence. For example, whether or not the defendant was at the victim's home on the night of a crime is a fact at issue; evidence (such as a fingerprint) is offered to prove or disprove the fact. The fingerprint is evidence; the fingerprint, while a fact, is not a fact at issue. The first hurdle for evidence is that it must be admissible. To gain admissibility, the evidence may not be irrelevant to the facts at issue, immaterial, or incompetent (impeachable). Prior to admissibility, the attorney must lay the foundation by demonstrating relevance, materiality, and competence (reliability). The threshold for relevance is that it must make a material fact more or less probable than without the evidence. Even relevant evidence, however, may be excluded from judicial proceedings if it is prejudicial, confusing, or misleading. Materiality refers to the potential impact that a piece of evidence may have. If the evidence has a tendency to affect the determination of the facts at issue, it is considered material. For evidence to be competent, it must be considered reliable. The ultimate value of any piece of evidence is in the eyes of the trier of fact (e.g., juror, judge, magistrate, etc.).

Real evidence is that evidence that "speaks for itself" and does not require explanatory testimony. A baseball bat with a victim's blood, hair, and DNA on it speaks for itself. To be admissible, real evidence must be authenticated. Authentication is a function of several attributes. First, the evidence must be collected properly. For example, investigators should not overtly mark evidence (it should be discretely done) or leave their fingerprints on it during collection. Once collected, the evidence must be preserved so that it is not altered or damaged. The evidence must be identifiable as it moves through the judicial system. One of the common elements is that the chain of custody must be preserved. Even though real evidence speaks for itself, it is still subject to interpretation. Simply because a baseball bat was used as a weapon to kill a person and a third party's fingerprints are on the bat does not make the third person the killer. One of the strengths of real evidence is that jurors, judges, and other triers of fact can see, touch, feel, smell, and possibly hear or taste the evidence.

Demonstrative evidence is any evidence that purports to educate, summarize, or amplify real evidence. PowerPoint slides, summary schedules, graphics, pictures, reenactments, models, etc. are all forms of demonstrative evidence. Demonstrative evidence tends to tell a story and complements other forms of evidence such as real and testimonial evidence. Some examples of demonstrative evidence include the following:

- Photographs and videotapes
- Maps, charts, diagrams, drawings
- Scale models
- Computer reconstructions or animations
- Scientific tests or experiments

Because demonstrative evidence is not real, it must not create prejudice and it must not materially alter any significant aspect of the facts at issue. Thus, demonstrative evidence is subject to examination for representational faithfulness.

As noted above, documentary evidence is at the heart of most fraud and forensic accounting investigations. Five considerations must be given to any piece of documentary evidence:

1. The document must not have been forged.
2. Original documents are preferable.
3. The document must not be hearsay or objectionable.
4. The document needs to be authenticated.
5. The document must be reliable.

While an original document is preferable, the *best evidence rule* allows copies to be presented at trial under certain circumstances. Mechanical copies of documents are generally allowed assuming that the copy can be authenticated. Note that copies can also qualify as real evidence if they are used to demonstrate that an original document was altered. Duplicates are typically accepted if they are copies of search warrants, mortgages, lease agreements, duplicate sales slips, official documents, public records, government sealed records, summaries, testimonies, and written admissions.

Chain of custody refers to those individuals who had possession of physical evidence and what they did with it. Essentially, fraud professionals and forensic accountants must be able to establish the origins of evidence and that the evidence has not been altered as a result of the investigation. The chain of custody protects against the possible corruption of evidence as a result of the investigators losing control of it. Close monitoring of all physical evidence is important in a fraud investigation. In civil litigation, much of the discovery work is done through copies transferred among parties. Although it is important to establish the integrity of evidence, generally, the chain of evidence does not normally play a central role in civil disputes. Attorneys for both sides typically stipulate that the evidence is valid.

Testimonial evidence brings about a discussion of hearsay. What happens if one person hears another person make a statement or one person makes a statement that so-and-so said something? Hearsay is a statement made other than those made during legal proceedings. Each person must testify based on his or her own first-hand experience. Presentation in court allows the jury to hear the evidence and allows opposing council to cross-examine the testimony. Despite the need to have live testimony, a number of hearsay exceptions exist. First, if the truth of the statement is not at issue and it does not impact actual guilt or innocence, the statement may be admissible. For example, a person's statements about his or her frustration levels heard by another person (first-hand) is admissible because it is not about guilt or innocence, it's about state of mind. Any statement, oral or written, that can be corroborated is generally admissible. Another interesting aspect of hearsay admissibility is *statements against interest*, defined as any statement that contradicts a prior statement. Such statements against interest are generally admissible. Other types of hearsay that are admissible include the following:

- Business and government records
- Absence of an entry in business records
- Recorded recollections
- Former testimony
- Present sense impressions
- Then existing mental, emotional, or physical condition
- Statements to medical personnel
- Printed matter, learned treatises, and refresher writings

CRIMINAL JUSTICE SYSTEM

As noted above, most cases never end up in the criminal justice system. Those that do, however, follow a relatively generic path. Readers should keep in mind that each jurisdiction, federal, state, and local, will have their own specific procedures and are advised to consult attorneys in that jurisdiction regarding specific issues and concerns that may impact the case.[7] Targets may enter the criminal justice system from

three routes: a warrantless arrest by the police based upon probable cause, an investigation that leads to the filing of an *Information* (a brief, written complaint in support of an arrest by law enforcement), or a grand jury proceeding that leads to an indictment and a subsequent arrest warrant issued by a judge. Assuming an arrest, law enforcement personnel provide the investigative outcomes and evidence to the prosecuting attorney, who decides whether charges will be filed against the target. Those persons formally charged by the prosecutor must appear before a judge "without unnecessary delay." Judges decide if probable cause exists to move forward. For less serious crimes, the judge may decide a verdict and penalty at this time. Another option is a diversion, where the defendant agrees to take some specified action to avoid prosecution.

For more serious crimes, a defense attorney may be assigned, or the defendant will be represented by an attorney of his or her choice. The following may also be evaluated at this time to determine pretrial release and bail: alleged drug use, residence, employment, family ties, and wealth. If the case comes to the criminal justice system through a grand jury, the jury panel decides if sufficient evidence exists to bring the case to trial. The choice of arrest or grand jury is a strategic one. In some cases, law enforcement and prosecutors may decide to let a grand jury prepare an indictment because of their subpoena power. The grand jury may also be used to investigate criminal activity, particularly in drug and other complex criminal organizations.

Assuming that the criminal case proceeds beyond the indictment stage where the defendant is officially charged, the next step is an arraignment hearing. During the arraignment, the defendant is informed of the crime and the charges against him, advised of his rights, and asked to enter a plea: guilty, not guilty, or *Nolo Contendere*, a plea in which the defendant accepts the penalty without admitting guilt. (A Nolo Contendere plea for all practical purposes is a plea of guilty.) If the judge accepts a guilty plea, a penalty will be issued and no trial will be scheduled. Assuming a "not guilty" plea or a plea of "guilty by reason of insanity," the judge will put a trial date on the court calendar.

Unless the defendant chooses a bench trial (one where the judge alone presides), a trial by jury ensues. During a jury trial, the judge still decides matters of law, but the jury decides whether the evidence as presented is sufficient to convict the defendant. If the jury acquits the defendant, the person goes free. If the person is found guilty, a sentencing hearing is scheduled. The sentence may be determined by the jury or the judge, depending on the jurisdiction. During a sentencing hearing, aggravating and/or mitigating circumstances are presented, and often a presentence investigation is undertaken to identify those circumstances that may warrant consideration. That presentence investigation may include victim impact statements. Sentences are tied to the offense and include death sentences (there is no death sentence for fraud in the United States), incarceration, probation, fines, restitution, and other penalties such as drug treatment, house arrest, electronic monitoring, sanctions, denial of federal benefits, community service, and boot camps. For some crimes, incarceration may be mandated.

Subsequent to the guilty verdict and sentence, the convicted person may appeal the verdict, the sentence, or both. Although not applicable in fraud cases, death sentences have automatic appeal. Jail is reserved for sentences of less than one year's duration, whereas prison is reserved for sentences greater than a year. The prison system has varying levels of custody, including community-based facilities, minimum security, medium security, and maximum security. Once a sentence has been fulfilled or is shortened for good behavior, the person is typically placed on parole. Often times, people confuse probation and parole. Probation is a penalty and is used as an alternative to prison, whereas parole is used to describe the corrections process subsequent to having served time in prison. Parole is often used as a reward for good behavior during time served. During the parole period, a parole officer is assigned.

Recidivism refers to the process in which a formerly convicted person reenters the criminal justice system. Unfortunately, many arrestees have a criminal history and the greater the number of prior arrests, the higher the probability of future arrests. Within the United States, more than half of convicted criminals will return to jail during their lifetime, frequently for more serious offenses. The criminal justice system is society and the government's response to an unfortunate fact of life: people commit crimes. Despite the impact on the victims and society in general, the Constitution and case law dictates that law enforcement and grand juries must respect the rights of individuals. Most criminal justice actions are handled at the state and local level. The U.S. Congress has established the federal response for crimes such as bank robbery, kidnapping, mail fraud, tax fraud, and interstate crimes, but state constitutions, counties, and municipalities further define and refine the criminal justice system. It must be understood that in criminal cases, dual jurisdiction often exists. For example, a bank fraud is a federal crime but also a local one. Law enforcement officials decide amongst themselves what agency will handle the investigation and prosecution.

The hallmark of the criminal justice system in the United States is discretion. At almost every level, people are the decision makers. For example, people, including victims, decide whether to report crimes;

law enforcement decides if a crime occurred and what the official response should be. This discretion is pervasive throughout the system: police, other law enforcement, prosecutors, judges and magistrates, correctional officials, and parole authorities. The discretion creates a professional level of responsibility on the part of participants including training, supervision, and periodic performance assessment and reviews.

In the criminal justice system, not only may individuals be named as defendants, but businesses and other organizations may be prosecuted as well. Prosecution can be used to obtain punishment for the wrongdoing entities, and as a means for changing future behavior and forcing cultural changes. Assuming that appropriate cases are prosecuted, entity prosecutions might result in deterrence on a very large scale, possibly industry wide. Prosecution of the entity still allows for prosecution of individuals as well, such as board members, officers, executives, shareholders, and employees. Generally, businesses may be held liable, assuming that the scope of the infraction was within the duties of the individual who committed the crime, and the individual was acting as an agent for the entity. In addition, the agent's action was intended to benefit the entity. Factors that affect the decision to prosecute an entity are similar to those for individual prosecution and include the sufficiency of evidence, likelihood of success at trial, probability of deterrence and rehabilitation, and adequacy of nonprosecutorial remediation options. Other factors are also considered:

- Nature and seriousness of offense
- Corporation's history
- Timely and voluntary disclosure
- Willingness to cooperate
- Corporate compliance program
- Corporate remedial action(s)
- Replacement of management
- Discipline/termination of wrongdoers
- Payment of restitution
- Disproportionate harm to employees, shareholders, pensioners
- Adequacy of prosecution for individuals
- Adequacy of other remedies: civil, regulatory

Consistent with the remainder of the criminal justice system, prosecutors have wide discretion in these types of situations.

CIVIL JUSTICE SYSTEM

As noted above, the government prosecutes criminal cases on behalf of society, including the victims. Private parties may also enter the justice system in an attempt to right a wrong or resolve a dispute through the civil justice system. Fraud is just one such wrong that may enter the civil justice system; others include torts, breach of contract, breach of implied contract, negligence, and misrepresentations. The primary purpose of a civil action is to recover losses and possibly reap punitive damages. In fact, money and other similar damages are the main outcome in the civil justice system. In civil cases, however, Cease and Desist Orders and similar penalties may be attached. The way a fraud perpetrator suffers the risk of incarceration is through the criminal justice system. Fraud examiners and forensic accountants often find their skills put to good use in the civil justice system, not only in matters where fraud claims are made but also where lost profits, wages, value, and other similar allegations are made on behalf of a victim plaintiff. Most civil actions are handled in state court in the jurisdiction of the plaintiff, the party prosecuting the civil case or the jurisdiction of the defendant. Federal courts may be used for larger cases (those involving more than $75,000 or those that are multi-jurisdictional) because the plaintiffs gain greater access to witnesses and documents due to the broad jurisdiction.

Complaints and Pre-trial Activity

Civil lawsuits begin when the plaintiff files a complaint in an appropriate jurisdiction. The complaint must provide assurance to the court that it has jurisdiction, outline the grounds for relief, and make a demand for judgment. Because the complaint is filed before the plaintiff may have all of its facts (i.e., before discovery,

which is discussed below), the complaint does not need to be overly particular. Interestingly, fraud civil complaints must be specific and outline the fraud misrepresentations (the act), to whom (the impacted victim), how the misrepresentations were false, and other particular details in order to understand the fraud act. Yet, because the plaintiff most likely does not have complete access to the defendant's information and records, the plaintiff may not have a complete story. Normally the defendant files an answer to the complaint, denies liability, and may add counterclaims against the plaintiff or even ask the court for a dismissal. The process to file a complaint and to await the defendant's response can be very time consuming, and in very larges cases can extend over a year or more. Of course, time is money so the more time spent, the greater the legal fees to the plaintiff and defense lawyers and others involved in the case.

Once the complaint and answer have been filed (and assuming that the case continues in the civil courts) discovery begins. Discovery is the process by which each side may explore the merits of the other side's arguments by obtaining documentary and testimonial evidence. Any matter or material relevant to the civil action that is not privileged is subject to discovery. Normally, discovery may take at least four forms.

Initially, interrogatories are passed to the opposing council. Interrogatories are questions that require answers and those answers become part of the testimonial record. As such, answers are provided under oath. Although interrogatories are one of the least expensive means to obtain evidence from the opposing party because of an inability to ask follow-up questions, except through additional interrogatories, they may not be effective. Opposing parties tend to provide truthful responses yet minimal information.

Subsequent to interrogatories, opposing parties submit "requests to produce documents" to one another. These requests may include copies of contracts, notes from meetings, calendars, invoices, and accounting records of all sorts including general ledgers, trial balances, journal entries, journal entry backup, financial statements, and tax returns. Just about any information that is captured in paper or electronic form is subject to discovery. In very complex cases, the review of discovered documents alone can take years. While attorneys and experts can become almost overwhelmed with produced documents, most are remiss to limit the amount of document production for fear of missing that critical piece of paper that blows their case wide open.

Third, attorneys start to take sworn testimony from opposing parties in the form of depositions. Depositions that are grounded in the evidence and documents are popular and provide very useful information. The format is that the deponent (the person being deposed) provides sworn testimony based on questions developed by opposing council. Assuming that the attorney is well prepared and accomplished, he or she can use the deposition exercise to evaluate a number of issues:

- How good of a witness will this person be; how good will they come across in front of a jury; can I get this person angry, aggressive, defensive, or emotional?

- What is the opposing side's theory of the case; what arguments are they likely to make in court; how deep is the evidence trail behind their theory of the case?

- Is their witness making informed statements grounded in the evidence, or is this person likely to shoot from the hip?

- How does this person react when I propose or suggest my side's theory of the case? Does this person refute my theory with evidence; are they dismissive; are they emotional?

Thus, the deposition process not only provides the opportunity to obtain additional evidence, it provides a good opportunity, especially with key witnesses, including fraud examiners and forensic accounting expert witnesses, to evaluate each side's case and their witness quality. As depositions proceed, it is often common for each side to develop additional requests for the production of documents based on deposition testimony of various parties. For example, a former accountant may know of the existence of a box of records in a storage area that was previously overlooked in a prior request for the production of documents.

The fourth and last stage of discovery is an attempt by counsel to get the other side to agree to certain basic aspects and facts of the case through "requests for admission." This process helps determine what issues are points of contention as the trial approaches, and what points can be agreed upon by both sides. Thus, a request for admission attempts to narrow the scope of the trial to its essential points of contention.

Negotiated Settlements

Once discovery is completed and before trial, judges will often attempt to cajole both sides into settling the case based on the relative merits of their evidence and legal positions. In fact, some attorneys estimate that fewer than five percent of civil actions ever come to trial. There are three major forms of negotiated remedies: out-of-court settlements, arbitration, and mediation. Out-of-court settlements occur when both

sides come to a settlement position after examination of their own clients, the evidence, the qualities of their fact witnesses, the strength of their expert opinions, and other important aspects of the case. Assuming that the two sides are reasonably close, the attorneys will confer with their clients and negotiate with the opposing attorney. This process can take weeks or months and may even start during the deposition phase. Normally a negotiated settlement will not be achievable prior to the end of, or near the end of, discovery.

If a negotiated settlement between opposing attorneys in concert with their clients does not work, a second approach is mediation. In this environment, an independent, objective mediator will work with both sets of opposing counsel to help reach a settlement between the two (and their clients). The mediator does not decide who should win, but his or her responsibility is to assist both sides to more objectively assess the merits of their case and work toward a mutually agreeable resolution. Since the mediator has no authority on which to decide cases, any settlement is voluntary on the part of the opposing parties.

A third possibility is arbitration. Like a mediator, an arbitrator is an independent third party who has the authority to determine the outcome of the case. Thus, the arbitrator acts like the judge and jury, listening to the primary aspects of each side's case and deciding what he or she believes to be the most appropriate outcome based on the merits of the cases presented. Arbitration may be binding, meaning that the "verdict" of the arbitrator is final, or it can be nonbinding. Even a nonbinding "verdict" may bring the parties closer together and may result in an out-of-court settlement because of the ability of the arbitrator to independently and objectively evaluate the merits of each side's case.

Pre-trial Motions and the Civil Trial

Assuming that the discovery process is complete and any out-of-court attempts to settle the case fail, a slew of pretrial motions are likely to follow:

- Writ of Attachments to prevent defendants from disposing of assets
- Sequestration, in which the court takes possession of certain assets pending the outcome of the trial
- Motions for Injunctive Relief to prevent a defendant from transferring or moving assets pending the trial's outcome
- Motions to Dismiss
- Motions to Make (some aspects of the civil action) More Definite and Certain
- Motions in Limine to prohibit reference to prejudicial matter
- Motions to Strike inflammatory, prejudicial, or irrelevant material from trial
- Motions for Continuance to postpone a hearing or trial
- Motions for Summary Judgment that request the judge to decide the merits of the case without a trial based on material and testimony submitted

Normally, counsel is going to object to motions proposed by the other side of the civil action and a judge will need to decide on the motions in advance of the trial.

It will take months, if not years, for a civil action to actually be heard in a court of law. While many aspects of the civil trial mirror that of a criminal trial, a few important differences exist. First, in most cases the jurors number six persons, and if the opposing attorneys agree, a unanimous verdict is not required. Furthermore, a civil action only requires a preponderance of the evidence, meaning that the evidence stacks up slightly more heavily on one side than the other. This contrasts with the criminal threshold of "beyond a reasonable doubt." During civil trials the plaintiff goes first, followed by the defense. Then the plaintiff gets a chance to rebut the defense's position. Once a verdict is received, either side may appeal the liability issues and/or the damages portion of the verdict. Furthermore, a plaintiff or defendant who wins monetary damages in a lawsuit will normally have to take additional steps to collect the award. Such steps may include obtaining a financial judgment, garnishing wages, and levying assets. A postjudgment discovery process may be necessary to locate assets available to satisfy a judgment or identify assets that have been moved or transferred in an attempt to avoid satisfying the judgment.

REGULATORY SYSTEM

An understanding of the regulatory system and entities such as the SEC and Public Company Accounting Oversight Board (PCAOB), laws such as the Sarbanes–Oxley Act (SOX), fraud prevention, deterrence and detection, and the auditor's responsibility for detecting fraud are important aspects of the fraud and

forensic professional's education. Basic accounting and bookkeeping involve the recording, classifying, and summarizing of economic events in a logical manner for the purpose of providing financial information for decision making. While accounting, per se, is not regulated, various aspects of the accounting profession and the financial reporting process come under the purview of various regulatory bodies.

Auditors are concerned with determining whether information recorded in the accounting books and records properly reflects the underlying economics of the transactions. Thus, auditors need to know how to audit and how to evaluate recorded activity for compliance with generally accepted accounting principles (GAAP). Like auditors, the fraud examiner and forensic professional needs to have some understanding of transactions and how those transactions are reflected in the books and records. If the facts at issue are associated with allegations of financial statement fraud the investigator needs to have a thorough understanding of GAAP, auditing procedures, and the impact of any applicable regulations. As noted in prior chapters and throughout this text, fraud examiners and forensic specialists must be able to follow the money. But they must also be able to recognize and identify red flags and anomalous situations where the accounting numbers and amount reflected in underlying accounting records do not make sense or do not seem to add up. Recognition and identification of red flags inherently assumes that the investigator has some expectation of how the numbers should look. This requires some knowledge of basic accounting as well as knowledge of expected relationships between accounts. Of course, the fraud examiner and forensic accountant must also possess expertise in accumulating and interpreting evidence. The fraud and financial forensics professional must design procedures to identify anomalies, investigate those anomalies, form and test hypotheses, and evaluate the evidence generated.

Basic Accounting Principles — A Survivor's Guide to Accounting

In this section we present an overview of the accounting system that every fraud examiner or forensic accountant needs to understand for successfully navigating financial books and records. Figure 6-1 depicts the flow of accounting information.

First, activities occur between the company and its stakeholders (board of directors, executive team, management, employees, creditors, bankers, suppliers, employee recruits, customers, suppliers, communities, government agencies, labor unions, etc.). Some of these activities are considered financial transactions, and from those various forms of paperwork are created: receipts, invoices, contracts, and other source documents. The paperwork captures the essential terms of the transactions and provides a primary means of inputting data into the formal accounting system. Transactions are input (recorded) into the accounting system through journal entries and electronic interfaces with nonaccounting information systems and posted into the general ledger. The general ledger is analogous to a series of buckets where the accounting transactions are organized and stored. Periodically, the information in the general ledgers is reconciled back to the underlying source documents as well as information provided by other nonaccounting systems and external stakeholders, such as banks. For example, banks provide monthly statements and the activities reflected on them can be reconciled to the cash "bucket" in the general ledger. The reconciliation process

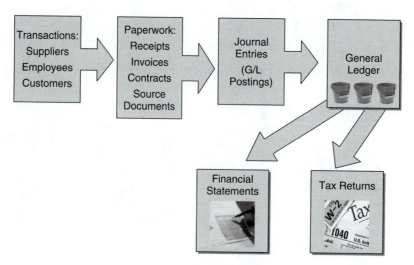

FIGURE 6-1 Accounting Flow through Books and Records

is conducted to ensure the integrity of the information in the general ledger. Once the entity's financial managers are satisfied with the integrity of the general ledger the financial statements, tax returns, and other summarized financial information can be created, distributed, and shared for the purposes of performance assessment and decision making.

One of the critical general ledger "buckets" for the fraud examiner and forensic accountant is the cash general ledger account. Most antifraud professionals follow the money. The company receives cash from its customers in the form of currency, checks directly from customers, and checks and electronic deposits from credit card companies. Although fewer in number, entities also receive cash from stockholder investments, loans from creditors, and from sales of old or used equipment. Entities disburse cash by writing checks and distributing them to employees, suppliers, creditors, and others. Cash disbursements can be made via the U.S. Postal Service, wire transfers, and through electronic funds transfer (EFT). All of these cash transactions are captured with various invoices and receipts and are input into the entity's accounting system and ultimately into the cash general ledger account ("bucket"). At the same time, the entity's bank is capturing and recording the transaction as well. Optimally, good accounting practice mandates that these two systems be checked for agreement each month through a formal reconciliation. Similar to cash, most transactions are tracked not only by the company, but by other parties to the transaction, such as customers. Thus, fraud examiners and forensic accountants review the company's accounting books and records as well as the corresponding information from third parties to look for discrepancies from which fraud investigations are often launched.

Not only do fraud examiners and forensic accountants need to monitor transactions from the perspective of the company and corresponding outsiders, they also need to ensure that the accounting information corresponds to the company's nonaccounting information, because many business activities are not captured in the accounting system. For example, a contract between a company and a customer to deliver goods and services next year is referred to as "backlog" and is not reflected in the accounting records. Figure 6-2 below depicts the information flow of nonaccounting information and data.

Notice how the information sources and flow is very similar to that of the accounting system flow. These management information systems (MIS) are used to provide the data required by managers to run their operations. For example, a petroleum plant would carefully monitor raw materials inventory levels, the transfers of raw materials into the manufacturing process, and various aspects of production to ensure quality, the amount of manufacturing output, and inventory levels of finished product. This data is critical for plant managers; they could not do their job without detailed and accurate information. In some systems, data from the nonaccounting systems is designed to interface directly with the accounting information systems. In others, data from the MIS systems is used as a manual input into the accounting system. In either case, antifraud professionals and forensic accountants will use data from nonaccounting sources as a means of looking for discrepancies with data reflected in the accounting records, a source of red flags.

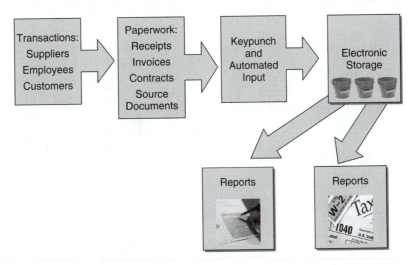

FIGURE 6-2 Nonfinancial Information Flow

Nonfinancial data can be generated from many sources. As an example, consider a bar owner who is suspected of underpaying taxes. A method commonly used is to look for data that is not normally captured in the accounting system. To illustrate, one crafty fraud examiner took all of the invoices supporting cost of goods sold, added up the quantities purchased, and multiplied the quantities by the selling prices on the bar's menu. The approach resulted in hundreds of thousands of dollars of underreported revenue. Because quantities presented on an accounting record (i.e., an invoice) are not captured by the accounting system, it becomes a nonfinancial information source upon which to identify discrepancies. To be successful, fraud examiners and forensic accountants need to continually seek out information sources from independent third parties and from internal sources that are not reflected in the accounting system as a means of evaluating data captured and reported in accounting reports, such as financial statements and tax returns. Even the reconciliation of tax returns to financial statements often reveals discrepancies between the two that serve as red flags that require additional investigative inquiry.

Other basic but critical aspects of the accounting process that fraud examiners and forensic accountants need to know include:

- Types of financial statements
- How cash transactions are categorized: operating, investing, and financing activities
- A second categorization approach: assets, liabilities, stockholders equity, revenues, and expenses
- Every transaction affects at least two general ledger "buckets" (accounts)
- Accrual accounting: the revenue recognition principle and the expense matching principle
- Accounting choices and exceptions: materiality and conservatism
- The importance of what's *not* on the financial statements

Consider the following example:

Value of Checking Account?

• Cash in from Owner	**$750**
• Loan from Bank	0
–Inflows	$750
• Purchase Office Equipment	$300
• Purchase Production Machine	250
• Rent	275
• Purchase Supplies	75
–Outflows	$900
• Inflows from Customers Sales	$300
• **Remaining cash in checking**	**$150**

The checking account for this start-up business has an initial deposit of $750 from the owner, pays for various items totaling $900, and collects $300 from sales to customers. These transactions leave a month-end checking account balance of $150. The ultimate question: Is the business owner better off at the end of the month than at the beginning? On the one hand, he started with $750 in cash but only has $150 now; that doesn't sound so good. On the other hand, the owner now has equipment and production machinery that have value and an ongoing business operation—also valuable. Another issue not addressed in the accounting system is the sales potential. Is a $300 sale per month a maximum or is that the result of a few days' sales at the end of the first month of business after the infrastructure was put in place? While this example has only a few transactions, what if the business had 100, 1,000, or 10,000 cash transactions? The point is that simply looking at checking account information is not enough. The accounting profession has responded to this anomaly by transferring the above information into a series of financial statements: balance sheet, income statement, and the cash flow statement. These documents meaningfully reorganize the above data for effective performance assessment and decision making.

Balance Sheet The balance sheet measures the financial condition of an entity at a point in time. It does this by measuring the resources that a business has, its assets, and compares the business'

resources (assets) to the sources from which those resources came. Resources are acquired with money provided from one of two sources: creditors (suppliers, banks, etc.) and the company's owners. Amounts owed to creditors are liabilities, and funds contributed by the owner are the stockholders' (or owner's) equity. Although a little confusing, the owner's contribution comes from two sources: investments of cash into the business and earnings (income) from prior periods that owners have left in the business (retained earnings) to fund additional investment and operational expansions. The balance sheet is set up in the fundamental accounting equation where assets must always equal liabilities plus owner's equity. From the balance sheet, the financial condition can be evaluated. Too many liabilities make the company vulnerable to bankruptcy. Liabilities, however, reflect the owner's ability to use "other people's money" to fund the business, suggesting that more liabilities are good. Simplistically, one challenge for business owners is to balance liabilities against owner's equity to maximize the use of other people's money without increasing the business' risk of bankruptcy. Of course, negative owner's equity suggests that liabilities exceed the value of the assets as recorded on the balance sheet and that is seldom, if ever, good news.

Income Statement The second major financial statement is the income statement. This summarizes information about a company's financial performance over a period of time (e.g., month, quarter, year). The income statement measures inflow from customers arising from sales of goods and services (revenue) versus outflow required to operate the business (expenses). The terms inflows and outflows are carefully chosen because sometimes sales to customers result in receivables, not cash. Similarly, outflows consider the fact that some items required to run the business are paid in advance (e.g., insurance is often paid in advance of a six-month or one-year policy), while others are paid after they are used (for example, employees are paid after they render services because it takes time to collect time cards, summarize the hours, input them into a payroll system, calculate taxes and other withholdings, and cut checks). We address the differences in timing between cash flows in more detail below (see accruals).

Statement of Cash Flows The third and final major financial statement is the statement of cash flows. This takes each "cash" transaction and categorizes it in one of three categories after considering how it affects the business. The three categories are cash flow from operating activities, investing activities, and financing activities. Operating cash flows are those cash transactions associated with day-to-day business activities: production and sales of goods and services and cash outflows to pay for operational expenses. Net operating cash flows are expected to be positive because a business should be taking in more cash from its customers than it is paying out to suppliers, employees, and for other expenses necessary to operate the business. The second category of cash flows includes payments for the acquisition of long-term assets and cash received from the sale of older or obsolete long-term assets. These are referred to as investing activities and, generally, the net of these types of cash transactions are expected to be negative because companies should be expending cash on long-term assets to secure a productive future.

The last category of cash flows includes receipts and payments associated with business financing choices and have four major types of activities:

1. Cash inflows from new loans.
2. Cash outflows from the repayment of loans (excluding interest which is categorized as operating).
3. Cash inflows from new stock investors.
4. Cash outflows to stock investors in the form of dividends.

Given these types of receipts and payments, financing cash flow could be negative or positive. In the early years in the life of a business, financing cash flows are more likely to be positive and, as a company matures, financing cash flows may turn toward the negative.

One of the challenges of accounting data is that it can be evaluated from multiple perspectives. As noted above, all cash transactions can be categorized as operating, investing, or financing. Since that categorization is associated only with the cash flow statement, those same transactions can also be categorized based on their effect on the other two statements: balance sheet and income statement. More interestingly, when evaluating the impact of a transaction on the balance sheet and income statement, each transaction has at least two effects. Some examples might help.

Example 1: A customer receives a service this month but will not pay for that service until next month, and the amount of the service is $100.

Assessment: Note that this transaction has no (zero) cash flow impact. It has two other effects:

- The business has a receivable amount of $100 from a customer (balance sheet)
- The business has made a sale of $100 (revenue on the income statement)

Example 2: A customer receives a service this month, paid cash at the time of the sale, and the amount of the service is $200.

Assessment: Note that this transaction has a $200 cash flow impact that is categorized as operating. It also has two other effects:

- The business has received cash of $200 (an asset on the balance sheet)
- The business has made a sale of $200 (revenue on the income statement)

Example 3: The company pays its one employee $25 on the twentieth of the month for the employee's work during the first half of the month.

Assessment: Note that this transaction has a $25 cash flow impact that is categorized as operating. It also has two other effects:

- The business has paid out cash of $25 (reducing the cash asset on the balance sheet)
- The business has a payroll expense of $25 (expense on the income statement)

Example 4: The company owes its one employee $30 as of the end of the month for the employee's work during the second half of the month.

Assessment: Note that this transaction has no (zero) cash flow impact. It has two other effects:

- As of month end, the business owes the employee $30 (liability on the balance sheet)
- The business has a payroll expense of $30 (expense on the income statement)

Example 5: During the month, the company pays its insurance company $120 for a twelve-month policy. Note that the company is trying to create financial statements for the current month only.

Assessment: Note that this transaction has a $120 cash flow impact that is categorized as operating. It also has three other effects:

- The business has paid out cash of $120 (reducing the cash asset on the balance sheet)
- The business has an insurance expense of $10 for the current month (expense on the income statement)
- The business has a resource that has future value (asset), totaling $110 for the remaining eleven months of the insurance policy (prepaid asset on the balance sheet)

Example 6: The company receives a check from a customer in the amount of $125 for services rendered during the previous month.

Assessment: Note that this transaction has a $125 cash flow impact that is categorized as operating. It has two other effects:

- The business' receivable amount has been reduced by $125 as a result of the customer payment (reducing a balance sheet asset)
- The business has additional cash of $125 (increasing the cash asset on the balance sheet)

Note that even though this transaction arose from a sale to a customer, sales were recorded in the prior month and there is no income statement impact in the current month.

Accrual Accounting Examples one, four, five, and six bring up the issue of accrual accounting. It recognizes the impact of a company's activities that affect its financial condition (balance sheet) or financial performance (income statements) that may not coincide with the timing of cash flows. Accruals are used to capture the financial impact of transactions for which the cash flows associated with the transaction are recorded in other periods (e.g., cash flows were in a prior month or year or the cash flow will occur in a future month or year). Whether or not a noncash transaction qualifies for treatment as an accrual transaction that must be recorded in the accounting books and records is determined by two matters: the revenue recognition principle and the matching principle.

The revenue recognition and matching principles are further refined through generally accepted accounting principles called Statements of Financial Accounting Standards, also known as SFASs, which are developed by the Financial Accounting Standards Board (FASB) as well as other authoritative guidance.[8] While the revenue recognition and matching principles provide conceptual guidelines, the guidance contained in the SFASs and other authoritative guidelines takes precedence. The revenue recognition principle requires that revenue be recorded in the period earned, and the expense matching principle requires that expenses be matched against the revenues they helped to generate. The intent of these two principles is that revenues and expenses are recorded in the proper period. More specifically, revenue is recognized when the following three criteria have been met:

1. Customers have received goods or services
2. All material uncertainty (risk) has been passed along to the customer
3. Collection of cash related to revenue is likely

Following revenue recognition, expenses are matched to revenue under three conditions:

1. Costs are incurred to generate revenue (e.g., wages)
2. Assets (capitalized costs) are no longer a resource with future value because they have been consumed to earn revenue (e.g., depreciation)
3. Assets (capitalized costs) are no longer a resource with future value due to obsolescence

Most people who are new to accounting believe that accounting is very rules driven and specific, and with regard to many aspects of accounting, they are correct. Such a belief, however, ignores the vast number of areas where management is required to exercise its judgment. The biggest problem area for accounting regulators is revenue recognition. Despite the above guidance, management has tremendous latitude related to the accounting principles they choose, the period that is most appropriate to record a specific type of transaction, the estimated useful life of an asset, and the estimated collectability of receivables from customers, to name a few.

Two additional conceptual principles provide accounting discretion. First, if a transaction or series of transactions are deemed "immaterial" the accountants can handle the transaction in any manner they wish. The theory is that if the amount is immaterial, how it is accounted for has little or no significant impact on decision making. While no specific number is agreed upon, some general rules of thumb are one percent of assets, one percent of revenues (sales), or five percent of pretax net income. For billion-dollar companies, transactions deemed immaterial can have very large dollar amounts associated with those thresholds.

A third and final area of discretion is related to a principle called conservatism. It suggests that if two outcomes are equally likely, the one that has the more negative effect is the better choice in situations where negative impact includes understating assets and revenues and overstating liabilities and expenses. Recently, standard setters and regulators seem more interested in determining the best estimate of financial condition and performance versus presenting the most pessimistic picture, but conservatism remains an influential concept.

The AICPA and Statement on Auditing Standards No. 99

While the FASB develops generally accepted accounting principles, the purview of auditing of nonpublic companies falls under the guidelines of the American Institute of Certified Public Accountants (AICPA).

Subsequent to the passage of the Sarbanes–Oxley Act of 2002 the auditing of public companies became the responsibility of the newly created Public Company Accounting Oversight Board (PCAOB). The AICPA has the authority to set standards and make rules in five major areas:

- Auditing standards (for nonpublic companies)
- Compilation and review standards
- Other attestation standards
- Consulting standards
- Code of professional conduct

An audit is performed to ensure that the financial statements are fairly presented. Inversely, an audit is conducted to ensure that the financial statements are free from material misstatement. Note that this does not imply that financial statements are correct or accurate. More specifically related to fraud, AICPA Statement on Auditing Standards (SAS) No. 99 directs that an audit should be planned and performed to obtain "reasonable assurance" about whether the financial statements are free of material misstatements, whether caused by error or fraud.

Furthermore, auditing standards require that an audit be completed with due professional care, which, in turn, requires that the auditor exercise professional skepticism. The causes of misstatements are errors and fraud. Fraud can arise from one of two sources: misappropriation of assets that rises to the level of materiality or (material) financial reporting fraud. (The ACFE lists three sources of what it defines as *occupational fraud*: asset misappropriations, fraudulent financial statements, and corruption. The latter category is distinguished from the first two in that it requires a coconspirator not employed by the entity.) Examples of financial reporting fraud include the falsification of underlying accounting books and records and omission of certain transactions.

Professional skepticism entails three overlapping concepts:

- An attitude that includes a questioning mind and a critical assessment of audit evidence
- Conducting of the engagement that recognizes the possibility of material misstatement due to fraud
- Dissatisfaction with less-than-persuasive evidence

Stated more succinctly, an auditor should have a questioning mind, recognize that financial statements may be materially misstated, and require persuasive evidence (evidence-based decision making).

FROM THE FRAUDSTER'S PERSPECTIVE

Adapted from the whitecollarfraud.com blog by Sam E. Antar
Sunday, March 4, 2007

White-Collar Crime: How Criminals Exploit Your Humanity

As a criminal, I considered your humanity as a weakness to be exploited in the commission of my crimes. I have often said that white-collar crime is a crime of deceit, and white-collar criminals are artful liars.

A great president, Ronald Reagan, once said, "Trust, but verify," when dealing with the Soviet Union during the cold war. However, as a criminal I took advantage of your initial inclination to trust me. I did everything in my power, to charm you by pointing out the good deeds I had done, in an effort to corrode your objectivity, professional skepticism, and cynicism.

During my many unpaid speaking engagements, people often ask if I am still a criminal today. My answer is that you do not know if I am a criminal today since I live with temptation and sin every day. Just because I travel the country and give unpaid presentations on white-collar crime and pay all travel expenses out of pocket, how do you know if I am building a false wall of integrity around me as I did during my criminal years at Crazy Eddie? You never know anyone's intentions.

SAS No. 99 specifically recognizes the importance of the fraud triangle: incentives (pressures), opportunity, and rationalization. SAS No. 99 offers an eight-step approach when considering the risk of materially misstated financial statements due to fraud. Step 1 is that auditors at the outset of an audit engagement should undertake a staff discussion concerning the risks of fraud. The staff discussion should consist of brainstorming as well as considering how and where the financial statements might be susceptible to fraud and emphasize the need for professional skepticism.

Step 2 involves gathering information necessary to identify fraud risks, including inquiries of management, the audit committee, internal auditors, and others; the results of analytical procedures; identified

fraud risk factors; and other information that may be suggestive of fraud. During step 3, auditors attempt to identify risks that may result in fraud, giving consideration to the types of risks, the significance or magnitude of the risk, the likelihood of the risk, and the pervasiveness of the risk.

In step 4, the auditor assesses fraud risks after consideration of programs and controls to prevent fraudulent financial reporting. The auditors must rely on their understanding of the systems of internal control and evaluate whether they actually address the fraud risks identified. Since internal controls are designed to reduce the opportunity for fraud, this reassessment after recognition of internal control policies and processes is an important step in the process.

Step 5 requires the auditor to develop specific responses to fraud risks. As the risk of materially misstated financial statements increases, the auditor may respond in several ways. For example, the auditor can assign more experienced staff to the engagement, give more attention to accounting policies and choices, and apply less predictable audit procedures. In short, the auditor needs to increase the amount and quality of audit evidence by altering the nature, timing, and extent of audit procedures. A critical aspect of step 5 is assessing the possibility of management override. Simplistically, despite a well-designed and implemented system of internal controls, certain persons in the management structure and executive suite have tremendous influence and control. At some point, the influence and control is so powerful that some managers may be able to override the system of internal controls. Essentially, the system of internal controls operates fine but for the actions of a few select, powerful individuals. The risk of management override should not be underestimated even in the most successful and well-run entities. To address the issue of management override, auditors should examine adjusting journal entries, support for adjusting journal entries, accounting estimates, underlying rationale and support for accounting estimates, and unusual (one time), significant transactions and the underlying rationale and support for the accounting treatment of these transactions.

Step 6 considers the audit evidence and requires auditors to continually assess fraud risk throughout the audit. The auditor needs to evaluate analytical procedures performed as substantive tests, evaluate risk of fraud near completion of fieldwork, and respond to identified material misstatements.

In step 7, the auditor must communicate his findings as follows:

- All fraud to an appropriate level of management
- All management fraud to the audit committee
- All material fraud to management and the audit committee

If reportable conditions related to the internal control environment have been identified, the auditor must communicate those to the audit committee.

Step 8 ensures that the auditor has documented each of these steps in the consideration of fraud:

- Staff discussion
- Information used to identify risk of fraud
- Fraud risks identified
- Assessed risks after considering programs and controls
- Results of assessment of fraud risk
- Evaluation of audit evidence
- Communications requirements

The Sarbanes–Oxley Act of 2002

The Sarbanes–Oxley Act of 2002 was signed into law on July 30, 2002 to address corporate governance and accountability as well as public accounting responsibilities in improving the quality, reliability, integrity, and transparency of financial reports. The Act provides sweeping measures aimed at

- Establishing higher standards for corporate governance and accountability
- Creating an independent regulatory framework for the accounting profession
- Enhancing the quality and transparency of financial reports
- Developing severe civil and criminal penalties for corporate wrongdoers
- Establishing new protections for corporate whistleblowers

The Act has authorized the SEC to issue implementation rules on many of its provisions intended to improve corporate governance, financial reporting, and audit functions. The SEC has issued the following implementation rules pertaining to the Act:

- New standards of professional conduct for attorneys
- Standards and procedures related to listed company audit committees
- Strengthening of the commission's requirements regarding auditor independence
- Disclosure in management's discussion and analysis about off-balance sheet arrangements and aggregate contractual obligations
- Disclosures regarding a Code of Ethics for Senior Financial Officers and Audit Committee Financial Experts
- Retention of records relevant to audits and reviews
- Insider trades during pension fund blackout periods
- Conditions for use of non-GAAP financial measures
- Certifications of disclosure in companies' quarterly and annual reports

These implementation rules are expected to create an environment that promotes strong marketplace integrity, new criminal and civil penalties for violations of securities laws, improve the probability of detection and deterrence of corporate misstatements, and restore public trust in the quality and transparency of financial information. Table 6-1 summarizes important provisions of the Act aimed at improving corporate governance, financial reports, and audit functions.

Certification Obligations for CEOs and CFOs   One of the most significant changes affected by the Sarbanes–Oxley Act is the requirement that the Chief Executive Officer and the Chief Financial Officer of public companies personally certify annual and quarterly SEC filings. These certifications essentially require CEOs and CFOs to take responsibility for their companies' financial statements, and prevent them from delegating this responsibility to their subordinates and then claiming ignorance when fraud is uncovered in the financial statements. There are two types of officer certifications mandated by Sarbanes–Oxley: criminal certifications, which are set forth in Section 906 of the act and codified at 18 USC § 1350; and civil certifications, which are set forth in Section 302.

Criminal Certifications (§ 906). Periodic filings with the SEC must be accompanied by a statement, signed by the CEO and CFO, which certifies that the report fully complies with the SEC's periodic reporting requirements and that the information in the report fairly presents, in all material respects, the financial condition and results of operation of the company. These certifications are known as *criminal certifications* because the act imposes criminal penalties on officers who violate the certification requirements. Corporate officers who *knowingly* violate the certification requirements are subject to fines of up to $1,000,000 and up to ten years imprisonment, or both. Corporate officers who *willfully* violate the certification requirements are subject to fines of up to $5,000,000 and up to twenty years imprisonment, or both.

Civil Certifications (§ 302). Section 302 of the Act requires the CEO and CFO to personally certify the following in their reports:

1. They have personally reviewed the report.
2. Based on their knowledge, the report does not contain any material misstatement that would render the financials misleading.
3. Based on their knowledge, the financial information in the report fairly presents in all material respects the financial condition, results of operations, and cash flow of the company.
4. They are responsible for designing, maintaining, and evaluating the company's internal controls; they have evaluated the controls within ninety days prior to the report; and they have presented their conclusions about the effectiveness of those controls in the report.
5. They have disclosed to the auditors and the audit committee any material weaknesses in the controls and any fraud, whether material or not, that involves management or other employees who have a significant role in the company's internal controls.
6. They have indicated in their report whether there have been significant changes in the company's internal controls since the filing of the last report.

TABLE 6-1 Corporate governance and accounting provisions of the Sarbanes–Oxley Act of 2002

Sec.	Provisions
101	**Establishment of Public Company Accounting Oversight Board (PCAOB)**
	1. The PCAOB will have five financially literate members.
	2. Members are appointed by the SEC for five-year terms, will serve on a full-time basis, and may be removed by the SEC "for good cause."
	3. Two of the members must be or have been CPAs, and the remaining three must not be or have been CPAs.
	4. The chair may be held by one of the CPA members, who must not have been engaged as a practicing CPA for five years.
103	**The PCAOB shall:**
	1. Register public accounting firms (foreign and domestic) that prepare audit reports for issuers.
	2. Establish, or adopt, by rule, auditing, quality control, ethics, independence, and other standards relating to the preparation of audit reports for issuers.
	3. Conduct inspections of registered public accounting firms.
	4. Conduct investigations and disciplinary proceedings and impose appropriate sanctions.
	5. Enforce compliance with the Act, the rules of the Board, and other applicable rules and regulations.
	6. Establish budget and manage the operations of the Board and its staff.
107	**Commission Oversight of the Board:**
	1. The SEC shall have oversight and enforcement authority over the PCAOB.
	2. The SEC can, by rule or order, give the PCAOB additional responsibilities.
	3. The PCAOB is required to file proposed rules and proposed rule changes with the SEC.
	4. The SEC may approve, reject, or amend such rules.
	5. The PCAOB must notify the SEC of pending investigations and coordinate its investigation with the SEC Division of Enforcement.
	6. The PCAOB must notify the SEC when it imposes any final sanction on any accounting firm or associated person.
	7. The PCAOB findings and sanctions are subject to review by the SEC which may enhance, modify, cancel, reduce, or require remission of such sanction.
108	**Accounting Standards:**
	1. The SEC may recognize as "generally accepted" any accounting principles that are established by a standard-setting body that meets the Act's criteria.
	2. The SEC shall conduct a study on the adoption of a principles-based accounting system.
201	**Auditor Independence: Services outside the Scope of Practice of Auditors:**
	1. Registered public accounting firms are prohibited from providing any nonaudit services to an issuer contemporaneously with the audit including but not limited to (1) bookkeeping or other services related to the accounting record or financial statement of the audit client, (2) financial information systems design and implementation, (3) appraisal or valuation services, (4) actuarial services, (5) internal audit outsourcing services, (6) management functions or human resources, (7) broker or dealer, investment advisor, or investment banking, (8) legal services and expert services unrelated to the audit, and (9) any other services that the PCAOB determines, by regulation, to be impermissible.
	2. The PCAOB may, on a case-by-case basis, exempt from these prohibitions any person, issuer, public accounting firm, or transaction, subject to review by the SEC.
	3. Nonaudit services not explicitly prohibited by the Act, such as tax services, can be performed upon preapproval by the audit committee and full disclosure to investors.
203	**Audit Partner Rotation:**
	The lead audit or coordinating partner and reviewing partner of the registered accounting firm must rotate off of the audit every five years.
204	**Auditor Reports to Audit Committees:**
	The registered accounting firm must report to the Audit Committee
	1. All critical accounting policies and practices to be used
	2. All alternative treatments of financial information within generally accepted accounting principles, ramifications of the use of such alternative disclosures and treatments, and the preferred treatment
	3. Other material written communication between the auditor and management

(Continued)

TABLE 6-1 (*Continued*)

206 **Conflicts of Interest:**

The registered accounting firm is prohibited from performing an audit for an issuer whose CEO, CFO, controller, chief accounting officer, or person in an equivalent capacity employed by the accounting firm during the one-year period preceding the audit.

207 **Study of Mandatory Rotation of Registered Public Accounting Firms:**

The Comptroller General of the United States will conduct a study on the potential effects of requiring the mandatory rotation of public accounting firms.

301 **Public Company Audit Committees:**

1. Each member of the audit committee shall be an independent member of the board of directors.
2. To be considered independent, the member of the audit committee should not receive any compensations other than for service on the board, not accept any consulting, advisory, or other compensatory fee from the company, and not be an affiliated person of the issuer or any subsidiary thereof.
3. The SEC may make exemptions for certain individuals on a case-by-case basis.
4. The audit committee shall be directly responsible for the appointment, compensation, and oversight of the work of any registered public accounting firm associated by the issuer.
5. The audit committee shall establish procedures for the receipt, retention, and treatment of complaints received by the issuer regarding accounting, internal accounting controls, or auditing matters, and the confidential, anonymous submission by employees of the issuer or concerns regarding questionable accounting or auditing matters.
6. The audit committee shall have the authority to engage independent counsel and other advisers necessary to carry out its duties.
7. The audit committee shall be properly funded.

302 **Corporate Responsibility for Financial Reports:**

1. The signing officers (e.g., CEO, CFO) shall certify in each annual or quarterly report filed with the SEC that (1) the report does not contain any untrue statement of a material fact or omitted material facts that cause the report to be misleading and that (2) financial statements and disclosures fairly present, in all material respects, the financial condition and results of operations of the issuer.
2. The signing officers are responsible for establishing and maintaining adequate and effective controls to ensure reliability of financial statements and disclosures.
3. The signing officers are responsible for proper design, periodic assessment of the effectiveness and disclosure of material deficiencies in internal controls to external auditors and the audit committee.

303 **Improper Influence on Conduct of Audits:**

It shall be unlawful for any officer or director of an issuer to take any action to fraudulently influence, coerce, manipulate, or mislead auditors in the performance of financial audit of the financial statements.

304 **Forfeiture of Certain Bonuses and Profits:**

1. CEOs and CFOs who revise company financial statements for the material noncompliance with any financial reporting requirements must pay back any bonuses or stock options awarded because of the misstatements.
2. CEOs and CFOs shall reimburse the issuer for any bonus or other incentive-based or equity-based compensation received or any profits realized from the sale of securities during that period for financial restatements due to material noncompliance with financial reporting and disclosure requirements.

306 **Insider Trades During Pension Fund Blackout Periods:**

1. It shall be unlawful for any directors or executive officers directly or indirectly to purchase, sell, or otherwise acquire or transfer any equity security of the issuer during any blackout periods.
2. Any profits resulting from sales in violation of this section shall inure to and be recoverable by the issuer.

401 **Disclosures in Periodic Reports:**

1. Each financial report that is required to be prepared in accordance with GAAP shall reflect all material correcting adjustments that have been identified by the auditors.
2. Each financial report (annual and quarterly) shall disclose all material off-balance-sheet transactions and other relationships with unconsolidated entities that may have a material current or future effect on the financial conditions of the issuer.

(*Continued*)

TABLE 6-1 *(Continued)*

2. The SEC shall issue final rules providing that pro forma financial information filed with the Commission (1) does not contain an untrue statement of a material fact or omitted material information and (2) reconciles with the financial condition and results of operations.
3. The SEC shall study the extent of off-balance sheet transactions, including assets, liabilities, leases, losses, and the use of special purpose entities, and whether the use of GAAP reflects the economics of such off-balance sheet transactions.

402   **Extended Conflict of Interest Provisions:**

It is unlawful for the issuer to extend credit to any directors or executive officers.

404   **Management Assessments of Internal Controls:**

1. Each annual report filed with the SEC shall contain an internal control report which shall (1) state the responsibility of management for establishing and maintaining an adequate internal control structure and procedures for financial reporting and (2) contain an assessment of the effectiveness of the internal control structure and procedures as of the end of the issuer's fiscal year.
2. Auditors shall attest to, and report on, the assessment of the adequacy and effectiveness of the issuer internal control structure and procedures as part of audit of financial reports in accordance with standards for attestation engagements.

406   **Code of Ethics for Senior Financial Officers:**

The SEC shall issue rules to require each issuer to disclose whether it has adopted a code of ethics for its senior financial officers and the nature and content of such code.

407   **Disclosure of Audit Committee Financial Expert:**

The SEC shall issue rules to require each issuer to disclose whether at least one member of its audit committee is a "financial" expert as defined by the Commission.

409   **Real Time Issuer Disclosures:**

Each issuer shall disclose information on material changes in the financial condition or operations of the issuer on a rapid and current basis.

501   **Treatment of Securities Analysts:**

Registered securities associations and national securities exchanges shall adopt rules designed to address conflicts of interest for research analysts who recommend equities in research reports.

601   **SEC Resource and Authority:**

SEC appropriations for 2003 are increased to $776,000,000, from which $98 million shall be used to hire an additional 200 employees to provide enhanced oversight of audit services.

602   **Practice before the Commission:**

1. The SEC may censure any person, or temporarily bar or deny any person the right to appear or practice before the SEC if the person does not possess the requisite qualifications to represent others, has willfully violated Federal Securities laws, or lacks character or integrity.
2. The SEC shall conduct a study of "Securities Professionals" (e.g., accountants, investment bankers, brokers, dealers, attorneys, investment advisors) who have been found to have aided and abetted a violation of Federal Securities laws.
3. The SEC shall establish rules setting minimum standards for professional conduct for attorneys practicing before the commission.

701   **GAO Study and Report Regarding Consolidation of Public Accounting Firms:**

The GAO shall conduct a study regarding consolidation of public accounting firms since 1989 and determine the consequences of the consolidation, including the present and future impact and solutions to any problems that may result from the consolidation.

802   **Criminal Penalties for Altering Documents:**

1. It is a felony to knowingly alter, destroy, falsify, cover up, conceal, or create documents to impede, obstruct, or influence any existing or contemplated federal investigation.
2. Registered public accounting firms are required to maintain all audit or review work-papers for five years.

(Continued)

TABLE 6-1   (*Continued*)

903 **904** **906**	**White Collar Crime Penalty Enhancements:** **1.** The maximum penalty for mail and wire fraud is ten years. **2.** The SEC may prohibit anyone convicted of securities fraud from being a director or officer of any public company. **3.** Financial reports filed with the SEC (annual, quarterly) must be certified by the CEO and CFO of the issuer. The certification must state that the financial statements and disclosures fully comply with provisions of Securities Acts and that they fairly present, in all material respects, financial results and conditions of the issuer. Maximum penalties for willful and knowing violations of these provisions of the Act are a fine of not more than $500,000 and/or imprisonment of up to five years.
1001	**Corporate Tax Returns:** The federal income tax return of public corporations should be signed by the CEO of the issuer.
1105	**Authority of the SEC:** The Commission may prohibit a person from serving as a director or officer of a publicly traded company if the person has committed securities fraud.

Note that in items two and three on p. 159 the CEO and CFO are not required to certify that the financials are accurate or that there is no misstatement. They are simply required to certify that *to their knowledge* the financials are materially representative and not misleading. This does not mean, however, that senior financial officers can simply plead ignorance about their companies' SEC filings in order to avoid liability. The term *fairly presents* in item three is a broader standard than what is required by GAAP. In certifying that their SEC filings meet this standard, the CEO and CFO essentially must certify that the company: (1) has selected appropriate accounting policies to ensure the material accuracy of the reports; (2) has properly applied those accounting standards; and (3) has disclosed financial information that reflects the underlying transactions and events of the company. Furthermore, the other new certification rules (see 1, and 4–6 above) mandate that CEOs and CFOs take an active role in their companies' public reporting, and in the design and maintenance of internal controls.

It is significant that in item four, the CEO and CFO not only have to certify that they are responsible for their companies' internal controls, but also that they have evaluated the controls *within ninety days prior to their quarterly or annual report*. Essentially, this certification requirement mandates that companies actively and continually reevaluate their control structures to prevent fraud.

Item five requires the CEO and CFO to certify that they have disclosed to their auditors and their audit committee any material weaknesses in the company's internal controls, and also any fraud, *whether material or not*, that involves management or other key employees. Obviously, this is a very broad reporting requirement that goes beyond the "material" standard contemplated in SAS 82. The CEO and CFO now must report to their auditors and audit committee *any fraud* committed by management. This places a greater burden on the CEO and CFO to take part in antifraud efforts and to be aware of fraudulent activity within their companies in order to meet this certification requirement.

Item six is significant because periodic SEC filings must include statements detailing significant changes to the internal controls of publicly traded companies.

Management Assessment of Internal Controls   In conjunction with the § 302 certification requirements on the responsibility of the CEO and CFO for internal controls, § 404 of SOX requires all annual reports to contain an internal control report that: (1) states management's responsibility for establishing and maintaining an adequate internal control structure and procedures for financial reporting; and (2) contains an assessment of the effectiveness of the internal control structure and procedures of the company for financial reporting. The filing company's independent auditor will also be required to issue an attestation report on management's assessment of the company's internal control over financial reporting. This attestation report must be filed with the SEC as part of the company's annual report.

New Standards for Audit Committee Independence   Section 301 of the Act requires that the audit committee for each publicly traded company shall be directly responsible for appointing, compensating, and overseeing the work of the company's outside auditors. The Act also mandates that the auditors must report directly to the audit committee—not management—and makes it the responsibility of the audit

committee to resolve disputes between management and the auditors. Section 301 also requires that the audit committee must have the authority and funding to hire independent counsel and any other advisors it deems necessary to carry out its duties.

Composition of the Audit Committee   The Sarbanes–Oxley Act mandates that each member of a company's audit committee must be a member of its board of directors and must otherwise be independent. The term *independent* means that the audit committee member can receive compensation from the company only for his or her service on the board of directors, the audit committee, or another committee of the board of directors. The company may not pay them for any other consulting or advisory work.

Financial Expert   Section 407 of the Act requires every public company to disclose in its periodic reports to the SEC whether or not the audit committee has at least one member who is a financial expert, and if not to explain the reasons why. The Act defines a *financial expert* as a person who, through education and experience as a public accountant or auditor, or a CFO, comptroller, chief financial officer or a similar position (1) has an understanding of generally accepted accounting principles and financial statements; (2) has experience in preparing or auditing financial statements of comparable companies and the application of such principles in accounting for estimates, accruals, and reserves; (3) has experience with internal controls; and (4) has an understanding of audit committee functions.

Establishing a Whistle-Blowing Structure   The Act makes it the responsibility of the audit committee to establish procedures (e.g., a hotline) for receiving and dealing with complaints and anonymous employee tips regarding irregularities in the company's accounting methods, internal controls, or auditing matters.

New Standards for Auditor Independence   Perhaps the greatest concern arising out of the public accounting scandals of 2001 and 2002 was the fear that public accounting firms that received multimillion-dollar consulting fees from their public company clients could not maintain an appropriate level of objectivity and professional skepticism in conducting audits for those clients. In order to address this concern, Congress, in § 201 of the Sarbanes–Oxley Act, established a list of activities that public accounting firms are now prohibited from performing on behalf of their audit clients. The prohibited services are:

- Bookkeeping services
- Financial information systems design and implementation
- Appraisal or valuation services, fairness opinions, or contribution-in-kind reports
- Actuarial services
- Internal audit outsource services
- Management functions or human resources
- Broker or dealer, investment adviser, or investment banking services
- Legal services and expert services unrelated to the audit
- Any other service that the Public Company Accounting Oversight Board proscribes

There are certain other nonaudit services—most notably tax services—that are not expressly prohibited by Sarbanes–Oxley. In order for a public accounting firm to perform these services on behalf of an audit client, however, that service must be approved in advance by the client's audit committee. Approval of the nonaudit services must be disclosed in the client's periodic SEC reports.

Mandatory Audit Partner Rotation   Section 203 of the act requires public accounting firms to rotate the lead audit partner or the partner responsible for reviewing the audit every five years.

Conflict of Interest Provisions   Another provision of Sarbanes–Oxley aimed at improving auditor independence is § 206, which seeks to limit conflicts or potential conflicts that arise when auditors cross over to work for their former clients. The Act makes it unlawful for a public accounting firm to audit a company if—within the prior year—the client's CEO, CFO, controller, or chief accounting officer worked for the accounting firm and participated in the company's audit.

Auditor Reports to Audit Committees Section 301 requires that auditors report directly to the audit committee, and § 204 makes certain requirements as to the contents of those reports. In order to help ensure that the audit committee is aware of questionable accounting policies or treatments that were used in the preparation of the company's financial statements, § 204 states that auditors must make a timely report of the following to the audit committee:

- All critical accounting policies and practices used
- Alternative GAAP methods that were discussed with management, the ramifications of the use of those alternative treatments, and the treatment preferred by the auditors
- Any other material written communications between the auditors and management

Auditors' Attestation to Internal Controls As was stated previously, § 404 of the Act requires every annual report to contain an internal control report which states that the company's management is responsible for internal controls and also assesses the effectiveness of the internal control structures. Section 404 requires the company's external auditors to attest to and issue a report on management's assessment of internal controls.

Improper Influence on Audits The Act also makes it unlawful for any officer or director of a public company to take any action to fraudulently influence, coerce, manipulate, or mislead an auditor in the performance of an audit of the company's financial statements. This is yet another attempt by Congress to ensure the independence and objectivity of audits in order to prevent accounting fraud and strengthen investor confidence in the reliability of public company financial statements.

Enhanced Financial Disclosure Requirements

Off-Balance Sheet Transactions As directed by § 401 of the Act, the rules require disclosure of

> *all material off-balance sheet transactions, arrangements, obligations (including contingent obligations), and other relationships the company may have with unconsolidated entities or persons that may have a material current or future effect on the company's financial condition, changes in financial condition, liquidity, capital expenditures, capital resources, or significant components of revenues or expenses.*

These disclosures are required in all annual and quarterly SEC reports.

Pro Forma Financial Information Section 401 also directs the SEC to issue rules on pro forma financial statements. These rules require that pro forma financials must not contain any untrue statements or omissions that would make them misleading, and that they are reconciled to GAAP. These rules apply to all pro forma financial statements that are filed with the SEC or that are included in any public disclosure or press release.

Prohibitions on Personal Loans to Executives Section 402 makes it illegal for public companies to make personal loans or otherwise extend credit, either directly or indirectly, to or for any director or executive officer. There is an exception that applies to consumer lenders if the loans are consumer loans of the type the company normally makes to the public, and on the same terms.

Restrictions on Insider Trading Section 403 establishes disclosure requirements for stock transactions by directors and officers of public companies, or by persons who own more than ten percent of a publicly traded company's stock. Reports of changes in beneficial ownership by these persons must be filed with the SEC by the end of the second business day following the transaction.

Under § 306, directors and officers are also prohibited from trading in the company's securities during any pension fund blackout periods. This restriction only applies to securities that were acquired as a result of their employment or service to the company. A blackout period is defined as any period of more than three consecutive business days in which at least fifty percent of the participants in the company's retirement plan are restricted from trading in the company's securities. If a director or officer violates this provision, he or she can be forced to disgorge to the company all profits received from the sale of securities during the blackout period.

Codes of Ethics for Senior Financial Officers Pursuant to § 406 of the Act, the SEC establishes rules that require public companies to disclose whether they have adopted a code of ethics for their senior financial officers and if not, to explain the reasons why. The new rules also require immediate public

disclosure any time there is a change of the code of ethics or a waiver of the code of ethics for a senior financial officer.

Enhanced Review of Periodic Filings Section 408 of the Act requires the SEC to make regular and systematic reviews of disclosures made by public companies in their periodic reports to the SEC. Reviews of a company's disclosures, including its financial statements, must be made at least once every three years. Prior to this enactment, reviews were typically minimal and tended to coincide with registered offerings.

Real Time Disclosures Under § 409, public companies must publicly disclose information concerning material changes in their financial condition or operations. These disclosures must be "in plain English" and must be made "on a rapid and current basis."

Protections for Corporate Whistle-Blowers under Sarbanes–Oxley

The Sarbanes–Oxley Act establishes broad new protections for corporate whistleblowers. There are two sections of the Act that address whistleblower protections: Section 806 deals with civil protections and Section 1107 establishes criminal liability for those who retaliate against whistleblowers.

Civil Liability Whistle-Blower Protection Section 806 of the Act, which is codified at 18 USC § 1514A, creates civil liability for companies that retaliate against whistle-blowers. It should be noted that this provision does not provide universal whistle-blower protection; it only protects employees of publicly traded companies. Section 806 makes it unlawful to fire, demote, suspend, threaten, harass, or in any other manner discriminate against an employee for providing information or aiding in an investigation of securities fraud. In order to trigger § 806 protections, the employee must report the suspected misconduct to a federal regulatory or law enforcement agency, a member of Congress or a committee of Congress, or a supervisor. Employees are also protected against retaliation for filing, testifying in, participating in or otherwise assisting in a proceeding filed or about to be filed relating to an alleged violation of securities laws or SEC rules.

The whistle-blower protections apply even if the company is ultimately found not to have committed securities fraud. As long as employees reasonably believe they are reporting conduct that constitutes a violation of various federal securities laws, then they are protected. The protections not only cover retaliatory acts by the company, but also by any officer, employee, contractor, subcontractor, or agent of the company.

If a public company is found to have violated § 806, the Act provides for an award of compensatory damages sufficient to "make the employee whole." Penalties include reinstatement; back pay with interest; and compensation for special damages including litigation costs, expert witness fees, and attorneys' fees.

Criminal Sanction Whistle-Blower Protection Section 1107 of Sarbanes–Oxley—codified at 18 USC § 1513—makes it a crime to knowingly, with the intent to retaliate, take any harmful action against a person for providing truthful information relating to the commission or possible commission of any federal offense. This protection is only triggered when information is provided to a law enforcement officer; it does not apply to reports made to supervisors or to members of Congress, as is the case under § 806.

In general, the coverage of § 1107 is much broader than the civil liability whistle-blower protections of § 806. While the § 806 protections apply only to employees of publicly traded companies, § 1107's criminal whistle-blower protections cover all individuals (and organizations) regardless of where they work. Also, § 806 only applies to violations of securities laws or SEC rules and regulations. Section 1107, on the other hand, protects individuals who provide truthful information about the commission or possible commission of *any federal offense*. Violations of § 1107 can be punished by fines of up to $250,000 and up to ten years in prison for individuals. Corporations that violate the Act can be fined up to $500,000.

Enhanced Penalties for White-Collar Crime

As part of Congress' general effort to deter corporate accounting fraud and other forms of white-collar crime, the Sarbanes–Oxley Act also enhances the criminal penalties for a number of white-collar offenses.

Attempt and Conspiracy The Act amends the mail fraud provisions of the United States Code (Chapter 63) to make attempt and conspiracy to commit offenses subject to the same penalties as the offense itself. This applies to mail fraud, wire fraud, securities fraud, bank fraud, and health care fraud.

Mail Fraud and Wire Fraud Sarbanes–Oxley amends the mail fraud and wire fraud statutes (18 USC § § 1341, 1343), increasing the maximum jail term from five to 20 years.

Securities Fraud Section 807 of the Act makes securities fraud a crime under 18 USC § 1348, providing for fines up to $250,000 and up to 25 years in prison.

Document Destruction Section 802 of the Act makes destroying evidence to obstruct an investigation or any other matter within the jurisdiction of any U.S. department illegal and punishable by a fine of up to $250,000 and up to 20 years in prison. This section also specifically requires that accountants who perform audits on publicly traded companies to maintain all audit or review work papers for a period of five years. Violations of this rule may be punished by fines up to $250,000 and up to ten years in jail for individuals, or fines up to $500,000 for corporations. (Although § 802 only requires work papers to be maintained for five years, keep in mind that under § 103 of the Act the Public Company Accounting Oversight Board is directed to set standards that require public accounting firms to maintain audit work papers for *seven* years. Accounting firms should design their document retention policies accordingly.)

Section 1102 of the Act makes it a criminal offense to corruptly alter, destroy, mutilate, or conceal a record or document with the intent to impair its integrity or use in an official proceeding or to otherwise obstruct, influence, or impede any official proceeding or attempt to do so. Violations of this section are punishable by fines up to $250,000 and imprisonment for up to twenty years.

Freezing of Assets During an investigation of possible securities violations by a publicly traded company or any of its officers, directors, partners, agents, controlling persons, or employees, the SEC can petition a federal court to issue a forty-five-day freeze on "extraordinary payments" to any of the foregoing persons. If granted, the payments will be placed in an interest-bearing escrow account when the investigation commences. This provision was enacted to prevent corporate assets from being improperly distributed while an investigation is underway.

Bankruptcy Loopholes Section 803 amends the bankruptcy code so that judgments, settlements, damages, fines, penalties, restitution, and disgorgement payments resulting from violations of federal securities laws are nondischargeable. This is intended to prevent corporate wrongdoers from sheltering their assets under bankruptcy protection.

Disgorgement of Bonuses One of the most unique aspects of the Sarbanes–Oxley Act is § 304, which states that if a publicly traded company is required to prepare an accounting restatement due to the company's material noncompliance, as a result of misconduct, with any financial reporting requirement under securities laws, then the CEO and CFO must reimburse the company for

- Any bonus or other incentive-based or equity-based compensation received during the twelve months after the initial filing of the report that requires restating
- Any profits realized from the sale of the company's securities during the same twelve-month period

While the Act requires the CEO and CFO to disgorge their bonuses if the company's financial statements have to be restated because of misconduct, it makes no mention of *whose* misconduct triggers this provision. There is nothing in the text of § 304 that limits the disgorgement provision to instances of misconduct by the CEO and CFO. Presumably then, the CEO and CFO could be required to disgorge their bonuses and profits from the sale of company stock even if they had no knowledge of and took no part in the misconduct that made the restatement necessary.

Now that we understand the underlying accounting principles that allow financial statement frauds to occur and the impact of the Sarbanes–Oxley Act to discourage these acts, in Chapter 14 we will turn to the mechanics of how such frauds are committed.

The Public Company Accounting Oversight Board (PCAOB)

Title I of Sarbanes–Oxley establishes the Public Company Accounting Oversight Board whose purpose is:

> *to oversee the audit of public companies that are subject to the securities laws, and related matters, in order to protect the interests of investors and further the public interest in the preparation of informative, accurate, and independent audit reports for companies the securities of which are sold to, and held by and for, public investors. (Section 101)*

In short, the Board is charged with overseeing public company audits, setting audit standards, and investigating acts of noncompliance by auditors or audit firms. The Board is appointed and overseen by the Securities and Exchange Commission. It is made up of five persons, two who are or have been CPAs and three who have never been CPAs. The Act lists the Board's duties, which include

- Registering public accounting firms that audit publicly traded companies
- Establishing or adopting auditing, quality control, ethics, independence, and other standards relating to audits of publicly traded companies
- Inspecting registered public accounting firms
- Investigating registered public accounting firms and their employees, conducting disciplinary hearings, and imposing sanctions where justified
- Performing such other duties as are necessary to promote high professional standards among registered accounting firms, to improve the quality of audit services offered by those firms, and to protect investors
- Enforcing compliance with the Sarbanes–Oxley Act, the rules of the Board, professional standards, and securities laws relating to public company audits

Registration with the Board   Public accounting firms must be registered with the Public Company Accounting Oversight Board in order to legally prepare or issue an audit report on a publicly traded company. In order to become registered, accounting firms must disclose, among other things, the names of all public companies they audited in the preceding year; the names of all public companies they expect to audit in the current year; and the annual fees they received from each of their public audit clients for audit, accounting, and nonaudit services.

Auditing, Quality Control, and Independence Standards and Rules   Section 103 of the Act requires the Board to establish standards for auditing, quality control, ethics, independence, and other issues relating to audits of publicly traded companies. On December 18, 2003, the Board adopted Auditing Standard No. 1, *References in Auditors' Reports to the Standards of the Public Company Accounting Oversight Board*. This standard requires that auditors' reports on engagements conducted in accordance with the Board's standards include a reference that the engagement was performed in accordance with the standards of the PCAOB. This supersedes historically requisite references to generally accepted auditing standards (GAAS). Adopted rules do not take effect until the SEC approves them, as detailed in Section 107 of the Act. Although the Act places the responsibility on the Board to establish audit standards, it also sets forth certain rules that the Board is required to include in those auditing standards. These rules include the following:

- Audit work papers must be maintained for at least seven years
- Auditing firms must include a concurring or second partner review and approval of audit reports, and concurring approval in the issuance of the audit report by a qualified person other than the person in charge of the audit
- All audit reports must describe the scope of testing of the company's internal control structure and must present the auditor's findings from the testing, including an evaluation of whether the internal control structure is acceptable, and a description of material weaknesses in internal controls and any material noncompliance with controls

Inspections of Registered Public Accounting Firms   The Act also authorizes the Board to conduct regular inspections of public accounting firms to assess their degree of compliance with laws, rules, and professional standards regarding audits. Inspections are to be conducted once a year for firms that regularly audit more than 100 public companies and at least once every three years for firms that regularly audit 100 or fewer public companies.

Investigations and Disciplinary Proceedings   The Board has the authority to investigate registered public accounting firms (or their employees) for potential violations of the Sarbanes–Oxley Act, professional standards, any rules established by the Board, or any securities laws relating to the preparation and issuance of audit reports. During an investigation, the Board has the power to compel testimony and document production.

The Board has the power to issue sanctions for violations or for noncooperation with an investigation. Sanctions can include temporary or permanent suspension of a firm's registration with the Board (which would mean that firm could no longer legally audit publicly traded companies), temporary or permanent suspension of a person's right to be associated with a registered public accounting firm, prohibition from auditing public companies, and civil monetary penalties of up to $750,000 for an individual and up to $15,000,000 for a firm.

Committee of Sponsoring Organizations' (COSO) Enterprise Risk Management Framework (ERM)

In September 2004, the Committee of Sponsoring Organizations (COSO) of the Treadway Commission released their ERM framework, recognized by the SEC as the critical methodology for Sarbanes–Oxley Section 404 compliance. It outlines the principles and components of effective risk management processes. Furthermore, the ERM framework describes how risks should be identified, assessed, and addressed. Interestingly, the framework emphasizes not only how effective risk management processes work but also emphasizes the possibility of enhanced profitability and return as a result of process evaluation and streamlining.

The fundamental purpose of the ERM framework approach is to help entities ensure that they will be able to achieve their operational and financial objectives and goals including:

- Achieving high-level strategic goals and the entity's mission
- Effective and efficient use of the company's operational resources
- Reliability of the company's financial reporting systems
- Compliance in meeting applicable laws and regulations
- Safeguarding of company resources by preventing loss through fraud, theft, waste, inefficiency, bad business decisions, etc.

In order to achieve its objectives, the ERM framework outlines the various components of good risk management processes. Some of those components consider an entity's risk tolerance and risk appetite. Other components evaluate the entity's internal environment; its ability to set objectives, the need to identify events that could have an effect on an entity's ability to achieve its objectives, its risk assessment including response, its control environment, information, communication, and its ability to monitor activities and events.

The COSO ERM Framework also has some specific suggestions for creating an antifraud environment:

- Consider and document fraud vulnerabilities
- Consider and document strategic objectives, the entity's risk appetite, risk tolerances, and consider them in the context of fraud probabilities
- Identify and document events that create risks of fraud
- Document enterprise risks by looking at the likelihood and impact of fraud vulnerabilities at all levels of the company
- Evaluate possible responses to fraud risks
- Implement and document antifraud control activities, policies, and procedures
- Communicate fraud prevention information, policies, and procedures throughout the company
- Monitor and document the success and failure of antifraud prevention controls and react to any findings

PCAOB's Auditing Standards Nos. 3[9] and 5

PCAOB Auditing Standard No. 3 (AS3), *Audit Documentation*, requires that audit engagement documentation should include a list of significant fraud risk factors, the auditor's response, and the results of the auditor's related procedures.

Auditing Standard No. 5 (AS5), *An Audit of Internal Control Over Financial Reporting That is Integrated with An Audit of Financial Statements*, superseded Auditing Standard No. 2 (AS2) and was

approved by the SEC on July 25, 2007. AS5 states that "the auditor should evaluate whether the company's controls sufficiently address identified risks of material misstatement due to fraud and controls intended to address the risk of management override of other controls."

Controls that mitigate these risks include

- Controls over significant, unusual transactions
- Controls over end-of-period adjusting journal entries
- Controls over related party transactions
- Controls related to significant management estimates
- Controls that mitigate management incentives and pressures to falsify or inappropriately manage financial results

Antifraud controls may be part of any of the five components of financial reporting internal controls:

- Control environment
- Risk assessment
- Control activities
- Information and communication
- Monitoring

Not surprisingly, internal controls related to the prevention and detection of fraud affect auditors' assessment of fraud risk for the entity under examination. Such controls include:

- Antifraud programs that address asset misappropriation that could be material in amount
- The company's internal risk assessment processes
- The company's code of ethics, especially those areas that address conflict of interest, related party dealings, illegal acts, and monitoring of company compliance in these areas by management and the audit committee
- The impact of internal audit on the fraud prevention environment, including ensuring that internal audit reports to the audit committee, and that the audit committee remains actively involved in internal audit examinations and findings
- The adequacy of the company's procedures and policies for handling complaints (e.g., whistle-blowing, maintaining confidentiality, etc.)

Management, executives, the board of directors, and the audit committee should set the proper tone at the top, create a culture of honesty, establish and maintain high ethical standards, and establish controls to prevent, detect, and deter fraud. The audit of internal controls is interrelated with the auditor's consideration of fraud in a financial statement audit (SAS no. 99). The audit of internal controls will often reveal issues that also impact the risk of financial reporting fraud. If auditors identify deficiencies in the internal controls designed to prevent and detect fraud during the internal control audit, the financial statement audit should consider altering the nature, extent, and timing of procedures to be performed during a financial statement audit to more carefully consider the impact of those control deficiencies.

IIA Practice Advisories 1210.A2-1 and 1210.A2-2

Internal Audit can be an integral resource in creating an antifraud environment. The Institute of Internal Auditors has issued Practice Advisories 1210.A2-1 and 1210.A2-2 that address identification of fraud and the internal auditors' responsibility for fraud detection, respectively. The IIA standards require the internal auditor to have sufficient knowledge to identify the indicators of fraud. The standards further recognize that fraud can be perpetrated for the benefit of or to the detriment of the organization and by individuals outside as well as inside the organization.

Examples of frauds designed to benefit the organization include:

- Sale or assignment of fictitious or misrepresented assets
- Improper payments such as illegal political contributions, bribes, kickbacks, and payoffs to government officials, intermediaries of government officials, customers, or suppliers
- Intentional improper representation or valuation of transactions, assets, liabilities, or income

- Intentional improper transfer pricing (e.g., valuation of goods exchanged between related organizations)
- Intentional improper related-party transactions
- Intentional failure to record or disclose significant information to outside parties
- Prohibited business activities such as those that violate government statutes, rules, regulations, or contracts
- Tax fraud

Examples of fraud perpetrated to the detriment of the organization include:

- Acceptance of bribes or kickbacks
- Diversion to an employee or outsider of a potentially profitable transaction
- Embezzlement, including efforts to falsify financial records to cover up the act
- Intentional concealment or misrepresentation of events or data
- Claims submitted for services or goods not actually provided to the organization

Management and internal audit have differing roles with respect to fraud detection. The normal course of work for the internal audit activity is to provide an independent appraisal, examination, and evaluation of an organization's activities as a service to the organization. The objective of internal auditing in fraud detection is to assist members of the organization in the effective discharge of their responsibilities by furnishing them with analyses, appraisals, recommendations, counsel, and information concerning the activities reviewed. The engagement objective includes promoting effective control at a reasonable cost. The IIA standards recognize that management has primary responsibility for the prevention, deterrence, and detection of fraud.

Nevertheless, in carrying out their responsibilities internal auditors should consider the following:

- Whether the organizational environment fosters control consciousness (tone at the top)
- Whether realistic organizational goals and objectives are set
- Written policies (e.g., code of conduct) and the response to policy violations
- Authorization for transactions, both existence and implementation
- Policies, practices, procedures, reports, and other mechanisms are developed to monitor activities and safeguard assets, particularly in high-risk areas
- Communication channels provide management with adequate and reliable information
- The response to recommendations to establish or enhance cost-effective antifraud controls

When red flags are identified and the internal auditor suspects that fraud may have occurred, the appropriate levels of corporate governance should be informed. The chief audit executive has the responsibility to report immediately any significant fraud to senior management and the board. When the incidence of significant fraud has been established to a reasonable certainty, senior management and the board should be notified immediately. When conducting fraud investigations, internal auditors should

- Assess the probable level and the extent of complicity in the fraud within the organization
- Determine the knowledge, skills, and other competencies needed to carry out the investigation effectively to ensure the appropriate types and levels of technical expertise
- Design procedures to identify the perpetrators, the extent of the fraud, the techniques used to perpetrate the fraud, and the underlying causes
- Coordinate activities with management personnel, legal counsel, and other specialists as appropriate
- Be cognizant of the rights of alleged perpetrators and personnel and the reputation of the organization itself

Once a fraud investigation is concluded, internal auditors should assess the facts known in order to determine if controls need to be implemented or strengthened to reduce future vulnerability and design engagement tests to help disclose the existence of similar frauds in the future. A draft of the proposed final communications on fraud should be submitted to legal counsel for review.

THE ROLE OF CORPORATE GOVERNANCE

The board of directors, the audit committee, executives, and management are responsible for the corporate governance environment in an organization. The primary role of corporate governance is to protect investors, create long-term shareholder value, ensure investor confidence, and support strong and efficient capital markets.[10] Most of the board's work regarding governance is discharged through committees. To effectively carry out its primary functions, a committee must ensure its independence. A good corporate governance environment will set the "tone at the top" by creating a culture of honesty and integrity, with the leadership of the organization practicing what they preach. As the saying goes, a fish starts to stink at the head, and if corporate leadership doesn't act in a responsible manner, it is doubtful that their subordinates will act differently.

Corporate leadership should also strive to create a positive work environment with efforts to increase employee morale, hiring and promoting employees who follow the company's ethical guidelines, providing adequate supervision and training, and creating and monitoring antifraud programs and controls. Effective corporate governance mechanisms include:

1. Organizational code of conduct supported by an embedded culture of honesty and ethical behavior.
2. An independent and empowered board of directors.
3. An independent and empowered audit committee.
4. Organizational policies and reward systems that are consistent with espoused ethical values.
5. Confidential disclosure methods.
6. Effective legal risk-assessment.

REVIEW QUESTIONS

6-1 What remedies are available through the civil and criminal justice systems?

6-2 Under what circumstances would a Miranda warning be required?

6-3 What constitutes "good cause" in the discharge of an employee?

6-4 What approaches are used by investigators to obtain documents?

6-5 What is meant by demonstrative evidence? Give examples.

6-6 In the criminal justice system, how is probation different from parole?

6-7 What are the factors that affect the decision to prosecute an entity?

6-8 What is the discovery process and how does it work?

6-9 What are the three major types of negotiated remedies and how do they differ?

6-10 How did the Sarbanes–Oxley Act address corporate governance and public accounting responsibilities?

ENDNOTES

1. Section 2.309, Fraud Examiner's Manual.
2. Fred E. Inbau et al., *Criminal Interrogations and Confessions, 4th Edition* (Gaithersburg, MD: Aspen Publishers Inc., 2001), 482.
3. Ibid., 486.
4. Section 2.310, Fraud Examiner's Manual.
5. Section 2.312, Fraud Examiner's Manual.
6. Section 2.317, Fraud Examiners Manual.
7. In addition, an entirely different system is available to juveniles.
8. In addition to SFASs, FASB issues Statements on Financial Accounting Concepts (SFAC); Interpretations, which clarify, explain, or elaborate on FASB Statements, Accounting Research Bulletins (ARB), or Accounting Principles Board (APB) Opinions; Technical Bulletins; Exposure Documents; and Discussion Papers.
9. Readers may also want to become familiar with SEC Staff Accounting Bulletin (SAB) No. 99 on materiality and International Auditing and Assurance Standards Board ISA 240, "The Auditor's Responsibility to Consider Fraud and Error in an Audit of Financial Statements."
10. Zabihollah Rezaee, *Corporate Governance Post-Sarbanes–Oxley: Regulations, Requirements, and Integrated Processes* (Hoboken, NJ: John Wiley & Sons, 2007).

DETECTION AND INVESTIGATIVE TOOLS AND TECHNIQUES

CHAPTER 7

FRAUD DETECTION: RED FLAGS AND TARGETED RISK ASSESSMENT

LEARNING OBJECTIVES

After completing this chapter, you should be able to

7-1 Describe management's primary responsibilities.

7-2 Discuss methods used to address management override and collusion.

7-3 Define the "expectations gap."

7-4 Describe the role of the external auditor in the financial reporting process.

7-5 Explain the concept of materiality.

7-6 Compare and contrast earnings management and fraud.

7-7 Recognize red flags for fraud.

7-8 Identify behavioral red flags.

7-9 Explain what is meant by an anomaly and give examples of certain types of anomalies.

7-10 Discuss the components that frame the fraud risk assessment process.

CRITICAL THINKING EXERCISE

A scientist has an unlimited water supply and two buckets; one holds four gallons and the other holds nine gallons. By using nothing but the buckets and water, how can she accurately measure seven gallons of water?

CORPORATE GOVERNANCE AND FRAUD

Management's Responsibility

Management is first and foremost responsible for ensuring that a corporation meets its strategic, operational, and performance objectives. To accomplish this, an organization's leadership must develop and implement strategies and procedures to manage the long-term economic stewardship of the organization rather than allow themselves to be viewed simply as agents of the owners—the shareholders—and responsible primarily for maximizing shareholder wealth.

Inherently, such responsibilities require that management establish some methodology for measuring performance and communicating the results of their efforts. Furthermore, management must protect the various resources controlled by the organization to meets its objectives. Statement on Auditing Standards (SAS) No. 1 states, "Management is responsible for adopting sound accounting policies and for establishing and maintaining internal control that will, among other things, initiate, authorize, record, process and report transactions (as well as events and conditions) consistent with management's assertions embodied in the financial statements."[1] More specifically, these latter obligations require management to design and implement a system of internal controls, processes, and procedures necessary to safeguard the resources of the entity and ensure relevant and reliable financial reporting. In many cases, the company falls under the purview of various regulatory and taxing authorities that also require compliance with their informational and reporting needs.

Overall, management must design, implement, and maintain internal controls and financial reporting processes to produce timely financial and nonfinancial information that reflects the underlying economics of the business. Accounting information and reporting must comply with generally accepted accounting principles as well as other necessary regulatory requirements. Because management is responsible for the fair presentation of the financial statements and to safeguard the assets of the business, they must also mitigate fraud within the organization by preventing, deterring, and detecting asset misappropriation, corruption, and fraudulent financial statements. Consistent with those objectives, management should design, maintain, and monitor a system of internal controls over assets, financial information, and the financial reporting process. Management is also responsible for providing information to the independent auditors so that they may complete the work necessary to render an opinion on the financial statements.

The Risk of Management Override and Collusion   Depending on the individuals involved, internal controls cannot prevent management override or collusive behavior by and among senior management. Because prevention (segregation of duties, approvals, and authorizations) is not possible in a collusive environment, the principal internal control procedures will be centered on detection. The fear of detection may be an effective deterrence mechanism, but that does not eliminate the concern that traditionally designed internal control systems centered on prevention will not be effective when management override or collusion is present. Thus, internal and external auditors, fraud examiners, and forensic accounting professionals must design procedures to detect such activity. Because management is in a unique position to override internal controls and collude with other top managers or outside third parties to work around the traditional control environment, auditors and anti-fraud professionals must design specific procedures to determine whether the system of internal controls that is otherwise operating effectively may be circumvented by a senior manager or group of managers.

Generally, three procedures are effective in identifying breakdowns in internal controls due to override and collusion. First, journal entries recorded in the books and records as well as other adjustments to financial information must be examined for symptoms of possible misstatement due to fraud. Fraud often results from adjustments to amounts recorded in the books and records, which misstate financial statements, even when there are effective controls in other areas of the organization. The auditor should obtain an understanding of the internal control processes regarding journal entries and other adjustments (such as consolidating entries that may appear only on an Excel spreadsheet) and determine whether the journal entries carry the proper authority, approvals, documentation, and sign-offs as required by organizational policies and procedures. Further, auditors should discuss journal entries with employees who are not senior managers and inquire about inappropriate or unusual activity regarding journal entries. Often, when intentionally inappropriate journal entries are recorded, they are approved by the individual who directed and authorized the journal entry. Auditors should consider examining the timing of journal entry activity, looking for journal entries that are recorded at odd hours, such as late at night and on weekends or holidays when such journal entries may not be expected. Also, they should consider investigating journal entries that are typically used to perpetrate fraud schemes, such as reductions in liabilities and increases in revenues, or reductions in period costs and increases in capital assets. SAS No. 99 requires testing of journal entries and other adjustments, and further details additional procedures the auditor should consider.

Second, significant accounting estimates need to be reviewed. Fraudulent financial reporting can be accomplished through manipulation of estimates that require judgment. Fabricated estimates can also be a source of concealment of other fraudulent activities. In some ways, accounting estimates may be a more effective source of fraud concealment than journal entries due to the professional judgment required to make the necessary calculations or determine the reasonableness of account balances. In many instances, underlying assumptions are not documented carefully or are documented with falsified or fictitious documents; these practices allow year-to-year modifications that could go unnoticed. SAS No. 99 requires auditors to consider the potential for bias when testing estimates. Included in the testing procedure should be a review of prior years' amounts to see if the methodology or underlying assumptions have changed, and if they have changed, a determination of the business rationale for the change in approach is in order.

Third, unusual "one-time" transactions should be scrutinized to ensure that they have an appropriate underlying business rationale. Understanding the business rationale is a SAS No. 99 requirement and is done to ensure that the financial statements are not subject to manipulation through the use of one-time, fraudulent transactions. The auditor has the responsibility to ensure that the accounting treatment is appropriate and that the transaction is properly supported, documented, and disclosed in the financial statements. Other procedures that may help identify breakdowns in internal controls include analytical reviews in which

anomalies are identified. One example is when gross margins are stable or increasing at a time when they should be decreasing, such as in a competitive environment or during an economic downturn.

The Role of the External Auditor

The perception of the public—particularly with regard to asset misappropriation, corruption, and misstated financial statements—is that independent auditors are responsible for fraud detection; however, an auditor's responsibility is to provide reasonable assurance that the financial statements are free from material misstatement whether caused by error or fraud. Auditors do not examine 100 percent of the recorded transactions; instead, they rely on sampling a portion of them to determine the probability that the transactions were recorded properly. Further, auditors also rely on high-level analytical procedures as well as interviews, inquiries, external confirmations, inspections, physical inventories, and other audit procedures to determine whether the financial statements are free from material misstatement. The difference between the public's perception of the role of the auditor and the role that audit professionals *actually* serve has led to an "expectations gap."

Management is responsible for the financial reporting process and its output: financial statements, disclosures, and related notes. Consequently, many might question what role the auditor plays. The auditor's role is to attest to the fairness of management's presentation of the financial information as well as the assertions inherent in the financial statements. When auditors have completed their work, they report their findings in an audit report. Auditors have several choices concerning the types of opinions that they may publish. First, auditors may conclude that the financial statements present fairly, in all material respects, the financial position (assets, liabilities, and stockholders equity), results of operations (income), and cash flows. This opinion is referred to as an unqualified opinion. The auditor may also publish a modified, unqualified opinion. This report is referred to as the "unqualified opinion with explanatory paragraph or modified wording." This type of opinion is issued when auditors feel that it is necessary to provide additional information that they believe needs to be understood by the financial statement users. Some examples of when an auditor may provide explanatory information include when substantial doubt exists about an entity's ability to continue as a going concern and when generally accepted accounting principles have not been consistently applied. Other opinions that an auditor may issue include a qualified opinion, when the auditor believes that some material aspect of the financial information is not presented fairly; a disclaimer opinion, when they cannot issue a report because of limitations on their work or when a lack of audit evidence that would provide a reasonable basis on which the auditors may draw conclusions; and an adverse opinion, when the auditor has concluded that the financial statements are essentially misleading.

SAS No. 99   Fraud, primarily financial statement fraud, has been a significant concern of the auditing profession, the Public Company Accounting Oversight Board (PCAOB), and the Securities Exchange Commission (SEC). The scandals of the late 1990s and the early 2000s, such as Enron, Adelphia, WorldCom, and Tyco, have increased the pressure on auditors to detect fraudulent financial reporting. The accounting profession responded in 2002 with Statement on Auditing Standard (SAS) No. 99: *Consideration of Fraud in a Financial Statement Audit*. The primary points of emphasis include enhanced professional skepticism, pre-audit fraud brainstorming, interviews with management concerning the risk and existence of fraud, and how to design audit tests to address the risk of management override of internal controls.

SAS No. 99 emphasizes that a material misstatement of financial information can result from fraud or error; intent will be the determining factor. Intent can be discerned by looking for evidence of concealment such as missing documents, altered documents, nonreconcilable items, misinformation obtained during management inquiries, and other indicators of concealment. Fraud—an intentional misstatement—can be achieved by (1) manipulation, falsification, or alteration of the underlying accounting data, records, and documentation; (2) misrepresentation or omission of events, transactions, or other significant information in the financial statements and/or related notes; or (3) intentional misapplication of accounting principles that guide the amounts, classification, presentation, or disclosure of financial information. Auditors need to be concerned about management override and also about the possibility of collusion, because both attributes are often observed as part of financial statement fraud. The auditing standard recognizes the fraud triangle and its elements of pressure, opportunity, and rationalization.

From there, SAS No. 99 can be summarized as involving eight steps in considering the risk of fraud:

1. *Staff discussion*—Auditors must brainstorm with the entire audit team at the beginning of the engagement to consider how and where financial statement fraud might occur.

2. *Obtain information needed to identify risks*—Auditors must conduct inquiries of management, the audit committee, internal auditors, and others, as well as consider the results of analytical procedures, fraud risk factors, and other information.

3. *Identify risks*—Based on the information and ideas gathered in steps 1 and 2, auditors must determine the type of fraud risks that exist, the significance of that risk (the magnitude), the likelihood of risk occurrence, and the pervasiveness of the risk (what accounts and balances could be affected).

4. *Assess identified risks and potential schemes after considering internal controls*—Auditors must utilize their understanding of the system of internal control, evaluate whether programs and controls address the identified risks from step 3, and reassess fraud risks taking into account this evaluation.

5. *Respond to the results of the risk assessment*—As the risk of fraud increases, auditors should consider using a fraud specialist on the engagement, determine the appropriate application of accounting policies, and employ less predictable procedures as well as increasing the amount of required audit evidence by modifying the nature, timing, and extent of audit procedures. Further, on all audits, the auditor should consider the possibility of management override of controls and examine nonstandard and standard journal entries, accounting estimates, and unusual significant transactions.

6. *Evaluate the audit evidence*—Throughout the audit, auditors must reassess the risk of fraud, evaluate analytical procedures performed, and respond to any identified misstatements.

7. *Communicate about fraud*—Auditors are required to report (1) all fraud to an appropriate level of management; (2) all management fraud to the audit committee; and (3) all material fraud to management and the audit committee. If reportable conditions (i.e., significant deficiencies and/or material weaknesses) exist concerning the system of internal controls, they should be communicated to the audit committee.

8. *The auditor should document the procedures undertaken in steps 1 through 7*

   a. Staff discussion

   b. Information used to identify the risk of fraud

   c. Any fraud risks identified

   d. The risks assessed after considering programs and controls

   e. Results of assessment of fraud risk

   f. Evaluation of audit evidence

   g. Communication requirements

Materiality   In the context of an audit, the auditor invokes a materiality threshold. FASB 2 defines materiality as the "magnitude of an omission or misstatement of accounting information that, in the light of surrounding circumstances, makes it probable that the judgment of a reasonable person relying on the information would have been changed or influenced by the omission or misstatement."[2] Thus, the auditor must apply judgment related to materiality, and that judgment has an impact on the information presented in the financial statements.

Materiality is a relative concept. A misstated amount that would be immaterial to a large company such as General Electric could be large enough to wipe out the net worth of most small companies. An amount material to a small company would likely be ignored at a larger company, other than obtaining an understanding of the nature of the misstatement. Some of the key financial statement attributes used by auditors to determine materiality include net income before taxes, revenues, gross profit, and assets. Further, the types of accounts (e.g., revenue, expense, asset, liability, and stockholder's equity) can have an impact on the auditor's judgment as well as the dollar impact on a particular financial statement line item.

When establishing materiality, auditors also consider profitability trends over time, situations where companies are experiencing a loss, financial performance that places the company in proximity of violating loan covenants or regulatory requirements, and financial performance that is relatively close to management compensation appraisal and bonus hurdles. For example, if an auditee's financial performance is such that management qualifies but just barely for annual bonuses and other short-term compensation, auditors are more likely to reduce their materiality threshold.

Similarly, company financial performance that just barely meets analysts' expectations may give rise to changes in materiality levels for audit purposes. Further, auditors rely not only on financial assessments,

they also consider various qualitative factors such as whether they have discovered fraud in prior audits or there are allegations of illegal acts or fraud.

Generally, illegal acts have no materiality threshold and require that auditors pay close attention to their nature and corresponding consequences to the company. For example, any violation of the Foreign Corrupt Practices Act (FCPA) may expose the client company to fines and penalties that may be material. The FCPA has far-reaching implications for a company because it's not just management that can get a company into trouble. An FCPA violation may also cover employees at any level or in any position in the organization, as well as agents, consultants, distributors, related parties, and other third parties associated with the company. Also, there could be significant legal exposure in the foreign country where a bribe has occurred because the country could revoke licenses and, therefore, the ability of the company to operate within their jurisdiction. This may require the auditor to assure that there is adequate disclosure as to possible material outcomes.

The materiality amount—once established—is not set in stone for the duration of the audit engagement. Auditors may become aware of new facts or circumstances that may cause them to reassess and adjust materiality. After a preliminary judgment about materiality has been made, auditors will then allocate that amount to various balance sheets and income statement account balances. The process of allocation determines tolerable risk of material misstatement for that account balance. SAS No. 111 limits the tolerable misstatement for any particular account balance to less than 100 percent of total materiality.

THE CPA JOURNAL

Determining Materiality: Relativity and Professional Judgment

AUGUST 2007—While returning home from a recent out-of-state conference, my flight was delayed by forty minutes. The person sitting next to me could see that I was frustrated, and sought to make me feel better by assuring me that forty minutes in a lifetime was "immaterial" and that I shouldn't allow it to bother me. Her words started me thinking.

Judgment and Expectations

Materiality is a concept that has caused much frustration and angst in the public accounting profession, primarily because it requires a substantial degree of auditor judgment regarding what's important to users of the financial statements when making economic decisions. To understand how any piece of information may influence an investor, supplier, creditor, or lender's decision-making process, an auditor needs to anticipate who the potential readers of the information may be and the range of decisions they may make. Although the number of possible decisions and assessments is endless, an auditor's judgment may be questioned and sometimes litigated in a court of law.

Although public accountants have been charged with stewardship in the financial reporting process, some in our profession still look for ways to avoid making the tough decisions that responsibility entails. One CPA wrote to me that when he was working for a major accounting firm in the 1960s, the ability to technically comply with financial statement disclosure requirements—while actually saying nothing—was a prized quality. So what has changed? In the past, many issues were overlooked with the excuse that they were immaterial. Yet some issues that an auditor deems to be immaterial may be very material to investors and others. The Sarbanes–Oxley Act made clear that the public expects the CPA to be a financial cop.

So CPAs are looking for guidance on the meaning of materiality. But despite accounting regulators' attempts to avoid bright-line rules and develop principles-based accounting standards, many in the profession consistently seek "definitions" and "examples" when it comes to materiality. This guidance inevitably turns into the detailed rules and checklists that we purport to disparage. The fundamental meaning of materiality continues to haunt regulators and practitioners.

The Problem with Quantification

The PCAOB recently adopted Auditing Standard No. 5 (AS5), *An Audit of Internal Control over Financial Reporting That Is Integrated with an Audit of Financial Statements*. This new standard, pending SEC approval, will replace AS2, which many critics contend was overly costly because it caused auditors to focus on minutiae when assessing risk and ignored the big picture that would be revealed by a top-down approach. AS5 encourages auditors to be consistent in the materiality measures they use for planning and performing audits of financial statements and internal controls; however, the standard stops short of providing a quantitative value.

But will anything other than a specific materiality number satisfy some auditors and business groups? Quantitative measures provide a deceptive sense of comfort, especially for those accustomed to dealing with numbers. In the past, a common practice was for audit firms to base the scope of their work on a numerical materiality threshold, such as 5 percent of net income. An auditor would then use this number to determine whether a misstatement should be reported. The profession has historically recognized that certain circumstances can render these strictly quantitative measures invalid. For example, is a 2 percent misstatement acceptable if it was caused by management fraud? The answer is that there is no such thing as "immaterial" fraud when it is committed by top executives.

The qualitative aspects of a misstatement cannot be disregarded or excused for merely quantitative reasons. The issues behind the numbers often tell us more than the numbers

alone. If CPAs ignore these clues, if they set aside their professional judgment, they do so at their own peril.

Materiality is relative. As a result of that forty-minute flight delay, I missed my connecting flight and spent an additional eight hours in the airport waiting on stand-by for another flight home. Put in this context, was the initial forty-minute delay really immaterial? I'll leave that to your judgment.

Mary-Jo Kranacher, MBA, CPA, CFE
Editor-in-Chief

Earnings Management and Fraud "Earnings management" involves deliberate actions by management to meet specific earnings objectives, generally for private gain.[3] An example of such an objective might be to enhance reported earnings to meet analysts' expectations. Earnings management may also involve building reserves during "good times" so that those reserves can be reversed during more difficult financial times. Some companies may even take a one-time "bath" in order to capture as much negative financial impact in one year to protect future earnings. Income smoothing is a specific type of earnings management whereby revenues or expenses are shifted between periods to minimize naturally occurring year-to-year fluctuations in net income. By enhancing the predictability of the organization's earnings stream, management believes that they can achieve higher market prices for the company's stock.

Auditors have many challenges with regard to earnings management. First, auditors have a materiality threshold, and as long as a transaction or group of transactions do not cross the materiality threshold, in theory any earnings management would be judged immaterial (at least when considered within the context of the year under evaluation) and thus would not have a significant impact on the judgment of users of the financial statements.

Second, accounting principles and policies were designed to provide some degree of choice. Management is given this flexibility to avoid a one-size-fits-all mentality for financial reporting and to ensure that the financial statements reasonably reflect the underlying economics and performance of the business. Nevertheless, management can use this latitude to manage earnings, and as long as the choices are considered "GAAP"-compliant, the auditor has little basis for recourse. Similarly, accounting procedures often require the development of underlying estimates to support the numbers in the financial statements.

There is no perfect advice for auditors and forensic accountants in this regard except that management may find itself on a slippery slope—an earnings management in one period may lead to fraud in the next. Any sign of deliberate efforts to manage earnings should be considered a red flag, and those performing the work should use their heightened sense of professional skepticism to be aware of other choices made by management, signs of management override (by carefully examining journal entries, estimates, and unusual transactions), and signs of collusion among the executive ranks. Managing earnings can be fraud, whether or not material. The primary issue is whether the independent auditor or forensic accountant has clear and convincing evidence that demonstrates that earnings have, in fact, been managed.

Boards of Directors and Audit Committees

The board of directors and/or an audit committee, if one exists, has a primary responsibility to oversee management and direct the internal audit and the external auditor with regard to the organization's internal controls over financial reporting and the company's internal control processes. One of the central duties of the audit committee with regard to fraud and fraudulent financial reporting is to carefully assure—with the assistance of the internal audit process—that management has adequately assessed the risk of management override or collusion among top-level managers and executives that may lead to asset misappropriation, corruption, or fraudulent financial statements.

The audit committee is an integral internal control mechanism with regard to management override and high-level management collusion. It is only by carrying out their responsibilities in concert with the internal and external auditors that management override and collusion can be detected and deterrence levels set high enough so that management's likelihood of attempting either method (override or collusion) is sufficiently reduced. Audit committees can signal their interest is this area by paying particular attention to the "tone at the top," anti-fraud programs, and ethics training, as well as by instituting a zero-tolerance policy toward fraud.

TABLE 7-2 Targeted Fraud Risk Assessment in Action

Fraud Risk	Revenue—"Roundtrip" Transactions—Inflating revenues	Revenue—Bill and Holds
Step 1. Identify, understand, and evaluate the company's operating environment and pressures that may exist.		
Operating Environment	The economy has been relatively weak with virtually no growth. The industry has been soft and generally follows the overall economy. The organization's primary competitors have reflected generally poor performance in the prior eight quarters of reported earnings. Despite the recent weak performance, the industry is considered healthy and the balance sheets of most competing organizations do not suggest a high risk of bankruptcy.	
Possible Pressures	The company has barely met analysts' expectations for the past six quarters. Despite some negative financial press concerning operational issues, particularly with regard to the organization's ability to tap into the Chinese market, the stock market has evaluated this company as positioned to outperform in the next four quarters. Most of the organizations' main competitors have been evaluated as below average expected performance.	
Step 2. Identify the business processes		
Process	Sales and Collection Cycle	Sales, Inventory, and Collection Cycle
Jurisdictions and Level of Control	The company sells product in the United States and China. Each jurisdiction has a regional vice president that reports to the Chief Operating Officer (COO). The COO reports to the CEO. The regional vice presidents have operational autonomy with respect to day-to-day operations (decentralized). The COO and CEO mainly concentrate on strategies for growth over the next two to five years. Operations in both the United States and China have regional accounting controllers. The organization has a corporate controller and a Chief Financial Officer (CFO).	
Step 3. Identify the "process owner" for each of the identified significant processes		
Process Owner	Regional Vice Presidents	
Process Sub-owner	Regional Director of Sales and Marketing	
Related Accounting Areas	Sales audit, inventory control, accounts receivables	
Journal Entry Control and Authority	Journal entries are initiated at the regional level. The corporate controller must approve the journal entry. The CFO has the ultimate approval, responsibility, and authority.	
Step 4. Review past fraud experience within the company for the process being evaluated		
Past Fraud Experience	None noted	None noted
Step 5. Identify how fraud may occur in each process at each location using fraud brainstorming techniques (Note: the risk of management override is evaluated separately and is not considered in this targeted fraud risk assessment)		
Cause of Fraud	Recording transactions that occur between two or more companies for which there is no business purpose or economic benefit to the companies involved in order to inflate revenues	When products have been booked as a sale but delivery and transfer of ownership has not occurred as of the date the sale recorded. The customer is not ready, willing, or able to accept delivery of the product at the time the sale is recorded. The customer may or may not have requested a bill and hold arrangement.
Step 6. Identify the parties who have the ability to commit the potential fraud		
May Involve	CEO, COO, regional vice president, and sales personnel. May or may not involve accounting personnel.	CEO, COO, CFO, regional vice president, other executives, customer, credit manager, sales personnel, inventory manager/personnel. Most likely must involve accounting personnel.
Step 7. Evaluate the likelihood that each of the identified frauds could occur and be significant as well as the persuasiveness of the potential fraud, without consideration of controls		
Significance	More than inconsequential, particularly in the Chinese operating environment because of a recent history of product defects.	Inconsequential due to the fact that demand currently outstrips supply.

(continued)

- What information systems are in place and does communication happen as designed and in a timely fashion?
- What monitoring activities are in place?
- What effective remediation and fraud investigation processes and procedures are designed and operational?

Note that these areas are consistent with COSO's five elements of internal controls: control environment, risk assessment, control activities, information and communication, and monitoring.

Step 9 requires the fraud examiner to investigate the characteristics of potential fraud manifestations within each process identified in which "residual fraud risk" exists:

- Design procedures to look for the fraud
- Consider data mining techniques
- Look for the fraud

In *Step 10*, the fraud examiner needs to reassess and quantify fraud risk given the findings from Steps 1–9. The fraud examiner needs to evaluate the results of the investigation and extrapolate each fraud manifestation over the entire population of possibilities, because the frauds that have been detected may be just the tip of the iceberg.

Table 7-2 includes two examples of targeted fraud risk assessment in actions: revenue "round-trip" transactions and revenue "bill and hold" schemes.

TARGETED FRAUD RISK ASSESSMENT IN A DIGITAL ENVIRONMENT[10]

We have all heard horror stories by fraud examiners of computer tests that result in the identification of hundreds, thousands, and possibly even millions of anomalous transactions that require further review. At these times, fraud examiners and investigators feel like throwing up their hands in frustration due to the sheer volume of exceptions. The main problem is that a targeted approach for the assessment of red flags or a targeted fraud risk assessment was not made in advance. As such, the digital assessment was also not targeted.

Prevention and Deterrence in a Digital Environment

In an electronic environment that captures millions of transactions annually, many transactions and data relationship anomalies appear to be a potential fraud or error. To utilize the computer environment effectively, the targeted fraud risk assessment process must be completed. This process will yield the highest probability of frauds that might manifest themselves and have a large enough magnitude to make a significant impact. Red flags and anomalous relationships require evidence to determine whether a fraud is ongoing, has occurred, or is not and never has happened. It is only by using a laser or rifle-shot approach that digital tools and techniques can be effective in preventing, deterring, and detecting fraud.

One of the acronyms related to fraud and forensic accounting in a digital environment is CAATTs, computer-aided auditing tools and techniques. CAATTs are used for data extraction and analysis. Auditors and other anti-fraud and forensic professionals often make use of this data for testing the information systems control environment as well as performing detail tests. Information systems and related technology, including the financial accounting system, are integral to an organization's success; they provide timely and essential information to facilitate achieving strategic objectives. These systems provide the information necessary to execute strategy and to achieve operational goals and objectives.

Because information is key to the successful operation and execution of strategy for any organization, information systems technology is central to many organizational transactions, beginning at a transaction's inception. If we use a purchase order for inventory as an example, this transaction flows through the information system to capture the receipt of the merchandise at a warehouse facility, payment via the cash disbursement system, and tracking through the inventory and merchandising systems. Some of these systems are part of or modules within the accounting information systems and others are periphery or separate and distinct information systems outside the normal accounting systems. In either case, this information is integral to producing fairly stated financial statements and strong systems of internal control.

Digital Evidence

A major challenge for the fraudster is to conceal their nefarious activities given that so much information is captured electronically and is available to monitor their activities during and after the perpetration of

TABLE 7-2 Targeted Fraud Risk Assessment in Action

Fraud Risk	Revenue—"Roundtrip" Transactions—Inflating revenues	Revenue—Bill and Holds
Step 1. Identify, understand, and evaluate the company's operating environment and pressures that may exist.		
Operating Environment	The economy has been relatively weak with virtually no growth. The industry has been soft and generally follows the overall economy. The organization's primary competitors have reflected generally poor performance in the prior eight quarters of reported earnings. Despite the recent weak performance, the industry is considered healthy and the balance sheets of most competing organizations do not suggest a high risk of bankruptcy.	
Possible Pressures	The company has barely met analysts' expectations for the past six quarters. Despite some negative financial press concerning operational issues, particularly with regard to the organization's ability to tap into the Chinese market, the stock market has evaluated this company as positioned to outperform in the next four quarters. Most of the organizations' main competitors have been evaluated as below average expected performance.	
Step 2. Identify the business processes		
Process	Sales and Collection Cycle	Sales, Inventory, and Collection Cycle
Jurisdictions and Level of Control	The company sells product in the United States and China. Each jurisdiction has a regional vice president that reports to the Chief Operating Officer (COO). The COO reports to the CEO. The regional vice presidents have operational autonomy with respect to day-to-day operations (decentralized). The COO and CEO mainly concentrate on strategies for growth over the next two to five years. Operations in both the United States and China have regional accounting controllers. The organization has a corporate controller and a Chief Financial Officer (CFO).	
Step 3. Identify the "process owner" for each of the identified significant processes		
Process Owner	Regional Vice Presidents	
Process Sub-owner	Regional Director of Sales and Marketing	
Related Accounting Areas	Sales audit, inventory control, accounts receivables	
Journal Entry Control and Authority	Journal entries are initiated at the regional level. The corporate controller must approve the journal entry. The CFO has the ultimate approval, responsibility, and authority.	
Step 4. Review past fraud experience within the company for the process being evaluated		
Past Fraud Experience	None noted	None noted
Step 5. Identify how fraud may occur in each process at each location using fraud brainstorming techniques (Note: the risk of management override is evaluated separately and is not considered in this targeted fraud risk assessment)		
Cause of Fraud	Recording transactions that occur between two or more companies for which there is no business purpose or economic benefit to the companies involved in order to inflate revenues	When products have been booked as a sale but delivery and transfer of ownership has not occurred as of the date the sale recorded. The customer is not ready, willing, or able to accept delivery of the product at the time the sale is recorded. The customer may or may not have requested a bill and hold arrangement.
Step 6. Identify the parties who have the ability to commit the potential fraud		
May Involve	CEO, COO, regional vice president, and sales personnel. May or may not involve accounting personnel.	CEO, COO, CFO, regional vice president, other executives, customer, credit manager, sales personnel, inventory manager/personnel. Most likely must involve accounting personnel.
Step 7. Evaluate the likelihood that each of the identified frauds could occur and be significant as well as the persuasiveness of the potential fraud, without consideration of controls		
Significance	More than inconsequential, particularly in the Chinese operating environment because of a recent history of product defects.	Inconsequential due to the fact that demand currently outstrips supply.

(continued)

because the productivity gains being realized outweighed any problems in the underlying economy. In fact, those productivity gains necessitated faster investment in technology in order to avoid being left behind in a difficult economic climate.

With this in mind, an assessment of the industry should be completed. The overall performance of the industry can be a key indicator of expectations of the organization. If the organization under study is not following the trends posted in the industry, an explanation of why this is occurring needs to be developed. Within any economy and in any industry there are always high-flyers and overachievers and there are also the laggards and underachievers. Some organization has to be first, and another has to be last. At the same time, there must be good business reasons for exemplary or inferior performance in an industry. Developing an understanding of the industry and how the organization under study compares is part of the fraud risk assessment that serves as a necessary basis for detecting fraud.

Similar to the overall industry, most organizations have one or two key competitors, similar organizations that compete in the same markets and for the same customers. A comparison of those competitors to the organization under study serves as a basis for looking for environments where fraud may be occurring. This analysis considers geographic and other demographics. For example, the first decade in the 2000s has been particularly difficult for Midwestern states such as Ohio and Michigan. Such a difficult climate may serve as the basis for a company to cook its books. At the same time, it may also serve as the backdrop for an employee or group of employees to commit fraud in order to maintain their lifestyles.

Finally, an evaluation of trends within an organization is required. Trends over time and across several different metrics including revenues, gross profits, and operating expenses, as well as assets, liabilities, and stockholders' equity are important points. The analysis of these trends needs to be both horizontal across time and vertical within a particular year.

Each of these techniques may be applied not only to an organization as a whole but also to specific units, divisions, and product lines. In fact, if an anti-fraud professional suspects an employee payroll scheme in a particular warehouse, the symptoms and the actual fraud scheme may only come to light through the comparison of this warehouse's operations to that of others in the same organization.

The purpose of this preliminary work is to develop a backdrop for evaluating the possibility of fraud. Another way of stating the same idea is to suggest that what has been created through this effort is a series of expectations. For example, a case was once noted in which a company claimed to be "put out of business by the actions of another." The actions of the other company had supposedly started in July, two years prior, and carried on for approximately eighteen months.

This claim suggested at least two expectations: (1) the performance of the failed company should have deteriorated over the eighteen-month period and (2) the failed company should have appeared reasonably healthy prior to July of two years prior. The first expectation held; the company's performance in fact deteriorated over the eighteen-month period, starting in July. The second expectation did not; the failed company was in horrendous financial condition at the beginning of the eighteen-month period. This necessitated additional work to understand how the company came to be in such a condition eighteen months prior to the alleged act and how a precarious starting point may have contributed to the failure.

The Internal Control Environment

In order to develop an approach to fraud detection, the second step is to develop an understanding of the control environment. The control environment consists of the policies, procedures, actions, and other activities that reflect the overall attitudes of the board of directors, the audit committee, and senior management concerning internal controls. Some of the attributes that should be considered include:[5]

1. Commitment to integrity and ethical and core values

2. Commitment to competence

3. An independent board of directors and audit committee that participates in the internal control process and oversees the process

4. Management's attitudes, philosophy, and operating style concerning important internal controls and operational issues ("tone at the top")

5. Organizational structure, including lines of responsibility and authority, particularly as it relates to the control environment and operational expectations

6. Communications about the importance of control-related matters, ethics, anti-fraud awareness and commitment, organizational and operating plans, employee job descriptions, and related policies

7. Human resource policies and practices

The anti-fraud professional or forensic accountant is hoping to see a clear and unwavering commitment to a culture of honesty, openness, and assistance. Optimally, the company is hiring honest employees and training them in all aspects of their duties and responsibilities, including fraud awareness and fraud risk assessment methodology. The company should also be creating a positive work environment with open door policies and a commitment to employee success. The company should have an up-to-date code of ethics that employees review and sign regularly that clarifies expectations concerning honesty.

With perceived pressure, employee assistance programs give people a place to go during difficult times. The company should not only expect its employees to be aware of its commitment to honest and ethical behavior, but it should also communicate its expectations to vendors, suppliers, customers, contractors, and others who do business with the organization. These communications, along with tip hotlines, create an environment in which whistleblowers feel free to leave tips concerning matters of questionable behavior.

The control environment is not only about openness and expectations; it also assumes that employees will be monitored, and that those who perpetrate fraud will be caught and those who engage in unacceptable behavior will suffer the consequences. Those consequences must be meted out regardless of the pressure or rationale behind such behavior. Of course, a good internal control environment must be supported by a system of internal controls that eliminates the opportunity to commit fraud, given sensible cost-benefit constraints.

While the above discussion suggests that the key to successful fraud prevention, deterrence, and detection is a solid control environment, missing or inadequate elements in a system of internal controls signal the possibility that fraud may be present and carry with it a heightened sense of awareness about the possibility of fraud.

The Use of Red Flags to Detect Fraud

Red flags—symptoms of fraud—often go unnoticed or are not vigorously pursued. This is not surprising given the number of red flags observed. The red flags that can lead to a formal fraud investigation include tips and complaints, behavioral red flags, analytical anomalies, accounting anomalies, and internal control irregularities and weaknesses. Each of these, when observed, needs to be evaluated with additional evidence to make a determination concerning fraud. Some of the questions that need to be answered include:

- Does the anomaly have supporting documentation?
- Does the documentation appear to be falsified, altered, or fictitious?
- Does the transaction and its reflection in the financial statements make sense?
- Does the transaction make sense in light of the company's operations, goals, and objectives?
- Does the totality of this and similar transactions make sense analytically when evaluated in comparison to the economy, the industry, key competitors, and other related accounting numbers within the organization?
- Does the transaction have proper approval and the proper authority levels?
- Does anything else about the transaction or its nature make it appear suspicious?

Asking follow-up questions and resolving those questions with evidence is one of the keys to professional skepticism and a key to successfully uncovering fraudulent activity, whether asset misappropriation, corruption, or financial statement fraud.

Tips and Complaints

The 2008 ACFE Report to the Nation noted (see Figure 7-1) that almost half of the frauds in the study were most commonly detected by *tips* (46.2 percent). It was also encouraging that the percentage of cases discovered by *accident* (20.0 percent) was five percent lower than in 2006. When combined, tips and accidental discovery account for 66.2 percent. This supports the contention that organizations need to do a better job of actively seeking out fraud. It also suggests that like it or not, employees, managers, co-workers, and colleagues outside the company, those closest to the day-to-day operations, are in the best position to detect and report fraud.

This also reinforces why the control environment is so critical to fraud detection. Without a visible commitment to fraud detection, prevention, investigation, and remediation, some frauds are likely to go unreported, and certainly some frauds will end up being far more costly than if they were discovered and resolved earlier in the process.

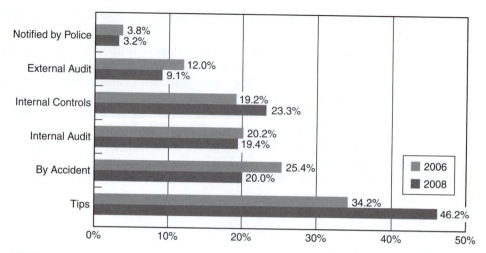

FIGURE 7-1 Initial Detection of Occupational Frauds

Source: 2008 ACFE Report to the Nation

At some level, these findings make sense. Because employees, co-workers, managers, and outside colleagues interact with the fraudster daily, weekly, or monthly, they are more likely to observe behavior that falls outside the norm. If they don't report it, we are left with other fraud detection methods that are more time-consuming and sometimes more invasive to discover the fraud. It should be noted that many times tips and complaints are false. At least one highly recognizable organization was noted as closing down their fraud hotline because most calls were bogus and the tips were made for purely vindictive reasons—to try to get an innocent person in trouble.

Another concern is that employees who suspect someone of doing something wrong or observe suspicious activity may not report it for fear of inappropriately getting someone in trouble. Knowing for certain is almost an impossible standard, and in some cases the suspicious employee is fearful of being labeled a tattletale. The person may even be fearful of the suspected perpetrator. For these reasons, some employees who know that something is going on do not come forward. The main lesson for companies is to make reporting suspected fraud easy and potentially anonymous.

The whistleblower needs to be able to feel safe and secure while providing the organization with the needed information. One alternative is a tip or fraud hotline. This approach is much more likely to be successful if an employee feels that the overall environment is one in which fraud and unethical behavior are frowned upon. The employee should always feel that going to a supervisor or manager is an option, but sometimes hotlines are the best alternative. The key to successful tip hotlines is to ensure that the tipster leaves enough detail so that the anomalous situation may be followed up on. In this regard, some hotlines are managed by third parties. This helps employees feel secure in their anonymity and allows the third party, through an interview-style inquiry, to ensure that all the necessary details have been gathered.

Behavioral Red Flags

Behavioral anomalies are exhibited in lifestyles and unusual behaviors. As suggested by the fraud triangle, many people who commit fraud do so first as a result of pressure. Beyond pressure, they then evaluate the perceived opportunity for success followed by a necessity to rationalize their actions. For many, pressure comes in the form of money or greed. They live a lifestyle beyond what their resources obtained through legal methods can achieve or have found themselves in a precarious financial condition due to living beyond their means in prior periods.

Lifestyle symptoms can be observed as cars, homes, boats, jewelry, clothing, and other material possessions an employee could not or should not be able to afford. As noted above, few perpetrators save what they steal; most spend their ill-gotten gains almost immediately. This psychological observation makes sense: those who can delay the gratification associated with their purchases need not steal because they can wait. Assuming that managers, employees, and co-workers pay attention, lifestyle red flags are relatively easy to observe. Just as easily, fraudsters often have a quick explanation: a recent inheritance,

winning the lottery, a promotion by a spouse, and so forth. Once identified these explanations are easily eliminated.

A second nonaccounting red flag revolves around unusual behaviors. Fear of getting caught and the ramifications associated with that can cause the person to act differently. The underlying cause may be guilt or fear, but either way, stress is created. That stress then causes changes in the person's behavior. Such changes include insomnia, alcohol abuse, drug abuse, irritability, paranoia, inability to relax, inability to look people in the eye, signs of embarrassment, defensiveness, argumentativeness, belligerence, confession to a trusted confidant, attributing failure to others (scapegoats), excessive smoking or starting smoking, and other anxiety-based symptoms.[6] These symptoms are similar to those that appear when a person or loved one suffers from a health or job-related crisis, for example. Unless the person is willing to talk, it can be difficult to discover a fraud from these clues alone. Still, when combined with other red flags, this can be one more piece of evidence to track down what is going on and who might be associated with the fraudulent activity.

Analytical Anomalies

Analytical anomalies are transaction or financial statement relationships that do not make sense. For example, one may notice transactions that are too small or too large when compared to normal activity; it's often about patterns and breaks in patterns. Some analytical anomalies include:

Unusual items

Missing items

Larger than usual items

No pattern when you would expect one

A break in a pattern that is unexpected

Round, even transaction amounts

Cash transactions instead of payments by check

Large consistent transactions

Unusual timing of transactions

Unexpected transaction recipients or beneficiaries

Unexplained cash shortages

Unexplained inventory shortages

Deviations from specifications

Increased scrap

Excessive purchases

Too many debit memos

Too many credit memos

Significant unexpected changes in account balances

Excessive late charges

Unreasonable expenses

Unusual expense reimbursements

Anomalies may also include strange relationships:

Revenues increasing	But inventory decreasing
	But accounts receivable decreasing
	But decreasing cash flows from operations
Inventory increasing	But accounts payable decreasing
	But decreasing warehouse costs
Increased volume	But increased cost per unit
	But decreased scrap[7]

These analytical anomalies are common in any organization, including those in which fraud is not present. Nevertheless, these preliminary symptoms of fraud should not be ignored and should be diligently pursued until fraud is discovered or a conclusion of no fraud is warranted.

Accounting Anomalies

Accounting anomalies are unusual activities that seem to violate normal expectations for the accounting system. For example, a fraud examiner may notice transactions being recorded in odd ways or at odd times during the month. In some cases, a transaction may be recorded by a person not expected to record such a transaction. For instance, the Chief Financial Officer may be logged as posting routine journal entries to Property, Plant, and Equipment accounts on a Sunday evening when these transactions are normally recorded by a clerical employee during regular business hours.

In some cases, irregularities in documentation may be observed. Some of these include:

- Missing documents
- Old items being carried on bank and other account reconciliations from one period to the next period
- Excessive voids or credit memos
- Common names, addresses, or phone numbers of payees or customers
- Names, addresses, or phone numbers that are the same as those of employees
- Increases in past due accounts receivables
- Increases in the number and amount of reconciling items
- Alterations on documents
- Duplicate payments
- Second endorsements on checks
- Breaks in check, invoice, purchase order, and other document number sequences
- Questionable handwriting
- Photocopied documents[8]

Irregular or undocumented journal entries are another accounting anomaly that may be observed. Also, unusual entries that reduce a liability while simultaneously increasing a revenue account are red flags that should be investigated. Journal entries may be a method fraudsters use to effect management override; unusual or problematic journal entries should be closely scrutinized. This includes journal entries with little, incomplete, or missing backup. Journal entries of concern are those by members of senior management as well as journal entries recorded by a person who does not have the required authority or entries for which expected approvals are missing. The following are some basic journal entry techniques for "cooking the books."

Journal Entry Example 1–Consider the following set of journal entries to record fraudulent revenues:

Fixed Asset	$350,000	
Cash		$350,000

This journal entry, although completely bogus, appears to be a normal acquisition of property, plant, and equipment.

Accounts Receivable	$350,000	
Sales		$350,000

The second journal entry, also bogus, looks like a normal sales transaction on credit.

Cash	$350,000	
Accounts Receivable		$350,000

This third bogus journal entry looks like a normal cash collection of accounts receivable.

Because all three journal entries are completely fictitious, let's see what's left:

Fixed Asset		$350,000
~~Cash~~		~~$350,000~~
~~Accounts Receivable~~		~~$350,000~~
Sales		$350,000
~~Cash~~		~~$350,000~~
~~Accounts Receivable~~		~~$350,000~~

The bottom line here is that through a series of seemingly reasonable, yet bogus, journal entries, fictitious sales have been recorded through the fictitious acquisition of property, plant, and equipment. The problem is that sales are not normally recorded through journal entry, unless it is a typical month-end accrual entry. Further, none of the journal entries would have proper documentation or backup. In addition, the bogus journal entries are likely to be recorded by someone who normally does not post journal entries to the general ledger.

Journal Entry Example 2—Consider the following timing difference:

Year 1—A contract is awarded

Cash	$500,000	
Sales		$500,000

In year 1, a company is paid $500,000 for work completed on a contract near year end. The journal entry to record the sale is consistent with generally accepted accounting principles, however, also in year 1, the company incurred expenses of $350,000 to fulfill the contract. Those expenses were paid in cash (via check) in year 2 and no accrual was recorded in year 1.

Year 2—Recognize expenses related to Year 1 contract

Operating Expense	$350,000	
Cash		$350,000

Year 2—Awarded new contract

Cash	$750,000	
Sales		$750,000

In year 2, the year 1 expenses are recorded. In addition, the company obtains and completes a new contract in year 2 but does not accrue any of the $450,000 of related expenses. The overall result of these three transactions is that year 1 income has been overstated by $350,000 and year 2 income has been understated by the same amount. Further, year 2 income has been overstated by the failure to accrue year 2 expenses of $450,000. Thus, in the net effect on year 2 is an overstatement of income in the amount of $100,000. In this case, all of the transactions have proper documentation but the expense transactions have been recorded in the wrong period, resulting in overstated income in years 1 and 2.

Journal Entry Example 3—Consider the following concealed liabilities and operating expenses:

Year 1—The proper accounting is to accrue normal period-end expenses

Operating Expense	$500,000	
Accounts Payable		$500,000

Year 1—However, no journal entry was made to accrue year 1 expenses

The net effect here is an overstatement of year 1 income of $500,000 and an understatement of income in year 2 by the same amount.

Journal Entry Example 4—Finally, consider the following attempt to treat operating expenses as capitalized property, plant, and equipment:

Year 1—The proper accounting is to accrue period-end expenses
Operating Expense	$500,000	
Accounts Payable		$500,000

Year 1—Instead of accruing the amount to expense, the amount was capitalized as a fixed asset
Fixed Assets	$500,000	
Accounts Payable		$500,000

The net effect in Example 4 is an overstatement of year 1 income of $500,000 and an understatement of income in future years as the fixed asset is depreciated.

In years gone by, it was possible for the general ledger not to balance, meaning that debits did not equal credits, and assets did not equal liabilities plus stockholders equity. In this day and age, most computerized accounting packages prevent one-sided and unbalanced journal entries from being recorded; however, professional skepticism requires the fraud examiner to test this assumption for veracity. Further, unbalanced entries are a real possibility in manual accounting systems and those maintained in spreadsheet software such as Excel. In electronic accounting software packages, it is far more likely that the general ledger subsidiary ledgers and other supporting documentation do not agree with or reconcile to the total reflected on the general ledger (and in the financial statements).

This is because many assume that most of a company's information systems feed directly into the general ledger and other aspects of the accounting system, but that is often not the case. It is common that payroll systems, marketing systems, inventory records, and accounts receivable details are independent of the main accounting system. As such, it is important to examine the underlying supporting details to ensure that the amounts agree with or reconcile to the general ledger totals. In addition, tests of the details need to be performed. This may include observation of physical inventory counts; confirmations with banks, customers, suppliers, and vendors; and other methods to verify that the supporting detail records are accurate and supported. Third-party independent verification is one of the best pieces of evidence unless persons in the third-party company are colluding with individuals in the organization under study.

Internal Control Irregularities and Weaknesses

The internal controls necessary to safeguard the assets and maintain the integrity of the financial reporting processes are beyond the scope of this text. Most companies of reasonable size often have several accounting information modules (possibly independent systems), including the following:

- Sales and accounts receivable collections
- Personnel and payroll
- Procurement (acquisition), accounts payable, and disbursements
- Inventory, warehousing, and distribution
- Capital acquisition, maintenance, retention (including depreciation), and payment
- Cash accounting and control

Additional controls are also required for prepaid assets; intellectual property; the acquisition, maintenance, and payment of short-term and long-term debt obligations; as well as others. Each of these processes, from the inception of any transaction through transaction completion and its proper reflection in the audited financial statements, has many steps, and each step has controls in place to ensure that the transaction (underlying activity) exists, is complete (detailed supporting documentation), accurate (properly valued), classified properly, recorded in the proper period, and posted and summarized properly in the financial statements (these are otherwise known as management's assertions concerning the attributes of amounts presented in the financial statements).

These controls not only safeguard the assets and facilitate accurate financial reporting, but are also integral to running an effective and efficient operation. They ensure that (1) customers receive high-quality goods and services; and (2) vendors, suppliers, and employees are paid accurately and on time. The Sarbanes–Oxley Act of 2002, particularly section 404, puts considerable emphasis on the system of internal

controls. Management is responsible for the system of internal controls, including their design, implementation, and maintenance. Auditors then must test management's assertions concerning the existence and operational effectiveness of that system of internal controls.

The normal internal control environment is expected to have several control activities, including:

1. Adequate separation of duties
2. Proper authorization of transactions and activities
3. Adequate documents and records
4. Physical control over assets and records
5. Independent checks on performance

While these characteristics are commonly presented in auditing texts and the auditing literature, from a fraud perspective, internal controls have at least three different objectives. The first line of defense related to internal controls is to prevent fraud. *Fraud prevention* refers to creating and maintaining an environment in which fraudulent activities are improbable or reduced to an acceptable level of risk of fraud and/or illegal activity. Along a similar vein, *fraud deterrence* involves creating an environment in which fraud is less likely to occur (e.g., by encouraging whistle blowing through hotlines).

Fraud deterrence creates an environment in which organizational stakeholders are discouraged from committing fraud. This is usually accomplished through a variety of efforts associated with internal controls and ethics programs that create a workplace of integrity, as well as by encouraging employees to report potential wrongdoing and promoting any actions that increase the perceived likelihood that an act of fraud will be detected and reported. Fraud deterrence can also be achieved through the use of continuous monitoring and auditing software tools. It is enhanced when potential perpetrators recognize that they will be punished when caught. *Fraud detection* is the process of discovering the presence or existence of fraud. Most often, this can be accomplished through the use of well-designed internal controls, supervision, monitoring, and the active search for evidence of potential fraud (e.g., fraud auditing).

Some internal controls are meant to prevent fraud, and this aspect is often the main focus that accountants place on internal controls and the main focus of items one through four above. Nevertheless, the second important goal of internal controls is also fraud deterrence. Creating the perception of detection, whether real or perceived, is an important goal of internal controls. In fact, this is critical given that the number of controls required to prevent every type of fraud would cost far more than the benefits achieved.

Finally, internal controls also need to be focused on fraud detection. This is the central goal of internal control area five, independent checks on performance. These independent checks, even if on a periodic or somewhat random basis, are designed, not to prevent fraud, but to deter or detect fraud. Thus, the fraud audit professional needs to not only consider and document those controls related to the prevention of fraud, but also those controls that increase the perception of detection and thus act as deterrents. Because independent checks are often periodic or random, it is precisely those checks that may not be operational, even though they have been designed and documented.

For example, let's consider the fraudster who cooked the accounts receivables, not directly to take the money but to keep his job. Because he was dedicated to his job and the organization, he not only cooked the accounts receivables in advance of credit meetings with the CEO, sales manager, and controller; he also attempted to reset the accounts receivable after each meeting to their original condition. Essentially, he hoped to find the time to make collection calls and get the accounts receivable details straightened out. To facilitate his efforts—prior to the weekly credit meeting—he "adjusted" the accounts receivable details using credit memos. And after the meeting, he restored the accounts receivable amounts by reversing the credit memos with debit memos. The pattern was clear and distinct.

The shortcoming in the company's internal control structure was that all accounts receivable debit and credit memos required supervisory approval. In fact, legitimate credit memos had been written up for management approval and had the appropriate sign-offs; however, the weekly credit meeting "adjustments" were not approved or signed-off. The internal control procedure to act as an independent check was in fact properly designed. The controller or CFO was supposed to review the accounts receivable system to ensure that all debit and credit memos were approved. Although part of the internal controls design for 3 1/2 years, the procedure had not been operationalized. This lack of independent check cost the company approximately $1 million in accounts receivable write-offs. The moral of the story is that fraud examiners need to pay as much attention to internal controls that act as independent checks as they do to those designed to prevent fraud.

Fraud examiners must document the system of internal controls to the level of detail necessary to complete their work. Assuming that the fraud examiner is using a targeted, red flag, scheme-oriented approach or a targeted, risk assessment, scheme-oriented approach, the documentation of the system of internal controls in and around the area of investigation is an integral step in fraud detection. The fraud examiner is looking for weaknesses in the design or deficiencies in the operations of the internal control system. This anti-fraud professional will also need to be aware of the possibilities of management override and/or collusion. Internal controls cannot prevent management override or collusion, but a properly designed system of internal controls should include detection controls that alert the proper individuals when anomalous situations occur.

Some typical internal control weaknesses include:

- Lack of segregation of duties
- Lack of physical safeguards
- Lack of independent checks
- Lack of proper authorization
- Lack of proper documentation and other records
- Override of existing internal controls
- Inadequate accounting system
- Inadequate employee education (expectations)
- Reactive fraud detection approach
- Inadequate surprise audits
- Inadequate whistleblower opportunities and protection[9]

The Power of Nonfinancial Numbers

Fraud examiners need to use not only data generated from the financial accounting systems, but also data from surrounding operational systems. The Internal Revenue Service's Fuels Excise Specialists will tell you that they spend as much time auditing the inventory, chemical processing, and distribution data as they do investigating the data generated from the subject organization's accounting system because fuels involve precise chemistry.

Thus, the managers working with the fuels cannot afford to have their nonfinancial systems corrupted with fraudulent data because of the effect on the quality of the product and the impact on end users (i.e., customers). The power of using nonfinancial data to corroborate financial information cannot be understated. Other examples of nonfinancial performance data may include:

Laundromat electricity usage

Laundromat cycle time

Gas produced

Tons of minerals mined (raw and processed)

Beer purchase quantities

Employee time records

Delivery records

Attorney hours charged

Travel (number of trips and average cost per trip)

The foundation behind the use of nonfinancial information is that the world revolves around quantities and prices. By breaking down the sum totals for a series of transactions into prices and quantities, a fraud examiner now has two additional pieces of data to evaluate. First, he or she can analyze the quantity. Does the total quantity make sense? How does it compare to other periods, divisions, the nonfinancial system's data, and so forth? How does it compare to prior periods? How does it compare to total capacity for the company under study? Similarly, the price per unit can be examined for reasonableness. Does the average price per unit make sense? How does the price compare to the average market price for the period and to other companies in the industry? How does the price compare to prior periods? How does the average price compare to published price lists for the company under study?

The nonfinancial data is then used to correlate with or reconcile to the numbers represented in financial statements and tax returns. Generally, any data generated outside of the financial accounting system will serve as a starting point for analysis. This does not mean that this data is never tainted, but if it is also impacted by the fraud, then the number of persons involved expands. The theory is that the nonfinancial data is generally not corrupted because companies always want to maximize operational performance. As such, operational managers need accurate and timely data in order to manage their portion of the business. If nonfinancial data cannot be reconciled to the related data in the financial systems, or the data is not correlated, additional examination is warranted.

Using Red Flags as a Basis for Further Investigation

It is impossible to completely list all of the red flags that may be observed when trying to detect fraud. Each fraud will have some unique attributes, and thus the related red flags will also be somewhat unique. Therefore, when considering red flags, it is important to think about the red flag in the context of the circumstances. Why does the transaction or transactions seem important? What causes this transaction or series of transactions to seem unusual or irregular? How does this red flag track into the company's control environment? Does the red flag fit a known fraud scheme, given the organization, its industry, its competition, and the current business environment? Finally, it is important to use evidence-based decision making to draw a conclusion that fraud is likely, or that this anomaly has another reasonable explanation. It is important to use evidence to see if you can develop other reasons for the suspicious activity.

In relation to observed red flags, the fraud examiner should consider possible motivations of specific individuals who might be involved. Each of the following should be documented:

The Elements of Fraud:

- Are cash or other assets missing (i.e., has a fraud act or financial crime possibly been committed)?
- What are the concealment possibilities?
- What are the conversion possibilities and have any conversion symptoms (e.g., lifestyle anomalies) been observed?

The Fraud Triangle:

- Which individuals have opportunity?
  - What are the key internal controls in this area?
  - Are key internal controls deficient or have they been violated?
- Have any individuals demonstrated signs of pressure?
- What potential rationalizations might be offered and is there any evidence of rationalization by particular individuals?

M.I.C.E.

- What might motivate the fraudster (money, ideology, coercion, or ego)?

Other Considerations:

- What are the most promising investigative techniques?
- What methods and approaches will most likely result in a successful investigation?
- Have any other related symptoms been observed?

TARGETED FRAUD RISK ASSESSMENT

Targeted fraud risk assessment starts with a foundation of solid knowledge, skills, and abilities in the areas of fraud detection and investigation. Further, the anti-fraud professional or forensic accountant must have a thorough knowledge of the various types of schemes used to perpetrate asset misappropriation, financial statement fraud, corruption activities, and financial crimes such as money laundering. They should be able to answer some basic questions, such as:

How is the scheme perpetrated?

Where would I find the fraud or where might it be located?

What attributes are involved in the act?

How would the act be concealed?

What symptoms (red flags) would be generated if the scheme were perpetrated?

How might the scheme be detected?

What controls need to be in place to prevent this particular scheme?

What controls might deter a fraudster due to increased perception of detection?

What controls would lead to detection of this scheme?

Are those controls in place?

Which employees, third parties, or management are likely to be involved, and could it be collusive?

By understanding the types of attributes of possible schemes, the fraud examiner is armed with a foundation upon which he or she can develop a targeted fraud risk assessment. When evaluating an organization, its industry, its key competition, its management structure, and its control environment for certain schemes, some will be more likely to show up than others. As noted in the red flag discussion, a typical audit of a large company may generate hundreds of red flags. What should an auditor do to address them? Using a targeted fraud risk assessment approach, some red flags (symptoms of fraud) are much more significant than others, and as such should be given more attention.

Likewise, clusters of red flags become valuable in the sense that where there is smoke, there is (usually) fire; therefore, where there is a lot of smoke, the likelihood of fire increases dramatically. Similarly, if there is a cluster of red flags, it increases the likelihood of a particular scheme's existence.

Also integral to the targeted fraud risk assessment methodology are a few overarching questions:

What is the likelihood of fraud occurring in this organization without consideration of controls?

What types of frauds would likely occur in this organization?

What types of frauds are likely to occur without consideration of the controls?

What types of frauds might be effective?

How large could the fraud be?

Would the fraud be large enough to generate the financial impact that allows the fraudster to achieve his or her goals?

By what process could the fraud be perpetrated without consideration of controls?

How strong is the anti-fraud control environment?

How well do the control systems appear to be working in the areas where the fraud would be perpetrated (including prevention, deterrence, and detection controls)?

Table 7-1 lists examples of recent fraud schemes. The fraud examiner categorizes schemes in three ways:

Category 1—Wrongdoing perpetrated *by an insider acting alone* with the principal *benefit to the individual* (examples include simple, one-person, garden-variety embezzlement schemes)

Category 2—Wrongdoing perpetrated by *more than one individual acting collusively* (possibly with individuals outside the company) with the principal *benefit to the individual perpetrators or the organization* (examples include sophisticated asset misappropriation, corruption, and/or financial statement fraud)

Category 3—Wrongdoing perpetrated *by an outside third party* against the organization with the principal *benefit to the third party* (examples include the sales of inferior goods that do not meet contract specifications)

Thus, the fraud examiner has a specific assessment of which accounts are most susceptible to manipulation, the likelihood of manipulation (remote, reasonably possible, or probable), and the magnitude of the likely scheme (inconsequential, more than inconsequential, or material), paying particular attention to accounts with high inherent risk (e.g., reserves, allowances, permanent impairments, etc.) and high control risk accounts. For example, in the area of revenues some of the preliminary questions might include the following:

- How would a person(s) perpetrate an over- or understatement of revenues?
- Who would be involved?

TABLE 7-1 Examples of Recent Fraud Schemes

• Vendor Allowance Manipulations	• Improper Asset Valuations
• Improper Bill and Holds	• Holding Periods Open
• Roundtrip Transactions	• Phony "Investment Deals"
• "Refreshed" Receivables	• Subscriber Count/Circulation Frauds
• "Off-Site" or Fake Inventory	• Provider Reimbursements
• Undocumented Rights of Return	• I/C Manipulations Affecting Other Accts
• Adjustments to Estimations	• Bribery, Corruption, and Kickbacks
• Quid-Pro-Quo Arrangements	• Agreements to "Sell Through" Product
• Phony Shipping Documentation	• Money Laundering
• Moving Inventory Between Locations	• Contributions
• Related Parties That "Create" Transactions	• Fraudulent Audit Confirmations
• Splitting of Multiple-Element Deals	• Early Rebates
• Unjustified Consolidation Entries	• Off-Balance Sheet Liabilities
• Adding Back O/S Checks to Cash	• Improper Capitalization of Expenses

- Would it be collusive between customers and sales and marketing?
- Which accounts would be affected?
- When would the scheme be perpetrated?
- Which quarter of the year is most at risk?
- Which financial statement assertions are at risk?

Targeted fraud risk assessment is consistent with the PCAOB's Auditing Standard No. 5 (AS5) that requires a top-down approach. First, the fraud examiner assesses fraud risk factors such as industry, competition, historical performance, management philosophy, and possible pressure concerns as well as geographic considerations. Then, the fraud examiner determines the fraud risks: which accounts would likely be utilized (revenue, expenses, liabilities, assets)? And further, which schemes could be used to perpetrate a fraud, including those who might be involved in the scheme?

The targeted fraud risk assessment approach assumes that there should be a direct relationship between the level of risk associated with a material weakness in a company's controls and the amount of attention devoted to that area during an audit. Further, an account can be significant based on the assessment of the risk that the account could contain misstatements that individually, or when aggregated with others, could have a material impact on the financial statements.

An overview of the fraud risk assessment process includes the following components:

- Evaluate the fraud risk factors
  - Identify, understand, and evaluate the company's operating environment, cultural tone, location, and existing pressures.
  - Identify which accounts might be used to perpetrate the frauds.
  - Identify relevant business processes, process owners, and related financial statement accounts.
  - Identify fraud risks for nonsignificant entities.

- Identify possible fraud schemes and scenarios
  - Brainstorm.
  - Identify how fraud may occur in each process by location.
  - Identify the parties who have the ability to commit a potential fraud.

- Prioritize individual fraud risks
  - Evaluate the likelihood, without consideration of controls, that each of the identified frauds could occur and the potential significance (in dollars) associated with the fraud risk.
  - Label the schemes by type of risk.
  - Identify the pervasiveness of the risk.

- Evaluate mitigating controls for those fraud schemes that are reasonably possible or probable and are more than inconsequential or material

  - Determine the level of mitigation to prevent, detect, and deter fraud.
  - Investigate the characteristics of potential fraud manifestations within each process identified.
  - Quantify and remediate fraud risk.

The following ten-step approach implements the targeted fraud risk assessment:

Step 1. Identify, understand, and evaluate the company's operating environment and the pressures that exist.

Step 2. Identify the business processes and consider differences in those processes in foreign operations, as well as between subsidiaries and decentralized divisions.

Step 3. Identify the "process owner" for each of the identified significant processes.

Step 4. Review past fraud experience within the company for the process being evaluated.

Step 5. Identify how fraud may occur in each process and at each location using fraud brainstorming techniques.

Step 6. Identify the parties who have the ability to commit the potential fraud.

Step 7. Evaluate the likelihood that each of the identified frauds could occur and be significant as well as the persuasiveness of the potential fraud without consideration of controls.

Step 8. Consider the likely methodology to commit and conceal the fraud to determine the level of mitigation to prevent, detect, and deter the fraud. The result is a determination of the existence of "Residual Fraud Risk."

Step 9. Investigate the characteristics of potential fraud manifestations within each process identified in which "Residual Fraud Risk" exists.

Step 10. Remediate fraud risk schemes by designing control activities to mitigate the unmitigated fraud scheme risk.

Step 1 evaluates the economic, operating, and competitive environment as well as the overall control environment. *Step 2* includes the identification of key business processes including sales, accounts receivable collections, personnel, payroll, procurement (acquisition), accounts payable, cash disbursements, inventory, warehousing, distribution, capital asset acquisition (including maintenance and depreciation) and cash accounting and control, licensing, intellectual property, investing, information and technology, marketing, and research and development. Step 2 also requires the fraud examiner to consider differences in the processes identified between local and foreign operations, as well as among subsidiaries or decentralized divisions. Some of the considerations include legal requirements across the various jurisdictions, cultural differences, staffing (expertise, experience, training, duration with the organization, etc.), processes for the approval of independent agents and contractors, the competency of management and supervisors, and the function of the operation within the organization.

To complete *Step 3*, the fraud examiner must identify the "process owner" for each of the identified processes within each major jurisdiction and/or operation. The process owner may be a senior level executive, subsidiary president, regional president, vice president, manager, or supervisor. The process owner is that individual who has the day-to-day authority and ability to alter standard operating procedures (management override) in order to accomplish the goals and objectives of the organization. Of course, being in a position to override normal operating procedures also places that person in a position in which he or she can alter those same procedures for personal benefit.

Step 4 requires an assessment of the organization's history with respect to fraud as well as experiences at lower levels of the organization and by process, geographic locale, and within specific jurisdictions. The fraud examiner needs to ask the following questions:

- What types of fraud have occurred in the past?
- Where (geographically and in which accounts) did the fraud occur?
- Where within the organizational structure did the fraud occur?
- Who committed the fraud?
- How was the fraud perpetrated?

- How could the fraud have been prevented?
- How could the fraud have been detected earlier?
- What may have deterred the commission of the fraud?

Step 5 investigates potential responses to the question, what could go wrong? This step requires process owners and their sub-process owners, in conjunction with the fraud examiner, to identify how fraud may occur in the respective process at each location using brainstorming techniques. The brainstorming process should focus on fraud risk factors by process, locale, and jurisdiction. Also, consideration should be given to fraud risks and fraud schemes that could be perpetrated and would be likely (probable) and significant (of large financial magnitude). Participants in the brainstorming process should identify control activities that would mitigate the identified fraud schemes, but only after the schemes have been identified and their likelihood and significance have been determined.

Only those schemes that are significant and likely should be evaluated to determine whether they are mitigated by control activities. Fraud risk assessment, after considering mitigating controls to prevent, deter, and detect fraud, leaves a remainder: residual fraud risk. Residual fraud risk includes those fraud schemes that are not adequately mitigated by control activities and, as such, require a fraud audit response. In that context, management override and collusion are only subject to fraud detection; in general, they cannot be prevented. Thus, the risk of management override and collusion are always residual fraud risks and require a specific audit response if detection control activities do not exist.

In *Step 6*, the identified parties who have the ability to commit the potential fraud need to be examined more closely. At this point, the fraud examiner needs to consider the elements of the fraud triangle: pressure, opportunity, and rationalization. Further, the fraud examiner needs to specifically consider the three categories of fraud discussed above. Individuals who are in a position to commit asset misappropriation, corruption, and financial statement fraud may include process owners, employees, agents (particularly in foreign countries), independent contractors, competitors, customers, vendors, and licensees.

During *Step 7*, process owners and the fraud examiner use the following descriptions to evaluate the likelihood that each of the identified frauds could occur: remote, reasonably possible, and probable. For each potential fraud, the following questions should be considered:

- What is the likelihood that this fraud will occur and be significant?
- How could this fraud manifest itself and where (which account and which process)?
- What would the fraud look like and where would it be found?
- What is the likelihood that the fraud will be perpetrated by an individual as compared to two or more individuals acting collusively?

Management should address those fraud risks that have more than a remote likelihood of having more than an inconsequential effect on the company's financial statements. The auditor should evaluate all controls specifically intended to address the risks of fraud that have at least a reasonably possible likelihood of having a material effect on the company's financial statements. The fraud examiner needs to make an assessment based on the scope of the engagement.

Step 8 requires the determination of the level of mitigation to prevent, detect, and deter each fraud scheme deemed significant and likely.

- Are entity level controls in place and operational?

  - How effectively is the anti-fraud message communicated throughout the organization?
  - Are there effective fraud awareness training programs?
  - Does the organization complete an effective fraud risk assessment?
  - Does the organization have effective ethics training and programs?
  - What ethics and core values seem to exist within the organization?
  - Do employees embrace the ethics and core values?
  - Does the organization have an effective "fraud hotline" and a reliable whistleblower protection policy?
  - Are allegations of fraud and wrongdoing investigated completely and in a timely fashion?

- What control activities are in place?

auditors often report directly to senior management with authority over a particular operation. Such reporting authority allows the internal auditor to be a mechanism for operational change.

On the other hand, in the financial reporting processes, including the evaluation of internal controls, such a reporting structure reduces the ability of the internal audit to offer criticisms or make recommendations due to the reporting lines that are established. Thus, for internal auditors to be objective and unbiased in assessing financial-reporting processes and evaluating the design and implementation of internal controls, they need to have a direct reporting line to the organization's audit committee. In fact, internal auditors are no longer allowed to complete any work for the external auditor unless their reporting structure is such that they report to the audit committee. In such circumstances, internal audit has the authority and independence necessary to carry out their assigned duties. The NYSE requires that all listed companies have an audit committee, and that the internal audit function report directly to them. NASDAQ also has a similar requirement.

The Institute of Internal Auditors (IIA) has few standards on fraud and those are vague concerning the specific responsibilities that internal auditors may have. Statement on Internal Auditing Standards (SIAS) No. 3 indicates that internal auditors have responsibility for fraud deterrence and should examine and evaluate the adequacy and effectiveness of the system of internal controls, commensurate with the extent of potential exposure or risk in the various segments of the organization's operations. During the detection phase of their work, internal auditors should identify conditions, red flags, and other symptoms that may be indicative of fraud. In addition, internal auditors need to be cognizant of the opportunities to perpetrate fraud, such as a lack of internal controls or the failure to observe them.

Upon discovering fraud, internal auditors have an obligation to notify management or the board when the incidence of significant fraud has been established to a reasonable degree of certainty. If the results of a fraud investigation indicate that previously undiscovered fraud materially and adversely affected previous financial statements for one or more periods, the internal auditor should inform management and the audit committee of the board of directors. A written report should include all findings, conclusions, recommendations, and corrective actions taken. Finally, a draft of the written report should be submitted to legal counsel for review, especially where the internal auditor chooses to invoke client privilege. On November 12, 2007, the IIA in conjunction with the AICPA and the ACFE issued an exposure draft titled "Managing the Business Risk of Fraud: A Practical Guide."

FRAUD DETECTION

> *A major difference between auditors and fraud examiners is that most auditors merely match documents to numbers to see whether support exists and is adequate. Fraud examiners and forensic accountants who detect fraud go beyond ascertaining the mere existence of documents. They determine whether the documents are real or fraudulent, whether the expenditures make sense and whether all aspects of the documentation are in order.[4]*

Fraud detection is challenging to say the least. At a minimum, the perpetrator has attempted to conceal the activity (the act) from those around him or her. Further, financial statement fraud is generally achieved through management override and collusion, which makes it even harder to detect. In most cases, asset misappropriation, corruption, and financial statement fraud last about twenty-four months from inception to conclusion. At some level, this observation reflects the nature of the average fraud and the average fraudster. Fraud perpetrators tend to be people who never stop.

In short, it's hard to be dishonest the first time; but once the fraudster crosses the line, he or she may never stop until caught. In addition, fraud perpetrators almost never save their stolen goods. This creates a necessity to continue perpetrating the fraud. Furthermore, fraudsters tend to get greedier and sloppier over time. Often, it is the sheer size of the fraud that ultimately takes the fraudster's proverbial "house of cards" down.

By the very title of this topic, "fraud detection," a fraud has already been perpetrated and is possibly ongoing. Thus, the internal control environment has either been violated or circumvented through collusion or management override. Thus, the internal control fabric of the organization has been compromised. Effective fraud detection is an attempt to identify the fraud as early as possible, in contrast to the optimal situation in which fraud is prevented or deterred.

The key to detecting fraud is to know where and under what circumstances to look. A targeted approach is necessary to improve the probability of discovering that a fraud has occurred or is occurring at the earliest possible moment. This makes sense since the average audit generates a large number of

red flags. Anomalies are part of the day-to-day operations of most organizations and are often observed by auditors. As such, anomalous transactions and activities generate anomalies in the underlying financial records and possibly the financial statements if the amount rises to the level of materiality.

The starting point for the anti-fraud professional or forensic accountant is an attitude of professional skepticism. Although outlined in auditing standards related to the traditional audit, such an approach applies to fraud and forensic accounting engagements as well. SAS No. 99 suggests that auditors approach audit engagements with an enhanced sense of professional skepticism.

Generally, enhanced skepticism has three defining elements. First, professional skepticism includes *recognition* that fraud may be present. Second, professional skepticism exemplifies itself in an auditors' *attitude*, an attitude that includes a questioning mind and a critical assessment of audit evidence. Thus, auditors need to be alert for red flags and other symptoms of fraud and "pull on those threads" to see if fraud may in fact be ongoing within an organization. Third, professional skepticism asks auditors to make a *commitment to persuasive evidence* to determine whether or not fraud is present. Auditors are expected to "go that extra mile" using evidence-based decision-making.

In addition, fraud detection techniques require that fraud and forensic accounting professionals pay particular attention to the possibility of concealment. It suggests deception, which comes in many forms: falsified, counterfeit, and altered documents; inappropriate general ledger activity; unauthorized journal entries (possibly without documentation and backup) and reconciling items that are false (do not have backup and supporting documentation or the backup and support is fraudulent); and tax returns that do not reconcile to the GAAP-based books and records.

Notwithstanding the above, there are two major approaches to fraud detection. The first is to detect fraud through the identification of red flags, anomalies that ultimately point to problems underlying the foundations upon which transactions have been recorded or a financial statement has been based. The second is to detect fraud through a targeted risk assessment. Both of these approaches are interrelated and both rely on a thorough understanding of the types of schemes (fraud schemes and financial crimes) that might be perpetrated.

In fact, throughout the major scheme-based chapters of this text, not only are the schemes outlined, but also the red flags are presented. Further, the steps necessary to prevent and detect the schemes are also identified. All of this information is necessary to give anti-fraud professionals and forensic accountants the knowledge, skills, and abilities necessary to successfully detect fraud early in the process. Because red flags are so prevalent and many times represent "false positives," it is only a targeted approach that considers the risk of fraud, likely fraud schemes, and the expected symptoms that will prove to be successful for anti-fraud professionals.

Fraud detection is the first sign or symptom that a fraud has occurred. It is the process of discovering the presence or existence of fraud. Fraud detection can be accomplished through the use of well-designed internal controls, supervision, and monitoring, as well as the active search for evidence of potential fraud (fraud auditing and related follow-through). However, the results of fraud detection are only symptoms and are not conclusive proof of fraud. Furthermore, the first signs of fraud often do not meet the threshold necessary for predication (the totality of circumstances that would lead a reasonable, professionally trained, and prudent individual to believe a fraud has occurred or is occurring).

Thus, more work needs to be done to ensure that other explanations—nonnefarious explanations—are not at the root of this particular symptom. With fraud detection, we continue to investigate until the anti-fraud professional believes that the predication threshold has been met. Fraud detection may be proactive fraud auditing, results of data interrogation based on predetermined parameters, or it may be a reaction to an anomaly found by the internal control system that requires additional explanation. In short, fraud detection is the first of several steps toward concluding that predication has been met but it is far from providing the evidence that will be needed to convince a jury that an actual fraud has occurred. That said, it is important to use a targeted approach when attempting to detect fraud to minimize the effort associated with false (fraud detection) positives.

Understanding the Business

The first step to detecting fraud is to build an understanding of the organization and the environment in which it operates. As a starting point, the performance of the overall economy and its effect on the industry and organization should be undertaken. Is the economy growing, stagnant, or shrinking, and what effect, if any, does the economy have on the particular industry and organization? For example, during the recession of the early 1980s, the overall economy had little noticeable effect on the fast-growing technology industry

TABLE 7-2 *(continued)*

Fraud Risk	Revenue—"Roundtrip" Transactions—Inflating revenues	Revenue—Bill and Holds
Likelihood	Probable in China; reasonably possible in the United States	Remote in both China and the United States
Pervasiveness	Risk is related to revenue, sales returns and allowances, and A/R accounts	Risk is related to revenue, sales returns and allowances, and A/R accounts

Step 8. Consider the likely methodology to commit and conceal the fraud to determine the level of mitigation so as to prevent, detect, and deter the fraud. The result is a determination of the existence of "Residual Fraud Risk."

Mitigating Control Activities	• Regular review of all sales contracts, with a focus on unusual terms and conditions for return policies, and a comparison to actual practice • Regular review of all sales returns for irregular returns patterns and inventory patterns • Regular review of A/R aging • Segregation of duties (sales and credit/order entry functions) • System of authorization and approval of transactions for sales, sales returns, and A/R write-offs • Where appropriate, standardization of sales terms • Existence of sales personnel confirmation/verification with customer for completeness and accuracy of recording of sales terms or conditions	• Checks to assure transfer of ownership (title, insurance, equipment installation, etc.) • Regular review of all sales contracts, with a focus on unusual terms and conditions, and a comparison to actual practice • Regular performance of physical inventory counts • Regular review of A/R aging • Segregation of duties (sales and credit/order entry functions) • System of authorization and approval of transactions for sales, sales returns, and A/R write-offs • Where appropriate, standardization of sales terms • Existence of sales personnel confirmation/verification with customer for completeness and accuracy of recording of sales terms or conditions
Mitigating Control Environment	• Regular ethics training/policies/adherence • Published code of ethics/conduct with provisions related to fraud and ethical behavior • Formal hiring and promotion standards • Tone at the top, including proper attitudes toward controls and corporate communication • Reporting and advice systems (hotlines for employees and separate hotlines for customers and vendors) • Regular measurement of achievement of ethics/compliance and fraud prevention goals • Investigation of suspected wrongdoing	
Determine Level of "Residual Fraud Risk"	The residual fraud risk was evaluated as potentially material. This is considered a collusive fraud and thus prevention controls would be expected to have minimal impact. Since the likelihood, significance, and pervasiveness were considered high, additional audit work was performed.	Due to the likelihood, significance, and pervasiveness being evaluated as low, combined with the mitigating controls and environment, the residual fraud risk was considered minimal.

Step 9. Determine the appropriate audit response and investigate the characteristics of potential fraud manifestations within each process identified, where "Residual Fraud Risk" exists

Additional Audit/ Investigational Procedures	In response to the high residual fraud risk, internal audit confirmed in writing directly with customers the amounts, dates, and shipping terms for all sales transactions, as well as the current A/R balance and items such as the payment due date, the details of	None required, and the normal audit procedures in the area of revenues, inventories, and A/R did not reveal any changes to the above assessment.

TABLE 7-2 *(continued)*

Fraud Risk	Revenue—"Roundtrip" Transactions—Inflating revenues	Revenue—Bill and Holds
	any right of returns, unrecorded terms and conditions, and any outside agreements not contained in the original written agreements. No exceptions were noted during these expanded procedures.	
Step 10. Remediate fraud risk schemes by designing control activities to mitigate the unmitigated fraud scheme risk		
Remediation	Recommending that internal audit regularly confirm with customers, not only account balances and transactions but also payment due date, the details of any right of returns, unrecorded terms and conditions, and any outside agreements not contained in the original written agreements	None required

a fraud act. Electronic storage is relatively inexpensive, and information systems house and manage this data. This means that the fraudster risks detection during the fraud act and as long as the data is stored. Stored data can be used to trace transactions, document approvals, and exceptions, as well as provide evidence of system override. This stored data can also be used with data mining software such as Access, ACL, or IDEA, which allow a large amount of data to be evaluated quickly for symptoms of fraud and provide evidence of the fraud act or concealment of the fraud.

Detection and Investigation in a Digital Environment

The importance of information systems as a mechanism for fraud prevention, deterrence, and detection cannot be understated. The value of these information systems to generate red flags for further investigation, to reconstruct actual data flow, and to provide a strong evidence trail is also of considerable value to the fraud and forensic specialist. That said, the most challenging issue with regard to fraud detection is the potential for an overwhelming number of fraud symptoms. Once preliminary symptoms are observed and documented, and the predication threshold has been met, the information systems serve as an important tool in the investigative process.

Additional discussion of fraud and forensic tools and techniques in a digital environment is presented in a separate chapter. The key to successful fraud detection and investigation using digital tools and techniques requires a targeted approach. The fraud examiner or investigator must have a sense of what could go wrong, what did go wrong, and how might it manifest itself in the information systems. This requires an understanding of the schemes, the industry, the organization, its IT control environments, its history of fraud, and other items outlined in the steps to develop a targeted risk assessment. With this foundation, the anti-fraud professional has a place to begin the fraud examination or financial forensic engagement.

REVIEW QUESTIONS

7-1 What are the primary responsibilities of management?

7-2 Generally, how is the problem of management override and collusion addressed?

7-3 What is the "expectations gap"?

7-4 What is the role of the external auditor in the financial reporting process?

7-5 How is materiality determined?

7-6 Is earnings management considered fraud?

7-7 What are some red flags that may indicate that fraud is occurring?

7-8 What is meant by behavioral red flags?

7-9 What are the similarities and differences between analytical and accounting anomalies?

7-10 What are the main components of the fraud risk assessment process?

ENDNOTES

1. The American Institute of Certified Public Accountant, "Consideration of Fraud in a Financial Statement Audit," AU Section 316, p. 169.
2. Financial Accounting Standards Board (FASB) (1980). "Qualitative Characteristics of Accounting Information," *Statement of Financial Accounting Concepts No. 2*. Stamford, CT: FASB, paragraph 132.
3. Katherine Schipper, "Commentary on Earnings Management," *Accounting Horizon* (December 1989), p. 92.
4. See Albrecht, "Fraud Examination," Thompson Southwestern (2003), p. 113.
5. See Alvin A. Arens, Mark S. Beasley, and Randal J. Elder, *Auditing and Assurance Services: An Integrated Approach*, 10th ed., (Upper Saddle River, NJ: Prentice Hall, 2004), 274–276.
6. See Albrecht, "Fraud Examination," Thompson Southwestern (2003), 126.
7. See Albrecht, "Fraud Examination," Thompson Southwestern (2003), 121.
8. See Albrecht, "Fraud Examination," Thompson Southwestern (2003), 114.
9. See Albrecht, "Fraud Examination," Thompson Southwestern (2003), 119–120.
10. The authors are grateful to Steve Silver for his contributions to this discussion on Targeted Risk Assessment. Steve Silver retired as a Director with Deloitte & Touche, Miami Office, February, 2007. Since the original writing of this chapter, the Institute of Internal Auditors, Association of Certified Fraud Examiners, American Institute of Certified Public Accountants created "Managing the Business Risk of Fraud: A Practical Guide," which champions a similar approach to that described herein.

CHAPTER 8

DETECTION AND INVESTIGATIONS

LEARNING OBJECTIVES

After completing this chapter, you should be able to:

8-1   Explain the threshold for predication.

8-2   Discuss the challenges associated with proving intent on the part of a fraudster.

8-3   Define evidence.

8-4   Describe the three types of evidence that may be offered at trial.

8-5   Explain what is meant by invigilation.

8-6   Compare and contrast witness interviewing and interrogation.

8-7   Describe some ways that documents may be altered.

8-8   Discuss ways by which assets may be hidden.

8-9   Explain when it is appropriate to use an indirect method for income reconstruction.

8-10 Identify places where fraud examiners and forensic accountants may find data.

CRITICAL THINKING EXERCISE

Five pieces of coal, a carrot, and a scarf are lying on the lawn. Nobody put them on the lawn, but there is a perfectly logical reason they should be there. What happened? How do you explain this?

INVESTIGATIONS: WHO, WHAT, WHERE, WHEN, HOW, AND WHY

To complete an investigation, the fraud examiner or forensic accountant needs to answer the essential questions of who, what, where, when, how, and why. Even in litigation support situations, the answers to these questions are required in order to convince a jury that you can explain each aspect of a case. In addition, the answers need to be woven into a coherent story. Critical thinking and analytical reasoning suggest that the fraud examiner or forensic accountant will have to make some intellectual leaps to pull the various pieces of evidence and the answers to these questions into a compelling case. However, evidence-based decision making suggests that investigators need to base their storyline on the evidence. A storyline grounded in the evidence is much more powerful to prosecutors, attorneys, judges, and juries.

Missing evidence is a fact of life. Another fact is that fraud examiners and investigators would always prefer more evidentiary material. How does the fraud examiner deal with situations where the evidence is less than perfect? The answer is that fraud and forensic professionals always face the prospect of less-than-perfect evidence, and they address potential evidentiary shortcomings or holes in the storyline through their consideration of the alternative hypotheses (alternative fraud theories). Using their commitment to critical thinking and analytical reasoning, these specialists attempt to identify all other hypotheses or theories that might fit at least some of the key pieces of evidence. Then the fraud examiner or forensic professional identifies flaws in the alterative hypothesis by examining the evidence and focusing on the evidence, suggesting that the alternative hypothesis does not withstand the scrutiny of the evidence.

Professionals in this field need to know that no one is better at generating alternative theories of the case than opposing attorneys. The question isn't *whether* opposing attorneys will develop alternative theories of the case, it's what theories they are mostly likely to create. Often, if a forensic accountant is deposed as part of the civil litigation process, the opposing attorney will develop new and novel theories

for trial, especially if the fraud or forensic professional has destroyed some of this attorney's alternative theories during the deposition. The authors of this text have participated in cases where opposing counsel modified their alternative theories of the case as often as most people change their underwear.

What tools are available to analyze evidence and develop a compelling storyline? First, the hypothesis–evidence matrix (analysis of competing hypotheses) should be used for considering alternative fraud theories in light of the evidence. By aligning alternative theories across the top of the matrix and considering each piece of evidence, the fraud examiner or forensic professional can highlight the flaws in the various alternative theories. In addition, fraud examiners and forensic accountants need to develop evidence, to the extent possible, around the elements of fraud: the act, concealment, and conversion; the fraud triangle (opportunity, perceived pressure, and rationalization); and M.I.C.E. (money, ideology, coercion, and ego). With regard to the fraud triangle and M.I.C.E., professionals know that, other than opportunity, they may never have compelling evidence of these aspects. That said, examiners and investigators need to explore and attempt to develop an evidentiary trail for pressure, rationalization, and M.I.C.E.

Predication

Prior to starting a fraud examination or forensic accounting investigation, the professional needs predication. *Predication* is defined as the totality of circumstances that would lead a reasonable, professionally trained, and prudent individual to believe that a fraud has occurred, is occurring, or is about to occur. Essentially, predication is the starting point for a formal fraud examination. Suspicion in the absence of any corroborating circumstantial evidence is not a sufficient basis for conducting a fraud examination. Something as innocuous as an anonymous tip or complaint with some supporting evidence to substantiate it may be enough to meet the predication threshold. In other cases, discovery of missing cash or other assets is usually sufficient grounds for launching an investigation.

What about red flags? Do red flags meet the requirement of predication? Typically, a few red flags are not in themselves sufficient as a basis for a fraud investigation. Especially when dealing with financial statement fraud, where a materiality threshold is required, red flags require additional audit work. A major obstacle is that many red flags have reasonable explanations and do not result in the auditor's discovering fraud or attempted fraudulent financial reporting. The approach to red flags is that they should be investigated to their logical conclusion, at which point the fraud examiner or forensic accountant can base a conclusion on evidentiary material. When verbal explanations are provided by employees, managers, and executives, such explanations need to be corroborated by supporting evidence.

The Fraud Triangle: Opportunity, Perceived Pressure, and Rationalization

The profile of the typical fraudster is basically that of the average American citizen. Most are not habitual criminals, and very few have any criminal history. Fraudsters do not usually fit the characteristics of street criminals. Further, common fraud perpetrators often are well-educated and respected members of their community, regularly attend church services, are married, and have children. Thus the critical question remains: what causes good people to turn bad?

The three key characteristics that enable any fraud are captured by the fraud triangle shown in Figure 8-1: opportunity, perceived pressure, and rationalization. The first predicate is opportunity—the

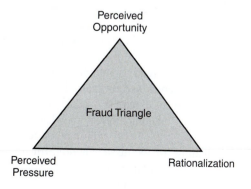

FIGURE 8-1 Fraud Triangle

opportunity to commit and conceal the fraud. Opportunity refers to a position of trust within an organization, and to the skill set required to carry out the fraud. Whether the issue is management override or another breakdown in internal controls, a fraudster requires opportunity. Without opportunity, fraud is highly improbable. Auditors and accountants often direct their fraud prevention and deterrence efforts toward using internal controls to minimize opportunity. Evidence of opportunity also encompasses training of clerical and supervisory personnel, supervision, executive-level management, monitoring by auditors, audit committees and boards of directors, assessment of the effectiveness of proactive anti-fraud programs, the ethical culture of the organization, results of fraud discovery audits, and tips from hotlines and whistleblowers. Many employees, with or without collusion, have the opportunity to take cash, checks, or other assets; yet many of those individuals never commit fraud.

Perceived pressure is necessary to supplement internal control weaknesses and other opportunities to enable fraud. The challenge here is that pressure, at least to some extent, is unique to each individual. The pressure that might push one employee "over the edge" to commit fraud may not be enough for someone else in similar circumstances. Nevertheless, to the extent possible, fraud examiners and forensic accountants should gather various types of evidence:

- Evidence of financial pressures, such as
  - living beyond one's means
  - greed
  - substantial debt
  - a poor credit rating
  - financial losses from unexpected sources—for example, health care expenses for a loved one
  - investment losses
  - the need to pay for a child's education at an expensive school
- Evidence of vices or similar problems, such as
  - gambling
  - drugs
  - marital discord
  - adultery
- Evidence of organizational pressure to achieve financial goals, such as
  - budget pressure
  - financial statement deadlines and year-end cutoff challenges
  - bonus opportunities
  - maintaining stock price
  - meeting analysts' expectations
- Evidence of the challenge of getting away with the fraud
- Evidence of excessive ego
- Evidence of family or peer pressure

It is important to understand that because pressure is fundamentally a factor unique to the individual, only indirect evidence can be gathered, and even that evidence is generally circumstantial. Thus, fraud examiners and forensic accountants must not only keep their eyes open for symptoms, they must keep their minds open as well.

The last condition facilitating fraud is rationalization. Because most fraudsters have no criminal history and do not think of themselves as criminals, fraud perpetrators typically have to develop some rationalization for their actions, at least initially. Like pressure, rationalization is an attribute unique to the individual. Rationalization is a manufactured, somewhat arbitrary justification for otherwise unethical or illegal behavior. In some cases, the fraud examiner or forensic accountant may be able to develop evidence of an employee's feelings of job dissatisfaction, frustration with job recognition, low salary and other perquisites, and attitudes such as "they owe me," "I am only borrowing the money," "nobody will get hurt," "they would understand if they only knew my situation," "it's for a good purpose," and "I just need the money to get over this hump."

M.I.C.E

Another approach to capturing the motivation of the typical fraudster is encapsulated in the acronym M.I.C.E.:

Money

Ideology

Coercion

Ego

Money and ego are self-explanatory, and are the two most commonly observed motivations. The roots of most fraud are the desires for greed (money) and power (ego). Less frequently, employees and others are victimized and unwillingly made part of a fraud scheme (coercion). Ideology is often an observed characteristic associated with taxpayer evasion schemes. In addition, ideology is often behind various kinds of terrorism—and even terrorists require money to further their causes. The M.I.C.E. heuristic complements the fraud triangle. Like pressure and rationalization, motivation is a personal attribute, but in some cases, evidence of M.I.C.E. can be documented during fraud and forensic accounting investigations.

The Problem of Intent: Investigations Centered on the Elements of Fraud

The fraud triangle provides the necessary conditions for fraud to occur. However, the investigator has to provide evidence of intent. Intent, like all aspects of the investigation, must be grounded in the evidence. Short of a confession by the fraudster or a coconspirator, evidence of intent is circumstantial. But intent is a legal attribute to proving fraud. The difference between a mistake and a fraud is intent. If the fraud examiner or forensic accountant cannot prove intent, a civil or criminal conviction for fraud cannot be sustained.

The elements of fraud as shown in Figure 8-2 include the act (e.g., fraud act, tort, and breach of contract), the concealment (i.e., hiding the act, or masking it to look like something different), and the conversion (i.e., the benefit to the perpetrator). The main benefit of using the elements of fraud in an investigation is that in virtually every fraud or financial crime, the evidence of each element can be developed.

More importantly, once the fraud examiner or forensic accountant has evidence that the alleged perpetrator (1) committed the act, (2) benefited from that act, and (3) concealed his or her activities, it becomes very difficult for the alleged perpetrator to make the case that he or she did not intend to do something that would cause harm or injury. In particular, evidence of concealment provides some of the best circumstantial evidence that the act and conversion (benefits) were intentional. An important element of intent can be inferred from repetitive similar acts. In the simplest example, an employee may be able to explain how one check from an employer might have "accidently" ended up in a suspect's personal bank account. It becomes much more difficult, though, to explain away multiple similar transactions. In civil litigation, especially damage claims based on torts and breaches of contract, the elements of fraud remain integral to any investigation. Reasoned evaluation of the evidentiary material often suggests that a tort or breach of contract occurred (the "act"): the tortuous actors benefited from the act and the tortuous actors concealed the activities. Below, we discuss the various methodologies used to answer the questions who, what, when, where, how, and why. Although these are centered on the elements of fraud—the act, concealment, and conversion—the same evidence can also shed light on the attributes of the fraud triangle and M.I.C.E.

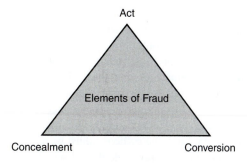

FIGURE 8-2 Elements of Fraud

Related to conversion, there is a current debate in the profession about whether tracing money to a perpetrator's bank account is sufficient evidence of conversion, or whether the fraud examiner or forensic accountant needs to show how the ill-begotten money was used. Legal precedent indicates that tracing the money into the hands of the perpetrator or his or her bank account is sufficient. However, showing how the money was used and how the perpetrator benefited from the act and concealment provides a more powerful case and can provide evidence of attributes of the fraud triangle, such as pressure and rationalization, and other motivations included in M.I.C.E. Generally, investigators should take the investigation as far as the evidence leads.

Examples of circumstantial evidence that may indicate the act, concealment, or conversion include the timing of key transactions or activities, altered documents, concealed documents, destroyed evidence, missing documents, false statements, patterns of suspicious activity, and breaks in patterns of expected activity.

THE DEFINITION OF EVIDENCE

Without evidence, there is no proof that a fraud has occurred, and neither criminal convictions nor civil verdicts are possible.

Evidence is defined as anything perceivable by the five senses, and any proof, such as testimony of witnesses, records, documents, facts, data, and tangible objects, legally presented at trial to prove a contention and to induce a belief in the minds of the jury.[1]

Working definition:

Anything legally admitted at trial that is relevant to the case.

Thus, just about anything may qualify as evidence, depending on the circumstances and what it is introduced to prove. Generally, evidence is admitted at trial provided that it is relevant to the issue at hand, that any probative effect outweighs any prejudicial effect, and that the evidence is trustworthy—meaning that it can withstand the scrutiny of examination and cross-examination.

The rules of evidence have been developed and refined over hundreds of years and are captured in the Federal Rules of Evidence as well as by states (where laws generally model those at the federal level). These intricate rules have the objective of ensuring that only relevant and probative evidence is admitted in court. Perhaps even more important, the rules of evidence seek to ensure that irrelevant, unreliable, and prejudicial evidence is excluded from the courtroom. The objective is to handle court cases (1) fairly and (2) expeditiously.

The rules of evidence not only qualify items as evidence, but they also govern how evidence is gathered and presented, as well as the chain of custody and other rules for handling evidence. Most law schools have entire courses on evidence, so although fraud examiners and forensic accountants need to be familiar with the rules of evidence, ultimately, lawyers and judges will make decisions about what constitutes evidence and what is admissible in legal actions.

Three types of evidence may be offered at trial:

- Testimony: are oral statements made by witnesses under oath
- Real: physical objects, such as documents, blood, footprints, fingerprints, or DNA, that are relevant to the facts at issue
- Demonstrative: items, generally tangible, incorporated by counsel to illustrate important points, having been created for presentation during a trial and often incorporating maps, charts, summaries, and PowerPoint presentations

Another way to evaluate evidence is by whether it is direct or circumstantial. Direct evidence includes direct testimony, an eyewitness, or a confession. Circumstantial evidence "tends to prove or disprove facts" and requires inference, judgment, and interpretation in order to draw meaning from the evidence. Most fraud cases are proved with circumstantial evidence. For example, pressure, rationalization, M.I.C.E., and intent are almost always circumstantial. Absent a confession or the testimony of a coconspirator, most frauds are resolved with the aid of circumstantial evidence.

As noted above, the rules of evidence are designed to minimize irrelevant, immaterial, and incompetent evidence in the courtroom. First, the evidence must be relevant, meaning that it has a tendency to make the existence of any fact more or less probable than it would be without the evidence. Relevance tends to prove or disprove an assertion that is a matter of concern to the court, such as action, motive, opportunity,

identity, and credibility. Not surprisingly, evidence that is judged relevant in one case may be irrelevant in another. Furthermore, evidence must be material—i.e., important (of consequence) to determining the fact at issue. Finally, evidence must be competent: it must be able to withstand the scrutiny of examination and cross-examination.

In order to be admitted at trial, evidence must be authenticated. In order to be considered authentic, the evidence must be shown to have unique identifiers (preferable), or it must be shown that the chain of evidence has been followed. Once authenticated, the evidence must be shown to have been unaltered since it was originally collected. For example, the act of turning on a computer changes the hard drive. This simple, yet inappropriate, act by an investigator would prohibit the use of any evidence found on the computer. To maintain the chain of custody, evidence collected must be tagged with the date and time of collection, the location of the article found, the name of the person collecting the evidence, and the person(s) with custody of the evidence at all "hand-off" points. To maintain the integrity of evidence, it should generally be

1. Unaltered from its original condition.
2. Logged for a chain of evidence or similar records to demonstrate chain of custody.
3. Stored in locked cabinets, preferably fireproof.
4. Secured with unauthorized access prevented, in the case of electronic files.
5. Backed up—copies, electronic and hard-copy, should be maintained in a separate location.
6. Inventoried—so that it can be located when necessary.

Investigators should always assume that the engagement will eventually go to trial. With such an assumption, the collection and preservation rules noted above are very important considerations. Furthermore, the amount of data collected can be quite large, so the investigator needs be very organized so that he or she can access data and review the types of data collected in summary fashion. In some civil litigation cases, Bates numbering will be used to ensure that paper documents are organized and inventoried. Bates numbers should only be applied to copies of originals.

FROM THE FRAUDSTER'S PERSPECTIVE

Adapted from the whitecollarfraud.com blog by Sam E. Antar
Saturday, December 13, 2008

Is there really more white-collar crime today?

Advice about white-collar crime from a convicted felon: A bad economy causes many white-collar crimes to float to the surface

Once, I asked a New York City police officer assigned to the harbor patrol why so many dead bodies are pulled out of the rivers around Manhattan every spring. He explained that many of these people did not actually die during the spring. Instead, they probably died the previous winter.

During the winter, if a person is killed and the dead body is dumped into the river, or if a person commits suicide—for example, by jumping into the river from a bridge—his or her body will sink to the bottom of the river, because the water is cold. When spring arrives, the water heats up, and the dead bodies float to the top of the river surface. The harbor police then retrieve these bodies, which are known as "floaters." Just because we find the dead bodies in spring doesn't mean they died in spring.

The same principle applies to white-collar crime. White-collar crime is always around, both in good and bad economic times. Such crimes are either less noticed during a good economic climate or more noticed during a bad economic climate such as the situation we face now. In a relatively good economy, white-collar crime is easier to execute and conceal. In a bad economy, many white-collar crimes implode, because they become unsustainable. Just as warm water brings bodies to the surface, a bad economy brings many white-collar crimes to the surface.

EVIDENCE SOURCES OF THE ACT, CONCEALMENT, AND CONVERSION

Documents

Documentary evidence is the backbone of most financial forensic investigations. Even investigations conducted using digital databases will need to be grounded in documentary and other physical evidence before the investigation concludes. At trial, documents can sometimes be more reliable and dependable than

eyewitnesses. Documents do not forget, cannot be cross-examined, cannot commit perjury, and—assuming the anti-fraud professional correctly interprets the meaning of their document content—tell the same story every time. In addition, documents provide the potential for fingerprints and other physical evidence.

Documentary evidence includes that gathered in both paper and electronic forms and includes invoices, contracts, deeds, titles, birth certificates, agreements, receipts, and forms. Documents may be collected from client company records, litigants, public records, and Internet searches, among many other sources. These records can become part of the evidentiary material or may become inputs for demonstrative evidence such as link charts, timelines, and flow diagrams. Documentary evidence also may become inputs for direct and indirect financial analysis. Once obtained, the document is not only examined for content, but also evaluated for authentication. Some items for which a document should be examined include:

Signatures (forged)

Handwriting (forged)

Alterations

Erasures

Eradications

Creation date

Counterfeiting

Indented writings

Paper examination

Ink examination

Source of paper (e.g., did two pieces of paper come from the same source?)

Folds

Tears and cuts

Restoration of damaged, burned, or charred documents

Photocopy or original

Facsimiles

Notary, seals, (rubber) stamps, and cachets

Envelope adhesives

Typewriter sources and marks

Sequence of creation

Numbering sequence on the documents

Documents can provide evidence related to the act, concealment, or conversion. Related to the act, bank statements can show that checks written to the company were in fact deposited into the perpetrator's or an accomplice's bank account. Bank statements can also be altered, for example by applying correction fluid to balances or adjusting amounts, thereby providing evidence of concealment. Finally, documents from public records, the Internet, and other sources may be included as part of an indirect financial profile method, such as the net worth method, to demonstrate that the person has income from unknown sources and thus has benefited from the act (conversion).

Bank, Credit Card, and Investment Statements

Bank, credit card, and investment statements can be integral evidence in almost every fraud case. One would think that smart fraudsters would be unlikely to run their ill-gotten gains through their checking account, but examination of monthly financial information for known bank accounts, credit cards, and investment accounts may provide clues and other investigative leads. For example, checking account activity may show deposits from sources other than known places of employment. Such deposits should be traced to determine whether additional, previously unknown sources of income exist.

In addition, bank account disbursements may be made to previously unknown credit cards, installment accounts, and investment accounts. These disbursements may become leads that the fraud or forensic professional can follow as they continue to follow the money. Credit card statements may demonstrate

that amounts spent far exceed the suspect's known sources of income, and that those credit card payments must be made from a previously unknown source.

Investment accounts need to be scrutinized for transactions, for money flows to other accounts (e.g., credit cards, checking accounts, other investment accounts), for new leads, and also to ensure that money that appears to be coming from unknown sources is not coming from the person's previously accumulated investment holdings. Thus, bank, credit card, investment, and other similar financial statements can provide evidence of the act and conversion and can provide additional clues regarding lifestyle and where the missing money may have flowed.

Generally, obtaining victim company bank statements and other pertinent documentary records is a basic requirement for initiating an investigation and providing evidence of the act. Evidence of concealment and conversion related to a fraud, financial crime, or civil matter is more difficult, because they require financial documents of the alleged perpetrator. In such cases, a subpoena or search warrant is often necessary, and that requires probable cause. While the probable cause threshold is not overly burdensome, it prevents investigators from going on fishing expeditions in an attempt to identify the perpetrator.

In addition to bank statements, deposit tickets, and cancelled checks, other items are sources of potentially useful investigative information:

- Account applications
- Signature cards
- Canceled check information beyond the payee, such as memo, endorsements, check cashing bank information, Magnetic Ink Character Recognition (MICR) information, numerical sequence, dates of transactions, wire transfers, electronic fund transfers (EFTs), ATM transactions, references to cashier's and traveler's checks, money orders, loans, mortgages, safe deposit boxes, certified checks, and bank drafts
- Credit card applications
- Mortgage applications
- Loan applications

Applications, in particular, provide useful information, including address, phone numbers, assets, liabilities, and associated persons such as spouses, parents, and other cosignatories.

Invigilation

Invigilation is an investigative technique that considers periods before, during, and after a suspected fraud has occurred. This method looks for changes in patterns of performance around the time that the suspicious activity occurred. It provides evidence of the act by helping to calculate how much money may be missing and helps to provide powerful visual evidence that a fraud has occurred.

In Table 8-1, consider the following example of invigilation. Jim is suspected of stealing money from a group of vending machines. Notice that the deposits decline during the period of Jim's employment until his termination at the end of 2006. In 2007, deposit levels rise almost to the level immediately prior to Jim's preemployment period. This pattern is clear and distinct, and it suggests a correlation between the pattern of deposits and the period of Jim's employment. This is a compelling piece of evidence.

The three years when Jim was not employed—2001, 2002, and 2007—can be used to estimate the amount of losses during Jim's watch over the vending machines. The expected annual deposits, assuming no increase in vending prices, is about $51,401 ([53, 064 + 49, 511 + 51, 630]/3). Next, expected deposits are compared to those actually made into the bank account. Based on this analysis, it appears that Jim did not steal any money during 2003, his first year on the job. However, more than $4,000 appears to be missing in 2004. Furthermore, the estimated amount of losses due to Jim's fraud rises to more than $22,000 in 2006. The total estimated amount of losses for the four-year period is approximately $38,800. Of course, additional evidence would need to be gathered. For example, who had keys and other access to the vending machines besides Jim? Were any of the deposit tickets altered? Was the same number of vending machines in use in all seven years? Were there periods of construction when a large number of machines were not available for use?

Invigilation becomes one piece of evidence that, when combined with additional evidence, can be presented as a compelling case.

TABLE 8-1   Example of Invigilation

MONTH	Prior to Hiring Jim		Period of Jim's Employment				After Jim
	2001	2002	2003	2004	2005	2006	2007
JAN	4,240	3,850	4,143	4,333	3,371	2,089	4,460
FEB	4,050	3,978	3,790	3,856	3,680	2,689	4,672
MAR	4,270	3,208	4,615	4,363	3,183	2,371	3,869
APRIL	4,481	3,751	4,049	3,585	3,316	2,331	3,989
MAY	4,462	4,291	4,209	3,230	2,497	2,174	4,131
JUNE	4,212	3,042	3,887	3,903	3,516	2,287	3,790
JULY	4,973	4,737	4,402	3,554	2,912	2,410	4,300
AUG	5,286	4,100	4,934	3,413	3,271	2,672	4,515
SEP	4,336	3,551	3,528	3,469	2,865	2,434	4,930
OCT	3,075	4,355	3,924	3,994	2,838	2,185	3,690
NOV	4,599	4,791	4,473	4,231	3,153	2,567	4,763
DEC	5,082	5,859	6,005	5,219	4,555	2,927	4,521
Actual	53,064	49,511	51,958	47,150	39,156	29,136	51,630
Expected			51,401	51,401	51,401	51,401	51,401
Estimated Overage (Shortage)			556	−4,252	−12,245	−12,226	229
Estimated Loss Dollars						−38,763	

Interviewing and Interrogation

Witness interviewing and interrogation can be integral aspects of a fraud and forensic accounting investigation. In a civil case, interviews are most often carried out in the form of depositions. This activity is used to find information and discover evidence in a case.

Although the common perception of an interrogation may conjure up images of bright lights and rubber hoses, an interrogation simply refers to an admission-seeking interview where the interviewer believes he or she has identified the perpetrator and is now attempting to get the subject to confess to the illegal activity.

Witness interviewing and interrogation skills are not normally developed in traditional accounting curricula. Because these skills are so important to fraud and forensic investigations, witness interviewing and interrogation are both covered in Chapter 9. Note that interviewing can be used to gather evidence pertinent to the act, concealment, and conversion.

Surveillance and Covert Operations

As financial crimes have become more sophisticated and investigators have sought to investigate nonfinancial crimes by following the money flow, investigators have adopted and adapted techniques to pursue white-collar criminals that have been traditionally associated with the pursuit of organized crime and drug trafficking. Such techniques include electronic surveillance, search warrants, and undercover operations. Thus, surveillance and convert operations are used as part of the investigative process for fraud and financial forensic investigations, although these methods tend to be reserved for more sophisticated frauds with law enforcement involvement. Some of the objectives of this type of work are to gather evidence, identify those engaged in illegal activities, identify coconspirators, recover money, and determine how an operation is conducted.

Generally, these techniques are not conducted by fraud examiners and financial forensic professionals, because they do not have the required training and skill set. Furthermore, such operations are more common when the activity is suspected to be complicated, involving multiple individuals, organizations, and jurisdictions. In these types of cases, surveillance and covert operations may be necessary to fully develop the case, identify all individuals involved, and understand how the operation is conducted. Many investigative operations are conducted by "private investigators" or law enforcement officers who have the necessary training and experience to engage in this type of activity. In fact, we recommend that the traditional fraud examiner and forensic accountant not perform these types of activities without proper training due to the dangers to both the professional and the outcome of the investigation.

Several types of surveillance are possible. First, fixed-point surveillance (e.g., stakeout) involves observing activity from a stationary, discreet location. These types of observation activities are relatively simple and require the use of detailed activity logs, photographs, and videos. A more difficult surveillance approach is to track people and goods using mobile surveillance. Mobile surveillance requires considerably more skill than fixed-point surveillance, and the risk of discovery is real, especially when the target is suspicious of those around him or her. Although the risks could be higher, the potential rewards might also be greater, because the investigator may discover how goods are transported, as well as learning about previously unknown linkages between people, places, and things.

Videography during surveillance provides a visible evidence log that can be shared with other investigators as well as with prosecutors, defense attorneys, judges, and juries. Keep in mind that if videos are used to document activity and linkages, sound features should be disabled. Generally, as long as an individual's reasonable expectation of privacy has not been violated, videography is legal. The theory is that what people do in public always has the possibility of being observed by others, and thus persons acting in public have a lowered expectation of privacy. However, if audio is also captured during the surveillance, different laws, rules, and regulations apply—audio surveillance has more stringent requirements.

Most people typically think of wiretapping in connection with audio or electronic surveillance. Generally, unless an individual is speaking loudly in public, most conversations are considered private. While electronic surveillance is permissible in fraud and forensic investigations, the investigator must obtain court permission before such activities are carried out. Under federal law, individuals are allowed to video- or audiotape conversations in which they are a part without telling the other party. State laws vary, so before recording your own conversations, check with counsel. Under no circumstances is it legal to tape-record a conversation between two or more persons if you are not a party to the conversation. Due to a person's reasonable expectation of privacy, the ability to convince a judge that electronic surveillance other than previously described can be quite challenging. If successful, the investigative technique can provide very valuable information, because people are generally more willing to discuss sensitive information in private conversations.

The most extreme level of surveillance is undercover operation. These operations are very costly due to the time commitment required, and they may put the investigator at personal risk. Generally, undercover operations are permissible as long as they are based on some reasonable level of probable cause and do not induce someone to commit a crime he or she would not otherwise commit (such an inducement, which is illegal, is called "entrapment"). Undercover operations are most effective with large-scale incidents, and when other methods fail to develop the case and the necessary evidence. Such operations should not be conducted unless the undercover work can be carefully monitored and the investigation can remain secret, and the undercover operative safe, until the investigation is completed. Typically, the undercover officer will face a variety of challenges related to legal and ethical conduct. The investigation should end when sufficient evidence has been collected.

Confidential Sources and Informants

Confidential sources and informants can be used to gather information and evidence about a case. Generally, sources have no criminal involvement in the case and are good citizens who are providing information. Informants are more culpable and typically have a direct or indirect role in the criminal activity. Sources and informants are usually considered confidential, so efforts should be made to maintain their confidentiality. Their information is independently verified, and documentary evidence and other witnesses are developed based on their leads. Good investigators evaluate the motives of their confidential sources and informants as well as the reliability and validity of their information.

CTRs, SARs, and FinCen 8300

Currency Transaction Reports (CTR), Suspicious Activity Reports (SAR), and FinCen Form 8300 are excellent sources of information for law enforcement officers trying to identify and follow the flow of money from illegal and illicit sources. The CTR, FinCen Form 104, was a direct result of the 1970 Bank Secrecy Act. CTRs must be filed by financial institutions when transactions include $10,000 or more in currency in a single banking day.

Financial institutions are broadly defined as banks, other depository institutions, brokers and dealers in securities, money transmitters, currency exchangers, check-cashing organizations, issuers and sellers of money orders, and traveler's checks. Casinos must file a form 103, rather than the normal CTR. Qualifying transactions include deposits, withdrawal, and currency exchange and wire transfers over the $10,000 limit.

Although privacy concerns were an issue for banks, this concern was alleviated in 1986 when the Money Laundering Control Act prevented banks from being held liable for releasing transaction information to law enforcement. In 2008, more than 15 million (15,449,549) CTRs were reviewed and posted into the Currency Banking and Retrieval System, as well as 733,543 SARs. Approximately 60 percent of financial institutions file their reports via magnetic tape that is uploaded directly into the Currency Banking and Retrieval System database. The remaining 40 percent arrive in paper format and are entered onto magnetic tapes by IRS personnel and then uploaded onto the database.[2]

SARs are used by financial institutions to report any suspicious activity or potentially suspicious activity to the Financial Crimes Enforcement Network (FinCen). If the suspected person is known and can be identified, the threshold to file a SAR is $5,000. If the suspicious activity is not associated with a known individual, the limit is raised to $25,000 of suspicious activity. SARs are particularly effective and are often used when currency transactions appear to be structured so that they fall just below the $10,000 reporting limit threshold for CTR reporting. The purpose of the SAR report is to help law enforcement identify individuals and organizations involved in money laundering, fraud, organized crime, drug trafficking, and terrorist financing. In order to protect themselves and limit liability, financial institutions often conduct due diligence work before filing a SAR to ensure that the transactions appear to be generated from illegal or illicit sources.

Form 8300 picks up where CTRs leave off, requiring any business receiving a cash payment in excess of $10,000 to report the transaction to FinCen using IRS Form 8300. Automobile dealers are one example of a business where a customer may pay for an expensive vehicle in cash, triggering the Form 8300 requirement. The Form 8300 instructions require businesses to accumulate multiple payments if in total the payments exceed the $10,000 threshold within a twenty-four-hour period.

The term "cash" means U.S. or foreign currency received in any transaction. Cash also includes a cashier's check, money order, bank draft, or traveler's check with a face amount of $10,000 or less and received in a designated reporting transaction, or any transaction in which the payer is attempting to avoid the filing of Form 8300. A cashier's check, money order, bank draft, or travelers check with a face amount of more than $10,000 is not considered cash, since the bank or financial institute that issued such monetary instruments is required to file a Currency Transaction Report (CTR). A personal check is not considered cash, regardless of the amount.

E-mail

Individuals will make statements, give instructions, and discuss many topics in an e-mail that they would never memorialize in written policies or procedures documents. As a result, the value of e-mail to include "smoking gun" evidence of financial crimes, fraud, motivations for activity, and other information cannot be understated. In general, external to an organization, e-mail is accessible only if the organization volunteers the information or it is gathered from a resulting subpoena or court authorized warrant. However, U.S. courts have generally held that e-mails within an organization that are generated by employees are not private, and that the employees have no reasonable expectation of privacy with regard to e-mail. However, there are exceptions. For example, some courts have held that it is illegal to intercept e-mail "in transit" to the recipient. Accordingly, it is best to review your procedures for accessing e-mails with legal counsel.

E-mail not only provides useful content, it also provides evidence of linkages among people and transactions or other activity. For example, an e-mail with the extension "wvu.edu" implies that the person has some association with an educational institution—and, more specifically, West Virginia University. In addition, e-mail headers contain information about the servers that have processed and transported the e-mail and can often be traced to the source. More sophisticated criminals can use anonymous re-mailers that prevent the source of the e-mail from being discovered.

Data Mining, Pattern Recognition, and Other Digital Tools

The world in which we live is impacted by digital information every day. Our names, addresses, phone numbers, and other personal information are captured in numerous databases around the world. In addition, cheap electronic storage has made the ability to capture more and more information less costly. This information, when sorted and analyzed in different ways, often has numerous uses. As a result, the amount of information captured electronically has ballooned to staggering levels.

This same phenomenon has also occurred in transaction detail captured by various organizations, whether for-profit or not-for-profit. Transactions that are coded for the general ledger for accounting

purposes also often have additional coding for costs centers and projects that allow the data to be pulled and analyzed after the fact. Large American corporations process billions of transactions annually. As a result, only through the use of effective and efficient digital tools and techniques can fraud examiners and forensic professionals complete their work.

Some of these tools include data mining software, software that looks for hidden patterns in data that can be used to predict future behavior. For example, data mining software can help retail companies find customers with common interests. The term is commonly misused to describe software that presents data in new ways. True data mining software doesn't just change the presentation, but actually discovers previously unknown relationships among the data. An important field of computer science concerns recognizing patterns. Such software is central to optical character recognition (OCR), voice recognition, and handwriting recognition but can also be applied to financial data to look for unusual activity that is suggestive of fraud.

In this regard, the results of pattern recognition searches and data mining software analyses provide additional evidence of who, what, where, when, how, and why. Like most evidence, individually, the data simply provides information, but in the context of other evidence gathered as part of the investigative process, the results of digital analysis might provide compelling and powerful insight into the act as well as how it was perpetrated. In organizations with large financial transaction databases, one way to analyze data is with sophisticated pattern recognition and data mining software. These application programs can "see" things in the data that the average investigator couldn't without extensive amounts of investigative time.

Other Physical Evidence

Although the bulk of the fraud examiner's and forensic accountant's work is usually completed using documents, other physical evidence is also important. For example, the Bureau of Alcohol, Tobacco, Firearms and Explosives (ATF) regularly works crime scenes along with other nonfinancial investigators. Although ATF financial investigative personnel are not normally first responders, they are knowledgeable about what financial documents should be bagged and tagged. ATF training for financial personnel includes crime scene investigation tools and techniques.

Other physical evidence may include fingerprints on documents to establish that a person has had contact with the document, and possibly even reviewed it. This would demonstrate that the individual has knowledge of the document's existence, and perhaps its content. Charred and partially burned financial books and records can provide valuable clues during an investigation. Phony documents, forgeries (including signatures), a typewriter's unique identifiers, photocopies, indentations, and paper age are some examples of physical evidence that may become part of a financial investigation.

Further, nonfinancial information can provide invaluable clues. Addresses and phone numbers can provide proof of linkages between people and organizations. For example, two businesses' using the same phone number suggests some association between those organizations. Dates and times can provide important evidence about who, when, where, what, why, and how. This sequencing of events is not financial evidence but can help put the financial investigation into context. For example, a timeline may show that an individual had nonsharable financial burdens from severe and costly health problems of a family member prior to a fraud. The existence of the medical condition is not financial evidence but could provide some insight into the financial pressure on the alleged perpetrator.

EVIDENCE SOURCES SPECIFIC TO CONCEALMENT

Concealment is the activity that is most closely associated with intent. Concealment can occur through the negligence of others or by direct intervention of the fraud perpetrator. When investigating an asset misappropriation, the investigation should be conducted in a way that does not arouse suspicion. The investigator should start as far away from the suspected target as possible and get closer as the investigation proceeds.

The investigation may start with public records searches. Once background data have been collected, the investigator should review the documents, including company personnel records and other company books and records. As evidence trails are developed and the investigator gathers clues, former employees

may be interviewed. Based on the evidence, internal witnesses may also be interviewed. Finally, when all possible evidence has been collected, all alternative hypotheses have been eliminated, and the evidence pointing to the suspect is seemingly conclusive, the investigator will interview the suspect and other investigative targets.

In contrast, with regard to financial statement fraud and tax fraud, the person responsible for the financial statements or tax return has already made a representation—that the financial statements are a reasonable reflection of the entity's underlying economic performance, or that the tax return presents a reasonable reflection of taxable income and taxes owed. In those situations, the financial statements or tax returns are part of the concealment activity.

In fact, the person responsible has gambled that (1) the auditor, examiner, or investigator is not going to identify red flags associated with his or her fraudulent representations and that (2) even if the red flags are identified, the auditor, examiner, or forensic accountant will not be able to ascertain what has happened. In such situations, the investigator should get the responsible person to verify his or her agreement with the accuracy of the financial statements and tax returns and then test those assertions. The representations made are an integral part of the fraud, particularly the concealment portion. In such cases, carefully document such statements (assertions) and then test the veracity of the assertions using documentary and other physical evidence.

Altered Documents

Accounting books and records that are found during the course of an investigation to have been altered provide compelling evidence of concealment. The methods by which documents can be altered are almost limitless, but include:

- Forged signatures
- Forged handwriting
- Restored erasures
- Erasures
- Eradications
- Recently created documents supposedly created years ago
- Counterfeiting of documents with copy machines
- Counterfeiting of documents with typewriters
- Counterfeiting of documents with (color) printers and matched paper

The methods by which documents can be examined for forgery include[3]:

- Examining signatures and handwriting
- Examining documents for erasures and eradications
- Determining document age
- Looking for telltale signs of copy machine use
- Looking for telltale signs of a typewriter's unique typing characteristics
- Looking for signs of printing, and for paper with characteristics different than expected
- Examining documents for indented writing
- Comparison of inks, paper, and writing style
- Determining whether separate papers came from the same source (e.g., the same writing pad)
- Examining paper folds
- Examining documents for tears and cuts, both expected and unexpected
- Restoring burned and partially burned documents
- Identifying the source typewriter, copying machine, or printer
- Examining facsimiles
- Examining notary seals and stamps
- Looking for envelopes that have been opened and subsequently resealed

- Looking for inserted text
- Looking for issues with numbering sequences (e.g., of checks)
- Examining rubber stamp impressions

Although fraud examiners and forensic accountants are not experts in these areas, they provide a first line of defense in an effort to identify possible alterations. If there is any indication that the books and records have been altered, anti-fraud professionals and forensic accountants should take steps to verify the alteration by having a qualified professional examine the documents in question.

General Ledger, Journal Entries, and Reconciling Items

The general ledger is an excellent resource for fraud examiners and forensic accountants, assuming that the transactions associated with the fraud have been processed through the entity's books and records. For example, disbursements must pass through the general ledger, so a money trail exists. Assuming that the fraudster wants to conceal his or her activity, he or she needs to post a debit to some account while the reduction in cash is posted via a credit to cash. Because stockholders equity accounts typically have very little activity, most fraud perpetrators would avoid these. However, no stone should be left unturned; balances and activity levels should be checked for all accounts, because even stockholders equity accounts can be used as a temporary hiding place.

Assuming that stockholders' equity is unlikely to be used to conceal fraudulent transactions, that leaves assets, liabilities, revenues, and expenses. Revenue accounts, other than returns and allowances, typically would not have debit entries. Thus debits to revenues would likely draw a great deal of attention. This being the case, any debit to revenues would and should be carefully scrutinized.

Debits to liabilities are a stronger possibility than to revenue or stockholders equity, and the effect would be an understatement of liabilities. Debits to specific liabilities may be caught through the audit confirmation process and by examining reconciliations of vendor subsidiary account balances to vendor statements. Journal entry debits to liability general ledger accounts should be examined for appropriate backup and approval to ensure that the transactions are legitimate.

Debits to assets and expense accounts are the most common places for concealment. Debits to assets create an overstatement of assets. Assuming that the victim company takes reasonable steps to verify and reconcile assets balances, this approach to conceal a fraud creates irreconcilable balances. Thus, to catch concealment on the asset side, the anti-fraud professional or forensic accountant needs to reconcile assets details to the general ledger balance. If reconciliations are prepared as part of the company's normal accounting procedures, reconciling items should be carefully scrutinized for appropriate backup and appropriate review and approval by management and by the age and size of the reconciling items.

Debits to expense accounts are the most common method of concealment. Assuming that expense account balances do not exceed budgeted amounts or exceed budgets by only a relatively small amount, the activity is not likely to be caught. Then, once expenses are closed into retained earnings as part of the annual closing process, the chance that the overstated expense balance will be caught decreases substantially. Whereas assets present an ongoing concealment problem for the fraud perpetrator, expenses are problematic for only one period. Some of the items that the anti-fraud professional and forensic accountant needs to scrutinize are the existence of reconciliations and reconciling items for source, backup, and approval.

Closely related to the general ledger, journal entries are a potential source of fraud concealment. Journal entries can be used to eliminate unreconciled balances and to hide inappropriate removal of cash and other entity resources. Thus, period-end and year-end journal entries also need to be examined. The review of journal entries includes looking for too many journal entries as well as too few—and for missing journal entries. Journal entries need to be scrutinized as to source, backup, and approval.

Tax Returns

Tax returns are an important source of information for fraud and forensic accounting engagements. Personal and business tax filings contain representations put forth by the taxpayer related to their taxable income. This information can be correlated with activity in bank accounts and corporate books and records and used as a source of investigative leads. Schedule M in corporate tax returns requires reconciliation between book income and taxable income. Then, book income on the tax return can be reconciled to financial

statement income. Furthermore, the new M-3 reconciliation for larger public companies provides a detailed reconciliation between book income and taxes. Schedule M-3 is required for corporations and partnerships with $10 million or more in assets. According to Deborah M. Nolan, IRS Large and Mid-Size Business Division Commissioner, quoted on the IRS Web site, "Schedule M-3 will enable the IRS to focus more quickly on high risk issues and taxpayers requiring our attention, and reduce our time spent with compliant taxpayers."

Tax returns may provide evidence of involvement in businesses not previous known or disclosed by the target. In addition, interest and dividend income may suggest investment, banking, hidden CDs, and other income-generating accounts of which the investigator was not aware. Deductions can also be a source of information. For example, deductions for real estate taxes may reveal ownership interests in property that were not previously disclosed. Furthermore, the amounts and types of deductions might raise questions about whether that particular business operation should need that level of support, a possible indicator of illegal or illicit payments. For example, a small laundry business paying large consulting fees does not make sense and serves as a clue that requires additional investigation. If warranted, in some cases, the tax preparer can be interviewed, and his or her work papers subpoenaed.

EVIDENCE SOURCES SPECIFIC TO CONVERSION

Locating Hidden Assets and Unknown Sources of Income

Assets can be hidden through several methods: hidden bank accounts, hidden investment accounts, purchasing of assets through straw men or front organizations, and transferring assets to individuals or accounts where detection can be difficult. The most common means for hiding real estate and business ownership is to transfer those assets to another party over which the person holding the assets has some element of control. Family members, such as a child or spouse, are a common technique used for hiding such ownership. Wives in particular make a good haven for hidden asset ownership, because they bring a maiden name to the marriage that has a complete history. Thus, investigators need to search for hidden assets using not only family members' names but also the spouse's maiden name. Identification of the spouse's maiden name can be made using voter registration and marriage records filed at the state and local levels.

To identify assets that may have been transferred, the investigator needs to carefully examine tax returns and business and personal financial records to look for transfer activity. When assets from one period disappear in the next period's records, the investigators have a clue that assets may have been transferred.

Another problem may be income that is diverted away from known accounts to unknown accounts. The investigator needs to search for transactions between the target's known accounts and accounts not previously identified by going through check registers, cancelled checks, account statements, and other records obtained during the investigation to identify suspicious activity that may suggest hidden assets or income diversion.

Other places where assets can be directed include children's trusts, mortgage payments, insurance policies, prepaid credit cards, savings bonds purchases, traveler's check purchases, and money order purchases. Money transferred directly into a child or family trust without passing through known bank accounts can be an effective tool for hiding income and assets, provided the investigator does not discover the existence of the trust. Another mechanism for hiding assets is to pay down mortgages without running the payments through known bank accounts. If the investigator does not inquire about the existence of mortgages or examine mortgage statements to tie the payment of interest and principle to known accounts, an important clue suggesting unknown income sources or hidden assets may be missed.

Insurance policies can be used to accumulate wealth that does not show up on most financial statements. An individual trying to hide income may make payments to insurance policies from unknown accounts and obtain good investment returns, and the investigator would be none the wiser. Prepaid credit cards, savings bonds, cashier's checks, traveler's checks, and money orders are assets that do not show up on traditional account statements, that take up little space, and that can be safely held in safety deposit boxes. Without appropriate inquiry and search for the existence of safety deposit boxes, the investigators may come up empty when it comes to hidden assets and concealed sources of income. Clues about the existence of safety deposit boxes can come from bank statements where annual fees may appear.

Concealed Offshore Financial Accounts, Transactions, and Loans

More sophisticated individuals with significant hoards of ill-gotten gains often use offshore bank accounts to hide assets and conceal sources of income. Typically offshore financial institutions are chosen for their favorable tax treatment and commitment to secrecy. For example, Nevis and its sister country St. Kitts form the Independent Federation of St. Kitts and Nevis. They are located in the Leeward Islands, approximately 1,200 miles southeast of Miami, Florida. St. Kitts–Nevis offer complete confidentiality if foreign authorities seek private banking and financial records. Prison terms are mandatory for violation of the statute. As another example, www.henleyglobal.com provides information on the best jurisdictions for companies, trusts, foundations, and private residences. This Web site reviews information on these types of services for over thirty countries. Favorite offshore countries change from time to time, so it is prudent for the investigator who needs such information to keep current.

Indirect Methods of Income Reconstruction

Using indirect methods to estimate assets controlled by an entity or income to an entity is referred to as "financial profiling." These analyses are methods for developing indicators of concealed income and hidden assets. In many cases, fraudsters or individuals subject to civil litigation, such as divorce, may not run all of their cash income through bank accounts or the books and records of companies. As such, indirect financial profiling may be the only means to establish illegal sources of income or the existence of hidden assets. Furthermore, prior court decisions have concluded that establishing illegal or illicit sources of income and hidden assets through the use of indirect methods can be admissible as evidence in court. Indirect approaches often provide circumstantial evidence.

Legitimate individuals generally run their income through one or more known bank accounts. Similarly, legitimate businesses not only utilize known bank accounts, but they also track financial transactions using detailed books and records and maintain backup documentation to support posted transactions. In many fraud and forensic accounting cases, the books and records are incomplete or otherwise inadequate. In such cases, the investigator must resort to other methods to establish estimated income levels and the existence of hidden assets.

An indirect method is generally used when

- The person or entity of interest has inadequate books and records
- The books do not clearly reflect taxable or other known income
- There is reason to believe that the taxpayer has omitted taxable income
- There appears to be a significant increase in year-to-year net worth
- Gross profit percentages appear to change significantly from period to period
- The person of interest's expenses (both business and personal) exceed known income, with no obvious cause for the difference

Other clues that may arise during an examination that suggest further work and the need to use the indirect method include

- Few or no original invoices or other supporting documentation
- Unusual or large transactions with little or no support
- A/P or A/R too large for the size of the business
- Missing check numbers
- Business checks that have been endorsed by individuals
- Business disbursements that have been used for personal expenses
- Checks to "cash" for large dollar amounts

The primary challenge related to using the financial profiling methods is the amount of legwork involved in developing sources of information. The investigator is likely to start with a tour of any known businesses, drive-bys of the home and other known real estate locations, and a review of any books and records that are available (e.g., tax returns). From there, the investigator can get an idea of income levels.

For example, suppose that a person of interest has reported taxable income of $50,000 and has corresponding bank account activity to support that income amount, but when the investigator drives by the person's home, he sees a Mercedes in the driveway of a $500,000 home. The investigator would rightly

conclude that something doesn't make sense. The investigator would likely go to the county courthouse to look for deeds of ownership, titles, liens, and UCC filings and could also visit the secretary of state's office to determine business ownership. Some of the sources for determining the inputs for the indirect methods include[4]:

- The subject of the investigation
- Informants and confidential sources
- Real estate records
- Judgment and lien records
- Bankruptcy records
- State motor vehicle records
- Loan applications
- Financial statements
- Accountant's work papers
- Lawsuits and depositions
- Surveillance
- Credit card applications or statements
- Tax returns
- Insurance records
- Child support and divorce records
- Employment applications, salary check stubs, and W-2s
- Companions and known associates
- Cancelled checks and deposit tickets

Net Worth Method Most simplistically, assets are resources owned or controlled by a business or individual. Liabilities are obligations owed by a business or individual, and owner's equity—sometimes referred to as stockholders' equity—is the difference between the two, and consists of contributions made by the owner(s) and their accumulated but undistributed profits. Assets, liabilities, and owner's equity are used to form the accounting equation in which assets equal liabilities plus owner's equity. This fundamental relationship implies that assets are provided by one of two sources: creditors (liabilities) or owners (owner's equity or stockholders' equity).

The easiest way to approach an analysis of net worth is to identify assets and the amounts paid for those assets and subtract obligations to creditors; whatever is left over is the owner's portion (also referred to as net worth). The accounting equation applies not only to corporations, but to individuals as well. The net worth method works by examining the change in net worth from one year to the next. Changes in net worth come from owners' or individuals' income sources' being used to purchase assets.

See Table 8-2 for examples of assets and Table 8-3 for examples of liabilities or obligations.

TABLE 8-2   Examples of Assets

Net Worth: Assets	
Resources or things of value owned (including cash)	
Individual	**Business**
• Cash in all accounts	• Cash, stocks, bonds, securities
• Personal property (vehicles, planes, boats, jewels, furs, collectibles, livestock, furniture, clothing)	• Accounts and notes receivable
	• Inventory
• Real property (residence, other houses, rental and commerical properties, vacant land, condos)	• Prepaid expenses
	• Real estate (property, structures)
• Securities (stocks and bonds, CDs, notes)	• Equipment (production machinery, office furniture and machines)
	• Vehicles of all types

TABLE 8-3 Examples of Liabilities/Obligations

Net Worth: Liabilities	
Financial obligations (debts) and claims on assets (liens)	
Individual	Business
• Mortgages	• Accounts payable (to vendors)
• Loans (personal, vehicle)	• Accrued expenses (those not yet paid salaries or wages)
• Credits cards and charge accounts	• Taxes payable
• Installment purchases	• Notes payable within the year
• Liens against property	• Mortgages/bonds payable in more than a year
• Alimony/child support	
• Past due payments (bills, taxes, alimony, child support)	

In this manner, the net worth method provides circumstantial evidence that amounts paid for assets and expenditures exceed income from known sources for a given period of time. Assuming that the investigator has made a thorough search for documentation, the net worth method provides a basis for estimating a person's income and cash flow from illicit, illegal, or unknown sources.

The steps for computing net worth are as follows:

1. Calculate net worth for a base year and each subsequent year.

2. Determine known income for each year after the base year.

3. Calculate the change in net worth. (Note: the change in net worth represents total estimated income for the year—i.e., the increase in yearly net worth (the growth of assets over liabilities) is considered income.)

4. Subtract income from known sources.

5. The remainder is income from unknown—and possibly illegal—sources.

Example of the net worth method Assume the following facts and circumstances, and the goal is to calculate the change in net worth for 2007, 2008, and 2009:

1. According to county courthouse records, the subject owns a residence at 101153 Grafton Road and paid $250,000 in 1997.

2. Brokerage statements indicate stock ownership in three companies:

   a. CompTech stock, with an original cost of $15,000 (owned in 2007 only)

   b. $30,000 in Wesleyan stock (purchase in 2008)

   c. $125,000 in WJU stock (purchased in 2009)

3. A credit card application found during the execution of a search warrant indicates that in 2007 and 2008, the subject owned two vehicles. Information from an interview with the subject indicates that both vehicles were sold in 2009.

   a. Chevy Truck (purchase price $32,000)

   b. Used Toyota Camry (purchase price $10,000)

   c. The application indicated that as of July 1, 2007, $24,600 was owed on the truck and $14,100 on a home equity loan—a portion of which was believed to have been used to purchase the car. Payments to principal were about $100 per month for each loan plus interest.

4. According to county courthouse records and a loan application obtained via subpoena from Bill's Boats and Jet Skis, the target owns a ski boat that was purchased in 2006 for $52,500. The boat loan was not listed on the credit card application noted above, but Bill's records helped estimate the December 31, 2007, loan at about $21,000, with payments to principal about $200 per month plus interest.

5. Testimony during a December 2009 divorce hearing indicates a savings account with amounts totaling $7,500 on December 31, 2007, and $12,500 on December 31, 2008, and with estimated balance of $0 on December 31, 2009.

6. In 2009, DMV records indicate that the subject purchased a Jaguar for $72,000. No record of any lien was discovered.

7. The secretary of state's records indicate that the subject incorporated a business in 2005. Company financial records indicate that the initial investment was $20,000.

8. Security records at the county court house suggest that the subject put down $50,000 to purchase the home on Grafton Road. Using the terms of the loan, the amounts owed were estimated (calculated) as about $152,000 in 2007, $140,000 in 2008, and $128,000 in 2009.

9. According to the loan application for the Jaguar, approximately $50,000 was owed at the time of purchase (near the end of 2009).

10. Divorce testimony indicated that the subject had a job that paid $62,500 in 2008, and that the subject normally receives a 5 percent annual raise. Subject tax records indicated that this estimate is reasonable. Divorce testimony further indicated that the subject spent about $40,000 in 2008 on nonasset purchases, and that the subject estimated $50,000 for similar purchases in 2009.

Notice that the identified expenses are added to the change in net worth to estimate total income. Based on this analysis, the subject has income from unidentified sources of almost $75,000 in 2008, and more than $126,000 in 2009. Preparers of net worth analyses should know that the calculation of net worth for the base year is very important. Further, this method works best when suspected income from unidentified sources is large. For a given period, the net worth analysis summarizes evidence of liabilities, ownership of assets, and expenditures and also provides additional leads on beneficial ownership of assets held by others for the subject, and expenditures made by others for the subject.

The Lifestyle Probe: Sources and Applications of Funds   The lifestyle probe, also called the sources and application of funds analysis, addresses the flow of funds for a given period. If more known expenditures exist than known sources of income and other known cash flow, there must be unknown sources of funds. Thus, the lifestyle of a subject of interest (e.g., a suspect employee) may give clues to the possibility of unreported income. Obvious lifestyle changes that may indicate fraud and unreported income include

- Lavish residence
- Expensive cars and boats
- Vacation home
- Private schools for children
- Exotic vacations

The calculation of unknown income using the lifestyle probe is as follows:

1. Gather information on amounts spent for a base year and each subsequent year.

2. Determine known income for each year.

3. Calculate the amount of all known expenditures (application of funds).

4. Subtract the estimate of all known income (sources of funds).

5. The difference equals income from unknown sources.

Example of the Lifestyle Analysis   Assume the following facts and circumstances, and that the goal is to estimate income from unknown sources for 2008 and 2009:

1. According to CTRs and SARs filed with FinCen, the subject made cash payments on his mortgage totaling $40,000 and $65,000 in 2008 and 2009, respectively.

2. Savings account records subpoenaed from the bank indicate that the target made deposits to the account as follows:

   a. In 2008, $12,000 was deposited and, according to testimony from her ex-husband, the source of that money was a gift from the target's parents.

   b. $20,000 was deposited in 2009.

3. Brokerage statement found in the target's trash indicated deposits to the account to purchase stocks of $20,000 in 2008.

4. According to the target's ex-husband, the target bought a Rolex watch in 2009 for $13,500.

5. The target was observed traveling to a cabin in a bordering state. Search of county records on the cabin's address revealed that the target purchased the cabin in 2008 for $75,000. No liens on the

cabin had been recorded with the county. Also on file at the county records office were 2009 building permits for the cabin totaling $25,000. All work at the cabin appears to have been completed.

6. The target was observed traveling to a home in Florida. Search of county records on the address revealed that the target purchased the home in 2009 for $155,500. No liens on the home had been recorded with the county.

7. The target was observed with a new car in January 2008. Records subpoenaed from the local BMW dealer indicated that the purchase price was $88,000 and that $53,000 was borrowed through the dealership. It is assumed that the target has been making monthly payments totaling $1,230.

8. In 2009, according to a salesperson at a marina near the Florida home, the target purchased a used sailboat from a convicted drug dealer for $19,000 in cash. The marina salesperson brokered the deal, was paid a $2,000 commission "under the table," and did not file a CTR for the cash transaction. The $19,000 was not recorded on the marina's books and records.

9. According to the ex-husband, his former wife spent at least $60,000 per year to maintain a lavish lifestyle.

10. According to the ex-husband, his wife is a computer programmer and was paid $65,000 in 2008. In 2009, the ex-wife was promoted to management and according to her ex-husband, her salary doubled. Analysis of W-2s and tax returns confirmed this amount.

11. The ex-husband and wife maintained separate financial lives. In 2009, the ex-husband loaned the wife $25,000 to "help her" out financially. According to deposition testimony, after being presented a clearer picture of his ex-wife's lifestyle, he now regrets that decision.

Financial Profile Worksheet
Net Worth Analysis

	Year			
Assets	**2007**	**2008**	**2009**	**Source**
Home	250,000	250,000	250,000	County Records
Comptech	15,000			Broker Records
Wesleyan		90,000	90,000	Broker Records
WJU			125,000	Broker Records
Chevy Truck	32,000	32,000		CC Application
Toyota Camry	10,000	10,000		CC Application
Ski Boat	52,500	52,500	52,500	Loan
Savings Account	7,500	12,500	–	Divorce Testimony
Jaguar			72,000	DMV/County Records
Contributed Capital	20,000	20,000	20,000	Secretary of State/F/S
Total	387,000	467,000	609,500	
Liabilities				
Home Mortage	152,000	140,000	128,000	Calculation/CR
Car Loan—Chevy Truck	24,000	22,800		CC Application
Home Equity Loan—incl. Toyota Camry	13,500	12,300		CC Application
Boat Loan	21,000	18,600	16,200	Loan
Car Loan—Jaguar			50,000	Creditor
Total	210,500	193,700	194,200	
Net Worth (Assets–Liabilities)	176,500	273,300	415,300	
Change in Net Worth		96,800	142,000	
Identified Expenses		40,000	50,000	Divorce Testimony
Estimated Total Income		136,800	192,000	
Income from Known Sources		62,500	65,625	Divorce Testimony/Tax Return
Income from Unidentified Sources		$ 74,300	$126,375	

Based on the above information and analysis, the target has unknown sources of income totaling $141,530 in 2008 and $239,760 in 2009. Notice that the analysis is not concerned about balances, but

rather cash flows or information that suggest cash flows were exchanged. Also notice that the sources and application of funds—the lifestyle analysis—made little use of bank statements or disbursement and deposit information. This method works best when the target operates mostly on a cash basis. In addition, the lifestyle analysis can be used to verify the accuracy of other techniques. It is useful when the target has little or no net worth but seemingly large cash expenditures. Also, it is easiest to use when there is little or no change in assets or liabilities. Like the net worth method, this approach is most useful when looking for large unknown sources of income.

The lifestyle analysis has some advantages over the net worth method:

1. It is easier to use and understand, because it deals with flows of money.

2. It can be calculated for periods shorter than a year.

3. It can be used to run a "quick-and-dirty" analysis with documents at hand to identify likely sources of income from unknown sources.

4. It can also be used to confront the target with other analytical results.

Bank Records Method   The bank records method is a hybrid between directly analyzing bank, savings, credit card, and brokerage account records and the net worth and sources and application of funds methods that rely very little on bank records. The bank deposit method assumes that when cash is received, it can either be deposited in the bank or spent. The basic formula for the bank records analysis is as follows:

1. Identify deposits to all known accounts.

2. Add known cash expenditures not paid by bank account check, ATM, or EFT.

3. Sum the total "spent" from all sources.

4. Subtract income from known sources.

5. The difference equals funds from unknown sources.

Financial Profile Worksheet
Sources and Application of Funds

	Year		
Application of Funds	**2008**	**2009**	**Source**
Home Mortgage Payments	40,000	65,000	CTRs/SARs
Savings Account Deposits	12,000		Savings Account
Savings Account Deposits		20,000	Savings Account
Stock	18,000		Brokerage
Watch		13,500	Ex-Husband
Purchase Cabin	65,000		County Records
Remodel Cabin		35,000	Building Permits
Florida Home		155,500	County Records
BMW 700 Series	35,000		Dealership
BMW Loan Payments	13,530	14,760	Dealership
Ocean Pacer Sailboat		21,000	Salesman
Annual Expenses	60,000	65,000	Ex-Husband
Total Known Expenditures	<u>243,530</u>	<u>389,760</u>	
Known Sources of Funds			
Employment Income	65,000	125,000	Tax Return
Gift from Parents	12,000		Ex-Husband
Downpayment on BMW	25,000		Dealership
Loan from ex-Husband		25,000	Ex-Husband
Total Known Inflows	<u>102,000</u>	<u>150,000</u>	
Funds from Unknown Sources	<u>141,530</u>	<u>239,760</u>	

Example of the Bank Records Analysis   Assume the following facts and circumstances, and that the goal is to estimate income from unknown sources for 2008 and 2009:

1. According to bank records subpoenaed from the target, total deposits made to the bank account are $115,000 for 2008 and $128,000 for 2009. These amounts were scheduled by month. (Note: in most cases, the investigator would want to list deposits individually, giving monthly subtotals; the monthly subtotals are presented here to conserve space.)

2. Savings account records subpoenaed from the bank indicate that the target made deposits of $5,000 and $2,000 for 2008 and 2009, respectively.

3. IRA account year-end correspondence indicates that the target made IRA deposits of $3,000 in 2008 and $4,000 in 2009.

4. The target also made several large cash payments in 2008 and 2009 that were not found in known checking, savings, and investment account records:

   a. According to CTRs filed with FinCen, the target purchased a Lexus in 2008 for $75,000 cash.

   b. The target purchased a home in 2009. County records indicate that the purchase price was $225,000, and the lien records indicate an original loan balance of $200,000. Mortgage payments of $1,350 were noted in the checking account subsequent to the home purchase.

   c. The target was followed to his mistress's condo. An interview with the mistress indicated that the target purchased her condo in 2009 for $80,000. No lien records were filed with the county.

5. Tax returns, W-2s, and consumer loan records found in the target's home office suggest that the target had income from known sources in 2008 of $95,000, income in 2009 of $115,000, and a consumer loan of $15,000.

Financial Profile Worksheet Bank Deposits Method

	Year:		Source
	2008	**2009**	
Statement Period / Deposit Date			
January	8,012	8,902	
February	6,097	6,774	
March	10,733	11,926	
April	3,803	4,226	
May	10,028	11,142	
June	12,705	14,117	
July	10,551	11,723	
August	12,491	13,879	
September	12,957	14,397	
October	11,647	12,941	
November	4,629	5,143	
December	11,347	12,830	
	115,000	128,000	Bank Statements
Known Savings and Loan Deposits	5,000	2,000	Bank Statement
Known Deposits to IRA Accounts	3,000	4,000	Brokerage
Total	123,000	134,000	
Cash Expenditures			
Lexus	75,000		CTR
Deposit on Purchase of Home		25,000	County Records
Purchase of Condo for Mistress		80,000	Interview
Total	75,000	105,000	
Total Cash Spent	$ 198,000	$ 239,000	

(Continued)

(*Continued*)

	Year:		Source
	2008	**2009**	
Known Sources of Income			
Consumer Loan	15,000		Loan Documents
Consulting Income	95,000	115,000	Tax Returns/W-2
Total	110,000	115,000	
Income from Unidentified Sources	88,000	124,000	

Based on the above information and analysis, the target has unknown sources of income totaling $88,000 in 2008 and $124,000 in 2009. Even though cash disbursements from the checking account and other known financial resources are effectively ignored for this analysis, the investigator should review this activity for additional leads and to better understand the buying habits and lifestyle of the target.

Upon completion, the results of financial profiling (i.e., net worth, sources and application of funds and bank records analysis) can be used as follows:

- Identify additional information needed
- Establish probable cause for search warrants
- Establish grounds for asset forfeiture
- Uncover useful leads:

  - Beneficial ownership of assets being held for the target by others
  - Expenditures made by others for the target
  - Ownership of long-term assets reported

- Identify indicators of financial difficulties
- Suggest money laundering activity
- Establish fraud within a business
- Uncover skimming, embezzlement, or other misappropriation of funds
- Indicate illegal income

Unknown Sources of Income: Defenses and Rebuttals   Given that the above analyses estimate income from unknown sources indirectly and provide circumstantial evidence, the investigator needs to be prepared for typical defenses raised by targets. In addition to being prepared, the investigator should, to the extent possible, have an evidence trail that suggests that the possible defenses are not feasible.

Defense #1: The estimated cash from unknown sources was accumulated in prior periods (e.g., cash hoard). The rebuttal, grounded in the evidence, can be

- Historical evidence suggests that the target is incapable of saving the amount specified
- The target has large existing debt whose terms are unfavorable, suggesting that prior cash hoards are not likely
- The target has made purchases using installment credit on generally unfavorable terms, suggesting that prior cash hoards are not likely
- The target's lifestyle is inconsistent with that of a person who saves money

During follow-up interviews, the subject could be asked the following questions; when appropriate, supporting evidence could be requested:

- Where was cash kept?
- Who knew about the cash savings?
- In what denominations were the savings kept?
- What records or other documents exist to suggest prior savings?

Defense #2: The estimated cash from unknown sources was obtained by gift or inheritance. The rebuttal and follow-up inquiry could include

- From whom was the gift or inheritance received?
- What was the motivation of the gift giver or deceased? Alternatively, why did the person give the gift or leave the inheritance to the target?
- Did the gift giver or deceased have the financial wherewithal to provide such large sums?
- What records of the gift were maintained?

In addition, the investigator should search for public records related to the inheritance and attempt to obtain tax records for large gifts.

Defense #3: The estimated cash from unknown sources were loan proceeds. The rebuttal and follow-up inquiry could include

- Where are the loan documents and other loan records?
- From whom was the loan received?
- What are the repayment terms of the loan?
- What is the interest rate on the loan?

In addition, the investigator should make an independent assessment of the target's borrowing capacity.

Defense #4: The estimated cash from unknown sources were lottery or other gambling winnings. The rebuttal and follow-up inquiry could include

- What lottery, casino, race track, or gambling establishment paid the amount(s) to the target?
- Where are the records for the winnings?
- If the winnings were from another citizen, what is that person's name?

Databases, Sources of Information, and Extra-organization Intelligence

Data availability increases every day. County courthouse records are being brought online. The number of electronic databases, whether free or by subscription, are ever increasing, as is the amount of data being tracked, gathered, organized, and made available for interested parties. The Internet has made access to public data easier than ever before. In fact, public data has become a controversial issue, because would-be perpetrators can easily access large quantities of sensitive data on the Internet during a single session online.

The primary benefit of using public sources of data such as the local county court house and extraorganizational sources of information are twofold. First, fundamental to an investigation—which is centered on the act, the concealment, and the conversion—is that open sources of data provide evidence of conversion. These sources of information contain data about addresses, home ownership, registered boats and motor vehicles, debts, and similar indicators of credit obligations and their status. In investigations in which traditional bank, credit card, and investment records are scarce, the best way to develop convincing circumstantial evidence that the target is spending more than amounts obtained from known sources is by piecing together assets and liabilities from external data sources. The same is true when the target operates almost exclusively with cash. Although often incomplete, if the evidence demonstrates higher net worth or spending patterns than that from known sources, the investigator can conclude that conversion (benefit) has occurred.

The second major advantage derived from database searches, Internet searches, and other extraorganizational sources of data is developing new leads. For example, the names of spouses, former spouses, business associates, and businesses where the perpetrator is named as an officer or director can all be discovered by searching open sources of data. Still other benefits include leverage during witness interviews and interrogations, because information helps the investigator listen better, and know what to listen for. Searching for data about targets provides a richer understanding of the target and often new investigative ideas. Investigators tend to be honest, but crooks are not! Although we practice thinking critically in order to think like a fraudster, using all our tools, including extraorganizational sources of data, makes critical thinking more productive, effective, and efficient. Places where fraud examiners and forensic accountants may find data include:

- Mail
- Newspapers

- Public records
- Conversations
- Documents
- Trash (public domain once on the curb)
- Computer files
- Internet sites and records sites

When gathering data, the issue of ethics arises. Data and information are ethically neutral! Where ethical conundrums arise depends on how you collect data and what you do with it once gathered. Just because you are able to get information doesn't mean you should. The bottom line is that investigators need to be ethical in how they use sensitive information.

The following tables (Tables 8-4 through 8-7) provide an overview of various sources of data. For a more detailed explanation of other types of data than those included here, please see section 3.4 of the ACFE's Fraud Examiners Manual. Fraud examiners and forensic accountants should understand that data sources and availability change constantly. This being the case, fraud and forensic professionals should make a habit of periodically looking for new sources, talking with fellow investigators about sources of data, and attending seminars to learn such things. Information is critical, so maintaining and improving knowledge of data information sources is essential to the long-term success of the investigator.

Although much data is available from various local, county, state, and federal governments, a challenge that the fraud examiner or forensic professional will encounter is the need for a subpoena to obtain the records. Another challenge is that publicly accessible data is disparate and located in many places, and thus requires significant time and expense to pull together. In response, commercial databases have been created to simplify and organize information, thereby making it easier to locate and obtain, provided that the investigator has the budget to pay for such resources. Some commercial sources of data and databases are listed in Table 8-8.

Internet Searching

Individuals are often shocked at the amount of data that is available about them on the Internet with just a few short keystrokes. With the addition of blogs, chat rooms, and Web sites such as MySpace, individuals provide sensitive information about themselves for anyone with the curiosity to read. Newsgroups and

TABLE 8-4   City Government

Building Inspector	Building permits, blueprints submitted with applications and building inspector's report
Health Department	Health violations Death certificates
Public Schools	Teacher biographies
Tax Assessor/Collector	Information on real property and tax status
Utility Company Records	These records include water, gas, and electricity usage and are generally restricted but can be subpoenaed under certain conditions

TABLE 8-5   County Government

Coroner	Records on deceased persons
Court Clerk	Criminal and civil court records that include the issue at question (e.g., divorce, accident, personal injury), as well as personal information about the litigants and other information pertinent to the case, such as assets owned or controlled
Public Schools	Teacher biographies
Registrar of Voters	Voter registration records, including addresses and phone numbers
County Recorder	Real estate transactions and ownership, mortgages, marriage records, wills admitted to probate, official bonds, mechanics liens, judgments, real estate attachments, and some bankruptcy papers
Welfare Commission	Information gathered by social workers, psychologists, and physicians (although such information is typically available only by subpoena)

TABLE 8-6 State Government

Business Filings Division—Secretary of State	Various business records concerning business ownership and important stakeholders, fictitious business names/DBAs (doing business as), and UCC (Uniform Commercial Code) filings
State Tax Department	Tax filings, inheritance and gift tax returns, some licenses and permits
Professional Associations and Licensing Boards	Doctors, dentists, nurses, social workers, attorneys, accountants (CPAs), real estate licensees, notaries, law enforcement personnel, firefighters, security guards, stockbrokers, teachers, insurance agents, private investigators, bail bond agents, travel agents, and some contractors, engineers, electricians, and architects
Bureau of Vital Statistics	Birth certificates, including parents' names
Department of Motor Vehicles (DMV)	Auto licenses, transfers, and sales and driver's licenses
Other, depending on jurisdiction	Health Department, Corrections (including parole and probation records), State Welfare Agency, Controller/Treasurer, Agriculture, Industrial Relations, Natural Resources, Horse Racing/Gambling Commission, Attorney General, Secretary of State, State Auditor, State Police, Department of Highways, State Securities Commissions, and State Utilities Commissions

chat rooms are worldwide electronic discussion groups and permit the sharing of information between people who share similar interests. Even for those individuals not participating in Internet discourse and information sharing, a tremendous amount of information is available from other public and private sources. Google and other search engines can be used to search an e-mail address, name, user name, nickname, address, or phone number. As a simple experiment, type a person's name in Google with quotation marks around it and see what comes up. This is easier for unique names than for those that are more common, but information abounds on the Internet regardless. By simply using various Internet search engines, anyone can create a profile for another individual, business, or organization by searching name, address, phone number, or e-mail address.

E-mail is the most widely used application of the Internet and may provide clues to an investigator about a subject's background. For example, joe@wvu.edu has some association with West Virginia University. Free e-mail is available from companies such as Yahoo!, Hotmail, and other e-mail service providers and may be used to engage in anonymous communications through the choice of the user portion of the e-mail address (i.e., user_portion@yahoo.com). Anonymous remailers can be used to send and receive e-mail communications around the world. Such services work by stripping all traces of the author's identity from the original e-mail before forwarding it through a series of anonymous servers. Sophisticated parties may hide behind a series of remailers.

Types of information available on the Internet:

- Corporate
- Criminal
- Licenses
- Sex offenders
- Court dispositions
- Financial
- SSDI
- Real estate records
- Personal property
- Military records
- Inmate records
- School information

Relevance, Reliability, and Validity

When one evaluates evidence, it may not be what it initially seems. As noted earlier in the chapter, documents may be altered. Furthermore, witnesses, informants, and confidential sources may not always tell the

TABLE 8-7 Federal Government

Inspectors General	Results of investigations and audits, although such information is typically available only by subpoena
Commodities Futures Trading Commission	Registration information concerning firms and individuals, administrative and injunctive actions, financial reports, and customer complaints
Department of Agriculture	Information concerning meat and poultry, feedlots, brokers, meat packers, canneries, farms, and ranches participating in USDA programs, food stamps, electric and telephone co-ops, applications for loans, grants, contracts from/with the USDA, crop insurance, logging, and import and export and personnel data
Department of Commerce	The department maintains data on international trade, social and economic conditions and trends, patents, trademarks, ocean studies, domestic economic development, and minority businesses
Social Security Administration	Original Social Security applications, including maiden and married names, date and place of birth, sex, race, parents' names, and address at time of application
Department of Defense	Military information for the Army, Navy, Air Force, and Marine Corps, including military pay, dependents, allotments, deposits, and other financial data
Department of Education	Financial aid applications and earnings statements
Department of Housing and Urban Development (HUD)	Includes the Federal Housing Administration and information on loans, cost certificates, mortgagees, mortgage companies, and developers, as well as investigation of HUD violations
Department of Justice	Extensive law enforcement activities and data both domestically and internationally, including by INTERPOL, in more than 155 countries
Department of Labor	Extensive information on labor-related issues, including occupational safety and health, mine safety, labor management, and the Employee Retirement Income Security Act of 1974 (ERISA)
Department of State	All diplomatic activity and import and export licenses
Department of Treasury: Bureau of Alcohol, Tobacco, Firearms and Explosives (ATF)	Extensive work in law enforcement financial investigations for products, services, and crimes falling under its jurisdiction (as denoted in its name), including data on businesses and business owners, manufacturers, importers, and exporters
Department of Treasury: Internal Revenue Service (IRS)	Tax investigations related to income tax, excise tax, currency transaction reports (CTR), and occupational tax
Department of Treasury: U.S. Customs Service	Import and export data, including narcotics, border issues, and drug enforcement
Department of Treasury: U.S. Secret Service	Responsibility for forgers, counterfeiters, and businesses reporting counterfeiting operations
Department of Treasury: Office of Foreign Asset Control (OFAC)	Maintains lists of individuals, government entities, companies, and merchant vessels that are known or suspected to engage in illegal activities including Specially Designated Nationals and Blocked Persons (SDNs)
Department of Veterans Affairs (VA)	Records of loans, tuition payments, insurance payments, and some medical data
Drug Enforcement Agency (DEA)	Licensed handlers of narcotics and criminal records of persons convicted of drug violations
Federal Aviation Administration (FAA)	Chain of ownership of all civil aircraft, including the manufacture, sale, transfer, inspection, modification of aircraft, bills of sale, sales agreements, mortgages and liens, as well as the listing of pilots, mechanics, flight engineers, and safety personnel
Federal Bureau of Investigation (FBI)	Extensive law enforcement data, including databases, fingerprints, and wanted, missing, or unidentified domestic and foreign persons
Federal Communications Commission (FCC)	Licensor of radio and television operators, including ownership and ownership changes
Federal Energy Regulatory Commission (FERC)	Data on electric and natural gas providers, including officers, directors, and 10 percent stockholders
Federal Maritime Commission	Data on oceangoing freight-forwarding licensees, including company history and officers, directors, and 10 percent stockholders

(Continued)

TABLE 8-7 (*Continued*)

General Services Administration (GSA)	Information on architects, engineers, property auctioneers, real estate appraisers, construction contractors, sales brokers, and GSA contract businesses
Interstate Commerce Commission (ICC)	Financial information on truck lines and other interstate shippers, including officers; ICC provides safety checks
National Aeronautics and Space Administration (NASA)	NASA contracts out the vast majority of its annual budget and maintains financial data and officer information on its contractors
National Railroad Passenger Corporation (Amtrak)	Information on passengers, the railroad industry, railroad contractors/subcontractors, train routes, and schedules
Nuclear Regulatory Commission (NRC)	Applications and licenses of persons and companies that export nuclear material and equipment
Securities and Exchange Commission (SEC)	Extensive information on public companies, the majority of which is available free at www.sec.gov
Small Business Administration (SBA)	Information on small businesses and their owner/officers for which it has guaranteed loans for business construction, expansion, equipment, facilities, material, and working capital
Bureau of Public Debt	Information on the purchase and redemption of public debt, including savings bonds, marketable securities, and other U.S. government–backed securities
Federal Highway Administration	Information on motor carriers, including licenses, inspections, registrations, and operating histories
U.S. Citizenship and Immigration Services	Formerly the INS, the organization maintains information in aliens, registration records, lists of passengers and crews on oceangoing vessels, naturalization records, deportation records, and financial data on aliens and their sponsors
U.S. Coast Guard	Names of merchant mariners and investigative records on smuggling and other criminal violations
U.S. Government Accountability Office	As the investigative arm of Congress charged with examining matters relating to the receipt and payment of public funds; GAO audit and other reports are offered at www.gao.gov
U.S. Postal Service	Extensive investigative work related to mail fraud, in addition to names and addresses of post office box holders and photocopies of postal money orders
Federal Procurement Data System	Summaries of transactions and services negotiated with the U.S. government
FedWorld Information Network	FedWorld provides government information and resources for consumers and search capabilities for over 30 million government Internet pages

truth. E-mail addresses made be faked or masked through programming tools and techniques. As such, all evidence must be evaluated for its information content. For example, what is the source of the information? Is the face value of the information reasonable or believable? Can the information be verified from another source? The axiom of data evaluation is that data must be relevant, reliable, and valid. Before information goes into an evidence gathering system, it should be reviewed for specific relevancy to the investigation and the issue at hand. Relevance means that the information will make a difference to a decision maker. Data must be relevant to constitute evidence. Reliability refers to the source providing the information. The following scale can be used to evaluate the reliability of information collected during an investigation.

Source	Rating
Reliable: Source's reliability is unquestioned.	A
Usually reliable: The majority of past information has proven to be reliable.	B
Unreliable: Source's reliability has been sporadic.	C
Unknown: Reliability of source unknown.	D

Validity refers to the underlying accuracy and integrity of the information. Interviewees can lie; documents can be altered; general ledgers and other financial data can be manipulated. Depending on

TABLE 8-8 Commercial Sources and Data Bases

Better Business Bureau	Chamber of Commerce
Abstract and title companies	Bonding companies
Western Union	Car Fax (auto histories)
International Air Transport Association (aviation security, including terrorism)	International Foundation for Art Research
National Association of Insurance Commissioners	Phonefiche (cross-referencing)
Switchboard.com	ChoicePoint
Phone numbers and addresses for business and individuals	Identification and credential verification services for business and government
CDB Infotek	DBT On-Line
Business-to-business provider of public record information products	Electronic information retrieval services and patent enforcement and exploitation services
Lexis-Nexis	USDataLink
Information and services solutions, including its flagship Web-based Lexis® and Nexis® research services, for a wide range of professionals in the legal, risk management, corporate, government, law enforcement, accounting, and academic markets	Employment screening and investigative services for asset protection, due diligence, and risk management
infoUSA.com	Diligenz
Mailing lists and e-mail lists of businesses	Due diligence for the lending, leasing, and legal industries through UCC searching, filing, tracking, and online portfolio management services from the online UCC database and film library
KnowX	Dialog Information Retrieval Service
Nationwide public records search, background checks, liens, bankruptcy public records, company background checks, real estate ownership information, and judgments	Alphanumeric and Boolean public records database search

the importance to the investigation, the fraud examiner or forensic accounting professional needs to take the necessary steps to ensure that the information, on its face, is what it seems. Similar to reliability, a four-category rating system can be used to rate the validity or truthfulness of the information:

Validity	Rating
Confirmed: The information has been corroborated.	1
Probable: The information is consistent with past accounts.	2
Doubtful: The information is inconsistent with past accounts.	3
Cannot be judged: The information cannot be evaluated.	4

WORK PAPERS: THE ORGANIZATION OF EVIDENCE AND ANALYSIS

Gathering, documenting, organizing, retaining, and retrieving data, information, and evidence is an important part of the investigative process. As one lawyer stated, "If it isn't written down, it didn't happen." The fraud examiner and forensic accounting professional should always "begin with the end in mind." The professional should always begin with the assumption that his or her work, report, and conclusions, as well as all other aspects of his or her investigation, will be presented and scrutinized in a court of law. Thus, careful attention to work paper detail and the gathering, documenting, organizing, and retention of work product is of critical importance. In that regard, the following outlines the requirements for gathering and organizing evidence:

1. Plan for the collection of the records.
2. Obtain and inventory the records.

3. Develop templates for financial records databases and analyses (manual or automated).

4. Enter data from the records into the templates.

5. Double- and triple-check records that are entered manually.

6. Review the records for investigative leads.

7. Sort and analyze the records

   - By date
   - By payees
   - By deposit amounts
   - By disbursement amounts
   - In combination (multisort/autofilter)

8. Review the records for patterns. Examples include:

   - Showing check-writing habits of the person in charge of the account
   - Checks routinely written on certain dates
   - Repetitions of checks written by date, by day of the week
   - Periodic times when an account balance was low
   - Performance of the business in terms of
     - Revenues
     - Gross profits
     - Net profits

9. Review the records for unusual activity, such as anomalous financial performance and uncharacteristic deposits or payments:

   - Changes in activity before/during/after alleged criminal activity
   - Unusual timing of checks written
   - Checks issued with greater frequency than expected for typical business
   - Widely varying amounts of deposits or payments

10. Analyze cash and transaction flows across multiple accounts.

11. Identify additional leads to investigate:

    - Money *leaving* the country may involve financial advisors, attorneys, investment brokers
    - Money *entering* the country may involve corporate salaries, consultant fees, fictitious loans, phantom (foreign) investors
    - Breaks in disbursement patterns
    - New payees or vendors

12. Graphically explore the data by using flowcharts, diagrams, link charts, timelines, etc.

13. Prepare a summary of the financial activities.

14. Develop conclusions from the records, graphics, and summaries.

    Other considerations related to gathering, organizing, and retaining evidence may include

    - Organizing all documents for easy retrieval
    - Identifying additional data that will need to be gathered, either by the investigator or via subpoena or search warrant
    - Maintaining the chain of custody, including keeping the records in a locked office or storage facility

Work papers will form the basis of conclusions, expert opinions, and testimony. As such, all analyses and databases should be referenced and cross-referenced to ensure that the underlying evidence for the fraud examiner's or forensic accountant's work can be entered into evidence, because it is the foundation upon which the case is built. Work papers should include accounting records, documents, public records searches, electronic files, correspondence, logs and other chain-of-custody proof, notes and summaries of interviews and inquiries, and court documents such as complaints, pleadings, and depositions.

REVIEW QUESTIONS

8-1   How is the threshold for predication determined?

8-2   What are the challenges associated with proving intent on the part of a fraudster?

8-3   What constitutes evidence?

8-4   What are the three types of evidence that may be offered at trial?

8-5   What is meant by invigilation?

8-6   How do witness interviewing and interrogation differ?

8-7   How might documents be altered?

8-8   What are some methods of hiding assets?

8-9   When is it appropriate to use an indirect method for income reconstruction?

8-10 Where may fraud examiners and forensic accountants find data?

ENDNOTES

1. See the Fraud Examiners Manual.

2. Dennis Crawford, "The Life and Times of a Currency Transaction Report," BankersOnline.com (Volume 8, No. 9, 9/98).

3. Fraud Examiners Manual, Section 3.105.

4. Fraud Examiners Manual, Section 3.728.

CHAPTER 9

EFFECTIVE INTERVIEWING AND INTERROGATION

LEARNING OBJECTIVES

After completing this chapter, you should be able to:

9-1 Describe the benefits of strong interviewing and interrogation skills.

9-2 Discuss the reasons why interviews in fraudulent financial statements and tax returns are handled differently than interviews in other fraud examinations.

9-3 Explain some suggested approaches for conducting interviews.

9-4 Identify the five types of interview and interrogation questions.

9-5 Discuss why introductory questions are so important to an interview's success.

9-6 Compare open, closed, and leading questions.

9-7 Explain the purpose of admission-seeking questions.

9-8 Explain why it is advisable to obtain a written confession from the subject of an investigation.

9-9 Identify some verbal clues to deception.

9-10 Describe some nonverbal clues to deception.

CRITICAL THINKING EXERCISE

A murderer is condemned to death. He has to choose between three rooms. The first is full of raging fires, the second is full of assassins with loaded guns, and the third is full of lions that haven't eaten in three years. Which room is safest for him?

FROM THE EXPERT'S PERSPECTIVE

Enhanced Interrogation Techniques
Joseph T. Wells

Much ado has been made recently about "enhanced interrogation techniques" such as "waterboarding" to obtain information from suspected terrorists. At this writing, the finger seems to point at former Vice-President Dick Cheney for approving these tactics; he has publicly and vigorously defended waterboarding. For those who may have been living in a bubble, it is a method whereby the subject is strapped down and water is poured through a cloth on his face to simulate drowning.

I'm not a political person, and what follows is not a political statement. My main connection to politics is that, as an FBI agent, I used to put crooked politicians in prison. This will doubtlessly offend some readers, but I am not a fan of Mr. Cheney; there are many differences between the former vice-president and me. The first is that I served my country honorably in the U.S. Navy. Mr. Cheney got five draft deferments to keep him from the war in Viet Nam. Yet he was instrumental in sending several thousand young American men and women to their deaths in Iraq and Afghanistan, while maiming tens of thousands more.

A second difference is that I lived abroad (nearly three years in Europe and the United Kingdom) and am well aware of how America can be viewed by others. The third difference is that I have actually conducted interrogations—hundreds of them—while Mr. Cheney has not. I've had many, many years of professional training and experience on how to elicit reliable information from people; the former vice-president has not.

A fundamental lesson I was taught at the FBI Academy was not to threaten, coerce, or torture people to get them to talk. There is a good reason for these prohibitions: statements by individuals under duress are highly unreliable. Whether or not these persons are American citizens is hardly the point. Former FBI agent Ali Soufan—who was heavily involved in the questioning of suspected terrorists—strongly condemned waterboarding and other "enhanced interrogation techniques," saying that such actions "... from an operational perspective, are ineffective, slow, and unreliable and harmful to our efforts to defeat al Qaeda."

The FBI didn't teach its agents how to waterboard; like most of you, I never even heard the term before the U.S. was accused of using this technique in violation of UN and other international treaties. You may be interested to know that this method of attempting to extract information was used back as far as the Spanish Inquisition when it was known as "tortura del agua"—literally, "water torture." It was also used by the Nazis in World War II, in the Algerian War, and in Viet Nam (by a few American soldiers who were court-martialed for it).

Only since about 2002 has the United States done an about-face and considered waterboarding acceptable; waterboarding was, and is, universally condemned by even America's strongest allies as torture. The term "waterboarding" is of relatively recent vintage, lifted from surfing terminology as a euphemism to mask the horrors of the procedure. If waterboarding actually worked, then why would it be necessary to use this method a combined 266 times on accused terrorists Abu Zubaydah and Khalid Shaikh Mohammed?

Is waterboarding torture? To quote a famous line in Shakespeare's *Romeo and Juliet*, "What's in a name? That which we call a rose by any other name would smell as sweet." But there is nothing sweet about waterboarding, regardless of whether it is torture. It, along with similar "enhanced interrogation techniques," is of dubious value; the interrogator is told what he or she wants to hear, whether it is the truth or not. And if an interrogation cannot elicit the truth, what is the point?

In conducting a fraud examination, it is highly unlikely that you will have the necessity to use these controversial methods. But there is still a very valuable lesson to be learned. In almost any investigation, there is an opportunity to step over the line—to do something illegal, immoral, or unethical. Experienced investigators know that not every case can be solved. Accept that fact and adhere to a high moral code, regardless of what is merely acceptable under current law. Let's work to ensure that the values we seek to protect are vigorously preserved.

INTRODUCTION TO INTERVIEWS AND INTERROGATIONS

In the fraud examination and forensic accounting professions, nothing is more important to the successful resolution of a case than the ability to conduct thorough interviews of witnesses, and interrogations (also known as admission-seeking interviews) of subjects and targets. While accountants and auditors routinely ask questions, the queries rarely are for the purposes of confronting a subject with wrongdoing. Interviewing is the systematic questioning of a person who has knowledge of events, people, evidence, and other details surrounding a fraud or forensic accounting issue. In contrast, interrogation generally involves the questioning of a suspect, target, or uncooperative witness to obtain evidence, to obtain an admission of guilt or complicity in an act, or to give the interviewee an opportunity to volunteer facts and circumstances that may eliminate them as a suspect or target of the investigation. (The terms "suspect," "subject," and "target" are used somewhat interchangeably, even by experienced interviewers, but they are not precisely the same. A *suspect* is just that—a person suspected of committing an offense. Once the investigator is fairly sure that the suspect has committed the fraud, the term changes to *subject* or *target*. However, *target* is more commonly used by prosecutors, who frequently send "target letters" to the subject of an investigation, putting the person(s) on notice that grand jury proceedings are likely imminent.)

Interviews and interrogations have many similarities: both require planning, controlled surroundings, some level of privacy, rapport between the interviewer and interviewee, and proper documentation upon completion. However, interviews contrast with interrogations in many ways. First, interrogations, being adversarial in nature, generally require more planning to be effective, as well as more control of the surrounding environment, and absolute privacy. In addition, whereas interviews are primarily an information-gathering exercise, interrogations act to test or confirm information already known or suspected by the investigator. Furthermore, in most situations, during an interrogation, especially by law enforcement, the interviewer must be vigilant of the rights of the interviewee. Interrogations can often generate a hostile reaction from the subject or suspect, whereas most interviews are conducted in a spirit of cooperation. Finally, the subject of an interrogation is suspected at some level of culpability in the act under investigation.

In civil litigation, interviews are critical. Generally, interviews are often conducted through deposition testimony, so the interview will not be conducted by an investigator, but by an attorney. However, even in those situations in which the fraud examiner or forensic accountant will not be asking the questions, he or she nonetheless plays a critical role. Attorneys often request that the fraud or forensic accounting professional provide an outline of topics that require inquiry. Furthermore, because many attorneys have no training in accounting and little experience with topics such as debits, credits, financial statements, revenues versus assets, liabilities versus expenses and so forth, they will request that their forensic accounting professional script a long series of questions in advance of the deposition. In those circumstances, the attorney

will be burdened with asking appropriate follow-up questions, looking for signs of deception and making sure that the topical area is exhausted prior to moving the deposition on to other topics. In that regard, the attorney will often request that the fraud professional or forensic accountant attend the deposition of key witnesses who have knowledge of, or should have knowledge of, the financial transactions and how they are reflected in the books and records. In those circumstances, the expert will need to treat the deposition as if he or she were conducting the interview themselves to ensure that the testimonial record is complete.

There are several benefits of effective interviewing and interrogation skills, including

- Reduced investigation time
- Increased probability of investigative success
- Improved confidence in investigative conclusions
- Direct evidence of culpability versus indirect evidence from examination of books, records, and other evidentiary forms
- The elimination of innocent subjects or targets

Interviews in Fraud Examinations

In a fraud examination, evidence is usually gathered in a manner that moves from the general to the specific, as illustrated in Figure 9-1. That rule applies both to gathering documentary evidence and to taking witness statements. Therefore, a fraud examiner would most likely start by examining appropriate documents and records, and then interview neutral third-party witnesses—persons who may have some knowledge about the fraud, but who are not involved in the offense. For example, the fraud examiner may start with a former employee of the company. Next, the fraud examiner would interview corroborative witnesses—those people who are not directly involved in the offense, but who may be able to corroborate specific facts related to it.

If after interviewing neutral third-party witnesses and corroborative witnesses it appears that further investigation is warranted, the fraud examiner proceeds by interviewing suspected coconspirators in the alleged offense. These people are generally interviewed in order, starting with those thought to be least culpable and proceeding to those thought to be most culpable. Only after suspected coconspirators have been interviewed is the person suspected of committing the fraud confronted. By arranging interviews in order of probable culpability, the fraud examiner is in a position to have as much information as possible by the time the prime target is interviewed. Moreover, if the interviews clear the target of the offense, an admission-seeking interview or interrogation can be avoided altogether.

Interviews in Fraudulent Financial Statements and Tax Returns

Interestingly, with fraudulent representations such as materially misstated financial statements and improper tax returns, the investigator starts with the suspected perpetrator. The logic of this is simple;

FIGURE 9-1 Evidence-Gathering Order in Fraud Examinations

assuming the person knowingly created false financial statements or tax returns, the act of falsifying is part of the concealment of the act. This being the case, the perpetrator has made one of the following assumptions: the auditor or investigator won't find the issue (or, if red flags related to the issue are identified, the auditor or investigator won't be skilled enough to unravel the underlying evidence to determine what really happened). Essentially, the alleged perpetrator is pitting his or her intellect against that of the auditor or investigator. Thus, by interviewing the suspected perpetrator at the inception of the audit, examination, or investigation, you are documenting his or her claim(s) that the financial statements are not materially misstated, or that the tax return properly reflects all items of taxable income and taxes owed. Thus, if the auditor subsequently finds fraudulent financial reporting, he or she has caught the perpetrator in a lie and has developed further evidence of concealment.

OVERVIEW OF THE INTERVIEW AND INTERROGATION PROCESS

Preparation and Planning

Preparation and planning are critical to successful interviews, interrogations, and depositions. Preparation includes knowing as much as you can about the witness, the crime (or forensic accounting issue), the victim or victim organization, and possible perpetrators in advance of the interview. In this regard, the fraud examiner or forensic accountant must pore over all the available evidence to identify what areas need to be covered in an interview, detect clues to deception in the interviewee's statements and nonverbal body language, and recognize unreasonable and inappropriate explanations for behavior and interpretations of the evidence by the interviewee. Most fraud professionals, forensic accountants, and attorneys will state that the outcome of the interview or interrogation can be determined before the first question is asked. Preparation is the primary key to success.

When planning an interview, the interviewer should have an understanding of the offense under investigation:

- What are the legal elements (i.e., is it a fraud charge, or a forensic accounting issue)?
- What are the details of the alleged issue under investigation:
  - Who?
  - What?
  - Where (place)?
  - When (date and time)?
  - How?
  - Why?
- What methodology was used to commit the offense?
- What methodology was used to conceal the offense?
- What benefit or conversion was there to the possible perpetrator(s)?
- What evidence of the act, concealment, and conversion has been obtained, and what evidence is needed to develop conclusions?
- Who had opportunity to commit the offense?
- Did the possible perpetrator(s) have access to other assets of the victim?

Interview and interrogation planning also considers the witness's personal background, including marital status, education, job history, and history with the entities involved in the suspected crime or civil offense. Furthermore, the fraud examiner or forensic professional should consider:

- Does the witness have any nonsharable financial needs (pressures)?
- What types of rationalizations might the witness or suspect have demonstrated?
- What other motivation might the witness have?
  - Money
  - Ideology
  - Coercion
  - Ego

Another planning consideration is the venue for the interview. When determining the location, consider the likelihood of distractions and interruptions as well the level of anxiety to the interviewee. With interrogations, the venue should be private and void of any distractions. This being the case, a location away from the interviewee's familiar surroundings is usually best; the ideal circumstance is to conduct the interrogation at a place selected by the investigator. When scheduling the interview or interrogation, allow sufficient time. Schedule the interview in advance to avoid time conflicts or constraints placed on the interview. However, interrogations should be conducted by surprise whenever possible. Finally, good interview preparation requires arriving at the interview early and reviewing notes one final time before meeting with the interviewee.

General Approach to Conducting Interviews

The following provides some guidelines for conducting the interview or interrogation. First, the room should be set up so that the interviewer can see the entire body of the interview subject. The interviewer's chair should be located about six feet in front of the interviewee. During the interview, the interviewer should be respectful and professional at all times. He or she should avoid technical terms and language that may confuse the interviewee, especially when the person does not have a financial background and is not familiar with fraud examination and forensic accounting terminology. The interviewer should avoid taking detailed notes during the interview, instead just jotting down key words. This may surprise some people, but a key to successful interviewing is listening and watching for body language that suggests discomfort and possibly deceit by the interviewee. Taking extensive notes distracts interviewers from their main responsibility to watch and listen.

Other considerations for conducting good interviews include

- Keeping questions reasonably short
- Keeping questions to the point
- Avoiding leading questions that suggest a specific answer
- Discouraging the interviewee from speculating too much in the absence of underlying facts
- Discouraging the interviewee from getting off-subject
- Making sure the interviewer understands the interviewee's response before moving on to new topics
- Maintaining control of the interview

Interviews of Witnesses

Witness interviewees are usually cooperative, but that is not always the case. In some instances, in an effort to calm the witness, the interviewer may assure the person that they are not a subject or a target of the investigation. At the same time, the interviewer needs to let the person know that their assumption is based on the evidence collected to date, and that if the direction of the investigation changes, it may be possible that the witness may at some point become a suspect, subject, or target. Some suggested approaches for interviewing witnesses are as follows:

- Start with background information. This will have a calming effect on the interviewee and will allow the interviewer to establish a baseline for evaluating deception during more difficult aspects of the interview as the interviewer drills down into details and gets closer to the fraud act.
- Organize interview questions in chronological order. Following a timeline provides a sense of organization to the interview and helps keep the witness on track.
- Document the witness' connection to suspects, subjects, or targets of the investigation. This may create some discomfort to the witness, because he or she may know some aspects of the act and may be concerned about their own culpability.
- Document discussions between the witness and any subjects or targets related to the specific issues under investigation.
- Determine whether the witness is in possession of any pertinent documents.
- Elicit any opinions that the witness may have about events and acts under investigation.
- Determine whether the witness has any other ideas, knows of other matters that should be looked into, or knows of other witnesses who may be of assistance in sorting through the issues at hand.

As the fraud examiner or forensic accountant moves away from witnesses and toward those with higher levels of culpability, the interviews are likely to be less friendly, and possibly adversarial. One of the reasons for this is that culpability and confrontation of the subject or target by the interviewer creates stress. Essentially, the possibility of getting caught creates a crisis for the subject or target. These individuals often react as most would react to crises—with denial, anger, rationalization, depression, and—finally—acceptance. Because of this, the tone of the interview with subjects and targets is likely to be strained. Although the content and goals of the interview of subjects and targets are the same as for those of any witness, the interviewer needs to be prepared for a more adversarial tenor to the conversation. Accordingly, the interviewer needs to manage the interview more carefully and have complete command of facts, events, dates, and all details in order to deflate attempts at misdirection and deception by the subject or target.

Three Stages of Interviewing: Introduction, Body, and Close

Interviews are conducted in three stages: the introduction, the body, and the close. During the introduction stage, the interviewer greets the interviewee and states the reason for the interview. (The reason should be simply stated, and not overly complicated—for example, "We are looking into a matter involving company assets.") Generally, the interviewer's tone during the introduction is nonconfrontational. At this point, the interviewer is trying to bring about a sense of rapport with the interviewee. Although this is more difficult with subjects and targets, the introduction will set the tone for all interview types. To the extent possible, it is important to start off on the right foot. During the introduction stage, the interviewer also maintains a professional tone but importantly solicits the cooperation of the witness, subject, or target. Although the subject or target may bristle at being asked to assist the investigator, setting the tone by requesting the help of each interviewee is important to successful interviews by helping establish rapport with the interviewee. This period is nonthreatening and allows the interviewer to assess the witness's spirit of cooperation. It also provides the beginnings of the baseline for assessment of misdirection and deceit.

The body of the interview is where most of the work gets done. In the last section of this chapter, a guide to the types of information solicited during interviews is provided. Although not every interview is going to solicit all of this information, the listing provides a comprehensive overview of areas that the interviewer should consider. During this phase, the facts and evidence of the case are reviewed with the interviewee. The interview tends to move from general topical areas to specific areas and issues of inquiry. The questions are generally open-ended; the interviewer should allow the interviewee to completely answer questions before asking any follow-up questions. Although keeping interviewees on subject is important, letting them talk often provides valuable tidbits of information. The interviewer should completely understand the witness's explanations and answers before moving on. Thus, one or two follow-up questions are usually necessary to arrive at a complete understanding. During the body of the interview, the interviewer needs to demonstrate patience, and should be sure not to interrupt the interviewee. It is also important for the interviewer to focus on listening, gathering information, and watching for misdirection and deceit.

One issue that arises is the use of checklists and prewritten questionnaires. The main benefit of checklists and questionnaires is that the interviewer will be well prepared, and less likely to miss important aspects of inquiry. However, checklists can create tunnel vision and inhibit the investigator's capacity for creative and critical thinking. If not used properly, checklists can also limit the discussion, distracting the interviewer from listening and looking for signs of deception. A compromise might be a list of topical areas that require exploration. Ultimately, the choice made by the interviewer should be that choice which makes him or her most effective at obtaining the necessary information. At all times, no matter what tools the interviewer chooses, he or she must remain flexible and maintain a commitment to critical thinking. Once the interview is complete, the fraud examiner or forensic accountant may not get another opportunity to question the witness, so it is important to be thorough, and not to terminate the interview before having obtained as much relevant information as possible.

The final stage of the interview is the close. At a minimum, during the close, the interviewer will review and summarize important aspects of the interview, clarifying when necessary and asking any final questions about the interviewee's responses. The interviewer should attempt to end the interview on a positive note by asking the following questions:

Is there anything that I have forgotten to ask?

Is there anything else you would like to add for the record?

Is there anyone else I should speak with about the issues we have covered?

Finally, the interviewer should leave the door open for future discussion.

Two Stages of Interrogations: Introduction and Admission-Seeking

Interrogations, or admission-seeking interviews, are reserved for obtaining confessions from those believed to be culpable for the acts under examination. This type of interview has two main phases: the introduction, and the process of obtaining a confession to the acts (discussed below in the admission-seeking questions section). The process seeks to soften the target's resistance to confessing by identifying a rationalization that is palatable to him. Rationalizations provide a morally justifiable reason for the target's actions. For example, he or she may justify the act as an appropriate response to bad treatment by his or her employer. Rationalization gives the person an excuse for his or her inappropriate behavior and helps "grease the skids" to gain the confession—however (importantly), the rationalization does not reduce the legal responsibility for the act.

FIVE TYPES OF INTERVIEW AND INTERROGATION QUESTIONS

Regardless of whom we interview, and about what, there are five general types of questions we can ask: introductory, informational, assessment, closing, and admission-seeking (interrogation). In routine interview situations, in which the object is to gather information from neutral or corroborative witnesses, only three of the five types of questions will normally be asked: introductory, informational, and closing. If you have reasonable cause to believe that the respondent is not being truthful, assessment questions can be asked. Finally, if you decide with reasonable cause that the respondent is responsible for misdeeds, admission-seeking questions can be posed.

Introductory Questions

Introductory questions serve four primary purposes: providing an introduction, establishing a rapport between you and the subject, establishing the theme of the interview, and observing the subject's reactions.

Provide the Introduction Indicate your name and company, but avoid using titles. As a general proposition, the more informal the interview, the more relaxed the respondent will be. This leads to better communication. You should also shake hands with the person. Making physical contact helps break down psychological barriers to communication. Be wary of invading the respondent's personal space; this might make the person uncomfortable. You generally should remain at a distance of four to six feet.

Once the respondent is seated, it is helpful to inquire whether the person would like something to drink, or whether he or she would like to remove a coat (and so forth). It is best to take care of these matters before beginning the interview, so that delays and interruptions can be minimized during the interview.

Establish Rapport Some common ground must be established before questioning begins. This is usually accomplished by engaging in "small talk" for a few minutes. This should not be overdone, but should be used as a means of breaking the ice and establishing a flow of communication between you and the interviewee.

Establish the Interview Theme The interview theme might be related only indirectly to the actual purpose of the interview. The goal of the theme is to get the respondent to "buy in" to assisting in the interview. The theme for the interview should be one that is logical for the respondent to accept, and easy for you to explain. One of the most effective interview themes is that you are seeking the subject's help. Nearly all human beings get satisfaction from helping others. Throughout the interview, it is important to include the subject as part of the process, rather than making him or her feel like a target of the inquiry. During this phase of the interview, the respondent must not feel threatened.

Observe Reactions You must be skilled in interpreting the respondent's reactions to questions. The majority of communication between individuals is nonverbal; the subject will provide clues about what he or she knows—consciously or subconsciously—with body language, tone of voice, and attitude. You must thus systematically observe the various responses the person gives during the course of the interview.

This is done by first posing nonsensitive questions while establishing rapport. By observing reactions to these kinds of questions, you can establish a baseline for the subject's verbal and nonverbal behavior. Later, when more sensitive questions are asked, you will observe the interviewee's response. If the respondent's verbal and nonverbal behavior significantly changes as particular questions are posed, you must attempt to determine why. (For more detailed discussion, see Judging Deception, below.)

General Rules for the Introductory Phase of the Interview

Don't Interview More Than One Person at a Time   One of the basic rules is to question only one person at a time. The testimony of one respondent will invariably influence the testimony of another. There are few hard-and-fast rules—but this is one of them.

Privacy   Another basic rule is to conduct interviews under conditions of privacy. The interview is best conducted out of sight and earshot of friends, relatives, or fellow employees. People are very reluctant to furnish information within the hearing of others.

Ask Nonsensitive Questions   Sensitive questions should be scrupulously avoided until well into the interview. Even then, such questions should be asked only after careful deliberation and planning. During the introductory phase, emotive words generally should be avoided. Such words normally put people on the defensive, making them more reluctant to answer and to cooperate.

EXAMPLE

Instead of	*Use*
Investigation	*Inquiry*
Audit	*Review*
Interview	*Ask a few questions*
Embezzle/steal/theft	*Shortage or paperwork problems*

Get a Commitment for Assistance   It is critical for you to obtain a commitment for assistance from the person being interviewed. The commitment must consist of some positive action on the part of the subject; remaining silent or simply nodding the head is not sufficient. You should ask for the commitment before the interview commences, and should encourage the interviewee to voice a positive, audible "yes" when asked if he or she will help. If you encounter silence the first time you ask for assistance, the question should be repeated in a slightly different way until the respondent verbalizes the commitment.

Make a Transitional Statement   Once you have gotten a commitment for assistance, you must describe the purpose of the interview in more detail. This is done with a transitional statement, which sets forth a legitimate basis for the questioning and explains to the subject how he or she fits into the inquiry. After making the transitional statement, you should seek a second commitment for assistance. Assume, for example, that we are interviewing Linda Reed Collins for the first time. If we don't know for sure that she has done anything wrong, we don't want to put her off; that would impede the information-gathering process. After you have introduced yourself and asked Ms. Collins for assistance, here is a way you might make a transitional statement:

EXAMPLE

Interviewer: "It's pretty routine, really. I'm gathering some information about the purchasing function and how it is supposed to work. It would be helpful to me if I could start by asking you to basically tell me about your job. Okay?"

Seek Continuous Agreement   Throughout the interview process—from the introduction to the close—you should attempt to phrase questions so that they can be answered "yes." It is easier for people to reply in the affirmative than the negative.

Do Not Promise Confidentiality   Some people may be hesitant to speak to you for fear that the information will not be confidential. They may request a promise of confidentiality for any statements made. When this happens, you should inform the individual that all information that is gathered will be provided only to others who have a "need to know." You should not make any promise that the matters discussed will be confidential. Any information gathered in an interview belongs to the client or employer, not you. You do not have the right to limit the use of the information or to decide how it will be used. Because of this, a promise that the information will be kept confidential is misleading, and may taint the information's subsequent use.

Negotiations   In some situations, a person may attempt to negotiate with you, offering information in exchange for something from the company or the client. If this happens, you should keep the discussion open and listen to what the individual may want. However, unless otherwise authorized to do so, you should not represent a "quid pro quo" with respect to cooperation. You should say that any information provided will be conveyed to the appropriate individual and will be taken into account. To negotiate is to lose control of the interview and investigation.

Discussing the Source of Allegations   In the event that you are following up on a complaint or allegation, you should not discuss the fact that there is an allegation, or whence the information originated. If Collins, for example, asks where the complaint or information originated, you should advise her that as a matter of policy, the basis for any inquiry is not discussed.

Informational Questions

Once the proper format for the interview has been set, you should turn to the fact-gathering portion. Informational questions should be nonconfrontational and nonthreatening and should be asked for the purpose of gathering unbiased, factual information. The great majority of your questions will fall into this category.

There are essentially three types of questions that can be asked: open, closed, and leading. These question types are discussed in more detail below. Each type of question is used in a logical sequence to maximize the development of information. If you have reason to believe that the respondent is being untruthful, then assessment questions can be posed. Otherwise, the interview is brought to a logical close at the end of the informational phase.

Open Questions   Open questions are those worded in a way that makes it difficult to answer "yes" or "no." The typical open question calls for a monologue response and can be answered in several different ways. During the information phase of the interview, you should endeavor to ask primarily open questions. This is to stimulate conversation and allow the subject to convey as much information as possible. An open question does not restrict the subject's response. So instead of asking, *"You are in charge of purchasing, aren't you?"* which directs the subject's response to one particular area, you might ask, *"Would you tell me about your job?"* The latter example allows a broad response in which more information will be conveyed. Later, you can go back and draw out more information about a particular topic.

Closed Questions   Closed questions are those that limit the possible responses by requiring a precise answer—usually "yes" or "no." (*"Did you approve this vendor?"*) Closed questions are also used to deal with specifics, such as amounts, dates, and times. (*"On what day of the week did it happen?"*) Generally, closed questions should be avoided in the informational part of the interview. (They are used extensively in the closing phase.)

Leading Questions   Leading questions contain the answer as a part of the question. They are usually used to confirm facts that are already known. An example of a leading question is: *"There have been no changes in the operation since last year, have there?"* This type of question gives the subject much less room to maneuver than an open question such as, *"What changes have been made in the operation since last year?"*

Notice how the leading question directs the subject to answer in a particular way. It implies that you already know the answer, and asks the subject to confirm it. The open question allows more latitude, allowing the subject to make any comments he or she wants about changes in the operation. The closed question narrows the subject's options a bit, but it still allows the subject to confirm or deny that changes have been made. Leading questions can be particularly effective in obtaining confessions or getting subjects to make unpleasant admissions.

Question Sequences   As a general rule, questioning should proceed from the general to the specific; it is best to gather general information before seeking details. A variation is to "reach backward" with the questions, beginning with known information and working toward unknown areas. An efficient method of doing this is to recount the known information and then frame the next question as a logical continuation of the facts previously related.

Informational Question Techniques Below are suggestions to improve the quality of the interview during the information-gathering phase.

- Begin by asking questions that are not likely to cause the respondent to become defensive or hostile.
- Ask the questions in a manner that will develop the facts in the order of their occurrence, or in some other systematic order.
- Ask only one question at a time, and frame the question so that only one answer is required.
- Ask straightforward and frank questions; generally avoid shrewd approaches.
- Keep interruptions to a minimum, and do not stop the subject's narrative without good reason.
- Give the respondent ample time to answer; do not rush.
- Try to help the respondent remember, but do not suggest answers, and be careful not to imply any particular answer by facial expressions, gestures, methods of asking questions, or types of questions asked.
- Repeat or rephrase questions, if necessary, to get at the facts.
- Be sure you understand the answers, and if they are not perfectly clear, have the respondent interpret them at that time instead of waiting until later.
- Give the person an opportunity to qualify his or her answers.
- Separate facts from inferences.
- Have the interviewee give comparisons by percentages, fractions, estimates of time and distance, and other such methods to ensure accuracy.
- After the respondent has given a narrative account, ask follow-up questions about key issues that have been discussed.
- Upon concluding the direct questioning, ask the respondent to summarize the information given. Then summarize the facts, and have the respondent verify that these conclusions are correct.

Methodology In order to begin the informational phase of the interview, you must first make a transition out of the introductory phase. The transition is a signal that you and the respondent are going to begin discussing the substantive issues that are the purpose of the interview. The transition usually is accomplished by asking people about themselves or their duties. It often begins with a restatement of the purpose of the interview—*"As I said, I am gathering information about the company's operations. Can you tell me about what you do on a day-to-day basis?"*

Begin with Background Questions Assuming the interviewee does not have a problem answering the transitional question, you should proceed with a series of easy, open questions designed to follow up on the subject's answer and to expand on the information already provided. Questions such as *"How long have you been working here?"* or *"What do you like best about your job?"* or *"What do your responsibilities involve?"* are good examples of background questions that will help you get a better understanding of what the person does and what information he or she might possess.

Observe Verbal and Nonverbal Behavior During the period when the respondent is talking, you should discreetly observe the person's verbal and nonverbal behavior. This will help you calibrate his or her mannerisms. Later, when more sensitive questions are posed, you can look for deviations in behavior that might indicate discomfort or deception.

Ask Nonleading (Open) Questions You should use open questioning techniques almost exclusively during the informational phase of the interview. The questions should not be accusatory. Once the respondent has answered open questions, you can go back and review the facts in greater detail. If the interviewee's answers are inconsistent, you should try to clarify them. But you should not challenge the honesty or integrity of the respondent at this stage of the interview. This can cause the person to become defensive, and reluctant to provide information.

Approach Sensitive Questions Carefully Words such as "routine questions" can be used to play down the significance of the inquiry. It is important for information-gathering purposes that you not react excessively to the respondent's statements. You should not express shock, disgust, or similar emotions during the interview; every answer given should be treated evenly.

Dealing with Difficult People   You will encounter some people who choose to be difficult during an interview. There are five common-sense steps to take in such situations.

Do Not React   A person might be belligerent or try to antagonize you, often for no apparent reason. There are three natural reactions for you in this situation: to strike back, to give in, or to terminate the interview. None of these tactics is satisfactory, for none leads to a productive interview. Instead, you should consciously ensure that you do not react to anger with hostility.

Disarm the Person   A common mistake is to try to reason with an unreceptive person. Instead, you should attempt to disarm them. The best tactic is surprise. If the person is stonewalling, he or she expects you to apply pressure; if attacking, he or she expects you to resist. To disarm the interviewee, listen, acknowledge the point, and agree whenever you can.

Change Tactics   In some situations, changing tactics to reduce hostility might be the only viable option. This means casting what the person says in a form that directs attention back to the problem and to the interests of both sides. An effective technique when faced with a hostile individual is to ask what he or she would do to solve the problem.

Volatile Interviews   A volatile interview is one that has the potential to bring about strong emotional reactions in the respondent. A typical scenario for a volatile interview occurs when you interview close friends or relatives of a suspect or subject. Some individuals, by nature, are resentful of authority figures, such as fraud examiners and law enforcement officers. It is important for you to know how to approach a volatile interview.

There should be two interviewers involved in potentially volatile situations. This procedure provides psychological strength for you. Additionally, the second person can serve as a witness in the event that the subject later makes allegations of improper conduct.

Potentially volatile interviews should be conducted on a surprise basis, meaning that the subject should be given little or no advance notice of the interview. If the interview is not conducted by surprise, you run the risk of the respondent not showing up, showing up with a witness, or being present with counsel.

In a potentially volatile interview, the order of questions should be out of sequence. This is to keep a volatile respondent from knowing the exact nature of the inquiry, and where it is leading. Although you are attempting to obtain the same information as in other interviews—who, what, why, when, where, and how—the order of the questions will vary. This is especially important in situations where the respondent is seeking to protect himself or herself.

A hypothetical question generally is considered to be less threatening, and is, therefore, ideally suited for the potentially volatile interview. For example, in an interview of Smith regarding Jones, rather than saying, *"Did Ms. Jones do it?"* ask, *"Is there any reason why Ms. Jones would have done it?"*

Closing Questions

In routine interviews, certain questions are asked at closing for the purposes of reconfirming the facts, obtaining previously undiscovered information, seeking new evidence, and maintaining goodwill.

Reconfirming Facts   It is not unusual for you to have misunderstood or misinterpreted statements made by the witness. Therefore, you should go over key facts to make certain they have been understood. You should not attempt to revisit all the information that has been provided. This is wasteful and unnecessary and may engender frustration or resentment in the interviewee. Instead, you need to identify the most relevant facts that have been provided, and go over each of them in summary form.

It is a good technique to pose leading questions at this phase of the interview. This allows you to state what you understood was said, and gives the person a chance to confirm or deny your interpretation— *"You knew Ms. Jones had some financial problems, is that right?"*

Gathering Additional Facts   The closing phase also can be used to obtain previously unknown facts. It provides the person further opportunity to say whatever he or she wants about the matter at hand. You should make it a point to ask if he or she knows of any other documents or witnesses that would be helpful to the investigation—such information is not always volunteered. The theme of the closing phase should be to provide the person with an opportunity to furnish any relevant facts or opinions that might have been overlooked.

To obtain additional facts, you can simply ask if there is anything else he or she would like to say. This gives the correct impression that you are interested in all relevant information, regardless of which side it favors. It can be helpful to involve the respondent in solving the case—*"If you were trying to resolve this issue, what would you do?"*

Concluding the Interview   At the conclusion of an interview, it is a good idea to ask respondents if they believe they have been treated fairly. This is particularly important at the conclusion of an admission-seeking interview, or when the person has been uncooperative. You generally should ask the question as if it were perfunctory—*"Ms. Collins, this is just a standard question. Do you feel that I have treated you fairly in this interview?"*

Before concluding, you should always ask the interviewee if he or she has anything else to say. This gives the person one final chance to add information. You should ask for permission to call the witness if you have any additional questions. This leaves the door open to additional cooperation. It is a good idea to give the person a business card or a telephone number and to invite a call if he or she remembers anything else that might be relevant. Finally, you should shake hands with the individual, thanking him or her for his or her time and information.

Assessment Questions

The purpose of assessment questions is to establish the credibility of the respondent. They are used only when you consider previous statements by the respondent to be inconsistent because of possible deception. By observing the verbal and nonverbal responses to these questions, you can assess the person's credibility with some degree of accuracy. That assessment will form the basis of your decision about whether to pose admission-seeking questions to obtain a legally binding admission of wrongdoing.

If the person has answered all informational questions about the event and you have reason to believe the answers are deceptive, a theme must be established to justify additional questions. This theme can ordinarily be put forth by saying, *"I have a few additional questions."* You should not indicate in any way that these questions are for a different purpose than seeking information.

Norming or Calibrating   *Norming* or *calibrating* is the process of observing behavior before critical questions are asked, as opposed to doing so during questioning. Norming should be a routine part of all interviews. People with truthful attitudes will answer questions one way; those with untruthful attitudes generally will answer them differently. Assessment questions ask the interviewee to agree with matters that go against the principles of most honest people. In other words, dishonest people are likely to agree with many of the statements, while honest people won't. Assessment questions are designed primarily to get a verbal or nonverbal reaction from the respondent. You will then carefully assess that reaction.

Methodology   Assessment questions should proceed logically from the least to the most sensitive. In most examples, the basis for the question should be explained before the question is asked. The following questions illustrate the pattern that an interviewer might take in questioning a witness when he has some reason to believe the respondent, a company employee, has knowledge of a suspected fraud.

EXAMPLE

Interviewer: "The company is particularly concerned about fraud and abuse. There are some new laws in effect that will cost the company millions if abuses go on and we don't try to find them. Do you know which law I am talking about?"

EXPLANATION

Most individuals will not know about the laws concerning corporate sentencing guidelines, and will, therefore, answer "no." The purpose of this question is to get the respondent to understand the serious nature of fraud and abuse.

EXAMPLE

Interviewer: "Congress passed a law that can levy fines of more than $200 million against companies that don't try to clean their own houses. $200 million is a lot of money, so you can understand why the company's concerned, can't you?"

EXPLANATION

The majority of people will say "yes" to this question. In the event of a "no" answer, you should explain the issue fully and, thereafter, attempt to get the respondent's agreement. If that agreement is not forthcoming, you should assess why not.

EXAMPLE

Interviewer: *"Of course, they are not talking about a loyal employee who gets in a bind. They're talking more about senior management. Have you ever read in the newspapers about what kind of people engage in company misdeeds?"*

EXPLANATION

Most people read the newspapers and are at least generally familiar with the problem of fraud and abuse. Agreement by the respondent is expected to this question.

EXAMPLE

Interviewer: *"Most of them aren't criminals at all. A lot of times, they're just trying to save their jobs or just trying to get by because the company is so cheap that they won't pay people what they are worth. Do you know what I mean?"*

EXPLANATION

Although the honest person and the dishonest person will both probably answer "yes" to this question, the honest individual is less likely to accept the premise that these people are not wrongdoers. Many honest people will reply to the effect that, while they might understand the motivation, that does not justify stealing.

EXAMPLE

Interviewer: *"Why do you think someone around here might be justified in making a secret arrangement with one of the company's vendors?"*

EXPLANATION

Because fraud perpetrators frequently justify their acts, the dishonest individual is more likely than the honest person to attempt a justification, such as, *"Everyone does it,"* or*"The company should treat people better if they don't want things like this to happen."* The honest person, on the other hand, is much less likely to offer a justification.

EXAMPLE

Interviewer: *"How do you think we should deal with someone who got in a bind and did something wrong in the eyes of the company?"*

EXPLANATION

Similar to other questions in this series, the honest person tends to want to punish the criminal, while the culpable individual will typically avoid suggesting a strong punishment—e.g., *"How should I know? It's not up to me,"* or, *"If they were a good employee, maybe we should give them another chance."*

EXAMPLE

Interviewer: *"Do you think someone in your department might have done something wrong because they thought they were justified?"*

EXPLANATION

Most people—honest or dishonest—will answer "no" to this question. However, when you get a "yes," the culpable person is more likely to do so without responding. The honest person, if answering "yes," will most likely provide details.

EXAMPLE

Interviewer: *"Have you ever felt yourself—even though you didn't go through with it—justified in taking advantage of your position?"*

EXPLANATION

Again, most people, both honest and dishonest, will answer this question "no." However, the dishonest person is more likely to acknowledge having at least "thought" of doing it.

EXAMPLE

Interviewer: *"Who in your department do you feel would think they were justified in doing something against the company?"*

EXPLANATION

The dishonest person will not likely furnish an answer to this question, frequently saying something to the effect that anyone could have a justification. Dishonest individuals will be reluctant to provide any answer that narrows the list of possible suspects. The honest individual, on the other hand, is more likely to name names—albeit reluctantly.

EXAMPLE

Interviewer: *"Do you believe that most people will tell their manager if they believed a colleague was doing something wrong, like committing fraud against the company?"*

EXPLANATION

The honest person is much more likely to report a misdeed and is more likely to respond "yes" to this question. The dishonest person, on the other hand, is more likely to say "no." When pressed for an explanation, the individual might qualify the "no" by adding that the information would be ignored or that it would not be believed.

EXAMPLE

Interviewer: *"Is there any reason why someone who works with you would say they thought you might feel justified in doing something wrong?"*

EXPLANATION

This is a hypothetical question designed to place the thought in the mind of a wrongdoer that someone has named him or her as a suspect. The honest person typically will say "no." The dishonest person is more likely to try to explain by saying something like, *"I know there are people around here that don't like me."*

EXAMPLE

Interviewer: *"What would concern you most if you did something wrong and it was found out?"*

EXPLANATION

The dishonest person is likely to accept the proposition of having done something wrong, and to focus on possible repercussions, for example: *"I wouldn't want to go to jail."* The honest person, on the other hand, is more likely to reject the notion of having committed a crime. If the honest person does address concerns about being caught in an illegal act, the concerns will usually be along the lines of disappointing friends or family; the dishonest person is more likely to discuss punitive measures.

Admission-Seeking Questions

Admission-seeking questions are reserved specifically for individuals whose culpability is reasonably certain. It is at this point that a *suspect* becomes a *subject*. These questions are posed in a precise order designed to (1) clear an innocent person or (2) encourage the culpable person to confess. Admission-seeking questions have at least three purposes. The first is to distinguish the innocent from the culpable. A culpable individual frequently will confess during the admission-seeking phase of an interview, while an innocent person will not do so unless threats or coercion are used. In some instances, the only way to differentiate the culpable from the innocent is to seek an admission of guilt.

The second purpose is to obtain a valid confession. Confessions, under the law, must be voluntarily obtained. The importance of a valid and binding confession to wrongdoing cannot be overstated.

The third purpose of the admission-seeking phase is to obtain from the confessor a written statement acknowledging the facts. Although oral confessions are legally as binding as written ones, the written statement has greater credibility. It also discourages a person from later attempting to recant.

Presence of Outsiders It is usually not necessary to inform the subject that he or she is entitled to have an attorney or other representative present. However, there are cases in which an employee may have the right to have a union representative or even a coworker present. Check with your lawyer if in doubt. Of course, even if the person has a right to have an attorney or other representative present, you should make it clear that the representative will be an observer only; representatives (even attorneys) should not ask questions or object.

Other than the subject and two investigators, no other observers should be permitted in the admission-seeking interview if at all possible. Having others in the room may present legal problems in "broadcasting" the allegation to a third party. Also, it is very difficult to obtain a confession with witnesses present. You should therefore consider whether the case can be proven without the admission-seeking interview.

Miranda Warnings As a general rule, private employers conducting an internal investigation are not required to give Miranda warnings; however, there are exceptions to the rule. You should consult with an attorney for details.

Theme Development People will confess to matters when they perceive that the benefits of confession outweigh the penalties. A good interviewer, through the application of sophisticated techniques, will be able to convince the respondent that the confession is in his or her best interest.

You must offer a morally acceptable reason for the confessor's behavior. You should not imply that the subject is a bad person, and you should never express disgust, outrage, or moral condemnation about the confessor's actions. Culpable people will almost never confess under these conditions. You must be firm, but must project compassion, understanding, and empathy to obtain a confession. The goal is to maximize sympathy and minimize the perception of moral wrongdoing.

It is important that you convey absolute confidence in the premise of the admission you seek from the subject—even if you are not fully convinced. People generally will not confess if they believe the accuser has doubts about their guilt. You should make his accusation in the form of a statement; the subject's guilt should already be assumed in the form of the question. Instead of asking, *"Did you do it?"* you ask, *"Why did you do it?"*

Remember that the first purpose of an admission-seeking question is to distinguish an innocent person from a culpable one. An innocent person generally will not accept the premise that he or she is responsible. The guilty person, on the other hand, knows he or she has committed the act, and is not shocked by the premise. The objection, if the person offers one, is more likely to focus on excuses for the conduct rather than outright denial.

Obviously, there is a danger during this phase that you will accuse an innocent person of a crime. This is regrettable, but there are some circumstances in which the only way to distinguish the innocent from the culpable is through the use of accusations. You must be careful, however, about opening yourself or your company up to legal liability for the accusation. In general, there is nothing illegal about accusing an innocent person of misdeeds as long as

- The accuser has reasonable suspicion or predication to believe the accused has committed an offense
- The accusation is made under conditions of privacy
- The accuser does not take any action likely to make an innocent person confess
- The accusation is conducted under reasonable conditions

Steps in the Admission-Seeking Interview (Interrogation)

Accuse the Subject of Committing the Offense During the admission-seeking interview, you must at some point make a direct accusation of the subject. The accusation should not be made in the form of a question, but rather as a statement. Emotive words such as "steal," "fraud," and "crime" should be avoided during the accusatory process. The accusation should be phrased as though the accused's guilt has already been established. Instead of saying, *"We have reason to believe that you..."* you should say, *"Our investigation has clearly established that you..."* The first statement leaves some ambiguity as to whether the accused really committed the act; the second affirmatively states that the accused committed the act.

Observe Reaction When accused of wrongdoing, the typical culpable person will react with silence. If the accused does deny culpability, those denials usually will be weak. In some cases, the accused will almost mumble the denial. It is common for the culpable individual to avoid outright denials. Instead, that person will give reasons why he or she could not have committed the act in question. The innocent person sometimes will react with genuine shock at being accused. It is not at all unusual for an innocent person, wrongfully accused, to react with anger. As opposed to the culpable person, the innocent person will usually strongly deny carrying out the act or acts in question.

Repeat Accusation If the accused does not strenuously object after the accusation is made, it should be repeated with the same degree of conviction and strength.

Interrupt Denials Both the truthful and untruthful person normally will object to the accusation and attempt to deny it. A culpable person more than an innocent one is likely to stop short of an outright denial (*"I didn't do it."*), and more apt to furnish you with explanations as to why he or she is not the responsible party. It is very important in instances where you are convinced of the individual's guilt that the denial be interrupted. An innocent person is unlikely to allow you to prevail in stopping the denial.

It becomes extremely difficult for the accused to change a denial once it has been uttered. If the subject denies the accusation and later admits it, he or she is admitting to lying. This is very hard to do. Therefore, your job is to prevent an outright denial, thereby making it easier for the subject to eventually confess to the act.

Both the innocent and the guilty person will make an outright denial if forced to do so. Accordingly, you should not solicit a denial at this stage of the admission-seeking interview. Instead of asking, *"Did you do this?"* which gives the subject a chance to say no, you should phrase the accusation as though the subject's wrongdoing has already been determined: *"Why did you do this?"*

DELAYS One of the most effective techniques for stopping or interrupting a denial is through the use of a delaying tactic. You should not argue with the accused, but rather attempt to delay the outright denial—*"I hear what you are saying, but let me finish first. Then you can talk."*

The innocent person usually will not allow you to continue to develop the theme.

INTERRUPTIONS Occasionally, it might be necessary to repeatedly interrupt the accused's attempts at denial. Because this stage is crucial, you should be prepared to increase the tone of the interruptions to the point at which the suspect is prepared to say, *"If you keep interrupting, I am going to have to terminate this conversation."* The culpable individual will find this threatening, since he or she wants to know the extent of incriminating evidence in your possession.

REASONING If the above techniques are unsuccessful, you might attempt to reason with the accused, and employ some of the tactics normally used for defusing alibis (see below). In this technique, the accused is presented with evidence implicating him or her in the crime. You should not disclose all the facts of the case, but rather small portions here and there.

Establish Rationalization Assuming the subject does not confess to the misconduct when faced with direct accusations, you should proceed to establish a morally acceptable rationalization that will allow the accused to square the misdeed with his or her conscience. It is not necessary that the rationalization be related to the underlying causes of the misconduct. It is acceptable for the accused to explain away the moral consequences of the action by seizing on any plausible explanation other than his or her being a "bad person."

If the accused does not seem to relate to one theme, you should go on to another and another until one seems to fit. Thereafter, that theme should be developed fully. Note that the rationalization explains away the moral—but not the legal—consequences of the misdeed. Do not to make any statements that would lead the accused to believe he or she will be excused from legal liability by cooperating!

Rather than being confrontational, constantly seek agreement from the accused. The goal is to remain in control of the interview while still appearing compassionate and understanding. Again, no matter what the accused has supposedly done, do not express shock, outrage, or condemnation.

UNFAIR TREATMENT   Probably the most common explanation for criminal activity in occupational fraud is the accused's attempt to achieve equity. As discussed in earlier chapters, studies have shown that counterproductive employee behavior—including stealing—is motivated primarily by job dissatisfaction. Employees and others feel that "striking back" is important to their self-esteem. The sensitive interviewer can capitalize on these feelings by suggesting to the accused that he or she is a victim—*"If you had been fairly treated, this wouldn't have happened, would it?"*

INADEQUATE RECOGNITION   Some employees might feel that their efforts have gone completely without notice by the company. As with similar themes, you should be empathetic: *"It looks to me that you have given a lot more to this company than they have recognized. Isn't that right?"*

FINANCIAL PROBLEMS   Occupational criminals, especially executives and upper management, frequently engage in fraud to conceal a problematic financial condition—either personal or business. You can exploit this theme by expressing sympathy and understanding for the subject's financial problems, as well as understanding for the misconduct—*"I know a lot of your investments have taken a beating. I don't know how you managed to keep everything afloat as well as you did. You just did this to stay alive financially, didn't you?"*

ABERRATION OF CONDUCT   Many fraudsters believe their conduct constitutes an aberration in their lives, and that it is not representative of their true character. You might establish this theme by agreeing that the misconduct was an aberration—*"I know this is totally out of character for you. I know that this would never have happened if something weren't going on in your life. Isn't that right?"*

FAMILY PROBLEMS   Some individuals commit fraud because of family problems—divorce, an unfaithful spouse, or demanding children. Men especially—who have been socially conditioned to tie their masculinity to earning power—might hold the notion that wealth connotes family respect. For their part, women have been found to commit white-collar crime in the name of their responsibility to the needs of their husbands and children. The skillful interviewer can convert this motive to his advantage— *"I know you have had some family problems. I know your divorce has been difficult for you. And I know how it is when these problems occur. You would have never done this if it hadn't been for family problems, isn't that right?"*

ACCUSER'S ACTIONS   You should not disclose the accuser's identity if it is not already known. But in cases where the accuser's identity is known to the accused, it can be helpful to blame the accuser for the problem. Or, the problem can be blamed on the company—*"I really blame a large part of this on the company. If some of the things that went on around this company were known, it would make what you've done seem pretty small in comparison, wouldn't it?"*

STRESS, DRUGS, ALCOHOL   Employees sometimes will turn to drugs or alcohol to reduce stress. In some instances, the stress itself will lead to aberrant behavior in some individuals. A rationalization established by you could play on the subject's substance abuse—*"You're one of the most respected people in this company. I know you have been under tremendous pressure to succeed. Too much pressure, really. That's behind what has happened here, isn't it?"*

REVENGE   Similar to other themes, revenge can be effectively developed as a justification for the subject's misconduct. In this technique, you attempt to blame the offense on the accused's feeling that he or she needed to "get back" at someone or something—*"Linda, what has happened is out of character for you. I think you were trying to get back at your supervisor because he passed you over for a raise. I would probably feel the same. That's what happened, isn't it?"*

DEPERSONALIZING THE VICTIM   In cases involving employee theft, an effective technique is to depersonalize the victim. The accused is better able to cope with the moral dilemma of her actions if the victim is a faceless corporation or agency—*"It's not like what you've done has really hurt a particular person. Maybe you thought of it this way: 'At most, I've cost each shareholder a few cents.' Isn't that the way it was?"*

MINOR MORAL INFRACTION   In many cases, you can reduce the accused's perception of the moral seriousness of the matter. This is not to be confused with the legal seriousness. Fraud examiners and interviewers should be careful to avoid making statements that could be construed as relieving legal responsibility. Instead, you should play down the moral seriousness of the misconduct. One effective way is through comparisons—*"This problem we have doesn't mean you're 'Jack the Ripper.' When you compare what you've done to things other people do, this situation seems pretty insignificant, doesn't it?"*

ALTRUISM   In many cases, the moral seriousness of the matter can be reduced by claiming the subject acted for the benefit of others. This especially is true if the accused views herself as a caring person—*"I know you didn't do this for yourself. I've looked into this matter carefully, and I think you did this to help your husband, didn't you?"*

GENUINE NEED   In some cases, employee fraud is predicated by genuine financial need. For example, the accused might be paying for the medical care of sick parents or a child. In those cases, the following techniques might be effective—*"You're like everyone else: you have to put food on the table. But in your position, it is very difficult to ask for help. You genuinely needed to do this to survive, didn't you?"*

Defuse Alibis   Even if the accused is presented with an appropriate rationalization, it is likely that he or she will continue to deny culpability. When you are successful in stopping denials, the accused will frequently present one or more reasons why he or she could not have committed the act in question. You must quickly and decisively defuse these alibis by convincing the accused of the weight of the evidence. Alibis generally can be defused using one of the methods listed below.

DISPLAY PHYSICAL EVIDENCE   It is common for most culpable people to overestimate the amount of physical evidence that you possess. You should try to reinforce this notion in the way the evidence is presented to the accused. The physical evidence—usually documents in fraud matters—generally should be displayed one piece at a time, in reverse order of importance. In this way, the full extent of the evidence is not immediately known by the accused. When the accused no longer denies culpability, you should stop displaying evidence.

Each time a document or piece of evidence is displayed, you should note its significance. During this phase, the accused is still trying to come to grips with being caught. You should, therefore, expect that the accused will attempt to lie. As with denials, you should stop the alibis and other falsehoods before they are fully articulated. Once the alibis are defused, you should return to the theme being developed.

DISCUSS WITNESSES   Another technique for defusing alibis is to discuss the testimony of witnesses. The objective is to give enough information about what other people would say without providing too much. Ideally, your statement will create the impression in the mind of the accused that many people are in a position to contradict his or her story.

You are again cautioned about furnishing enough information to the accused to identify the witnesses. This might place the witness in a difficult position, and the accused could contact the witness in an effort to influence testimony. The accused could make reprisals against potential witnesses, though this is rare.

DISCUSS DECEPTIONS   The final technique is to discuss the accused's deceptions. The purpose is to appeal to the person's logic, not to scold or degrade. This technique is sometimes the only one available if physical evidence is lacking. As in other interview situations, the word "lying" should be avoided.

PRESENT THE ALTERNATIVE   After the accused's alibis have been defused, he or she normally will become quiet and withdrawn. Some people in this situation might cry. (If so, be comforting. Do not discourage the accused from showing emotion.) In this stage the accused is deliberating whether or not to confess. You at this point should present an alternative question to the accused. The alternative question forces the accused to make one of two choices. One alternative allows the accused a morally acceptable reason for the misdeed; the other paints the accused in a negative light. Regardless of which answer the accused chooses, he or she is acknowledging guilt—*"Did you plan this deliberately, or did it just happen?"* or *"Did you just want extra money, or did you do this because you had financial problems?"*

Obtain the Benchmark Admission Either way the accused answers the alternative question—either yes or no—he or she has made a culpable statement, or *benchmark admission*. Once the benchmark admission is made, the subject has made a subconscious decision to confess. The questions above are structured so that the negative alternative is presented first, followed by the positive alternative. In this way, the accused only has to nod or say "yes" for the benchmark admission to be made. The accused might also answer in the negative—*"I didn't do it deliberately."*

In the cases where the accused answers the alternative question in the negative, you should press further for a positive admission—*"Then you did it to take care of your financial problems?"*

Should the accused still not respond to the alternative question with a benchmark admission, you should repeat the questions or variations thereof until the benchmark admission is made. It is important for you to get a response that is tantamount to a commitment to confess. The questions for the benchmark admission should be constructed as leading questions, so that they can be answered "yes" or "no" without requiring any sort of explanation. That will come later.

REINFORCE RATIONALIZATION   Once the benchmark admission has been made, you should reinforce the confessor's decision by returning to the theme for the rationalization. This will help the confessor feel comfortable and will let the person know that you do not look down on him or her. After reinforcing the subject's rationalization, you should make the transition into the verbal confession, where the details of the offense will be obtained.

Transition to the Verbal Confession The transition to the verbal confession is made when the accused furnishes the first detailed information about the offense. Thereafter, it is your job to probe gently for additional details—preferably those that would be known only to the perpetrator. As with any interview, there are three general approaches to obtaining the verbal confession: chronologically, by transaction, or by event. The approach to be taken should be governed by the circumstances of the case.

During the admission-seeking interview or interrogation, it is best to first confirm the general details of the offense. For example, you will want the accused's estimates of the amounts involved, other parties to the offense, and the location of physical evidence. After these basic facts are confirmed, you can then return to the specifics, in chronological order. It is imperative that you obtain an early admission that the accused knew the conduct in question was wrong. This confirms the essential element of intent.

Because of the nature of the psychology of confessions, most confessors will lie about one or more aspects of the offense, even though confirming overall guilt. When this happens during the verbal confession, you should make a mental note of the discrepancy and proceed as if the falsehood had been accepted as truthful.

Such discrepancies should be saved until all other relevant facts have been provided by the accused. If the discrepancies are material to the offense, then you should either resolve them at the end of the verbal confession or wait and correct them in the written confession. If not material, the information can be omitted altogether from the written confession.

You should focus on obtaining the following items of information during the verbal confession:

- That the accused knew the conduct was wrong
- Facts known only to the perpetrator
- An estimate of the number of instances or amounts
- A motive for the offense
- When the misconduct began
- When/if the misconduct was terminated
- Others involved
- Physical evidence
- Disposition of proceeds
- Location of assets
- Specifics of each offense

THE ACCUSED KNEW THE CONDUCT WAS WRONG   Intent is an essential element in all criminal and civil actions involving fraud. Not only must the confessor have committed the act, he or she must have intended to commit it—*"As I understand it, you did this, and you knew it was wrong, but you didn't*

really mean to hurt the company, is that right?" (Note that the question is phrased so that the confessor acknowledges intent, but "didn't mean to hurt" anyone. Make sure the question is not phrased so that the confessor falsely says that he or she "didn't mean to do it.")

FACTS KNOWN ONLY TO PERPETRATOR   Once the intent question has been solved, the questioning turns to those facts known only to the person who committed the crime. These facts include—as a minimum—the accused's estimates of the number of instances of wrongful conduct, as well as the total amount of money involved. It is best to use open questions here to force the subject to provide as much information about the offense as possible.

ESTIMATE OF NUMBER OF INSTANCES/AMOUNTS   In fraud matters in particular, it is common for the accused to underestimate the amount of funds involved as well as the number of instances. This is probably because of a natural tendency of the human mind to block out unpleasant matters. You should consider the figures provided by the confessor with a grain of salt. If the accused's response is "I don't know," start with high amounts and gradually work down.

MOTIVE FOR OFFENSE   Motive is an important element of establishing the offense. The motive might be the same as the theme you developed earlier—or it might not. The most common response when a subject is asked about his or her motive is *"I don't know."* You should probe for additional information, but if it is not forthcoming, then attribute the motive to the theme developed earlier. The motive should be established along the lines below.

WHEN OFFENSE COMMENCED   You will need to determine the approximate date and time that the offense started—*"I am sure you remember the first time this happened."* Once the subject has admitted to remembering the first instance (which will usually play into the motive), you should simply ask him or her to *"tell me about it."* This is phrased as an open question to get the subject to provide as much information as possible.

WHEN/IF OFFENSE WAS TERMINATED   In fraud matters, especially occupational fraud, the offenses usually are ongoing. That is, the fraudster seldom stops before he or she is discovered. If appropriate, you should seek the date the offense terminated.

OTHERS INVOLVED   Most frauds are solo ventures—committed without the aid of an accomplice. However, you should still seek to determine whether other parties were involved. It is best to use soft language—*"Who else knew about this besides you?"*

By asking who else "knew," you are in effect not only asking for the names of possible conspirators, but also about others who might have known what was going on but failed to report it. This question should be leading—not *"did someone else know?"* but rather *"who else knew?"*

PHYSICAL EVIDENCE   Physical evidence—regardless of how limited it might be—should be obtained from the confessor. In many instances, illicit income from fraud is deposited directly in the bank accounts of the perpetrator. You should ask the confessor to surrender banking records voluntarily for review. It is recommended that you obtain a separate written authorization or that language be added to the confession noting the voluntary surrender of banking information. The first method generally is preferable. If there are other relevant records that can be obtained only with the confessor's consent, permission to review those records should also be sought during the oral confession.

DISPOSITION OF PROCEEDS   If it has not come out earlier, you should find out in general what happened to any illicit income derived from the misdeeds. It is typical for the money to have been used for frivolous or ostentatious purposes. It is important, however, that the confessor casts the confessor's actions in a positive light.

LOCATION OF ASSETS   In appropriate situations, you will want to find out whether there are residual assets that the confessor can use to reduce losses. Rather than ask the accused, *"Is there anything left?"* the question should be phrased as *"What is left?"*

SPECIFICS OF EACH OFFENSE   Once the major hurdles have been overcome, you should then return to the specifics of each offense. Generally, it is best to start with the first instance and work forward chronologically.

Because this portion of the interview is information-seeking in nature, you should use open questions. It is best to seek the independent recollections of the confessor first before displaying physical evidence. If the confessor cannot independently recall something, documents can be used to refresh her recollection. It generally is best to resolve all issues relating to a particular offense before proceeding to the next.

Obtain a Signed Statement   At the conclusion of the admission-seeking interview, it is best for you to obtain a written confession from the subject, if possible. As was discussed earlier, a written statement has greater credibility than an oral confession, and it discourages a culpable person from later attempting to recant. The information to be included in the signed statement is essentially the same as that which you should obtain in an oral confession. There are, however, a few extra inclusions that should be made in a written confession.

VOLUNTARY CONFESSIONS   The general law of confessions requires that they be completely voluntary. The statement should contain language expressly stating that the confession is being made voluntarily.

INTENT   There is no such thing as an accidental fraud or crime. Both require as part of the elements of proof the fact that the confessor knew the conduct was wrong and intended to commit the act. This can best be accomplished by using precise language in the statement that clearly describes the act (e.g., *"I wrongfully took assets from the company that weren't mine,"* versus *"I borrowed money from the company without telling anyone"*).

As a general rule, strong emotive words, such as "lie" and "steal," should be avoided, as the confessor might balk at signing the statement. Still, the wording must be precise. Following are suggested wordings:

EXAMPLE

Instead of	Use the Following
Lie	*I knew the statement/action was untrue.*
Steal	*Wrongfully took the property of _____ for my own benefit.*
Embezzle	*Wrongfully took _____'s property, which had been entrusted to me, and used it for my own benefit.*
Fraud	*I knowingly told _____ an untrue statement, and he/she/they relied on it.*

APPROXIMATE DATES OF OFFENSE   Unless the exact dates of the offense are known, the word "approximately" must precede any dates of the offense. If the confessor is unsure about the dates, language to that effect should be included.

APPROXIMATE AMOUNTS OF LOSSES   Include the approximate losses, making sure they are labeled as such. It is satisfactory to state a range ("probably not less than $_____ or more than $_____").

APPROXIMATE NUMBER OF INSTANCES   Ranges also are satisfactory for the number of instances. The number is important because it helps establish intent by showing a repeated pattern of activity.

WILLINGNESS TO COOPERATE   It makes it easier for the confessor when he or she perceives that the statement includes language portraying her in a more favorable light. The confessor can convert that natural tendency by emphasizing cooperation and willingness to make amends—*"I am willing to cooperate in helping undo what I have done. I promise that I will try to repay whatever damages I caused by my actions."*

EXCUSE CLAUSE   The confessor's moral excuse should be mentioned. You should make sure that the confessor's excuse does not diminish his or her legal responsibility for the actions. Instead of using language like, *"I didn't mean to do this,"* which implies lack of intent, you should focus on an excuse that provides only a moral explanation for the misconduct—*"I wouldn't have done this if it had not been for pressing financial problems. I didn't mean to hurt anyone."*

HAVE THE CONFESSOR READ THE STATEMENT   The confessor must acknowledge that he or she read the statement and should initial all the pages of the statement. It might be advisable to insert intentional errors in the statement so that the confessor will notice them. The errors are crossed out, the correct information is inserted, and the confessor is asked to initial the changes. Whether this step is advisable depends on the likelihood that the confessor will attempt to retract the statement or claim it was not read.

TRUTHFULNESS OF STATEMENT   The written statement should state specifically that it is true. However, the language also should allow for mistakes. Typical language reads, "This statement is true and complete to the best of my current recollection."

PREPARING A SIGNED STATEMENT   There is no legal requirement that a statement must be in the handwriting or wording of the subject. In fact, it is generally not a good idea to let a confessor draft the statement. Instead, you should prepare the statement for the confessor to sign.

The confessor should read and sign the statement without undue delay. Instead of asking the confessor to sign the statement, you should say, "Please sign here." Although there is no legal requirement, it is a good idea to have two people witness the signing of a statement.

There should not be more than one written statement for each offense. If facts are inadvertently omitted, they can later be added to the original statement as an addendum. For legal purposes, you should prepare separate statements for unrelated offenses. This rule applies because the target might be tried separately for each offense.

You should preserve all notes taken during an interview, especially those concerning a confession. Having access to pertinent notes can aid in a cross-examination regarding the validity of a signed statement. Stenographic notes, if any, also should be preserved. Once a confession has been obtained, you should substantiate it through additional investigation, if necessary.

Here is a sample of the way the confession of Linda Reed Collins might be worded.

St. Augustine, Florida

May 1, 2010

I, Linda Reed Collins, furnish the following free and voluntary statement to Loren D. Bridges and Tonya Vincent of Bailey Books, Incorporated. No threats or promises of any kind have been used to induce this statement.

I am Senior Purchasing Agent for Bailey Books, Incorporated, and have been employed by Bailey Books since 2003. My job is to oversee the purchase of merchandise and other supplies for Bailey Books Incorporated. As part of my job, I am to ensure that Bailey Books Incorporated receives the highest-quality products at the lowest possible cost.

Commencing in approximately February 2008, and continuing through the current time, I have accepted money from James Nagel, Sales Representative for Orion Corporation, St. Augustine, Florida. Nagel offered me money to ensure that his company received preferential treatment in supplying Bailey Books with stationery and paper products.

On those occasions that I accepted money, I was aware that Bailey Books Incorporated was not obtaining the best product at the lowest possible price. The price charged for products delivered during the time I accepted money was substantially higher than market value.

On two occasions in April 2008, I authorized the payment of invoices of $102,136 and $95,637, respectively. These invoices were paid without the receipt of any merchandise. Nagel and I subsequently split the proceeds of these invoices equally between us.

I estimate that I have received in excess of $150,000 in connection with Mr. Nagel. I am not sure whether anyone at Orion Corporation knew of our arrangement. No one at Bailey Books had knowledge of, or participated in, my scheme.

I am aware that my conduct was illegal and violated Bailey Books' policies. I participated in this scheme because my husband and I were having severe financial problems due to his business. My husband is not aware of this matter. I am truly sorry for my conduct, and I promise to repay any resulting damages.

I have read this statement, consisting of this page. I now sign my name below, because this statement is true and correct to the best of my knowledge.

Witnesses:

Loren D. Bridges

Tonya Vincent

Signature:

Linda Reed Collins

JUDGING DECEPTION

Physiology of Deception

It is said that everyone lies, and does so for one of two reasons: to receive rewards or to avoid punishment. In most people, lying produces stress. The human body will attempt to relieve this stress (even in practiced liars) through verbal and nonverbal cues. A practiced interviewer will be able to draw inferences about the honesty of a subject's statements from his or her behavior.

When pushed into a corner, a subject or witness will often react to the stress created by deception. Some signs of stress that may accompany deception include

- Vague answers to questions
- Evasive answers to questions
- Distancing themselves from the act under examination
- An unwillingness to suspect anyone of committing the act under examination
- Being relatively silent when considering answers to questions
- Avoiding eye contact with the interviewer
- Acting tired and bored
- Hostility toward the interviewer
- Casting guilt to others in general, but not specifically
- Being indignant
- Being arrogant
- Attempting to interrupt the interview
- Erratic physical movements during the interview
- Exemplifying a "holier-than-thou" attitude
- Arguing that they never act unethically
- Arguing that they are (always) an honest person
- Arguing that they attend church

These types of actions and others are explored in more detail below, but all are indicators of stress. Although stress indicators are not always associated with deception, the interviewer needs to be vigilant that these mechanisms may foreshadow attempts to deceive or may be used as part of the deception. Deceit

can take on multiple forms: outright lying, omission of information, misdirection, and attempts to manage the interviewer's perceptions.

Conclusions concerning behavior must be tempered by a number of factors. The physical environment in which the interview is conducted can affect behavior. If the respondent is comfortable, fewer behavior quirks might be exhibited. The more intelligent the respondent, the more reliable verbal and nonverbal clues will be. If the respondent is biased toward you, or vice versa, this will affect behavior. People who are mentally unstable or are under the influence of drugs will be unsuitable for interviewing. Behavior symptoms of juveniles generally are unreliable. Ethnic and economic factors should be carefully noted. Some cultures, for example, discourage looking directly at someone. Other cultures use certain body language that might be misinterpreted. Because pathological liars often are familiar with advanced interview techniques, they are less likely to furnish observable behavioral clues. You must take all relevant factors into account before drawing any conclusions about the meaning of the verbal and nonverbal signals demonstrated by a subject.

Verbal Cues to Deception

Changes in Speech Patterns Deceptive people often speed up or slow down their speech or speak louder. There might be a change in the voice pitch; as a person becomes tense, the vocal chords constrict. Deceptive people also have a tendency to cough or clear their throats during times of deception.

Repetition of the Question Liars frequently will repeat your question to gain more time to think of how to respond. The deceptive individual will say, *"What was that again?"* or use similar language.

Comments Regarding Interview Deceptive people often will comment on the physical environment of the interview room, complaining that it is too hot, too cold, etc. As they come under increasing stress, they may frequently ask how much longer the interview will take.

Selective Memory In some cases, a deceptive person will have a fine memory for insignificant events, but will claim to be unable to remember important facts.

Making Excuses Dishonest people frequently make excuses about things that look bad for them, such as, *"I'm always nervous; don't pay any attention to that."*

Oaths On frequent occasions, dishonest people will add what they believe to be credibility to their lies by use of emphasis. Expressions such as *"I swear to God,"* or *"Honestly,"* or *"Frankly,"* or *"To tell the truth,"* are frequently used.

Character Testimony A liar often will request that you *"Check with my wife,"* or *"Talk to my minister."* This is done to add credibility to the false statement.

Answering with a Question Rather than deny allegations outright, a deceptive person frequently answers with a question such as, *"Why would I do something like that?"* As a variation, the deceptive person sometimes will question the interview procedure by asking, *"Why are you picking on me?"*

Overuse of Respect Some deceptive people go out of their way to be respectful and friendly. When accused of wrongdoing, it is unnatural for an honest person to react in a friendly and respectful manner.

Increasingly Weaker Denials When an honest person is accused of something he or she did not do, that person is likely to become angry or forceful in making the denial. The more the person is accused, the more forceful the denial becomes. The dishonest person, on the other hand, is likely to make a weak denial. Upon repeated accusations, the dishonest person's denials become weaker, to the point that the person becomes silent.

Failure to Deny Honest people are more likely than dishonest people to deny an event directly. An honest person might offer a simple and clear *"no,"* whereas the dishonest person will qualify the denial:

"No, I did not take a kickback on June 27." Other qualified denial phrases include, *"To the best of my memory"* and *"As far as I recall,"* or similar language.

Avoidance of Emotive Words

A liar often will avoid emotionally provocative terms such as "steal," "lie," and "crime." Instead, the dishonest person frequently prefers "soft" words, such as "borrow," and "it" (referring to the misdeed in question).

Refusal to Implicate Other Suspects

Both the honest respondent and the liar will have a natural reluctance to name others involved in misdeeds. However, the liar frequently will refuse to implicate possible suspects, no matter how much pressure is applied by you. This is because the culpable person does not want the circle of suspicion to be narrowed.

Tolerant Attitudes

Dishonest people typically have tolerant attitudes toward illegal or unethical conduct. In an internal theft case, you might ask, *"What should happen to this person when he or she is caught?"* The honest person usually will say, *"They should be fired/prosecuted."* The dishonest individual, on the other hand, is much more likely to reply, *"How should I know?"* or, *"Maybe it is a good employee who got into problems. Perhaps the person should be given a second chance."*

Reluctance to Terminate Interview

Dishonest people generally will be more reluctant than honest ones to terminate the interview. The dishonest individual wants to convince you that he or she is not responsible, so that the investigation will not continue. The honest person, on the other hand, generally has no such reluctance.

Feigned Unconcern

The dishonest person often will try to appear casual and unconcerned, and might react to questions with nervous or false laughter or feeble attempts at humor. The honest person, on the other hand, typically will be very concerned about being suspected of wrongdoing, and will treat your questions seriously.

Nonverbal Cues to Deception

For decades communications researchers have found that approximately two-thirds of communication is nonverbal. This suggests that effective listening includes not only listening for verbal cues of deception, but also watching for nonverbal cues as well.

Full Body Motions

When asked sensitive or emotive questions, the dishonest person typically will change his or her posture completely—as if moving away from you. The honest person frequently will lean forward toward you when questions are serious.

Anatomical Physical Responses

Anatomical physical responses are those involuntary reactions by the body to fright, such as increased heart rate, shallow or labored breathing, or excessive perspiration. These reactions are typical of dishonest people accused of wrongdoing.

Illustrators

Illustrators are the motions made primarily with the hands to demonstrate points when talking. During nonthreatening questions, the illustrators will be used at one rate. During threatening questions, the use of illustrators might increase or decrease.

Hands over the Mouth

Frequently, dishonest people will cover the mouth with the hand or fingers during deception. This reaction goes back to childhood, when many children cover their mouths when telling a lie. It is done subconsciously to conceal the false statement.

Manipulators

Manipulators are those motions such as picking lint from clothing, playing with objects such as pencils, or holding one's hands while talking. Manipulators are displacement activities, done to reduce nervousness.

Fleeing Positions During the interview, dishonest people often will posture themselves in a "fleeing position." While the head and trunk might be facing you, the feet and lower portion of the body might be pointing toward the door in an unconscious effort to flee from you.

Crossing the Arms Crossing one's arms over the middle zones of the body is a classic defensive reaction to difficult or uncomfortable questions. A variation is crossing the feet under the chair and locking them. These crossing motions occur mostly when a person is being deceptive.

Reaction to Evidence While trying to be outwardly unconcerned, the guilty person will have a keen interest in implicating evidence. The dishonest person often will look at documents presented by you, attempt to be casual about observing them, and then shove them away, as though wanting nothing to do with the evidence.

Fake Smiles Genuine smiles usually involve the whole mouth; false ones are confined to the upper half. People involved in deception tend to smirk rather than to smile.

Ability to Judge Deception

Despite the differences in attitudes displayed by truthful versus untruthful respondents (Table 9-1), the average persons' ability to judge deception is relatively poor. Some studies have indicated that interviewers fail to identify lies as much as 50 percent of the time. That said, good interviewers with proper training and experience can develop a strong skill set for judging deception. The bottom line is that identifying lies can be challenging. Lies are often interspersed with the truth, and many times lies are subtle variations of the truth. Furthermore, research in Europe (England and Italy) found that truthful subjects displayed more verbal and nonverbal cues of deceit than liars.[1] Some of the reasons that persons often fail to identify lies include

- A tendency to believe people. Fraud professionals and forensic accountants tend to be honest, and they may inflict their value system on others who are more comfortable lying.
- Behaviors are incorrectly judged: deceitful behaviors are labeled as truthful, while truthful behaviors are labeled as deceitful.
- Failure to recognize reliable cues to deception.
- Truthful behavior is relatively easy to imitate if you have knowledge of behavioral cues.
- Deceitful behavior is actually the response to stress, not deceit. Thus, simply because the interviewee exhibits symptoms of stress does not mean that they will follow the stress-inducing stimulus with a lie.

Developing skills to more accurately detect deceit is important. First, the interviewer should ignore truthful behavioral cues. Since truthful behavior cues can be imitated, truthful behavior has little meaning and, if focused upon, can give a false sense of security and distract the interviewer from observation of deceitful cues. Generally, truthful behavior includes direct answers that give the impression that the interviewee has nothing to hide, spontaneous answers that indicate that the interviewee has nothing to think about, a perception by the interviewee of attentiveness and interest in the interview outcomes, an orientation toward the interviewer, and behavioral consistency between verbal and nonverbal cues.

TABLE 9-1 Typical Attitudes Displayed by Respondents

Truthful	Untruthful
Calm	Impatient
Relaxed	Tense
Cooperative	Defensive
Concerned	Outwardly unconcerned
Sincere	Overly friendly, polite
Inflexible	Defeated
Cordial	Surly

Deceitful behavior, on the other hand, is generally a response to some stimuli, a question, or the release of stress. Identifying deceitful behavior requires that the interviewer both listen and watch at the same time because the interviewer must listen to the answer, assess verbal cues, and assess nonverbal cues. Deceptive behavior typically begins within a few seconds of the question that gave rise to the stress. This is because the mind moves more quickly than the mouth can speak, so the working of the brain means that stress symptoms will quickly follow the stress-inducing stimulus. Deceptive behavior also typically occurs in clusters. Thus, when questions induce stress, it is likely that the interviewer will observe not just a single stress response, but multiple stress responses at the same time. To improve the interviewer's probabilities of identifying deceit, single behaviors should be ignored; however, clusters of behavioral cues are more suggestive of deceit—the greater the number of indicators, the higher the probability of deceit.

In conclusion, it cannot be stressed enough that no single symptom or behavior proves anything, because even truthful subjects can generate a random symptom of stress that is of no consequence. Second, the interviewer should look for "clusters" of symptoms—two or more behaviors occurring at approximately the same moment. Finally, any cues should be timely and thus should occur at the same moment the mental and emotional stress level of the subject either peaks or dramatically ceases.

JOE WELLS' TEN COMMANDMENTS FOR EFFECTIVE INTERVIEWS[2]

The following provide a best practices overview for maximizing interview outcomes.

1. Preparation is the key to success. The outcome of the interview is determined before the introduction is made and the first question is asked.

2. Think as you go. Although question outlines, checklists, and other preparation tools are important planning devices, the value of planning is in the exercise itself, not in the actual plan. Interviews and interrogations will never proceed as planned; the interviewer needs to think on his or her feet and follow the direction of the interview where it leads. This does not mean to imply that the interviewer is relinquishing control of the interview. In contrast, it means that the interviewer cannot know in advance what interview outcomes will occur. Because of this, the interviewer needs to be flexible and think as the interview proceeds in order to ensure that all possible information has been gathered and accurately understood.

3. Watch nonverbal behavior. Although common sense suggests that good listening skills are crucial to success, nonverbal communication accounts for much more than half of all communication. Thus, the interviewer needs to watch as carefully as he or she listens.

4. Set the tone for the interview. First impressions are lasting impressions. The interviewer needs to approach the interview in a professional, nonthreatening manner, giving the appearance of being objective. The interviewer is interested in the truth—finding the guilty party—not in pinning the fraud or forensic accounting issue on the most likely suspect.

5. Set the pace for the interview. The interview should proceed from easy material to more difficult questions, and from the general to the specific. The interviewer should maintain a natural flow to the interview, maintaining control and moving the interview toward the intended outcomes.

6. Keep quiet. The interviewer should let the interviewee talk while he or she listens and watches.

7. Be straightforward. Most people enjoy the drama created on television, but in the real world, successful interviewing is the result of good preparation and thorough examination of the issues. There is no need for the interviewer to be cagey; simply ask the questions, make sure that the interviewee's answers are completely understood, and ensure that each issue is carefully and meticulously discussed.

8. Patience. The interviewer should schedule ample time to ask all of his or her questions and should leave time for follow-up questions and other areas of inquiry. Assuming that the schedule allows plenty of time, the interviewer should be patient and explore each issue carefully and thoroughly. The longer the interview, the more likely the witness is to provide helpful information: subjects will provide information that implicates a target, and guilty targets will make a mistake and implicate themselves with their own words.

9. Circle back. During the closing, the interviewer should circle back to double-check, summarize, and review important facts, figures, and other important details. Reconfirming details increases the interviewer's confidence that he or she has accurate information and minimizes the probability that at a later date the interviewee will contradict your understanding with an alternative, yet reasonable explanation, for their previous statements.

10. Get it in writing. Assuming that an interview or interrogation (admission-seeking interview) reveals important facts, figures, and other details, the interviewer should attempt to get the interviewee to document important statements in writing. This is particularly important when a confession of wrongdoing has been obtained.

COMPREHENSIVE GUIDELINES: INFORMATION COLLECTED IN INTERVIEWS[3]

The following summarizes the important information that an interviewer should consider soliciting during an interview, interrogation, or deposition related to financial aspects of a fraud or forensic accounting issue.

Identification

Full name

Alias

Reason for alias

Birth

Date and place of birth

Citizenship

Father's name (Living? If deceased, when?)

Mother's name (Living? If deceased, when?)

Address during Pertinent Years

Resident address; phone number

Business address; phone number

Other present or prior addresses

Marital status (if married, date and place of marriage; if divorced, when and where)

Spouse's maiden name

Spouse's parents (Living? If deceased, when?)

Children's names and ages; other dependents

Occupation

Present occupation

Company name and address

Present salary

Length of time employed

Additional employment

Prior occupations

Spouse's occupation

General Background

Physical health

Mental health

Education

Professional qualifications

Military service

Passport, Social Security, and/or Social Insurance numbers

Ever been investigated for financial crime?

Ever been arrested?

Ever filed bankruptcy? If so, who acted as receiver/trustee?

Hobbies, interests

Financial Institutions (Business and Personal)

Financial institutions accounts

Safety deposit boxes (request inventory); in whose name; content; who has access?

Credit cards

Trusts; beneficiary, donor, or trustee

Mutual funds or other securities owned

Brokers; currency exchanges used

Life insurance

Indirect dealings—e.g., through lawyers or accountants

Cashier's checks

Money orders, bank drafts, traveler's checks

Sources of Income

Salaries, wages, business receipts

Interest and dividends

Sales of securities

Rents and royalties

Pensions, trusts annuities, etc.

Gifts

Inheritances

Loans

Mortgages

Sales of assets

Municipal bond interest

Insurance settlements

Damages from legal actions

Any other source of funds; when?

Net Income and Expenditures

Cash in currency on hand, including in safety deposit boxes; location(s)?

Largest amount of currency on hand, ever?

End-of-year cash

Notes receivable

Mortgages receivable

Life insurance policies

Automobiles

Real estate

Stocks, bonds, and other securities

Jewelry, furs

Airplanes, boats

Any other assets of value; where?

Liabilities

    Payables

    Loans

    Assets purchased by financing

    Mortgages

    Bonds

Expenditures

    Debt reduction

    Insurance premiums

    Interest expense

    Contributions

    Medical

    Travel

    Real estate and other taxes

    Household wages (e.g., babysitter, housekeeper, gardener, etc.)

    Casualty losses

Business Operations

    Name and address

    Date organized

    Nature of business

    Type of business (corporation, partnership)

    Company or business registration numbers

    Tax identification numbers

    Title and duties

    Reporting arrangements; to and from whom; terms?

    Banking and cash handling arrangements

    Investments; when, where, amounts?

    Subsidiaries

    Associates

    Key personnel

Books and Records

    Nature of accounting system—cash or accrual

    Period books and records are kept

    Location

    Name(s) of persons maintaining and controlling

    External auditors

Business Receipts

    Form—electronic, cash, or check

    Where are receipts deposited?

    Are business receipts separated from personal transactions?

    Are expenses ever paid in cash? If so, are receipts obtained and retained?

    Do you have any transactions with foreign entities?

    Do you have any transactions in foreign currencies?

    Trade financing arrangements

    Letters of credit

REVIEW QUESTIONS

9-1 What are the benefits of strong interviewing and interrogation skills?

9-2 Why are interviews in fraudulent financial statements and tax returns handled differently than interviews in other fraud examinations?

9-3 What are some suggested approaches for conducting interviews?

9-4 What are the five types of interview and interrogation questions?

9-5 Why are introductory questions so important to an interview's success?

9-6 Why shouldn't an interviewer use closed or leading questions during the information-gathering phase of the interview?

9-7 What is the primary purpose of admission-seeking questions?

9-8 Why is it advisable to obtain a written confession from the subject of an investigation?

9-9 What are some of the verbal clues to deception?

9-10 What are some nonverbal clues to deception?

ENDNOTES

1. See BBC News, "Liars 'Too Self Aware to Twitch,'" 2006.

2. Adapted from Joseph T. Wells, "Ten Steps to a Top-Notch Interview," *Journal of Accountancy,* November 2002.

3. Fraud Examiners Manual, Section 3.701.

CHAPTER 10

USING INFORMATION TECHNOLOGY FOR FRAUD EXAMINATION AND FINANCIAL FORENSICS

LEARNING OBJECTIVES

After completing this chapter, you should be able to do the following:

10-1 Discuss the two major approaches for testing IT system controls.

10-2 Describe CAATTs and explain what they are used for.

10-3 Explain the purpose of computer forensics.

10-4 Identify some computer functions that can make recovering deleted files more difficult.

10-5 Describe how e-discovery rules impact the storage of e-mail and other electronic files.

10-6 Identify functions used by data extraction and analysis software to highlight red flags of fraud.

10-7 Recognize the two categories of data mining and knowledge discovery software.

10-8 Explain the role that graphics play in an investigation.

10-9 Describe the purpose of timelines in an investigation.

10-10 Discuss how case management software may be used in an investigation.

CRITICAL THINKING EXERCISE

A married couple goes to a movie. During the movie, the husband strangles the wife. He is able to get her body home without attracting attention.

How is this possible?

THE DIGITAL ENVIRONMENT

The purpose of this chapter is to provide an overview of the information systems control environment, as well as data extraction and analysis tools and techniques. Technology is a specialized area and, as a result, the auditor, fraud examiner, or forensic accountant needs to solicit the assistance of a professional with expertise in digital environments, tools, and techniques. Of course, determining the required level of expertise is similar to other tasks that arise in many areas of the fraud examination or forensic accounting engagement—it requires judgment on the part of the professional involved.

The starting point for the use of electronic data in the fraud or forensic accounting area, as a means of fraud prevention and deterrence, is the examination of the integrity of the data and their related systems. Many have heard the acronym GIGO, "garbage-in, garbage-out." If the data going into the information system lack integrity, or the information processes somehow destroy the integrity of the data, any information subsequently extracted similarly lacks integrity. Similar to the chain of custody concepts, good audit trails that allow the data to be tracked through the systems are also important, again, with the goal of maintaining data integrity and, just as important, being able to prove the origins and credibility of the data.

Overview of Information Technology Controls

Many of the process controls applicable to paper-based information systems are analogous to the internal controls surrounding digital information systems. An information technology (IT) audit consists of (1) planning, (2) tests of controls, and (3) substantive tests. Further, the IT audit requires an understanding

of the control environment related to IT; risk assessment of the things that could go wrong in an IT environment; information, communications, monitoring, and independent checks of the IT systems' internal controls. Some of the control activities in an IT environment that parallel those in the world of paper include proper authorization and access controls, segregation of IT duties, IT supervision, adequate record keeping, and independent supervision and verification.

More specific to IT, the general framework for viewing IT risks and controls include the following:[1]

- IT Operations
- Data Management Systems
- New Systems (Software) Development and Integration
- Systems Maintenance
- Systems Backup and Contingency Planning
- Electronic Commerce
- Control over Computer Operations (Hardware, Software, and User Access)

Each of these areas has particular control issues and needs to be examined carefully because data integrity issues can arise in any area.

CAATTs (Computer-Aided Audit Tools and Techniques) can assist with the testing of the IT systems control environment. One of the necessary areas of concern is applications controls. Applications are systems or subsystems in the areas of accounting, finance, marketing, sales, warehousing, distribution, payroll, personnel, etc. Application controls are designed to address risks that threaten the processing and storage of data in these application areas.

The first application control applies to the initial input of data. A transaction must start somewhere, and someone must have the authority to initiate that transaction. The important financial and operational attributes of that transaction must then be captured by the digital system. This is accomplished by first writing the transaction on paper, such as preparing an invoice, or the transaction can be entered directly into the computer system. In some cases, such as e-commence, transactions are entered directly into the computer by participants to the transaction who are not employees of the company. Ordering a product on Amazon.com is an example. In such cases, little or no traditional source documents exist. In other cases, a paper trail is created.

Similar to paper-based information systems, the source documents that support the electronic data systems should be pre-numbered and used in sequence. Supporting source documents should be audited periodically and should be retained, because they can include transaction information; sign-offs for those who prepared the document; required approvals and other authorizations; and the identity of the person who input the information into the application system.

Once documents or transactions are entered into the application systems, data coding controls can be used to identify transcription and transposition errors. In some cases, check digits may accompany transactions as a means of authenticating those transactions as they move throughout the system.

Batch controls are used when groups of documents are entered in batches. Batch controls may consist of a document count or a manual sum of all the transactions to be entered, which is later compared to the electronic batch total from the computer system after entry.

Validation controls detect input errors by flagging those transactions that fall outside accepted ranges. These controls may look for numeric, alphabetical, or alpha-numeric data in a particular field, as an example. They attempt to identify and isolate errors as early in the data processing effort as possible, so that the error can be addressed before those data are further processed. Validation controls can also be established to ensure that the correct file is being accessed.

Record validation is another technique that ensures that data relationships within a record make sense. It can include reasonableness checks, sequence checks, and other checks. An important application control is input error correction. This control requires that all errors be properly addressed prior to the data being processed further in the system.

Finally, the application input system needs to be examined as a whole, to ensure that input errors can be identified and addressed as quickly as possible.

Once the transaction data are "inside" the application system(s), they are available for further processing and transfer to other application systems. Processing controls are necessary to ensure that processed data maintain integrity as they move within the system. These include run-to-run controls that monitor various batch totals as data move from procedure to procedure and recalculate control totals, transaction

codes, and sequence checks. Some data processing requires systems operator intervention to initiate further action. Operator intervention increases the chances of human error, so controls need to be in place to minimize this. As data are processed by the system, an audit trail also needs to be developed. The data audit trail usually includes transaction logs, logs of automated transactions, a listing of automated transactions, unique transaction identifiers, and error logs.

Once the data have been sufficiently processed, they are available for output in the form of reports, as well as for transfer to other systems for additional processing. Output controls are established for spooling (how outputs move through the system and address output backlogs) and print programs and bursting (separating and collating printed pages). Output controls also address how to monitor waste and how to identify who is responsible for data accuracy and maintenance, report distribution, and end-user controls.

IT Audits and Assurance Activities

Auditors, fraud auditors, and forensic accountants who specialize in IT audit and assurance can approach IT system controls testing by one of two major approaches. First, the IT systems can be audited around. This is often referred to as the "black-box" approach, according to which the professional relies on interviews and flow charts to develop an understanding of the systems but primarily tests the integrity of the data and the system by reconciling inputs to outputs. The second alternative is the "white-box" approach, which utilizes a relatively small dataset to test the system. Some of the tests performed include authenticity, accuracy, completeness, redundancy, access audit trail, and rounding error tests. CAATTs can facilitate the white-box approach by creating test data and performing electronic systems walk-throughs (tracing). Computer forensic professionals may employ integrated test facilities by which the auditor examines the applications and their logic during normal operations by running parallel simulations.

These examinations are necessary to ensure that the data used by the auditor, fraud examiner, or forensic accountant have integrity. Various levels of assurance are necessary, depending on the engagement. Professionals in this environment need to be cognizant of the fact that one or more of the IT systems personnel may be colluding with others to commit or conceal fraud. As such, fraud and forensic accounting professionals need to remain alert to the human side of fraud, the fraud triangle (pressure, opportunity, and rationalization) as well as M-I-C-E (motivations such as money, ideology, coercion, and ego). In fact, the IT professional may be in a unique position to commit and conceal a fraud, simply because so few others understand IT and how it can be manipulated.

The prior discussion focused mainly on the integrity of data entered into, processed by, and output from the digital environment. However, other risks may be present. For example, the data may accurately go through the system as programmed in the software, but an IT professional periodically substitutes an inappropriate version of the software into the digital environment. Thus, in this example, most transactions are handled correctly and according to system design and company policy. However, some legitimate data are processed by the inappropriate software and, as a result, are not accurate. Searching for those exceptional transactions requires sifting through the remainder, but it can be approached more effectively with some of the following data extraction and analysis tools.

The IT auditors or assurance professionals need to ensure that they examine the entire control environment, including controls that address other aspects of the computer operation—such as IT operational policies and procedures; data management systems; systems development and integration into the digital environment; system maintenance policies and procedures, including backup and contingency planning; electronic commerce; and daily, weekly, monthly, and annual computer operations—with regard to hardware, software, and IT personnel and user access.

DIGITAL EVIDENCE

Auditors solicit, obtain, evaluate, and develop audit evidence in order to test management's assertions concerning the fairness of the presentation of the financial statements and to ensure that they are free from material misstatement, whether as a result of error or irregularity. The assertions of management related to financial statements include the following:

1. The existence of assets and transactions.
2. The completeness of the transactions reflected in the financial statements and related notes.

3. Proper disclosure of all rights and obligations associated with assets and liabilities.

4. The valuation of transactions and balances reflected in the financial statements are reasonable.

5. Proper financial statement presentation and disclosure of the related notes.

As part of their work, forensic accountants and fraud examiners use information technology to gather, manage, and analyze evidence. Digital evidence analysis is particularly beneficial when the professional must sift through, organize, and analyze large amounts of evidence. Given Internal Revenue Service cycle times, audit engagement budgets, and cost-benefit considerations in litigation support engagements, large amounts of data, evidence, and information must be examined with speed and accuracy. Electronic imaging is a technique for scanning evidence and case documents into an electronic format for easy storage and retrieval. This process normally entails some coding to facilitate ease of access. Once the material has been captured and coded in electronic format, the professional can sort, analyze, and retrieve the data.

Computer forensics involves using specialized tools and techniques to image and capture data and information, housed on computer hardware and embedded in software applications, so that the integrity and chain of custody of such evidence is protected and can be admitted into a court of law. Electronic evidence refers to any evidence captured by computers and electronic devices. As such, it can be captured from desktop computers, notebook computers, network servers, backup storage medium, cell phones, personal digital assistants (PDAs), handheld computers, CDs, DVDs, digital cameras, stick drives, or any other electronic device or storage medium. Electronic e-mail is a rich source of digital evidence. Persons often put in e-mail comments and information that they might never say out loud or include in a formal memo or letter. As with other digitized information, the challenge with e-mail is the sheer volume of exchanges. It is only through electronic searches that the benefits of these data are available to the investigator. Generally, a warrant or subpoena is required to obtain digital evidence. In order to obtain a warrant, the professional must show probable cause.

One of the main concerns in the digital environment is related to the initial acquisition of the evidence. Auditors, fraud auditors, and forensic accountants may attempt to "do too much" when they first encounter digital evidence. For example, the simple act of turning on a confiscated computer, digital camera, cell phone, PDA, etc. may make all the evidence on that digital device inadmissible in a courtroom. That is because, as soon as a device is turned on, it starts writing logs and performing other activities that alter the structure of the hard drives where data are stored (the defense would say the alterations show that the digital evidence had been tampered with). If this is the situation, it can't be proven beyond a reasonable doubt what the data looked like before the device was booted up. Forensic accountants and fraud examiners seldom perform the work that is within the expertise of computer forensic professionals—usually computer and electrical engineers and management information systems (MIS) personnel who have specialized training and experience in fraud and forensic accounting. It is not only the need to protect the integrity of the data that justifies the use of the specialized knowledge, skills, and abilities of the computer forensic specialist but also their ability to find hidden information, deal with encrypted data, and retrieve previously deleted or erased files.

When the traditional forensic accountant or fraud examiner receives data in electronic format, they assume that digital evidence was obtained through legal means and was extracted in accordance with methodologies that are acceptable in a manner that protects its admissibility in a court of law. Students should understand that, with regard to digital evidence, only those persons with specialized training, experience, and appropriate professional certifications should initially handle digital evidence. Once the digital evidence has been made available to auditors, fraud auditors, and forensic accountants, they may work with the tools discussed in the following section to conduct audit procedures and detect and investigate fraud.

Consistent with other aspects of the fraud and forensic accounting engagement, professionals should maintain good work papers and be able to demonstrate the foundations of their work. In an electronic world, audit trails and logs are especially helpful. As an example, if the data extraction and analysis require multiple steps, each step and its results should be documented.

Tools Used to Gather Digital Evidence

Numerous tools have been developed to gather and protect digital evidence, some of which are described as follows.

Road MASSter   Road MASSter can be described as a portable computer (digital) forensic lab. It is housed in a metal briefcase-type container on wheels; inside is a keyboard, a color LCD display, and data-copying devices. Road MASSter can be used in the field (e.g., at crime scenes or search warrant locations) to acquire and analyze electronic data and preview and image hard drives. The system can copy the hard drive to a number of different formats for subsequent data extraction and analysis, including Microsoft Windows XP (Access and Excel), Linux, EnCase, Safe Back, ICS, or other imaging file formats. Road MASSter's tools are designed to perform quick, reliable hard drive imaging and data analysis. The device can be used to image hard drives of any kind, as well as capturing data from other media (e.g., CDs, stick drives, flash drives, etc.) and unopened computers. IT computer forensics professionals can also copy and analyze information stored on hard drives and devices such as cell phones and BlackBerrys, for example. Investigators can save or print audit trail reports for use as evidence in court. Finally, Road MASSter can also be used to write-protect and sanitize hard drives.

EnCase   EnCase is another tool for digital imaging of hard drives and other storage media. EnCase acquires data in a forensically sound manner that has generally been accepted in courtrooms. Like Road MASSter, EnCase can be used to investigate and analyze data on multiple platforms, including Windows, Linux, AIX, OS X, Solaris, and others. This software also provides tools to identify information stored on hard drives despite efforts to hide, cloak, or delete the data. It is also designed to manage large volumes of computer evidence and to view relevant file types, including so-called deleted files, file slack, and unallocated space. Once the data have been properly and legally obtained, they can be transferred as evidence files.

Recovering Deleted Files

Computer forensic specialists may discover that files have been deleted from a hard drive. Generally, recovering deleted files is not considered difficult, provided that the file has not been overwritten or corrupted and that the drive has not been repartitioned or reformatted. A number of software tools, for example, Uneraser for Windows and Data Rescue II for Apple Computers, are commercially available. Recovering deleted files is considered a separate task from restoring overwritten or corrupted files. The reason is that when a file is deleted from your computer, it has not been removed from the hard drive. The delete function simply removes the file from the list of files in a particular folder. The first step to recovering a deleted file is to look in the Recycle Bin. With Windows, deleted file names are simply moved there. While the file resides in Window's Recycle Bin, the file can be restored by "right-clicking" on the file name and choosing "restore."

If the deleted file is not in the Recycle Bin, it may still be recoverable. When a file is deleted or the Recycle Bin has been emptied, the file name is removed from the list of files in the folder. The risk is that the space where the file resides was made available for reuse. Until the computer reuses the space where the file resides, the data contained in the file remain intact. Obviously, the more time that passes, the lower the chances are of recovering a deleted file intact, because it becomes increasingly likely that the computer will reuse all or part of the file's disk space for another task.

Another activity that can severely reduce the ability to recover deleted files is the "Defrag" command. Defrag, or defragmenting the hard drive, is a method of reorganizing the computer hard drive so that the unused space is allocated for the most efficient data storage. For example, over time, as the computer user creates and deletes files, adds and removes software, etc., computer programs and files get spread over the available hard drive. This creates pockets of used and unused space. The result is that large contiguous storage space is no longer available, and the computer has to store files in pieces. Thus, the computer has to spend time searching for space to save new files and programs, and large files or programs may need to be stored in more than one place on the hard drive. When a computer has a fragmented hard drive, computer operations slow down. Defrag reorganizes the files, placing files together and creating as much contiguous unused storage space as possible. Because defragmenting the hard drive moves the files around, the probabilities of recovering deleted files is reduced. In the Defrag process, all of the computer's file pointers to the location of the deleted files are overwritten. After the Defrag command, even undelete software tools have a difficult time restoring deleted files.

Assuming that Recycle Bin recovery is not successful, that the Defrag command has not been run, and that a limited amount of time has passed since a particular file was deleted, third-party undelete software can be acquired to attempt to recover the deleted files. Undelete software understands the internal system of pointers used by the computer to store files. With this knowledge, it searches for clues as to the location of the disk space where the deleted file resides. Undelete software can also examine the unallocated disk space, that is, space where the deleted files had been located but which the computer has not yet chosen to reuse. If a number of files are to be recovered, recovered files should be stored on a separate hard drive, stick drive, or some storage space, where the save action will not impair the recovery of other deleted files on the hard drive. The separate hard drive or other external storage device can also be used as the location for the undelete programs for the same reason.

Some of the third-party software available for recovering deleted files include DiskInternal's Uneraser, Office Recovery (Microsoft Office documents), Word Recovery (Word DOC, DOT, and RTF files), DOC Regenerator (Microsoft Word documents), Excel Recovery (Excel spreadsheets and worksheets), XLS Regenerator (Excel spreadsheets), Flash Recovery (digital image recovery, including photos, from hard drives and memory cards), Music Recovery (MP3, WMA, and other music files from hard drives, memory cards, and other music players).

Recovering Deleted E-mail

E-mails are stored in mail folders (not individually as separate files), and each mail folder is considered as a separate file. Some e-mail systems have a recycle bin feature that is analogous to Window's Recycle Bin for deleted files. If the e-mail software system has a recycle bin, that is the first place to attempt e-mail recovery. However, most e-mail recycle bins have some time limit or some other "auto-empty recycle bin" feature that periodically clears the deleted e-mail. For example, Outlook Express provides an option to empty the Deleted Items folder when the user exits the program. In such cases, recovery of deleted e-mail becomes more difficult.

Normally, even after an e-mail has been deleted from a mail folder or from the recycle bin, the space it occupied is left empty until the mail program compacts the folder. Prior to compaction, deleted e-mail messages may be recovered using special e-mail recovery software. Some of the e-mail recovery tools include Mail Recovery (for Outlook Express and Windows Mail) and Advanced Outlook Repair (for Microsoft Outlook PST files). Another option for deleted e-mail is to restore it from backup tapes or another backup storage medium. New e-discovery rules require organizations to be able to provide e-mail and other electronic files that go back in time in a manner similar to that of paper files. So the probability of e-mail and other deleted file recovery in an e-discovery environment is greatly enhanced.

Restoring Data

Restoring data and files is a more sophisticated approach to recovering deleted files and is used to restore lost files under more challenging circumstances, such as the following:

- Lost files, photos, or documents
- Deleted files or folders where the Recycle Bin has been emptied
- Irreplaceable files that cannot be found and may have accidentally been deleted
- Archived files or photos (e.g., to CD or DVD) where the CD or DVD has been corrupted or tagged unreadable
- Files deleted some time ago, but which are now needed
- A hard drive that has failed
- A hard drive that has been reformatted
- A hard drive that has been damaged (some files in the damaged area will be lost)

Assuming that techniques to recover deleted files do not work, it is important to stop writing to the drive as soon as the possibility of missing or unrecoverable deleted files exists. This increases the probability of recovering whatever is left of previously deleted files. At this point, third-party

software is most likely necessary to facilitate the restoration process. Some common software includes the following:

- CD & DVD Recovery to restore files burned to CD or DVD
- DOC Regenerator to restore Microsoft Word documents
- Excel Recovery or XLS Regenerator to recover Microsoft Excel files
- Flash Recovery, FAT Recovery, or Partition Recovery to restore files from pen drives, flash drives, memory sticks, and other removable drives. (FAT Recovery is for external storage in FAT or FAT32 format)
- HDD Regenerator to restore files from hard drives where "read errors" have been generated by the operating system
- Mail Recovery for deleted e-mails from Outlook Express or Windows Mail
- Music Recovery to restore music (MP3, WMA, RA, etc.); Tune Tech for iPod (Apple/Macintosh)
- Office Recover to restore Microsoft Office files
- Partition Recovery to recover lost files from hard drives
- Word Recovery to restore Microsoft Word documents
- Uneraser for recovering deleted files

Third-party software is not as readily available for Apple Macintosh computers. However, one such software package for Macintosh is Data Rescue II.

In some cases, the undelete utility from the software package may appear to restore a file, but it is evaluated as corrupt when the user attempts to open it. It may be that the contents of the file are unrecoverable. It may also be that some restoration software tools are better than others. Not surprisingly, some of the more effective data recovery tools cost more. Nevertheless, if the restoration project is important and one software package fails, others may be attempted until the file can be fully restored.

If third-party software restoration fails but provides some results, in some cases, software engineers and computer forensic specialists can manually search for lost files. The human brain can often solve difficult tasks. Software programs can replicate the ability to solve complex problems if properly designed and programmed. However, some recovery can be so unpredictable and difficult that even the best software programs cannot anticipate all possible restoration solutions. For example, assume that a computer forensic analyst has a partially recovered Microsoft Word document and that the language of the document stops halfway through a sentence (and the rest of the file starting with the unfinished sentence is missing). In such a case, the computer forensic specialist can search the entire hard disk for clusters that may contain what are likely to be the next words in the document (i.e., those words that might complete the sentence) and piece together files from fragments of data. In other cases, the data recovery specialist can restore files by taking the magnetic platters out of the drive, casing and reading them using special equipment. Of course, it's not surprising that manual (intervention) restoration is far more expensive than recovery or restoration using third-party software; however, in some situations, the cost-benefit may warrant the application of manual restoration activities.

The good news for fraud examiners and forensic accountants is that files deleted from a computer are not actually deleted and can be recovered and restored relatively easily. For perpetrators, this is not good news at all for someone who is relying on the deletion of the data for concealment of his or her scheme. For high-security needs, data security software and privacy tools, such as Privacy Guardian or Privacy Suite, are available. These do more than delete files; they overwrite the disk sectors that held the data. Once these sectors have been overwritten, generally, even a computer forensic specialist cannot recover the files. Because some application software programs write data to temporary locations during use, the high-security packages also erase and overwrite known temporary storage locations and other unused disk space. If a tool of this type has been used, the chance of restoring files is essentially nonexistent. However, depending on the nature, size, or other attributes of an investigation and the importance of the digital evidence, computer forensic tools and techniques may be worth a try. Traces of the sensitive data may remain. Even if all of the files cannot be recovered, enough pieces may be available that vital evidence can be developed. Like other cases previously described, if high-security or privacy software has been used, a computer forensic specialist is likely going to need to examine the storage device manually to determine what can be recovered.

General knowledge of tools and techniques used by forensic computer scientists for retrieving files from seized computers—and of how the work of forensic accountants must be coordinated with forensic computer specialists—is an important aspect of fraud examination and forensic accounting engagements. In addition, fraud examiners and forensic accountants need to be able to identify situations in which a forensic computer specialist should be employed, and they need to understand how legal proceedings against a perpetrator can be jeopardized if evidence is gathered by one who lacks appropriate skills.

DETECTION AND INVESTIGATION IN A DIGITAL ENVIRONMENT

In recent years, computer companies and programmers have developed software that enables users to sift through large volumes of information and transactions. These programs identify customers, suppliers, vendors, and employees and can be used to analyze performance, trends, and other important attributes related to a company. They can also be configured to identify control weaknesses in application programs, as well as anomalies in accounting books and records. Fraud examiners and auditors use data analysis software as the ultimate system of red flags, detecting a potential fraud in situations for which manual examination would prove extremely difficult or impossible.

Because of the sheer size of some databases and the amount of information stored in electronic media, the key to successful fraud detection and investigation using digital tools and techniques is a targeted approach. The fraud auditor or investigator must have an understanding of what could go wrong, what did go wrong, and how those concerns would manifest in the information system. This requires knowledge of the schemes, the industry, the organization, its IT control environments, its history of fraud, and other aspects outlined in the steps to develop a targeted risk assessment. With this foundation, the anti-fraud professional has an idea of what he or she is looking for.

As a starting point for digital analysis, whether for fraud detection or investigation, the electronic data must be obtained and delivered in some kind of file structure. Optimally, the data have been converted in advance to a text, ASCII, Microsoft Access, Excel, or some format that can be read and analyzed by some of the more popular programs for data extraction and analysis. From there, the data can be analyzed in the format received or converted for use in programs such as ACL, IDEA, or Picalo. However, the data often come in some other format and must be prepared for use in one of the many programs available for analysis. Data files normally come in either a "flat file" or "hierarchical and network database" structure. Some of the flat file structures include sequential, indexed, hashing, and pointer file structures. With "hierarchical and network database" structures, the database is relational. Relational databases often incorporate some aspects of the flat file structures and incorporate linkages between the data as well. These need to be converted for use in programs such as Excel, Access, IDEA, ACL, and Picalo. This can only be done by knowing the type of database and its accompanying file structure. Each of the previously discussed programs that are often used by fraud examiners and forensic accountants have "import" functionality embedded in the program. This allows the program to access and read data from various formats for later use. In most cases, the files to be exported from a source computer system, program, or database—whether flat, hierarchical, or network—need to be converted to a file format that can be read by Excel, Access, IDEA, ACL, or Picalo, for example. In other cases, the extraction process creates a generic file structure that most programs can read. No matter how the data are exported from a computer system and subsequently imported for use by the fraud examiner or forensic accountant, data and file integrity measures must be in place to ensure completeness and accuracy.

A continued point of emphasis is this idea that a targeted approach is required. There are horror stories of IT specialists running programs that kick out thousands of anomalies that may be indicative of fraud. However, the exceptions are so numerous that no one from the audit team has the time to examine each anomaly. Such an approach may even create liability exposure for the financial statement auditor, because a smart lawyer may subpoena such records and take the time to sift through the anomalies to locate the few that were indicative of a much larger problem. Although the action or inaction of the auditors with respect to such an extensive number of anomalies makes sense and is justifiable, a jury may take a different position if a significant (material) fraud is subsequently discovered when, all the while, the auditors had the red flags right there in front of them. In contrast, a targeted risk assessment, followed by incorporating IT tools and techniques that search for specific anomalies, is likely to yield far fewer exceptions and a far higher probability that the red flags deserve additional attention and work on the part of the auditor. Conan Albrecht and Steve Silver have each referred to this as a "rifle shot" approach, as opposed to a "shotgun" approach to data extraction and analysis.

Data Extraction and Analysis Software Functions

Computer software using a targeted risk assessment can be utilized to scan the database information for several different types of information, resulting in output that highlights red flags. To perform this, most software packages use a combination of functions, including the following:

- Sorting: arranging the data in some meaningful order, such as customer name, number, amount, date, etc.

- Record selection and extraction: querying (requesting) that the computer find occurrences of items or records in a field that match some criteria of interest to the investigator. This type of request only returns (extracts) instances where the record occurred, effectively reducing large amounts of information into concise lists. Often, additional criteria placed on the record selection or query reveal a more pertinent list of information.

- Joining files: gathering together the specified parts of different data files. Joining files uses a common attribute between files to combine fields from two input files to create a third file that consists of selected data from the original files. For example, the join function can be used to match data in a transaction file with records in a master file, such as matching invoice data in an accounts receivable file to the name and address of the customer.

- Multi-file processing: relating multiple files by defining relationships between those files, without the use of the join command. An example of a common data relationship might be to relate an outstanding customer invoice file to an accounts receivable file based on customer number.

- Correlation analysis: determining statistical relationships between different variables in a dataset. Investigators can learn a lot about data by observing how variables move together, disparately, or have little to no relationship with one another. For example, employee hotel expenses should increase as the number of days traveled increases for a given time period. Similarly, gallons of paint used should increase as the number of houses built increases. Investigators look for correlations where none had existed previously, as well as correlations that no longer exist. Such anomalies, within a targeted risk assessment framework, may suggest further investigative steps.

- Verifying multiples of a number: examining the relationship between quantities and prices. For example, an invoice total can be recalculated based on the quantity ordered and the price per the published price lists. Exceptions require investigation. Other examples of inquiries related to multiplication expectations include reimbursement rates for mileage, pay check amounts for hours worked (with or without overtime), etc. For instance, a mileage reimbursement check that does not compute, given the current per mile rate and the number of miles driven, can be a red flag.

- Compliance verification: using the software functionality to determine whether employee transactions are in compliance with company policies. For example, company policy may require that customers seeking high credit limits obtain the approval of the accounts receivable manager or some other high-ranking official. If the computer captures the approval function, a query can be set up to search for large credit invoices and accounts receivable balances where both approvals were not present (input). In some instances, fraud examiners can find early indications of fraud by testing detail data for values above or below specified amounts. As another example, when employees are out of town, do they adhere to company policy of spending not more than the per diem amount for meals? As a starting point, a query can identify all expense report data where meal expense per day exceeds the per diem. Even though the identified variances may be small ($2 and $3), the time taken to perform further research with respect to small variances can be well invested. Small anomalies may be the "tip of the iceberg" and might lead to something larger.

- Duplicate searches: querying the database for the observance of duplicates in a database where none are expected. For example, a search for the same or similar mailing addresses for different suppliers, vendors, or employees. As a further example, fraud examiners and auditors can perform searches on invoice disbursements numerically to determine whether any invoices have been paid twice. By cross-checking the invoices with vendor payments, they can catch duplicate billings.

- Vertical ratio analysis: analyzing the relationships between the items on an income statement, balance sheet, or statement of cash flows by expressing each line item as a percentage of a selected total. For example, in a vertical analysis of an income statement, net sales are usually 100 percent, and each income statement includes line items presented as a percentage of net sales; on a balance sheet, total

assets, liabilities, or equity is often assigned on the basis of 100 percent. For instance, an investigator may be able to determine whether paid expenditures over multiple periods are reasonable. If one area of company expenses seems abnormally large or growing/declining in a manner that is unexpected, a red flag could be raised and further investigation might be appropriate.

- Horizontal ratio analysis: analyzing the percentage change in individual financial statement line items from one year to the next. With horizontal analysis, the first year is considered the base year. In subsequent years, changes from the prior year are computed and expressed as a percentage of the base year or the most recent prior year. This function determines the trends over time (e.g., expenses, inventory, etc.). Discrepancies and unexpected trends may suggest further inquiry.

- Date functions: querying the database based on dates. This function can be used to identify discrepancies in dates across database files; for example, invoice dates in the accounts receivable files may not agree with invoice dates in the customer history file. By using the software to verify that dates are consistent, the fraud examiner or forensic accountant can extract suspicious transactions where the dates are inconsistent. Other date functions include aging of data and looking for transaction dates outside of expected date ranges.

- Recalculations: checking the accuracy of amounts by recomputing those amounts using quantities and prices/dollar rates. For example, employee paycheck amounts can be examined by pulling hours data from the manufacturing data capture files and pulling the employee's wage rate from the employee master file. Amounts that do not agree with the paycheck amount could be flagged for further investigation.

- Transactions and balances exceeding expectations: checking to ensure that transaction amounts and balances (conglomerations of transactions) do not exceed expected limits. For example, a 24-hour per day, seven-day work week is 168 hours. Clearly, no employee should be paid for more hours than there are in a week. Likewise, a salaried employee should be paid his or her salary amount for the pay period. Notwithstanding bonuses, the paycheck amount should not exceed the salary amount based on the employee master file.

Given the functions previously described, the following are some examples of data analysis queries that can be performed by most data analysis software:[2]

General Ledger Analysis

- Select specific journal entries for analysis
- Create actual to budget comparison reports
- Analyze and confirm specific ledger accounts for legitimate transaction activity
- Speed account reconciliation through specialized account queries
- Calculate financial ratios
- Calculate percentage comparison ratios between accounts
- Prepare custom reports, cash flow, profit/loss, and asset and liability total reports
- Compare summaries by major account in any order (low to high, high to low)
- Create reports in any format by account, division, department, etc.

Accounts Receivable

- Create a list of customer limit increases and decreases
- Age accounts receivable in various formats
- Identify gaps in sequential forms such as invoices
- Identify duplicate invoices or customer account number entries
- Show specified reports on credits taken by customers
- Report customer summaries by invoice, product, etc.
- Identify customer activity by age, product, etc.
- Compare customer credit limits and current or past balances

Sales Analysis

- Create a report of all system overrides and sales exceptions
- Analyze returns and allowances by store, department, or other areas

- Create descriptive statistics
- Perform Benford's Law analyses
- Locate

  - Data matching specified criteria
  - Data not matching specified criteria
  - Unordered data items
  - Duplicates
  - Gaps in the dataset

- Create a column for Z-scores and identify, include, or exclude outliers
- Perform trend analyses using regression, high to low, and handshaking slope techniques

Like other similar programs, Picalo also has an expression builder and some detectlets (see Figure 10-7).

In addition to the data extraction tools and techniques previously discussed, the following features are somewhat unique to Picalo:

- Picalo is an open-source framework where users either utilize the software "as-is" or write programs of their own (detectlets). Those users who choose to write detectlets can share their software with the Picalo community. Picalo's scripting is based on Python, a programming language. Those who choose to write detectlets need some knowledge of Python to accomplish that goal.

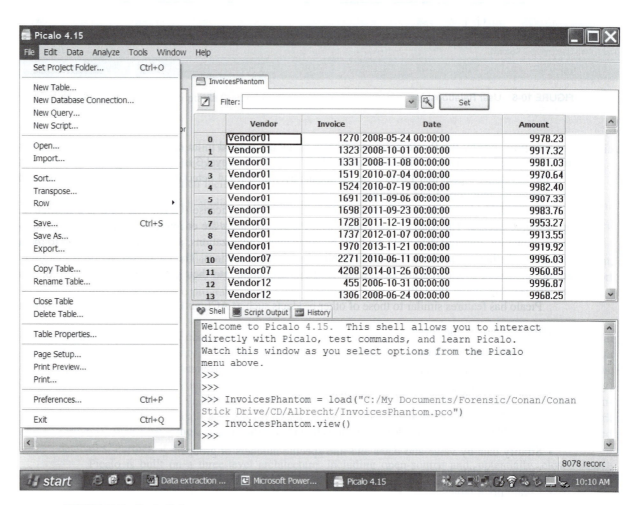

FIGURE 10-7 Picalo Software

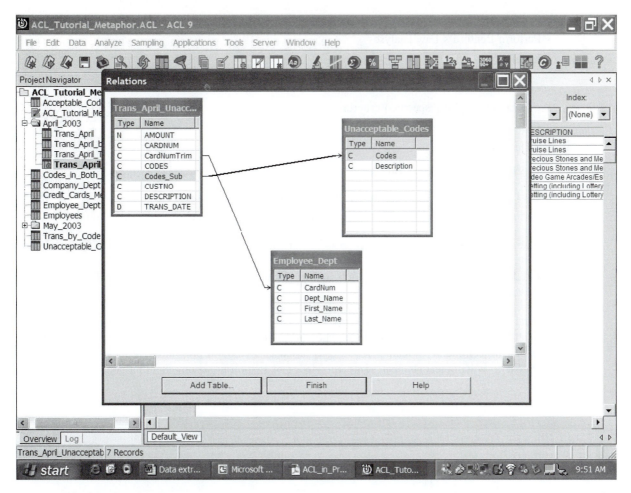

FIGURE 10-6 User Relationships

are set up for use by the Picalo software. Because they are created in an open-source environment, users are encouraged to make their detectlets available to other users. Level 3 is still in the planning stages, but it is the developer's goal that Level 3 be the means by which fraud detection detectlets can be automated for continuous monitoring and auditing.

Most of Picalo is released under the GNU General Public License (GPL). The GPL is a restrictive, open-source license. The source code comes with Picalo, and users are encouraged to improve and add to its functionality. Because detectlets are built by companies, organizations, and individuals, it is up to them to decide whether to open source, sell, or public domain their routines. The Picalo restriction is that users are not permitted to incorporate any Picalo programming code into their products unless those products are also released under the GPL.

Picalo has features similar to those of other products such as ACL and IDEA, including the following:

- Import various file formats
- Sort and transpose data
- Manually insert data items
- Find and replace data meeting specified criteria
- Select and extract data
- Join tables by value, soundex, fuzzy match, and specified expression
- Stratify data by value and dates and into specific numbers of groups
- Summarize data values and dates
- Create pivot tables
- Upload tables to a database

- Create descriptive statistics
- Perform Benford's Law analyses
- Locate

  - Data matching specified criteria
  - Data not matching specified criteria
  - Unordered data items
  - Duplicates
  - Gaps in the dataset

- Create a column for Z-scores and identify, include, or exclude outliers
- Perform trend analyses using regression, high to low, and handshaking slope techniques

Like other similar programs, Picalo also has an expression builder and some detectlets (see Figure 10-7).

In addition to the data extraction tools and techniques previously discussed, the following features are somewhat unique to Picalo:

- Picalo is an open-source framework where users either utilize the software "as-is" or write programs of their own (detectlets). Those users who choose to write detectlets can share their software with the Picalo community. Picalo's scripting is based on Python, a programming language. Those who choose to write detectlets need some knowledge of Python to accomplish that goal.

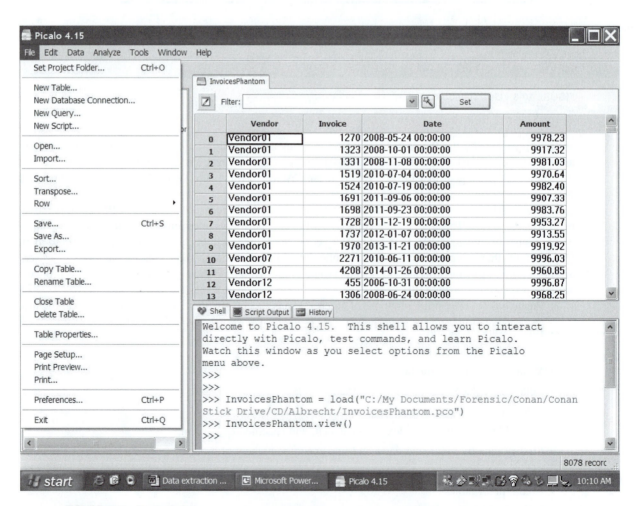

FIGURE 10-7 Picalo Software

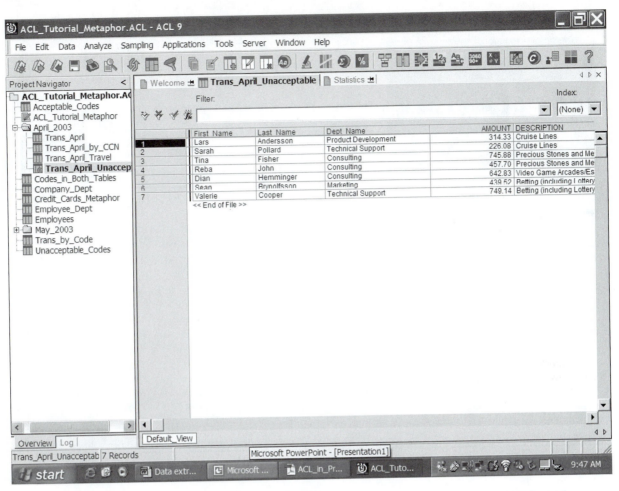

FIGURE 10-5   ACL Unacceptable Credit Card Transactions

- Dialog builder, allowing users to custom design a dialog box for variables, files, and selection criteria during an interactive batch.
- Oversampling, which includes the selection order number of randomly sampled items.
- If Command, which applies a condition to an entire file before command execution within a batch.
- Set Filter command, which enables commands after Set Filter to be applied only to the filtered records in a batch.
- Display options, which allow users to create many different types of graphs from the Histogram, Stratify, Classify, Age, and Benford commands. These graphs can be saved as bitmap files for import into other software programs and/or investigation reports.

Picalo   Picalo is a collaborative, open-source effort started in 2000 by Conan C. Albrecht, Professor at Brigham Young University, to produce data extraction and analysis tools for auditors, fraud examiners, data miners, and other data analysts. Picalo can be used to analyze financial information, employee records, purchasing systems, accounts receivable and payables, sales, marketing, and merchandising (inventory) systems. Data from Excel, XML, EBCDIC, CSV, and TSV can be imported into Picalo for further examination and analysis. Picalo also has an added feature in that it can be programmed to analyze network activities, Web server logs, and system log-in records and to import e-mail into relational or text-based databases. Further, it has data analysis tools for fraud detection and investigation.

Picalo is built on a three-level architecture, including open-source and, potentially, closed-source parts of the software. The open-source level, Level 1, includes the basic data structures and the tools needed for extraction and analysis. Level 2 permits nontechnical people to run more advanced analyses without having to script or write programs—by incorporating detectlets (analogous to Excel macros) that

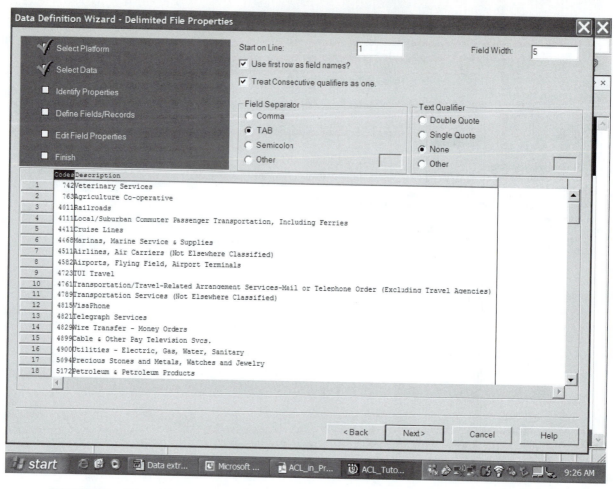

FIGURE 10-4 ACL and Data Definition Wizard

Chapters 4, 5, and 6 of "ACL in Practice" are centered on analyzing the imported data. Some of the tasks related to the employee credit cards include the following:

- Determining the total credit card liability
- Extracting credit card numbers that meet specified criteria
- Locating transactions by customer number
- Filtering credit card balances that exceed the card's credit limit
- Summarizing total expenses by expense category
- Extracting transactions that meet specified expense category criteria
- Isolating recreational expenses
- Identifying unacceptable transactions

As a result of this work, seven of 200 employees have unacceptable credit card transactions, as follows in Figure 10-5.

This exercise not only requires importing files from various formats, it also requires users to join tables based on relationships. The joining function is relatively easily accomplished, as can be seen in Figure 10-6.

In the final chapter, "ACL in Practice" brings in the May data, and students are asked to replicate many of the tasks completed in Chapter 4 on April's credit card transactions. The software also has a reporting function that facilitates the writing of investigative reports.

Advanced users can take advantage of ACL features, including the following:

- Batches, a series of ACL commands stored in an ACL project. This series of commands can be executed repeatedly and automatically. Any command can be stored in a batch.

- Search for duplicate records
- Examine employee salaries and bonuses
  - Developing control totals
  - Sorting records
  - Filtering records
  - Using mathematical functions to create and analyze new data.

For example, in Figure 10-3, columns for "Bonus," "Percent," and "Salary" were created and added to the dataset.

In Chapter 3, several files and file types are accessed:

Acceptable_Codes.mdb (database file)

Credit_Cards_Metaphor.xls (Excel)

Company_Departments.txt (tab delimited text file)

Employees.cvs (comma delimited text file)

Trans_April.xls (Excel)

Unacceptable_Codes.txt (tab delimited text file)

The ACL tutorial has students work through importing these various file formats using the Data Definition Wizard (see Figure 10-4).

Once imported, each file is checked to verify the completeness of the data and accuracy of the import functions. The ACL "project notes" feature allows users to document their work so that they have an audit trail and can replicate the results of their work if needed.

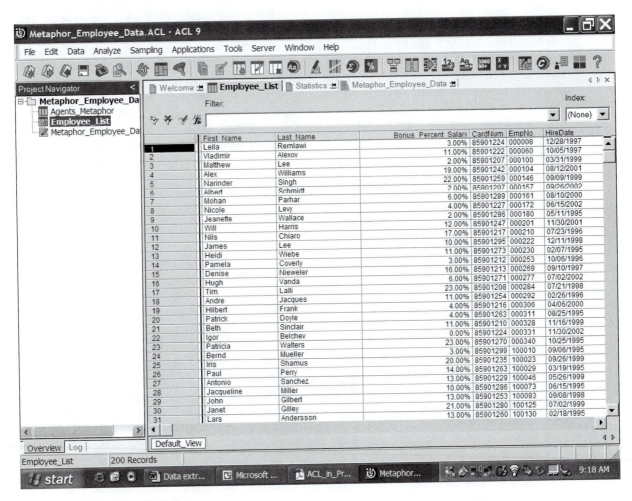

FIGURE 10-3 ACL Software

- Copying data files
- Searching for data files
- Renaming a database

Each of the audits/investigations in the workbook increases in complexity in using IDEA's functions and tests, building on the experience learned in earlier sections. The data files provided for use in the IDEA workbook were created in a variety of formats, to provide experience in importing data from a number of different file types. The screen shots and check figures facilitate quick and independent development of the skills needed to use the software to its fullest. In summary, IDEA can read, display, analyze, manipulate, sample, and extract data from files obtained from many sources in many formats.

ACL   ACL Services Ltd. provides audit analytics and continuous monitoring software. The software provided by ACL can be used to ensure internal controls compliance, thereby reducing the risk of fraud, and to detect and investigate seemingly fraudulent activity. ACL facilitates organization-wide testing and monitoring of internal controls through independent verification of transactional data. ACL can be used for audit analytics and controls monitoring on a continuous basis (continuous auditing). ACL can be used for the following activities in a digital environment:

- Audit analytics
- Continuous auditing and monitoring
- Fraud detection and investigation
- Regulatory compliance
- Secure data access

ACL stands for Audit Control Language, a phrase that points to the early roots of the software. This software package is PC-based and permits data importation from differing file formats. Once the data files have been imported, ACL can be used to examine file characteristics, visually examine the raw data, and create various analyses and statistics that can be used as audit and investigative evidence. Imported data can be reviewed, searched, sorted, indexed, and extracted. Users can also search for duplicate records and for unexpected gaps in the data. Finally, ACL summarizes and stratifies and can be used to export files to other formats, such as Excel.

Like Excel, ACL data are presented in rows and columns. ACL has equation editors to create mathematical formulas that can generate new data for further analysis. ACL equations can also be set up to filter and extract data, and ACL users can also perform additional functions such as these:

- Aging analyses (e.g., accounts receivables and payables)
- Benford's Law analyses
- Draw samples
- Statistically evaluate audit findings
- Import and join multiple files
- Append and compare files

The user's activities are automatically captured in a log to create an audit trail. Like IDEA, ACL provides a comprehensive tutorial, in this case, a 76-page PowerPoint document called "ACL in Practice." The tutorial is set up around Metaphor Corporation and walks new users through the tasks addressed by the software. In addition to some background data about Metaphor Corporation, the tutorial reviews the company's policies with regard to company-backed but employee-held credit cards. Employees can use their credit cards to cover travel, entertainment, and office and professional expenses incurred for the benefit for Metaphor. Accounting coding policies are captured in a separate Word file that students access during the tutorial. In Chapter 2, the tutorial begins by familiarizing users with some of the basic functions of the software by analyzing employee salaries and bonuses and hiring dates, as well as the incorporation of human resources data. Tutorial users complete the following tasks:

- Import the employee list, review the data, and ensure that the record count is accurate
- Develop a statistical view of the data

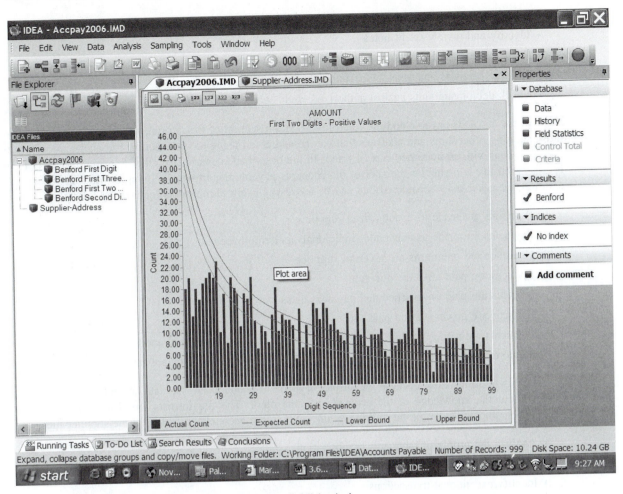

FIGURE 10-2 IDEA: Benford's Law "first-two digit" Analysis

that may also have an impact on the amounts reflected in the financial statements. Then students examine the inventory attributes as follows:

- Identify obsolete inventory items
- Calculate usage ratios
- Estimate the obsolescence provision
- Estimate the obsolescence provision by depot (location)
- Test the accuracy of the automatic reordering system
- Analyze selling prices and related margins
- Analyze payments by suppliers

The IDEA tutorial then has students work through a number of useful tasks that apply to most data extraction and analysis projects:

- Designing reports
- Printing
- Rerunning analyses
- Housekeeping activities
  - Reviewing and documenting analysis outcomes
  - Managing folders and projects
  - Backing up and restoring data files
  - Deleting data and other files

- Extract old unpaid accounts receivable items
- Identify and review credit notes
- Recalculate transaction amounts
- Analyze balances and taxes by account
- Check debtors/amounts against authorized credit limits from another file

In the accounts payable and the fraud investigation section of the tutorial, students not only identify those auditing procedures and analyses that can be addressed using data extraction and analysis tools, but they also deal with an increased risk of fraud. In the described scenario, the chief financial officer (CFO) is concerned that a particular member of the accounts payable department is living beyond his means. In addition, the other risks considered that can be addressed using digital tools include the following:

- Payments are made to unauthorized suppliers
- Payments are made to nonvendor individuals and employees
- Unauthorized premiums are given to suppliers
- Invoices are paid after the due date
- Invoices are paid on unscheduled payment dates
- Invoices are processed and paid twice
- Payments are made "off-line" so that they are not detected by normal audit procedures
- Supporting documentation items, such as POs, delivery receipts, etc., are missing

In this fictitious case, because the suspicion of fraud is enhanced, the data are obtained through the CFO without the knowledge of the accounts payable clerk. The file formats are ASCII Delimited and Excel. Then students examine the following attributes in the accounts payable and the supplier files:

- Analyze the profile of payments (stratification)
- Identify large and unusual payments (by dollar amount)
- Identify exceptional transactions

  - "Cash" as the payee
  - Round sum payments
  - Payments authorized by the suspected manager
  - Payments processed on Sunday
  - Amounts that appear to violate Benford's Law

- Test for duplicate payments
- Search for gaps in check number sequence
- Search for gaps in the date sequence
- Analyze payment days to identify favorable terms to suppliers
- Test payments to unauthorized suppliers
- Analyze payments by suppliers

The following are the results of the Benford's Law "first-two digit" analysis presented in Figure 10-2.

The third section of the tutorial addresses issues associated with inventory. More specifically, the CFO has identified problems with the underlying inventory system and needs assistance to identify those issues and make recommendations for corrective action. Some of the anomalies include the following:

- The listing of obsolete items seems to have too few items and to be incomplete
- The business is suffering from frequent stock-outs
- The margins on products do not seem to be reflective of the economics of some products

Thus, this section is more of a consulting-type of engagement, where the power and strength of data extraction and analysis tools can facilitate a more comprehensive identification and examination of issues

screen shots to coach new users into the appropriate use of the IDEA software. Tutorial users perform three separate audits/investigations: one each into accounts receivable, accounts payable/fraud investigation, and inventory analysis.

In the accounts receivable section (shown in Figure 10-1), the tutorial requires students to identify the potential risks, the business implications of those risks (e.g., the inability to collect accounts receivables from customers who do not meet credit standards), and the audit objectives of the audit tests (such as completeness, accuracy, valuation, existence, validity, and presentation). Students must also provide an overview of the types of tests required, such as mechanical accuracy and valuation, analysis, exception testing, gap and duplicate analysis, matching records across files, and comparison tests and sampling. Next, students are provided with an eight-step audit program to work through.

From there, users need to set up the engagement in IDEA and import the data files, given the formats received from the fictitious client. Step-by-step instructions, explanations, and screen shots are provided, to give users comfort that they are taking the correct actions. Once the files are imported, users work with control total functions to ensure that the import is successful. Then students complete the following tasks in the accounts receivable and related files:

- Examine field statistics
- Develop and complete reconciliations
- Randomly sample records
- Develop and analyze the accounts receivable aging
- Extract transactions and balances with high values

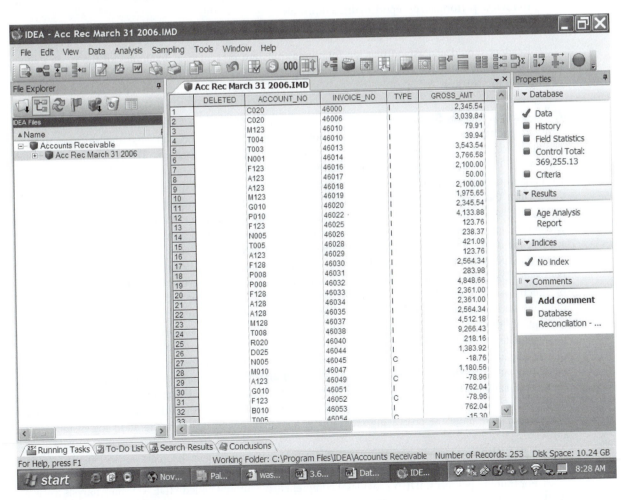

FIGURE 10-1 IDEA Software

- Monitoring choices. Consider the various levels of aggregation in the data and their impact on the ability of digital tools and techniques to monitor exceptional transactions (red flags and other anomalies) successfully. The lowest level of monitoring is often at the transaction level, whereas the highest level of monitoring is account balances and financial statement totals. Between transactions and financial statement amounts are various intervening layers. How to monitor these layers effectively and efficiently is often dictated, at least in part, by the targeted risk assessment—the likelihood of a particular fraud scheme and its relative magnitude. As discussed throughout the text, the fraud and forensic accounting professional not only needs to be cognizant of the sole fraudster but also of predator fraudsters and collusion and management override schemes that can be more difficult to detect and investigate and more costly to the organization.

Data Extraction and Analysis Software

There are many types of data analysis software on the market, with new products and new versions of old products emerging. Because every fraud examination or forensic accounting engagement is different, choosing a data analysis tool is something that the fraud examiner should consider in each individual case, to decide which package is most appropriate for the current investigation.

Data mining and knowledge discovery software is generally classified into two general categories:

- Public domain/shareware/freeware: available free, or for a nominal charge, through Web sites, ftp sites, and newsgroups. Some of the more common freeware includes Picalo, SAOimage, Super-Mongo, Tiny Tim, and xv. Many shareware programs, such as WINKS v4.62, allow users a trial period, after which a fee must be paid to reactivate the software. Freeware and shareware programs can be located through Internet search engines and through software download services. In some cases—research prototypes/beta versions or free software in the development stages—users are asked to review performance, report malfunctions, etc.

- Commercial applications: general release products, usually with technical support and warranty.

Readers should understand that the following tools are presented as examples of the types that are available, that the listing of available tools is not complete, and that the authors are not promoting the use of any specific software.

IDEA Data Analysis Software

IDEA is an acronym for Interactive Data Extraction & Analysis. This software package is a PC-based file interrogation package that allows accountants, auditors, and financial managers to view, sample, and analyze data from other computerized systems. IDEA is generalized audit software. IDEA is able to import data in differing file formats. For audit trail purposes, IDEA field statistics are created during the import function, which creates the working files that IDEA then analyzes.

Once the data are imported, IDEA can be used to examine file statistics and observe the raw data values underlying those statistics. Users can browse through the data; search for records meeting specified attributes; sort and index the records; extract records meeting specified criteria; search for duplicates and gaps in the data; summarize, stratify, and export files to other formats, such as Excel.

IDEA has many of the data analysis features of a product such as Excel, Quatro, or other spreadsheet packages. Data are presented in rows and columns, and IDEA can be used with mathematical formulas or functions (e.g., statistics) to analyze the data presented in columns and rows or to create new data columns for further analysis. For example, IDEA can be used to test invoice totals, by picking up prices and quantities from their respective columns and multiplying those together in a new column. Then, the calculated (extended) invoice amount can be compared to the invoice total to ensure that the two match. In addition, IDEA users can make pivot tables, aging analyses (e.g., accounts receivables and payables), and conduct Benford's Law analyses, plan and draw samples, and statistically evaluate audit findings in sampled transactions. When the user imports several files, IDEA can join, append, and compare them and create action fields, i.e., those from one file that have relationship to a field of another IDEA file. Information about the processing measures is automatically recorded in the audit log history of this software.

IDEA also supports the organization of work by allowing users to create to-do lists and folders, move and copy files, and create macros.

For training purposes, IDEA provides a comprehensive tutorial called "IDEA: Data Analysis Software Workbook." It is an easy-to-use, intuitive 270-page tutorial, with step-by-step instructions, solutions, and

assets, liabilities, or equity is often assigned on the basis of 100 percent. For instance, an investigator may be able to determine whether paid expenditures over multiple periods are reasonable. If one area of company expenses seems abnormally large or growing/declining in a manner that is unexpected, a red flag could be raised and further investigation might be appropriate.

- Horizontal ratio analysis: analyzing the percentage change in individual financial statement line items from one year to the next. With horizontal analysis, the first year is considered the base year. In subsequent years, changes from the prior year are computed and expressed as a percentage of the base year or the most recent prior year. This function determines the trends over time (e.g., expenses, inventory, etc.). Discrepancies and unexpected trends may suggest further inquiry.

- Date functions: querying the database based on dates. This function can be used to identify discrepancies in dates across database files; for example, invoice dates in the accounts receivable files may not agree with invoice dates in the customer history file. By using the software to verify that dates are consistent, the fraud examiner or forensic accountant can extract suspicious transactions where the dates are inconsistent. Other date functions include aging of data and looking for transaction dates outside of expected date ranges.

- Recalculations: checking the accuracy of amounts by recomputing those amounts using quantities and prices/dollar rates. For example, employee paycheck amounts can be examined by pulling hours data from the manufacturing data capture files and pulling the employee's wage rate from the employee master file. Amounts that do not agree with the paycheck amount could be flagged for further investigation.

- Transactions and balances exceeding expectations: checking to ensure that transaction amounts and balances (conglomerations of transactions) do not exceed expected limits. For example, a 24-hour per day, seven-day work week is 168 hours. Clearly, no employee should be paid for more hours than there are in a week. Likewise, a salaried employee should be paid his or her salary amount for the pay period. Notwithstanding bonuses, the paycheck amount should not exceed the salary amount based on the employee master file.

Given the functions previously described, the following are some examples of data analysis queries that can be performed by most data analysis software:[2]

General Ledger Analysis

- Select specific journal entries for analysis
- Create actual to budget comparison reports
- Analyze and confirm specific ledger accounts for legitimate transaction activity
- Speed account reconciliation through specialized account queries
- Calculate financial ratios
- Calculate percentage comparison ratios between accounts
- Prepare custom reports, cash flow, profit/loss, and asset and liability total reports
- Compare summaries by major account in any order (low to high, high to low)
- Create reports in any format by account, division, department, etc.

Accounts Receivable

- Create a list of customer limit increases and decreases
- Age accounts receivable in various formats
- Identify gaps in sequential forms such as invoices
- Identify duplicate invoices or customer account number entries
- Show specified reports on credits taken by customers
- Report customer summaries by invoice, product, etc.
- Identify customer activity by age, product, etc.
- Compare customer credit limits and current or past balances

Sales Analysis

- Create a report of all system overrides and sales exceptions
- Analyze returns and allowances by store, department, or other areas

- Summarize trends by customer type, products, salesperson, etc.
- Compare ratios of current sales to outstanding receivables or other variables
- Generate reports on a correlation between product demand or supply and sales prices

Accounts Payable

- Audit paid invoices for manual comparison with actual invoices
- Summarize large invoices by amount, vendor, etc.
- Identify debits to expense accounts outside of set default accounts
- Reconcile check registers to disbursements by vendor invoice
- Verify vendor 1099 requirements
- Create vendor detail and summary analysis reports
- Review recurring monthly expenses and compare to posted/paid invoices
- Generate a report on specified vouchers for manual audit or investigation

Asset Management

- Generate depreciation to cost reports
- Compare book and tax depreciation and indicate variances
- Sort asset values by asset type or dollar amount
- Select samples for asset existence verification
- Recalculate expense and reserve amounts using replacement costs

Cash Disbursement

- Summarize cash disbursements by account, bank, department, vendor, etc.
- Verify audit trail for all disbursements by purchase order, vendor, department, etc.
- Generate vendor cash activity summary for analysis
- Identify disbursements by department, supervisor approval, or amount limits

Payroll

- Summarize payroll activity by specific criteria for review
- Identify changes to payroll or employee files
- Compare time card and payroll rates for possible discrepancies
- Prepare check amount reports for amounts over a certain limit
- Check proper supervisory authorization on payroll disbursements

Purchasing

- Track scheduled receipt dates versus actual receipt dates, summary, and detail
- Compare vendor performance by summarizing item delivery times and amounts
- Isolate purchase order types for analysis
- Analyze late shipments

The following are some key issues to address as data analysis is completed in a digital environment:

- Data validity and data integrity. As data are moved or transferred from one file or storage location to another, data validity and integrity must be verified. The first step in data analysis is to ensure the validity and integrity of the data.
- Data format and structure. Data format and structure have an impact on the ability to import and export data to and from computers and software programs.
- Magnitude. Targeted risk assessment is not only concerned with the probability of a fraud scheme, but also its relative size. Preliminary targeted risk assessment and related analyses ensure that the potential issue is a reasonable and proper utilization of fraud examination and forensic accounting resources.

- The detectlet framework means that users within an organization can share with others in their organizations. This permits less technologically savvy users to harness the power of the software tool without having to learn how to operate the software in great detail.
- Picalo includes some advanced analysis tools not available in other products:
  - Picalo supports grouping activities by a number of days for analysis of labor and timecard data.
  - Picalo can also automatically group records to achieve smoothness in data.

GRAPHICS AND GRAPHICS SOFTWARE

It is said that a picture is worth a thousand words. Data analysis programs and graphics software packages can provide numerous pictorial representations of the data. Graphics have at least three distinct roles in an investigation. First, they can be used as an investigative tool. By visually putting together linkages, flows, timelines, and other graphics, the investigator can gain insight into the case, possibly seeing the case in ways that he or she had not previously considered. Second, graphics can also help the investigator to identify holes in the case or problem areas where further investigation is required. For example, the graphics might suggest that persons with opportunity have not been properly eliminated as suspects. Similarly, graphics can be used to identify questions that need to be answered in order to wrap up a case. Graphical representations of the data, like spreadsheets and examination of raw data, such as source documents, can facilitate critical thinking by facilitating consideration of the case from differing perspectives.

Third, graphics can be useful to communicate investigative findings, conclusions, and results. Although individuals with a mathematical or accounting background are perfectly comfortable looking at spreadsheets to derive meaning and interpret their importance to an investigation, most people are overwhelmed by a page of numbers (or pages of numbers) with subtotals, totals, columns, rows total, rows of data, etc. Translating numerical and other important data from a case into graphics allows those with less experience and less comfort with numbers to better understand the findings of the fraud examiner or forensic accountant. Case outcomes often hinge on the ability of the professional to take complex ideas, relationships, and the results of detailed data extraction and analysis activities and express them in a simpler, more meaningful manner so that a greater number of people, including juries, are likely to understand what the professional is trying to communicate.

Recognizing that the professional needs (1) to answer the questions who, what, when, where, why, and how; (2) to address the fraud triangle to the extent that evidence is available; and (3) to be centered on the elements of fraud: the act, the concealment, and conversion; as well as (4) the motivations for fraudulent activities, such as money, ideology, coercion, and ego (M-I-C-E), graphics help represent the findings and help investigators draw meaning from their work.

The Association Matrix

One of the first graphical tools is an association matrix for identifying major players who are central to an investigation and to identify linkages between those players. Linkages can take the form of names, places, addresses, phone numbers, etc. Although all of these data are documented as preliminary evidence electronically in some software tool, such as Excel, Access, or even Word, the association matrix is a starting point for reflecting some of the most important data in a simplified format. These matrices often serve as an intermediate format that organizes observed relationship material into a compact arrangement—to facilitate review and as a basis for creating more complex charts.

The format for the association matrix, including an example, is presented in Figure 10-8.

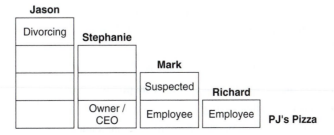

FIGURE 10-8 Association Matrix

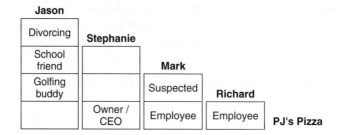

FIGURE 10-9 Updated Association Matrix

Notice that, on each line in the association matrix, the name of an important person, place, address, business, organization, etc. is written, followed by the boxes with the relationship that exists between the entities (as known from the evidence). In this example, Stephanie and Jason are divorcing. The divorce is being contested by Jason, who has a reputation as a playboy. Stephanie started and developed the 54-store PJ's Pizza chain, named after her little sister, who has Lyme disease. Stephanie has been hands-off, pursuing charity work for the last couple of years, and has entrusted the day-to-day operations of the pizza chain to her chief operating officer and friend of thirty years, Alexandria. Alexandria has been with the company since day one, owns 20 percent of the stock, and is considered a genius at marketing and store location, but her financial and accounting background is judged to be very weak.

Recently, Stephanie discovered enough evidence to suspect strongly that someone is embezzling reasonably large sums of money from her company. Mark is the treasurer and accounting manager located at corporate headquarters, and Richard is a regional manager of fifteen stores. Preliminary evidence suggests that the fraud is isolated to Richard's region. Further, the fraud appears to be concealed by person(s) with access to operational data, cash, and the accounting records. Initially, the divorce seemed to have no relation to the possible fraud. However, surveillance conducted by a licensed private investigator revealed that two of the key suspects have very close ties to Jason, Stephanie's estranged husband; he has been seen with one or the other at least one time during each of the past five weeks. At no time were the three seen together. As a result, the association matrix was updated as shown in Figure 10-9.

In this example, the major players have been listed and their relationships described. Although no proof exists that Mark and Richard are in collusion to perpetrate a fraud, based on the graphic, it appears that Jason seems to be the common link. Given the impending divorce, he and his close friends may be trying to damage Stephanie and generate some cash in the process. This graphic helps the investigator see important links. In addition, this association matrix may be useful in communicating with lawyers, judges, and jury members, if such a need arises. From the information in the matrix, investigators can develop more complex graphics, such as a link chart.

Link Charts

Link charts are another way to represent the associations, linkages, and other important relationships graphically. They help graphically describe linkages between entities: people, businesses, and "organizations" (in quotes because some organizations, including gangs, consortiums of drug dealers, and organized criminal enterprises, are probably not listed with the Secretary of State's records but may act and operate like many legitimate business entities). Link charts therefore create a graphic representation of known and suspected associations among businesses, individuals, organizations, telephone numbers, addresses, e-mail accounts, Web sites, etc. that are potentially involved in criminal activity.

Link charts are more complex than association matrices and, as such, follow rules to ensure that viewers understand the graphics and are to interpret their meaning with a minimum of error. The rules of link charting include the following:

- Each person has one link chart symbol and location on the chart
- The chart should be developed as simply as possible, while remaining accurate
- The chart cannot be misleading
- Evidence and other documentation should be maintained as backup
- Preferably no linkage lines should cross (although this is not always practicable)

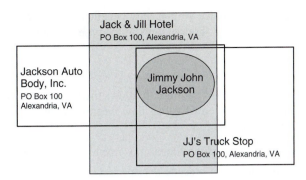

FIGURE 10-10 Link Chart Example

- The date and important references should be printed on the chart
- A legend should be used that describes the meaning of symbols, colors, shapes, and lines
- Symbols and other aspects of the link chart should be used consistently

In Figure 10-10, you can see the linkages between Jimmy John Jackson and several business enterprises.

In this example, three businesses are presented: Jackson Auto Body, Inc., JJ's Truck Stop, and Jack & Jill Hotel. The Secretary of State's records database indicates that Jimmy John Jackson has an ownership role in all three. Assume further that evidence indicates that a supplier fraud is occurring at a trucking company, and it appears that the three companies presented are receiving payments for services not rendered. Also assume that the evidence indicates that no actual businesses exist, and yet the mailing addresses are the same. If a criminal activity is suspected and these three businesses are involved, it appears that Jimmy John Jackson is at the center of everything. Armed with this information and a pictorial representation, the investigator is able to concentrate his or her effort and can easily communicate findings. Along a similar line, the association matrix previously discussed can be converted into a link chart (see Figure 10-11).

Notice that the picture here is clearer and easier to read and understand than the association matrix previously presented. Further, notice that a dashed line exists between Mark and Richard, because the evidence does not yet suggest that the two have a known relationship. Also note that no line is presented to connect Stephanie with Mark or Richard. This is because she is generally a hands-off owner/CEO and thus may not know either of them. These possible relationships need to be investigated further. At this point, a fraud may have been committed by Richard and Mark, and one of the other beneficiaries could be Jason. However, what if Stephanie is purposely taking money out of the company to lower its value so that her divorce payout to Jason is lower? This could only be determined through further investigation.

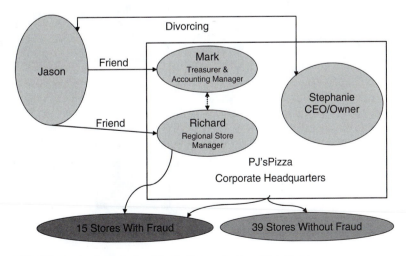

FIGURE 10-11 Association Matrix Converted to a Link Chart

Thus, link charts and other graphics are not only beneficial as investigative and communication tools but can also be helpful in identifying shortcomings in the case and areas where further work is necessary.

Flow Diagrams

The next type of graphic is the flow diagram. It allows the investigator to analyze the movement of events, activities, and commodities—to see what that flow means in relation to a suspected criminal activity. The flow diagram can be used for the following:

- To illustrate the operation of the illegal movement of goods, services, people, money, etc.
- To present the activities that precede a suspected criminal act
- To show the flow of criminal goods, cash flows, and profits
- To illustrate and describe a money-laundering scheme
- To present changes in organizational structure over time
- To illustrate the flow of cash, information, or documents through an organization

The general purpose is to discover the meaning of those activities and their importance to the investigation. For example, the following flow diagram (Figure 10-12) can be used to show how transactions are captured and how they flow through the accounting system into the periodic financial statements and tax returns.

In this example, transactions take place between the suspect entities (and their representatives) and others: suppliers, vendors, customers, employees, etc. The essence of these transactions is captured in paper format. Examples of paper documents include receipts, invoices, purchase orders, delivery receipts, bills of lading, contracts, and other sources. Certain information presented on the paper documents is captured in journal entries. The journal entries are then posted to the general ledger, which acts like a series of buckets where transactions are categorized and sorted. The general ledger amounts—the sum total of the transactions in a particular bucket—are then summarized and presented in periodic financial statements and tax returns.

In Figure 10-13, a kickback scheme is outlined graphically. In this case, evidence suggests that the investigators know everything about the scheme except how the inside kickback recipient received his or her payoff. The investigators are considering three options:

Option 1: Third-party merchandiser writes a check to kickback recipient.

Option 2: Third-party merchandiser writes checks to cash and gives cash to kickback recipient.

Option 3: Third-party merchandiser writes a check to fictitious company controlled by the kickback recipient.

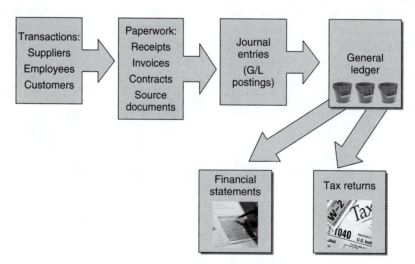

FIGURE 10-12   Flow Chart: Review of Suspect Company's Books and Records

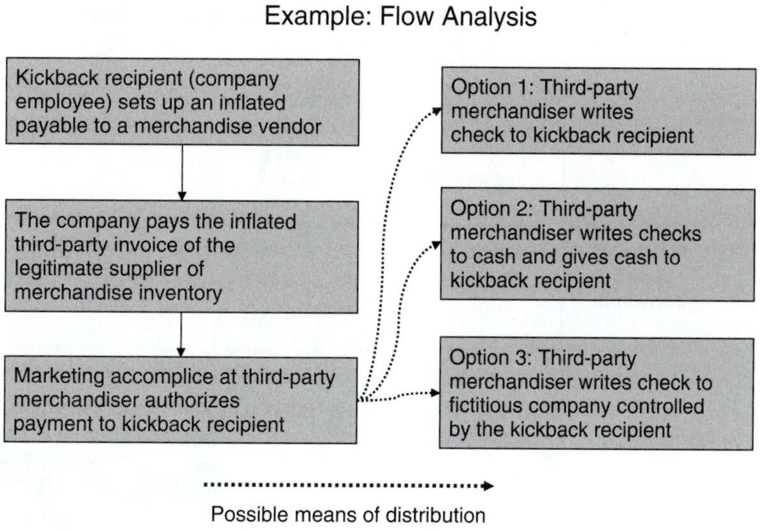

Example: Flow Analysis

FIGURE 10-13   Kickback Scheme Illustration

At this point, the investigators can see that more work needs to be done related to the conversion aspect of the case. Because the actual kickback aspect of the scheme is unknown, dotted instead of solid lines are used in the presentation. The movement of commodities lends itself particularly well to flow diagrams. Examples include the following:

Money laundering (flow of cash)

Stolen goods

Narcotics trafficking

Smuggling

Timelines

The next type of graphical analysis is that of a timeline, which organizes information about events or activities chronologically to determine what has or may have occurred and the impact that these actions have had on the activity under investigation. In the following example (see Figure 10-14), Seth purchases a sales and marketing company from Vance. Further, by 2004, Seth is bankrupt and is now complaining that he was sold a failing company by Lance. However, Seth knew very little about the sales and marketing business when he purchased the company, with newly inherited wealth from his father, except that Vance drove a Mercedes and lived in a large house. Seth seems to have assumed that he could do the same. However, Vance claims that the success of the company under his ownership was his ability to secure large contracts with successful clients. As seen from the following timeline, after purchasing the company, Seth negotiated no new contracts. If additional evidence supports Vance's contention, it appears that the demise of Seth's company is due to his own inability to secure new sales and marketing contracts.

The break in the pattern of new sales and marketing contracts is clear and distinct, especially when presented in graphical form.

Other Graphical Formats

As stated, graphics can be a simple, clear, and concise method of presenting case material to communicate outcomes. They can be developed in nearly any manner and for almost any purpose that appears to further the investigation. For example, in Figure 10-15, you can see the impact of a person selling a company in a sham transaction and establishing himself during the sales transaction as a secured creditor. As can be seen in the left-hand column, the former owner was "last in line" before the company was sold. However, after the sale, the former owner was now first in line and moved ahead of every other creditor. If the former

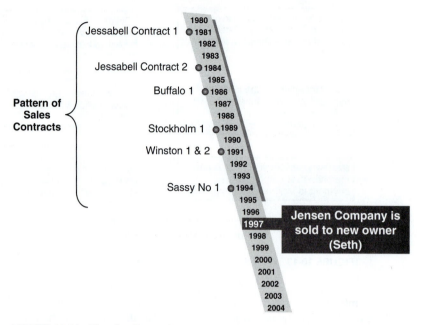

FIGURE 10-14 Timeline Example

owner has the right contractual relationship with his former company, he or she could milk the company of all cash and profits and effectively bankrupt it. Because of a position as secured creditor, unsecured creditors (examples include off-balance sheet liability holders, such as a plaintiff to a lawsuit against the company) have little recourse unless it could be proven that the sales transaction was a sham.

The result of graphical analysis and presentation can be a number of outcomes:

Critical questions need to be answered:

- What actions are critical to the activity under investigation?
- Who are the key people involved?
- Who appears to guide the activity?
- What is the net result of the activities?
- Who appears to benefit?

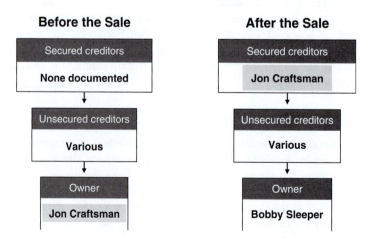

FIGURE 10-15 Defendant's Company Financial Structure before and after the Sale in 2007

Work and additional follow-up is needed to finalize the case:

- Re-interview suspect to determine possible motivation for the fraud.
- Subpoena bank records.
- Trace laundered money to source.
- Need undercover agent to pose as vendor of questionable ethical character to develop evidence of a kickback scheme.

CASE MANAGEMENT SOFTWARE

Case management software can be used in a number of situations to manage cases and case data, organize it in meaningful ways, and even present information for use in reports or during testimony. Sophisticated, complicated, and complex cases can benefit from the use of case management software, including the following:

- Complex fraud schemes: examples include insurance schemes, health care frauds, investment schemes, credit card scams, identity theft rings.
- Money laundering: organize and investigate large databases of suspicious activities, movements of money around the world, and other sophisticated financial crimes.
- Compliance: internal investigations and risk management, such as Sarbanes–Oxley compliance.
- Complex and complicated financial statement frauds: multiple participating persons and possibly multiple schemes.
- Organized criminal operations: complex organizational structures and related activities, such as money laundering, movement of contraband, and cash flows.
- Drug trafficking: loosely knit but fluid organizational structures that include the movement of narcotics and the flow of money back to the persons controlling the activity.
- Terrorism financing: the perpetrators exist in semiautonomous cells, operating in various localities around the world.

Case management software can be used to initiate investigations that can evolve into complex cases. New investigations can be initiated, and evidence collected and organized when it is developed through various channels—including detectives, forensic accountants, computer forensic specialists, internal audit and other experts, as well as from employees, vendors, customers, and other participating persons and organizations.

Most case management software has workflow rules, so that leads, evidence, and next-steps can be prioritized, and investigative approaches can be tasked to the most appropriate people. With some software packages, investigators are able to send and receive e-mails within the system and record notes, evidence, activities, and investigative outcomes. Another feature of case management software tools is the ability to organize and present data graphically so they can be reported.

Readers should understand that the following tools are presented as examples of the types that are available, that the listing of commercially available tools is not complete, and that the authors are not endorsing the tools described.

Analyst's Notebook i2   One of the case management software tool options is Analyst's Notebook i2. It is one of the leading providers of visual investigative analysis software for law enforcement, intelligence, military, and business enterprises. i2 allows investigators and analysts to visualize complex schemes and to organize and analyze large volumes of seemingly unrelated data. Upon completion and at appropriate times during the investigation, the results can be efficiently communicated to attorneys, other investigators, superiors, judges, juries, and grand juries. As previously discussed, visual analysis can bring clarity to complex investigations, schemes, and scenarios. This software can generate timelines, flow charts, activities matrices, link charts, and other graphics to help investigators better understand the schemes, who is involved, and how participants benefit from their activities.

All data are gathered and stored in various databases that the software can access. From those, the evidence can be searched, analyzed, and visualized from multiple perspectives and given various alternative assumptions, with the goal of resolving the case. The main advantage is that less time is required to manage,

organize, and process data, which are then analyzed and housed in one comprehensive locale. With more efficient evidence management for complex cases, more time can be spent on analysis and on drawing conclusions from the complete set of evidence, enabling investigators to uncover, interpret, and display complex information about seemingly unrelated persons, places, and events in an intuitive visual format.

LexisNexis CaseMap CaseMap® by LexisNexis makes it easy to organize, evaluate, and explore evidence, the list of potential suspects and other witnesses, and case issues; it is designed for litigators and investigators. CaseMap is a central repository for case knowledge. The software can be used to organize information, facts, evidence, documents, people, case issues, and applicable law. CaseMap files include spreadsheets, documents, and PDF files. Every CaseMap spreadsheet can be sorted, filtered, and tagged for later use. CaseMap details can be sent to the TimeMap® tool to create timeline graphics. CaseMap software also evaluates relationships between different attributes of the case information. For example, CaseMap can be structured to connect facts to applicable case law that supports a particular position on an issue.

CaseMap is not only supported by TimeMap but also by several other related packages, including TextMap® for transcription summary, NoteMap® for creating outlines, and DepPrep® for preparing witnesses for deposition and courtroom testimony. CaseMap and its suite of related products also have a reporting feature so that outcomes can be exported to other software packages.

REVIEW QUESTIONS

10-1 What are the two major approaches for testing IT system controls?

10-2 What is meant by the acronym CAATTs and what are they used for?

10-3 What is computer forensics?

10-4 What computer functions can make recovering deleted files more difficult?

10-5 How do e-discovery rules have an impact on the storage of e-mail and other electronic files?

10-6 What functions are used by data extraction and analysis software to highlight red flags of fraud?

10-7 What are the two categories of data mining and knowledge discovery software?

10-8 What role do graphics play in an investigation?

10-9 What is the purpose of timelines in an investigation?

10-10 How is case management software used in an investigation?

ENDNOTES

1. See James A. Hall and Tommie Singleton, *Information Technology Auditing and Assurance*, South-Western, 2005, p. 30.

2. ACFE, *Fraud Examiners Manual*, 3.60.

FRAUD SCHEMES

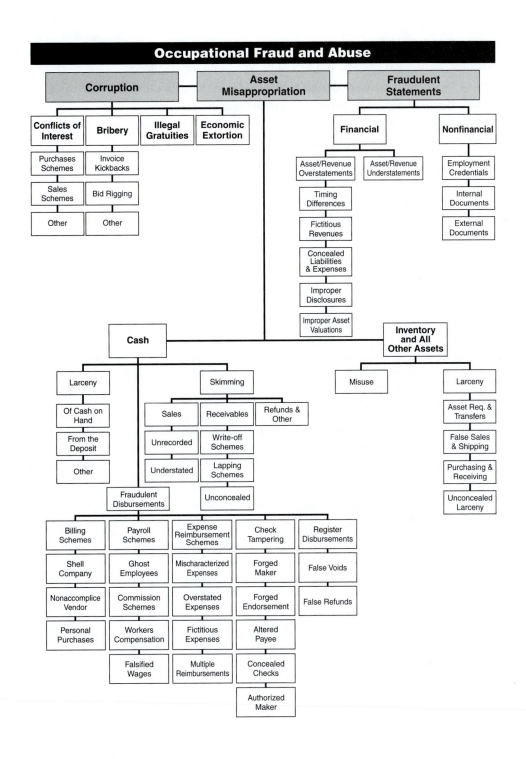

CHAPTER 11

CASH RECEIPT SCHEMES AND OTHER ASSET MISAPPROPRIATIONS

LEARNING OBJECTIVES

After completing this chapter, you should be able to do the following:

11-1 Describe the two principal categories of skimming schemes.

11-2 Discuss how sales skimming is committed and concealed.

11-3 Discuss how the skimming of receivables is committed and concealed.

11-4 Explain the techniques used to detect skimming.

11-5 Compare and contrast skimming and cash larceny.

11-6 Explain the techniques used to detect cash larceny.

11-7 Give examples of noncash misappropriation schemes.

11-8 Describe what is meant by the misuse of noncash assets.

11-9 Discuss how inventory shrinkage is concealed.

11-10 Explain the techniques used to detect noncash misappropriations.

CASE STUDY: TAKING FROM THE POOR TO GIVE TO THE RICH

After the 2001 terrorist attack on the World Trade Center in New York City, a thirty-year-old Section 501(c)(3) nonprofit organization established a means of raising money for the families of 9/11 victims. The entity already had established contacts with vendors and a method of distributing its products to support the venture. Most of the sales were transacted in cash. The organization planned to donate a large portion of its sales revenue from specific products to the 9/11 families.

Several years later, an anonymous tip was received by the Board of Directors, alerting them to a possible misappropriation of funds. The allegation was vague and suggested that the organization's corporate officers were using the organization's income for personal use. The allegations were taken seriously because it was widely known that the entity was among the top fund raisers in the area for 9/11 victims, yet the financial records revealed minimal sales revenue. Questions also were raised about the lack of funds transmitted to the intended recipients.

A preliminary examination of the journal and ledgers was conducted, and the initial findings indicated that, although the records had a few immaterial misstatements, proper record keeping was followed. Interviews with vendors revealed inconsistent information regarding accounts. Several of the vendors confirmed transactions with the entity only after they were shown receipts maintained by the organization under investigation. One vendor firmly refused to confirm any transactions with the entity, stating that all records for the period had been destroyed in a fire. Not surprisingly, no official

record of a fire could be found. Another vendor confirmed that the entity in question was one of its largest customers and also served as a distribution center; however, the only records that they maintained were hard copies of invoices that had been thrown into several cardboard boxes. There were no computerized records for transactions with the entity in question.

After sorting through boxes of invoices at the vendor's site, entity-related transactions were discovered. Many of the recovered records did not match the financial records maintained by the nonprofit organization. Also discovered during the search was information that indicated the entity used several different names to purchase goods, including those of the corporate officers. Payment for invoices was frequently made in cash.

Working with the newly disclosed information about how the entity conducted its operations, investigators began to reconstruct the books and conducted a surprise visit to the entity. A second set of financial records was discovered.

Bank statements that were obtained directly from the bank showed additional transactions that did not appear in the original journals and ledgers. Several credit cards issued to the officers of the corporation were also discovered. A detailed examination of the credit card statements disclosed unauthorized personal purchases that were made during the period for which the records were missing. The credit card vendors provided additional information related to the delivery of goods—many of them to the homes of the officers of

the corporation. Because of the nature of the goods purchased, they were easily identifiable and even easier to locate.

When the goods were located, law enforcement was notified, and the evidence was legally seized by court order.

The investigation and a reconstruction of the financial statements showed that the organization received significantly more income than was reported, indicating a cash skimming scheme. Several officers of the corporation were criminally and civilly prosecuted.

CRITICAL THINKING EXERCISE

Far off in the woods, there is a cabin. The cabin contains three people. Two are in one room; the other is alone in another room. All doors to the cabin are locked tight and have not been opened. All three people are dead. There was no sign of violence in this cabin. How did they die?

The Fraud Tree, as shown on page 293, was developed as a classification system to identify occupational frauds and abuses by the methods used to commit them. By categorizing schemes into different classifications, researchers can identify common methods used by perpetrators and typical vulnerabilities in victim organizations that allow these schemes to succeed.

SKIMMING SCHEMES

Skimming is the theft of cash from a victim entity prior to its entry in an accounting system. Because the cash is stolen before it has been recorded in the victim company's books, skimming schemes are known as "off-book" frauds, and, because the missing money is never recorded, skimming schemes leave no direct audit trail. Consequently, it may be very difficult to detect that the money has been stolen. This is the principal advantage to the fraudster of a skimming scheme.

Skimming can occur at any point where funds enter a business, so almost anyone who deals with the process of receiving cash may be in a position to skim money. This includes salespeople, tellers, wait staff, and others who receive cash directly from customers. In addition, employees whose duties include receiving and logging payments made by customers through the mail perpetrate many skimming schemes. These employees are able to slip checks out of the incoming mail for their own use, rather than posting the checks to the proper revenue or customer accounts. Those who deal directly with customers or who handle customer payments are obviously the most likely candidates to skim funds.

Skimming schemes all follow the same basic pattern as shown in Figure 11-1: an employee steals incoming funds before they are recorded in the victim organization's books. Within this broad category, skimming schemes can be subdivided based on whether they target sales or receivables. The character of the incoming funds has an effect on how the frauds are concealed, and concealment is the crucial element of most occupational fraud schemes. All of the following case examples come from various research projects by the ACFE; the latest is the *2008 Report to the Nation on Occupational Fraud and Abuse*.

Sales Skimming

The most basic skimming scheme occurs when an employee makes a sale of goods or services to a customer, collects the customer's payment at the point of sale, but makes no record of the transaction. The employee pockets the money received from the customer, instead of turning it over to his employer.

In order to discuss sales skimming schemes more completely, let us consider one of the simplest and most common sales transactions, a sale of goods at the cash register. In a normal transaction, a customer purchases an item—such as a pair of shoes—and an employee enters the sale on the cash register. The register tape reflects that the sale has been made and shows that a certain amount of cash (the purchase price of the item) should have been placed in the register. By comparing the register tape to the amount of money on hand, it may be possible to detect thefts. For instance, if $500 in sales is recorded on a particular register on a given day, but only $400 cash is in the register, someone has obviously stolen $100 (assuming there was no beginning cash balance).

When an employee skims money by making off-book sales of merchandise, however, the theft cannot be detected by comparing the register tape to the cash drawer because the sale was never recorded on the register. Return to the example in the preceding paragraph. Assume a fraudster wants to steal $100 and

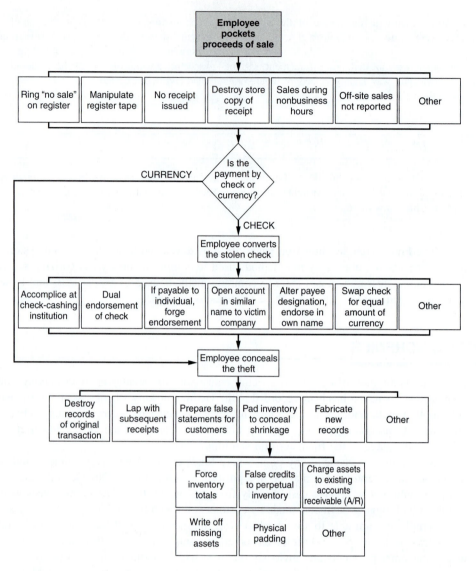

FIGURE 11-1 Unrecorded Sale

that there are $500 worth of sales at that employee's cash register through the course of the day. Also assume one sale involves a $100 pair of shoes. When the $100 sale is made, the employee does not record the transaction on his or her register. The customer pays $100 and takes the shoes home, but instead of placing $100 in the cash drawer, the employee pockets it. Because the employee did not record the sale, at the end of the day, the register tape reflects only $400 in sales. There will be $400 on hand in the register ($500 in total sales minus the $100 that the employee stole), so the register balances. By not recording the sale, the employee was able to steal money without the missing funds appearing on the books.

Cash Register Manipulation The most difficult part in a skimming scheme at the cash register is that the employee must commit the overt act of taking money. If the employee takes the customer's money and shoves it into his or her pocket without entering the transaction on the register, the customer may suspect that something is wrong and report the conduct to another employee or manager. It is also possible that a manager, a fellow employee, or a surveillance camera will spot the illegal conduct.

In order to conceal their thefts, some employees might ring a "no sale" or other noncash transaction on their cash registers to mask the theft of sales. The false transaction is entered on the register so that it appears a sale is being rung up, when in fact the employee is stealing the customer's payment. To the casual observer, it looks as though the sale is being properly recorded.

In other cases, employees have rigged their cash registers so that sales are not recorded on their register tapes. With modern cash registers, this is difficult to do. As we have stated, the amount of cash

on hand in a register may be compared to the amount showing on the register tape in order to detect employee theft. It is therefore not important to the fraudster what is keyed into the register, but rather what shows up on the tape. If employees can rig their register so that sales do not print, they can enter a sale that they intend to skim yet ensure that the sale never appears on the books. Anyone observing the employee sees the sale entered, and the cash drawer open, and so forth, yet the register tape does not reflect the transaction. How is this accomplished? In one fraud, a service station employee hid stolen gasoline sales by simply lifting the ribbon from the printer. He then collected and pocketed the sales that were not recorded on the register tape. The fraudster then rolled back the tape to the point where the next transaction should appear and replaced the ribbon. The next transaction was printed without leaving any blank space on the tape, apparently leaving no trace of the fraud. However, in this case, the fraudster had overlooked the fact that the transactions on his register were pre-numbered. Even though he was careful in replacing the register tape, he failed to realize that he was creating a break in the sequence of transactions. For instance, if the perpetrator skimmed sale #155, the register tape would show only transactions #153, #154, #156, #157, and so on. The missing transaction numbers, which were omitted because the ribbon was lifted when they took place, indicated fraud.

Special circumstances can lead to more creative methods for skimming at the register. In another situation, for instance, a movie theater manager figured out a way around the theater's automatic ticket dispenser. In order to reduce payroll hours, this manager sometimes worked as a cashier, selling tickets. He made sure, at these times, that there was no one checking patrons' tickets outside the theaters. When a sale was made, the ticket dispenser fed out the appropriate number of tickets, but the manager withheld tickets from some patrons and allowed them to enter the theater without them. When the next customer made a purchase, the manager sold her one of the excess tickets, instead of using the automatic dispenser. Thus, portions of the ticket sales were not recorded. At the end of the night, there was a surplus of cash, which the manager removed and kept for himself. Although the actual loss was impossible to measure, it was estimated that this manager stole over $30,000 from his employer.

After-Hours Sales Another way to skim unrecorded sales is to conduct sales during nonbusiness hours. For instance, some employees have been caught running their employers' stores on weekends or after hours without the knowledge of the owners. They were able to pocket the proceeds of these sales because the owners had no idea that their stores were even open. One manager of a retail facility in an unusual fraud case went to work two hours early every day, opening his store at 8:00 a.m. instead of 10:00 a.m., and pocketed all the sales made during these two hours. Talk about dedication! He rang up sales on the register as if it were business as usual, but then he removed the register tape and all the cash that he had accumulated. The manager then started from scratch at 10:00, as if the store were just opening. The tape was destroyed, so there was no record of the before-hours revenue.

Skimming by Off-Site Employees Although we have discussed skimming so far in the context of cash register transactions, skimming does not have to occur at a register or even involve hard currency. Employees who work at remote locations or without close supervision perpetrate some of the most costly skimming schemes. This can include independent salespeople who operate off-site and employees who work at branches or satellite offices. These employees have a high level of autonomy in their jobs, which often translates into poor supervision and, in turn, to fraud.

Several cases involved the skimming of sales by off-site employees. Some of the best examples of this type of fraud occur in the apartment rental industry, where apartment managers handle the day-to-day operations without much oversight. A common scheme, as evidenced by a bookkeeper in one fraud, is for the perpetrator to identify the tenants who pay in currency and remove them from the books. This causes a particular apartment to appear as vacant on the records, although, in fact, it is occupied. Once the currency-paying tenants are removed from the records, the manager can skim their rental payments without late notices being sent to the tenants. As long as no one physically checks the apartment, the fraudster can continue skimming indefinitely.

Another rental skimming scheme occurs when apartments are rented out, but no lease is signed. On the books, the apartment still appears to be vacant, even though there are rent-paying tenants on the premises. The fraudster can then steal the rent payments, which are not missed. Sometimes the employees in these schemes work in conjunction with the renters and give a "special rate" to these people. In return, the renters' payments are made directly to the employee, and any complaints or maintenance requests are directed only to that employee, so that the renters' presence remains hidden.

Instead of skimming rent, the property manager in another case skimmed payments made by tenants for application fees and late fees. Revenue sources such as these are less predictable than rental payments, and their absence may therefore be harder to detect. The central office knew when rent was due and how many apartments were occupied, but it had no control in place to track the number of people who filled out rental applications or how many tenants paid their rent a day or two late. Stealing only these nickel-and-dime payments, the property manager in this case was able to make off with approximately $10,000 of her employer's money.

A similar revenue source that is unpredictable and therefore difficult to account for is parking lot collection revenue. In one example, a parking lot attendant skimmed approximately $20,000 from his employer, simply by not preparing tickets for customers who entered the lot. He would take the customers' money and wave them into the lot, but because no receipts were prepared by the fraudster, there was no way for the victim company to compare tickets sold to actual customers at this remote location. Revenue sources that are hard to monitor and predict, such as late fees and parking fees in the preceding examples, are prime targets for skimming schemes.

Another off-site person in a good position to skim sales is the independent salesperson. A prime example is the insurance agent who sells policies but does not file them with the carrier. Most customers do not want to file claims on a policy, especially early in the term, for fear that their premiums will rise. Knowing this, the agent keeps all documentation on the policies, instead of turning it in to the carrier. The agent can then collect and keep the payments made on the policy, because the carrier does not know the policy exists. Customers continue to make their payments, thinking that they are insured, when in fact the policy is a ruse. Should a customer eventually file a claim, some agents are able to backdate the false policies, submit them to the carrier, and then file the claim so that the fraud remains hidden.

Poor Collection Procedures Poor collection and recording procedures can make it easy for an employee to skim sales or receivables. In one case, for instance, a governmental authority that dealt with public housing was victimized because it failed to itemize daily receipts. This agency received payments from several public housing tenants, but, at the end of the day, money received from tenants was listed as a whole. Receipt numbers were not used to itemize the payments made by tenants, so there was no way to pinpoint which tenant had paid how much. Consequently, the employee in charge of collecting money from tenants was able to skim a portion of their payments. She simply did not record the receipt of over $10,000. Her actions caused certain accounts receivable to be overstated, where tenant payments were not properly recorded.

Understated Sales The prior cases dealt with purely off-book sales. Understated sales work differently, in that the transaction is posted to the books, but for a lower amount than the perpetrator collected from the customer (see Figure 11-2). For instance, an employee wrote receipts to customers for their purchases, but she removed the carbon-paper backing on the receipts so that they did not produce a company copy. The employee then used a pencil to prepare company copies that showed lower purchase prices. For example, if the customer had paid $100, the company copy might reflect a payment of $80. The employee skimmed the difference between the actual amount of revenue and the amount reflected on the fraudulent receipt. This can also be accomplished at the register when the fraudster under-rings a sale, by entering a sale total that is lower than the amount actually paid by the customer. The employee skims the difference between the actual purchase price of the item and the sales figure recorded on the register. Rather than reduce the price of an item, an employee might record the sale of fewer items. If 100 units are sold, for instance, a fraudster might only record the sale of 50 units and skim the excess receipts.

Check-for-Currency Substitutions Another common skimming scheme is to take unrecorded checks that the perpetrator has stolen and substitute them for receipted currency. This type of scheme is especially common when the fraudster has access to incoming funds from an unusual source, such as refunds or rebates that have not been accounted for by the victim organization. The benefit of substituting checks for cash, from the fraudster's perspective, is that stolen checks payable to the victim organization may be difficult to convert. They also leave an audit trail showing where the stolen check was deposited. Currency, on the other hand, disappears into the economy once it has been spent.

An example of a check-for-currency substitution was found in a fraud where an employee responsible for receipting ticket and fine payments on behalf of a municipality abused her position and stole incoming revenues for nearly two years. When this individual received payments in currency, she issued receipts, but, when checks were received, she did not. The check payments were therefore unrecorded revenues—ripe

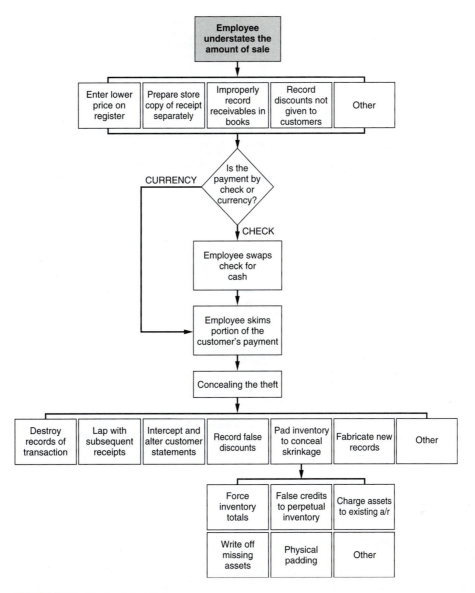

FIGURE 11-2 Understated Sales

for skimming. These unrecorded checks were then placed in the days' receipts, and an equal amount of cash was removed. The receipts matched the amount of money on hand, except that payments in currency had been replaced with checks.

Theft in the Mailroom—Incoming Checks Another common form of skimming occurs in the mailroom, where employees charged with opening the daily mail simply take incoming checks instead of processing them. The stolen payments are not posted to the customer accounts, and, from the victim organization's perspective, it is as if the check had never arrived (see Figure 11-3). When the task of receiving and recording incoming payments is left to a single person, it is all too easy for that employee to slip an occasional check into his or her pocket.

An example of a check theft scheme is where a mailroom employee stole over $2 million in government checks arriving through the mail. This employee simply identified and removed envelopes delivered from a government agency that was known to send checks to the company. Using a group of accomplices, acting under the names of fictitious persons and companies, this individual was able to launder the checks and divide the proceeds with his cronies.

Preventing and Detecting Sales Skimming Perhaps the biggest key to preventing skimming of any kind is to maintain a viable oversight presence at any point where cash enters an organization. Recall that the second leg of Cressey's fraud triangle involved a perceived opportunity to commit the fraud and get

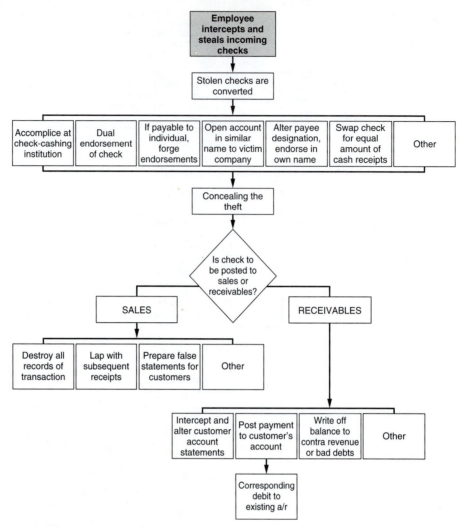

FIGURE 11-3   Theft of Incoming Checks

away with it. When an organization establishes an effective oversight presence, it diminishes the perception among employees that they would be able to steal without getting caught. In other words, employees are less likely to try to steal.

Therefore, it is important to have a visible management presence at all cash entry points, including cash registers and the mailroom. This is not to say that a manager must hover over cashiers and mailroom clerks at all times—too much oversight can actually produce a negative effect on employees, causing them to feel mistrusted or resentful of management. But managers should routinely check on all cash entry points—not just to look out for signs of fraud, but also to ensure proper customer service, monitor productivity, and so forth.

Instead of a physical management presence, video cameras can be installed at cash entry points to serve essentially the same purpose. The principal benefit to the use of video cameras is not that the cameras might detect theft (which they might), but that their use might dissuade employees from attempting to steal. Incidentally, a 24-hour video monitoring system can also deter any off-hours sales of the kind that were discussed earlier in this chapter.

Organizations do not have to rely solely on management to oversee cash collections. In retail organizations that utilize several cash registers, the registers are frequently placed in one "cluster" area, rather than spread out through the store. One reason for this is so that cashiers are working in full view of other employees, as well as customers. Again, this serves to deter attempts at skimming.

Customers can also be utilized in the monitoring function. Have you ever seen a sign at a retail establishment offering a discount to any customer who does not get a receipt at the time of his purchase? The purpose for these programs is to force employees to ring up sales, thereby making it more difficult to commit an unrecorded sales scheme. In addition, customer complaints and tips are a frequent source of detection for all types of occupational fraud, including skimming. Calls from customers for whom there is

no record, for example, are a clear red flag of unrecorded sales. Customer complaints should be received and investigated by employees who are independent of the sales staff.

All cash registers should record the log-in and log-out time of each user. This simple measure makes it easy to detect off-hours sales by comparing log-in times to the organization's hours of operation. In addition, if a theft occurs, the user log is helpful in identifying the potential culprit.

Off-site sales personnel should also be required to maintain activity logs accounting for all sales visits and other business-related activities. These logs should include information such as the customer's name, address, and phone number; the date and time of the meeting; and the result of the meeting (e.g., was a sale made?). Employees independent of the sales function can spot-check the veracity of the entries by making "customer satisfaction calls," in which the customer is asked to verify the information recorded in the activity log.

In addition to monitoring, organizations can take other steps to reduce employees' perceived opportunity to steal. For example, it is advisable, particularly in busy retail establishments, to maintain a secure area where cashiers are required to store coats, hats, purses, and so on. The idea is to eliminate potential hiding places for stolen money.

In the mailroom, employees who open incoming mail should do so in a clear, open area that is free from blind spots. Preferably, to deter thefts, there should be a supervisory presence or video monitoring in place when mail is opened. At least two employees should be involved with opening the organization's mail and logging incoming payments, so that one is not able to steal incoming checks without the other noticing.

Receivables Skimming

Skimming receivables is more difficult than skimming sales. Incoming receivables payments are expected, so the victim organization is likely to notice if these payments are not received and logged into the accounting system. As receivables become past due, the victim organization sends notices of nonpayment to its customers. Customers complain when they receive a second bill for a payment that has already been made. In addition, the customer's cashed check serves as evidence that the payment was made. When fraudsters attempt to skim receivables, they generally use one of the following techniques to conceal the thefts:

- Lapping
- Force balancing
- Stolen statements
- Fraudulent write-offs or discounts
- Debiting the wrong account
- Document destruction

Lapping   Lapping customer payments is one of the most common methods of concealing receivables skimming. Lapping is the crediting of one account through the abstraction of money from another account. It is the fraudster's version of "robbing Peter to pay Paul." Suppose a company has three customers, A, B, and C. When A's payment is received, the fraudster takes it for himself instead of posting it to A's account. Customer A expects that his account will be credited with the payment he has made, but this payment has actually been stolen. When A's next statement arrives, he sees that his check was not applied to his account, and he complains. To avoid this, some action must be taken to make it appear that the payment was posted.

When B's check arrives, the fraudster takes this money and posts it to A's account. Payments now appear to be up-to-date on A's account, but B's account is short. When C's payment is received, the perpetrator applies it to B's account. This process continues indefinitely until one of three things happens: (1) someone discovers the scheme, (2) restitution is made to the accounts, or (3) some concealing entry is made to adjust the accounts receivable balances.

It should be noted that, although more commonly used to conceal skimmed receivables, lapping could also be used to disguise the skimming of sales. In one actual situation, a store manager stole daily receipts and replaced them with the following day's incoming cash. She progressively delayed making the company's bank deposits, as more and more money was taken. Each time a day's receipts were stolen, it took an extra day of collections to cover the missing money. Eventually, the banking irregularities became so great that an investigation was commenced. It was discovered that the manager had stolen nearly $30,000 and concealed the theft by lapping her store's sales.

A Ponzi scheme, such as the one Bernard Madoff perpetrated, contains the essential elements of lapping in that money from new investors was used to pay off what was "owed" to earlier investors.

Because lapping schemes can become very intricate, fraudsters sometimes keep a second set of books on hand, detailing the true nature of the payments received. In many skimming cases, a search of the fraudster's work area reveals a set of records tracking the actual payments made and how they have been misapplied to conceal the theft. It may seem odd for someone to keep on hand records of his or her illegal activity, but many lapping schemes become complicated, as more and more payments are misapplied. The second set of records helps the perpetrator keep track of what funds he or she has stolen and what accounts need to be credited to conceal the fraud. Uncovering these records, if they exist, greatly aids the investigation of a lapping scheme.

Force Balancing

Among the most dangerous receivables skimming schemes are those where the perpetrator is in charge of collecting and posting payments. If a fraudster has a hand in both ends of the receipting process, he or she can falsify records to conceal the theft of receivables payments. For example, the fraudster might post an incoming payment to a customer's receivables account, even though the payment is never deposited. This keeps the receivable from aging, but it creates an imbalance in the cash account. The perpetrator hides the imbalance by forcing the total on the cash account, overstating it to match the total postings to accounts receivable.

Stolen Statements

Another method used by employees to conceal the misapplication of customer payments is the theft or alteration of account statements. If a customer's payments are stolen and not posted, his or her account becomes delinquent. When this happens, the customer should receive late notices or statements showing that the account is past due. The purpose of altering customers' statements is to keep them from complaining about the misapplication of their payments.

To keep customers unaware about the true status of their accounts, some fraudsters intercept their account statements or late notices. This might be accomplished, for instance, by changing the customer's address in the billing system. The statements are sent directly to the employee's home or to an address where he or she can retrieve them. In other cases, the address is changed so that the statement is undeliverable, which causes the statements to be returned to the fraudster's desk. In either situation, once the employee has access to the statements, he or she can do one of two things. The first option is to throw the statements away. This is not particularly effective, especially if customers ever request information on their accounts after not having received a statement.

Therefore, the fraudster may instead choose to alter the statements or to produce counterfeit statements to make it appear that the customers' payments have been properly posted. The fraudster then sends these fake statements to the customers. The false statements lead the customers to believe that their accounts are up-to-date and thus keep them from complaining about stolen payments.

Fraudulent Write-Offs or Discounts

Intercepting the customers' statements keeps them in the dark as to the status of their accounts, but the problem still remains that as long as the customers' payments are being skimmed, their accounts are slipping further and further past due. The fraudster must find some way to bring the accounts back up-to-date in order to conceal his or her crime. As we have discussed, lapping is one way to keep accounts current as the employee skims from them. Another way is to write off the customers' accounts fraudulently. For example, an employee skimmed cash collections and wrote off the related receivables as "bad debts." Similarly, in another case, a billing manager was authorized to write off certain patient balances as hardship allowances. This employee accepted payments from patients and then instructed billing personnel to write off the balance in question. The payments were never posted, because the billing manager intercepted them. She covered approximately $30,000 in stolen funds by using her authority to write off patients' account balances.

Instead of writing off accounts as bad debts, some employees cover their skimming by posting entries to contra revenue accounts, such as "discounts and allowances." If, for instance, an employee intercepts a $1,000 payment, he or she might create a $1,000 "discount" on the account to compensate for the missing money.

Debiting the Wrong Account

Fraudsters also debit existing or fictitious accounts receivable in order to conceal skimmed cash. As an example, an office manager in a health care facility took payments from patients for herself. To conceal her activity, the office manager added the amounts taken to the accounts of other patients that she knew would soon be written off as uncollectable. The employees who use this method generally add the skimmed balances to accounts that are either very large or are aging and about

to be written off. Increases in the balances of these accounts are not as noticeable as in other accounts. In this case, once the old accounts were written off, the stolen funds were written off along with them.

Rather than existing accounts, some fraudsters set up completely fictitious accounts and debit them for the cost of skimmed receivables. The employees then simply wait for the fictitious receivables to age and be written off, knowing that they are uncollectible. In the meantime, they carry the cost of a skimming scheme where it is not detected.

Destroying or Altering Records of the Transaction

Finally, when all else fails, a perpetrator may simply destroy an organization's accounting records in order to cover his or her tracks. For instance, we have already discussed the need for a salesperson to destroy the store's copy of a receipt in order for the sale to go undetected. Similarly, cash register tapes may be destroyed to hide an off-book sale. In one situation, two management-level employees skimmed approximately $250,000 from their company over a four-year period. These employees tampered with cash register tapes that reflected transactions in which sales revenues had been skimmed. The perpetrators either destroyed entire register tapes or cut off large portions where the fraudulent transactions were recorded. In some circumstances, the employees then fabricated new tapes to match the cash on hand and make their registers appear to balance.

Discarding transaction records is often a last-ditch method for a fraudster to escape detection; the fact that records have been destroyed may itself signal that fraud has occurred. Nevertheless, without the records, it can be very difficult to reconstruct the missing transactions and prove that someone actually skimmed money. Furthermore, it may be difficult to prove who was involved in the scheme.

Preventing and Detecting Receivables Skimming

Receivables skimming schemes typically succeed when there is a breakdown in an organization's controls, particularly when one individual has too much control over the process of receiving and recording customer payments, posting cash receipts, or issuing customer credits. If the accounting duties associated with accounts receivable are properly separated, so that there are independent checks of all transactions, skimming of these payments is very difficult to commit and very easy to detect. For example, when force balancing is used to conceal skimming of receivables, it causes a shortage in the organization's cash account, because incoming payments are not deposited. By simply reconciling its bank statement regularly and thoroughly, an organization ought to be able to catch this type of fraud. Similarly, when an individual skims receivables but continues to post the payments to customer accounts, postings to accounts receivable exceeds what is reflected in the daily deposit. If an organization assigns an employee to verify independently that deposits match accounts receivable postings, this type of scheme ought to be quickly detected, or, more likely, it is not attempted at all. It is also a good idea to have that employee spot-check deposits to accounts receivable, to ensure that payments are being applied to the proper accounts. If a check was received by customer A, but the payment was posted to customer B's account, this indicates a lapping scheme.

As discussed earlier, lapping schemes can become very complicated, and they may require the perpetrator to spend long hours at work, trying to shift funds around in order to conceal the crime. Ironically, it is actually very common in these cases for the perpetrator to develop a reputation as a model employee, because of all the overtime that he or she puts in at the office. After the frauds come to light, the employers frequently express shock—not only because they were defrauded, but also because they had considered the perpetrator to be one of their best employees. The point is that a lapping scheme can only succeed through the constant vigilance of the perpetrator. Because of this fact, many organizations mandate that their employees take a vacation every year or regularly rotate job duties among employees. Both of these tactics can be successful in uncovering lapping schemes, because they effectively take control of the books out of the perpetrator's hands for a period of time, and, when this happens, the lapping scheme quickly becomes apparent.

It is also important to mandate supervisory approval for write-offs or discounts to accounts receivable. As we have seen, fraudulent write-offs and discounts are a common means by which the skimming of receivables is concealed; they enable the fraudster to wipe the stolen funds off the books. However, if the person who receives and records customer payments has no authority to make these adjustments, the perceived opportunity to commit the crime is severely diminished.

Although strong internal controls are a valuable preventative tool, the fact remains that fraud can and does continue to occur, regardless of the existence of controls designed to prevent it. Organizations must also be able to detect fraud once it has occurred. Some detection methods are very simple. For example, fraudsters sometimes conceal the theft of receivables by making alterations or corrections to books and records. Physical alterations to financial records, such as erasures or cross-outs, are often a sign of fraud, as are irregular entries to miscellaneous accounts. Audit staff should be trained to investigate these red flags.

It is also important for organizations to search out proactively the accounting clues that point to fraud. This can be tedious, time-consuming work, but computerized audit tools allow organizations to automate many of these tests and greatly aid in the process of searching out fraudulent conduct.

The key to using automated tests successfully is in designing them to highlight the red flags that are typically associated with a particular scheme. For example, we have seen that fraudsters often conceal the skimming of receivables by writing off the amount of funds they have stolen from the targeted account. To detect this kind of activity, organizations can run reports summarizing the number of discounts, adjustments, returns, write-offs, and so on that have been generated by location, department, or employee. Unusually high levels may be associated with skimming schemes and could warrant further investigation. Because some fraudsters conceal their skimming by debiting accounts that are aging or that typically have very little activity, it may also be helpful to run reports looking for unusual activity in otherwise dormant accounts.

Trend analysis on aging of customer accounts can likewise be used to highlight a skimming scheme. A significant rise in the number or size of overdue accounts could be a result of an employee who has stolen customer payments without ever posting them, thereby causing the accounts to run past due. If skimming is suspected, an employee who is independent of the accounts receivable function should confirm overdue balances with customers.

There are several audit tests that can be used to help detect various forms of occupational fraud. In each chapter of this book where fraud schemes are examined, we provide a set of proactive computer audit tests that are tailored to that particular category of fraud. These tests were developed and accumulated by Richard Lanza, working through the Institute of Internal Auditors Research Foundation.

Proactive Computer Audit Tests for Detecting Skimming

Title	Category	Description	Data file(s)
Summarize net sales by employee and extract top ten employees with low sales.	All	Employees with lower sales may be a suspect. This test may also prove more valuable when executed over a trend in time.	• Sale System Register
Summarize by location discounts, returns, inventory adjustments, accounts receivable write-offs, and voids charged.	All	Locations with high adjustments may signal actions to hide skimming schemes.	• Sale System Register • Invoice Sales Register • Inventory Adjustments
Summarize by employee discounts, returns, inventory adjustments, accounts receivable write-offs, and voids charged.	All	Employees with high adjustments may signal actions to hide skimming schemes.	• Sale System Register • Invoice Sales Register • Inventory Adjustments
List top 100 employees by dollar size (one for discounts, one for refunds, one for inventory adjustments, one for accounts receivable write-offs, and one for sale voids).	All	Employees with high adjustments may signal actions to hide skimming schemes.	• Sale System Register • Invoice Sales Register • Inventory Adjustments
List top 100 employees who have been on the top 100 list for three months (one for discounts, one for refunds, one for inventory adjustments, one for accounts receivable write-offs, and one for sale voids).	All	Employees with high adjustments may signal actions to hide skimming schemes.	• Sale System Register • Invoice Sales Register • Inventory Adjustments
List top ten locations that have been on the top ten list for three months (one for discounts, one for refunds, one for inventory adjustments, one for accounts receivable write-offs, and one for sale voids).	All	Locations with high adjustments may signal actions to hide skimming schemes.	• Sale System Register • Invoice Sales Register • Inventory Adjustments

Title	Category	Description	Data file(s)
Compute standard deviation for each employee for the last three months, and list those employees that provided three times the standard deviation in the current month (one for discounts, one for refunds, one for inventory adjustments, one for accounts receivable write-offs, and one for sale voids).	All	Employees with high adjustments may signal actions to hide skimming schemes.	• Sale System Register • Invoice Sales Register • Inventory Adjustments
Compare adjustments to inventory to the void/refund transactions summarized by employee.	All	First, a summary of adjustments by inventory number (SKU number) and employee is completed, which is then compared to credit adjustments (to decrease inappropriately inventory that was supposedly returned) by inventory number.	• Sales System Register • Inventory Detail Register
Summarize user access for the sales, accounts receivable, inventory, and general ledger systems for segregation of duties reviews.	All	User access to systems may identify segregation of duties issues. For example, if an employee can make changes to the accounts receivable system and then post other concealment entries in the general ledger, such nonsegregation of duties would allow an employee to hide his or her actions. User access should be reviewed from the perspective of adjustments within the application and adjustments to the data themselves.	• System User Access Logs or • System User Access Master File
Summarize user access for the sales, accounts receivable, inventory, and general ledger systems in nonbusiness hours.	All	Many times, concealment adjustments are made in nonbusiness hours. User access should be reviewed from the perspective of adjustments within the application and adjustments to the data themselves.	• System User Access Logs
Compute the percentage of assigned to unassigned time for employees.	All	Service employees that have a high majority of unassigned time may be charging the customer and pocketing the proceeds.	• Employee Timecard System
Review telephone logs for calls during nonbusiness hours.	All	Service employees that are completing transactions during nonbusiness hours probably use company lines to effectuate their services.	• Detail Telephone Record
Extract sales with over X percent discount and summarize by employee.	Understated sales	Employees with high discount adjustments may signal actions to hide understated sales schemes.	• Sale System Register
Extract invoices with partial payments.	Understated and refunds & other	Employees who are using lapping to hide their skimming scheme may find it difficult to apply a payment from one customer to another customer's invoices in a fully reconciled fashion.	• Invoice Sales Register

(Continued)

duties. If someone noticed that a shipment was short, the fact that the merchandise was sitting out in the open made it appear that the omission had been an oversight rather than an intentional removal. In most cases, however, no one noticed that shipments were short, and the excess inventory was available for the perpetrator to take. If customers complained about receiving short shipments, the company sent the missing items without performing any follow-up to determine where the missing inventory had gone. The culprit was eventually caught when someone noticed that he was involved in the preparation of an inordinate number of short shipments.

When we speak of inventory theft, we tend to conjure up images of late-night rendezvous at the warehouse or merchandise stuffed hastily under clothing as a nervous employee beats a path to his or her car. Sometimes this is how employees go about stealing inventory and other assets, but, in many instances, fraudsters do not have to go to these extremes. In several of the cases in our study, employees took items openly, during business hours, in plain view of their co-workers. How does this happen? The truth is that people tend to assume that their friends and acquaintances are acting honestly. When they see a trusted co-worker taking something out of the office, people are likely to assume that the culprit has a legitimate reason for removing the asset. In most cases, people just don't assume that fraud is going on around them. Such was the situation in another fraud, where a university faculty member was leaving his offices to take a position at a new school. This person was permitted to take a small number of items to his new job, but he certainly exceeded the intentions of the school when he loaded two trucks full of university lab equipment and computers worth several hundred thousand dollars. The perpetrator simply packed up these stolen assets along with his personal items and drove away.

Even though it is true that employees sometimes misappropriate assets in front of co-workers who do not suspect fraud, it is also true that employees may be fully aware that one of their co-workers is stealing, yet they refrain from reporting the crime. There are several reasons that employees might ignore illegal conduct, such as a sense of duty to their friends, a "management versus labor" mentality, intimidation of honest employees by the thief, or poor channels of communication—or the co-workers may be assisting in the theft. When high-ranking personnel are stealing from their companies, employees often overlook the crime because they fear they will lose their jobs if they report it. For example, a school superintendent was not only pilfering school accounts but also stealing school assets. A search of his residence revealed a cellar filled with school property. A number of school employees knew or suspected the superintendent was involved in illegal dealings, but he was very powerful, and people were afraid to report him for fear of retaliation. As a result, he was able to steal from the school for several years. Similarly, in another fraud, a city manager ordered subordinates to install air conditioners—known to be city property—in the homes of several influential citizens, including his own. Although there was no question that this violated the city's code of ethics, no one reported the manager because of a lack of a proper whistleblowing procedure in the department.

Ironically, employees who steal company property are often highly trusted within their organizations. This trust can provide employees with access to restricted areas, safes, supply rooms, or even keys to the business. Such access, in turn, makes it easy for employees to misappropriate company assets. One embezzlement scheme, in particular, provides an example of how an employee abused his position of trust to misappropriate noncash assets. In this case, a long-term employee of a contractor was given keys to the company parts room. It was his job to deliver parts to job sites. This individual used his access to steal high-value items that he then sold to another contractor. The scheme itself was uncomplicated, but, because the employee had a long history of service to the company and because he was highly trusted, inventory counts were allowed to lapse, and his performance went largely unsupervised. As a result, the scheme continued for over two years and cost the company over $200,000.

Employees with keys to company buildings are able to misappropriate assets during nonbusiness hours, when they can avoid the prying eyes of their fellow employees, as well as management and security personnel. The ACFE study revealed several schemes in which employees entered their places of business to steal assets during weekends, as well as before or after normal working hours. In one scheme, two employees in management positions at a manufacturing plant set finished items aside at the end of the day and then returned the next day an hour before the morning shift and removed the merchandise before other employees arrived. These perpetrators had keys to the plant's security gate, which allowed them to enter the plant before normal hours. Over the course of several years, these two fraudsters removed and sold approximately $300,000 worth of inventory from their company.

It can be unwise for fraudsters to carry inventory and other assets physically off the company's premises. This practice carries with it the inherent risk and potential embarrassment of being caught red-handed with stolen goods on one's person. Some fraudsters avoid this problem by mailing company assets

On the other hand, misuse schemes can be very costly. Take, for example, situations discussed previously in which an employee uses company equipment to operate a side business during work hours. Because the employee is not performing his or her work duties, the employer suffers a loss in productivity. If the low productivity continues, the employer might have to hire additional employees to compensate, which means more capital diverted to wages. If the employee's business is similar to the employer's, lost business could be an additional cost. If the employee had not contracted work for his or her own company, the business would presumably have gone to the employer. Unauthorized use of equipment can also mean additional wear and tear, causing the equipment to break down sooner than under normal business conditions. Additionally, when an employee "borrows" company property, there is no guarantee that he or she will bring it back. This is precisely how some theft schemes begin. Despite some opinions to the contrary, asset misuse is not always a harmless crime.

Unconcealed Larceny Schemes

Although the misuse of company property might be a problem, the theft of company property is obviously of greater concern. As we have seen, losses resulting from larceny of company assets can run into the millions of dollars. The means employed to steal noncash assets range from simple larceny—just walking off with company property—to more complicated schemes involving the falsification of company documents and ledgers.

The textbook definition of larceny is too broad for our purposes, because it would encompass every kind of theft. In order to gain a more specific understanding of the methods used to steal noncash assets, we have narrowed the definition of larceny. For our purposes, larceny is the most basic type of theft, the schemes in which an employee simply takes property from the company premises without attempting to conceal it in the books and records (see Figure 11-6). In other fraud schemes, employees may create false documentation to justify the shipment of merchandise or tamper with inventory records to conceal missing assets. Larceny schemes are more brazen. The culprits in these crimes take company assets without trying to "justify" their absence.

Most noncash larceny schemes are not very complicated. They are typically committed by employees (such as warehouse personnel, inventory clerks, and shipping clerks) with access to inventory and other assets. A typical example of this type of scheme was committed by a warehouse clerk who simply removed inventory from outgoing shipments and left it in plain sight on the warehouse floor as he went about his

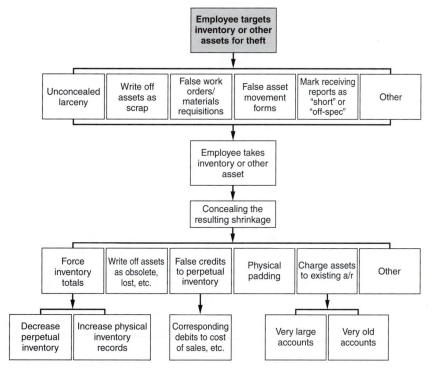

FIGURE 11-6 Noncash Larceny

duties. If someone noticed that a shipment was short, the fact that the merchandise was sitting out in the open made it appear that the omission had been an oversight rather than an intentional removal. In most cases, however, no one noticed that shipments were short, and the excess inventory was available for the perpetrator to take. If customers complained about receiving short shipments, the company sent the missing items without performing any follow-up to determine where the missing inventory had gone. The culprit was eventually caught when someone noticed that he was involved in the preparation of an inordinate number of short shipments.

When we speak of inventory theft, we tend to conjure up images of late-night rendezvous at the warehouse or merchandise stuffed hastily under clothing as a nervous employee beats a path to his or her car. Sometimes this is how employees go about stealing inventory and other assets, but, in many instances, fraudsters do not have to go to these extremes. In several of the cases in our study, employees took items openly, during business hours, in plain view of their co-workers. How does this happen? The truth is that people tend to assume that their friends and acquaintances are acting honestly. When they see a trusted co-worker taking something out of the office, people are likely to assume that the culprit has a legitimate reason for removing the asset. In most cases, people just don't assume that fraud is going on around them. Such was the situation in another fraud, where a university faculty member was leaving his offices to take a position at a new school. This person was permitted to take a small number of items to his new job, but he certainly exceeded the intentions of the school when he loaded two trucks full of university lab equipment and computers worth several hundred thousand dollars. The perpetrator simply packed up these stolen assets along with his personal items and drove away.

Even though it is true that employees sometimes misappropriate assets in front of co-workers who do not suspect fraud, it is also true that employees may be fully aware that one of their co-workers is stealing, yet they refrain from reporting the crime. There are several reasons that employees might ignore illegal conduct, such as a sense of duty to their friends, a "management versus labor" mentality, intimidation of honest employees by the thief, or poor channels of communication—or the co-workers may be assisting in the theft. When high-ranking personnel are stealing from their companies, employees often overlook the crime because they fear they will lose their jobs if they report it. For example, a school superintendent was not only pilfering school accounts but also stealing school assets. A search of his residence revealed a cellar filled with school property. A number of school employees knew or suspected the superintendent was involved in illegal dealings, but he was very powerful, and people were afraid to report him for fear of retaliation. As a result, he was able to steal from the school for several years. Similarly, in another fraud, a city manager ordered subordinates to install air conditioners—known to be city property—in the homes of several influential citizens, including his own. Although there was no question that this violated the city's code of ethics, no one reported the manager because of a lack of a proper whistleblowing procedure in the department.

Ironically, employees who steal company property are often highly trusted within their organizations. This trust can provide employees with access to restricted areas, safes, supply rooms, or even keys to the business. Such access, in turn, makes it easy for employees to misappropriate company assets. One embezzlement scheme, in particular, provides an example of how an employee abused his position of trust to misappropriate noncash assets. In this case, a long-term employee of a contractor was given keys to the company parts room. It was his job to deliver parts to job sites. This individual used his access to steal high-value items that he then sold to another contractor. The scheme itself was uncomplicated, but, because the employee had a long history of service to the company and because he was highly trusted, inventory counts were allowed to lapse, and his performance went largely unsupervised. As a result, the scheme continued for over two years and cost the company over $200,000.

Employees with keys to company buildings are able to misappropriate assets during nonbusiness hours, when they can avoid the prying eyes of their fellow employees, as well as management and security personnel. The ACFE study revealed several schemes in which employees entered their places of business to steal assets during weekends, as well as before or after normal working hours. In one scheme, two employees in management positions at a manufacturing plant set finished items aside at the end of the day and then returned the next day an hour before the morning shift and removed the merchandise before other employees arrived. These perpetrators had keys to the plant's security gate, which allowed them to enter the plant before normal hours. Over the course of several years, these two fraudsters removed and sold approximately $300,000 worth of inventory from their company.

It can be unwise for fraudsters to carry inventory and other assets physically off the company's premises. This practice carries with it the inherent risk and potential embarrassment of being caught red-handed with stolen goods on one's person. Some fraudsters avoid this problem by mailing company assets

NONCASH MISAPPROPRIATION SCHEMES

To this point in the chapter, our discussion of asset misappropriations has focused on cash receipts schemes. Although the vast majority of asset misappropriation schemes involve cash, other assets can be stolen as well. Schemes involving the misappropriation of inventory and other assets are not as common as cash schemes, but they are nevertheless potentially disastrous. The remainder of this chapter will discuss the ways in which employees misappropriate inventory, supplies, equipment, and other noncash assets.

Noncash assets, such as inventory and equipment, are misappropriated by employees in a number of ways. These schemes can range from taking a box of pens home from work to the theft of millions of dollars worth of company property. In general, noncash misappropriations fall into one of the following categories:

- Misuse
- Unconcealed larceny
- Asset requisitions and transfers
- Purchasing and receiving schemes
- Fraudulent shipments

Misuse of Noncash Assets

There are basically two ways a person can misappropriate a company asset: the asset can be misused (or "borrowed"), or it can be stolen. Simple misuse is obviously the less egregious of the two. Assets that are misused but not stolen typically include company vehicles, company supplies, computers, and other office equipment. For example, an employee made personal use of a company vehicle while on an out-of-town assignment. The employee provided false information, both written and verbal, regarding the nature of his use of the vehicle. The vehicle was returned unharmed, and the cost to the perpetrator's company was only a few hundred dollars. Nevertheless, such unauthorized use of a company asset amounts to fraud when a false statement accompanies the use.

Computers, supplies, and other office equipment are also used by some employees to do personal work on company time. For instance, employees might use their computers at work to write letters, print invoices, or do other work connected with a business that they run on the side. In many instances, these side businesses are of the same nature as the employer's business, so the employees are essentially competing with their employer and using the employer's equipment to do it. An example of how employees misuse company assets to compete with their employers involved a group of employees who not only stole company supplies but also used the stolen supplies and their employer's equipment to manufacture their own product. The fraudsters then removed the completed product from their work location and sold it in competition with their employer. In a similar scheme, the perpetrator used his employer's machinery to run his own snow removal and excavation business for approximately nine months. He generally did his own work on weekends and after hours, falsifying the logs that recorded mileage and usage on the equipment. The employee had formerly owned all the equipment himself, but then he had sold it in order to avoid bankruptcy. As a term of the sale, he had agreed to go to work for the new owner who was operating the equipment, but, in truth, he never stopped running his old business.

The preceding cases offer a good illustration of how a single scheme can encompass more than one type of fraud. Even though the perpetrators in these schemes were misusing company materials and equipment—a case of asset misappropriation—they were also competing with their employers for business—a conflict of interest. The categories ACFE researchers have developed for classifying fraud are helpful in that they allow us to track certain types of schemes, noting common elements, victims, methods, and so on; but those involved in fraud prevention should remember that every crime does not fall neatly into one category. Frauds often expand as opportunity and need allow, and a scheme that begins as something small may grow into a massive crime that can cripple a business.

The Costs of Inventory Misuse The costs of noncash asset misuse are difficult to quantify. To many individuals, this type of fraud is viewed not as a crime, but rather as "borrowing." In truth, the cost to a company from this kind of scheme may often be immaterial. When perpetrators borrow a stapler for the night or take home some tools to perform a household repair, the cost to their company is negligible, as long as the assets are returned unharmed.

Title	Category	Description	Data file(s)
List top 100 employees by dollar size (one for discounts, one for refunds, one for cash receipt adjustments, one for accounts receivable write-offs, and one for sale voids).	All	Employees with high adjustments may signal actions to hide cash larceny schemes.	• Sales System Register • Invoice Sales Register • Cash Receipts Register
List top 100 employees who have been on the top 100 list for three months (one for discounts, one for refunds, one for cash receipt adjustments, one for accounts receivable write-offs, and one for sale voids).	All	Employees with high adjustments may signal actions to hide cash larceny schemes.	• Sales System Register • Invoice Sales Register • Cash Receipts Register
List top ten locations that have been on the top ten list for three months (one for discounts, one for refunds, one for cash receipt adjustments, one for accounts receivable write-offs, and one for sale voids).	All	Locations with high adjustments may signal actions to hide cash larceny schemes.	• Sales System Register • Invoice Sales Register • Cash Receipts Register
Compute standard deviation for each employee for the last three months and list those employees who provided three times the standard deviation in the current month (one for discounts, one for refunds, one for cash receipt adjustments, one for accounts receivable write-offs, and one for sale voids).	All	Employees with high adjustments may signal actions to hide cash larceny schemes.	• Sales System Register • Invoice Sales Register • Cash Receipts Register
Compare adjustments to inventory to the void/refund transactions summarized by employee.	All	First, a summary of adjustments by inventory item number and employee is completed, which is then compared to credit adjustments (to decrease inappropriately any inventory that was supposedly returned) by inventory number.	• Sales System Register • Inventory Detail Register
Review unique journal entries in cash accounts.	All	All journal entries in cash accounts, especially those that appear to be unique adjustments, should be reviewed as concealment actions to a cash larceny scheme.	• General Ledger Detail
Summarize user access for the sales, accounts receivable, cash receipt, and general ledger systems for segregation of duties reviews.	All	User access to systems may identify segregation of duties issues. For example, if an employee can make changes to the accounts receivable system and then post other concealment entries in the general ledger, such nonsegregation of duties allows an employee to hide his or her actions. User access should be reviewed from the perspective of adjustments within the application and adjustments to the data themselves.	• System User Access Logs or System User Access Master File
Summarize user access for the sales, accounts receivable, cash receipt, and general ledger systems in nonbusiness hours.	All	Concealment adjustments often are made in nonbusiness hours. User access should be reviewed from the perspective of adjustments within the application and adjustments to the data themselves.	• System User Access Logs

performed independently of one another. As long as this separation is maintained, shortages in the deposit should be quickly detected.

All incoming revenues should be delivered to a centralized department, where an itemized deposit slip is prepared, listing each individual check or money order, along with currency receipts. Itemizing the deposit slip is a key anti-fraud control. It enables the organization to track specific payments to the deposit and may help detect larceny, as well as lapping schemes and other forms of receivables skimming. It is very important that the person who prepares the deposit slip be separated from the duty of receiving and logging incoming payments, so that he or she can act as an independent check on these functions. Before it is sent to the bank, the deposit slip should be matched to the remittance list to ensure that all payments are accounted for.

Typically, the cashier delivers the deposit to the bank, and a cash-receipts clerk posts the total amount of receipts in the cash receipts journal. In some cases, the cashier does the posting, and a separate individual delivers the deposit. In either case, the duties of posting cash receipts and delivering the deposit should be separated. If a single person performs both functions, that individual can falsify the deposit slip and/or cash receipts postings to conceal larceny from the deposit.

Once the deposit has been totaled and matched to the remittance list, it should be secured and taken immediately to the bank, along with two copies of the deposit slip (one of which is retained by the bank). A third copy of the deposit slip should be retained by the organization. When the deposit is made, one copy of the deposit slip is stamped (authenticated) by the bank as received. The bank then delivers this copy back to the depositing organization.

The authenticated deposit slip should be compared with the organization's copy of the deposit slip, the remittance list, and the general ledger posting of the day's receipts. If all four totals match, this verifies that the deposit was properly made. It is critical that someone other than the person who prepared the deposit reconcile the authenticated deposit slip. If the cashier, for example, is allowed to prepare and reconcile the deposit, the control function designed to prevent cash larceny at this stage is effectively destroyed. The cashier could falsify the deposit slip or force totals to conceal larceny. If fraud is suspected, verify each deposit prior to dispatch without the suspect's knowledge; then call the bank to verify that the entire deposit was made.

In order to further safeguard against larceny, two copies of the bank statement should be delivered to different persons in the organization. Each person should verify deposits on the bank statement to postings in the general ledger and to receipted deposit slips. If deposits in transit show up on a bank reconciliation, they should clear within two days of the date of reconciliation. Any instance in which a deposit in transit exceeds the two-day clearance should be investigated.

To prevent deposit lapping, organizations can require that deposits be made in a night drop at the bank and that each deposit be verified at the beginning of the next day's business.

Proactive Computer Audit Tests for Detecting Cash Larceny

Title	Category	Description	Data file(s)
Summarize by employee the difference between the cash receipt report and the sales register system.	All	Focus should be given to employees with high-dollar differences, especially high occurrences of small-dollar differences.	• Sales System Register • Cash Receipts Register
Summarize by employee by day the difference between the cash receipt report and the sales register system.	All	Focus should be given to employees with high-dollar differences, especially high occurrences of small-dollar differences.	• Sales System Register • Cash Receipts Register
Summarize by location discounts, returns, cash receipt adjustments, accounts receivable write-offs, and voids charged.	All	Locations with high adjustments may signal actions to hide cash larceny schemes.	• Sales System Register • Invoice Sales Register • Cash Receipts Register
Summarize by employee discounts, returns, cash receipt adjustments, accounts receivable write-offs, and voids charged.	All	Employees with high adjustments may signal actions to hide cash larceny schemes.	• Sales System Register • Invoice Sales Register • Cash Receipts Register

Similarly, in a retail store where cash registers were not used, sales were recorded on pre-numbered invoices. The controller of this organization was responsible for collecting cash receipts and making the bank deposits. This controller was also the only person who reconciled the totals on the pre-numbered receipts to the bank deposit. Therefore, he was able to steal a portion of the deposit with the knowledge that the discrepancy between the deposit and the day's receipts would not be detected.

Another oversight in procedure is failure to reconcile the bank copy of the deposit slip with the office copy. When persons making the deposit know that their company does not reconcile the two deposit slips, they can steal cash from the deposit on the way to the bank and alter the deposit slip so that it reflects a lesser amount. In some cases, sales records are also altered to match the diminished deposit.

When cash is stolen from the deposit, the receipted deposit slip is, of course, out of balance with the company's copy of the deposit slip (unless the perpetrator also prepared the deposit). To correct this problem, some fraudsters alter the bank copy of the deposit slip after it has been validated. This brings the two copies back into balance. For example, an employee altered twenty-four deposit slips and validated bank receipts in the course of a year to conceal the theft of over $15,000. These documents were altered, with correction fluid or ballpoint pen, to match the company's cash reports. Of course, cash having been stolen, the company's book balance does not match its actual bank balance. If another employee regularly balances the checking account, this type of theft should be easily detected.

Another mistake that can be made in the deposit function, one that is a departure from common sense, is entrusting the deposit to the wrong person. For instance, a bookkeeper who had been employed for only one month was put in charge of making the deposit. She promptly diverted the funds to her own use. This is not to say that all new employees are untrustworthy, but it is advisable to have some sense of a person's character before handing that person a bag full of money.

Still another common sense issue is the handling of the deposit on the way to the bank. Once prepared, the deposit should be immediately put in a safe place until it is taken to the bank. In a few of the cases we studied, the deposit was carelessly left unattended. In another fraud, for example, a part-time employee learned that it was the bookkeeper's habit to leave the bank bag in her desk overnight before taking it to the bank the following morning. For approximately six months, this employee pilfered checks from the deposit and got away with it. He was able to endorse the checks at a local establishment, without using his own signature, in the name of the victim company. The owner of the check-cashing institution did not question the fact that this individual was cashing company checks; as a pastor of a sizable church in the community, the fraudster's integrity was thought to be above reproach.

As with other cash larceny schemes, stealing from the company deposit can be rather difficult to conceal. In most cases, these schemes are successful for a long term only when the person who counts the cash also makes the deposit. In any other circumstance, the success of the scheme depends primarily on the inattentiveness of those charged with preparing and reconciling the deposit.

Deposit Lapping   One method the ACFE study has identified that, in some cases, is successfully used to evade detection is the lapping method. Lapping occurs when an employee steals the deposit from day one and then replaces it with day two's deposit. Day two is replaced with day three, and so on. The perpetrator is always one day behind, but, as long as no one demands an up-to-the-minute reconciliation of the deposits to the bank statement and if the size of the deposits does not drop precipitously, he or she may be able to avoid detection for a period of time. For example, a company officer stole cash receipts from the company deposit and withheld the deposit for a time. Eventually, the deposit was made, and the missing cash was replaced with a check received at a later date.

Deposits in Transit   A final concealment strategy with stolen deposits is to carry the missing money as deposits in transit. In one instance, an employee was responsible for receiving collections, issuing receipts, posting transactions, reconciling accounts, and making deposits. Such a lack of separation of duties leaves a company extremely vulnerable to fraud. This employee took over $20,000 in collections from her employer over a five-month period. To hide her theft, the perpetrator carried the missing money as deposits in transit, meaning that the missing money would appear on the next month's bank statement. Of course, it never did. The balance was carried for several months as a "deposit in transit," until an auditor recognized the discrepancy and put a halt to the fraud.

Preventing and Detecting Cash Larceny from the Deposit   The most important factor in preventing cash larceny from the deposit is separating duties. Calculating daily receipts, preparing the deposit, delivering the deposit to the bank, and verifying the receipted deposit slip are duties that should be

office manager stole approximately $75,000 in customer payments from her employer. Her method, in a number of these instances, was to post the payment to the customer's account and then later reverse the entry on the books with unauthorized adjustments such as "courtesy discounts."

Destruction of Records A less elegant way to hide a crime is simply to destroy all records that might prove that the perpetrator has been stealing. Destroying records en masse does not prevent the victim company from realizing that it is being robbed, but it may help conceal the identity of the thief. A controller in one fraud used this "slash-and-burn" concealment strategy. The controller, who had complete control over the books of her employer, stole approximately $100,000. When it became evident that her superiors were suspicious of her activities, the perpetrator entered her office one night after work, stole all the cash on hand, destroyed all records, including her personnel file, and left town.

Cash Larceny from the Deposit

At some point in every revenue-generating business, someone must physically take the company's currency and checks to the bank. This person or persons, literally holding the bag, has an opportunity to take a portion of the money prior to depositing it into the company's accounts.

Typically, when a company receives cash, someone is assigned to tabulate the receipts, list the form of payment (currency or check), and prepare a deposit slip for the bank. Then another employee, preferably one who was not involved in the preparing of the deposit slip, takes the cash and deposits it in the bank. The person who made out the deposit generally retains one copy of the slip. This copy is matched to a receipted copy of the slip stamped by the bank when the deposit is made.

This procedure is designed to prevent theft of funds from the deposit, but thefts still occur, often because the process is not adhered to (see Figure 11-5). For instance, an employee in a small company was responsible for preparing and making the deposits, recording the deposits in the company's books, and reconciling the bank statements. This employee took several thousand dollars from the company deposits and concealed it by making false entries in the books that corresponded to falsely prepared deposit slips.

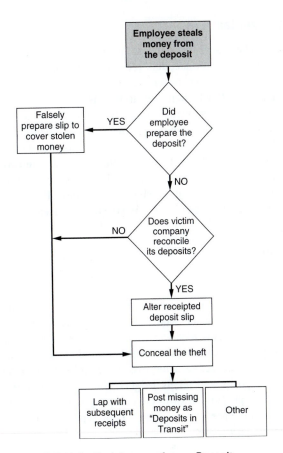

FIGURE 11-5 Cash Larceny from a Deposit

Preventing and Detecting Cash Larceny at the Point of Sale   Most cash larceny schemes only succeed because of a lack of internal controls. In order to prevent this form of fraud, organizations should enforce separation of duties in the cash receipts process and make sure there are independent checks over the receipting and recording of incoming cash.

When cash is received over the counter, the employee conducting the transaction should record each transaction. The transaction is generally recorded on a cash register or on a pre-numbered receipt form. At the end of the business day, each salesperson should count the cash in his or her cash drawer and record the amount on a memorandum form.

Another employee then removes the register tape or other records of the transactions. This employee also counts the cash to make sure the total agrees with the salesperson's count and with the register tape. By having an independent employee verify the cash count in each register or cash box at the end of each shift, an organization reduces the possibility of long-term losses resulting from cash theft. Cash larceny through the falsification of cash counts can be prevented by this control, and suspicions of fraud are immediately raised if sales records have been purposely destroyed.

Once the second employee has determined that the totals for the register tape and cash on hand reconcile, the cash should be taken directly to the cashier's office. The register tape, memorandum form, and any other pertinent records of the day's transactions are sent to the accounting department, where the totals are entered in the cash receipts journal.

Obviously, to detect cash larceny at the point of sale, the first key is to look for discrepancies between sales records and cash on hand. Large differences normally draw attention, but those who reconcile the two figures should also be alert to a high frequency of small-dollar occurrences. Fraudsters sometimes steal small amounts, hoping that they will not be noticed or will be too small to review. A pattern of small shortages may indicate the presence of this type of scheme.

Organizations should also periodically run reports showing the number of discounts, returns, adjustments, write-offs, and other concealing transactions issued by employee, department, and/or location. These transactions may be used to conceal cash larceny. Similarly, all journal entries to cash accounts could be scrutinized, because these are often used to hide missing cash.

Larceny of Receivables

Not all cash larceny schemes occur at the point of sale. As discussed earlier, employees frequently steal incoming customer payments on accounts receivable. Generally, these schemes involve skimming—the perpetrator steals the payment but never records it. In some cases, however, the theft occurs after the payment has been recorded, which means it is classified as cash larceny. For example, an employee posted all records of customer payments to date but stole the money received. In a four-month period, this employee took over $200,000 in incoming payments. Consequently, the cash account was significantly out of balance, which led to discovery of the fraud. This was one of the cases in the ACFE study, incidentally, in which the employee justified the theft by saying that she planned to pay the money back. This case illustrates the central weakness of cash larceny schemes—the resulting imbalances in company accounts. In order for an employee to succeed at a cash larceny scheme, he or she must be able to hide the imbalances caused by the fraud. Larceny of receivables is generally concealed through one of three methods:

1. Force balancing
2. Reversing entries
3. Destruction of records

Force Balancing   Those fraudsters who have total control of a company's accounting system can overcome the problem of out-of-balance accounts. In another example, an employee stole customer payments and posted them to the accounts receivable journal in the same manner as the fraudster discussed in the prior case. As in the previous case, this employee's fraud resulted in an imbalance in the victim company's cash account. The difference between the two frauds is that the perpetrator in the first case had control over the company's deposits and all its ledgers. She was therefore able to conceal her crime by force balancing: making unsupported entries in the company's books that produced a fictitious balance between receipts and ledgers. This case illustrates how poor separation of duties can allow the perpetuation of a fraud that is ordinarily easy to detect.

Reversing Entries   In circumstances in which payments are stolen but nonetheless posted to the cash receipts journal, reversing entries can be used to balance the victim company's accounts. For instance, an

- Reversing transactions
- Altering cash counts or register tapes
- Destroying register tapes

Thefts from Other Registers   One basic way for an employee to disguise the fact that he or she is stealing currency is to take money from someone else's cash register. In some retail organizations, employees are assigned to certain registers. Alternatively, one register is used and each employee has an access code. When cash is missing from a cashier's register, the most likely suspect for the theft is obviously that cashier. Therefore, by stealing from another employee's register, or by using someone else's access code, the fraudster makes sure that another employee will be the prime suspect in the theft. In the prior case, the employee who stole money did so by waiting until another teller was on break and then logging onto that teller's register, ringing a "no sale," and taking the cash. The resulting cash shortage therefore appeared in the register of an honest employee, deflecting attention from the true thief. In another case that the ACFE reviewed, a cash office manager stole over $8,000, in part by taking money from cash registers and making it appear that the cashiers were stealing.

Death by a Thousand Cuts   A very unsophisticated way to avoid detection is to steal currency in very small amounts over an extended period of time. This is the "death by a thousand cuts" larceny scheme: $15 here, $20 there, and, slowly, the culprit bleeds his or her company. Because the missing amounts are small, the shortages may be credited to errors rather than theft. Typically, the fraudulent employees become dependent on the extra money that they are pilfering, and their thefts increase in scale or become more frequent, which causes the scheme to be uncovered. Most retail organizations track overages or shortages by employee, making this method largely ineffectual.

Reversing Transactions   Another way to conceal cash larceny is to use reversing transactions, such as false voids or refunds, which cause the register tape to reconcile to the amount of cash on hand after the theft. By processing fraudulent reversing transactions, an employee can reduce the amount of cash reflected on the register tape. For instance, a cashier received payments from a customer and recorded the transactions on her system. She later stole those payments and then destroyed the company's receipts that reflected the transactions. To complete the cover-up, the cashier went back and voided the transactions, which she had entered when the payments were received. The reversing entries brought the receipt totals into balance with the cash on hand. (These schemes are discussed in more detail in Chapter 12.)

Altering Cash Counts or Cash Register Tapes   A cash register is balanced by comparing the transactions on the register tape to the amount of cash on hand. Starting at a known balance, sales, returns, and other register transactions are added to or subtracted from the balance to arrive at a total for the period in question. The actual cash is then counted, and the two totals are compared. If the register tape shows that there should be more cash in the register than is present, it may be because of larceny. To conceal cash larceny, some fraudsters alter the cash counts from their registers to match the total receipts reflected on their register tape. For example, if an employee processes $1,000 worth of transactions on a register and then steals $300, there is only $700 left in the cash drawer. The employee can falsify the cash count, by recording that $1,000 is on hand, so that the cash count balances to the register tape. This type of scheme occurred in one case when a fraudster not only discarded register tapes to conceal her thefts, but also erased and rewrote cash counts for the registers from which she pilfered. The new totals on the cash count envelopes were overstated by the amount of money she had stolen, reflecting the actual receipts for the period and balancing with the cash register tapes. Under the victim company's controls, this employee was not supposed to have access to cash. Ironically, co-workers praised her dedication for helping them count cash when it was not one of her official duties.

Instead of altering cash counts, some employees manually alter the register tape from their cash registers. Again, the purpose of this activity is to force a balance between the cash on hand and the record of cash received. In one fraud, for instance, a department manager altered and destroyed cash register tapes to help conceal a fraud scheme that had gone on for four years.

Destroying Register Tapes   If the fraudster cannot make the cash and the tape balance, the next best thing is to prevent others from computing the totals and discovering the imbalance. Employees who are stealing at the point of sale sometimes destroy detail tapes that might implicate them in a crime.

Larceny at the Point of Sale

A large percentage of the cash larceny schemes in our research occurred at the point of sale, and for good reason—that's where the money is. The cash register (or similar cash collection points, such as cash drawers or cash boxes) is usually the most common point of access to ready cash for employees, so it is understandable that larceny schemes frequently occur there. Furthermore, there is often a great deal of activity at the point of sale—particularly in retail organizations—with multiple transactions requiring the handling of cash by employees. This activity can serve as a cover for the theft of cash. In a flurry of activity, with cash being passed back and forth between customer and employee, a fraudster is more likely to be able to slip currency out of the cash drawer and into his or her pocket without getting caught.

This is the most straightforward scheme: the fraudster opens up the register and removes currency (see Figure 11-4). It might be done as a sale is being conducted to make the theft appear to be part of the transaction, or perhaps when no one is around to notice the perpetrator digging into the cash drawer. For instance, a teller simply signed onto a cash register, rang a "no sale," and took currency from the drawer. Over a period of time, the teller took approximately $6,000 through this simple method.

Recall that the benefit of a skimming scheme is that the transaction is unrecorded, and the stolen funds are never entered on company books. Employees who are skimming either under–ring the register transaction so that a portion of the sale is unrecorded, or they completely omit the sale by failing to enter it at all on their register. This makes the skimming scheme difficult to detect, because the register tape does not reflect the presence of the funds that have been taken. In a larceny scheme, on the other hand, the funds that the perpetrator steals are already reflected on the register tape. As a result, an imbalance results between the register tape and the cash drawer. This imbalance should be a signal that alerts a victim organization to the theft.

The actual method for taking money at the point of sale—opening a cash drawer and removing currency—rarely varies. But the methods used by fraudsters to avoid getting caught are what distinguish larceny schemes. Oddly, in many cases, the perpetrator has no plan for avoiding detection. A large part of fraud is rationalizing; fraudsters convince themselves that they are somehow entitled to what they are taking or that what they are doing is not actually a crime. Cash larceny schemes frequently begin when perpetrators convince themselves that they are only "borrowing" the funds to cover a temporary monetary need. These people might carry the missing cash in their registers for several days, deluding themselves in the belief that they will one day repay the funds and hoping that their employers will not perform a surprise cash count until the missing money is replaced.

Employees who do nothing to camouflage their crimes are easily caught; more dangerous are those who take active steps to hide their misdeeds. In the cash larceny schemes reviewed, there were several methods used to conceal larceny that occurred at the point of sale:

- Thefts from other registers
- Death by a thousand cuts

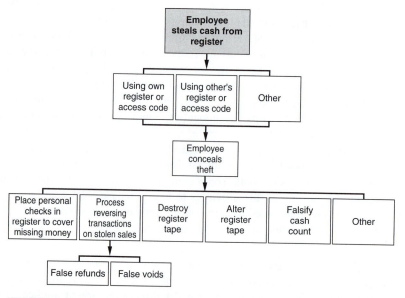

FIGURE 11-4 Cash Larceny from the Register

Title	Category	Description	Data file(s)
Compute standard deviation for each employee for the last three months, and list those employees that provided three times the standard deviation in the current month (one for discounts, one for refunds, one for inventory adjustments, one for accounts receivable write-offs, and one for sale voids).	All	Employees with high adjustments may signal actions to hide skimming schemes.	• Sale System Register • Invoice Sales Register • Inventory Adjustments
Compare adjustments to inventory to the void/refund transactions summarized by employee.	All	First, a summary of adjustments by inventory number (SKU number) and employee is completed, which is then compared to credit adjustments (to decrease inappropriately inventory that was supposedly returned) by inventory number.	• Sales System Register • Inventory Detail Register
Summarize user access for the sales, accounts receivable, inventory, and general ledger systems for segregation of duties reviews.	All	User access to systems may identify segregation of duties issues. For example, if an employee can make changes to the accounts receivable system and then post other concealment entries in the general ledger, such nonsegregation of duties would allow an employee to hide his or her actions. User access should be reviewed from the perspective of adjustments within the application and adjustments to the data themselves.	• System User Access Logs or • System User Access Master File
Summarize user access for the sales, accounts receivable, inventory, and general ledger systems in nonbusiness hours.	All	Many times, concealment adjustments are made in nonbusiness hours. User access should be reviewed from the perspective of adjustments within the application and adjustments to the data themselves.	• System User Access Logs
Compute the percentage of assigned to unassigned time for employees.	All	Service employees that have a high majority of unassigned time may be charging the customer and pocketing the proceeds.	• Employee Timecard System
Review telephone logs for calls during nonbusiness hours.	All	Service employees that are completing transactions during nonbusiness hours probably use company lines to effectuate their services.	• Detail Telephone Record
Extract sales with over X percent discount and summarize by employee.	Understated sales	Employees with high discount adjustments may signal actions to hide understated sales schemes.	• Sale System Register
Extract invoices with partial payments.	Understated and refunds & other	Employees who are using lapping to hide their skimming scheme may find it difficult to apply a payment from one customer to another customer's invoices in a fully reconciled fashion.	• Invoice Sales Register

(*Continued*)

(*Continued*)

Title	Category	Description	Data file(s)
Join the customer statement report file to accounts receivable and review for balance differences.	Understated and refunds & other	Through the matching of the customer statement report file (file that is used to print customer statements) and the open invoices to that customer, any improper changes to customer statements to mask skimming schemes are detected.	• Customer Statement Report File • Invoice Sales Register
Extract customer open invoice balances that are in a credit position.	Understated and refunds & other	Customers with a credit position account may be due to improper credit entries posted to the customer account to hide cash skimming.	• Invoice Sales Register
Extract customers with no telephone or tax ID number.	Understated and refunds & other	Customers without this information may have been created for use in posting improper entries to hide a skimming scheme.	• Customer Master File
Identify customers added during the period under review.	Understated and refunds & other	The issuers of new customer additions should be reviewed, using this report to determine whether an employee is using phony customer accounts as part of a lapping scheme by crediting their account for cash misappropriation.	• Customer Master File
Match the customer master file to the employee master file on various key fields.	Understated and refunds & other	Compare telephone number, address, tax ID numbers, numbers in the address, PO box, and zip code in customer file to employee file, especially those employees working in the accounts receivable department. Questionable customer accounts should be reviewed, using this report to determine whether an employee is using phony customer accounts as part of a lapping scheme by crediting their account for cash misappropriation.	• Customer Master File • Employee Master File

CASH LARCENY SCHEMES

In the occupational fraud setting, a cash larceny may be defined as the intentional taking away of an employer's cash (the term *cash* includes both currency and checks) without the consent and against the will of the employer.

Cash receipts schemes are what we typically think of as the outright stealing of cash. The perpetrator does not rely on the submission of phony documents or the forging of signatures; he or she simply grabs the cash and takes it. The cash receipts schemes fall into two categories: skimming, which we have already discussed, and cash larcenies. Remember that skimming was defined as the theft of off-book funds. Cash larceny schemes, on the other hand, involve the theft of money that has already appeared on a victim company's books.

A cash larceny scheme can take place in any circumstance in which an employee has access to cash. Every company must deal with the receipt, deposit, and distribution of cash (if not, it certainly will not be a very long-lived company!), so every company is potentially vulnerable to this form of fraud. Although the circumstances in which an employee might steal cash are nearly limitless, most larceny schemes involve the theft of cash:

- At the point of sale
- From incoming receivables
- From the victim organization's bank deposits

to a location where they can pick them up without having to worry about security, management, or other potential observers. For instance, a spare-parts custodian took several thousand dollars' worth of computer chips and mailed them to a company that had no business dealings with the custodian's employer. He then reclaimed the merchandise as his own. By taking the step of mailing the stolen inventory, the fraudster allowed the postal service to do his dirty work for him unwittingly.

The Fake Sale Asset misappropriations are not always undertaken solely by employees of the victim organization. In many cases, corrupt employees utilize outside accomplices to help steal an organization's property. The fake sale is one method that depends on an accomplice for its success. Like most larceny schemes, the fake sale is not complicated. As reflected in one fraud, a fake sale occurs when the accomplice of the employee-fraudster "buys" merchandise, but the employee does not ring up the sale, and the accomplice takes the merchandise without making any payment. To a casual observer, it appears that the transaction is a normal sale. The employee bags the merchandise and may act as though a transaction is being entered on the register, but, in fact, the "sale" is not recorded. The accomplice may even pass a nominal amount of money to the employee to complete the illusion. The perpetrator went along with these fake sales in exchange for gifts from her accomplice, although in other cases the two might split the stolen merchandise.

Accomplices are also sometimes used to return the inventory that employees have stolen. This is an easy way for employees to convert the inventory into cash when they do not have a need for the merchandise itself and have no means of reselling it on their own.

Preventing and Detecting Larceny of Noncash Assets In order to prevent larceny of noncash assets, the duties of requisitioning, purchasing, and receiving these assets should be segregated. The payables function should be segregated from all purchasing and receiving duties, to provide additional checks and balances. In addition, physical controls are a key to preventing theft of noncash assets. All merchandise should be physically guarded and locked, with access restricted to authorized personnel only. Access logs can be used to track those who enter restricted areas, or each authorized individual could be given a personalized entry code. In either case, a log is created that shows who had access to restricted assets and at what times. Not only does this help identify the perpetrator if a theft occurs, but, more important, it helps deter employees from attempting to steal company merchandise.

Another deterrence method that can be effective is the installation of security cameras in warehouses or on sales floors. If security cameras are to be used, their presence should be made known to employees, in an effort to deter misconduct. Security guards can also be utilized to serve the same function.

In order to help detect inventory thefts in a timely manner, organizations should periodically conduct physical inventory counts. Someone independent of the purchasing and warehousing functions should conduct these counts. Physical counts should be comprehensive. Check boxes to make sure they actually contain inventory, and do not rely on assurances by warehouse personnel regarding the existence of inventory. Physical inventory counts should be subject to recounts or spot-checks by independent personnel. Also, shipping and receiving activities should be suspended during physical counts, to ensure a proper cut-off. Significant discrepancies between physical counts and perpetual inventory (shrinkage) should be investigated before adjustments are made to inventory records.

One common way to commit inventory theft is to remove items from outgoing shipments of merchandise. It is therefore important for organizations to have in place a mechanism for receiving customer complaints regarding, among other things, "short" shipments. An employee who is independent of the purchasing and warehousing functions should be assigned to follow up on complaints. If a large number of complaints are received, the dates of shipment can be compared to employee work schedules to help identify suspects.

Asset Requisitions and Transfers

Asset requisitions or other documentation that enables noncash assets to be moved from one location in a company to another can be used to facilitate the misappropriation of those assets. Fraudsters use these internal documents to gain access to merchandise that they otherwise might not be able to handle without raising suspicion. Transfer documents do not account for missing merchandise the way false sales do, but they allow fraudsters to move assets from one location to another. In the process of this movement, fraudsters take the merchandise for themselves (see Figure 11-6).

The most basic scheme occurs when an employee requisitions materials to complete a work-related project and then steals the materials. In some cases, fraudsters simply overstate the amount of supplies or equipment needed to complete their work and pilfer the excess. In more extreme cases, fraudsters might completely fabricate a project that necessitates the use of certain assets that they intend to steal. For instance, an employee of a telecommunications company used false project documents to request approximately $100,000 worth of computer chips, allegedly to upgrade company computers. Knowing that this type of requisition required verbal authorization from another source, the employee set up an elaborate phone scheme to get the "project" approved. The fraudster used his knowledge of the company's phone system to forward calls from four different lines to his own desk. When the confirmation call was made, it was the perpetrator who answered the phone and authorized the project.

Dishonest employees sometimes falsify property transfer forms so that they can remove inventory or other assets from a warehouse or stockroom. Once the merchandise is in their possession, the fraudsters simply take it home with them. For example, a manager requested merchandise from the company warehouse to be displayed on a showroom floor. The pieces he requested never made it to the showroom, because he had loaded them into a pickup truck and taken them home. In some instances, he actually took the items in broad daylight, with the help of another employee. The obvious problem with this type of scheme is that the person who orders the merchandise is usually the primary suspect when it turns up missing. In many cases, fraudsters simply rely on poor communication between different departments in their company and hope that no one pieces the crime together. The individual in this case, however, thought that he was immune from detection because the merchandise was requested via computer, using a management-level security code. The code was not specific to any one manager, so there would be no way of knowing which manager had ordered the merchandise. Unfortunately for the thief, the company was able to record the computer terminal from which the request originated. The manager had used his own computer to make the request, which led to his undoing.

Where inventory is stored in multiple locations, the transfer of assets from one building to another can create opportunities for employees to pilfer.

Purchasing and Receiving Schemes

The purchasing and receiving functions of a company can also be manipulated by dishonest employees to facilitate the theft of noncash assets (see Figure 11-6). It might at first seem that any purchasing scheme falls under the heading of false billings. There is, however, a distinction between the purchasing schemes that are classified as false billings and those that are classified as noncash misappropriations. If employees cause their company to purchase merchandise that the company does not need, this is a false billing scheme. The harm to the company comes in paying for assets for which it has no use. For instance, a carpenter was allowed control over the ordering of materials for a small construction project. No one bothered to measure the amount of materials ordered against the size of the carpenter's project. The carpenter was therefore able to order excess, unneeded lumber, which was then delivered to his home in order to build a fence for his own residence. The essence of the fraud in this case was the purchase of unneeded materials.

On the other hand, if the assets are intentionally purchased by the company but simply misappropriated by the fraudster, this is classified as a noncash scheme. In the preceding example, assume that the victim company wanted to keep a certain amount of lumber on hand for odd jobs. If the carpenter took this lumber home, the crime is a theft of lumber. The difference is that, in the second example, the company is deprived not only of the cash it paid for the lumber but also of the lumber itself. It then has to purchase more lumber to replace what is missing. In the first example, the company's only loss was the cash paid in the fraudulent purchase of the unneeded materials.

Falsifying Incoming Shipments One of the most common ways for employees to abuse the purchasing and receiving functions is for a person charged with receiving goods on behalf of the victim company—such as a warehouse supervisor or receiving clerk—to falsify the records of incoming shipments. In one case, for instance, two employees conspired to misappropriate incoming merchandise by marking shipments as short. If 1,000 units of a particular item were received, for example, the fraudsters indicated that only 900 were received. They were then able to steal the 100 units that were unaccounted for.

The obvious problem with this kind of scheme is that, if the receiving report does not match the vendor's invoice, there is a problem with payment. In the prior example, if the vendor bills for 1,000 units, but the accounts payable voucher shows receipt of only 900 units of merchandise, someone has to explain where the extra 100 units went. Obviously, the vendor indicates that a full shipment was made, so the victim company's attention likely turns to whoever signed the receiving reports.

In the preceding case, the fraudsters attempted to avoid this problem by altering only one copy of the receiving report. The copy that was sent to accounts payable indicated receipt of a full shipment, so the vendor would be paid without any questions. The copy used for inventory records indicated a short shipment, so that the assets on hand would equal the assets in the perpetual inventory.

Instead of marking shipments short, the fraudster might reject portions of a shipment as not being up to quality specifications. The perpetrator then keeps the "substandard" merchandise, rather than sending it back to the supplier. The result is the same as if the shipment had been marked short.

False Shipments of Inventory and Other Assets

To conceal thefts of inventory, fraudsters sometimes create false shipping documents and false sales documents to make it appear that missing inventory was not actually stolen but was instead sold (see Figure 11-7). The document that tells the shipping department to release inventory for delivery is usually the packing slip. By creating a false packing slip, corrupt employees can cause inventory to be delivered to themselves or an accomplice fraudulently. The "sales" reflected in the packing slips are typically made to a fictitious person, a fictitious company, or an accomplice of the perpetrator. For instance, an inventory control employee used his position to create fraudulent paperwork that authorized the shipment of over $30,000 worth of inventory to his accomplices. The fraudsters were then able to sell the inventory for their own profit.

One benefit to using false shipping documents to misappropriate inventory or other assets is that someone other than the fraudsters can remove the product from the warehouse or storeroom. The perpetrators of the scheme do not have to risk being caught stealing company inventory. Instead, the victim company unknowingly delivers the targeted assets to them.

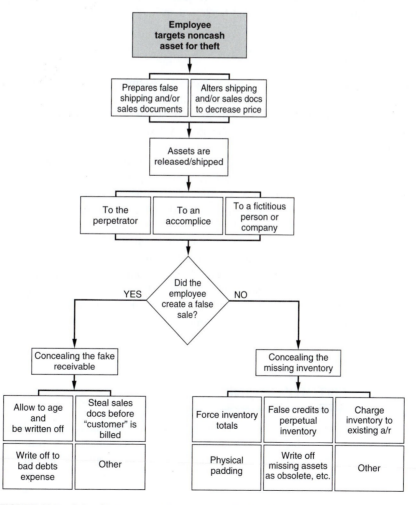

FIGURE 11-7 False Shipments of Inventory and Other Assets

Packing slips allow inventory to be shipped from the victim company to the perpetrator, but alone they do not conceal the fact that inventory has been misappropriated. In order to hide the theft, fraudsters may create a false sale, so it appears that the missing inventory was shipped to a customer. In this way, the inventory is accounted for. Depending on how the victim organization operates, the fraudster may have to create a false purchase order from the "buyer," a false sales order, and a false invoice along with the packing slip to create the illusion of a sale.

The result is that a fake receivable account goes into the books for the price of the misappropriated inventory. Obviously, the "buyer" of the merchandise never pays for it. How do fraudsters deal with these fake receivables? In some cases, fraudsters simply let the receivable age on their company's books until it is eventually written off as uncollectable. In other instances, the employee may take steps to remove the sale—and the delinquent receivable that results—from the books. For instance, in Case 1683, the perpetrator generated false invoices and delivered them to the company warehouse for shipping. The invoices were then marked "delivered" and sent to the sales office. The perpetrator removed all copies of the invoices from the files before they were billed to the fictitious customer. In other scenarios, the perpetrator might write the receivables off, as did a corrupt manager in another case. In that five-year scheme, the perpetrator took company assets and covered up the loss by setting up a fake sale. A few weeks after the fake sale went into the books, the perpetrator wrote off the receivable to an account for "lost and stolen assets." More commonly, the fake sale is written off to discounts or allowances or to a bad debts expense account.

Instead of completely fabricated sales, some employees understate legitimate sales so that an accomplice is billed for less than delivered. The result is that a portion of the merchandise is sold at no cost. In one instance, a salesman filled out shipping tickets, which he forwarded to the warehouse. After the merchandise was delivered, he instructed the warehouse employees to return the shipping tickets to him for "extra work" before they went to the invoicing department. The extra work that the salesman did was to alter the shipping tickets, reducing the quantity of merchandise on the ticket so that the buyer (an accomplice of the salesman) was billed for less than he received.

Other Schemes

Because employees tailor their thefts to the security systems, record-keeping systems, building layout, and other day-to-day operations of their companies, the methods used to steal inventory and other assets vary. The preceding categories comprised the majority of schemes in our study, but there were a couple of other schemes that did not fit any established category, yet which merit discussion.

Write-offs are often used to conceal the theft of assets after they have been stolen. In some cases, however, assets are written off in order to make them available for theft. For example, a warehouse foreman abused his authority to declare inventory obsolete. He wrote off perfectly good inventory and then "gave" it to a dummy corporation that he secretly owned. This fraudster took over $200,000 worth of merchandise from his employer. Once assets are designated as "scrap," it may be easier to conceal their misappropriation. Fraudsters may be allowed to take the "useless" assets for themselves, buy or sell them to an accomplice at a greatly reduced price, or simply give the assets away.

One final unique example was presented in a scheme where a low-level manager convinced his supervisor to approve the purchase of new office equipment to replace existing equipment, which was to be retired. When the new equipment was purchased, the perpetrator took it home and left the existing equipment in place. His boss assumed that the equipment in the office was new, even though it was actually the same equipment that had always been there. If nothing else, this case illustrates that sometimes a little bit of attentiveness by management is all it takes to halt fraud.

CONCEALING INVENTORY SHRINKAGE

When inventory is stolen, the key concealment issue for the fraudster is shrinkage. Inventory shrinkage is the unaccounted-for reduction in the company's inventory that results from theft. For instance, assume a computer retailer has 1,000 computers in stock. After work one day, an employee loads ten computers into a truck and takes them home. Now the company only has 990 computers, but, because there is no record that the employee took ten computers, the inventory records still show 1,000 units on hand. The company has experienced inventory shrinkage in the amount of ten computers.

Shrinkage is one of the red flags that signal fraud. When merchandise is missing and unaccounted for, the obvious question is "Where did it go?" The search for an answer to this question can uncover fraud. The goal of fraudsters is to proceed with their scheme undetected, so it is in their best interest to prevent anyone from looking for missing assets. This means concealing the shrinkage that occurs from theft.

Inventory is typically tracked through a two-step process. The first step, the perpetual inventory, is a running count that records how much should be on hand. When new shipments of supplies are received, for instance, these supplies are entered into the perpetual inventory. Similarly, when goods are sold, they are removed from the perpetual inventory records. In this way, a company tracks its inventory on a day-to-day basis.

Periodically, companies should make a physical count of assets on hand. In this process, someone actually goes through the storeroom or warehouse and counts everything that the company has in stock. This total is then matched to the amount of assets reflected in the perpetual inventory. A variation between the physical inventory and the perpetual inventory totals is shrinkage. Although a certain amount of shrinkage may be expected in any business, large shrinkage totals may indicate fraud.

Altered Inventory Records

One of the simplest methods for concealing shrinkage is to change the perpetual inventory record so that it matches the physical inventory count. This is also known as a forced reconciliation of the account. Basically, the perpetrator just changes the numbers in the perpetual inventory to make them match the amount of inventory on hand. As an illustration, a supervisor involved in the theft of inventory credited the perpetual inventory and debited the cost of sales account to bring the perpetual inventory numbers into line with the actual inventory count. Once these adjusting entries were made, a review of inventory would not reveal any shrinkage. Rather than use correcting entries to adjust perpetual inventory, some employees simply alter the numbers by deleting or covering up the correct totals and entering new numbers.

There are two sides to the inventory equation: the perpetual inventory and the physical inventory. Instead of altering the perpetual inventory, fraudsters who have access to the records from a physical inventory count can change those records to match the total of the perpetual inventory. Going back to the computer store example, assume the company counts its inventory every month and matches it to the perpetual inventory. The physical count should come to 990 computers, because that is what is actually on hand. If the perpetrator is someone charged with counting inventory, he or she can simply write down that there are 1,000 units on hand.

Fictitious Sales and Accounts Receivable

We have already discussed how fraudsters create fake sales to mask the theft of assets. When the perpetrator made an adjusting entry to the perpetual inventory and cost of sales accounts in the prior case, the problem was that there was no sales transaction on the books that corresponded to these entries. Had the perpetrator wished to fix this problem, he would have entered a debit to accounts receivable and a corresponding credit to the sales account to make it appear that the missing goods had been sold.

Of course, the problem of payment then arises, because no one is going to pay for the goods that were "sold" in this transaction. There are two routes that a fraudster might take in this circumstance. The first is to charge the sale to an existing account. In some cases, fraudsters charge fake sales to existing receivables accounts that are so large that the addition of the assets they have stolen is not noticed. Other corrupt employees charge the "sales" to accounts that are already aging and will soon be written off. When these accounts are removed from the books, the fraudster's stolen inventory effectively disappears.

The other adjustment that is typically made is a write-off to discounts and allowances or bad debt expense. To illustrate, an employee with blanket authority to write off up to $5,000 in uncollectable sales per occurrence used this authority to conceal false sales of inventory to nonexistent companies. The fraudster bilked his company out of nearly $180,000 using this method.

Write-Off Inventory and Other Assets

We have already discussed the case where a corrupt employee wrote off inventory as obsolete and then "gave" the inventory to a shell company that he controlled. Writing off inventory and other assets is a relatively common way for fraudsters to remove assets from the books before or after they are stolen. Again, this is beneficial to the fraudster because it eliminates the problem of shrinkage that inherently exists in every case of noncash asset misappropriation. Examples of this method include a manager who wrote supplies off as lost or destroyed and then sold the supplies through his own company; in another

case, a director of maintenance disposed of fixed assets by reporting them as broken and then took the assets for himself.

Physical Padding

Most methods of concealment deal with altering inventory records, either changing the perpetual inventory or miscounting during the physical inventory. In the alternative, some fraudsters try to make it appear that there are more assets present in the warehouse or stockroom than there actually are. Empty boxes, for example, may be stacked on shelves to create the illusion of extra inventory. For example, employees stole liquor from their stockroom and restacked the containers for the missing merchandise. This made it appear that the missing inventory was present when, in fact, there were really empty boxes on the stockroom shelves. In a period of approximately eighteen months, this concealment method allowed employees to steal over $200,000 worth of liquor.

The most egregious case of inventory padding in our study occurred when the fraudsters constructed a facade of finished product in a remote location of a warehouse and cordoned off the area to restrict access. Although there should have been a million dollars' worth of product on hand, there was actually nothing of finished product behind the wall, which was constructed solely to create the appearance of additional inventory.

PREVENTING AND DETECTING NONCASH THEFTS THAT ARE CONCEALED BY FRAUDULENT SUPPORT

In the purchasing function, it is important to separate the duties of ordering goods, receiving goods, maintaining perpetual inventory records, and issuing payments. Invoices should always be matched to receiving reports before payments are issued, in order to help prevent schemes where inventory is stolen from incoming shipments.

To prevent fraudulent shipments of merchandise, organizations should make sure that every packing slip (sales order) is matched to an approved purchase order and that every outgoing shipment is matched to the sales order before the merchandise goes out. Shipments of inventory should be periodically matched to sales records to detect signs of fraud. Whenever a shipment shows up that cannot be traced to a sale, this should be investigated. Another red flag that may indicate a fraudulent shipping scheme is an increase in bad debt expense. As discussed earlier, some employees create a fraudulent sale to justify a shipment of merchandise and then either cancel the sale or write it off as a bad debt after the goods have left the victim organization. Customer shipping addresses can also be matched against employee addresses to find schemes in which employees have had inventory or equipment delivered to their home address.

Carefully review any unexplained entries in perpetual inventory records. Make sure all reductions to the perpetual inventory records are supported by proper source documents. Look for obvious signs of alterations. Make sure that the beginning balance for each month's inventory ties to the ending balance from the previous month. Also determine that the dollar value of ending inventory is reasonably close to previous comparable amounts. Reconcile inventory balance on the inventory report to inventory balance in the general ledger. Investigate any discrepancies.

Another fairly common scheme involves employees who overstate the amount of materials needed for a project and steal the excess materials. To prevent this kind of fraud, organizations should reconcile materials ordered for projects to the actual work done. Make sure all materials requisitions are approved by appropriate personnel and require both the requestor and the approver to sign materials requisitions, so that, if fraud occurs, the culprit can be identified.

In some circumstances, employees write off stolen inventory or equipment as "scrap"—either to make it easier to steal (because the organization has fewer safeguards over its scrap items) or to account for the missing assets on the organization's books. In either case, organizations should periodically perform trend analysis on the amount of inventory that is being designated as scrap. Significant increase in scrap levels could indicate an inventory theft scheme. Similarly, look for unusually high levels of reorders for particular items, which could indicate that a particular item of inventory is being stolen.

Assets should be removed from operations only with the proper authority. For example, if a journal entry is used to record abandonment of a fixed asset, the journal entry should be supported by the responsible

person's approval. Control should be maintained over assets during disposal. If the organization sells assets that have been designated as scrap, they should be turned over to the selling agent on approval of the disposal. The asset custodian should maintain contact with the selling agent to report on the disposition of the asset in question. Proceeds from the sale of scrap items should follow normal cash receipt operations. The person responsible for asset disposition should not be responsible for receipt of the proceeds.

Proactive Computer Audit Tests for Detecting Noncash Misappropriations

Title	Category	Description	Data file(s)
Identify delivery of inventory to employee address by joining employee address to shipment address file.	All	Inventory may be shipped directly to an employee address.	• Shipment Register • Employee Address
Identify delivery of inventory to address that is not designated as a business address.	All	Inventory may be shipped to an employee address that is entered into the system to appear as a regular business address. The identification of whether an address is legitimately a business one can be done with software databases such as Select Phone Pro.	• Shipment Register
Inventory actual to standard price.	All except larceny	Inventory prices may be adjusted in an attempt to conceal inventory larceny schemes.	• On-Hand Inventory
List top 100 employees by dollar size (one for inventory adjustments, asset transfers, and accounts receivable write-offs).	All except larceny	Employees with high adjustments may signal actions to hide inventory larceny schemes.	• Invoice Sales Register • Inventory Adjustments • Shipment Register
List top 100 employees who have been on the top 100 list for three months (one for inventory adjustments, asset transfers, and accounts receivable write-offs).	All except larceny	Employees with high adjustments may signal actions to hide inventory larceny schemes.	• Invoice Sales Register • Inventory Adjustments • Shipment Register
List top ten locations that have been on the top ten list for three months (one for inventory adjustments, asset transfers, and accounts receivable write-offs).	All except larceny	Locations with high adjustments may signal actions to hide inventory larceny schemes.	• Invoice Sales Register • Inventory Adjustments • Shipment Register
Compute standard deviation for each employee for the last three months and list those employees who provided three times the standard deviation in the current month (one for inventory adjustments, asset transfers, and accounts receivable write-offs).	All except larceny	Employees with high adjustments may signal actions to hide inventory larceny schemes.	• Invoice Sales Register • Inventory Adjustments • Shipment Register
Summarize user access for the receiving, inventory adjustments, shipping, and customer account systems for segregation of duties reviews.	All except larceny	User access to systems may identify segregation-of-duties issues. For example, if employees post fraudulent shipments to their home address and then write off the receivable, this nonsegregation facilitates the fraud. User access should be reviewed from the perspective of adjustments within the application and adjustments to the data themselves.	• System User Access Logs or • System User Access Master File

(Continued)

(*Continued*)

Title	Category	Description	Data file(s)
Duplicate inventory listing by amount and description, as well as quantity and amount.	All except larceny	Inventory may be fraudulently listed in duplicate in the on-hand register to appear on hand, concealing the inventory larceny.	• On-Hand Inventory
Inventory price greater than retail price.	All except larceny	Inventory prices may be adjusted in an attempt to conceal inventory larceny schemes.	• On-Hand Inventory
Extract all inventory coded as obsolete that possesses reorder points within the inventory system.	Purchasing and receiving schemes	Inventory that has been written off as obsolete while also having reorder points may be a sign that the items were written off fraudulently to conceal an inventory larceny.	• Inventory Master File • Inventory Adjustments
Receipts per receiving report in the receiving system that do not agree to the receipts per the accounts payable invoice.	Purchasing and receiving schemes	Receipts per the receiving log may be fraudulently lowered to conceal an inventory larceny and then increased when passed to accounts payable to effectuate the payment to the vendor.	• Receiving Log • Invoice Payment
Inventory receipts per inventory item that exceed the economic order quantity or maximum for that item.	Purchasing and receiving schemes	Overordering of product so that it may be taken fraudulently may be detected through this analysis.	• Receiving Log • Inventory Master File
Inventory with a negative quantity balance.	False shipments	Employees posting fraudulent shipments may erroneously enter more shipments than there are in the inventory for a stated inventory item.	• On-Hand Inventory
Dormant customer accounts for the past six months that post a sale in the last two months of the year.	False shipments	Customers that have been dormant may be used as accounts to post fraudulent sales, concealing an inventory larceny.	• Sales Register
Calculate the ratio of the largest sale to next-largest sale by customer.	False shipments	By identifying the largest sale to a customer and the next-largest sale, any large ratio difference may identify a fraudulently recorded "largest" sale. This is essentially made to conceal an inventory larceny.	• Sales Register
Shipping documents with no associated sales order.	False shipments	A false shipment, concealing inventory larceny, may be posted to the sales journal with no corresponding shipment entry, thereby avoiding detection of the entry.	• Sales Register • Shipment Register

REVIEW QUESTIONS

11-1 Why is sales skimming called an "off-book" fraud?

11-2 What techniques are generally used to conceal a receivables skimming scheme?

11-3 Which is the most effective control to prevent receivables skimming?

11-4 What is the difference between skimming and cash larceny?

11-5 In cash larceny schemes, what methods may be used to conceal these schemes at the point of sale?

11-6 How are noncash assets misappropriated?

11-7 What types of company assets are typically misused?

11-8 How may the larceny of noncash assets be prevented?

11-9 What is meant by inventory "shrinkage"?

11-10 What steps should an organization take to prevent fraudulent shipments of merchandise?

CHAPTER 12

CASH DISBURSEMENT SCHEMES

LEARNING OBJECTIVES

After completing this chapter, you should be able to:

12-1 Identify the five major categories of fraudulent disbursements.

12-2 Describe a shell company and explain how it is formed.

12-3 Discuss how pay-and-return schemes work.

12-4 Identify the five principal categories of check tampering.

12-5 Differentiate between forged maker and forged endorsement schemes.

12-6 Discuss ways to prevent and detect the theft and alteration of outgoing company checks.

12-7 Explain what is meant by a ghost employee, and describe the four steps needed to make this scheme work.

12-8 Describe the methods employees use to overstate legitimate expenses on their expense reports.

12-9 Identify red flags that are commonly associated with fictitious expense schemes.

12-10 Compare and contrast fraudulent disbursements at the cash register with other register frauds.

CRITICAL THINKING EXERCISE

A clerk in the butcher shop is 5′ 10″ tall. What does he weigh?

BILLING SCHEMES

In a billing scheme, the perpetrator uses false documentation—such as an invoice, purchase order, or credit card bill—to cause his employer to issue a payment for some fraudulent purpose. The actual disbursement of funds is performed by the organization in the same manner as would be a legitimate disbursement. The crux of the fraud is not that a bogus check is issued; instead, the key to these schemes is that the fraudster is able to deceive his employer so that the organization willingly and unwittingly issues the bogus check.

Billing schemes generally fall into one of three categories:

1. Shell company schemes
2. Nonaccomplice vendor schemes
3. Personal purchases schemes

Shell Company Schemes

Shell companies, for the purposes of our discussion, are fictitious entities created for the sole purpose of committing fraud. They may be nothing more than a fabricated name and a post office box that an employee uses to collect disbursements from false billings. However, since the checks received will be made out in the name of the shell company, the perpetrator will normally also set up a bank account in his new company's name, listing himself as an authorized signer on the account (see Figure 12-1).

Forming a Shell Company In order to open a bank account for a shell company, a fraudster will probably have to present the bank with a certificate of incorporation or an assumed-name certificate. These are documents that a company must obtain through a state or local government. These documents can

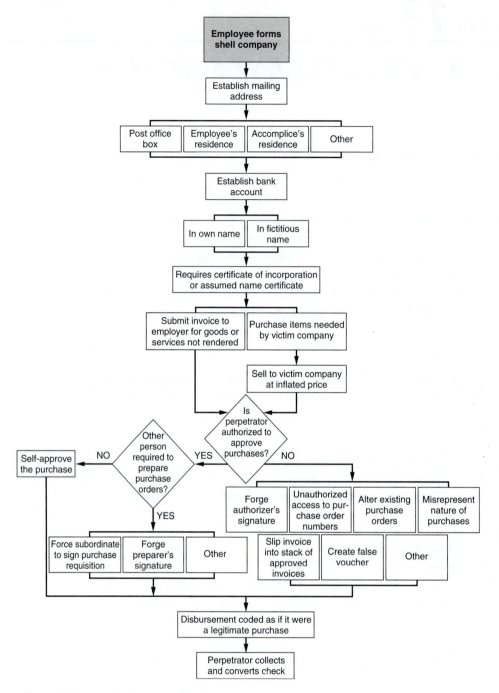

FIGURE 12-1 False Billings from Shell Companies

be forged, but it is more likely that the perpetrator will simply file the requisite paperwork and obtain legitimate documents from his state or county. This can usually be accomplished for a small fee, the cost of which can be more than offset by a successful fraud scheme.

If it is discovered that a company is being falsely billed by a vendor, fraud examiners for the victim company may try to trace the ownership of the vendor. The documents used to start a bank account in a shell company's name can sometimes assist examiners in determining who is behind the fraudulent billings. If the corrupt employee formed his shell company under his own name, a search of public records at the local court house may reveal him as the fraudster.

For this reason, the corrupt employee will sometimes form his shell company in the name of someone other than himself. For example, in one case, an employee stole approximately $4 million from his company via false billings submitted from a shell company set up in his wife's name. Using a spouse's name adds

a buffer of security to an employee's fraud scheme. When a male employee sets up a shell company, he sometimes does so in his wife's maiden name to further distance himself from the fictitious company.

A more effective way for a fraudster to hide his connection to a false company is to form the company under a fictitious name. In another case, an employee used a coworker's identification to form a shell vendor. The fraudster then proceeded to bill his employer for approximately $20,000 in false services. The resulting checks were deposited in the account of the shell company, and currency was withdrawn from the account through an ATM.

The other issue involved in forming a shell company is the entity's address—where fraudulent checks will be collected. Often, an employee rents a post office box and lists it as the mailing address of his shell company. Some employees list their home address instead. In one instance, a department head set up a dummy company using his residence as the mailing address. Over a two-year period, this man submitted over $250,000 worth of false invoices. Eventually, the scheme was detected by a newly hired clerk. The clerk was processing an invoice when she noticed that the address of the vendor was the same as her boss's address. (By a lucky coincidence, the clerk had typed a personal letter for her boss earlier that day and remembered his address.) Had the department head used a post office box instead of his home address on the invoices, his scheme might have continued indefinitely.

One reason employees might be hesitant to use post office boxes in shell company schemes is that some businesses are especially wary of sending checks to vendors that do not have street addresses. Such an address, as we have already discussed, can signal fraud. For this reason, fraudsters may use the address of a relative, friend, or accomplice as a collection point for fraudulent checks.

Submitting False Invoices   Once a shell company is formed and a bank account has been opened, the corrupt employee is in a position to begin billing his employer. Invoices can be manufactured by various means such as a professional printer, a personal computer, or a typewriter. False invoices do not always have to be of professional quality to generate fraudulent disbursements.

Self-Approval of Fraudulent Invoices   The difficulty in a shell-company scheme is not usually in producing the invoices, but in getting the victim company to pay them. Authorization for the fictitious purchase (and therefore payment of the bill) is the key. In a large percentage of the shell company cases in ACFE studies, the fraudster was in a position to approve payment on the very invoices he was fraudulently submitting. For example, a manager authorized payment of $6 million worth of phony invoices from a dummy company he had formed. Similarly, another employee set up a bogus freight company and personally approved $50,000 worth of bogus invoices from it. It is only logical that those with authority to approve purchases would be among the most likely to engage in billing schemes, since they have fewer hurdles to overcome than other employees.

A slight twist to this method was used in another case. The victim organization in this case properly required vouchers to be prepared and approved by different persons. The fraudster in this case had approval authority, but was not allowed to prepare the vouchers that he approved. Therefore, this person created false vouchers and forged a coworker's initials as the preparer. Then the perpetrator approved the voucher for payment under his own authority. It therefore appeared that two employees had signed off on the voucher (as mandated by the organization's controls).

Not all companies require the completion of payment vouchers before they will issue checks. In some enterprises, checks are written based on less formal procedures. For example, the CEO of a nonprofit company simply submitted "check requests" to the accounting department. As the CEO, his "requests" obviously carried great weight in the organization. The company issued checks to whatever company was listed on the request in whatever amount was specified. The CEO used these forms to obtain over $35,000 in payments for fictitious services rendered by a shell company he had formed. In this case, invoices were not even required to authorize the payments. The check request forms simply listed the payee, the amount, and a brief narrative regarding the reason for the check. This made it so easy for the CEO to generate fraudulent disbursements that he eventually had three separate companies billing the victim company at the same time. It is obvious that, as CEO, the fraudster in this case had a wide degree of latitude within the company and was unlikely to be obstructed by one of his subordinates. Nevertheless, this case should illustrate how the failure to require proper support for payments can lead to fraud.

"Rubber-Stamp" Supervisors   If an employee cannot authorize payments himself, the next best thing is if the person who has that authority is inattentive or overly trusting. "Rubber-stamp" supervisors like this are destined to be targeted by unethical employees. For example, an employee set up a fake computer

supply company with an accomplice and "sold" parts and services to his employer. The perpetrator's supervisor did not know much about computers and therefore could not accurately gauge whether the invoices from the dummy company were excessive or even necessary. The supervisor was therefore forced to rely on the perpetrator of the scheme to verify the authenticity of the purchases. Consequently, the victim company suffered approximately $20,000 in losses.

Reliance on False Documents   When an employee does not have approval authority for purchases and does not have the benefit of a rubber-stamp supervisor, he or she must run his or her vouchers through the normal accounts payable process. The success of this kind of scheme will depend on the apparent authenticity of the false voucher she creates. If the fraudster can generate purchase orders and receiving reports that corroborate the information on the fraudulent invoice from a shell company, he or she can fool Accounts Payable into issuing a check.

Collusion   Collusion among several employees is sometimes used to overcome well-designed internal controls of a victim company. For example, in a company with proper separation of duties, the functions of purchasing goods or services, authorizing the purchase, receiving the goods or services, and making the payment to the vendor should be separated. Obviously, if this process is strictly adhered to, it will be extremely difficult for any single employee to commit a false-billing scheme. As a result, ACFE studies included several schemes in which employees conspired to defeat the fraud prevention measures of their employer. For example, a warehouse foreman and a parts-ordering clerk conspired to purchase approximately $300,000 of nonexistent supplies. The parts-ordering clerk would initiate the false transactions by obtaining approval to place orders for parts he claimed were needed. The orders were then sent to a vendor who, acting in conjunction with the two employee fraudsters, prepared false invoices that were sent to the victim company. Meanwhile, the warehouse foreman verified receipt of the fictitious shipments of incoming supplies. The perpetrators were therefore able to compile complete vouchers for the fraudulent purchases without overstepping their normal duties. Similarly, in another case, three employees set up a shell company to bill their employer for services and supplies. The first employee, a clerk, was in charge of ordering parts and services. The second employee, a purchasing agent, helped authorize these orders by falsifying purchasing reports regarding comparison pricing, and so on. The clerk was also responsible for receiving the parts and services, while a third conspirator, a manager in the victim company's accounts payable department, ensured that payments were issued on the fraudulent invoices.

The cases above illustrate how collusion among several employees with separate duties in the purchasing process can be very difficult to detect. Even if all controls are followed, at some point a company must rely on its employees to be honest. One of the purposes of separating duties is to prevent any one person from having too much control over a particular business function. It provides a built-in monitoring mechanism where every person's actions are in some way verified by another person. But if everyone is corrupt, even proper controls can be overcome.

Purchases of Services Rather than Goods   Most of the shell company schemes in our survey involved the purchase of services rather than goods. Why is this so? The primary reason is that services are not tangible. If an employee sets up a shell company to make fictitious sales of goods to his employer, these goods will obviously never arrive. By comparing its purchases to its inventory levels, the victim company might detect the fraud. It is much more difficult, however, for the victim company to verify that the services were never rendered. For this reason, many employees involved in shell company schemes bill their employers for things like "consulting services."

Pass-Through Schemes   In the schemes discussed so far, the victim companies were billed for completely fictitious goods or services. This is the most common formula for a shell company fraud, but there is a subcategory of shell company schemes in which actual goods or services are sold to the victim company. These are known as pass-through schemes.

Pass-through schemes are usually undertaken by employees in charge of purchasing on behalf of the victim company. Instead of buying merchandise directly from a vendor, the employee sets up a shell company and purchases the merchandise through that fictitious entity. He then resells the merchandise to his employer from the shell company at an inflated price, thereby making an unauthorized profit on the transaction.

One of the best examples of a pass-through scheme came from a case in an ACFE study in which a department director was in charge of purchasing computer equipment. Because of his expertise on the

subject and his high standing within the company, he was unsupervised in this task. The director set up a shell company in another state and bought used computers through the shell company, then turned around and sold them to his employer at a greatly exaggerated price. The money from the victim company's first installment on the computers was used to pay the shell company's debts to the real vendors. Subsequent payments were profits for the bogus company. The scheme cost the victim company over $4 million.

Preventing and Detecting Shell Company Schemes   Shell company schemes are among the most costly of all forms of occupational fraud, so it is imperative that organizations have controls in place to prevent these frauds. As is the case in regard to all forms of billing fraud, it is critical that duties in the purchasing process be separated. Most billing schemes succeed when an individual has control over one or more aspects of purchasing, authorizing purchases, receiving and storing goods, and issuing payments. If these duties are strictly segregated, it will be very difficult for an employee to commit most forms of billing fraud, including shell company schemes.

Because shell company schemes, by definition, involve invoicing from fictitious vendors, one of the best ways to counter this type of fraud is to maintain and regularly update an approved vendor list. The legitimacy of all vendors on the list should be verified by someone independent of the purchasing function, and whenever an invoice is received from a vendor not on the list, independent verification of that company should be required before the invoice is paid.

Identifying Shell Company Invoices   In addition to controls aimed at generally preventing billing fraud, auditors, accounting personnel, and other employees should be trained to identify fraudulent invoices. One common red flag is a lack of detail on the fraudulent invoice. For example, the invoice might lack a phone number, fax number, invoice number, tax identification number, and/or other information that usually appears on legitimate invoices. Another common sign of fraud is an invoice that lacks detailed descriptions of the items for which the victim organization is being billed. Finally, the mailing address on an invoice can indicate that it is fraudulent. In most shell company schemes, the mailing address for payments is a mail drop or a residential address. Any invoice that calls for a payment to one of these locations should be scrutinized, and the existence of the vendor should be verified before a check is mailed.

In some cases, a fraudster will print or create several invoices and then submit them to her employer one at a time over an extended period so that the amount she is stealing will be spread out and less noticeable. These schemes can sometimes be detected because the invoices used by the perpetrator will be consecutively numbered. In other words, the invoice numbers might be 4002, 4003, 4004, and so forth. This is clearly a sign of a shell company, because it indicates that the vendor in question is only sending invoices to the victim. Suppose, for example, that an organization receives invoice #4002 from a vendor on September 1, and receives invoice #4003 on October 1. This would indicate that the vendor issued only a single invoice in September—the invoice received by the company in question. Obviously, a legitimate company could not operate this way and survive.

Organizations can detect this sort of anomaly by regularly reviewing the payables account and sorting payments by vendor and invoice number. Also, in many shell company schemes, the perpetrator will repeatedly bill for the same or similar amounts. If the perpetrator has purchase authority, these amounts will tend to be just below the perpetrator's approval limit. So if Employee X is committing a shell company scheme and he is authorized to approve purchases up to $10,000, his shell company invoices might tend to fall in the $9,000 to $9,999 range. This can be detected by sorting payments by vendor and amount.

Testing for Shell Company Schemes   As discussed above, sorting payments by vendor, amount, and invoice number is one way to search out red flags that might indicate a shell company scheme. There are a number of other trends and red flags that are frequently associated with these frauds, and organizations should regularly test for them as part of a proactive fraud detection program.

Billing schemes will typically cause an organization's expenses to exceed budget projections, so organizations should be alert to large budget overruns and departments that regularly exceed their budgets. Billing schemes will also tend to cause an increase in expenses from previous years. In a small company a billing scheme could significantly affect the financial statements and could be detected through horizontal analysis (comparison of financials on a year-to-year basis). In a very large company, a billing scheme might not have a significant impact on the overall financials, but it could still be detected by analyzing expense trends on a departmental or project basis. Obviously, by fraudulently increasing purchasing expenses, billing schemes will also tend to cause an increase in cost of goods sold relative to sales, and therefore will tend to negatively impact profits.

Because billing schemes generally involve the purchase of fictitious goods or services, a review of purchase levels can help detect this form of fraud. As we have stated, most shell company schemes involve purchases of fictitious services, because these "soft account" items cannot be traced to inventory, meaning there will be no physical evidence that the transaction was fraudulent. However, these schemes will cause an increase in service-related expenses. So, for instance, a large, unexplained rise in consulting or training expenses could indicate a shell company scheme. When this red flag shows up, the underlying purchases should be reviewed and both the performance of the service and the legitimacy of the provider should be confirmed. By tracking approval authority for all purchases, organizations can also run comparison reports looking for employees or managers who approve an unusually high level of services based on their job function.

In cases where a shell company bills for goods, these goods either will be nonexistent or will be overpriced as part of a pass-through scheme. In either case, this will cause expenses and cost of goods sold to rise, as discussed above. Furthermore, if an individual causes her organization to buy nonexistent goods, the quantity of items purchased will increase by the number of fictitious items bought from the shell company. Unexplained increases in the quantity of goods purchased should be investigated, particularly when the increase does not translate to increased sales. Purchases of nonexistent goods will also cause inventory shortages, because the purchased items will be added to the organization's perpetual inventory system but will never enter the physical inventory. Purchases that cannot be traced to inventory are a clear red flag of shell company schemes.

If, on the other hand, the shell company sells existing goods as part of a pass-through scheme, then the price for these items will be substantially marked up. Organizations should monitor trends in average unit price of goods purchased. Significant increases could signal not only pass-through schemes, but also kickback schemes and other types of billing fraud. If prices on a particular transaction or set of transactions seem out of line, other vendors should be contacted to determine the industry norm. Assuming the pricing is way out of line, the organization should review the transaction to determine how the vendor was approved, and what employees were involved in the transaction. In addition, steps should be taken to confirm that the vendor is legitimate, as discussed below.

In addition to reviewing *quantities* purchased, organizations should also pay attention to *types of goods and services* that are purchased. In many shell company schemes and other forms of billing fraud, the nature of the purchases is patently unreasonable, but the invoices in question are nevertheless rubber-stamped. For instance, when a law firm buys a truckload of gravel, red flags should immediately go up. This kind of test is really a common sense issue and requires that auditors, managers, and accounting personnel have a good understanding of how their organizations function.

Because employees sometimes run shell company schemes using their home address to collect payments, organizations should periodically run comparison reports for vendor addresses and employee addresses. If a match occurs, the employee in question is probably engaging in a shell company scheme.

Fraudulent vouchers are also generally run through the payables system more quickly than legitimate ones. The employees who commit these schemes try to get their bogus invoices paid as quickly as possible, because they want their money immediately—and once the invoice is paid, the likelihood of the scheme being detected drops considerably. A report showing the average turnaround time on invoices sorted by vendor might show that a particular company tends to have its invoices paid much more quickly than other vendors. If so, steps should be taken to confirm that the company exists, and that the purchases were appropriate.

Verifying Whether a Shell Company Exists   It is usually fairly simple to determine whether a particular vendor is legitimate. A good first step is to simply look up the vendor in the phone book. The absence of a phone number for a vendor is generally an indication that the company is a shell. It is also a good idea to contact others in your industry to determine whether they are familiar with the vendor. If the vendor only appears to have billed your company, or if no one else in your community seems to have heard of it, this would tend to indicate that the company does not actually exist. Finally, if questions persist about whether the vendor is a shell, someone from the victim organization should visit its address to see whether business is actually conducted there.

Identifying the Employee behind a Shell Company   Even if a company has been identified as a shell, there is still the matter of determining who is behind the scheme. In most cases, the perpetrator will have been involved in selecting the vendor or approving the purchase. However, it may be necessary to gather independent verification to prove the identity of the fraudster. This can make it easier to obtain

a confession during an investigative interview, and it will also serve as useful evidence if the matter eventually goes to trial, a possibility that exists in any fraud investigation. There are a number of ways to verify the identity of the person or persons operating a shell company.

In many cases, the person who creates a shell company will register the company with the appropriate government authority, because this registration is necessary to open a bank account in the shell's name. These documents require the name, address, and signature of the person who is forming the company. Therefore, a search of the company's registration, which is a public record, may indicate who committed the fraud. Articles of incorporation are maintained by the secretary of state (or the state corporation bureau or corporate registry office) in every state. DBA (Doing Business As) information can usually be obtained at the county level. These public records can be obtained without a subpoena.

When conducting a records search, it is important to remember that fraudsters might set up a company under a false name to avoid being identified with the shell. One common technique is to establish the shell in the name of a relative or accomplice who does not work for the victim organization. If the perpetrator is male and is married, he might also form the shell under his wife's maiden name. When checking public records, investigators should be alert for related names, as well as addresses, phone numbers, Social Security numbers, or other identifiers that may match an employee's personnel information.

Rather than conduct a records search, it may be possible to confirm the identity of the fraudster based on other factors. For instance, a company could match checks that have been converted by the shell company with payroll checks that have been deposited by a suspect employee. Matching endorsements, account numbers, or handwriting would indicate that the checks were deposited into the same bank account. Similarly, handwriting samples on business filings and/or communications from the suspected vendor can be matched against the handwriting of suspected employees.

Another way to identify the perpetrator behind a shell company scheme is to conduct surveillance of the mail drop to determine who collects checks on behalf of the shell company. Finally, if a suspect or suspects have been identified, a search of their office or workspace might also reveal trash. Many shell company schemes are detected when a vendor's invoices or letterhead are discovered in an employee's work area. However, any workplace search must be done carefully so that the employee's privacy rights are not violated. Workplace searches should be conducted only after consulting with an attorney.

Billing Schemes Involving Nonaccomplice Vendors

Pay-and-Return Schemes   Rather than using shell companies as vessels for overbilling schemes, some employees generate fraudulent disbursements by using the invoices of nonaccomplice vendors. In pay-and-return schemes, these employees do not prepare and submit the vendor's invoices; rather, they intentionally mishandle payments that are owed to the legitimate vendors (see Figure 12-2). One way to do this is to purposely double-pay an invoice. For instance, a secretary was responsible for opening mail, processing claims, and authorizing payments. She intentionally paid some bills twice, then requested that the recipients return one of the checks. She intercepted these returned checks and deposited them into her own bank account.

Another way to accomplish a pay-and-return scheme is to intentionally pay the wrong vendor. In another case, an accounts payable clerk deliberately put vendor checks in the wrong envelopes. After they had been mailed, she called the vendors to explain the "mistake," and requested that they return the checks to her. She deposited these checks into her personal bank account and ran the vouchers through the accounts payable system a second time to pay the appropriate vendors.

Finally, an employee might pay the proper vendor, but intentionally overpay him. In one instance, an employee intentionally caused a check to be issued to a vendor for more than the invoice amount, then requested that the vendor return the excess. This money was taken by the fraudster and deposited into her own account. Similarly, an employee might intentionally purchase excess merchandise, return the excess, and pocket the refund.

Overbilling with a Nonaccomplice Vendor's Invoices   In some cases, employees use invoices in the name of existing vendors to generate fraudulent payments. This occurs in kickback schemes when the vendor is an accomplice in the fraud, but it can also occur when the vendor is unaware of the crime. The perpetrator either manufactures a fake invoice for a vendor who regularly deals with the victim organization or reruns an invoice that has already been paid. The perpetrator submits the fraudulent invoice and intercepts the resulting payment. Since the bill is fictitious, the existing vendor is not out of any money. The only victim is the employer's organization, which pays for goods or services that it does not receive.

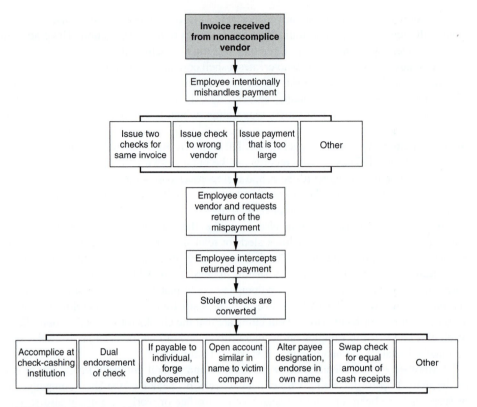

FIGURE 12-2 Pay-and-Return Schemes

Preventing and Detecting Fraudulent Invoices from a Nonaccomplice Vendor Prevention of nonaccomplice vendor invoicing schemes is largely dependent on the purchasing function controls already discussed in this chapter. Efforts at detecting these schemes should focus on several red flags that are common to nonaccomplice vendor invoicing. For example, if an employee produces invoices designed to mimic those of a known vendor, the mailing address might differ from that of the real vendor. This variation is necessary so that the perpetrator can collect the check. As discussed previously, organizations should maintain up-to-date approved vendor lists that include contact and mailing information for approved vendors. Deviations from this information, such as a change in mailing address, should be flagged and the changes verified as legitimate before a disbursement is issued. In addition, a fraudulent invoice prepared by an employee to mimic that of a legitimate vendor might have an invoice number that is significantly out of sequence. A sort of disbursements by vendor, date, and invoice number could reveal this type of anomaly.

Instead of producing fraudulent vendor invoices, some employees simply rerun invoices from existing vendors and steal the checks that result from the second run. This type of fraud should be easily detectable if an organization has an effective duplicate checking system to ensure that the same invoice cannot be run through the payables system twice. In manual systems, every paid voucher should be clearly marked "paid" to prevent reprocessing. In an electronic system, duplicate invoice numbers should be automatically flagged. In order to dodge a duplicate checking system, some fraudsters will slightly alter the invoice number. For instance, invoice #44004 might be changed to #44004a, or a zero in the number might be changed to the letter *O* so that the number will look the same to the naked eye but will not show up as a duplicate in the accounting system. However, a sort of invoice numbers from a particular vendor in ascending or descending order will reveal these as out of sequence.

Pay-and-return schemes can be mostly prevented if the duties of purchasing, authorizing, and distributing payments are separated and if all invoices are matched to purchase orders before payments are issued. Incoming mail should also never be delivered directly to an employee. All incoming mail should be opened by mailroom personnel to ensure that every incoming check is recorded. In addition, each incoming check should be photocopied, with the copy attached to the remittance advice. This will help prevent a dishonest employee from being able to recover a check that was intentionally double-paid.

When the targeted vendor in a pay-and-return scheme sends an overpayment back to the fraudster, the check is often payable to the victim organization. To make it more difficult to convert such a check, organizations should instruct their banks not to cash checks payable to the organization.

Finally, if a pay-and-return scheme is suspected, organizations should spot-check past accounts payable files for overpayments. Identify all persons involved in processing any overpayment, and review their transactions for similar "mistakes."

Personal Purchases with Company Funds

Instead of undertaking billing schemes to generate cash, many fraudsters simply purchase personal items with their company's money. Company accounts are used to buy items for fraudsters, their businesses, their families, and so on. In one case, a supervisor started a company for his son and directed work to the son's company. In addition, the supervisor saw to it that his employer purchased all the materials and supplies necessary for the son's business, and he purchased materials through his employer that were used to add a room to his own house. All in all, the perpetrator bought nearly $50,000 worth of supplies and materials for himself using company money.

Conceptually, one might wonder why a purchasing fraud is not classified as a theft of inventory or other assets rather than a billing scheme. After all, in purchasing schemes the fraudster buys something with company money and then takes the purchased item for himself. In the case discussed above, for example, the supervisor took building materials and supplies. How does this differ from those frauds where employees steal inventory, supplies, and other materials? At first glance, the schemes appear very similar. In fact, the perpetrator of a purchases fraud is stealing inventory just as he would in any other inventory theft scheme. Nevertheless, the heart of the scheme is not the *taking* of the inventory but the *purchasing* of the inventory. In other words, when an employee steals merchandise from a warehouse, he is stealing an asset that the company needs, an asset that it has on hand for a particular reason. The harm to the victim company is not only the cost of the asset, but also the loss of the asset itself. In a purchasing scheme, on the other hand, the asset that is taken is superfluous. The perpetrator causes the victim company to order and pay for an asset that it does not really need, so the only damage to the victim company is the money lost in purchasing the particular item. This is why purchasing schemes are categorized as billing frauds.

Personal Purchases through False Invoicing

Most of the employees in our study who undertook purchasing schemes did so by running unsanctioned invoices through the accounts payable system. The fraudster in this type of fraud buys an item and submits the bill to his employer as if it represented a purchase on behalf of the company (see Figure 12-3). The goal is to have the company pay the invoice. Obviously, the invoice that the employee submits to his company is not legitimate. The main hurdle for a fraudster to overcome, therefore, is to avoid scrutiny of the invalid invoice and obtain authorization for the bill to be paid.

The Fraudster as Authorizer of Invoices

As was the case in the shell company schemes we reviewed, the person who engages in a purchases scheme is often the very person in the company whose duties include *authorizing* purchases. Obviously, proper controls should preclude anyone from approving his own purchases. Such poorly separated functions leave little other than his conscience to dissuade an employee from fraud.

Nevertheless, we saw several examples of organizations in which this lapse in controls existed. As we continue to point out, fraud arises in part because of a perceived opportunity. An employee who sees that no one is reviewing his actions is more likely to turn to fraud than one who knows that his company diligently works to detect employee theft.

An example of how poor controls can lead to fraud was found in one case in which a manager of a remote location of a large, publicly traded company was authorized to both order supplies and approve vendor invoices for payment. For over a year, the manager routinely added personal items and supplies for his own business to orders made on behalf of his employer. The orders often included a strange mix of items; technical supplies and home furnishings might, for instance, be purchased in the same order. Because the manager was in a position to approve his own purchases, he could get away with such blatantly obvious frauds. In addition to ordering personal items, the perpetrator changed the delivery address for certain supplies so that they would be delivered directly to his home or side business. This scheme cost the victim company approximately $300,000 in unnecessary purchases. In a similar case, an employee with complete control of purchasing and storing supplies for his department bought approximately $100,000 worth of unnecessary supplies using company funds. The employee authorized both the orders and the payments. The excess supplies were taken to the perpetrator's home, where he used them to manufacture a product for his own business. It should be obvious from the examples cited above that not only do poor

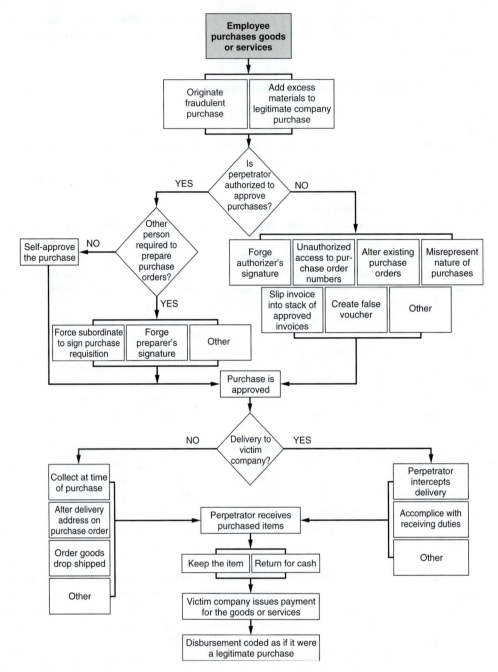

FIGURE 12-3 Invoice Purchasing Schemes

controls pave the way for fraud, but a lack of oversight regarding the purchasing function can allow an employee to take huge chunks out of his company's bottom line.

In some situations, the perpetrator is authorized to approve purchases, but controls prevent him from also initiating purchase requests. This procedure is meant to prevent the kinds of schemes discussed above. Unfortunately, those with authority to approve purchases are often high-level employees with a good deal of control over their subordinates. These persons can use their influence to force subordinates to assist in a purchases scheme. In one case, for example, purchases under $1,000 at a certain utility company could be made with limited-value purchase orders (LPOs), which required two signatures—the originator of a purchase request and the approver of the request. An LPO attached to an invoice for less than $1,000 would be paid by the accounts payable department. In this case, a manager bought goods and services on company accounts, and prepared LPOs for the purchases. (In some cases, the LPO would falsely describe the item to conceal the nature of the purchase.) Once the LPO was prepared, the manager forced a clerk in his department to sign the document as the originator of the transaction. The clerk, intimidated by her

boss, did not question the authenticity of the LPOs. With two signatures affixed, the LPO appeared to be legitimate, and the bills were paid. The scheme cost the victim company at least $25,000.

Falsifying Documents to Obtain Authorization   Not all fraudsters are free to approve their own purchases. Those who cannot must rely on other methods to get their personal bills paid by the company. The chief control document in many vouchers is the purchase order. When an employee wants to buy goods or services, he submits a purchase requisition to a superior. If the purchase requisition is approved, a purchase order is sent to a vendor. A copy of this purchase order, retained in the voucher, tells accounts payable that the transaction has been approved. Later, when an invoice and receiving report corresponding to this purchase order are assembled, accounts payable will issue a check.

Thus, in order to make their purchases appear authentic, some fraudsters generate false purchase orders. For example, in one case an employee forged the signature of a division controller on purchase orders, so the purchase orders appeared to be authentic; the employee was able to buy approximately $3,000 worth of goods at his company's expense. In another instance, a part-time employee at an educational institution obtained unused purchase order numbers and used them to order computer equipment under a fictitious name. The employee then intercepted the equipment as it arrived at the school and loaded the items into his car. Eventually, the employee began using fictitious purchase order numbers instead of real ones. The scheme came to light when the perpetrator inadvertently selected the name of a real vendor. After scrutinizing the documents, the school knew that it had been victimized. In the meantime, the employee had bought nearly $8,000 worth of unnecessary equipment.

Altering Existing Purchase Orders   Purchase orders can also be altered by employees who seek to obtain merchandise at their employer's expense. In one case in the ACFE studies, several individuals conspired to purchase over $2 million worth of materials for their personal use. The ringleader of the scheme was a low-level supervisor who had access to the computer system that controlled the requisition and receipt of materials. This supervisor entered the system and either initiated orders of materials that exceeded the needs of a particular project or altered existing orders to increase the amount of materials being requisitioned. Because the victim organization had poor controls, it did not compare completed work orders on projects to the amount of materials ordered for those projects. This allowed the inflated orders to go undetected. In addition, other employees involved in the scheme were in charge of receiving deliveries. These employees were able to divert the excess materials and falsify receiving reports to conceal the missing items. In addition, the victim institution did not enforce a central delivery point, meaning that employees were allowed to pick up materials from the vendors in their personal vehicles. This made it very easy to misappropriate the excess merchandise. The supervisor's ability to circumvent controls and initiate false orders or alter genuine ones, though, was the real key to the scheme.

False Purchase Requisitions   Another way for an employee to get a false purchase approved is to misrepresent the nature of the purchase. In many companies, those with the power to authorize purchases are not always attentive to their duties. If a trusted subordinate vouches for an acquisition, for instance, busy supervisors often give rubber-stamp approval to purchase requisitions. Additionally, employees sometimes misrepresent the nature of the items they are purchasing in order to pass a cursory review by their superiors. For example, an engineer bought over $30,000 worth of personal items. The engineer dealt directly with vendors and was also in charge of overseeing the receipt of the materials he purchased. He was therefore able to misrepresent the nature of the merchandise he bought, calling it "maintenance items." Vendor invoices were altered to agree to this description.

Of course, the problem with lying about what he is buying is that when delivery occurs, it is the perpetrator's personal items that arrive, not the business items listed on the purchase requisition. In the case discussed above, the problem of detection at this stage of the crime was avoided, because the engineer who made the fraudulent purchases was also in charge of receiving the merchandise. He could therefore falsify receiving reports to perpetuate the fraud. We have also encountered cases in which fraudsters in the purchasing department enlisted the aid of employees in the receiving department to conceal their crimes.

Another way to avoid detection at the delivery stage is to change the delivery address for purchases. Instead of being shipped to the victim company, the items that the employee buys are sent directly to his home or business. In a related scenario, an accounts payable supervisor purchased supplies for her own business by entering vouchers in the accounts payable system of her employer. Checks were cut for the expenses during normal daily check runs. To avoid problems with receiving the unauthorized goods, the perpetrator ordered the supplies from the vendor and had them shipped directly to a client of her side business.

Personal Purchases on Credit Cards or Other Company Accounts Instead of running false invoices through accounts payable, some employees make personal purchases on company credit cards or running accounts with vendors. As with invoicing schemes, the key to getting away with a false credit card purchase is avoiding detection. Unlike invoicing schemes, however, prior approval for purchases is not required. An employee with a company credit card can buy an item merely by signing her name (or forging someone else's) at the time of purchase. Later review of the credit card statement, however, may detect the fraudulent purchase. In invoicing schemes we saw how those who committed the frauds were often in a position to approve their own purchases. The same is often true in credit card schemes. A manager in one case, for example, reviewed and approved his own credit card statements. This allowed him to make fraudulent purchases on the company card for approximately two years.

Of course, only certain employees are authorized to use company credit cards. The manager in the case above, for instance, had his own company card. Employees without this privilege can make fraudulent purchases with a company card only if they first manage to get hold of one. To this end, company cards are sometimes stolen or "borrowed" from authorized users. A more novel approach was used by an accountant, who falsely added her name to a list of employees to whom cards were to be issued. She used her card to make fraudulent purchases, but forged the signatures of authorized cardholders to cover her tracks. Since no one knew she even had a company card, she would not be a prime suspect in the fraud even if someone questioned the purchases. For over five years this employee continued her scheme, racking up a six-figure bill on her employer's account. In addition, she had control of the credit card statement and was able to code her purchases to various expense accounts, thereby further delaying detection of her crime.

An executive secretary in another case used her access to the statement for a different purpose. After making hundreds of thousands of dollars' worth of fraudulent purchases on corporate cards, this employee destroyed both the receipts from her purchases and the monthly credit card statements. Eventually, duplicate statements were requested from the credit card company, and the fraud was discovered. The fact that no statements were received by the company therefore led to detection of the scheme. Some fraudsters, having destroyed the real copies of credit card statements, produce counterfeit copies on which their fraudulent purchases are omitted. By taking this extra step, the fraudster is able to keep his employer in the dark about the true activity on the account.

Charge Accounts Some companies keep charge accounts with vendors with whom they do regular business. Office supply companies are a good example of this kind of vendor. Purchases on charge accounts may require a signature or other form of authorization from a designated company representative. Obviously, that representative is in a position to buy personal items on the company account. Other employees might do the same by forging the signature of an authorized person at the time of a fraudulent purchase. In some informal settings, purchases can be verified by as little as a phone call, making it very easy to make fraudulent purchases.

Returning Merchandise for Cash The cases we have discussed in the fraudulent purchases section to this point have all involved the false purchase of merchandise for the sake of obtaining the merchandise. In some cases, however, the fraudster buys items and then returns them for cash. The best example of this type of scheme in our survey was a case in which an employee made fraudulent gains from a business travel account. The employee began by purchasing tickets for herself and her family through her company's travel budget. Poor separation of duties allowed the fraudster to order the tickets, receive them, prepare claims for payments, and distribute checks. The only review of her activities was made by a busy and rather uninterested supervisor who approved the employee's claims without requiring support documentation. Eventually, the employee's scheme evolved. She began to purchase airline tickets and return them for their cash value. An employee of the travel agency assisted in the scheme by encoding the tickets as though the fraudster had paid for them herself. That caused the airlines to pay refunds directly to the fraudster rather than to her employer. In the course of two years, this employee embezzled over $100,000 through her purchasing scheme.

Preventing and Detecting Personal Purchases on Company Credit Cards The most important step in preventing credit card fraud is conducting thorough reviews of each credit card statement. This duty should be performed by someone independent of those with signature authority on the account. During review, a business purpose should be verified for each listing on the statement, and the person who incurred the expense should be required to provide original support for the expense.

To prevent falsifications of the statement, organizations should direct the credit card issuer to send two copies of the statement to two different individuals within the organization. Both individuals should reconcile the statements separately and then compare the results. To prevent large abuses, it is advisable to establish spending limits for credit card users.

Credit card statements should be compared with employee expense vouchers for duplications, and credit card expenses should be monitored for any unexplained increase in purchasing levels. Excess purchases can be traced to a particular cardholder and that person can be interviewed to determine the reason for the increase.

Proactive Computer Audit Tests for Detecting Billing Schemes

Title	Category	Description	Data file(s)
Perform a trend analysis of vendor payments.	All	Special note should be given to vendors that had minimal purchases in prior periods, yet have large payments in current periods.	• Invoice Payment
Identify duplicate payments based on various means.	All	Duplicate payment tests can be enacted on the vendor, invoice number, and amount. More complicated tests can look for instances in which the same invoice and amount are paid, yet the payment is made to two different vendors. Another advanced test would be to search for same vendor and invoice when a different amount is paid.	• Invoice Payment
Summarize debit memos by vendor, issuer, and type.	All	Debit memo trends that appear unusual should be investigated as attempts to cover unauthorized payments.	• Invoice Payment
Summarize accounts payable activity by general ledger account, sort from high to low, and review for reasonableness.	All	Expense account trends that appear unusual should be investigated as attempts to cover unauthorized payments.	• Invoice Payment • General Ledger Distribution
Extract manual checks and summarize by vendor and issuer.	All	Manual checks are more prone to abuse and therefore should be scrutinized, especially if a particular issuer is drafting the majority of manual checks.	• Check Register
Extract all purchases with no purchase orders and summarize by vendor and issuer.	All	Purchases with no purchase orders are more prone to abuse and therefore should be scrutinized, especially if a particular issuer is drafting the majority of payments without purchase orders.	• Invoice Payment
Extract all round-dollar payments.	All	Round-dollar payments have a higher likelihood of being fabricated and, therefore, fraudulent.	• Invoice Payment
Calculate the ratio of the largest purchase to next-largest purchase by vendor.	All	By identifying the largest purchase to a vendor and the next-largest purchase, any large ratio difference may identify a fraudulently issued "largest" check.	• Invoice Payment
Compare check register to invoice payment file to identify any checks with no related system invoices.	Shell company	Check payments that do not appear on the invoice register may be an attempt to hide unauthorized payments.	• Invoice Payment • Check Register

(Continued)

(*Continued*)

Title	Category	Description	Data file(s)
Match vendor master file to the accounts payable invoice file.	Shell company	Identify payments to a potentially unapproved vendor by joining the vendor to the invoice file on vendor number. The joining of these two files should be done in an "unmatched" format so that only those vendor numbers in the invoice file not appearing in the vendor file are shown.	• Vendor Master • Invoice Payment
Extract vendors with no telephone or tax ID number.	Shell company	Vendors without this information are more prone to abuse and should be scrutinized.	• Vendor Master
Identify vendors added during the period under review.	Shell company	The issuers of new vendor additions should be reviewed using this report to determine whether a particular issuer is drafting the majority of vendor additions.	• Vendor Master
List all vendors with an address that is not designated as a business address.	Shell company	The identification of whether an address is legitimately a business one can be done through some software databases.	• Vendor Master
List all vendors who had multiple invoices immediately below an approval limit (e.g., many $999 payments to a vendor when there is a $1,000 approval limit), highlighting a circumvention of the established control.	Shell company	Invoices below an approval limit may be an attempt to circumvent a management review.	• Invoice Payment
Match the vendor master file to the employee master file on various key fields.	Shell company	Compare telephone number, address, tax ID numbers, numbers in the address, ZIP code, and post office box in vendor file to employee file, especially those employees working in the accounts payable department.	• Vendor Master • Employee Master
Review payments with little or no sequence between invoice numbers.	Shell company	Employees developing shell companies many times will invoice the company with no gaps in invoice sequence, highlighting that the victim company is the shell company's only customer.	• Invoice Payment
List payments to any vendor that exceed the twelve-month average payments to that vendor by a specified percentage (i.e., 200 percent).	Shell company and non-accomplice vendor	Large payments are unusual and should be scrutinized as being potentially fraudulent.	• Invoice Payment
Extract vendor payments where the payment is a specified percentage (i.e., 200 percent) greater than the last largest payment to that vendor.	Shell company and non-accomplice vendor	Large payments are unusual and should be scrutinized as being potentially fraudulent.	• Invoice Payment
Sample vendor open invoices for confirmation with vendor.	Nonaccomplice vendor	Vendor invoices may remain open on the subledger when the vendor believes such invoices have been paid.	• Invoice Payment
Extract SIC codes from credit card payments normally associated with personal purchases.	Personal purchases	Personal purchases with company cards may be a sign of abuse.	• Procurement Card

Title	Category	Description	Data file(s)
Extract multiple charges of the same product type (using SIC code) below a predefined credit card expense limit.	Personal purchases	Charges below an approval limit may be an attempt to circumvent a management review.	• Procurement Card
Summarize credit card use by employee and sort from high to low.	Personal purchases	High usage of credit cards by certain employees may be a sign of abuse.	• Procurement Card
List all vendors with a billing address that is different from their delivery address.	Personal purchases	Company purchases sent to a different delivery address from where they are paid may signal personal purchases made on account of the company.	• Vendor Master
Extract all delivery addresses that do not correspond to company locations.	Personal purchases	Company purchases should normally be sent to known company locations. Shipments to other locations are a potential sign of fraud.	• Vendor Master

CHECK TAMPERING SCHEMES

Check tampering is unique among fraudulent disbursements because it is the one group of schemes in which the perpetrator physically prepares the fraudulent check. In most fraudulent disbursement schemes, the culprit generates a payment to himself by submitting some false document to the victim company such as an invoice or a timecard. The false document represents a claim for payment and causes the victim company to issue a check that the perpetrator then converts. These frauds essentially amount to trickery; the perpetrator fools the company into handing over its money.

Check tampering schemes are fundamentally different. In these frauds, the perpetrator takes physical control of a check and makes it payable to himself through one of several methods. Check tampering schemes depend on factors such as access to the company checkbook, access to bank statements, and the ability to forge signatures or alter other information on the face of the check. There are five principal methods used to commit check tampering:

1. Forged maker schemes
2. Forged endorsement schemes
3. Altered payee schemes
4. Concealed check schemes
5. Authorized maker schemes

Forged Maker Schemes

The legal definition of forgery includes not only the signing of another person's name to a document (such as a check) with a fraudulent intent, but also the fraudulent alteration of a genuine instrument. This definition is so broad that it would encompass all check tampering schemes, so we have narrowed the term to fit our needs. Because we are interested in distinguishing the various methods used by individuals to tamper with checks, we will constrain the concept of "forgeries" to those cases in which an individual signs another person's name on a check.

The person who signs a check is known as the "maker" of the check. A forged maker scheme, then, may be defined as a check tampering scheme in which an employee misappropriates a check and fraudulently affixes the signature of an authorized maker thereon (see Figure 12-4). Frauds that involve other types of check tampering, such as the alteration of the payee or the changing of the dollar amount, are classified separately.

As one might expect, forged check schemes are usually committed by employees who lack signature authority on company accounts. In order to forge a check, an employee must have access to a blank check, he must be able to produce a convincing forgery of an authorized signature, and he must be able to conceal

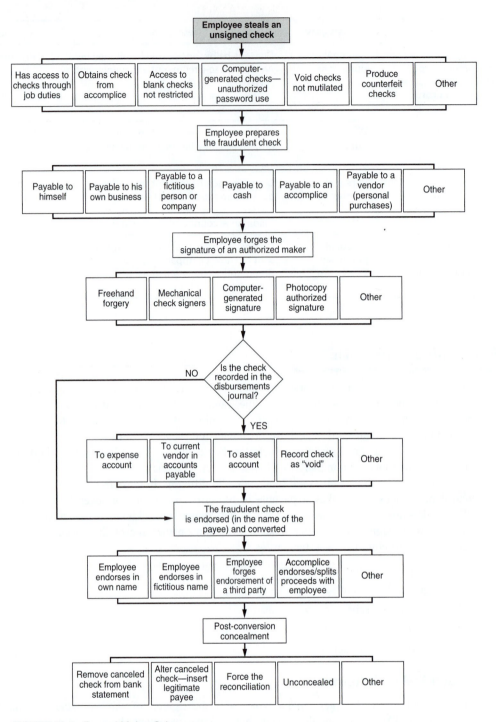

FIGURE 12-4 Forged Maker Schemes

his crime. If the fraudster cannot hide his crime from his employer, his scheme is sure to be short-lived. Concealment is a universal problem in check tampering schemes; the methods used are basically the same for all categories of check tampering. Therefore, concealment issues will be discussed as a group at the end of the chapter.

Obtaining the Check

Employees with Access to Company Checks One cannot forge a company check unless one first possesses a company check. The first hurdle that a fraudster must overcome in committing a forgery scheme is to figure out how to get his hands on a blank check. Most forgery schemes are committed by accounts payable clerks, office managers, bookkeepers, or other employees whose duties typically include the preparation of company checks. These are people who have access to a company's check stock on

a regular basis and are therefore in the best position to steal blank checks. If an employee spends his workday preparing checks on behalf of his company, and if that employee has some personal financial difficulty, it takes only a small leap in logic (and a big leap in ethics) to see that his financial troubles can be solved by writing fraudulent checks for his own benefit. Time and again we see that employees tailor their fraud to the circumstances of their jobs. It stands to reason that those who work around the checkbook would be prone to committing forgery schemes.

Employees Lacking Access to Company Checks   If the perpetrator does not have access to the check stock through her work duties, she will have to find other means of misappropriating a check. The way a person steals a check depends largely on how blank checks are handled within a particular company. In some circumstances checks are poorly guarded, left in unattended areas where anyone can get to them. In other companies the checkbook may be kept in a restricted area, but the perpetrator may have obtained a key or combination to this area, or may know where an employee with access to the checks keeps his own copy of the key or combination. An accomplice may provide blank checks for the fraudster in return for a portion of the stolen funds. Perhaps a secretary sees the checkbook left on a manager's desk or a custodian comes across blank checks in an unlocked desk drawer.

In some companies, checks are computer generated. When this is the case, an employee who knows the password that allows checks to be prepared and issued may be able to obtain as many unsigned checks as he desires. There are an unlimited number of ways to steal a check, each dependent upon the way in which a particular company guards its blank checks.

A fraudster may also be able to obtain a blank check when the company fails to properly dispose of unused checks. In one case, for example, a company used voided checks to line up the printer that ran payroll checks. These voided checks were not mutilated. A payroll clerk collected the voided checks after the printer was aligned and used them to issue herself extra disbursements through the payroll account.

Producing Counterfeit Checks   In more sophisticated forgery schemes, the perpetrator may produce counterfeit check stock with the organization's bank account number on the counterfeit checks. These counterfeit checks can be practically indistinguishable from the company's legitimate stock. In another case, for example, the perpetrator had an accomplice who worked for a professional check-printing company and who printed blank checks for the bank account of the perpetrator's employer. The perpetrator then wrote over $100,000 worth of forgeries on these counterfeit checks.

Safeguarding the Organization's Check Stock   Organizations should take steps to safeguard their check stock and proactively seek out stolen and forged checks. These goals can be achieved through a number of relatively simple prevention and detection techniques that may avert a very large fraud scheme.

Obviously, blank checks should be maintained under lock and key, and access should be strictly limited to those whose duties include check preparation. (If checks are computer-generated, access to the code or password that allows issuance of checks should likewise be restricted.) Boxes of blank checks should be sealed with security tape to make it obvious when a new box has been opened, and on a periodic basis, someone independent of the check preparation function should verify the security of unused checks. Organizations should also promptly destroy any voided checks. These checks, if carelessly discarded, may be stolen and forged by employees.

The type of paper a check is printed on can sometimes help distinguish a legitimate check from a counterfeit. Organizations should print their checks on watermark paper supplied by a company independent of its check printer. (This will prevent a dishonest employee of the printer from using the company's watermarked paper.) Security threads or other markers can also be incorporated to help verify that company checks are legitimate. If an organization uses high-quality, distinctly marked paper for its checks, counterfeits will be easier to detect. In addition, it is a good idea to periodically rotate check printers and/or check stock to help make counterfeits stand out.

There are certain indicators that organizations can look for to help spot stolen or forged checks. Obviously, as stated above, if checks are noticed missing or there are signs of tampering with unused check stock, this is a clear indicator of theft. In addition, out-of-sequence checks or duplicate check numbers that show up on an organization's bank statement may signal theft. When employees steal blank checks, they will often take them from the bottom of the box with the hope that the missing check will not be noticed for some time. When these checks are converted, they should be noted as out-of-sequence on the bank statement. Employees who reconcile the statement should be trained to look for this red flag.

Similarly, counterfeit checks often have numbers that are completely out of sequence or that duplicate numbers of checks that were already issued.

Employees who steal blank checks often do so after hours, because there are fewer people around to witness the theft. As a matter of practice, at the start of each business day, organizations should reconcile the first check in the checkbook to the last check written on the previous day. If there is a gap, it should be promptly investigated.

To Whom Is the Check Made Payable?

Payable to the Perpetrator   Once a blank check has been obtained, the fraudster must decide to whom it should be made payable. He can write the check to anyone, although in most instances forged checks are payable to the perpetrator himself so that they are easier to convert. A check made payable to a third person, or to a fictitious person or business, may be difficult to convert without false identification. The tendency to make forged checks payable to oneself seems to be a result of fraudsters' laziness rather than a decision based on the successful operation of their schemes. Checks payable to an employee are obviously more likely to be recognized as fraudulent as compared to checks made out to other persons or entities.

If the fraudster owns his own business or has established a shell company, he will usually write fraudulent checks to these entities rather than himself. When the payee on a forged check is a "vendor" rather than an employee of the victim company, the checks are not as obviously fraudulent on their faces. At the same time, these checks are easy to convert, because the fraudster owns the entity to which the checks are payable.

Payable to an Accomplice   If a fraudster is working with an accomplice, she can make the forged check payable to that person. The accomplice then cashes the check and splits the money with the employee-fraudster. Because the check is payable to the accomplice in her true identity, it is easily converted. An additional benefit to using an accomplice is that a canceled check payable to a third-party accomplice is not as likely to raise suspicion as a canceled check to an employee. The obvious drawback to using an accomplice in a scheme is that the employee-fraudster usually has to share the proceeds of the scheme.

In some circumstances, however, the accomplice may be unaware that she is involved in a fraud. An example of how this can occur was found in a case in which a bookkeeper wrote several fraudulent checks on company accounts, and then convinced a friend to allow her to deposit the checks in the friend's account. The fraudster claimed the money was revenue from a side business she owned and that the subterfuge was necessary to prevent creditors from seizing the funds. After the checks were deposited, the friend withdrew the money and gave it to the fraudster.

Payable to "Cash"   The fraudster may also write checks payable to "cash" in order to avoid listing himself as the payee. Checks made payable to cash, however, must still be endorsed. The fraudster will have to sign his own name or forge the name of another in order to convert the check. In addition, checks payable to "cash" are usually viewed more skeptically than checks payable to persons or businesses.

Payable to a Vendor   The employee who forges company checks may do so not to obtain currency, but to purchase goods or services for his own benefit. When this is the case, forged checks are made payable to third-party vendors—such as airlines or hotels—that are uninvolved in the fraud.

Forging the Signature

After the employee has obtained and prepared a blank check, he must forge an authorized signature in order to convert the check. The most obvious method, and the one that comes to mind when we think of the word *forgery*, is to simply take pen in hand and sign the name of an authorized maker.

Free-Hand Forgery   The difficulty a fraudster encounters when physically signing the authorized maker's name is in creating a reasonable approximation of the true signature. If the forgery appears authentic, the perpetrator will probably have no problem cashing the check. In truth, the forged signature may not have to be particularly accurate. Many organizations do not verify the signatures on cancelled checks when they reconcile their bank statements, so even a poorly forged signature may go unnoticed.

Photocopied Forgeries   To guarantee an accurate forgery, some employees make photocopies of legitimate signatures and affix them to company checks. The fraudster is thus assured that the signature appears authentic. This method was used by a bookkeeper in one case to steal over $100,000 from

her employer. Using her boss's business correspondence and the company Xerox machine, she made transparencies of his signature. These transparencies were then placed in the copy machine so that when she ran checks through the machine the boss's signature was copied onto the maker line of the check. The bookkeeper now had a signed check in hand. She made the fraudulent checks payable to herself, but falsified the check register so that the checks appeared to have been written to legitimate payees.

Automatic Check-Signing Instruments Companies that issue a large number of checks sometimes utilize automatic check-signing instruments in lieu of signing each check by hand. Automated signatures are either produced with manual instruments like signature stamps or are printed by computer. Obviously, a fraudster who gains access to an automatic check-signing instrument will have no trouble forging the signatures of authorized makers. Even the most rudimentary control procedures should severely limit access to these instruments. Nevertheless, several of the forged maker schemes the ACFE reviewed were accomplished through the use of a signature stamp. In one case, for instance, a fiscal officer maintained a set of manual checks that were unknown to other persons in the company. The company used an automated check signer, and the custodian of the signer let the officer have uncontrolled access to it. Using the manual checks and the company's check signer, the fiscal officer was able to write over $90,000 worth of fraudulent checks to himself over a period of approximately four years.

The same principle applies to computer-generated signatures. Access to the password or program that prints signed checks should be restricted, specifically excluding those who prepare checks and those who reconcile the bank statement. The fraudster in another case, for example, was in charge of preparing checks. The fraudster managed to obtain the issuance password from her boss, then used this password to issue checks to a company she owned on the side. She was able to bilk her employer out of approximately $100,000 using this method.

The beauty of automated check signers, from the fraudster's perspective, is that they produce perfect forgeries. Nothing about the physical appearance of the check will indicate that it is fraudulent. Of course, forged checks are written for illegitimate purposes, so they may be detectable when the bank statement is reconciled or when accounts are reviewed. The ways in which fraudsters avoid detection through these measures will be discussed later in this chapter.

Preventing and Detecting Forged Maker Schemes Obviously, a key to preventing forgeries is to maintain a strict set of procedures for the handling of outgoing checks, which includes safeguarding blank check stock, establishing rules for custody of checks that have been prepared but not signed, and separating the duties of check preparation and check signing. Organizations should establish a restrictive list of authorized check signers and see to it that checks that have been prepared are safeguarded until they are presented to these signatories.

To the extent possible, organizations should rotate authorized check signers and keep track of who is approved to sign checks during a given period. Rotating this duty can help prevent abuse by an authorized signatory, but also, if a canceled check shows a signature from the wrong signer for the date of the disbursement, this could indicate fraud. Also, on a periodic basis an organization should have authorized check signers verify their signatures on returned checks or another employee should be required to spot-check signatures against an established signature file.

In organizations that use a signature stamp, access to the stamp should be strictly limited, and a custodian should maintain a log of who uses the signature stamp, and at what time. If it is suspected that someone is misusing the signature stamp, temporarily suspend use of the stamp and instruct the bank to honor only checks with original signatures.

Miscoding Fraudulent Checks Miscoding a check is actually a form of concealment, a means of hiding the fraudulent nature of the check. We will discuss the ways fraudsters code their forged checks in the concealment section at the end of this chapter. It should be noted here, however, that miscoding is typically used as a concealment method only by those employees with access to the checkbook. If a forged maker scheme is undertaken by an employee without access to the checkbook, she usually makes no entry whatsoever in the disbursements journal.

Converting the Check In order to convert the forged check, the perpetrator must endorse it. The endorsement is typically made in the name of the payee on the check. Since identification is generally required when one seeks to convert a check, the fraudster usually needs fake identification if he forges

checks to real or fictitious third persons. As discussed earlier, checks payable to "cash" require the endorsement of the person converting them. Without fake ID, the fraudster will likely have to endorse these checks in his own name. Obviously, an employee's endorsement on a canceled check is a red flag.

Forged Endorsement Schemes

Forged endorsement frauds are those check tampering schemes in which an employee intercepts a company check intended for a third party and converts the check by signing the third party's name on the endorsement line of the check (see Figure 12-5). In some instances the fraudster also signs his own name as a second endorser. The term *forged endorsement schemes* would seem to imply that these frauds should be categorized along with the forged maker schemes discussed in the previous section. It is true that both kinds of fraud involve the false signing of another person's name on a check, but there are certain distinctions that cause forged endorsement schemes to be categorized here rather than with the other forgeries.

In classifying fraud types, we look to the heart of the scheme. What is the crucial point in the commission of the crime? In a forged maker scheme, the perpetrator is normally working with a blank check. The trick to this kind of scheme is in gaining access to blank checks and producing a signature that appears authentic.

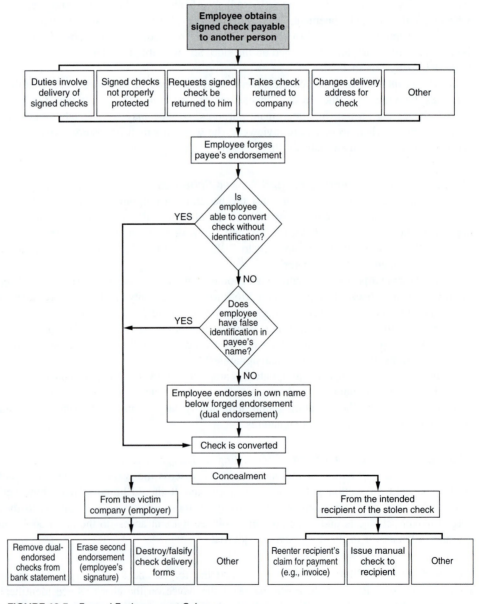

FIGURE 12-5 Forged Endorsement Schemes

In a forged endorsement scheme, on the other hand, the perpetrator is tampering with a check that has already been written, so the issues involved in the fraud are different. The key to these schemes is obtaining the checks after they are signed but before they are properly delivered. If this is accomplished, the actual forging of the endorsement is somewhat secondary.

A fraudster's main dilemma in a forged endorsement case is gaining access to a check after it has been written and signed. The fraudster must either steal the check between the point where it is signed and the point where it is delivered, or he must reroute the check, causing it to be mailed to a location where he can retrieve it. The manner used to steal a check depends largely on the way the company handles outgoing disbursements. Anyone who is allowed to handle signed checks may be in a good position to intercept them.

Intercepting Checks before Delivery

Employees Involved in Delivery of Checks   Obviously, the employees in the best position to intercept signed checks are those whose duties include the handling and delivery of signed checks. The most obvious example would be a mailroom employee who opens outgoing mail containing signed checks and steals the checks. Other personnel with access to outgoing checks might include accounts payable employees, payroll clerks, secretaries, and so forth.

Poor Control of Signed Checks   Unfortunately, fraudsters are often able to intercept signed checks because of poor internal controls. For instance, in one case, signed checks were left overnight on the desks of some employees, because processing on the checks was not complete. One of the janitors on the overnight cleaning crew found these checks and took them, forged the endorsements of the payees, and cashed them at a liquor store. Another example of poor observance of internal controls appeared in a case in which a high-level manager with authority to disburse employee benefits instructed accounts payable personnel to return signed benefits checks to him instead of immediately delivering them to their intended recipients. These instructions were not questioned despite the fact that they presented a clear violation of the separation-of-duties concept due to the manager's level of authority within the company. The perpetrator simply took the checks that were returned to him and deposited them into his personal bank account, forging the endorsements of the intended payees.

This case represents what seems to be the most common breakdown of controls in forged endorsement frauds. We have seen repeated occurrences of signed checks being returned to the employee who prepared the check. This typically occurs when a supervisor signs a check and hands it back to the clerk or secretary who presented it to the supervisor; it is done either through negligence or because the employee is highly trusted and thought to be above theft. Adequate internal controls should prevent the person who prepares company disbursements from having access to signed checks. This separation of duties is elemental; its purpose is to break the disbursement chain so that no one person controls the entire payment process.

Theft of Returned Checks   Another way to obtain signed checks is to steal checks that have been mailed but that have been returned to the victim company for some reason, such as an incorrect address. Employees with access to incoming mail may be able to intercept these returned checks from the mail and convert them by forging the endorsement of the intended payee. In one case, for example, a manager took and converted approximately $130,000 worth of checks that were returned due to noncurrent addresses. (He also stole outgoing checks, cashed them, and then declared them lost.) The fraudster was well known at his bank and was able to convert the checks by claiming that he was doing it as a favor to the real payees, who were "too busy to come to the bank." The fraudster was able to continue with his scheme because the nature of his company's business was such that the recipients of the misdelivered checks were often not aware that the victim company owed them money. Therefore, they did not complain when their checks failed to arrive. In addition, the perpetrator had complete control over the bank reconciliation, so he could issue new checks to those payees who did complain, then "force" the reconciliation, making it appear that the bank balance and book balance matched when in fact they did not. Stealing returned checks is obviously not as common as other methods for intercepting checks, and it is more difficult for a fraudster to plan and carry out on a long-term basis. However, it is also very difficult to detect and can lead to large-scale fraud.

Rerouting the Delivery of Checks   The other way an employee can go about misappropriating a signed check is to alter the address to which the check is to be mailed. The check either is delivered to a place where the fraudster can retrieve it, or is purposely misaddressed so that he can steal it when

it is returned, as discussed above. As we have said before, proper separation of duties should preclude anyone who prepares disbursements from being involved in their delivery. Nevertheless, this control is often overlooked, allowing the person who prepares a check to address and mail it as well.

In some instances in which proper controls are in place, fraudsters are still able to cause the misdelivery of checks. In one case, for instance, the fraudster was a clerk in the customer service department of a mortgage company where her duties included changing the mailing addresses of property owners. She was assigned a password that gave her access to make address changes. The clerk was transferred to a new department where one of her duties was the issuance of checks to property owners. Unfortunately, her supervisor forgot to cancel her old password. When the clerk realized this oversight, she began to request checks for certain property owners, then sign onto the system with her old password and change the addresses of those property owners. The check would be sent to her. The next day, the employee used her old password to reenter the system and reinstate the proper address so that there would be no record of where the check had been sent. This fraudster's scheme resulted in a loss of over $250,000 to the victim company.

Converting the Stolen Check

Once the check has been intercepted, the perpetrator can cash it by forging the payee's signature, hence the term *forged endorsement scheme*. Depending on where he tries to cash the check, the perpetrator may or may not need fake identification at this stage. As we alluded to earlier, many fraudsters cash their stolen checks at places where they are not required to show an ID.

If a fraudster is required to show identification in order to cash his stolen check, and if he does not have a fake ID in the payee's name, he may use a dual endorsement to cash or deposit the check. In other words, the fraudster forges the payee's signature as though the payee had transferred the check to him, then the fraudster endorses the check in his own name and converts it. When the bank statement is reconciled, double endorsements on checks should always raise suspicions, particularly when the second signer is an employee of the company.

Preventing and Detecting the Theft of Outgoing Company Checks

It is very important that the functions of cutting, signing, and delivering checks be separated. If a check preparer is also allowed to have custody of signed checks, it is easy to commit check tampering. The individual can draft a check for a fraudulent purpose, wait for it to be signed, and simply pocket it. However, if the individual knows he or she will not see the check again after it has been signed, then that person is less likely to attempt this kind of scheme, because of the diminished perceived opportunity for success.

In addition to establishing controls designed to prevent the theft of outgoing checks, organizations should train their employees to look for this kind of scheme and should establish routine procedures designed to help detect it if and when it does occur. These proactive detection techniques are generally not very complicated and do not require sophisticated procedures or investigative methods; all that is required is that an organization devote a minimal amount of time to routinely checking for thefts.

If an employee steals a check payable to a vendor and does not issue a replacement, the vendor will almost certainly complain about the nonpayment. This is the point at which most forged endorsement schemes should be detected. Every organization should have a structure in place to handle both vendor and customer complaints. All complaints should be investigated by someone independent of the payables function so that the fraudster will not be able to cover his or her own tracks. When a complaint regarding nonpayment is received, it should be a relatively simple matter to track the missing check and identify when it was converted, and by whom. As a proactive measure, it may be advisable—particularly in organizations where check theft has been a problem—to have independent personnel randomly contact vendors to confirm receipt of payments.

As was previously discussed, some employees who steal outgoing checks will cause a replacement check to be issued so that the vendor will not complain. In order to detect these schemes, an organization's accounting system should be set up to detect duplicate payments. Paid vouchers should immediately be stamped "paid," and computerized systems should automatically flag duplicate invoice numbers. In addition, payables reports sorted by payee and amount should be periodically generated in order to detect duplicates when invoice numbers have been altered for the second check.

Instead of stealing checks on the company premises, some employees will cause them to be misdelivered by changing the mailing address of the intended recipient in the organization's payables system. For this reason, authority to make changes to vendor records should be restricted, and the organization's accounting system should automatically track who makes changes to vendor records. This will make it easier to identify the perpetrator if an outgoing check is stolen. Periodically, a report listing all changes to

vendor addresses, payment amounts, payees, and so on can be generated to check for an inordinate amount of changes, especially those in which a vendor's address is temporarily changed when a check is issued, then restored after the check has been mailed.

To convert an intercepted check, the perpetrator may have to use a dual endorsement. Any canceled checks with more than one endorsement should be investigated, as should any nonpayroll check that an employee has endorsed. The employee or employees reconciling the bank statement should be required to review the backs of canceled checks for suspicious endorsements as a matter of course.

Another procedure that all organizations should have in place is to chart the date of mailing for every outgoing check. In the event that a signed check is stolen, the date of mailing can be compared to work records of mailroom personnel and other employees who have contact with outgoing checks to determine a list of possible suspects.

Finally, organizations should consider installing surveillance cameras in their mailrooms. Mailroom personnel are in a good position to steal outgoing checks and to skim incoming revenues or merchandise shipments. If a theft is discovered, security camera tapes may help identify the wrongdoer. More important, the presence of surveillance cameras can help deter employees from stealing.

Altered Payee Schemes

The second type of intercepted check scheme is the altered payee scheme. This is a type of check tampering fraud in which an employee intercepts a company check intended for a third party and alters the payee designation so that the check can be converted by the employee or an accomplice (see Figure 12-6). The fraudster inserts his own name, the name of a fictitious entity, or some other name on the payee line of the check. Altering the payee designation eliminates many of the problems associated with converting the check that would be encountered in a forged endorsement fraud. The alteration essentially makes the check payable to the fraudster (or an accomplice), so there is no need to forge an endorsement and no need to obtain false identification. The fraudster or his accomplice can endorse the check in his own name and convert it.

Of course, if canceled checks are reviewed during reconciliation of the bank statement, a check made payable to an employee is likely to cause suspicion, especially if the alteration to the payee designation is obvious. This is the main obstacle that must be overcome by fraudsters in altered payee schemes.

Altering Checks Prepared by Others: Inserting a New Payee The method used to alter the payee designation on a check depends largely on how that check is prepared and intercepted. (Incidentally, the amount of the check may also be altered at the same time, and by the same method as the payee designation.) Checks prepared by others can be intercepted by any of the methods discussed in the forged endorsements section above. When the fraudster intercepts a check that has been prepared by someone else, there are basically two methods that may be employed. The first is to insert the false payee's name in place of the true payee's. This is usually done by rather unsophisticated means. The true name might be scratched out with a pen or covered up with correction fluid. Another name is then entered on the payee designation. These kinds of alterations are usually simple to detect.

A more intricate method occurs when the perpetrator of the fraud enters the accounts payable system and changes the names of payees. An accounts payable employee in one case was so trusted that her manager allowed her to use his computer password in his absence. The password permitted access to the accounts payable address file. This employee waited until the manager was absent, and then selected a legitimate vendor with whom her company did a lot of business. She held up the vendor's invoices for the day, and after work used the manager's log-on code to change the vendor name and address to that of a fictitious company. The new name and address were run through the accounts payable cycle with an old invoice number, causing a fraudulent check to be issued. The victim company had an automated duplicate invoice test, but the fraudster circumvented it by substituting "1" for I and "0" (zero) for capital O. The next day, the employee replaced the true vendor's name and address, and mutilated the check register so that the check payable to the fictitious vendor was concealed. Approximately $300,000 in false checks was issued using this method.

Altering Checks Prepared by Others: "Tacking On" The other method that can be used by fraudsters to alter checks prepared by others is "tacking on" additional letters or words to the end of the real payee designation. This rather unusual approach to check tampering occurred in a case in which an employee took checks payable to "ABC" company and altered them to read "A.B.Collins." She then

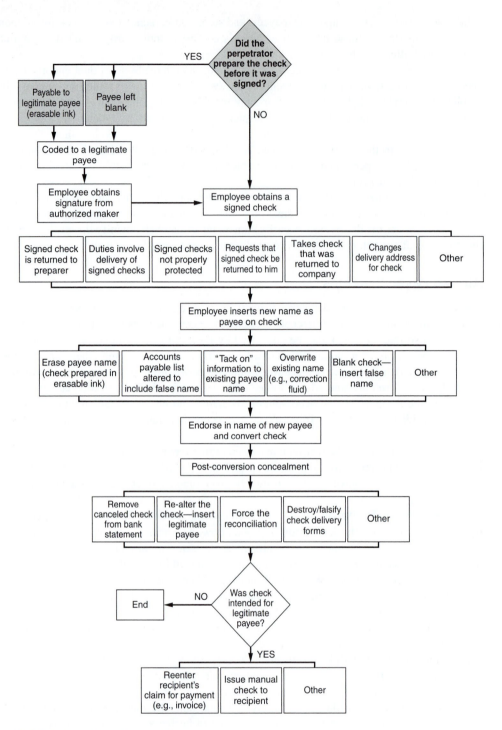

FIGURE 12-6   Altered Payee Schemes

deposited these checks in an account that had been established in the name of A.B. Collins. The simple inclusion of a filler line after the payee designation would have prevented the loss of over $60,000 in this case. In addition to altering the payee designation, the amount of the check can be altered by tacking on extra numbers if the person preparing the check is careless and leaves space for extra numbers in the "amount" portion of the check.

Altering Checks Prepared by the Fraudster: Erasable Ink   When the fraudster prepares the check that is to be altered, the schemes tend to be a bit more sophisticated. The reason for this is obvious: when the perpetrator is able to prepare the check himself, he can prepare it with the thought of how the payee

designation will be altered. But if the perpetrator is preparing the check, why not make the check payable to himself or an accomplice to begin with? In order to get an authorized maker to sign the check, the fraudster must make it appear that the check is made out to a legitimate payee. Only after a legitimate signature is obtained does the fraudster in an altered payee scheme set about tampering with the check.

One of the most common ways to prepare a check for alteration is to write or type the payee's name (and possibly the amount) in erasable ink. After the check is signed by an authorized maker, the perpetrator retrieves the check, erases the payee's name, and inserts his own. One example of this type of fraud was found in which a bookkeeper typed out small checks to a local supplier and had the owner of the company sign them. The bookkeeper then used her erasing typewriter to lift the payee designation and amount from the check. She entered her own name as the payee and raised the amount precipitously. For instance, the owner might sign a $10 check that later became a $10,000 check. These checks were entered in the disbursements journal as payments for aggregate inventory to the company's largest supplier, who received several large checks each month. The bookkeeper stole over $300,000 from her employer in this scheme. The same type of fraud can be undertaken using an erasable pen. In some cases fraudsters have even obtained signatures on checks written in pencil.

We have already discussed how with a proper separation of duties, a person who prepares a check should not be permitted to handle the check after it has been signed. Nevertheless, this is exactly what happens in most altered payee schemes. When fraudsters prepare checks with the intent of altering them later, those fraudsters obviously have a plan for re-obtaining the checks once they have been signed. Usually, the fraudster knows that there is no effective separation of controls in place. He knows that the maker of the check will return it to him.

Altering Checks Prepared by the Fraudster: Blank Checks The most egregious example of poor controls in the handling of signed checks is one in which the perpetrator prepares a check, leaves the payee designation blank, and submits it to an authorized maker, who signs the check and returns it to the employee. Obviously, it is quite easy for the fraudster to designate himself or an accomplice as the payee when this line has been left blank. Common sense tells us that one should not give a signed, blank check to another person. Nevertheless, this happened in several cases in our study, usually when the fraudster was a long-time, trusted employee. In one case, for example, an employee gained the confidence of the owner of his company, whom he convinced to sign blank checks for office use while the owner was out of town. The employee then filled in his own name as the payee on one of the checks, cashed it, and altered the check when it was returned, along with the bank statement. The owner's blind trust in his employee cost him nearly $200,000.

Converting Altered Checks As with all other types of fraudulent checks, conversion is accomplished by endorsing the checks in the name of the payee. Conversion of fraudulent checks has already been discussed in previous sections and will not be reexamined here.

Preventing and Detecting the Alteration of Company Checks Most successful altered payee schemes occur when the person who prepares checks also has access to those checks after they have been signed. As with all forms of check tampering, altered payee schemes can usually be prevented by separating the duties of check preparation, signing, and delivery. It is also critical that the duty of reconciling the bank statement be separated from other check-preparation functions. Altered payee schemes should be very simple to detect during reconciliation, simply because the name or amount on the fraudulent check will not match the entry in the books or the support for the check. In almost all successful altered payee schemes, the perpetrator was able to prepare checks and reconcile the bank statement.

In addition to diligently matching all bank statement items to canceled checks, organizations might consider the use of carbon copy checks. Even if these instruments are altered after they have been cut, the copy will still reflect the intended payee and amount. Another simple method is to require that all checks be drafted in permanent ink to prevent schemes in which the payee and amount are erased and rewritten after a check is signed.

Concealed Check Schemes

Another scheme that requires a significant breakdown in controls and common sense is the concealed check scheme. These are check tampering frauds in which an employee prepares a fraudulent check and submits it along with legitimate checks to an authorized maker who signs it without a proper review (see

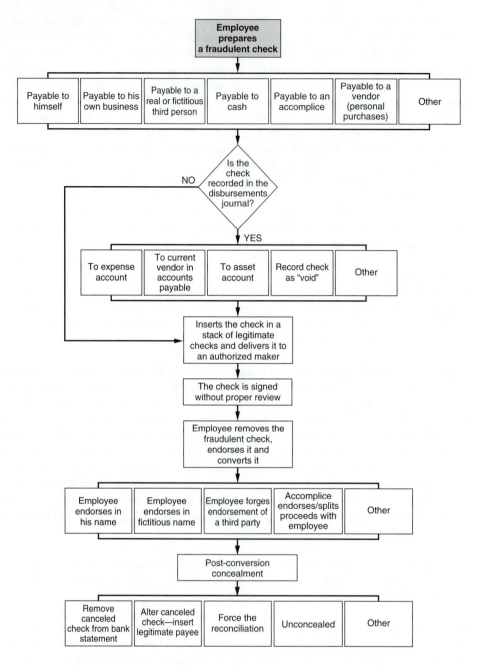

FIGURE 12-7   Concealed Check Schemes

Figure 12-7). Although not nearly as common as the other check tampering methods, it is worth mentioning for its simplicity, its uniqueness, and the ease with which it could be prevented.

The perpetrator of a concealed check scheme is almost always a person responsible for preparing checks. The steps involved in a concealed check scheme are similar to those in a forged maker scheme, except for the way in which the employee gets the fraudulent check signed. These schemes work as follows: The perpetrator prepares a check made out to himself, an accomplice, a fictitious person, and so on. Instead of forging the signature of an authorized maker, the employee takes the check to the authorized maker, usually concealed in a stack of legitimate checks awaiting signatures. The checks are typically delivered to the signer during a busy time of day, when he is rushed and will be less likely to pay close attention to them. Generally, the checks are fanned out on the signer's desk so that the signature lines are exposed but the names of the payees are concealed. If a particular authorized maker is known to be inattentive, the checks are given to him.

The maker signs the checks quickly and without adequate review. Because he is busy or generally inattentive or both, he simply does not look at what he is signing. He does not demand to see supporting documentation for the checks, and does nothing to verify their legitimacy. Once the checks have been signed they are returned to the employee, who removes his check and converts it. This appears to be one of the methods used by Ernie Philips in a case study later in this chapter. Philips slipped several checks payable to himself into a stack of company checks, then took them to the operations manager, who was designated to sign checks when the business's owner was out of town. The operations manager apparently did not check the names of the payees and unknowingly signed several company checks to Philips.

A similar example of the concealed check method took place in a case where a bookkeeper took advantage of the owner of her company by inserting checks payable to herself into batches of checks given to the owner for signature. The owner simply never looked at whom he was paying when he signed the checks.

The perpetrator of a concealed check scheme banks on the inattentiveness of the check signer. If the signer were to review the checks he was signing, he would certainly discover the fraud. It should be noted that the fraudster in these cases could make the fraudulent check payable to an accomplice, a fictitious person, or a fictitious business instead of payable to himself. This is more common and certainly a lot less dangerous for the employee (but not nearly as exciting).

Authorized Maker Schemes

The final check tampering scheme, the authorized maker scheme, may be the most difficult to defend against. An authorized maker scheme is a type of check tampering fraud in which an employee with signature authority on a company account writes fraudulent checks for his own benefit and signs his own name as the maker (see Figure 12-8). The perpetrator in these schemes can write and sign fraudulent checks without assistance. He does not have to alter a pre-prepared instrument or forge the maker's signature.

Overriding Controls through Intimidation When a person is authorized to sign company checks, preparing the checks is easy. The employee simply writes and signs the instruments the same way he would with any legitimate check. In most situations, check signers are owners, officers, or otherwise high-ranking employees who have or can obtain access to all the blank checks they need. Even if company policy prohibits check signers from handling blank checks, the perpetrator's influence normally can be used to overcome this impediment. What employee is going to tell the CEO that he can't have a blank check?

The most basic way an employee accomplishes an authorized maker scheme is to override controls designed to prevent fraud. We have already stated that most authorized signatories have high levels of influence within their companies. This influence may be used by the perpetrator to deflect questions about fraudulent transactions. The most common example is one in which a majority owner or sole shareholder uses his company as a sort of alter ego, paying personal expenses directly out of company accounts. If this arrangement is disclosed and agreed to by other owners, there may be nothing illegal about it. After all, one cannot steal from oneself. On the other hand, in the absence of an agreement between all owners, these disbursements amount to embezzlement. Instead of paying personal expenses, the fraudster might cut checks directly to himself, his friends, or family. Using fear for job security as a weapon, the owner can maintain a work environment in which employees are afraid to question these transactions.

High-level managers or officers may also use their authority to override controls in those companies whose ownership is either absent or inattentive. Intimidation can play a large part in the commission and concealment of any type of occupational fraud where powerful individuals are involved. In one case, for example, the manager of a sales office stole approximately $150,000 from his employers over a two-year period. This manager had primary check-signing authority and abused this power by writing company checks to pay his personal expenses. The manager's fraudulent activities were well known by certain members of his staff, but these employees' careers were controlled by the perpetrator. Fear of losing their jobs, combined with lack of a proper whistleblowing structure, prevented the manager's employees from reporting his fraud.

Poor Controls Although overriding controls is the most blatant way to execute an authorized maker scheme, it is not the most common. Far more of these schemes occur because no one is paying attention to the accounts and few controls are present to prevent fraud. For instance, a manager of a small business wrote company checks to purchase assets for his own business. He took approximately $800,000 from his employer, hiding the missing money in accounts receivable because he knew that those accounts were

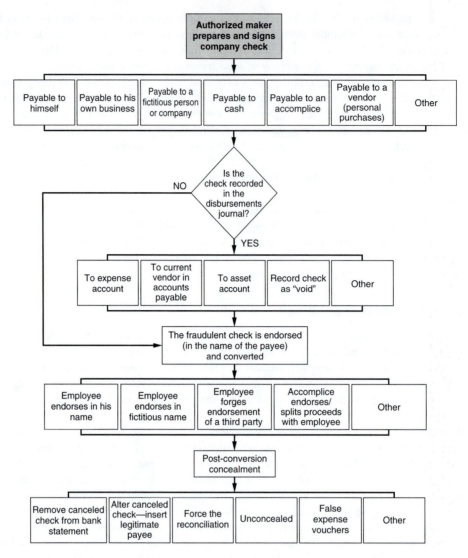

FIGURE 12-8 Authorized Maker Schemes

reviewed only once a year. Before audits, the manager would borrow money from the bank to replace the missing funds, and then begin the whole process again when the books were closed. This unfortunate scheme ended in tragedy as the manager and his wife committed suicide when the fraud came to light. Setting aside the personal catastrophe that occurred in this case, it is obvious that if the books had been more closely monitored, or if there had been a threat of surprise audits in addition to the regularly scheduled reviews, this fraud might not have gotten so far out of hand.

The failure to closely monitor accounts is supplemented by lack of internal controls, specifically the absence of separation of duties in the cash disbursements process. In one case, for instance, the perpetrator was in charge of signing all company checks, as well as reconciling the bank accounts for a small business. This put the fraudster in a perfect position to write fraudulent checks to herself and her husband. Similarly, in another case, the bookkeeper of a medium-sized company was charged with paying all bills and preparing the company payroll. She had access to an automatic check signer and total control over company bank accounts. The bookkeeper wrote extra checks to herself, coded the expenditures to payroll, and destroyed the canceled checks when they were returned with the bank statement. Had the duties of preparing checks and reconciling accounts been separated, as they should be, the fraudster would not have been able to complete her scheme.

Preventing and Detecting Check Tampering by Authorized Makers

Check tampering committed by authorized signers can be among the most difficult forms of occupational fraud to prevent, simply because the check signer is relied on by an organization to serve as a control against fraud by reviewing

prepared checks and affixing her signature only to legitimate disbursements. When the check signer is herself a part of the fraud, this control evaporates.

As with all forms of check tampering, the most important preventative measure is to establish a firm separation of duties in the check-writing function, specifically to separate the duties of preparing and signing checks, and to ensure that check signers do not have access to blank checks. If an authorized maker has access only to checks that have already been prepared by someone else, then she cannot create a fraudulent check on her own.

Another control that can help limit losses caused by authorized maker schemes is to require dual signatures for disbursements over a threshold amount. This will not prevent fraudulent checks below the threshold, but it will limit the damage a single fraudster can do by abusing his or her check-signing authority.

Organizations should also maintain up-to-date vendor lists and confirm all disbursements to the list, giving scrutiny to checks written to unknown vendors. Payments to known vendors in unusual amounts or at unusual times should also be investigated. In addition, canceled checks should be spot-checked for proper support and to verify the business purpose of the disbursements. Obviously, all of these tests should be performed by persons who are independent of the disbursements function.

Concealing Check Tampering

Since most check tampering schemes do not consist of a single occurrence but instead continue over a period of time, concealing the fraud is arguably the most important aspect of the scheme. If a fraudster intended to steal a large sum of money and skip to South America, hiding the fraud might not be so important. But the vast majority of occupational fraudsters remain employees of their companies as they continue to steal from them. Therefore, hiding the fraud is extremely important. Concealment of the fraud entails not only hiding the identity of the criminal, but in most cases hiding the fact that the fraud occurred. The most successful frauds are those in which the victim company is unaware that it is being robbed. Obviously, once a business learns that it is being victimized it will take steps to stanch its bleeding, and the end of the fraudster's scheme will be at hand.

Check tampering schemes can present especially tricky concealment problems for fraudsters. In other types of fraudulent disbursements such as invoice or payroll schemes, the fraudulent payment is entered in the books as a legitimate transaction by someone other than the fraudster. Remember that the payments in those schemes are generated by the production of false documents that cause accounts payable personnel to think that money is owed to a particular person or vendor. When accounts payable issues a disbursement for a bogus invoice, it does so because it believes the invoice to be genuine. The payment is then entered in the books as a legitimate payment. In other words, the perpetrator generally does not have to worry about concealing the payment in the books, because someone else unwittingly does it for him.

Check tampering schemes do not always afford this luxury to the fraudster. In forgery and authorized maker schemes, the perpetrator is the one writing the check, and he is usually the one coding the check in the disbursements journal. He must "explain" the check on the books. Forged endorsement schemes and altered payee schemes are different, because they involve the alteration of checks that were already prepared and coded by someone else. Nevertheless, they create a problem for the fraudster, because the intercepted check was intended for a legitimate recipient. In short, someone is out there waiting for the check that the fraudster has taken. The culprit in these schemes must worry not only about hiding the fraud from his employer, but also about appeasing the intended payee. If the intended recipient of the check does not receive his payment, he will complain to the fraudster's employer about the nonpayment. This could trigger an investigation into the whereabouts of the missing check, something the fraudster definitely wants to avoid.

The Fraudster Reconciling the Bank Statement   Many of those who perpetrate check tampering frauds are involved in reconciling the company's bank statement. The bank statement that a company receives normally includes the canceled checks that have been cashed in the preceding period. A person who reconciles the accounts is therefore in a position to hide the existence of any fraudulent checks that he has written to himself. He can remove the fraudulent checks or doctor the bank statement or both.

We said earlier that in forged maker and authorized maker schemes, the perpetrator usually has to code the check in the disbursements journal. The most fundamental way to hide the check is to code it as "void," or to include no listing at all in the journal. Then, when the bank statement arrives, the perpetrator

removes the fraudulent check from the stack of returned checks and destroys it. Now there is no record of the payment in the journal and no physical evidence of the check on hand. Of course, the bank will have a copy of the check, but unless someone questions the missing check, there will be little chance that the company will routinely discover the problem. And since the perpetrator is the one who reconciles the account, it is unlikely that anyone will even notice that the check is missing.

The problem with simply omitting the fraudulent check from the disbursements journal is that the bank balance will not reconcile to the book balance. For instance, if the fraudster wrote a $25,000 check to himself and did not record it, then the book balance will be $25,000 higher than the bank balance ($25,000 was taken out of the bank account by the fraudster, but was not credited out of the company's cash account). Fraudsters usually omit their illicit checks from the disbursements journal only in situations where they personally reconcile the bank statement and no one reviews their work. This allows the fraudster to force the reconciliation. In other words, the fraudster reports that the bank balance and book balance match, when in fact they do not. These are circumstances in which the employer basically takes the perpetrator's word that the book balance and bank balance reconcile.

Some of the victim companies in our study simply did not reconcile their accounts regularly. Because no one was reconciling the book balance and the bank balance, the fraudster was able to write checks without recording them. In a system where controls are so lax, almost any concealment method will be effective to disguise fraud. In fact, no effort to conceal the crime may even be necessary in these circumstances.

Fraudsters might physically alter the bank statement to cause it to match the company's book balance. For instance, a person engaging in a forged maker scheme may decide to steal blank checks from the back of the checkbook. These checks are out of sequence and therefore will be listed last on the bank statement. The employee then deletes this clump of checks and alters the final total to match the victim company's books. We will see this method of concealment used in the following case study.

In some cases, an employee's duties do not include reconciling the bank accounts, but he is nevertheless able to intercept bank statements and alter them to hide his crimes. In the following case study, Ernie Philips was able to persuade his company's bank to send the bank statements directly to him instead of his boss. Philips then altered the bank statements to conceal his fraudulent activities. This case describes how CFE James Sell put an end to Philips' scheme.

CASE STUDY: WHAT ARE FRIENDS FOR?

[Several names have been changed to preserve anonymity.]

Ernie Philips had fallen on hard times. Several back operations left him barely able to move around. He became addicted to the pills that made the pain bearable. His CPA practice was going under. He and his wife had six adopted children to support. Not surprisingly, he suffered from depression and chronic anxiety. But Ernie's luck changed when he ran into his old friend, James Sell. The two men had worked together at a federal agency and had known each other over 20 years. Ernie talked about the trouble he was having and James said he could help. At the time, Ernie was in a rehabilitation program for his substance abuse, so James told him, "Let me know when you're finished with that, and I'll have some work for you."

James rented Ernie an office and started sending a few small projects his way. "I wanted to try him out, see how he would do," Sell remarks. "He seemed like he was trying to get himself together." Ernie completed the work on time, and performed well, so when James got a big account with the Arizona and Nevada governments, he brought his friend into the main office. They agreed on a salary just over $38,000 a year, which James upped to $42,000 after six months.

Sell was appointed receiver for CSC Financial Services in Arizona and Nevada. CSC owners had been caught diverting $5.5 million of customer escrow funds from its operations in Arizona and Nevada. The computer equipment used in the operation dated from the 1960s, and a lack of supervision and

proper controls had obviously allowed the embezzlement to take place. The company didn't use a double-entry system, so management could alter ending totals with a wide latitude. Even after a regulatory audit discovered that things were in disarray at CSC, the Arizona administrators had allowed the offending owners to continue operating for a year and a half. So when Sell finally took over, he found a rather large mess. That's part of the game, he says. "When you get a company as receiver, you try to survive with what you inherit." The receivership involved more than 15,000 active accounts, with about $285 million in-house payments each year, and over 30,000 transactions a month. Sorting out the trouble wouldn't be easy. Sell knew Ernie had experience, and so tapped him for the job. "One of the reasons I brought him in," Sell says, "was to establish controls where there were none before."

But Ernie had little respect for controls. When James asked the mailroom clerk about the bank statements for a particular month, he told him that Ernie had them. "Why is that?" James asked. "He knows those are supposed to come to me unopened. He shouldn't have them." The clerk said Ernie needed the statements to do a reconciliation. James didn't want to overreact, but he was nervous. "There's limited control over any position and even less over a key financial position," he says, "and any time you lose a control point, you're in jeopardy. So you have to take a strong position in order to restore the process." He discussed the matter with Ernie and thought they had an understanding.

Ernie was having problems with other people in the company, too. He and the operations manager had a heated exchange when the manager retrieved some account papers from Ernie's desk. Ernie had been out, and the papers were needed right away. When Ernie aired his grievance, James sided with the operations manager. There shouldn't be any problem, James said. It wasn't like anyone was rifling Ernie's desk. Besides that, Sell traveled frequently, and spent a lot of time in the Nevada office, so having open access in the Arizona office allowed for informal oversight. Sell muses, "One of the best controls in the world is to create an atmosphere of uncertainty. Usually embezzlement doesn't occur unless the person thinks he can hide what he's doing. So I figured this would be a way to keep things on the up and up."

The uncertainty didn't prevent the fraud, but it did help detect what was going on. The operations manager discovered Ernie's sting during a search for accounting records. He brought Sell a company check from Ernie's desk, made out in the name of Ernie Philips for $2,315. It wasn't Ernie's payroll check, so what was it? The check hadn't been cashed, but Sell's signature had been forged. Not sure yet about the situation, Sell arranged to meet Ernie away from the main office.

Sell had been out of town and needed some updates on the escrow operations, so he dropped by Ernie's private office one afternoon. After they finished their discussion, James said, "There's one more thing I wanted to ask you about." He pulled a copy of the check from his briefcase and told Ernie, "I was hoping you could explain this."

There was a long silence. Ernie stared at the check, pursing his lips and scratching his hands across the desktop. The pause stretched into what seemed like minutes. Finally he confessed, "I've been taking money."

"I could tell from the look on his face this was trouble," Sell reports. The worst was confirmed. He had been hoping there was an explanation, an innocuous one, despite all the signs. Still, he had come prepared. "I wanted to confront him away from the main office so if there was anything he could get to and destroy, I'd be protected." James had also brought a copy of the check so it wouldn't be apparent when he showed the check to Ernie that it wasn't cashed. "I wanted to make him believe I knew more than I did. Nailing down this operation would have meant reviewing pages and pages of bank statements, verifying checks and payments. Before I went to that trouble, I wanted to know there was a reason to look."

Sell barred Ernie from both his offices, and began tracing his friend's activities over the past seven months. In some cases, Sell's name was forged onto the checks in handwriting that wasn't his and which bore a resemblance to Ernie's. Others were marked with the signature stamp that was supposed to remain locked in a clerk's office except when she was using it for a very limited set of transactions. Somehow, Ernie had been able to slip the stamp away and mark his checks.

He covered his tracks by taking checks out of sequence so they would show up at the end of the bank statement. Then he intercepted the statement and altered the report at the end, returning a copy of the statement to the clerk for filing. After the clerk told Sell about Ernie having the statement, Ernie arranged with the bank for the statements to come addressed to his attention. Without getting authorization, the bank agreed; Ernie could then doctor the statement, copy it, and send it down the line. If someone did ask about an unidentified disbursement, Ernie told them the money went to a supply vendor and, since he was the controller, he was taken at his word. He even managed on a couple of occasions to slip checks made out to himself into a regular batch, which the operations manager—who was authorized to sign checks in Sell's absence—signed.

Sell was, to put it mildly, chagrined. He had believed that his office was set up to avoid the kind of flagrant defalcation he was facing now. But, he admits, "No matter how good a system you design, one knowledgeable person can circumvent it.... The trick is to make sure the procedures you set up are followed. I don't know if there's a system in the world that's immune. The key is to limit and control the extent of any one person's action, so you can at least detect when things go awry."

Sell figured his losses at about $109,000. He got a complete run of the bank statements from Ernie's tenure, identified checks out of sequence, or gaps in issued checks, and then verified to whom they were payable and the stated purpose. The scheme had required some footwork, but wasn't terribly sophisticated. The checks were written in odd amounts, $4,994.16 for example, but Ernie had made the payments in his own name. He had left behind some of his personal bank statements, which showed deposits correlated with the money he'd taken from Sell. (The amounts didn't always match, because Ernie would take cash back from the deposit, but they were close enough to link the transactions.)

Ernie's brief era of good feelings had ended. He had used the proceeds from his finagling for a lavish family vacation, a new car, a new computer, and improvements on the house where he lived with his wife and their adopted family, but in the fallout of his dismissal, Ernie's house went into foreclosure. He was charged around the same time with driving under the influence. The CPA board revoked his license and fined him for ethics violations. He made no defense at his civil trial, where a judgment was rendered against him for the $109,000 he took, plus treble damages. While he was out on bail for the criminal charges against him, Ernie took his family and fled. Sell was able to locate him through an Internet search service. Ernie died in May 1996. "He threw everything away," Sell laments. "For $109,000 he fouled up his life, and his family."

Sell takes the matter philosophically. There are plenty of cases that echo Ernie's. For example, Sell just investigated a paralegal who not only wrote company checks to herself, but also sent one to the County Attorney's office—to pay the fine she owed for writing bad checks. "Typically, these people don't take the time to set up a new identity or a dummy company," James says. "They just want the money fast and grab it the easiest way they can."

"And often enough," he adds, "they want to get caught.... Ernie knew he was out of control; we had been friends for so long. He knew he was doing more than just breaking the law. During one of our conversations after this he told me, 'You know, the first check was real hard to write. But I had clients I had borrowed from, I owed money all over the place, I had a family. As it went on, writing the checks just got easier.'"

Re-Altering Checks In altered payee schemes, remember that it is common for the perpetrator to take a check intended for a legitimate recipient and then doctor the instrument so that he is designated as the payee. A company check payable to an employee will obviously raise suspicions of fraud when the canceled check is reconciled with the bank statement. To prevent this, some employees re-alter their fraudulent checks when the bank statement arrives. We have already discussed how some fraudsters alter checks by writing the payee's name in erasable ink or type when the check is prepared. These employees obtain a signature for the check, then erase the true payee's name and insert their own. When these checks return with the statement, the employee erases his own name and reenters the name of the proper payee. Thus there will be no appearance of mischief. The fraudster in one case used the re-alteration method to hide over $185,000 in fraudulent checks.

The re-alteration method is not limited to altered payee schemes. The concealment will be equally effective in forged maker schemes, authorized maker schemes, and concealed check schemes. Re-altered checks will match the names of legitimate payees listed in the disbursements journal.

Falsifying the Disbursements Journal Rather than omit a fraudulent check from the disbursements journal or list it as void, the perpetrator might write a check payable to himself but list a different person as the payee on the books. Usually, the fake payee is a regular vendor—a person or business that receives numerous checks from the victim company. Employees tend to pick known vendors for these schemes because one extra disbursement to a regular payee is less likely to stand out.

The false entry is usually made at the time the fraudulent check is written, but in some cases the fraudster makes alterations to existing information in the books. Obviously, alterations found in a company's books should be carefully scrutinized to make sure they are legitimate.

The fraudster can also conceal a fraudulent check by falsely entering the amounts of legitimate checks in the disbursements journal. He overstates the amounts of legitimate disbursements in order to absorb the cost of a fraudulent check. For instance, assume that a company owes $10,000 to a particular vendor. The fraudster would write a check to the vendor for $10,000 but enter the check in the disbursements journal as a $15,000 payment. The company's disbursements are now overstated by $5,000. The fraudster can write a $5,000 check to himself and list that check as void in the disbursements journal. The bank balance and the book balance will still match, because the cost of the fraudulent check was absorbed by overstating the amount of the legitimate check. Of course, the fact that the canceled checks do not match the entries in the journal should indicate potential fraud. This type of concealment is really effective only when the bank accounts are not closely monitored or where the employee is in charge of reconciling the accounts.

If possible, fraudsters will try to code their fraudulent checks to existing accounts that are rarely reviewed or to accounts that are very active. In one case, for instance, the perpetrator charged his checks to an intercompany payables account, because it was reviewed only at the end of the year, and not in great detail. The perpetrator in this case might also have coded his checks to an account with extensive activity in the hopes that his fraudulent check would be lost in the crowd of transactions on the account. In the cases the ACFE researchers reviewed, most checks were coded to expense accounts or liability accounts.

This particular method can be very effective in concealing fraudulent checks, particularly when the victim company is not diligent in reconciling its bank accounts. For instance, in one case, the victim company reconciled its accounts by verifying the amount of the checks with the check numbers, but did not verify that the payee on the actual check matched the payee listed in the disbursements journal. As a result, the company was unable to detect that the checks had been miscoded in the disbursements journal. As we discussed in the previous section, the fraudster might also intercept the bank statement before it is reconciled and alter the payee name on the fraudulent check to match the entry he made in the disbursements journal.

Reissuing Intercepted Checks We mentioned before that in intercepted check schemes, the employee faces detection not only through his employer's normal control procedures, but also from the intended recipients of the checks he steals. After all, when these people do not receive their payments from the victim company, they are likely to complain. These complaints, in turn, could trigger a fraud investigation.

Some employees head this problem off by issuing new checks to the people whose initial checks they stole. For instance, an employee would steal checks intended for vendors and deposit them into her checking account. She would then take the invoices from these vendors and reenter them in the company's accounts payable system, adding a number or letter to avoid the computerized system's duplicate check controls. This assured that the vendors received their due payment, and therefore would not blow the whistle on her scheme, which netted approximately $200,000.

Another example of reissuance was provided by an accounts payable troubleshooter. The employee in this case was in charge of auditing payments to all suppliers, reviewing supporting documents, and mailing checks. Once in a while, she would purposely fail to mail a check to a vendor. The vendor, of course, would call accounts payable about the late payment and would be told that his invoice had been paid on a certain date. Since the accounts payable staff could not locate a copy of the canceled check (because the fraudster was still holding it), they called the troubleshooter to research the problem. Unfortunately for the company, the troubleshooter was the one who had stolen the check. She would tell accounts payable to issue another check to the vendor while she stopped payment on the first check. Thus the vendor received his payment. Meanwhile, instead of stopping payment on the first check, the troubleshooter deposited it into her own account.

The difference between these two schemes is that in the latter, two checks were issued for a single invoice. The troubleshooter in this case did not have to worry about this problem because she performed the bank reconciliations for her company and was able to force the totals. Once again we see how access to the bank statement is a key to concealing a check tampering scheme.

Bogus Supporting Documents   While some fraudsters attempt to wipe out all traces of their fraudulent disbursements by destroying the checks, forcing the bank reconciliation, and so on, others opt to justify their checks by manufacturing fake support for them. These fraudsters prepare false payment vouchers, including false invoices, purchase orders, and/or receiving reports, to create an appearance of authenticity. This concealment strategy is practical only when the employee writes checks payable to someone other than himself (e.g., an accomplice or a shell company). A check made payable to an employee may raise suspicions regardless of any supporting documents he manufactures.

Conceptually, the idea of producing false payment vouchers may seem confusing in a chapter on check tampering. If the fraudster is using fake vouchers, shouldn't the crime be classified as a billing scheme? Not necessarily. In a check tampering scheme, the fraudster generates the disbursement by writing the check himself. He may create fake support to justify the check, but the support—the voucher—had nothing to do with the disbursement being made. Had the fraudster not created a fake invoice, he would still have had a fraudulent check.

In a billing scheme, on the other hand, the fraudster uses the false voucher to *cause a payment to be generated*. Without a fake voucher in these schemes, there would be no fraudulent disbursement at all, because the employee depends on someone else to actually cut the check. In other words, the false voucher is a means of creating the unwarranted payment in these schemes, rather than an attempt to hide it.

Proactive Computer Audit Tests for Detecting Check Tampering Schemes

Title	Category	Description	Data file(s)
Extract all voided checks and summarize by issuer for reasonableness.	All	Checks may be voided in the system and then cashed (which requires another entry in the bank reconciliation to conceal the fraud).	• Check Register*
Extract all reconciling items per the bank reconciliation and summarize for reasonableness.	All	Most of the concealment of check tampering is done between the bank balance and the general ledger. Therefore, these adjusting entries should be closely scrutinized.	• General Ledger Detail
Summarize debit memos by vendor, issuer, and type.	All	Debit memo trends that appear unusual should be investigated as attempts to cover unauthorized payments.	• Invoice Payment
Identify duplicate payments based on various means.	All	Duplicate payments are made to properly pay down open vendor balances when another check, intended for the vendor, is stolen. Duplicate payment tests can be enacted on the vendor, invoice number, amount. More complicated tests can look for instances in which the same invoice and amount are paid, yet the payment is made to two different vendors. Another advanced test would be to search for same vendor and invoice when a different amount is paid.	• Invoice Payment

(Continued)

(*Continued*)

Title	Category	Description	Data file(s)
Summarize accounts payable activity by general ledger account, sort from high to low, and review for reasonableness.	All	Expense account trends that appear unusual should be investigated as attempts to cover unauthorized payments.	• Invoice Payment G/L Distribution
Compare balance per accounts payable subledger to vendor account balances per their accounts receivable system.	All	Vendors that are not paid will show their customer account from the defrauded company as an old receivable. In order to obtain an electronic file of all customer account statements, it may be necessary to request statements and enter them into a spreadsheet. Note that even vendors with no balance should be requested to provide customer statements.	• Accounts Payable Subledger • Customer Account Statements (from all vendors)
Extract users who can write checks and also post entries to the general ledger.	All	Users who can write checks and also subsequently conceal the misappropriation through adjustments to the general ledger cash accounts would be taking advantage of a nonsegregation of duties to conceal their fraud. User access should be reviewed from the perspective of adjustments within the application and adjustments to the data itself.	• Check Register User Access Master File • General Ledger User Access Master File • Check Register* User Access Log File • General Ledger User Access Log File
Extract all employee payments equal to zero in any given pay period.	All	Reports unusual check amounts to employees for review. Check amounts may be written in after printing.	• Check Register*
Extract all checks payable to "cash" and summarize by issuer for reasonableness.	Forged maker	Checks issued to "cash" have a higher incidence of fraud.	• Check Register*
Extract manual checks and summarize by vendor and issuer.	Forged maker	Manual checks are more prone to abuse and therefore should be scrutinized, especially if a particular issuer is drafting the majority of manual checks.	• Check Register*
Extract all purchases with no purchase orders and summarize by vendor and issuer.	Forged maker	Purchases with no purchase orders are more prone to abuse and therefore should be scrutinized, especially if a particular issuer is drafting the majority of payments without purchase orders.	• Invoice Payment
Sequence gaps in checks.	Forged maker	Checks that are stolen will not normally appear in the check register and thus will be seen as a gap in the check sequence.	• Check Register*
Extract checks that are out of the normal sequence.	Forged maker, concealed check, and authorized maker	Checks that are fabricated or stolen will, at many times, not be in the same general sequence as the company's normal check sequence.	• Check Register*
Sample vendor open invoices for confirmation with vendor.	Forged maker, concealed check, and authorized maker	Similar to the above comparison test, vendor invoices may appear paid on the subledger when the vendor believes such invoices have not been paid.	• Invoice Payment

*Please note that the file "Check Register" may designate the vendor check register but could also refer to the payroll check register.

PAYROLL SCHEMES

Payroll schemes are similar to billing schemes in that they are based on a fraudulent claim for payment that causes the victim company to unknowingly make a fraudulent disbursement. In billing schemes, the false claim is usually based on an invoice (coupled, perhaps, with false receiving reports, purchase orders, and purchase authorizations) that shows the victim organization owes money to a vendor. Payroll schemes are typically based on fraudulent timecards or payroll registers, and they show that the victim organization owes money to one of its employees.

Payroll schemes may be defined as occupational frauds in which a person who works for an organization causes that organization to issue a payment by making false claims for compensation. There are three main categories of payroll fraud:

1. Ghost employee schemes
2. Falsified hours and salary schemes
3. Commission schemes

Ghost Employees

The term *ghost employee* refers to someone on the payroll who does not actually work for the victim company. The ghost employee may be a fictitious person, or a real individual who simply does not work for the victim employer. When the ghost is a real person, it is often a friend or relative of the perpetrator. In some cases, the ghost employee is an accomplice of the fraudster who cashes the fraudulent paychecks and splits the money with the perpetrator.

Through the falsification of personnel or payroll records, a fraudster causes paychecks to be generated to a ghost. Then, the paychecks are converted by the fraudster or an accomplice (see Figure 12-9). Use of a ghost employee scheme by a fraudster can be like adding a second income to his household.

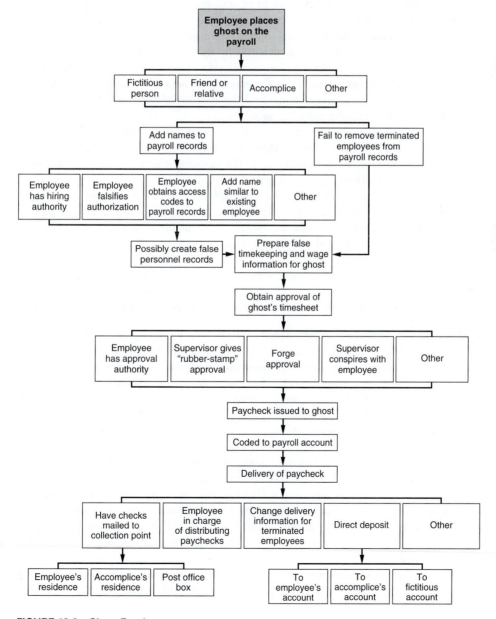

FIGURE 12-9 Ghost Employees

In order for a ghost employee scheme to work, four things must happen: (1) the ghost must be added to the payroll, (2) timekeeping and wage rate information must be collected, (3) a paycheck must be issued to the ghost, and (4) the check must be delivered to the perpetrator or an accomplice.

Adding the Ghost to the Payroll   The first step in a ghost employee scheme is entering the ghost on the payroll. In some businesses, all hiring is done through a centralized personnel department, while in others the personnel function is spread over the managerial responsibilities of various departments. Regardless of how hiring of new employees is handled within a business, it is the person or persons with authority to add new employees that are in the best position to put ghosts on the payroll. In one case, for example, a manager who was responsible for hiring and scheduling janitorial work added over 80 ghost employees to his payroll. The ghosts in this case were actual people who worked at other jobs for different companies. The manager filled out timesheets for the fictitious employees and authorized them, then took the resulting paychecks to the ghost employees, who cashed them and split the proceeds with the manager. It was this manager's authority in the hiring and supervision of employees that enabled him to perpetrate this fraud.

Another area where the opportunity exists to add ghosts is payroll accounting. In a perfect world, every name listed on an organization's payroll would be verified against personnel records to make sure that those persons receiving paychecks actually work for the company, but in practice this does not always happen. Thus, persons in payroll accounting may be able to generate fraudulent paychecks by adding fictitious employees to the roll. Access to payroll records is usually restricted, so it may be that only managers have access to make changes to payroll accounting records, making these managers the most likely suspects in a ghost employee scheme. On the other hand, lower-level employees often gain access to payroll records, either through poor observance of controls or by surreptitious means. In one case, for instance, an employee in the payroll department was given the authority to enter new employees into the payroll system, make corrections to payroll information, and distribute paychecks. This employee's manager gave rubber-stamp approval to the employee's actions because of a trusting relationship between the two. The lack of separation of duties and the absence of review made it simple for the culprit to add a fictitious employee into the payroll system.

One way to help conceal the presence of a ghost on the payroll is to create a fictitious employee with a name very similar to that of a real employee. The name on the fraudulent paycheck, then, will appear to be legitimate to anyone who glances at it. The perpetrator of another case, a bookkeeper who made off with $35,000 in fraudulent wages, used this method.

Instead of adding new names to the payroll, some employees undertake ghost employee schemes by failing to remove the names of terminated employees. Paychecks to the terminated employee continue to be generated even though he or she no longer works for the victim company. The perpetrator intercepts these fraudulent paychecks and converts them to his own use. For instance, in one case, an accountant delayed the submission of resignation notices of certain employees, and then she falsified timesheets for these employees to make it appear that they still worked for the victim company. This accountant was in charge of distributing paychecks to all employees of the company, so when the fraudulent checks were generated, she simply took them out of the stack of legitimate checks and kept them for herself.

Collecting Timekeeping Information   The second thing that must occur in order for a paycheck to be issued to a ghost employee, at least in the case of hourly employees, is the collection and computation of timekeeping information. The perpetrator must provide payroll accounting with a timecard or other instrument showing how many hours the fictitious employee worked over the most recent pay period. This information, along with the wage rate information contained in personnel or payroll files, will be used to compute the amount of the fraudulent paycheck.

Timekeeping records can be maintained in a variety of ways. Employees might manually record their hours on timecards or punch time clocks that record the time at which a person starts and finishes his or her work. In more sophisticated environments, computer systems can track an employee's hours.

When a ghost employee scheme is in place, someone must create documentation for the ghost's hours. This essentially amounts to preparing a fake timecard showing when the ghost was allegedly present at work. Depending on the normal procedure for recording hours, a fraudster might write up a fake timecard and sign it in the ghost's name, punch the time clock for the ghost, or so on. The preparing of the timecard is not a great obstacle to the perpetrator. The real key to the timekeeping document is obtaining approval of the timecard.

A supervisor should approve timecards of hourly employees. This verifies to the payroll department that the employee actually worked the hours that are claimed on the card. A ghost employee, by definition,

does not work for the victim company, so approval will have to be fraudulently obtained. Often, the supervisor himself is the one who creates the ghost. When this is the case, the supervisor fills out a timecard in the name of the ghost, and then affixes his approval. The timecard is thereby authenticated, and a paycheck will be issued. When a nonsupervisor is perpetrating a ghost employee scheme, he will typically forge the necessary approval and then forward the bogus timecard directly to payroll accounting, bypassing his supervisor.

In computerized systems, a supervisor's signature might not be required. In lieu of this, the supervisor inputs data into the payroll system, and the use of his password serves to authorize the entry. If an employee has access to the supervisor's password, he or she can input any data desired, and it arrives in the payroll system with a seal of approval.

If the fraudster creates ghost employees who are salaried rather than hourly employees, it is not necessary to collect timekeeping information. Salaried employees are paid a certain amount each pay period regardless of how many hours they work. Because the timekeeping function can be avoided, it may be easier easy for a fraudster to create a ghost employee who works on salary. However, salaried employees typically are fewer, and are more likely to be members of management. The salaried ghost may therefore be more difficult to conceal.

Issuing the Ghost's Paycheck   Once a ghost is entered on the payroll and his timecard has been approved, the third step in the scheme is the actual issuance of the paycheck. The heart of a ghost employee scheme is in the falsification of payroll records and timekeeping information. Once this falsification has occurred, the perpetrator does not generally take an active role in the issuance of the check. The payroll department prints the check—based on the bogus information provided by the fraudster—as it would any other paycheck.

Delivery of the Paycheck   The final step in a ghost employee scheme is the distribution of the checks to the perpetrator. Paychecks might be hand-delivered to employees while at work, mailed to employees at their home addresses, or direct-deposited into the employees' bank accounts. Distribution is almost always conducted in person and on-site when employees are paid in currency rather than by check.

Ideally, those in charge of payroll distribution should not have a hand in any of the other functions of the payroll cycle. For instance, the person who enters new employees in the payroll system should not be allowed to distribute paychecks, because this person can include a ghost on the payroll and then simply remove the fraudulent check from the stack of legitimate paychecks he or she handles while disbursing pay. Obviously, when the perpetrator of a ghost employee scheme is allowed to mail checks to employees or pass them out at work, he is in the best position to ensure that the ghost's check is delivered to himself.

In most instances, the perpetrator does not have the authority to distribute paychecks, and so must make sure that the victim employer sends the checks to a place where he can recover them. When checks are not distributed in the workplace, they are either mailed to employees or deposited directly into those employees' accounts.

If the fictitious employee was added into the payroll or personnel records by the fraudster, the problem of distribution is usually minor. When the ghost's employment information is input, the perpetrator simply lists an address or bank account to which the payments can be sent. In the case of purely fictitious ghost employees, the address is often the perpetrator's own residence (the same goes for bank accounts). The fact that two employees (the perpetrator and the ghost) are receiving payments at the same destination may indicate that fraud is afoot. Some fraudsters avoid this problem by having payments sent to a post office box or a separate bank account. For example, a perpetrator in one case set up a fake bank account in the name of a fictitious employee and arranged for paychecks to be deposited directly into this account.

As we have said, the ghost is not always a fictitious person. It may instead be a real person who is conspiring with the perpetrator to defraud the company. For instance, an employee listed both his wife and his girlfriend on the company payroll. When real persons conspiring with the fraudster are falsely included on the payroll, the perpetrator typically sees to it that checks are sent to the homes or accounts of these persons. In this way, the fraudster avoids the problem of duplicating addresses on the payroll.

Distribution is a more difficult problem when the ghost is a former employee who was simply not removed from the payroll. In one case, for instance, a supervisor continued to submit timecards for employees who had been terminated. Payroll records will obviously reflect the bank account number or address of the terminated employee in this situation. The perpetrator then has two courses of action. In companies where paychecks are distributed by hand or are left at a central spot for employees to collect, the perpetrator can ignore the payroll records and simply pick up the fraudulent paychecks. If the paychecks

are to be distributed through the mail or by direct deposit, the perpetrator will have to enter the terminated employee's records and change their delivery information.

Preventing and Detecting Ghost Employee Schemes It is very important to separate the hiring function from other duties associated with payroll. Most ghost employee schemes succeed when the perpetrator has the authority to add employees to the payroll and approve the timecards of those employees; it therefore follows that if all hiring is done through a centralized human resources department, an organization can substantially limit its exposure to ghost employee schemes.

Personnel records should be maintained independently of payroll and timekeeping functions, and the personnel department should verify any changes to payroll. The personnel department should also conduct background checks and reference checks on all prospective employees in advance of hire. These simple verification procedures should eliminate most ghost employee schemes, because it would make it impossible for a single individual to add a ghost to an organization's payroll. If employees know that payroll changes are verified against personnel records, this will deter most ghost employee schemes. Furthermore, if personnel and payroll records are maintained separately, a simple comparison report should identify persons on the payroll who have no personnel file. Organizations should also periodically check the payroll against personnel records for terminated employees, and unauthorized wage or deduction adjustments.

Another way to proactively test for ghost employees is to have someone in the organization independent of the payroll function periodically run a report looking for employees who lack Social Security numbers, who have no deductions on their paychecks for withholding taxes or insurance, or who show no physical address or phone number. Fraudsters who create ghost employees often fail to attend to these details, the omission of which is a clear red flag. Similarly, reports should be run periodically looking for multiple employees who have the same Social Security number, bank account number, or physical address. All of these conditions would tend to indicate the presence of a ghost on the payroll.

A comparison of payroll expenses to production schedules might also uncover a ghost employee scheme. The distribution of hours to activity or departments should be reviewed by supervisors in those departments, and payroll expenses should be compared to budgeted amounts. Significant budget overruns could signal payroll fraud.

Finally, by simply keeping signed paychecks in a secure location and by verifying that they are properly distributed, an organization can thwart most ghost employee schemes. The employee or manager who adds a ghost to the payroll must be able to collect the ghost's check. In most cases, they are able to do that because the perpetrator has access to payroll checks prior to distribution, or because the perpetrator is in charge of distributing paychecks himself. If an organization assigns the task of distributing paychecks to a person who is independent of the payroll functions and who has no authority to add personnel, this can make it difficult for the perpetrator to obtain the ghost's paycheck. The duty of distributing paychecks should be rotated among several employees to further guard against fraud. Employees should be required to provide identification to receive their paychecks so that every employee receives only his or her own check, and if pay is deposited directly into bank accounts, a report should be run every pay period searching for multiple employees who share an account number.

Falsified Hours and Salary

The most common method of misappropriating funds from the payroll is through the overpayment of wages. For hourly employees, the size of a paycheck is based on two essential factors: the number of hours worked and the rate of pay. It is therefore obvious that for an hourly employee to fraudulently increase the size of his paycheck, he must either falsify the number of hours he has worked or change his wage rate (see Figure 12-10). Since salaried employees do not receive compensation based on their time at work, in most cases these employees generate fraudulent wages by increasing their rates of pay.

When we discuss payroll frauds that involve overstated hours, we must first understand how an employee's time at work is recorded. As we have already discussed, time is generally kept by one of three methods. Time clocks may be used to mark the time when an employee begins and finishes work. The employee inserts a card into the clock at the beginning and end of work, and the time is imprinted on that card. In more sophisticated systems, computers may track the time employees spend on the job based on log-in codes or a similar tracking mechanism. Finally, timecards showing the number of hours an employee worked on a particular day are often prepared manually by the employee, and approved by his or her manager.

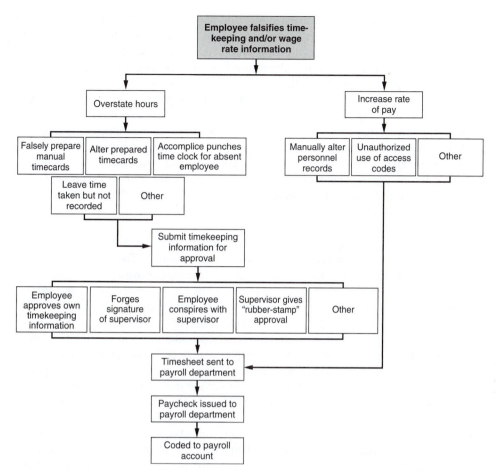

FIGURE 12-10 Falsified Hours and Salary

Manually Prepared Timecards When hours are recorded manually, an employee typically fills out his timecard to reflect the number of hours he has worked and then presents it to his supervisor for approval. The supervisor verifies the accuracy of the timecard, signs or initials the card to indicate his approval, and then forwards it to the payroll department so that a paycheck can be issued. Most of the payroll frauds we encountered in our study stemmed from abuses of this process.

Obviously, if an employee fills out his own timecard, it may be easy to falsify his hours worked. He simply writes down the wrong time, showing that he arrived at work earlier or left later than he actually did. The difficulty is not in falsifying the timecard, but in getting the fraudulent card approved by the employee's supervisor. There are basically four ways for the employee to obtain the authorization he needs.

Forging a Supervisor's Signature When using this method, an employee typically withholds his timecard from those being sent to the supervisor for approval, forges the supervisor's signature or initials, and then adds the timecard to the stack of authorized cards that are sent to payroll. The fraudulent timecard arrives at the payroll department with what appears to be a supervisor's approval, and a paycheck is subsequently issued.

Collusion with a Supervisor The second way to obtain approval of a fraudulent timecard is to collude with a supervisor who authorizes timekeeping information. In these schemes, the supervisor knowingly signs false timecards and usually takes a portion of the fraudulent wages. In some cases, the supervisor may take the entire amount of the overpayment. In one case, for example, a supervisor assigned employees to better work areas or better jobs, but in return she demanded payment. The payment was arranged by the falsification of the employees' timecards, which the supervisor authorized. The employees were paid for fictitious overtime, which was then kicked back to the supervisor. It may be particularly difficult to detect payroll fraud when a supervisor colludes with an employee, because managers are often relied on as a control to assure proper timekeeping.

In payroll collusion schemes, the supervisor does not necessarily take a cut of the overpayment. One such case involved a temporary employee who added fictitious hours to her timesheet. Rather than get the approval of her direct supervisor, the employee obtained approval from an administrator at another site. The employee was a relative of this administrator, who authorized her overpayment without receiving any compensation for doing so. In another case, a supervisor needed to enhance the salary of an employee in order to keep him from leaving for another job. The supervisor authorized the payment of $10,000 in fictitious overtime to the employee. Two part-time employees, who did not even bother to show up for work, committed perhaps the most unique case in the ACFE studies. One of the fraudsters did not perform any verifiable work for nine months, and the other was apparently absent for *two years!* The timecards for these employees were completed by a timekeeper based on their work schedules, and a supervisor approved the timecards. This supervisor was also a part-time employee who held another job, in which he was supervised by one of the fraudsters. Thus, the supervisor was under pressure to authorize the fraudulent timecards in order to keep his second job.

Rubber-Stamp Supervisors

The third way to obtain approval of fraudulent timecards is to rely on a supervisor to approve them without reviewing their accuracy. The "lazy manager" method seems risky, and one would think that it would be uncommon, but the truth is that it occurs quite frequently. A recurring theme in our study is the reliance of fraudsters on the inattentiveness of others. When an employee sees an opportunity to make a little extra money without getting caught, that employee is more likely to be emboldened to attempt a fraud scheme. The fact that a supervisor is known to rubber-stamp timecards or even ignore them can be a factor in an employee's decision to begin stealing from his company.

For instance, in one case a temporary employee noticed that his manager did not reconcile the expense journal on a monthly basis. Thus, the manager did not know how much was being paid to the temporary agency. The fraudster completed fictitious time reports that were sent to the temporary agency and that caused the victim company to pay over $30,000 in fraudulent wages. Since the fraudster controlled the mail and the manager did not review the expense journal, this extremely simple scheme went undetected for some time. In another example of poor supervision, a bookkeeper whose duties included the preparation of payroll checks inflated her checks by adding fictitious overtime. This person added over $90,000 of unauthorized pay to her wages over a four-year period before an accountant noticed the overpayments.

Poor Custody Procedures

One form of control breakdown that occurred in several cases in our study was the failure to maintain proper control over authorized timecards. In a properly run system, once management authorizes timecards, they should be sent directly to payroll. Those who prepare the timecards should not have access to them after they have been approved. When this procedure is not observed, the person who prepared a timecard can alter it after his supervisor has approved it but before it is delivered to payroll. This is precisely what happened in several cases in our study.

Another way hours are falsified is in the misreporting of leave time. This is not as common as timecard falsification, but nevertheless can be problematic. Incidentally, this is the one instance in which salaried employees commit payroll fraud by falsifying their hours. The way a leave scheme works is very simple. An employee takes a certain amount of time off from work as paid leave or vacation, but does not report the absence. Employees typically receive a certain amount of paid leave per year. If a person takes a leave of absence but does not report it, those days are not deducted from his allotted days off. In other words, he gets more leave time than he is entitled to. The result is that the employee shows up for work less, yet still receives the same pay.

An example of this type of scheme was found where a senior manager allowed certain persons to be absent from work without submitting leave forms to the personnel department. Consequently, these employees were able to take excess leave amounting to approximately $25,000 worth of unearned wages.

Time Clocks and Other Automated Timekeeping Systems

In companies that use time clocks to collect timekeeping information, payroll fraud is usually uncomplicated. In the typical scenario, the time clock is located in an unrestricted area, and a timecard for each employee is kept nearby. The employees insert their timecards into the time clock at the beginning and end of their shifts and the clock imprints the time. The length of time an employee spends at work is thus recorded. Supervisors should be present at the beginning and end of shifts to assure that employees do not punch the timecards of absent coworkers, but this simple control is often overlooked.

AFCE researchers encountered very few time clock fraud schemes, and those they did come across followed a single, uncomplicated pattern. When one employee is absent, a friend of that person punches

his timecard so that it appears the absent employee was at work that day. The absent employee is therefore overcompensated on his next paycheck.

Rates of Pay While the preceding discussion focused on how employees overstate the number of hours they have worked, it should be remembered that an employee could also generate a larger paycheck by changing his pay rate. An employee's personnel or payroll records reflect his rate of pay. If an employee can gain access to these records, or has an accomplice with access to them, he can adjust his pay rate to increase his compensation.

Preventing and Detecting Falsified Hours and Salary Schemes As with most other forms of occupational fraud, falsified hours and salaries schemes generally succeed because an organization fails to enforce proper controls. As a rule, payroll preparation, authorization, distribution, and reconciliation should be strictly segregated. In addition, the transfer of funds from general accounts to payroll accounts should be handled independently of the other functions. This will prevent most instances of falsified hours and salary schemes.

The role of the manager in verifying hours worked and authorizing timecards is critical to preventing and detecting this form of payroll fraud. Organizations should have a rule stating that no overtime will be paid unless a supervisor authorizes it in advance. This control is not only a good anti-fraud mechanism; it is essential to maintaining control over payroll costs. Sick leave and vacation time should also not be granted without a supervisor's review. Leave and vacation time should be monitored for excesses by an independent human resources department.

A designated official should verify all wage rate changes. These changes should be administered through a centralized human resources department. Any wage rate change not properly authorized by a supervisor and recorded by human resources should be denied.

After a supervisor has approved timecards for her employees, those timecards should be sent directly to the payroll department, and employees should not have access to their timecards after they have been approved. One of the most common falsified hours and salary schemes is to simply alter a timecard after it has been approved. Maintaining proper custody of approved timecards will mostly eliminate this type of fraud.

If a time clock is used, timecards should be secured, and a supervisor should be present whenever timecards are punched. This supervisor should work independently of hiring and other payroll functions. A different supervisor should approve timecards.

In addition to controls aimed at preventing payroll fraud, organizations should run tests that actively seek out fraudulent payroll activity. For example, supervisors should maintain copies of their employees' timecards. These copies can be spot-checked against a payroll distribution list or against timecards on file in the payroll department. Any discrepancies would tend to indicate fraud.

Because most falsified hours and salary schemes involve fraudulent claims for overtime pay, organizations should actively test for overtime abuses. Comparison reports can illustrate where a particular individual has been paid significantly more overtime than other employees with similar job duties, or where a particular department tends to generate more overtime expenses than are warranted. Other tests can highlight falsified hours and salary schemes:

- Perform a trend analysis comparing payroll expenses to budget projections or prior years' totals. This analysis can be done by company or by department.

- Generate exception reports that test for any employee whose compensation has increased from the prior year by a disproportionately large percentage. For example, if an organization generally awards raises of no more than 3 percent, then it would be advisable to double-check the records of any employee whose wages have increased by more than 3 percent.

- Verify that payroll taxes for the year equal federal tax forms.

- Compare net payroll-to-payroll checks issued.

Commission Schemes

Commission is a form of compensation calculated as a percentage of the amount of sales a salesperson or other employee generates. It is a unique form of compensation that is not based on hours worked or a set yearly salary, but rather on an employee's revenue output. A commissioned employee's wages are based on two factors: the amount of sales he generates and the percentage of those sales he is paid. In other

words, there are two ways an employee on commission can fraudulently increase his pay: (1) falsify the amount of sales made, or (2) increase the rate of commission (see Figure 12-11).

Fictitious Sales An employee can falsify the amount of sales he has made in two ways, the first being the creation of fictitious sales. In one case, for example, an unscrupulous insurance agent took advantage of his company's incentive commissions that paid $1.25 for every $1.00 of premiums generated in the first year of a policy. The agent wrote policies to fictitious customers, paid the premiums, and received his commissions, which created an illicit profit on the transaction. For instance, if the fraudster paid $100,000 in premiums, he would receive $125,000 in commissions, a $25,000 profit. No payments were made on the fraudulent policies after the first year.

The way in which fictitious sales are created depends on the organization for which the fraudster works. A fictitious sale might be constructed by the creation of fraudulent sales orders, purchase orders, credit authorizations, packing slips, invoices, and so on. On the other hand, a fraudster might simply ring up a false sale on a cash register. The key is that a fictitious sale is created, that it appears to be legitimate, and that the victim company reacts by issuing a commission check to the fraudster.

Altered Sales The second way for a fraudster to falsify the value of sales he has made is to alter the prices listed on sales documents. In other words, the fraudster charges one price to a customer, but records a higher price in the company books. This results in the payment of a commission that is larger than the fraudster deserves. In one situation, a salesman quoted a certain rate to his customers, billed them at this rate and collected their payments, but overstated his sales reports. The fraudster intercepted and altered the outgoing invoices from these transactions so that his customers would not detect the fraud. He also overstated the revenues received from his customers. Since the fraudster's commissions were based on the amount of revenues he billed out, he was overcompensated.

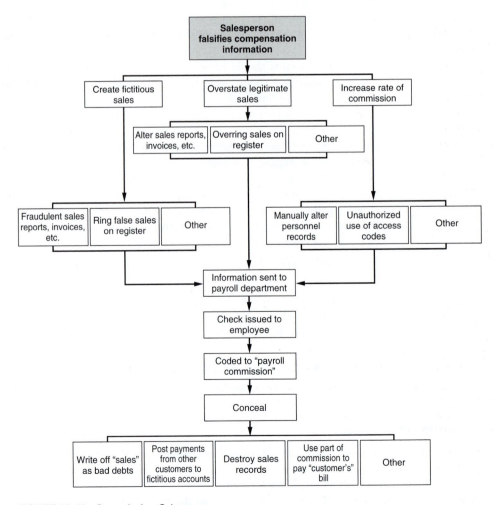

FIGURE 12-11 Commission Schemes

As mentioned above, the other way to manipulate the commission process is to change the employee's rate of commission. This would likely necessitate the alteration of payroll or personnel records, which should be off-limits to the sales staff.

Detecting Commission Schemes   Generally, there should be a linear correlation between sales figures and commission expenses. Periodic reports should be run to confirm this relationship. If commission expenses increase as a percentage of total sales, this might indicate fraud. An employee independent of the sales department should investigate the reason for the increase.

If a salesperson is engaged in a commission scheme, his commissions earned will tend to rise compared to other members of the sales department. Organizations should routinely test for this type of fraud by running a comparative analysis of commission earned by each salesperson verifying rates and calculation accuracy.

In addition, organizations should track uncollected sales generated by each member of their sales department. One of the most common commission schemes involves the creation of fictitious sales to bolster commission earnings. Obviously, these fictitious sales will most likely go uncollected. Therefore, if an employee tends to generate a much higher percentage of uncollected sales than his coworkers, this could indicate fraud. A review of the support for the uncollected sales should be conducted to verify that they were legitimate transactions.

Overstated sales or fictitious sales can also be detected by conducting a random sample of customers. Verify that the customer exists, that the sale is legitimate, and that the amount of the sale corresponds to the customer's records. Someone independent of the sales force must perform this confirmation.

Proactive Computer Audit Tests for Detecting Payroll Fraud

Title	Category	Description	Data file(s)
Age employee payments by check date.	All	Focuses audit efforts on periods of increased activity.	• Payroll Register
Stratify on hourly rates, hours worked, net pay amount, commission amount, overtime hours.	All	Focuses audit efforts on high rates.	• Payroll Register
Compare salaried employee gross pay from one pay period to the next.	All	Review changes in salaried payroll for areas of potential fraud.	• Payroll Register
Age customer open invoices by salesperson.	Commission	Identifies salespeople that have unusually old receivable balances, which may be phony invoices used to bolster commission payments.	• Sales Register (Open Invoices Designated)
Extract all round-dollar payments.	All	Round-dollar payments have a higher likelihood of being fraudulent.	• Invoice Payment
Compare current year to prior year payroll file to detect additional/terminated employees.	Ghost employees	Highlights new and terminated employees for agreement to authorization records. New employees should be reviewed closely to determine whether ghost employees accepting fraudulent payments exist.	• Payroll Register • Employee Master File
Compare employees reported per timecard system to payroll system.	Ghost employees	Isolates differences between the employee register in the timecard system and the payroll register. Focus should be on employees in the payroll register who do not appear in the timecard system and who thus may have been fraudulently added.	• Payroll Register • Timecard System

(Continued)

(*Continued*)

Title	Category	Description	Data file(s)
Compare payroll data files to human resource data files to test for differences between the files.	Ghost employees	Ensures agreement between human resource and payroll records. Isolate potential unauthorized payroll payments. Detect new or terminated employees for agreement to authorized forms.	• Payroll Register • Employee Master File
Extract all employee payments with no deductions/taxes withheld.	Ghost employees	Highlights payments without taxes/deductions, which are, by their nature, more prone to fraud.	• Payroll Register
Extract all employees without an employee number or Social Security number.	Ghost employees	Reports potential ghost employees who may have unauthorized payments. Please note that this field may be blank or filled with "999999999."	• Payroll Register • Employee Master File
Extract employee payments with payment dates after termination dates.	Ghost employees	Reports potentially unauthorized payments to terminated employees that may be made by an employee and later intercepted.	• Payroll Register • Employee Master File
Extract employees without names.	Ghost employees	Reports potential ghost employees who may have unauthorized payments or payments made with payees being written in after check printing.	• Payroll Register • Employee Master File
Sequence duplicate Social Security numbers paid in the same pay period.	Ghost employees	Lists possible duplicate payments to employees, which are highly prone to fraud.	• Payroll Register • Employee Master File
Sequence duplicate direct deposit numbers paid in the same pay period.	Ghost employees	Lists possible duplicate payments to employees, which are highly prone to fraud.	• Payroll Register • Employee Master File
Sequence possible duplicate payments based on the absolute value of the net pay and the check date.	Ghost employees	Lists possible duplicate payments to employees, which are highly prone to fraud.	• Payroll Register
Sequence duplicate mailing address numbers paid in the same pay period.	Ghost employees	Lists possible duplicate payments to employees, which are highly prone to fraud.	• Payroll Register • Employee Master File
Extract users who can write checks and also add new employees in the payroll and timecard system.	Ghost employees and falsified hours and salary	Users who can enter new employees, enter time, and write a fraudulent check would be taking advantage of nonsegregation of duties to commit their fraud. User access should be reviewed from the perspective of adjustments within the application and adjustments to the data itself.	• Payroll Register User Access Master File • Timecard User Access Master File • Payroll Register User Access Log File • Timecard User Access Log File
Calculate the percentage of bonus to gross pay (on a person-by-person basis) and sort from high to low.	Falsified hours and salary	Reports high and potentially unauthorized bonus payments.	• Payroll Register
Calculate the percentage of fringe expense to the gross pay (on a person-by-person basis) and sort from high to low.	Falsified hours and salary	Reports unusually high fringe payments. Also, payments with fringe payments equal to zero are, by their nature, more prone to fraud.	• Payroll Register
Calculate the percentage of overtime to gross pay (on a person-by-person basis) and sort from low to high.	Falsified hours and salary	Reports high and potentially unauthorized overtime expenses.	• Payroll Register

Title	Category	Description	Data file(s)
Calculate the average payroll per employee and sort from high to low.	Falsified hours and salary and commission schemes	Reports high and potentially unauthorized employee payments.	• Payroll Register
Compare bonus payments to budget or prior year on an employee-by-employee basis.	Falsified hours and salary	Reports large changes and potentially unauthorized bonus payments.	• Payroll Register
Compare current year to prior year payroll file to detect changes in pay rates.	Falsified hours and salary	Highlights changes in rates that can be reviewed for unusual trends, exceptions, and unauthorized changes.	• Payroll Register • Employee Master File
Compare hours reported per timecard system to payroll system.	Falsified hours and salary	Isolates differences between the hours worked and the hours paid to employees. Overpayments may be detected if more hours are paid for than worked or unauthorized deductions of hours may be occurring.	• Payroll Register • Timecard System
Compare overtime hours to budget or prior year by department.	Falsified hours and salary	Reports large changes and potentially unauthorized overtime payments.	• Payroll Register
Compare payroll data files to human resource data files to test for differing salary rates.	Falsified hours and salary	Ensures agreement between human resource and payroll records. Isolates potential unauthorized payroll payments. Detects new or terminated employees for agreement to authorized forms.	• Payroll Register • Employee Master File
Extract all employees paid more than 25 percent of their gross pay in overtime.	Falsified hours and salary	Reports large and potentially unauthorized overtime payments.	• Payroll Register
Extract all employees with over x hours per pay period.	Falsified hours and salary	Reports large and potentially unauthorized hours charged by employees. One popular test is to review any employees with over 168 hours (more hours than there are in a week).	• Payroll Register
Recalculate gross pay.	Falsified hours and salary	Recalculate gross pay for agreement to company records. Any differences may signal a control weakness in the computer system or fraudulently adjusted payment.	• Payroll Register
Recalculate net pay.	Falsified hours and salary	Recalculate net pay for agreement to company records. Any differences may signal a control weakness in the computer system or fraudulently adjusted payment.	• Payroll Register
Recalculate the hours reported per the timecard system by employee.	Falsified hours and salary	Recalculate hours per timecard system for agreement to payroll check-writing system. Any differences may signal a control weakness in the computer system or fraudulently adjusted payment.	• Timecard System
Summarize commissions paid by product line, region, and salesperson.	Commission schemes	Focus should be on areas of high ratios for potential fraudulently inflated sales/commissions.	• Payroll Register

(Continued)

(*Continued*)

Title	Category	Description	Data file(s)
Complete a trend analysis of commission to sale ratios by salesperson.	Commission schemes	Sales and commission ratios should work in a linear fashion over time and should not appear overstated in relation to the sales.	• Payroll Register • Sales Register
Recalculate commissions based on current year sales and other required performance measures.	Commission schemes	Recalculate commissions for agreement to company records. Any differences may signal a control weakness in the computer system or fraudulently adjusted payment.	• Payroll Register • Sales Register
Classify sales prices by salesperson and calculate an average price per salesperson.	Commission schemes	Focus should be on areas of high sales prices for potential fraudulently inflated sales/commissions.	• Sales Register
Sequence possible duplicate sales invoices based on the absolute value of the invoice and customer.	Commission schemes	Lists possible duplicate invoices that may be used to inflate sales and associated commissions.	• Sales Register
Dormant customer accounts for the past six months that post a sale in the last two months of the year.	Commission schemes	Customers that have been dormant may be used as accounts to post fraudulent activity, increasing any associated commissions.	• Sales Register
Calculate the ratio of the largest sale to next largest sale by customer.	Commission schemes	By identifying the largest sale to a customer and the next largest sale, any large ratio difference may identify a fraudulently recorded "largest" sale. This would essentially be made to increase any associated commissions.	• Sales Register
Extract customer sales that exceed the twelve-month average sales from that customer by a specified percentage (i.e., 200 percent).	Commission schemes	This test may identify a large fraudulently recorded sale. This would essentially be made to increase any associated commissions.	• Sales Register
Extract customer sale balances that exceed the customer credit limit.	Commission schemes	This test may identify a large fraudulently recorded sale. This would essentially be made to increase any associated commissions.	• Sales Register • Customer Master File
Compare the Customer Master File to the Sales Register for phony customers.	Commission schemes	Phony customers added could be used to post fraudulent invoices that would be used to inflate commissions.	• Sales Register • Customer Master File
Extract customers with no telephone or tax ID number.	Commission schemes	Customers without this information are more prone to abuse and should be scrutinized as possible phantom customers.	• Customer Master File
Identify customers added during the period under review.	Commission schemes	New customer additions should be reviewed using this report to determine whether any phantom customers are being created.	• Customer Master File
Extract any salesperson users who can enter sales orders/adjustments and also can create customer accounts.	Commission schemes	Users who can create new customers and then post orders/adjustments to those customers would be taking advantage of nonsegregation of duties to commit their fraud. User access should be reviewed from the perspective of adjustments within the application and adjustments to the data itself.	• Sales Register User Access Master File • Customer Master User Access Master File • Sales Register User Access Log File • Customer Master Access Log File

EXPENSE REIMBURSEMENT SCHEMES

Expense reimbursement schemes, as their name implies, occur when employees make false claims for reimbursement of fictitious or inflated business expenses. This is a very common form of occupational fraud and one that, by its nature, can be extremely difficult to detect. Employees who engage in this type of fraud generally seek to have the company pay for their personal expenses, or they pad the amount of business expenses they have incurred in order to generate excess reimbursements. In most cases, the travel and entertainment expenses at issue were incurred away from the office, where there was no direct supervision and no company representative (other than the fraudster) present to verify that the expenses were, indeed, incurred. Thus, these frauds generally are detected through indirect means—trend analysis, comparisons of expenses to work schedules, and so forth. If a fraudster is smart and does not get too greedy, it can be virtually impossible to catch an expense reimbursement scheme. But then, most fraudsters eventually get greedy.

Expense reimbursements are usually paid by organizations in the following manner: An employee submits a report detailing an expense incurred for a business purpose, such as a business lunch with a client, airfare, or hotel bills associated with business travel. In preparing the expense report, the employee usually must explain the business purpose for the expense, as well as the time, date, and location in which it was incurred. Attached to the report should be supporting documentation for the expense, typically a receipt. In some cases canceled checks written by the employee or copies of a personal credit card statement showing the expense are allowed. The report usually must be authorized by a supervisor in order for the expense to be reimbursed.

There are four methods by which employees typically abuse this process to generate fraudulent reimbursements:

1. Mischaracterized expense reimbursements
2. Overstated expense reimbursements
3. Fictitious expense reimbursements
4. Multiple reimbursements

Mischaracterized Expense Reimbursements

Most companies reimburse only certain expenses of their employees. Which expenses a company will pay depends to an extent on policy, but in general, business-related travel, lodging, and meals are reimbursed. One of the most basic expense schemes is perpetrated by simply requesting reimbursement for a personal expense, claiming that it is business-related (see Figure 12-12). Examples of mischaracterized expenses include claiming personal travel as a business trip, listing dinner with a friend as "business development," and so on. Fraudsters may submit the receipts from their personal expenses along with their reports and provide business reasons for the incurred costs.

The false expense report induces the victim company to issue a check, reimbursing the perpetrator for his personal expenses. A mischaracterization is a simple scheme.

In cases involving airfare and overnight travel, a mischaracterization can sometimes be detected by simply comparing the employee's expense reports to his or her work schedule. Often, the dates of the so-called "business trip" coincide with a vacation or day off. Detailed expense reports allow a company to make this kind of comparison and are therefore very helpful in preventing expenses schemes.

Requiring detailed information means more than just supporting documents; it should mean precise statements of what was purchased, as well as when and where. In one case, a fraudster submitted credit card statements as support for expenses, but he submitted only the top portion of the statements, not the portion that describes what was purchased. Over 95 percent of his expenses that were reimbursed were of a personal rather than a business nature. Of course, in this particular example, the scheme was made easier because the perpetrator was the CEO of the company, making it unlikely that anyone would challenge the validity of his expense reports.

For whatever reason, most of the mischaracterized expense schemes in ACFE studies were undertaken by high-level employees, owners, or officers. Many times, the perpetrator actually had authority over the account from which expenses were reimbursed. Another common element was the failure to submit detailed expense reports, or any expense reports at all. Obviously, when a company is willing to reimburse employee expenses without any verifying documentation, it is easy for an employee to take advantage of the system. Nevertheless, there does not seem to be anything inherent in the nature of a mischaracterization scheme that would preclude its use in a system where detailed reports are required. As an example, suppose a traveling

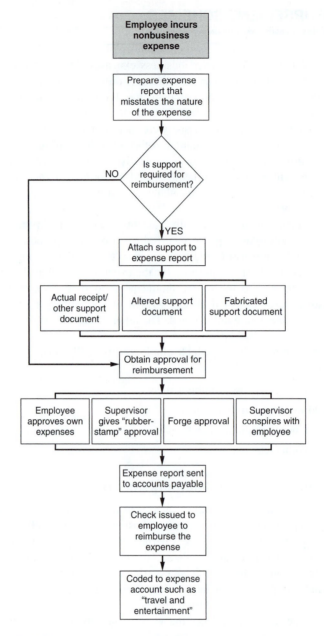

FIGURE 12-12 Mischaracterized Expenses

salesman goes on a trip and runs up a large bar bill one night in his hotel, saves his receipt, and lists this expense as "business entertainment" on an expense report. Nothing about the time, date, or nature of the expense would readily point to fraud, and the receipt would appear to substantiate the expense. Short of contacting the client who was allegedly entertained, there is little hope of identifying the expense as fraudulent.

One final note is that mischaracterization schemes can be extremely costly. They do not always deal with a free lunch here or there, but instead may involve very large sums of money. One case involved two mid-level managers who ran up $1 million in inappropriate expenses over a two-year period. Their travel was not properly overseen, and their expense requests were not closely reviewed, allowing them to spend large amounts of company money on international travel, lavish entertainment of friends, and the purchase of expensive gifts. They simply claimed that they incurred these expenses entertaining corporate clients. While this was certainly more costly than the average mischaracterization scheme, it should underscore the potential harm that can occur if the reimbursement process is not carefully tended.

Preventing and Detecting Mischaracterized Expense Reimbursements Expense reimbursement fraud is very common and can be difficult to detect. It is important for organizations to focus on preventing these crimes by establishing and adhering to a system of controls that makes fraud more

difficult to commit. As a starting point, every organization should require detailed expense reports that include original support documents, dates and times of business expenses, method of payment, and descriptions of the purpose for the expenses. All travel and entertainment expenses should be reviewed by a direct supervisor of the requestor. In no circumstance should expenses be reimbursed without an independent review.

Organizations should establish a policy that clearly states what types of expenses will and will not be reimbursed, that explains what are considered nonvalid reasons for incurring business expenses, and that sets reasonable limits for expense reimbursements.

This policy must be publicized to all employees, particularly those who are likely to incur travel and entertainment expenses, and employees should sign a statement acknowledging that they understand the policy and will abide by it. This serves two purposes: (1) it educates employees about what are considered acceptable reimbursable expenses, and (2) in the event that an employee tries to claim reimbursement for personal or nonreimbursable expenses, the signed statement will provide evidence that the employee knew the company's rules, which will help establish that the expense report in question was intentionally fraudulent and not the result of an honest mistake.

In some cases, fraud perpetrators try to get personal expenses approved by having their expense reports reviewed by a supervisor outside their department. The idea is that these supervisors will not be as familiar with the employee's work schedule, duties, and so on, so for instance, if the perpetrator is claiming expenses for dates when she was on vacation, a direct supervisor might spot this anomaly, but a supervisor from another department might not. Therefore, organizations should scrutinize any expense report that was approved by a supervisor outside the requestor's department.

Because so many mischaracterized expense schemes involve personal expenses incurred during nonworking hours, one way to catch these crimes is to compare dates of claimed expenses to work schedules. For example, an organization could set up its accounting system so that any payment coded as an expense reimbursement is automatically compared to vacation or leave time requested by the employee in question. Expenses incurred on weekends or at unusual times could also be flagged for follow-up.

Organizations can also use trend analysis to detect these frauds. Current expense reimbursement levels should be compared to prior years and to budgeted amounts. If travel and entertainment expenses seem to be excessive, attempt to identify any legitimate business reasons for the increase. Also compare expense reimbursements per employee, looking for particular individuals whose expense reimbursements seem excessive.

Overstated Expense Reimbursements

Instead of seeking reimbursement for personal expenses, some employees overstate the cost of actual business expenses (see Figure 12-13). This can be accomplished in a number of ways.

Altered Receipts The most fundamental example of overstated expense schemes occurs when an employee doctors a receipt or other supporting documentation to reflect a higher cost than what he actually paid. The employee may use correction fluid, a ball-point pen, or some other method to change the price reflected on the receipt before submitting his expense report. If the company does not require original documents as support, the perpetrator generally attaches a copy of the receipt to his expense report. Alterations are usually less noticeable on a photocopy than on an original document. For precisely this reason, many businesses require original receipts and ink signatures on expense reports.

As with other expense frauds, overstated expense schemes often succeed because of poor controls. In companies where supporting documents are not required, for example, fraudsters simply lie about how much they paid for a business expense. With no support available, it may be very difficult to disprove an employee's false expense claims.

Over purchasing One case illustrated another way to overstate a reimbursement form, the "overpurchasing" of business expenses. An employee purchased two tickets for his business travel, one expensive and one cheap. He returned the expensive ticket, but retained the passenger-receipt coupon and used it to overstate his expense reports. Meanwhile, he used the cheaper ticket for his trip. In this manner, he was able to be reimbursed for an expense that was larger than what he had actually paid.

Overstating Another Employee's Expenses Overstated expense schemes are not only committed by the person who incur the expenses. Instead, they may be committed by someone else who handles or processes expense reports. An example occurred in a case where a petty cashier used correction fluid on

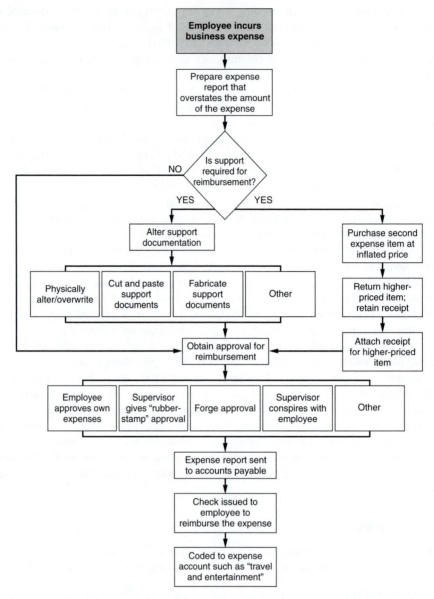

FIGURE 12-13 Overstated Expenses

other employees' requests for travel advances and inserted larger amounts. The cashier then passed on the legitimate travel advances and pocketed the excess.

This kind of scheme is most likely to occur in a system where expenses are reimbursed in currency rather than by a check, since the perpetrator would be unable to extract her "cut" from a single check made out to another employee.

Orders to Overstate Expenses Finally, AFCE researchers have seen a few cases where employees knowingly falsified their own reports, but did so at the direction of their supervisors. For instance, a department head forced his subordinates to inflate their expenses and return the proceeds to him. The employees went along with this scheme, presumably for fear of losing their jobs. The fraud lasted for ten years and cost the victim company approximately $6 million. Similarly, in another case, a sales executive instructed his salesmen to inflate their expenses in order to generate cash for a slush fund. This fund was used to pay bribes and to provide improper forms of entertainment for clients and customers.

Preventing and Detecting Overstated Expense Reimbursement Schemes In addition to the prevention and detection methods that have already been discussed, it is particularly important in dealing with overstated expense reimbursement schemes that an organization require *original* receipts

for all expense reimbursements. Alterations to original receipts should be very obvious, whereas it can be difficult to detect alterations to photocopies. Any policy on expense reimbursements should clearly state that expenses will be reimbursed only when supported by original receipts. For example, organizations should require employees to supply original ticket stubs when reimbursing airline and rail travel. If an employee does supply a photocopied receipt in support of claimed travel and entertainment expenses, the expense should be independently verified before it is reimbursed. Itineraries or travel agency receipts are not sufficient, because these do not prove that the tickets were actually used (see over purchasing schemes).

Comparison reports that show reimbursed expenses can be useful in detecting overstated expense reimbursement schemes. If one employee's travel and entertainment expenses are consistently higher than those of co-workers who have similar travel schedules, this would be a red flag. Also, a comparison of similar expenses incurred by different individuals may highlight fraud. For example, if two salespeople regularly fly to the same city, does one tend to seek higher levels of reimbursement?

If an organization has had problems with expense reimbursement fraud, it may be helpful to spot-check expense reports with customers, confirming business dinners, meetings, and so forth.

Fictitious Expense Reimbursement Schemes

Expense reimbursements are sometimes sought by employees for wholly fictitious items. Instead of overstating a real business expense or seeking reimbursement for a personal expense, an employee just invents a purchase that needs to be reimbursed (see Figure 12-14).

Producing Fictitious Receipts One way to generate a reimbursement for a fictitious expense is to create bogus support documents, such as false receipts. The emergence of personal computers has enabled some employees to create realistic-looking counterfeit receipts at home. Such was the scheme in one case in which an employee manufactured fake receipts using his computer and laser printer. These counterfeits were very sophisticated, even including the logos of the stores where he had allegedly made business-related purchases.

Computers are not the only means for creating support for a fictitious expense. Another fraudster used several methods for justifying fictitious expenses as his scheme progressed. He began by using calculator printouts to simulate receipts, then advanced to cutting and pasting receipts from suppliers before finally progressing to the use of computer software to generate fictitious receipts.

Obtaining Blank Receipts from Vendors If receipts are not created by the fraudster, they can be obtained from legitimate suppliers in a number of ways. A manager in one case simply requested blank receipts from waiters, bartenders, and so on. He then filled in these receipts to "create" business expenses, including the names of clients whom he allegedly entertained. The fraudster usually paid all his expenses in cash to prevent an audit trail. One thing that undid this culprit was the fact that the last digit on most of the prices on his receipt was usually a zero or a five. This detail, which was noticed by an astute employee, raised questions about the validity of his expenses.

A similar scheme was found in a case in which an employee's girlfriend worked at a restaurant near the victim company. This girlfriend validated credit card receipts and gave them to the fraudster so that he could submit them with his expense reports.

Instead of asking for blank receipts, some employees simply steal them. In some cases a fraudster will steal an entire stack of blank receipts and over time submit them to verify fictitious business expenses. This type of fraud should be identifiable by the fact that the perpetrator is submitting consecutively numbered receipts from the same establishment despite the fact that his expense reports are spread out over time.

Claiming the Expenses of Others Another way fraudsters use actual receipts to generate unwarranted reimbursements is by submitting expense reports for expenses that were paid by others. For instance, an employee claimed hotel expenses that had actually been paid by his client. Photocopies of legitimate hotel bills were attached to the expense report as though the employee had paid for his own room.

As we have stated, not all companies require receipts to be attached to expense reports. Checks written by the employee or copies of his personal credit card bill might be allowed as support in lieu of a receipt. In one case, a person wrote personal checks that appeared to be for business expenses, then photocopied these checks and attached them to reimbursement requests. In actuality, nothing was purchased with the checks; they were destroyed after the copies were made. This enabled the fraudster to receive a

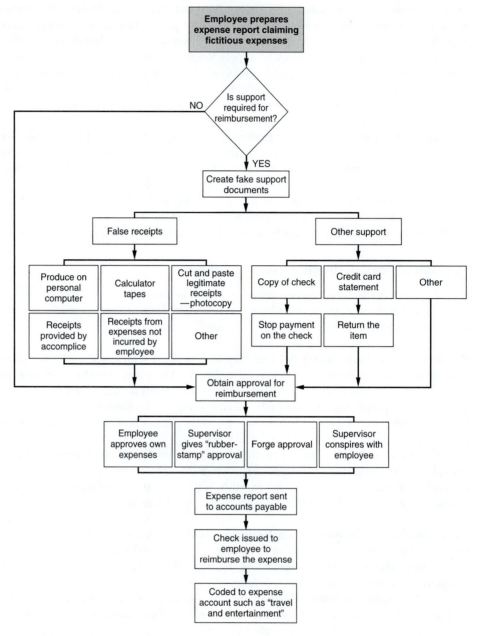

FIGURE 12-14 Fictitious Expenses

reimbursement from his employer without ever actually incurring a business expense. The same method can be used with credit cards, where a copy of a statement is used to support a purchase. Once the expense report is filed, the fraudster returns the item and receives a credit to his account.

In many expense reimbursement schemes the perpetrator is not required to submit any support at all. This makes it much easier to create the appearance of an expense that does not actually exist.

Preventing and Detecting Fictitious Expense Reimbursement Schemes There are a number of red flags that may indicate an employee is seeking reimbursement for fictitious travel and entertainment expenses. One of the most common is the employee who claims items—particularly high-dollar items—were paid for in cash. The reason an employee would claim an expense was paid in cash is because this allows him to explain why there is no audit trail for the expense (i.e., why the item did not show up on his company credit card statement). Organizations should be alert for patterns in which an employee uses credit cards for low-dollar expenses but pays cash for high-dollar expenses. Other common red flags include the following:

EXPENSE REIMBURSEMENT SCHEMES

- Expenses that are consistently rounded off, ending with a "0" or a "5," which tends to indicate that the employee is fabricating the numbers.

- Patterns in which expenses are consistently for the same amount (i.e., a salesperson's business dinners always cost $120).

- Reimbursement requests from an employee that consistently fall at or just below the organization's reimbursement limit.

- Receipts from a restaurant that are submitted over an extended period of time, yet are consecutively numbered. This tends to indicate that the employee has obtained a stack of blank receipts and is using them to support fictitious expenses.

- Receipts or other support that does not look professional or lacks information about the vendor, such as phone numbers, physical addresses, or logos.

Multiple Reimbursement Schemes

The least common of the expense reimbursement schemes as revealed in the ACFE's studies are the multiple reimbursement schemes. This type of fraud involves the submission of a single expense several times to receive multiple reimbursements. The most frequent example of a duplicate reimbursement scheme is the submission of several types of support for the same expense. An example arose in a case in which an employee used, for example, an airline ticket stub and a travel agency invoice on separate expense reports so that he could be reimbursed twice for the cost of a single flight. The fraudster would have his division president authorize one report and have the vice president approve the other, so that neither would see both reports. Additionally, the perpetrator allowed a time lag of about a month between the filing of the two reports so that the duplication would be less noticeable.

In cases where a company does not require original documents as support, some employees even use several copies of the same support document to generate multiple reimbursements.

Rather than file two expense reports, employees may charge an item to the company credit card, saving the receipt and attaching it to an expense report as if they paid for the item themselves. The victim company therefore ends up paying twice for the same expense.

Perhaps the most interesting case of duplicated expenses in our study involved a government official who had responsibilities over two distinct budgets. The perpetrator of this case would take a business trip and make expense claims to the travel funds of each of his budgets, thereby receiving a double reimbursement. In some cases the culprit charged the expenses to another budget category and still submitted reports through both budgets, generating a triple reimbursement. Eventually this person began to fabricate trips when he was not even leaving town, which led to the detection of his scheme.

Preventing and Detecting Multiple Reimbursement Schemes   Organizations should enforce a policy against accepting photocopies as support for business expenses. This practice will help prevent schemes where copies of the same receipt are submitted several times. If photocopies are submitted, verify the expense and check it against previous requests before issuing a reimbursement. An organization's accounting system should be set up to flag duplicate payment amounts that are coded as travel and entertainment expense.

It is also important to clearly establish what types of support will be accepted with an expense report. For instance, some fraudsters use a restaurant receipt to claim reimbursement for a business dinner, and then use their credit card statement to claim reimbursement for the meal a second time. If the organization accepts only original receipts, this scheme will not succeed.

Expense reports that are approved by supervisors outside the requestor's department should be carefully scrutinized, and in general, organizations should require that expense reports be reviewed and approved by a direct supervisor. Employees may take an expense report to a manager from another department because they know that manager will not be familiar enough with their work schedule to spot an inconsistency on the report, or they may try to have two managers approve the same report as part of a multiple reimbursement scheme.

Some employees obtain reimbursement for a business expense, maintain a copy of the receipt, and resubmit the expense after a few weeks. Organizations should establish a policy whereby expenses must be submitted within a certain time frame. Any expenses more than sixty days old, for example, would be denied.

Proactive Computer Audit Tests for Detecting Expense Reimbursement Schemes

Title	Category	Description	Data file(s)
Age employee payments by check date.	All	Focuses audit efforts on periods of increased activity.	• Invoice Payment
Stratify by expense payment amount.	All	Focuses audit efforts on high invoice payments.	• Invoice Payment
Extract multiple charges of the same product type (using SIC code) below a predefined credit card expense limit.	All	Charges below an approval limit may be an attempt to circumvent a management review.	• Procurement Card
Summarize credit card use by employee and sort from high to low.	All	High usage of credit cards by certain employees may be a sign of abuse.	• Procurement Card
Extract all round-dollar payments.	All	Round-dollar payments have a higher likelihood of being fraudulent.	• Invoice Payment
Extract payments to employees for expenses that were incurred during time periods when the employee was on vacation.	Mischaracterized expenses	Expenses for business are rarely charged when the employee is also on vacation.	• Invoice Payment • Procurement Card
Extract SIC codes from credit card payments normally associated with personal purchases.	Mischaracterized expenses	Personal purchases with company cards may be a sign of abuse.	• Procurement Card
Sequence possible duplicate expenses based on the absolute value of the amount and receipt date.	Multiple reimbursements	Lists possible duplicate invoices that may be used to inflate sales and associated commissions.	• Invoice Payment

REGISTER DISBURSEMENT SCHEMES

In Chapter 11, we discussed two ways in which fraud is committed at the cash register—skimming and cash larceny. These schemes are what we commonly think of as outright theft. They involve the surreptitious removal of money from a cash register. When money is taken from a register in a skimming or larceny scheme, there is no record of the transaction; the money is simply missing.

Fraudulent disbursement schemes differ from the other register frauds in that when money is taken from the cash register, the removal of money is recorded on the register tape. A false transaction is recorded as though it were a legitimate disbursement to justify the removal of money.

There are two basic fraudulent disbursement schemes that take place at the cash register: *false refunds* and *false voids*. Although the schemes are largely similar, there are a few differences between the two that merit discussing them separately.

False Refunds

A refund is processed at the register when a customer returns an item of merchandise purchased from that store. The transaction that is entered on the register indicates that the merchandise is being replaced in the store's inventory and the purchase price is being returned to the customer. In other words, a refund shows a disbursement of money from the register as the customer gets his money back (see Figure 12-15).

Fictitious Refunds In a fictitious refund scheme, a fraudster processes a transaction as if a customer were returning merchandise, even though there is no actual return. Two things result from this fraudulent transaction. The first is that the fraudster takes cash from the register in the amount of the false return. Since the register tape shows that a merchandise return has been made, it appears that the disbursement is legitimate. The register tape balances with the amount of money in the register, because the money that was taken by the fraudster was supposed to have been removed and given to a customer as a refund.

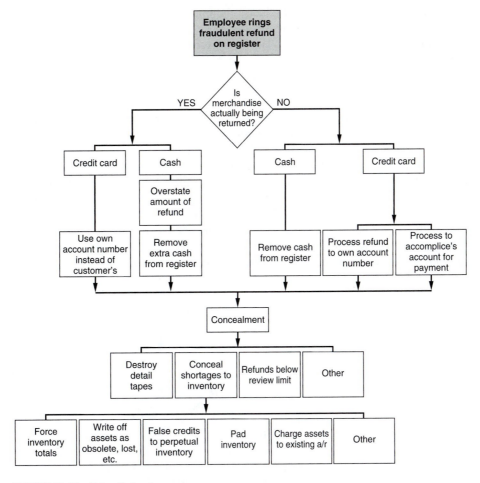

FIGURE 12-15 False Refunds

The second thing that happens in a fictitious refund scheme is that a debit is made to the inventory system showing that the merchandise has been returned to the inventory. Since the transaction is fictitious, no merchandise is actually returned. The result is that the company's inventory is overstated. For instance, in one case, a manager created $5,500 worth of false returns, resulting in a large shortage in the company's inventory. He was able to carry on his scheme for several months, however, because (1) inventory was not counted regularly, and (2) the perpetrator, a manager, was one of the people who performed inventory counts.

Overstated Refunds Rather than create an entirely fictitious refund, some fraudsters merely overstate the amount of a legitimate refund and steal the excess money. This occurred in another case, where an employee sought to supplement his income through the processing of fraudulent refunds. In some cases he rang up completely fictitious refunds, making up names and phone numbers for his customers. In other instances he added to the value of legitimate refunds. He would overstate the value of a real customer's refund, pay the customer the actual amount owed for the returned merchandise, and then keep the excess portion of the return for himself.

Credit Card Refunds When purchases are made with a credit card rather than cash, refunds appear as credits to the customer's credit card rather than as cash disbursements. Some fraudsters process false refunds on credit card sales in lieu of processing a normal cash transaction. One benefit of the credit card method is that the perpetrator does not have to physically take cash from the register and carry it out of the store. This is the most dangerous part of a typical register scheme, because managers, co-workers, or security cameras may detect the culprit in the process of removing the cash. By processing the refunds to a credit card account, a fraudster reaps an unwarranted financial gain and avoids the potential embarrassment of being caught red-handed taking cash.

In a typical credit card refund scheme, the fraudster rings up a refund on a credit card sale, though the merchandise is not actually being returned. Rather than use the customer's credit card number on the refund, the employee inserts his own. The result is that the cost of the item is credited to the perpetrator's credit card account.

False Voids

False voids are similar to refund schemes in that they generate a disbursement from the register. When a sale is voided on a register, a copy of the customer's receipt is usually attached to a void slip, along with the signature or initials of a manager that indicate that the transaction has been approved (see Figure 12-16). In order to process a false void, then, the first thing the fraudster needs is the customer's copy of the sales receipt. Typically, when an employee sets about processing a fictitious void, he simply withholds the customer's receipt at the time of the sale. If the customer requests the receipt, the clerk can produce it, but in many cases customers simply do not notice that they didn't receive a receipt.

With the customer copy of the receipt in hand, the culprit rings a voided sale. Whatever money the customer paid for the item is removed from the register as though it were being returned to a customer. The copy of the customer's receipt is attached to the void slip to verify the authenticity of the transaction.

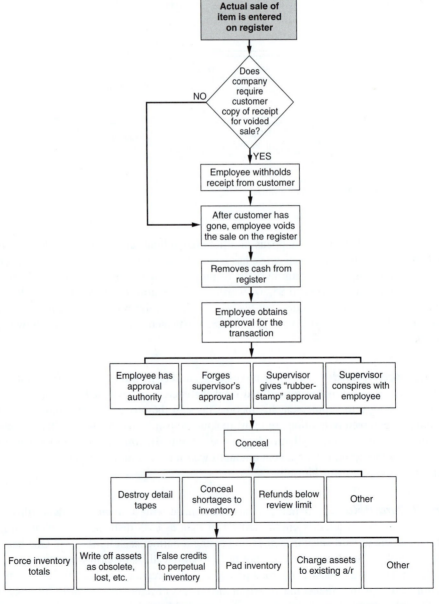

FIGURE 12-16 False Voids

Before the voided sale will be perceived as valid, a manager generally must approve it. In many of the cases in ACFE studies, the manager in question simply neglected to verify the authenticity of the voided sale. These managers signed almost anything presented to them and thus left themselves and their organizations vulnerable to a voided sales scheme. An example of this kind of managerial disinterest occurred in a case in which a retail clerk kept customer receipts and "voided" their sales after the customers left the store. The store manager signed the void slips on these transactions without taking any action to verify their authenticity. A similar breakdown in review was detected in another case in which an employee processed fraudulent voids, kept customer receipts, and presented them to her supervisors for review at the end of her shift, long after the alleged transactions had taken place. Her supervisors approved the voided sales, and the accounts receivable department failed to notice the excessive number of voided sales processed by this employee.

It was not a coincidence that the perpetrators of these crimes presented their void slips to a manager who happened to be lackadaisical about authorizing them. Rather, it is generally the case that these kinds of managers are essential to the employee's schemes.

Since not all managers are willing to provide rubber-stamp approval of voided sales, some employees take affirmative steps to get their voided sales "approved." This usually amounts to forgery, whereby the fraudster forges his supervisor's signature.

Finally, it is possible that a manager will conspire with a register employee and approve false voids in return for a share of the proceeds. While ACFE researchers did not encounter any cases like this in their study, they did come across several examples of managers helping employees to falsify timecards or expense reimbursement requests. There is no logical reason why the same kind of scheme would not work with false voids.

Concealing Register Disbursements

As we discussed above, when a false refund or void is entered into the register, two things happen. The first is that the employee committing the fraud removes cash from the register, and the second is that the item allegedly being returned is debited back into inventory. This leads to shrinkage: a situation in which there is less inventory actually on hand than the inventory records reflect. A certain amount of shrinkage is expected in any retail industry, but too much of it raises concerns of fraud.

Inventory, remember, is accounted for by a two-step process. The first part of the process is the perpetual inventory, which is essentially a running tabulation of how much inventory *should be on hand*. When a sale of merchandise is made, the perpetual inventory is credited to remove this merchandise from the records. The amount of merchandise that should be on hand is reduced. Periodically, someone from the company takes a physical count of the inventory, going through the stockroom or warehouse and counting the amount of inventory that *is actually on hand*. The two figures are then compared to see if there is a discrepancy between the perpetual inventory (what should be on hand) and the physical inventory (what is on hand). When a fraudulent refund or void has been recorded, the amount of inventory that is actually on hand will be less than the amount that should be on hand.

Typically, fraudsters do not make any effort to conceal the shrinkage that results from their schemes. In many register disbursement cases, the amount of shrinkage is not large enough to raise a red flag. However, in large-scale cases the amount of shrinkage caused by a fraudster can be quite significant. An excessive number of reversing transactions, combined with increased levels of shrinkage, would generally be considered a strong indicator of register disbursement fraud. For a discussion of how fraudsters attempt to conceal shrinkage, please see Chapter 11.

Aside from shrinkage, a register disbursement scheme leaves the victim organization's books in balance. The whole purpose of recording a fraudulent refund or void, after all, is to account for the stolen funds and justify their removal from the cash drawer. Therefore, fraudsters will often take no further steps to conceal a register disbursement scheme. However, a register disbursement scheme can still be detected if someone notices abnormal levels of refunds or voids. There are two methods that fraudsters often use to avoid this form of detection.

Small Disbursements   One common concealment technique is to keep the sizes of the disbursements low. Many companies set limits below which management review of a refund is not required. Where this is the case, fraudsters simply process copious numbers of small refunds that are small enough that they do not have to be reviewed. In one case, for example, an employee created over 1,000 false refunds, all under the review limit of $15. He was eventually caught because he began processing refunds before store hours and

another employee noticed that refunds were appearing on the system before the store opened. Nevertheless, before the fraudster's scheme was detected, he made off with over $11,000 of his employer's money.

Destroying Records One final means of concealing a register scheme, as with many kinds of fraud, is to destroy all records of the transaction. Most concealment methods are concerned with keeping management from realizing that fraud has occurred. When an employee resorts to destroying records, however, he typically has conceded that management will discover his theft. The purpose of destroying records is usually to prevent management from determining who the thief is. In one case, for example, a woman was creating false inventory vouchers that were reflected on the register tape. She then discarded all refund vouchers, both legitimate and fraudulent. Because documentation was missing on all transactions, it was extremely difficult to distinguish the good from the bad. Thus it was hard to determine who was stealing.

Preventing and Detecting Register Disbursement Schemes

The best way for organizations to prevent fraudulent register disbursements is to always maintain appropriate separation of duties. Management approval should be required for all refunds and voided sales in order to prevent a rogue employee from generating fraudulent disbursements at his cash register. Access to the control key or management code that authorizes reversing transactions should be closely guarded, and cashiers should not be allowed to reverse their own sales.

In addition to management review, voided transactions should be properly documented. Require a copy of the customer's receipt from the initial purchase, which should be attached to a copy of a void slip or other documentation of the transaction. This documentation should be retained on file.

Every cashier or sales clerk should be required to maintain a distinct log-in code for work at the register. This allows voids and refunds to be traced back to the employee who processed them. Periodically, organizations should generate reports of all reversing transactions at the register, looking for employees who tend to process an inordinate number of these transactions. Recurring transaction amounts, particularly round numbers such as $50, $100, and so on, are also common indicators of register disbursement fraud.

If the organization requires management approval only for voids and refunds above a certain amount, look for large numbers of transactions just below this amount. For instance, if the minimum review amount is $20, fraudsters may process multiple refunds for $19 in order to avoid review.

One way to help deter register disbursements is to place signs or institute store policies encouraging customers to ask for and examine their receipts. For example, offer a discount to any customer who does not receive a receipt. This will prevent employees from retaining customer receipts to use as support for false voids or refunds.

Random customer service calls can also be made to customers who have returned merchandise or voided sales as a way of verifying that these transactions actually took place. This type of verification is effective only if the persons who make the customer service calls are independent of the cash receipts function.

Proactive Computer Audit Tests for Detecting Register Disbursement Schemes

Title	Category	Description	Data file(s)
Summarize by location refunds and voids charged.	All	Locations with high adjustments may signal actions to hide register disbursement schemes.	• Sales System Register
Summarize by employee refunds and voids charged.	All	Employees with high adjustments may signal actions to hide register disbursement schemes.	• Sales System Register
List top 100 employees by dollar size (one for refunds and one for sale voids).	All	Employees with high adjustments may signal actions to hide register disbursement schemes.	• Sales System Register
List top 100 employees who have been on the top 100 list for three months (one for refunds and one for sale voids).	All	Employees with high adjustments may signal actions to hide register disbursement schemes.	• Sales System Register

Title	Category	Description	Data file(s)
List top ten locations that have been on the top ten list for three months (one for discounts and one for sale voids).	All	Locations with high adjustments may signal actions to hide register disbursement schemes.	• Sales System Register
Compute standard deviation for each employee for the last three months and list those employees that provided 3 × the standard deviation in the current month (one for discounts and one for sale voids).	All	Employees with high adjustments may signal actions to hide cash larceny schemes.	• Sales System Register
Compare adjustments to inventory to the void/refund transactions summarized by employee.	All	First, a summary of adjustments by inventory number (SKU number) and employee is completed, which is then compared to credit adjustments (to inappropriately decrease inventory that was supposedly returned) by inventory number.	• Sales System Register • Inventory Detail Register
Extract users who can enter and approve void and refund transactions.	All	Users who can enter the void/refund and subsequently approve it have a nonsegregation of duties that gives an opportunity for fraud.	• Sales System User Access Master File • Sales System User Access Log File
Extract users who can post refunds and voids as well as inventory adjustments.	All	Users who can enter the void/refund and subsequently conceal the misappropriation through adjustments to the inventory system have a nonsegregation of duties that gives an opportunity to fraud. User access should be reviewed from the perspective of adjustments within the application and adjustments to the data itself.	• Sales System User Access Master File • Inventory System User Access Master File • Sales System User Access Log File • Inventory System User Access Log File
Compare customer sales and refunds within the same day.	All	Although possible, it is improbable that a customer would return a product in the same day. Such refund transactions may be fraudulently invoked.	• Sales System Register
Compare customer sales posted to one card and refunds posted to another card.	Credit card refunds	A common fraud is to have a customer make a purchase of a product and then fraudulently charge the refund to a fraud perpetrator or accomplice's credit card.	• Sales System Register

REVIEW QUESTIONS

12-1 What are the five major categories of fraudulent disbursements?

12-2 What is a shell company, and how is it formed?

12-3 How do pay-and-return schemes work?

12-4 What are the five principal categories of check tampering?

12-5 What are the differences between forged maker and forged endorsement schemes?

12-6 How may theft and alteration of outgoing company checks be prevented and detected?

12-7 What is a ghost employee, and what are the four steps needed to make such a scheme work?

12-8 How do employees overstate legitimate expenses on their expense reports?

12-9 What red flags are commonly associated with fictitious expense schemes?

12-10 How do fraudulent disbursements at the cash register differ from other register frauds?

CHAPTER 13

CORRUPTION AND THE HUMAN FACTOR

LEARNING OBJECTIVES

After completing this chapter, you should be able to:

13-1   Identify and explain the different types of corruption schemes.

13-2   Compare and contrast bribery and illegal gratuities.

13-3   Explain what is meant by a conflict of interest.

13-4   Describe the notion of "something of value."

13-5   Discuss how to prevent and detect conflicts of interest.

13-6   Describe kickback schemes and how they are committed.

13-7   Discuss the types of abuses that are committed at each stage of the bidding process.

13-8   Explain what is meant by the human factor.

13-9   Discuss the significance of the "perception of detection."

13-10 Compare and contrast fraud prevention and fraud deterrence.

CRITICAL THINKING EXERCISE

A woman had two sons who were born on the same hour of the same day of the same year, but they were not twins. How could this be?

Black's Law Dictionary defines *corruption* as "an act done with an intent to give some advantage inconsistent with official duty and the rights of others. The act of an official or fiduciary person who unlawfully and wrongfully uses his station or character to procure some benefit for himself or for another person, contrary to duty and the rights of others."[1] This definition strikes at the heart of what corruption is: an act in which a person uses his or her position to gain some personal advantage at the expense of the organization he or she represents.

CASE STUDY: WHY IS THIS FURNITURE FALLING APART?

A number of years ago, the *Washington Post* ran a series of articles detailing charges of waste, fraud, and abuse in the General Services Administration (GSA), the federal government's housekeeping agency. In particular, for more than a decade a furniture manufacturer in New Jersey had churned out $200 million worth of defective and useless furniture that GSA purchased.

Despite years of complaints from GSA's customers about the shoddiness of the furniture and equipment, the GSA had done little to investigate the contractor, Art Metal U.S.A. Government agencies that had been issued the furniture, like the Internal Revenue Service, the Central Intelligence Agency, and the State Department, told horror stories about furniture that fell apart, desks that collapsed, and chairs with one leg shorter than the others.

Several names have been changed to preserve anonymity.

When federal employees complained to the GSA, they were ignored or rebuffed. "You didn't fill out the right form," GSA would say, or "You have to pay to ship it back to the contractor and wait two years and you might get a replacement."

After several years, this behavior naturally gave rise to the speculation that bribery and corruption were the cause of the problem.

A series of articles in the *Washington Post* led to a congressional investigation. Peter Roman, then chief investigator for a subcommittee of the U.S. Senate Committee on Government Affairs, recalled when Senator Lawton Chiles of Florida, chairman of the subcommittee, called him to his office. "He wanted a full investigation into all the practices of GSA," Roman said. Unlike a private audit, a congressional investigation involves a thorough review of financial and

operational records, interviews, and sworn testimony, when necessary. If there is enough evidence to show a crime has been committed, then the U.S. Justice Department prosecutes. Roman said this was "one of the few white-collar fraud investigations the Senate had done in years, with the exception of the Investigation Subcommittee's organized crime inquiries."

The first step in such an analysis involved general oversight hearings for the Subcommittee on Federal Spending Practices and Open Government. At one of the first hearings, Mr. Phillip J. Kurans, president of the Art Metal furniture company, appeared, uninvited, and demanded an opportunity to testify. He told Senator Chiles that his company produced good-quality furniture at bargain prices and challenged the subcommittee to prove otherwise. He invited the senator to the plant in Newark, New Jersey, to inspect their records.

"Chiles had me in his office the next morning," Roman recalls. "He said, 'Tell them we accept their offer. Get up to New Jersey and find out what happened.'"

Roman assembled an investigation team borrowed from other federal agencies. The principals were Dick Polhemus, CFE, from the Treasury Department; Marvin Doyal, CFE, CPA; and Paul Granetto from the U.S. General Accounting Office. "We agreed that the logical approach was to do a cash flow analysis," Roman recalls. "If the furniture was defective, then someone had to generate cash to bribe somebody else to accept it. All of us had experience in following the money, so we went off to Newark to look for it."

Together, they paid a visit to Art Metal U.S.A. on behalf of the senator. Kurans grudgingly sent them into a large room filled with 30 years of financial records. In the past, the sheer volume of paper had caused two GSA investigations to end without incident and the company's own auditors to find nothing untoward. Half the team began controlling the checks, separating them out into operations and payroll, while the others reviewed the canceled checks to do a pattern analysis.

"Marvin Doyal and I still argue over which one of us first found the checks to a subcontractor that had been cashed rather than deposited," Roman says.

"As we began to review the operational checks," he remembers, "one of the items that stood out were checks made out to one company, but under three different names: I. Spiegel, Spiegel Trucking Company, and Spiegel Trucking, Inc." Were the bookkeepers careless in writing the wrong name? The investigators discovered that the checks made out to I. Spiegel (which were folded into threes, like one would fold a personal check and place it in his wallet) were cashed by one Isador Spiegel. These checks were not run through any Spiegel Trucking Co. business account and had been used solely for cash. The checks to Spiegel Trucking Co., on the other hand, "looked like they had been used for actual delivery of furniture to various GSA depots or customers," Roman said.

The other item that caught the investigators' eyes involved checks made out simply to "Auction Expenses" for even sums of money. Kurans told them that the company bought used machinery for cash at auctions throughout the East Coast. That was the reason, he said, that the company spent large amounts of cash.

Yet when the team called operators of furniture auctions they found that auctions required the buyer to show up with a certified check for 10 percent of the amount bought. The rest was also to be paid with certified checks. Over four years, Art Metal generated $482,000 in cash through so-called "auction expenses." More than $800,000 flowing to Spiegel was converted into cash. This was enough evidence to garner Kurens a subpoena to appear before the subcommittee. The subpoena enabled investigators to obtain "literally a truckfull of documents" from Art Metal, Roman said, "which filled a whole room in the basement of the Russell Senate Office Building."

With over $1 million in cash discovered, the next step for the investigating team was to look for evidence of bribery. They painstakingly interviewed every furniture inspector in GSA's Region Two, eventually focusing on a former regional inspector of the GSA. Over the past four years, this man had bought eleven racehorses at an average price of $13,000 each—much more money than a GSA furniture inspector could afford. At this point, Senator Chiles authorized bringing in a special counsel. This was Charles Intriago, Esq., a former Miami Strike Force prosecutor. When confronted, the inspector availed himself of his Fifth Amendment rights, and the search for another witness continued. They found one: Louis Arnold, a retired bookkeeper at Art Metal. Arnold would testify that Art Metal management was paying off GSA inspectors. Arnold revealed a third source of cash, a petty cash fund, totaling about $100,000, which was used to pay for the inspectors' lunches and hotel expenses.

Based on Arnold's testimony, investigators subpoenaed three banks that had photographed all of their cash transactions. "We found pictures of the treasurer, the plant manager, and occasionally one of the partners cashing these 'auction expense' checks, and taking the money in twenties."

During the Senate hearings, several senior agency officials testified to the shoddiness of the furniture. Roman, who spent some time on the floor of the plant, saw many examples of shabby workmanship. For example, although plant managers claimed they had bought a quality paint machine to paint filing cabinets, Roman said all he ever saw was a man wearing a gas mask, with a hand-held paint sprayer, wildly spraying at cabinets that darted past him on a conveyor belt. "It was like seeing a little kid playing laser tag, and the target appears for half a second, and he takes a wild shot at it and hopes he hits the target," he said.

Marvin Doyal testified to the generation of $1.3 million in cash, a company official testified that the money had been used to bribe (unnamed) GSA inspectors, and company officials and GSA inspectors availed themselves of their Fifth Amendment rights. Interagency problems between the subcommittee and the Justice Department played a major role in a failed plea bargain with a former GSA official. At this point, Senator Chiles and the staff decided that the subcommittee had gone as far as it could.

Why did Art Metal not make an attempt to hide their fraud? "In the first place," Roman said, "they thought nobody would ever come. Secondly, they had been the subject of two GSA-appointed investigations that uncovered nothing."

The result of the investigations proved disappointing to Senator Chiles and the subcommittee staff. "In the end, however," Senator Chiles later said, "we achieved our legislative mission. We were disappointed that the plea bargain and other subcommittee efforts didn't pay off as fully as they might have, but we sure got GSA's attention."

Embarrassed by the subcommittee disclosures, GSA

stopped awarding government furniture contracts to Art Metal U.S.A. Having lost what amounted to its sole customer, Art Metal soon went bankrupt. Its plant manager and general counsel were convicted of related offenses within two years. The investigations into the GSA prompted a housecleaning of that agency. At the time of the hearings, GSA had 27,000 employees; today, it employs about 13,000. GSA's role as the federal government's chief purchasing agent has been greatly diminished. The Art Metal case showed that centralized purchasing is not always a good idea.

CORRUPTION SCHEMES

Corruption schemes in ACFE studies are broken down into four classifications:

1. Bribery
2. Illegal gratuities
3. Economic extortion
4. Conflicts of interest

Before discussing how corruption schemes work, we must understand the similarities and differences that exist among bribery, illegal gratuities, and extortion cases. Bribery may be defined as the offering, giving, receiving, or soliciting anything of value to influence an official act. The term *official act* means that traditional bribery statutes proscribe only payments made to influence the decisions of government agents or employees.

Many occupational fraud schemes, however, involve *commercial bribery*, which is similar to the traditional definition of bribery except that something of value is offered to influence a business decision rather than an official act of government. Of course, payments are made every day to influence business decisions, and these payments are perfectly legal. When two parties sign a contract agreeing that one will deliver merchandise in return for a certain sum of money, this is a business decision that has been influenced by the offer of something of value. Obviously, this transaction is not illegal. In a commercial bribery scheme, the payment is received by an employee without his or her employer's consent. In other words, commercial bribery cases deal with the acceptance of under-the-table payments in return for the exercise of influence over a business transaction. Notice also that *offering* a payment can constitute a bribe, even if the illicit payment is never actually made.

Illegal gratuities are similar to bribery schemes, except that something of value is given to an employee to *reward* a decision rather than influence it. In an illegal gratuities scheme, a decision is made that happens to benefit a certain person or company. This decision is not influenced by any sort of payment. The party who benefited from the decision then rewards the person who made the decision. For example, in one case, an employee of a utility company awarded a multimillion-dollar construction contract to a certain vendor and later received an automobile from that vendor as a reward.

At first glance, it may seem that illegal gratuities schemes are harmless if the business decisions in question are not influenced by the promise of payment. But most company ethics policies forbid employees from accepting unreported gifts from vendors. One reason is that illegal gratuities schemes can (and do) evolve into bribery schemes. Once an employee has been rewarded for an act, such as directing business to a particular supplier, an understanding might be reached that future decisions beneficial to the supplier will also be rewarded. Additionally, even though an outright promise of payment has not been made, employees may direct business to certain companies in the hope that they will be rewarded with money or gifts.

Economic extortion cases are the "pay up or else" corruption schemes. Whereas bribery schemes involve an offer of payment intended to influence a business decision, economic extortion schemes are committed when one person demands payment from another. Refusal to pay the extorter results in some harm, such as a loss of business. For instance, in another case, an employee demanded payment from suppliers and in return awarded those suppliers subcontracts on various projects. If the suppliers refused to pay the employee, the subcontracts were awarded to rival suppliers or held back until the fraudster got his money.

Bribery, illegal gratuities, and economic extortion cases all bear a great deal of similarity in that they all involve an illicit payment from one party to another, either to influence a decision or as a reward for a decision already made. Conflicts of interest are different in nature. A conflict of interest occurs when an employee, manager, or executive has an undisclosed economic or personal interest in a transaction that adversely affects the organization. The key word here is *undisclosed*. If the company is aware of a

personal interest in a transaction that may adversely affect the organization, no conflict exists. As with other corruption cases, conflict schemes involve the exertion of an employee's influence to the detriment of his or her employer. But whereas in bribery schemes a fraudster is paid to exercise his or her influence on behalf of a third party, in a conflict of interest scheme the perpetrator engages in *self*-dealing. The distinction between conflicts of interest and other forms of corruption will be discussed in more detail later in this chapter.

Bribery

At its heart, a bribe is a business transaction, albeit an illegal or unethical one. As in the GSA case discussed above, a person "buys" something with the bribes he pays. What he buys is the influence of the recipient. Bribery schemes generally fall into two broad categories: *kickbacks* and *bid-rigging schemes*.

Kickbacks are undisclosed payments made by vendors to employees of purchasing companies. The purpose of a kickback is usually to enlist the corrupt employee in an overbilling scheme. Sometimes vendors pay kickbacks simply to get extra business from the purchasing company. Bid-rigging schemes occur when an employee fraudulently assists a vendor in winning a contract through the competitive bidding process.

Kickback Schemes   Kickback schemes are usually very similar to the billing schemes described in Chapter 12. They involve the submission of invoices for goods and services that are either overpriced or completely fictitious (see Figure 13-1).

Kickbacks are classified as corruption schemes rather than asset misappropriations because they involve collusion between employees and vendors; in an asset misappropriation, no outsiders are knowing participants. In a common type of kickback scheme, a vendor submits a fraudulent or inflated invoice to the victim company and an employee of that company helps make sure that a payment is made on the false invoice. For his assistance, the employee/fraudster receives some form of payment from the vendor. This payment is the kickback.

Kickback schemes almost always attack the purchasing function of the victim company, so it stands to reason that these frauds are often undertaken by employees with purchasing responsibilities. Moreover, these schemes are naturally more common when the purchasing decision is ultimately made by one person. That is why the usual kickback suspect is the head of the purchasing department. Purchasing employees often have direct contact with vendors and therefore have an opportunity to establish a collusive relationship. In one case, for example, a purchasing agent redirected orders to a company owned by a supplier with whom he was conspiring. In return for the additional business, the supplier paid the purchasing agent over half the profits from the additional orders. Remember, the funds for the kickback are coming directly from the victim company and not from the entity paying the kickback to the employee.

Diverting Business to Vendors   In some instances, an employee/fraudster receives a kickback simply for directing excess business to a vendor. There might be no overbilling involved in these cases; the vendor simply pays the kickbacks to ensure a steady stream of business from the purchasing company. In one instance, the president of a software supplier offered a percentage of ownership in his company to an employee of a purchaser in exchange for a major contract. Similarly, a travel agency in another case provided free travel and entertainment to the purchasing agent of a retail company. In return, the purchasing agent agreed to book all corporate trips through the travel agent. Because these transactions do not require the direct payment of cash, they can be particularly difficult to detect.

If no overbilling is involved in a kickback scheme, one might wonder where the harm lies. Assuming the vendor simply wants to get the buyer's business and does not increase his prices or bill for undelivered goods and services, how is the buyer harmed? The problem is that, having bought off an employee of the purchasing company, a vendor is no longer subject to the normal economic pressures of the marketplace. This vendor does not have to compete with other suppliers for the purchasing company's business, and so has no incentive to provide a low price or quality merchandise. In these circumstances the purchasing company almost always ends up overpaying for goods or services, or getting less than it paid for. Those who accept kickbacks are effectively making a pact with the Devil. The kickback recipient is hardly in a position to complain about higher prices or lower quality. In the case described above, the victim company estimated that it paid $10,000 more for airfare over a two-year period by booking through the corrupt travel agency than if it had used a different company.

Once a vendor knows he or she has an exclusive purchasing arrangement, his or her incentive is to raise prices to cover the cost of the kickback. Most bribery schemes end up as overbilling schemes even if

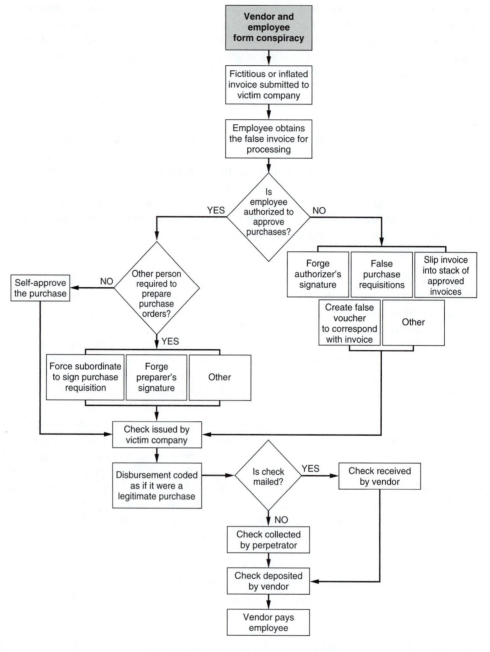

FIGURE 13-1 Kickbacks/Overbilling

they do not start that way. This is one reason why most business codes of ethics prohibit employees from accepting undisclosed gifts from vendors. In the long run, the employee's company is sure to pay for his or her unethical conduct.

Overbilling Schemes

EMPLOYEES WITH APPROVAL AUTHORITY   In most instances, kickback schemes begin as overbilling schemes in which a vendor submits inflated invoices to the victim company. The false invoices either overstate the cost of actual goods and services or reflect fictitious sales. In a case in which an employee had complete authority to approve vouchers from a certain vendor, she authorized payment on over 100 fraudulent invoices in which the vendor's rates were overstated. Because no one was reviewing her decisions, the employee could approve payments on invoices at above-normal rates without fear of detection.

As stated, the ability to authorize purchases (and thus to authorize fraudulent purchases) is usually a key to kickback schemes. For example, in one case the fraudster was a nonmanagement employee who had approval authority for purchases made from the vendor with whom she colluded. She authorized

approximately $300,000 worth of inflated billings in less than two years. Similarly, in another case, a manager was authorized to purchase fixed assets for his company as part of a leasehold improvement. The assets he ordered were of a cheaper quality and lower price than what was specified, but the contract he negotiated did not reflect this. Therefore, the victim company paid for high-quality materials but received low-quality materials. The difference in price between what the company paid and what the materials actually cost was diverted back to the manager as a kickback.

The existence of purchasing authority can be critical to the success of kickback schemes. The ability of a fraudster to authorize payments himself means he does not have to submit purchase requisitions to an honest superior who might question the validity of the transaction.

FRAUDSTERS LACKING APPROVAL AUTHORITY   Although the majority of the kickback schemes the ACFE researchers reviewed involved people with authority to approve purchases, this authority is not an absolute necessity; in these cases, the lack of authority makes the illegal activity more complicated for the fraudster. When an employee cannot approve fraudulent purchases himself or herself, he or she can still orchestrate a kickback scheme if he or she can circumvent purchasing controls. In some cases, all that is required is the filing of a false purchase requisition. If a trusted employee tells his or her superior that the company needs certain materials or services, this is sometimes sufficient to get a false invoice approved for payment. Such schemes are generally successful when the person with approval authority is inattentive or when he or she is forced to rely on his or her subordinates' guidance in purchasing matters.

Corrupt employees might also prepare false vouchers to make it appear that fraudulent invoices are legitimate. Where proper controls are in place, a completed voucher is required before accounts payable will pay an invoice. One key is for the fraudster to create a purchase order that corresponds to the vendor's fraudulent invoice. The fraudster might forge the signature of an authorized party on the purchase order to show that the acquisition has been approved. Where the payables system is computerized, an employee with access to a restricted password can enter the system and authorize payments on fraudulent invoices.

In less sophisticated schemes, a corrupt employee might simply take a fraudulent invoice from a vendor and slip it into a stack of prepared invoices before they are input into the accounts payable system. A more detailed description of how false invoices are processed is found in Chapter 12.

Kickback schemes can be very difficult to detect. In a sense, the victim company is being attacked from two directions. Externally, a corrupt vendor submits false invoices that induce the victim company to unknowingly pay for goods or services that it does not receive. Internally, one or more of the victim company's employees waits to corroborate the false information provided by the vendor.

Other Kickback Schemes   Bribes are not always paid to employees to process phony invoices. In some circumstances outsiders seek other fraudulent assistance from employees of the victim company. In other cases, bribes come not from vendors who are trying to sell something to the victim company, but rather from potential purchasers who seek a lower price from the victim company. In one case, for instance, an advertising salesman not only sold ads, but was also authorized to bill for and collect on advertising accounts. He was also authorized to issue discounts to clients. In return for benefits such as free travel, lodging, and various gifts, this individual either sold ads at greatly reduced rates or gave free ads to those who bought him off. His complete control over advertising and a lack of oversight allowed this employee to "trade away" over $20,000 in advertising revenues. Similarly, in another case, the manager of a convention center accepted various gifts from show promoters. In return, he allowed these promoters to rent the convention center at prices below the rates approved by the city that owned the center.

Slush Funds   Every bribe is a two-sided transaction. In every case where a vendor bribes a purchaser, there is someone on the vendor's side of the transaction who is making an illicit payment. It is therefore just as likely that your employees are paying bribes as accepting them.

In order to obtain the funds to make these payments, employees usually divert company money into a slush fund, a noncompany account from which bribes can be made. Assuming that the briber's company does not authorize bribes, he must find a way to generate the funds necessary to illegally influence someone in another organization. Therefore, the key to the crime from the briber's perspective is the diversion of money into the slush fund. This is a fraudulent disbursement of company funds, which is usually accomplished by the writing of company checks to a fictitious entity or the submitting of false invoices in the name of the false entity. In one case, an officer in a very large health care organization created a fund to pay public officials and influence pending legislation. This officer used check requests for several different expense codes to generate payments that went to one of the company's lobbyists, who

placed the money in an account from which bribe money could be withdrawn. Most of the checks in this case were coded as "fees" for consulting or other services.

It is common to charge fraudulent disbursements to nebulous accounts like "consulting fees." The purchase of goods can be verified by a check of inventory, but there is no inventory for these kinds of services. It is therefore more difficult to prove that the payments are fraudulent. The discussion of exactly how fraudulent disbursements are made is found in Chapter 12.

Preventing and Detecting Kickback Schemes   Kickback schemes are in most respects very similar to billing schemes, which were discussed in Chapter 12, with the added component that they include the active participation of a vendor in the fraud. Because of their similarity to billing schemes, the controls discussed earlier relating to billing fraud—separation of purchasing, authorization, receiving and storing goods, and cash disbursements; maintenance of an updated vendor list; proper review and matching of all support in disbursement vouchers—may be effective in detecting or deterring some kickback schemes.

These controls, however, do not fully address the threat of kickback fraud because they are principally designed to ensure the proper accounting of purchases and to spot abnormalities in the purchasing function. For example, separation of duties will help prevent a billing scheme in which an employee sets up a shell company and bills for nonexistent goods, because independent checks in authorization, receiving, and disbursements should identify circumstances in which a vendor does not exist or goods or services were never received. But this is not an issue in most kickback schemes, because the vendors in these frauds do exist, and in most cases these vendors provide real goods or services, albeit at an inflated price. Similarly, because the vendor is conspiring with a purchasing agent or other employee of the victim, the fraudulent price will usually be agreed to by both parties at the outset, so that the terms on the vendor's invoices will match the terms on purchase orders, receiving reports, and so forth. On the face of the documents in the disbursements voucher there will be no inconsistency or abnormality.

Many kickback schemes begin as legitimate, nonfraudulent transactions between the victim organization and an outside vendor. It is only after a relationship has been established between the vendor and an employee of the victim organization (e.g., a purchasing agent) that the conspiracy to overbill the victim organization begins. Because the vendors in these schemes were selected for legitimate reasons, controls such as independent verification of new vendors or independent approval of purchases will not help detect or deter many kickback schemes.

In working to prevent and detect kickbacks, organizations must tailor their efforts to the specific red flags and characteristics of kickback schemes. For example, the key component to most kickback schemes is price inflation; the vendor fraudulently increases the price of goods or services to cover the cost of the kickback. Organizations should routinely monitor the prices paid for goods and services, and should compare them to market rates. If more than one supplier is used for a certain type of good or service, prices should be compared among these suppliers as well. If a certain vendor is regularly charging above-market rates, this could indicate a kickback scheme.

Organizations should also monitor trends in the cost of goods and services that are purchased. If a supplier raises its prices to cover the cost of kickbacks, this will obviously cause an increase in prices. Furthermore, kickbacks, like most other fraud schemes, often start small and increase over time as the fraudsters become emboldened by their success. Kickback schemes often start with relatively small 5 percent or 10 percent overcharges, but as these frauds progress the supplier and corrupt employee may begin to bill for several times the legitimate purchase price.

In order to help detect overcharges, price thresholds should be established for materials purchases. Deviations from these thresholds should be noted and the reasons for the deviations verified in advance of payment. In addition, organizations should maintain an up-to-date vendor list, and purchases should be made only from suppliers who have been approved. As part of the approval process, organizations should take into account the honesty, integrity, and business reputation of prospective vendors.

Kickback schemes not only frequently result in overcharges, they may also result in the purchase of excessive quantities of goods or services from a corrupt supplier. Organizations should track purchase levels by vendor and routinely monitor these trends for excessive purchases from a certain supplier or deviations from a standard vendor rotation, if one exists. Unusually high-volume purchases from a vendor that do not appear to be justified by business need are frequently a sign of fraud.

It is important to monitor not only the number of transactions per vendor, but also the amount of materials being ordered in any given transaction. Purchases should be routinely reviewed to make sure materials are being ordered at the optimal reorder point. If inventory is overstocked with materials provided by a particular vendor, this may indicate a kickback scheme.

On the other hand, some kickback schemes progress to the point at which a corrupt employee will pay invoices without any goods or services actually being delivered by the vendor. In these cases, inventory shortages—purchases that cannot be traced to inventory—can also signal fraud.

Another potential sign of fraud is the purchase of inferior-quality inventory or merchandise. This may result from kickback schemes in which a corrupt employee initiates a purchase of premium-quality merchandise from a vendor, but the vendor delivers lower-quality (less expensive) merchandise. The difference in price between the materials that were contracted for and those that were actually delivered is kicked back to the corrupt purchasing agent or split between the purchasing agent and the vendor.

As with any form of billing fraud, kickback schemes have the potential to create budget overruns, either because of overcharges or excessive quantities purchased, or both. Actual expenditures should be compared to budgeted amounts and to prior years, with follow-up for significant deviations.

As a preventative measure, organizations should assign an employee who is independent of the purchasing function to routinely review the organization's buying patterns for signs of fraud such as those discussed above. In order to provide an appropriate audit trail for this type of review, organizations should require that all purchase decisions be adequately documented, showing who initiated the purchase, who approved it, who received the materials, and so on.

Because any investigation of a kickback scheme will likely necessitate a review of the corrupt vendor's books, all contracts with suppliers should contain a "right-to-audit" clause. This is a standard provision in many purchasing contracts that requires the supplier to retain and make available to the purchaser support for all invoices issued under the contract. In short, a right-to-audit clause gives an organization the right to review the supplier's internal records to determine whether fraud occurred.

Finally, organizations should establish written policies prohibiting employees from soliciting or accepting any gift or favor from a customer or supplier. These policies should also expressly forbid employees from engaging in any transaction on behalf of the organization when they have an undisclosed personal interest in the transaction. This should be a standard part of any organizational ethics policy, and it serves two purposes: (1) it clearly explains to employees what types of conduct are considered to be improper; and (2) it provides grounds for termination if an employee accepts a bribe or kickback while preventing the employee from claiming that she did not know such conduct was prohibited.

Bid-Rigging Schemes   As we have said, when one person pays a bribe to another, he does so to gain the benefit of the recipient's influence. The competitive bidding process, in which several suppliers or contractors are vying for contracts in what can be a very cutthroat environment, can be tailor-made for bribery. Any advantage one vendor can gain over his competitors in this arena is extremely valuable. The benefit of "inside influence" can ensure that a vendor will win a sought-after contract. Many vendors are willing to pay for this influence.

In the competitive bidding process, all bidders are legally supposed to be placed on the same plane of equality, bidding on the same terms and conditions. Each bidder competes for a contract based on the specifications set forth by the purchasing company. Vendors submit confidential bids stating the price at which they will complete a project in accordance with the purchaser's specifications.

The way competitive bidding is rigged depends largely on the level of influence of the corrupt employee. The more power a person has over the bidding process, the more likely the person can influence the selection of a supplier. Therefore, employees involved in bid-rigging schemes, like those in kickback schemes, tend to have a good measure of influence or access to the competitive bidding process. Potential targets for accepting bribes include buyers, contracting officials, engineers and technical representatives, quality or product assurance representatives, subcontractor liaison employees, or anyone else with authority over the awarding of contracts.

Bid-rigging schemes can be categorized based on the stage of bidding at which the fraudster exerts his or her influence. Bid-rigging schemes usually occur in the pre-solicitation phase, the solicitation phase, or the submission phase of the bidding process (see Figure 13-2).

The Pre-Solicitation Phase   In the pre-solicitation phase of the competitive bidding process— before bids are officially sought for a project—bribery schemes can be broken down into two distinct types. The first is the need recognition scheme, in which an employee of a purchasing company is paid to convince his company that a particular project is necessary. The second reason to bribe someone in the pre-solicitation phase is to have the specifications of the contract tailored to the strengths of a particular supplier.

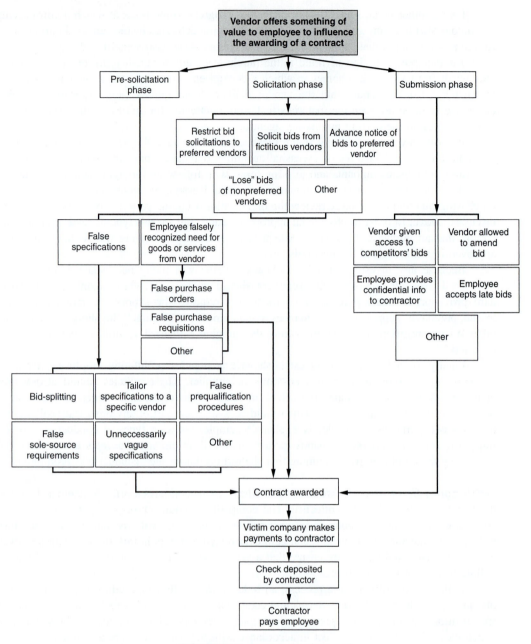

FIGURE 13-2 Bid Rigging (Bribery)

NEED RECOGNITION SCHEMES The typical fraud in the need recognition phase of the contract negotiation is a conspiracy between the buyer and contractor in which an employee of the buyer receives something of value and in return recognizes a "need" for a particular product or service. The result of such a scheme is that the victim company purchases unnecessary goods or services from a supplier at the direction of the corrupt employee.

There are several trends that may indicate a need recognition fraud. Unusually high requirements for stock and inventory levels may reveal a situation in which a corrupt employee is seeking to justify unnecessary purchase activity from a certain supplier. An employee might also justify unnecessary purchases of inventory by writing off large numbers of surplus items to scrap. As these items leave the inventory, they open up spaces to justify additional purchases. Another indicator of a need recognition scheme is the defining of a "need" that can be met only by a certain supplier or contractor. In addition, the failure to develop a satisfactory list of backup suppliers may reveal an unusually strong attachment to a primary supplier—an attachment that is explainable by the acceptance of bribes from that supplier.

SPECIFICATIONS SCHEMES   The other type of pre-solicitation fraud is a specifications scheme. The specifications of a contract are a list of the elements, materials, dimensions, and other relevant requirements for completion of the project. Specifications are prepared to assist vendors in the bidding process, telling them what they are required to do and providing a firm basis for making and accepting bids.

One corruption scheme that occurs in this process is the fraudulent tailoring of specifications to a particular vendor. In these cases, the vendor pays off an employee of the buyer who is involved in the preparation of specifications for the contract. In return, the employee sets the specifications of the contract to accommodate that vendor's capabilities. In one case, for instance, a supplier paid an employee of a public utility company to write contract specifications that were so proprietary that they effectively eliminated all competition for the project. For four years, this supplier won the contract, which was the largest awarded by the utility company. The fraud cost the utility company in excess of $2 million.

The methods used to restrict competition in the bidding process may include the use of "prequalification" procedures that are known to eliminate certain competitors. For instance, the bid may require potential contractors to have a certain percentage of female or minority ownership. There is nothing illegal with such a requirement, but if it is placed in the specifications as a result of a bribe rather than as the result of other factors, then the employee has sold his influence to benefit a dishonest vendor, a clear case of corruption.

Sole-source or noncompetitive procurement justifications may also be used to eliminate competition and steer contracts to a particular vendor. For example, a requisitioner distorted the requirements of a contract up for bid, claiming the specifications called for a sole-source provider. Based on the requisitioner's information, competitive bidding was disregarded and the contract was awarded to a particular supplier. A review of other bids received at a later date showed that certain materials were available for up to $70,000 less than what the company paid in the sole-source arrangement. The employee had helped divert the job to the contractor in return for a promise of future employment. Competitive bidding was also disregarded in another case, where management staff of a state entity took bribes from vendors to authorize purchases of approximately $200,000 in fixed assets. Sole-source contracts, by their nature, are ripe for corruption and this fact should be always considered in evaluating these kinds of arrangements.

Another type of specifications scheme is the deliberate writing of vague specifications. In this type of scheme, a supplier pays an employee of the purchasing company to write specifications that will require amendments at a later date. This will allow the supplier to raise the price of the contract when the amendments are made. As the buyer's needs become more specific or more detailed, the vendor can claim that, had he known what the buyer actually wanted, his bid on the project would have been higher. In order to complete the project as defined by the amended specifications, the supplier will have to charge a higher price. These vague specification schemes are particularly problematic for defense and other government contracts.

Another form of specifications fraud is bid splitting. In one instance, a manager of a federal employer split a large repair job into several component contracts in order to divert the jobs to his brother-in-law. Federal law required competitive bidding on projects over a certain dollar value. The manager broke the project up so that each smaller project was below the mandatory bidding level. Once the contract was split, the manager hired his brother-in-law to handle each of the component projects. Thus, the brother-in-law got the entire contract while avoiding competitive bidding.

An egregious and unfair form of bid rigging occurs when a vendor pays an employee of the buyer for the right to see the specifications earlier than his or her competitors. The employee does not alter the specifications to suit the vendor, but instead simply gives him or her a head start on planning his or her bid and preparing for the job. The extra planning time gives the vendor an advantage over his or her competitors in preparing a bid for the job.

The Solicitation Phase   In the solicitation phase of the competitive bidding process fraudsters attempt to influence the selection of a contractor by restricting the pool of competitors from whom bids are sought. In other words, a corrupt vendor pays an employee of the purchasing company to assure that one or more of the vendor's competitors do not get to bid on the contract. In this manner, the corrupt vendor is able to improve his chances of winning the job.

One type of scheme involves the sales representative who deals on behalf of a number of potential bidders. The sales representative bribes a contracting official to rig the solicitation, ensuring that only those companies represented by him get to submit bids. It is not uncommon in some sectors for buyers to "require" bidders to be represented by certain sales or manufacturing representatives. These representatives pay a kickback to the buyer to protect their clients' interests. The result of this transaction is that the purchasing

company is deprived of the ability to get the best price on its contract. Typically, the group of "protected" vendors will not actually compete against each other for the purchaser's contracts, but instead engage in "bid pooling."

BID POOLING   Bid pooling is a process by which several bidders conspire to split up contracts and ensure that each gets a certain amount of work. Instead of submitting confidential bids, the vendors decide in advance what their bids will be so they can guarantee that each vendor will win a share of the purchasing company's business. For example, if vendors A, B, and C are up for three separate jobs, they may agree that A's bid will be the lowest on the first contract, B's bid will be the lowest on the second contract, and C's bid will be the lowest on the third contract. None of the vendors gets all three jobs, but on the other hand, they are all guaranteed to get at least one. Furthermore, since they plan their bids ahead of time, the vendors can conspire to raise their prices. Thus the purchasing company suffers as a result of the scheme. In one case, it was standard practice for bidders on highway contracts to meet in a hotel the night before bids were announced for projects and decide among themselves who would be the low bidder and high bidder on each deal. That way, the highway construction companies were always sure of getting exactly the jobs they wanted at the prices they wanted to get. This resulted in the state overpaying on highway construction by over $150 million.

FICTITIOUS SUPPLIERS   Another way to eliminate competition in the solicitation phase of the selection process is to solicit bids from fictitious suppliers. In the bid-splitting case discussed above, the brother-in-law submitted quotes in the names of several different companies and performed work under these various names. Although confidential bidding was avoided in this case, the perpetrator used quotes from several of the brother-in-law's fictitious companies to demonstrate price reasonableness on the final contracts. In other words, the brother-in-law's fictitious price quotes were used to validate his actual prices.

OTHER METHODS   In some cases, competition for a contract can be limited by severely restricting the time for submitting bids. Certain suppliers are given advance notice of contracts before bids are solicited. These suppliers are therefore able to begin preparing their bids ahead of time. With the short time frame for developing bid proposals, the supplier with advance knowledge of the contract will have a decided advantage over his competition.

Bribed purchasing officials can also restrict competition for their co-conspirators by soliciting bids in obscure publications where other vendors are unlikely to see them. Again, this is done to eliminate potential rivals and create an advantage for the corrupt suppliers. Some schemes have also involved the publication of bid solicitations during holiday periods when those suppliers not "in the know" are unlikely to be looking for potential contracts. In more blatant cases, the bids of outsiders are accepted but are "lost" or improperly disqualified by the corrupt employee of the purchaser.

Typically, when a vendor bribes an employee of the purchasing company to assist him in any kind of solicitation scheme, the cost of the bribe is included in the corrupt vendor's bid. Therefore, the purchasing company ends up bearing the cost of the illicit payment in the form of a higher contract price.

The Submission Phase   In the actual submission phase of the process, where bids are proffered to the buyer, several schemes may be used to win a contract for a particular supplier. The principal offense tends to be abuse of the sealed-bid process. Competitive bids are confidential; they are, of course, supposed to remain sealed until a specified date at which all bids are opened and reviewed by the purchasing company. The person or persons who have access to sealed bids are often the targets of unethical vendors seeking an advantage in the process. In one example, gifts and cash payments were given to a majority owner of a company in exchange for preferential treatment during the bidding process. The supplier who paid the bribes was allowed to submit his bids last, knowing what prices his competitors had quoted, or in the alternative, he was allowed to actually see his competitors' bids and adjust his own accordingly.

Vendors also bribe employees of the purchaser for information on how to prepare their bids. In another case, the general manager for a purchasing company provided confidential pricing information to a supplier that enabled the supplier to outbid his competitors and win a long-term contract. In return, both the general manager and his daughter received payments from the supplier. Other reasons to bribe employees of the purchaser include to ensure receipt of a late bid or to falsify the bid log, to extend the bid opening date, and to control bid openings.

Preventing and Detecting Bid-Rigging Schemes Since bid rigging is a form of bribery similar to the kickback schemes already mentioned, many of the anti-fraud measures discussed earlier under the heading "Preventing and Detecting Kickback Schemes" will also be effective in dealing with bid-rigging frauds. In addition, there are a number of prevention and detection methods that are specifically applicable to the competitive bidding process.

Bid-rigging schemes are often uncovered because of unusual bidding patterns that emerge during the process. Perhaps the most common indicator of collusive bidding practices is an unusually high contract price. For example, if two or more contractors conspire with an employee in the bidding process, or if an employee incorporates bids from fictitious vendors to artificially inflate the contract price, the result will be that the winning bid (or in some cases all bids submitted) is excessively high compared to expected prices, previous contracts, budgeted amounts, and so on. Organizations should monitor price trends for this type of circumstance.

Another red flag sometimes arises in bid-rigging cases when low-bid awards are frequently followed by change orders or amendments that significantly increase payments to the contractor. This may indicate that the contractor has conspired with somebody in the purchasing organization who has the authority to amend the contract. The contractor submits a very low bid to ensure that it will win the contract, knowing that the final price will be inflated after the award.

Very large, unexplained price differences among bidders can also indicate fraud. As noted in the preceding paragraph, this condition may arise when one supplier submits a very low bid with the understanding that the final contract price will later be inflated. Significant cost differences among bidders can also occur when an honest bidder submits a proposal in a competitive bidding process that was previously dominated by a group of suppliers who were conspiring in a bid-pooling scheme to keep prices artificially high.

Red flags might also appear from certain patterns within the bidding process. For example, if the last contractor to submit a bid repeatedly wins the contract, this would tend to indicate that an employee of the purchasing organization is allowing vendors to see their competitors' bids. The corrupt supplier would wait until all other bids have been submitted, then would use its inside knowledge to narrowly undercut the competition with a last-minute proposal. This narrow margin of victory can itself be a sign of fraud. If the winning bidder repeatedly wins contracts by a very slim margin, this could also indicate that the bidder has an accomplice working within the purchasing organization.

In bid-pooling schemes, as discussed above, several vendors conspire to fix their bids so that each one wins a certain number of contracts, thereby removing the competitive element of the bidding prices and enabling the corrupt suppliers to inflate their prices. These schemes may result in a predictable rotation of bid winners, which would not be expected in a truly competitive bidding process. Any sort of predictable pattern of contract award that is based on a factor other than price or quality should be investigated.

Another red flag consistent with collusive bidding occurs when losing bidders frequently appear as subcontractors on the project. This tends to indicate that the suppliers conspired to divide the proceeds of the contract, agreeing that one would win the award while others would receive a certain portion of the project through subcontracting arrangements. In some cases, the low bidder will withdraw and subsequently become a subcontractor after the job has been awarded to another supplier.

A corrupt employee or vendor will sometimes submit bids from fictitious suppliers to create the illusion of competition where none really exists. In some cases, these frauds have been detected because the same calculations or errors occurred on two or more bids, or because two or more vendors had the same address, phone number, officer, and so forth.

Fraud may be indicated by a situation in which qualified bidders fail to submit contract proposals, or in which significantly fewer bidders than expected respond to a request for proposals. This type of red flag is consistent with schemes in which a corrupt employee purposely fails to advertise the contract up for bid. This eliminates competition and helps ensure that a certain supplier will be awarded the contract. Similarly, the number of bids might be reduced because a corrupt employee has destroyed or fraudulently disqualified the bids of contractors who submitted more favorable proposals than the employee's co-conspirator.

Finally, bid rigging may be indicated by the avoidance of competitive bidding altogether, such as occurs when an employee splits a large project into several smaller jobs that fall beneath a bidding threshold, then makes sole-source awards to favored suppliers.

Something of Value Bribery was defined at the beginning of this chapter as "offering, giving, receiving, or soliciting *anything* of value to influence an official act." A corrupt employee helps the briber obtain something of value, and in return the employee gives something of value. There are several ways for a

vendor to "pay" an employee to surreptitiously aid the vendor's cause. The most common, of course, is money. In the most basic bribery scheme, the vendor simply gives the employee currency. This is what we think of in the classic bribery scenario—an envelope stuffed with currency being slipped under a table or a roll of bills hastily stuffed into a pocket. These payments are preferably made with currency rather than checks, because the cash payment is harder to trace. Currency may not be practical, however, when large sums are involved. When this is the case, slush funds can be set up to finance the illegal payments. In other cases, checks may be drawn directly from company accounts. As mentioned previously, these disbursements are usually coded as "consulting fees," "referral commissions," or the like.

Instead of cash payments, some employees accept promises of future employment as bribes. In one instance, a government employee gave a contractor inside information in order to win a bid on a multimillion-dollar contract in return for the promise of a high-paying job. This has been a problem with Pentagon procurement contracts. As with money, the promise of employment might be intended to benefit a third party rather than the corrupt employee. In another case, a consultant who worked for a particular university hired the daughter of one of the university's employees.

We also discussed how a corrupt individual diverted a major purchase commitment to a supplier in return for a percentage of ownership in the supplier's business. This is similar to a bribe affected by the promise of employment, but also contains elements of a conflict of interest scheme. The promise of part ownership in the supplier amounts to an undisclosed financial interest in the transaction for the corrupt employee.

Gifts of all kinds may also be used to corrupt an employee. The types of gifts used to sway an employee's influence can include free liquor and meals, free travel and accommodation, cars, other merchandise, and even sexual favors.

Other inducements include the paying off of a corrupt employee's loans or credit card bills, the offering of loans on very favorable terms, and transfers of property at substantially below market value. These kinds of payments are sometimes quite difficult to detect. The list of things that can be given to an employee in return for the exercise of his influence is almost endless. Anything that the employee values is fair game and may be used to sway his loyalty.

Illegal Gratuities

As stated previously, illegal gratuities are similar to bribery schemes except there is not necessarily intent to influence a particular business decision. An example of an illegal gratuity was found in a case in which a city commissioner negotiated a land development deal with a group of private investors. After the deal was approved, the commissioner and his wife were rewarded with a free international vacation, all expenses paid. Although the promise of this trip may have influenced the commissioner's negotiations, this would be difficult to prove. On the other hand, merely accepting such a gift amounts to an illegal gratuity—an act that is prohibited by most government and private company codes of ethics.

Economic Extortion

Economic extortion is basically the flip side of a bribery scheme. Instead of a vendor offering a payment to an employee to influence a decision, the employee demands a payment from a vendor in order to make a decision in that vendor's favor. In any situation in which an employee might accept bribes to favor a particular company or person, the situation could be reversed to a point at which the employee extorts money from a potential purchaser or supplier. In one example, a plant manager for a utility company started his own business on the side. Vendors who wanted to do work for the utility company were forced by the manager to divert some of their business to his own company. Those who did not "play ball" lost their business with the utility company. Economic extortion is common in bank loans, when the banker demands a payment for granting the loan.

Conflicts of Interest

As stated earlier in this chapter, a conflict of interest occurs when an employee, manager, or executive has an undisclosed economic or personal interest in a transaction that adversely affects the company. To repeat for emphasis, the key word in this definition is *undisclosed*. The crux of a conflict case is that the fraudster takes advantage of his employer; the victim organization is unaware that its employee has divided loyalties. If an employer knows of the employee's interest in a business deal or negotiation, there can be no conflict of interest, no matter how favorable the arrangement is for the employee.

Most conflict cases occur because the fraudster has an undisclosed *economic* interest in a transaction. But the fraudster's hidden interest is not necessarily economic. In some scenarios an employee acts in a manner detrimental to his employer in order to provide a benefit to a friend or relative, even though the fraudster receives no financial benefit from the transaction himself. As previously illustrated, a manager split a large repair project into several smaller projects to avoid bidding requirements. This allowed the manager to award the contracts to his brother-in-law. Though there was no indication that the manager received any financial gain from this scheme, his actions nevertheless amounted to a conflict of interest.

Any bribery scheme could potentially be considered a conflict of interest—after all, an employee who accepts a bribe clearly has an undisclosed economic interest in the transaction (in the form of the bribe he or she is paid), and he or she is clearly not working with his or her employer's best interests at heart. If an employee approves payment on a fraudulent invoice submitted by a vendor in return for a kickback, this is bribery. If, on the other hand, an employee approves payment on invoices submitted by his or her own company (and if the ownership is undisclosed), this is a conflict of interest. This was the situation in a case in which an office service employee recommended his own company to do repairs and maintenance on office equipment for his employer. The fraudster approved invoices for approximately $30,000 in excessive charges.

The distinction between the two schemes is obvious. In the bribery case the fraudster approves the invoice in return for a kickback, whereas in a conflict case he or she approves the invoice because of his or her own hidden interest in the vendor. Aside from the employee's motive for committing the crime, the mechanics of the two transactions can be practically identical. The same duality can be found in bid-rigging cases in which an employee influences the selection of a company in which he or she has a hidden interest instead of influencing the selection of a vendor who has bribed him.

Conflict schemes do not always simply mirror bribery schemes, though. There are vast numbers of ways in which an employee can use his or her influence to benefit a company in which he or she has a hidden interest. The majority of conflict schemes fit into one of two categories: purchasing schemes and sales schemes.

In other words, most conflicts of interest arise when a victim company unwittingly buys something at a high price from a company in which one of its employees has a hidden interest, or unwittingly sells something at a low price to a company in which one of its employees has a hidden interest. Most of the other conflict cases the ACFE researchers reviewed involved employees who stole clients or diverted funds from their employers.

Purchasing Schemes The majority of conflict schemes in ACFE studies were purchasing schemes and the most common of these was the overbilling scheme. We have already briefly discussed conflict schemes that involved false billings. These frauds are very similar to the billing schemes discussed in Chapter 12 of this book, so it will be helpful at this point to discuss the distinction between traditional billing schemes and purchasing schemes that are classified as conflicts of interest.

Though it is true that any time an employee assists in the overbilling of his or her company there is probably some conflict of interest (the employee causes harm to his or her employer because of a hidden financial interest in the transaction), this does not necessarily mean that every false billing will be categorized as a conflict scheme. In order for the scheme to be classified as a conflict of interest, the employee (or a friend or relative of the employee) must have some kind of ownership or employment interest in the vendor that submits the invoice. This distinction is easy to understand if we look at the nature of the fraud. Why does the fraudster overbill his or her employer? If he or she engages in the scheme only for the cash, the scheme is a fraudulent disbursement billing scheme. If, on the other hand, he or she seeks to better the financial condition of his or her business at the expense of his or her employer, this is a conflict of interest. In other words, the fraudster's *interests* lie with a company other than his or her employer. When an employee falsifies the invoices of a third-party vendor to whom he or she has no relation, this is not a conflict of interest scheme because the employee has no interest in that vendor. The sole purpose of the scheme is to generate a fraudulent disbursement.

One might wonder, then, why shell company schemes are classified as fraudulent disbursements rather than conflicts of interest. After all, the fraudster in a shell company scheme owns the fictitious company and therefore must have an interest in it. Remember, though, that shell companies are created for the sole purpose of defrauding the employer. The company is not so much an entity in the mind of the fraudster as it is a tool. In fact, a shell company is usually little more than a post office box and a bank account. The fraudster has no interest in the shell company that causes a division of loyalty; he or she

simply uses the shell company to bilk his or her employer. Shell company schemes are therefore classified as false billing schemes.

A short rule of thumb can be used to distinguish between overbilling schemes that are classified as asset misappropriations and those that are conflicts of interest: if the bill originates from a *real company* in which the fraudster has an economic or personal interest, and if the fraudster's interest in the company is undisclosed to the victim company, then the scheme is a conflict of interest.

Now that we know what kinds of purchasing schemes are classified as conflicts of interest, the question is: How do these schemes work? After our lengthy discussion about distinguishing between conflicts and fraudulent disbursements, the answer is somewhat anticlimactic. The schemes work the same either way. The distinction between the two kinds of fraud is useful only to distinguish the status and purpose of the fraudster. The mechanics of the billing scheme, whether conflict or fraudulent disbursement, do not change (see Figure 13-3). In one case, a purchasing superintendent defrauded his employer by purchasing items on behalf of his employer at inflated prices from a certain vendor. The vendor in this case was owned by the purchasing superintendent but established in his wife's name and run by his brother. The perpetrator's interest in the company was undisclosed. The vendor would buy items on the open market, then inflate the prices and resell the items to the victim company. The purchasing superintendent used his influence to ensure that his employer continued doing business with the vendor and paying the exorbitant prices. A more detailed analysis of overbilling frauds is found in Chapter 12.

Fraudsters also engage in bid rigging on behalf of their own companies. The methods used to rig bids were discussed in detail earlier in this chapter. Briefly stated, an employee of the purchasing company is in a perfect position to rig bids because he or she has access to the bids of his or her competitors. Because he or she can find out what prices other vendors have bid, the fraudster can easily tailor his or her own company's bid to win the contract. Bid waivers are also sometimes used by fraudsters to avoid competitive bidding outright. In one instance, a manager processed several unsubstantiated bid waivers in order to direct purchases to a vendor in which one of his employees had an interest. The conflict was undisclosed and the scheme cost the victim company over $150,000.

In other cases a fraudster might ignore his or her employer's purchasing rotation and direct an inordinate number of purchases or contracts to his or her own company. Any way in which a fraudster exerts his or her influence to divert business to a company in which he or she has a hidden interest is a conflict of interest.

Not all conflict schemes occur in the traditional vendor–buyer relationship. Several of the cases in our survey involved employees negotiating for the purchase of some unique, typically large asset such as land or a building in which the employee had an undisclosed interest. It is in the process of these negotiations that the fraudster violates his or her duty of loyalty to his or her employer. Because he or she stands to profit from the sale of the asset, the employee does not negotiate in good faith on behalf of his or her employer; he or she does not attempt to get the best price possible. The fraudster will reap a greater financial benefit if the purchase price is high.

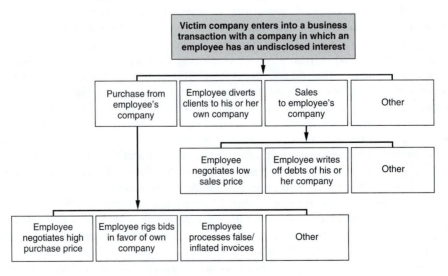

FIGURE 13-3 Conflicts of Interest

An example of this type of scheme was found in which a senior vice president of a utility company was in charge of negotiating and approving mineral leases on behalf of his company. Unbeknownst to his employer, the vice president also owned the property on which the leases were made. The potential harm in this type of relationship is obvious. There was no financial motive for the vice president to negotiate a favorable lease for his employer.

Turnaround Sales   A special kind of purchasing scheme encountered in ACFE studies is called the turnaround sale or flip. In this type of scheme, an employee knows his or her employer is seeking to purchase a certain asset and takes advantage of the situation by purchasing the asset himself or herself (usually in the name of an accomplice or shell company). The fraudster then turns around and resells the item to his or her employer at an inflated price. We have already seen one example of this kind of scheme in a previous case discussed above in which a purchasing supervisor set up a company in his wife's name to resell merchandise to his employer. Another interesting example of the turnaround method occurred in another case, in which the CEO of a company, conspiring with a former employee, sold an office building to the CEO's company. What made the transaction suspicious was that the former employee had purchased the building on the same day that it was resold to the victim company, and for $1.2 million less than the price charged to the CEO's company.

Sales Schemes   ACFE studies identified two principal types of conflict schemes associated with the victim company's sales. The first and most harmful is the underselling of goods or services. Just as a corrupt employee can cause his or her employer to overpay for goods or services sold by a company in which he or she has a hidden interest, so too can he or she cause the employer to undersell to a company in which he or she maintains a hidden interest (see Figure 13-3).

Underbillings   In an underbilling scheme the perpetrator sells goods or services below fair market value to a vendor in which he or she has a hidden interest. This results in a diminished profit margin or even a loss on the sale, depending on the size of the discount. Using this method, two employees sold their employer's inventory to their own company at off-spec prices, causing a loss to the employer of approximately $100,000. Another example is a case in which an employee disposed of his employer's real estate by selling it below fair market value to a company in which he had a hidden interest, causing a loss of approximately $500,000.

Writing-Off Sales   The other type of sales scheme involves tampering with the books of the victim company to decrease or write off the amount owed by an employee's business. For instance, after an employee's company purchases goods or services from the victim company, credit memos may be issued against the sale, causing it to be written off to contra accounts such as Discounts and Allowances. A plant manager in one case used this method. This fraudster assisted favored clients by delaying billing on their purchases for up to 60 days. When the receivable on these clients' accounts became delinquent, the perpetrator issued credit memos against the sales to delete them.

A large number of reversing entries to sales may be a sign that fraud is occurring in an organization. The fraudster in another case avoided the problem of too many write-offs by issuing new invoices on the sales after the "old" receivables were taken off the books. In this way, the receivables could be carried indefinitely on the books without ever becoming past due.

In other cases the perpetrator might not write off the scheme, but simply delay billing. This is sometimes done as a favor to a friendly client and is not an outright avoidance of the bill but rather a dilatory tactic. The victim company eventually gets paid, but loses time value on the payment that arrives later than it should.

Other Conflict of Interest Schemes
Business Diversions   In one instance, an employee started his own business that would compete directly with his employer. While still employed by the victim company, this employee began siphoning off clients for his own business. This activity clearly violated the employee's duty of loyalty to his employer. There is nothing unscrupulous about free competition, but while a person acts as a representative of his employer it is certainly improper to try to undercut the employer and take his clients. Similarly, the fraudster in another case steered potential clients away from his employer and toward his own business. There is nothing unethical about pursuing an independent venture (in the absence of restrictive employment

covenants such as noncompete agreements), but if the employee fails to act in the best interests of his employer while carrying out his duties, then this employee is violating the standards of business ethics and his fiduciary responsibility to his employer.

Resource Diversions Finally, some employees divert the funds and other resources of their employers to the development of their own businesses. In one example, a vice president of a company authorized large expenditures to develop a unique type of new equipment used by a certain contractor. Another firm subsequently took over the contractor, as well as the new equipment. Shortly after that, the vice president retired and went to work for the firm that had bought out the contractor. The fraudster had managed to use his employer's money to fund a company in which he eventually developed an interest. This scheme involves elements of bribery, conflicts of interest, and fraudulent disbursements. In this particular case, if the vice president had financed the equipment in return for the promise of a job, his actions might have been properly classified as a bribery scheme. This case, nevertheless, illustrates a potential conflict problem. The fraudster could just as easily have authorized the fraudulent expenditures for a company in which he secretly held an ownership interest.

Though these schemes are clearly corruption schemes, the funds are diverted through the use of a fraudulent disbursement. The money could be drained from the victim company through a check tampering scheme, a billing scheme, a payroll scheme, or an expense reimbursement scheme. For a discussion of the methods used to generate fraudulent disbursements, please refer to Chapter 12.

Financial Disclosures Management has an obligation to disclose to the shareholders fraud committed by officers, executives, and others in positions of trust. Management does not have the responsibility of disclosing *uncharged* criminal conduct of its officers and executives. Nevertheless, if and when officers, executives, or other persons in trusted positions become subjects of a criminal indictment, disclosure is required.

The inadequate disclosure of conflicts of interest can be among the most serious of frauds. Inadequate disclosure of related-party transactions is not limited to any specific industry; it transcends all business types and relationships.

Preventing and Detecting Conflicts of Interest Conflict of interest schemes are violations of the rule that a fiduciary, agent, or employee must act in good faith, with full disclosure, in the best interest of the principal or employer. Most schemes are a violation of the legal maxim that a person cannot serve "two masters." Some of the more common schemes involve an employee's, manager's, or executive's interest in a customer or supplier and receipt of gifts. As in other situations, the employee, manager, or executive is compensated for his or her interest in the form of "consulting fees."

The prevention of conflicts of interest can be difficult. The primary resource for heading off this complex act is a company ethics policy that specifically addresses the problems and illegalities associated with conflicts of interest and related offenses. The purpose of the policy is to make the position of the company absolutely clear, to define what constitutes a conflict or an improper relationship, and to express in no uncertain terms that conflicts are not appropriate and will not be tolerated. The absence of a clear policy leaves an opportunity for a perpetrator to rationalize his or her behavior or to claim ignorance of any wrongdoing.

A policy requiring employees to complete an annual financial disclosure statement is also an excellent proactive approach to preventing conflicts of interest. Comparing the disclosed names and addresses with the vendor list may reveal real and potential conflicts of interest. Communication with employees regarding their other business interests is also advisable. In cases in which public state records reveal the key officers of all corporations, a name search of these records compared to company employees could be revealing.

In order to detect conflicts of interest, organizations should concentrate on establishing an anonymous reporting mechanism to receive tips and complaints. This is how most conflict of interest cases are detected. Complaints typically come from employees who are aware of a co-worker's self-dealing, or from vendors who have knowledge that a competing vendor with ties to an employee of the organization is being favored.

Another detection method that can be helpful is to periodically run comparisons between vendor and employee addresses and phone numbers. Obviously, if a vendor is owned or run by an employee of the organization without that fact having been disclosed, this would constitute a conflict of interest.

Proactive Computer Audit Tests for Detecting Corruption

Title	Category	Description	Data file(s)
Stratify vendor payments by approval limits, especially directly under (i.e., 5 percent) the approval limit.	All	A high incidence of invoice payments directly below an approval limit may be an attempt to circumvent a management review.	• Paid Invoice
Stratify inventory actual to standard price.	All	Inventory prices may be agreed to that are higher than normal as part of the fraud schemes. This stratification will direct audit efforts on those parts exceeding the standard price.	• On-Hand Inventory
Identify trends in obsolete inventory over two or more periods.	All	Over-purchased inventory, which generally ends in obsolescence, will be identified through trend analysis.	• On-Hand Inventory
Age inventory by the date of last part issuance.	All	Over-purchased inventory, which generally ends in obsolescence, will be identified through trend analysis.	• On-Hand Inventory
Calculate number of months of inventory that is on hand (on a part-by-part basis) and extract those with high number of months.	All	Over-purchased inventory, which generally ends in obsolescence, will be identified through trend analysis.	• On-Hand Inventory • Shipment Log
Extract all parts greater than zero in cost that have had no usage in the current year.	All	Over-purchased inventory, which generally ends in obsolescence, will be identified through trend analysis.	• On-Hand Inventory • Shipment Log
Identify inventory price greater than retail price (if inventory is for sale).	All	Inventory prices may be agreed to that are higher than normal as part of the fraud schemes.	• On-Hand Inventory
Identify inventory receipts per inventory item that exceed the economic order quantity or maximum for that item.	All	Inventory quantities may be agreed to that are higher than normal as part of the fraud schemes.	• Receiving Log • Inventory Master File
Identify duplicate payments based on various means that would be made with intent by the employee and accepted with intent by the vendor.	All	Duplicate payment tests can be enacted on the vendor, invoice number, amount. More complicated tests can look where the same invoice and amount are paid yet the payment is made to two different vendors. Another advanced test would be to search for same vendor and invoice when a different amount is paid.	• Paid Invoice
Calculate the ratio of the largest purchase to the next-largest purchase by vendor.	All	By identifying the largest purchase to a vendor and the next-largest purchase, any large ratio difference may identify a fraudulently issued "largest" purchase.	• Paid Invoice
Calculate the annualized unit price changes in purchase orders for the same product in the same year.	All	Assesses price changes in purchases for potential fraudulent company purchases and employee payments.	• Purchase Order
List all vendors who had multiple invoices immediately below an approval limit (e.g., many $999 payments to a vendor when there is a $1,000 approval limit), highlighting a circumvention of the established control.	All	Multiple invoices below an approval limit may be an attempt to circumvent a management review.	• Paid Invoice
Extract round-dollar payments and summarize by vendor.	All	Payments made in round dollars have a higher incidence of being fraudulent and should be scrutinized closely.	• Paid Invoice

(*Continued*)

(*Continued*)

Title	Category	Description	Data file(s)
Review payments with little or no sequence between invoice numbers.	All	Vendors issuing phony invoices many times will invoice the company with no gaps in invoice sequence.	• Paid Invoice
List payments to any vendor that exceed the twelve-month average payments to that vendor by a specified percentage (i.e., 200 percent).	All	Large payments are unusual and should be scrutinized as potentially being fraudulent.	• Paid Invoice
List payments to any vendor that exceed the twelve-month average payments to any vendor within the purchase category (i.e., supplies, fixtures, etc.) by a specified percentage (i.e., 200 percent).	All	Large payments are unusual and should be scrutinized as potentially being fraudulent, especially when analyzed in relation to other vendors of similar products.	• Paid Invoice
Summarize invoice payment general ledger activity by type of purchase and identify areas with fewer than three vendors.	All	By summarizing general ledger activity, the vendors can be identified by type of purchase (i.e., fixtures, transportation, etc.). Types with fewer than three vendors could identify an area where few vendors are being used, reducing competitive influence and providing the opportunity for fraudulent activity.	• Paid Invoice • General Ledger Distribution
Calculate the average payment by general ledger activity type and review for payments made that exceed that average by a large percentage (i.e., 100 percent).	All	By summarizing general ledger activity by type of purchase (i.e., fixtures, transportation, etc.) high value payments may be identified to fraudulent vendors.	• Paid Invoice • General Ledger Distribution
Summarize by vendor the number of inferior goods based on number of returns.	All	Inferior quality may be reduced to companies with employees receiving fraudulent payments.	• Receiving Log
Identify delivery of inventory to employee address by joining employee address to shipment address file.	All	Inventory may be shipped directly to an employee address to act as consideration to the employee for fraudulent activity.	• Shipment Register • Employee Address
Identify delivery of inventory to address that is not designated as a business address.	All	Inventory may be shipped to an employee address that is entered into the system to appear as a regular business address. Such a shipment would act as consideration to the employee for fraudulent activity. The identification of whether an address is legitimately a business one can be done via software databases such as Select Phone Pro.	• Shipment Register
Match the vendor master file to the employee master file on various key fields.	All	Compare telephone number, address, tax ID numbers, numbers in the address, PO box, and ZIP code in vendor file to information in employee files, especially those employees working in the accounts payable department.	• Vendor Master • Employee Master
Identify vendor address that is not designated as a business address.	All	The identification of whether an address is legitimately a business one can be done via software databases such as Select Phone Pro.	• Vendor Master
Review Internet resources, online newspaper archives, background check, and commercial credit databases for related parties of employees.	All	Review of Internet resources such as AuditNet.Org, online newspapers such as newyorktimes.com and wsj.com, and other online background databases may identify employee-related parties.	• N/A

THE HUMAN FACTOR

We cannot eliminate the problem of fraud in the workforce without eliminating people. The human race is notoriously subject to periodic fits of bad judgment. Anyone in fraud detection or deterrence who is aiming for perfection from the workforce will not only be disappointed, but also find that such attitudes invariably increase the problem.

To quote Dr. Steve Albrecht, "If you set standards too high, you may be inadvertently giving an employee two choices in his mind—to fail or to lie." Your job in establishing anti-fraud standards, then, is to make them clear and reasonable.

The diverse case studies in this book have one common element. That is, of course, the human failings that led trusted people to violate that trust. Were these employees, from the mailroom to the boardroom, all simply greedy? Were they all simply liars? Did they always have defective morals that just surfaced when their honesty was tested? Or were they mistreated, underpaid, and only taking what they considered to be rightfully theirs?

The answer, of course, is that it depends. Crime is a complex tapestry of motive and opportunity. The Sultan of Brunei, one of the world's richest men, may have unlimited opportunity to defraud people. But does he have the motive? Contrarily, the minimum wage cashier may be very motivated to steal in order to keep his lights turned on. But if he is constantly aware his cash drawer may be counted unexpectedly he may not perceive the opportunity to do so. In any anti-fraud effort, we must always keep in mind that no one factor alone will deter occupational fraud; we must attack the problem on several fronts.

Greed

Michael Douglas uttered the now-famous line from the movie *Wall Street*: "Greed is good." While some may debate whether that is true, there is little debate that greed is certainly a factor in occupational fraud. Indeed, students of this subject are most likely to describe embezzlers and their ilk by one single word: *greedy*.

The problem with that definition of a fraud motivator is that it is subjective, and begs for the response, "Greedy? Compared to what?" Most of us consider ourselves greedy to some extent; it is, after all, a very human trait. But there are many greedy people who do not steal, lie, and cheat to get what they want. And how can we measure the amount of greed in any way that will become a predictor of behavior? In sum, there is little we can say about greed as a motive that will help us detect or deter occupational fraud.

Wages in Kind

In nearly all the case studies in this book, one common thread prevails: Those who chose to commit fraud against their employers felt justified in doing so. A perfect example is the case of Bob Walker, the cashier who began stealing to get even with his employer. Walker had been demoted from a management position to head cashier at his store, a move that included a $300 a month pay cut. Feeling morally justified in his theft, Walker went on to process over $10,000 in false refunds, more than twenty-five times what his demotion cost him in lost wages.

For the purpose of detecting and deterring occupational fraud, it does not matter whether the employee is *actually* justified, but whether he *perceives* that he is. Your prevention efforts must begin with education of employees and staff, and attack this misperception on all fronts—the morality, legality, and negative consequences of committing occupational fraud and abuse.

Employers must also understand the concept of *wages in kind*. Joseph T. Wells recounts a perfect illustration from his days as an anti-fraud consultant in the 1980s.

> A local banker heard me give a speech on fraud prevention, and he later called me. "We have a hell of a time with teller thefts," he confidentially admitted. "I would like to hire you to evaluate the problem and give us some solutions."
>
> I spent several days in the bank, going over the accounting procedures, the history of teller thefts, the personnel policies, and the internal controls. I also interviewed bank supervisors, head tellers, and the rank-and-file. The interviews were particularly revealing.
>
> When it came time to give my report, the banker requested I meet with his entire board to deliver my conclusions orally and be able to respond to questions. I tried to be as diplomatic as I could, but when the veneer was stripped away, it wasn't a pretty picture. The reason the bank was having problems with teller thefts was because they (1) had inadequate personnel screening procedures, (2) had no anti-fraud training whatsoever, (3) paid inadequate wages to persons entrusted with drawers full of money, and (4)

were perceived by the employees as cheap and condescending. When I finished my presentation to the board, I asked for questions. The silence was deafening.

After standing there for what seemed like eternity, my banker colleague meekly thanked me for my suggestions and told me they would call. They didn't.

So employers must be educated in the concept of wages in kind. There are three basics that are absolutely necessary to minimizing (not eliminating) occupational fraud and abuse. First, hire the right people. Second, treat them well. Third, don't subject them to unreasonable expectations.

Unreasonable Expectations

If you have carefully evaluated the cases in this book, you should have empathy with at least some of the situations that led to an employee deciding to commit fraud. Employers sometimes have unreasonable expectations of their employees that may contribute to occupational fraud and abuse. First, employers frequently expect their employees to be honest in all situations. That belies the human condition. According to Patterson and Kim in *The Day America Told the Truth*, a full 91 percent of people surveyed admitted to lying on a regular basis. Thankfully, most of these lies have nothing to do with fraud. But it must be remembered that while all liars are not fraudsters, all fraudsters are liars. Our approach to deterrence therefore must be not to eliminate lying (since it can't be done), but to keep lies from turning into frauds.

It is easy to see how anyone can confuse the two concepts of lying and fraud. When we lie to our family, our co-workers, our superiors, and our customers, these are typically deceptions motivated by the human desire to tell people what they want to hear: "My, you look nice today!" So keep your eye on the ball: We want to deter fraud specifically; we don't have quite the time to reform humanity, even though that is a lofty goal. And to deter fraud requires some understanding.

Understanding Fraud Deterrence

Deterrence and prevention are not the same, although we frequently use the terms interchangeably. Prevention, in the sense of crime, involves removing the root causes of the problem. In this case, to prevent fraud, we would have to eliminate the motivation to commit it, such as the societal injustices that lead to crime. We fraud examiners must leave that task to the social scientists. Instead, we concentrate on *deterrence*, which can be defined as the modification of behavior through the perception of negative sanctions.

Fraud offenders are much easier to deter than run-of-the-mill street criminals. Much violent crime is committed in the heat of the moment, and criminologists agree that those crimes are very difficult to stop in advance. But fraud offenders are very deliberate people, as you have seen in this book. At each stage of the offense, they carefully weigh—consciously or subconsciously—the individual risks and rewards of their behaviors. For that reason, their conduct can be more easily modified.

The Impact of Controls   Throughout this book, you have witnessed situations that could have been prevented with the most basic control procedure: separating the money from the record-keeping function. However, it is likely that accountants and auditors expect controls to do too much. After all, many internal controls have nothing to do with fraud. And still others are only indirectly related. Our view is that internal controls are only part of the answer to fraud deterrence. However, not everyone else shares that view. Others argue that if the proper controls are in place, occupational fraud is almost impossible to commit without being detected.

The Perception of Detection   As alluded to throughout this book, the deterrence of occupational fraud and abuse begins in the employee's mind. The perception of detection axiom is as follows:

> Employees who perceive that they will be caught engaging in occupational fraud and abuse are less likely to commit it.

The logic is hard to dispute. Exactly how much deterrent effect this concept provides will be dependent on a number of factors, both internal and external. But as you can see, internal controls can have a deterrent effect only when the employee perceives such a control exists, and exists for the purpose of uncovering fraud. "Hidden" controls have no deterrent effect. Conversely, controls that are not even in place—but are perceived to be—will have the same deterrent value.

How does an entity raise the perception of detection? That, of course, will vary from organization to organization. But the first step is to bring occupational fraud and abuse out of the closet and deal with

the issue in an open forum. Companies and agencies must be cautioned that increasing the perception of detection, if not handled correctly, will smack of "Big Brother" and can cause more problems than it solves. There are at least six positive steps organizations can employ to increase the perception of detection.

Employee Education   Unless the vast majority of employees are in favor of reducing occupational fraud and abuse, any proactive fraud deterrence program is destined for failure. It is therefore necessary that the entire workforce be enlisted in this effort. Organizations should provide at least some basic anti-fraud training at the time workers are hired. In this fashion, the employees become the eyes and ears of the organization, and are more likely to report possible fraudulent activity.

Education of employees should be factual rather than accusatory. Point out that fraud—in any form—is eventually very unhealthy for the organization and the people who work there. Fraud and abuse cost raises, jobs, benefits, morale, profits, and one's integrity. The fraud-educated workforce is the fraud examiner's best weapon—by far.

Proactive Fraud Policies   When we ask most people how to deter fraud, they typically say something like this: "In order to prevent fraud, we must prosecute more people. That will send a message." There are at least three flaws in this well-meaning argument. First, there is nothing proactive about prosecuting people. As some in Texas would say, it is like closing the barn door after the cows have escaped. Second, whether it really sends much of a message is debatable. This concept is called "general deterrence" by criminologists. As logical as the idea sounds on its face, there is little data—out of scores of studies—that show it actually works.

Without getting into the intricacies of criminological thought, punishment is believed by many experts to be of little value in deterring crime, because the possibilities of being punished are too remote in the mind of the potential perpetrator. Think about it for a second. If you were debating whether to commit a crime (of any kind) the first question that comes into your mind is: "Will I be caught?" not "What is the punishment if I am caught?" If you answer yes to the first question, you are very unlikely to commit the offense. That makes the punishment moot, no matter how severe it is.

The foregoing is not to say that crime should not be punished. Quite the opposite—it is something that must be done in a civilized society. But remember that the primary benefit of any type of punishment is society's retribution for the act, not that punishment will deter others.

A Higher Stance   Proactive fraud policies begin simply with a higher stance by management, auditors, and fraud examiners. That means, as previously stated, bringing fraud out of the closet. At every phase of a routine audit or management review, the subject of fraud and abuse should be brought up in a nonaccusatory manner. People should be asked to share their knowledge and suspicions, if any. They should be asked about possible control and administrative weaknesses that might contribute to fraud. What we are trying to accomplish through this method is to make people subtly aware that if they commit illegal acts, others will be looking over their shoulders.

A higher stance also means making sure that "hidden" controls don't remain that way. Auditors may have a peculiar image to the uninformed. Employees know auditors are there, but many are not quite sure what the auditors actually do. While this attitude can obviously bring benefits if you are trying to conduct your activities in secret, it is counterproductive in proactive fraud deterrence. You must let employees know you are looking.

Increased Use of Analytical Review   If an employee embezzles $100,000 from a Fortune 500 corporation, it will not cause even a blip in the financial statements. And in large audits, the chance of discovering a bogus invoice is remote at best. That is because of the sampling techniques used by auditors—they look at a relatively small number of transactions in total.

But as you can see from the cases in this book, the real risks are in asset misappropriations in small businesses. These of course can be and frequently are very material to the bottom line. And the smaller businesses are those that benefit the most from the increased use of analytical review. Throughout this book we have presented dozens of proactive computer-aided audit tests that are specifically tailored to the various forms of occupational fraud that we have discussed. These audit tests were accumulated and organized by Richard B. Lanza in his publication *Proactively Detecting Occupational Fraud Using Computer Audit Reports*, and have been reprinted here with his permission. These tests should be a part of any organization's proactive fraud program.

Surprise Audits Where Feasible The threat of surprise audits, especially in businesses that are currency-intensive, may be a powerful deterrent to occupational fraud and abuse. In case after case, all too many fraud perpetrators were aware that audits were coming, so they had time to alter, destroy, and misplace records and other evidence of their offenses. Obviously, surprise audits are more difficult to plan and execute than a normal audit that is announced in advance. But considering the impact of the perception of detection, surprise audits may certainly be worth the trouble.

Adequate Reporting Programs As many of the cases in this book illustrate, adequate reporting programs are vital to serious efforts to detect and deter occupational fraud and abuse. In situation after situation we encountered, employees suspected that illegal activity was taking place, but they had no way to report this information without the fear of being "dragged into" the investigation.

Reporting programs should emphasize at least six points: (1) fraud, waste, and abuse occur at some level in nearly every organization; (2) this conduct costs jobs, raises, and profits; (3) the organization actively encourages employees to come forward with information; (4) there are no penalties for furnishing good-faith information; (5) there is an exact method for reporting, such as a telephone number or address; and (6) a report of suspicious activity does not have to be made by the employee to his immediate supervisor.

A hotline is considered by most professionals to be the cornerstone of an employee reporting program. According to some studies, about 5 percent of hotline calls are actually developed into solid cases. In many instances, these schemes would not have been discovered by any other method. And as the data from ACFE studies show, tips from various sources (employees, vendors, customers, and anonymous) are the most common means by which occupational fraud is detected.

Hotlines also help to increase the perception of detection. An employee who is aware that his nefarious activities might be reported by a co-worker will be less likely to engage in such conduct.

Behaviorists tell us that the vast majority of our personality has been formed by the age of three. A large part of our personality relates to the values we have, which are instilled in us by our parents and mentors. Without being cynical (which we admit to), it is highly unlikely that ethical policies—no matter how strong they are—will seriously deter those sufficiently motivated to engage in occupational fraud and abuse.

There is no ethical policy stronger than the leadership provided by the head of the organization. Modeling of behavior occurs with strong influences such as the boss. Indeed, the Treadway Commission specifically commented on the importance of the "tone at the top." Unfortunately, the formal ethics policies in place right now are thought to exist mostly in large organizations. In the small business—which is much more vulnerable to going broke from asset misappropriations—few of the bosses victimized seem to realize the importance of their own personal example.

When employees hear their leaders telling the customer what he wants to hear, when the small business boss fudges on the myriad taxes he must pay, when the chief executive officer lies to the vendors about when they will be paid, nothing good can possibly result. So setting an example is the *real* ethical connection.

FROM THE FRAUDSTER'S PERSPECTIVE

Adapted from the WhiteCollarFraud.com blog by Sam E. Antar
Monday, December 25, 2006

The Art of Spinning: How to Identify Possible White-Collar Criminals—or, at Least, Unethical and Deceitful People Whom You Should Avoid

White-collar crime is a crime of persuasion and deceit. Since the white-collar criminal uses persuasion and deceit to commit crimes, it follows that such felons are artful liars.

People often ask me what characteristics I look for in other people to alert me to possible criminal activity, or at least to unethical and deceitful behavior.

Not all questionable conduct is illegal. A person can be unethical or deceitful without committing any illegal acts, as the law defines them.

However, most criminals use tools like spinning in the conduct of their crimes.

The Art of Spinning:

- Sell people hope. My cousin "Crazy Eddie" Antar taught me that "people live on hope," and their hopes and dreams must be fed through our spinning and lies. In any situation, if possible, accentuate the positive.

- Make excuses as long as you can. Try to have your excuses based on at least one truthful fact, even if the fact is unrelated to your actions and argument.

- When you cannot dispute the underlying facts, accept them as true, but rationalize your actions. You are allowed to make mistakes as long as you have no wrongful intent. Being stupid is not a crime.

- Always say in words that you "take responsibility," but try to indirectly shift the blame to other people and factors. You need to portray yourself as a "stand-up" guy or gal.

- When you cannot defend your actions or arguments, attack the messenger to detract attention from your questionable actions.
- Always show your kindness by doing people favors. You will require the gratitude of such people to come to your aid and defend you.
- Build up your stature, integrity, and credibility by publicizing the good deeds you have done in areas unrelated to the subject of scrutiny.
- Build a strong base of support. Try to have surrogates and the beneficiaries of your largess stand up for you and defend you.
- If you can, appear to take the "high road" and have your surrogates do the "dirty work" for you. After all, you cannot control the actions of your zealots.
- When you can no longer spin, shut up. For example, offer no guidance to investors, or resign for "personal reasons." Your surrogates and so-called friends can still speak on your behalf and defend you.
- If you are under investigation, always say you will "cooperate." However, use all means necessary legal or otherwise to stifle the investigators. Remember that "people live on hope," and their inclination is to believe you.
- When called to testify under oath (if you do not exercise your Fifth Amendment privilege against self-incrimination) exhibit selective memory about your questionable actions. It is harder to be charged with perjury if you cannot remember what you have done rather than testify but lie about it.
- However, before you testify, have other friendly witnesses testify before you to defend you. You need to "lock in" their stories first (before they change their minds) so that your testimony does not conflict with their testimony; this will make your story appear more truthful.
- Try not to have your actions at least appear to rise to the level of criminal conduct or a litigable action. Being stupid or being unethical is not always a crime or a tort action.
- One last rule: to be a most effective spinner, always keep your friends close and your enemies closer. The kindness you show your enemies will reduce their propensity to be skeptical of you.

If you see some of the above similarities in people who are in authority such as executives, politicians, and others, you are forewarned: watch out. Before a person can be a white-collar criminal, he or she must be deceitful and be able to follow most of the above rules of spinning.

Another thing I learned as a criminal is that "it takes one to know one."

Sam E. Antar (former Crazy Eddie CFO and convicted felon)

REVIEW QUESTIONS

13-1 What are the different types of corruption schemes?

13-2 How do bribery and illegal gratuities differ?

13-3 What is meant by a conflict of interest?

13-4 What is defined as "something of value?"

13-5 How can conflicts of interest be prevented and detected?

13-6 What is a kickback scheme, and how is it committed?

13-7 What type of abuses may occur at the pre-solicitation stage of the bidding process?

13-8 Why is it problematic for an organization to set standards that are too high?

13-9 How does the "perception of detection" impact fraud deterrence?

13-10 What is the difference between fraud prevention and fraud deterrence?

ENDNOTE

1. Henry Campbell Black, *Black's Law Dictionary*, 5th ed., West Publishing Co., 1979.

CHAPTER 14

FINANCIAL STATEMENT FRAUD

LEARNING OBJECTIVES

After completing this chapter, you should be able to:

14-1 Identify some common reasons why senior management might overstate or understate business performance.

14-2 Describe the ways in which financial statement fraud is committed.

14-3 Discuss the conceptual framework for financial reporting.

14-4 Identify and describe the five classifications of financial statement fraud.

14-5 Explain how fictitious revenue schemes are committed.

14-6 List the four criteria necessary for a sale to be complete.

14-7 Describe how understating liabilities and expenses can make a company appear more profitable.

14-8 Identify the issues generally involved in improper disclosures.

14-9 Discuss how improper asset valuation may inflate the current ratio.

14-10 Explain how financial statement fraud may be deterred.

CRITICAL THINKING EXERCISE

A woman shoots her husband. Then she holds him underwater for over five minutes. Finally, she hangs him. But five minutes later they both go out together and enjoy a wonderful dinner together. How can this be?

ACCOUNTING PRINCIPLES AND FRAUD

Fraud in Financial Statements

In this chapter, we will examine some of the principles underlying financial statement frauds. These frauds are caused by a number of factors occurring at the same time, the most significant of which is the pressure on upper management to show earnings. Preparing false financial statements is made easier by the subjective nature of book- and record-keeping. The accounting profession has long recognized that accounting is a somewhat arbitrary process, subject to differences in judgment. The profession also indirectly recognizes that numbers are subject to manipulation. After all, a debit on a company's books can be recorded as either an expense or an asset. A credit can be a liability or equity. Therefore, there can be tremendous temptation—when a strong earnings showing is needed—to classify expenses as assets and liabilities as equity.

Later in this chapter, we will explore the five major methods by which financial statement fraud is committed, but it is important to first consider three general questions that go to the heart of these crimes:

1. Who commits financial statement fraud?

2. Why do people commit financial statement fraud?

3. How do people commit financial statement fraud?

Who Commits Financial Statement Fraud? There are three main groups of people who commit financial statement fraud. In descending order of likelihood of involvement, they are as follows:

1. *Senior management.* According to a 1999 study of approximately 200 financial statement frauds from 1987 to 1997 conducted by the Committee of Sponsoring Organizations of the Treadway Commission (COSO), senior management is the most likely group to commit financial statement fraud. The CEO was involved in 72 percent of the frauds and the CFO was involved in 43 percent. Either the CEO or the CFO was involved in 83 percent of the cases. Motives for senior managers to commit financial statement fraud are varied and are described below.

2. *Mid- and lower-level employees.* This category of employees may falsify financial statements for their respective area of responsibility (subsidiary, division, or other unit) to conceal their poor performance or to earn bonuses based on higher performance.

3. *Organized criminals.* This group may use such a scheme to obtain fraudulent loans from a financial institution, or to hype a stock they are selling as part of a "pump-and-dump" scheme.

Why Do People Commit Financial Statement Fraud? Senior managers (CEOs, CFOs, etc.) and business owners may "cook the books" for any of several key reasons:

- *To conceal true business performance.* The objective may be to overstate or understate results
- *To preserve personal status/control.* Senior managers with strong egos may be unwilling to admit that their strategy has failed and that business performance is bad, since it may lead to their termination
- *To maintain personal income/wealth* flowing from salary, bonus, stock, and stock options

We can better deter and detect fraud if we understand the different pressures senior managers and business owners face that might drive them to commit fraud. If we understand the motivating factors behind these crimes, it stands to reason we will be in a better position to recognize the circumstances that might lead people to commit financial statement fraud. We will also increase our likelihood of detecting these crimes by knowing the most likely places to find fraud in an organization's financials.

As with other forms of occupational fraud, financial statement schemes are generally tailored to the particular circumstances in the organization. This means that the evaluation criteria used by those with power over management tend to drive management behavior in fraud cases. For example, during the Internet boom investors pressured dot-com companies to grow revenues rather than to achieve high profits. This type of pressure might drive senior managers to overstate revenues, without necessarily overstating earnings. Some Internet companies did this by recording advertising revenue from barter transactions even where no market value for the advertising could be identified. Tight loan covenants might drive managers to misclassify certain liabilities as long-term rather than current in order to improve the entity's current ratio (current assets to current liabilities), without affecting reported earnings.

Following are some of the more common reasons senior management *overstate* business performance:

- To meet or exceed the earnings or revenue growth expectations of stock market analysts
- To comply with loan covenants
- To increase the amount of financing available from asset-based loans
- To meet a lender's criteria for granting/extending loan facilities
- To meet corporate performance criteria set by the parent company
- To meet personal performance criteria
- To trigger performance-related compensation or earn-out payments
- To support the stock price in anticipation of a merger, acquisition, or sale of personal stockholding
- To show a pattern of growth to support a planned securities offering or sale of the business

Alternatively, senior management may *understate* business performance to meet certain objectives:

- To defer "surplus" earnings to the next accounting period. If current period budgets have been met and there is no reward for additional performance, corporate managers may prefer to direct additional earnings into the next period to help meet their new targets
- To take all possible write-offs in one "big bath" now so future earnings will be consistently higher
- To reduce expectations now so future growth will be better perceived and rewarded

- To preserve a trend of consistent growth and avoid volatile results
- To reduce the value of an owner-managed business for purposes of a divorce settlement
- To reduce the value of a corporate unit whose management is planning a buyout

How Do People Commit Financial Statement Fraud? The mechanics of the major types of financial statement fraud will be discussed in the next chapter. As you review that material, keep in mind that, regardless of method, there are three general ways in which fraudulent financial statements can be produced. By being aware of these three approaches, those who investigate financial statement fraud can remain alert for evidence of attempts to manipulate the accounting and financial reporting process or to go outside it. Financial statement frauds may involve more than one of these three methods, though perpetrators commonly start with the first method and incorporate the other two methods as the fraud grows. The three general methods are as follows:

1. *Playing the accounting system.* In this approach, the fraudster uses the accounting system as a tool to generate the desired results. For example, to increase or decrease earnings to a selected figure, a fraudster might manipulate the assumptions used to calculate depreciation charges, allowances for bad debts, or allowances for excess and obsolete inventory. If the goal is to avoid recognizing expenses and liabilities, vendor invoices might not be recorded on a timely basis, or genuine sales might be recorded prematurely. Transactions recorded in the accounting system have a basis in fact, even if they are improperly recorded. There is a documentary trail to support the results reported in the financial statements, though the assumptions shown in some of those documents may be questionable.

2. *Beating the accounting system.* In this approach, the fraudster feeds false and fictitious information into the accounting system to manipulate reported results by an amount greater than can be achieved by simply "playing the accounting system." Fictitious sales may be recorded to the accounts of legitimate or phony customers. Inventory and receivables figures may be fabricated, with documents later forged to support the claimed numbers. Senior financial management might determine allowances for bad debts and for excess and obsolete inventory without regard to the formulae or methods historically used in the entity to determine these amounts. Journal entries might be disguised in an attempt to conceal their fraudulent intent (e.g., splitting big round-sum adjustments into many smaller entries of odd amounts), or transactions may be hidden through the use of intercompany accounts to conceal the other side of a transaction. Some transactions recorded in the accounting system may have no basis in fact, and some that do may be improperly recorded. There will be no documentary trail to support certain transactions or balances unless the fraudster prepares forged or altered documents to help support the fraud.

3. *Going outside the accounting system.* In this approach, the fraudster produces whatever financial statements he or she wishes, perhaps using just a typewriter or a personal computer. These financial statements could be based on the results of an accounting and financial reporting process for an operating entity, with additional manual adjustments to achieve the results desired by the fraudster. Alternatively, they could just be printed using phony numbers supplied by the fraudster. In some cases, fraudsters may go back and enter false data in the accounting system to support the phony financial statements. In other cases, they may not bother or there might be no accounting system. Not all transactions may be recorded in an accounting system, and some or all transactions may have no basis in fact. To catch this type of fraud, it is usually necessary to start by tracing the published financial statements back to the output of the accounting system. As in the previous situation, there will be no documentary trail to support certain transactions or balances reported in the financial statements unless the fraudsters prepare forged or altered documents to help support this fraud.

Conceptual Framework for Financial Reporting

Over the years, businesses have found numerous ingenious ways to overstate their true earnings and assets. As a result, a number of accounting guidelines, or generally accepted accounting principles (GAAP), have developed. The Financial Accounting Standards Board (FASB), an independent public watchdog

organization responsible for standard setting, has codified most historic accounting principles. Statement on Auditing Standards (SAS) No. 69, "The Meaning of Present Fairly in Conformity with Generally Accepted Accounting Principles," indicates the primary sources of generally accepted accounting principles—FASB Standards and Interpretations, APB Opinions, and American Institute of Certified Public Accountants (AICPA) Accounting Research Bulletins. Although accounting students should be familiar with these concepts, we will review them here with the emphasis on fraud. The following is a conceptual framework for financial reporting:

I. Recognition and Measurement Concepts

    A. Assumptions
        i. Economic entity
        ii. Going concern
        iii. Monetary unit
        iv. Periodicity

    B. Principles
        i. Historical cost
        ii. Revenue recognition
        iii. Matching
        iv. Full disclosure

    C. Constraints
        i. Cost-benefit
        ii. Materiality
        iii. Industry practice
        iv. Conservatism

II. Qualitative Characteristics

    A. Relevance and Reliability

    B. Comparability and Consistency

Economic Entity   The premise of the economic entity assumption is that the activity of a business enterprise should be kept separate and distinct from its owners and other business entities. The entity concept does not rely on legal criteria but rather on substance. The concept of the entity is becoming ever more difficult to define. Companies with subsidiaries, joint ventures, or special-purpose entities (SPEs), such as those established by Enron, have raised further questions about how to account for the entity in order to prevent fraudulent manipulation of the financial statements.

Going Concern   In valuing a firm's assets for financial statement purposes, it is assumed that the business is one that will continue into the future. That is because the worth of any good business will be higher than the value of its hard assets. For example, if you wanted to buy a business that paid you a 10 percent return, then you would pay up to a million dollars for an investment that earned $100,000 a year. The value of the actual assets underlying the business, if they were sold at auction, would typically not total nearly a million dollars. The going-concern concept assumes that the business will go on indefinitely into the future. If there is serious doubt about whether a business can continue, this must be disclosed as a footnote in the financial statements.

Fraud in the going-concern context usually results from attempts by an entity to conceal its terminal business condition. For example, assume a company is in the computer parts manufacturing business. Last year the company earned $100,000 after taxes. This year management is aware that new technology will make its business totally obsolete, and that by next year the business will likely close. The company's auditors might not know this. And when they prepare the financial statements for their company, management has the duty to inform the accountants of the business's future ability to earn money. The auditors, in turn, will insist that the financial statements for the current period reflect this future event.

Monetary Unit To measure and analyze financial transactions, a common standard is necessary. In our society, that common denominator is money. The U.S. dollar has remained reasonably stable, but some countries, as a result of persistent economic volatility, use "inflation accounting" to adjust for price-level changes in their currency. International companies that deal with foreign currency transactions may be subject to fraudulent abuse of monetary exchange rates.

Periodicity This "time period" assumption uses the principle of dividing economic activity into specific time intervals, such as monthly, quarterly, and annually. With shorter reporting periods, however, the data tend to be subject to greater human error and manipulation and, therefore, are less reliable.

Historical Cost Generally accepted accounting principles require that assets be carried on the financial statements at the price established by the exchange transaction. This figure is referred to as historical or acquisition cost, and this is generally the most conservative and reliable method. However, there are some exceptions to the historical-cost principle. For example, if inventory is worth less than its cost, this lower value is to be reported on the financials. This approach is referred to as the lower of cost or market. Furthermore, although many investments are reported at fair value, there are other methods of valuation. The net realizable value of an asset is the amount of money that would be realized upon the sale of the asset, less the costs to sell it. The problem arises in attempting to establish a sales value for the asset without selling it. If a company was required to place a sales value on every asset in order to determine net income, the resulting figure would be materially affected by opinion. The potential for fraud, in this case, is evident. Similar arguments have been made against using replacement value.

Revenue Recognition According to generally accepted accounting principles, the accrual basis of accounting should be used for financial reporting. In this method, revenues are recognized and reported in the period in which they are earned. Intentional manipulation of the timing for revenues earned is a potential area for fraudulent abuse.

Matching The matching concept requires that the books and records and the resultant financial statements match revenue and expense in the proper accounting period. Fraud can occur when purposeful attempts are made to manipulate the matching procedure. For example, through controlling the year-end cut-off in financial figures, many companies boost their current net income by counting revenue from the following year early, and by delaying the posting of this year's expenses until the following year. This is a fairly common method of financial statement manipulation. As a routine test, auditors examine the cut-off dates of significant transactions of income and expense to see that they are recorded in the proper period.

Full Disclosure The principle behind full disclosure, once again, is that any material deviation from generally accepted accounting principles must be explained to the reader of the financial information. In addition, any known event that could have a material impact on future earnings must be explained or disclosed. For example, as discussed earlier, suppose a company is aware that competitors are making its principal manufacturing method for computer parts obsolete. Such a state of affairs must be disclosed. If the company is being sued and is in danger of a material monetary judgment, that too must be disclosed. In actuality, any potential adverse event of a material nature must be disclosed in the financials. Many major financial frauds have been the result of purposeful omission of footnote disclosures to the statements.

Cost-Benefit In formulating standards for financial reporting, the FASB considers the trade-off between the cost of providing certain information and the related benefit to be derived by the users of the information. The specific costs and benefits, however, are not always readily apparent. Some costs, such as the cost to collect, distribute, and audit data, are more easily measured than, for example, the costs associated with disclosure when important information may be used by competitors to gain an unfair advantage. This

limitation should not be construed as an excuse to purposely and fraudulently omit material information from the financial statements.

Materiality   Financial statements are not meant to be perfect, only reasonable and fair. There are doubtless many small errors in the books of corporations of all sizes, but what does it really mean in terms of the big picture? The answer is that it depends on who is looking at the financial statements and making decisions based on them. If a company's estimated earnings are given as $1 million a year on its financial statements, and it turns out that the figure is actually $990,000 (or $1,010,000), who cares? Probably not many people. But suppose that $1 million in purported earnings on the financial statements is actually $500,000—half of what the company shows. Then a lot of people—investors and lenders, primarily—would care a great deal.

Materiality, then, according to GAAP, is a user-oriented concept. If a misstatement is so significant that reasonable, prudent users of the financial statements would make a different decision than they would if they had been given correct information, then the misstatement is material and requires correction.

A typical issue involving materiality and fraud is asset misappropriations. Taken separately, they may be quite small and not material to the financial statements as a whole. But what of the aggregate? If many small amounts are stolen, the result could indeed be material.

Industry Practice   Reporting practices within certain industries may deviate from generally accepted accounting principles as a matter of fair and clear presentation. For example, the utility industry, due to its highly capital-intensive nature, lists noncurrent assets first on the balance sheet rather than listing the assets in order of liquidity. In the event of deviations from GAAP, a determination should be made regarding whether there is justification for the departure.

Conservatism   The conservatism constraint requires that, when there is any doubt, one should avoid overstating assets and income. The purpose of this principle is to provide a reasonable guideline in a questionable situation. If there is no doubt concerning the accuracy of a valuation, this constraint need not be applied. An example of conservatism in accounting is the use of the "lower of cost or market" rule as it relates to inventory valuation. That simply means that if a company paid one dollar for a widget and at a later date the price fell to fifty cents, then the lower of those two prices should be carried on the balance sheet; the resulting price fall should then be recorded on the income statement. If a company's financial statements violate the conservatism constraint, they could be fraudulent.

Relevance and Reliability   "Qualitative Characteristics of Accounting Information," outlined in Statement of Financial Accounting Concepts No. 2, identifies relevance and reliability as two primary qualities of usefulness for decision making. Relevance implies that certain information will make a difference in arriving at a decision. Reliability, on the other hand, means that the user can depend on the factual accuracy of the information. It is precisely when the accuracy of information is intentionally compromised, to influence a decision by the user of the financial statements, that fraud occurs.

Comparability and Consistency   In order for financial information to be useful for analytical purposes, it must possess the secondary qualitative characteristics of comparability and consistency. For example, one easy way for the value of assets and income to be inflated is through the depreciation methods that companies use on their books. Assume a valuable piece of equipment was purchased by a company for $99,000 and was expected to last three years, with no salvage value at the end of its useful life. That means under *straight-line* depreciation, the write-off in the first year would be $33,000. Using the *double-declining-balance* method of depreciation, the write-off would be $66,000 in the first year. By switching depreciation methods from one year to the next, the company could influence its net income by as much as $33,000. By manipulating income in this manner, the user is comparing apples and oranges. So if a company changes the way it keeps its books from one year to the next, and if these changes have a material impact on the financial statements, they must be disclosed in a footnote. Fraud occurs when consistency is intentionally avoided to show false profits.

Responsibility for Financial Statements

Financial statements are the responsibility of company management. Therefore, it is hard to believe that financial statement fraud can be committed without some knowledge or consent of management. However, financial statement fraud can be perpetrated by anyone who has the opportunity and the motive to omit or misstate data in furtherance of his or her own purpose. For example, a department manager whose compensation is based partly on the sales of his unit might be motivated to falsely increase his department's sales in order to get paid more.

Recall that fraud is generally instigated by members of management or, at the least, by persons under the direction and control of management. If management does not investigate suspected frauds, how can management assure itself that fraud will be deterred and, if fraud does occur, that it will be detected?

A company's board of directors and senior management are supposed to set the code of conduct for the company. This code is often referred to as the company's "ethic," the standard by which all employees should conduct themselves. It stands to reason, therefore, that if the company's ethic is one of high integrity, the company's employees will operate in a more honest manner. If the ethic is corrupt, the employees will view that as a license to be dishonest. An unimpeachable company ethic does not, in and of itself, ensure that financial statement fraud will not occur. Additional measures are required in order for management to discharge its responsibilities with respect to deterrence and detection of fraudulent financial reporting.

Users of Financial Statements

As we have made clear, financial statement fraud schemes are most often perpetrated against potential users of financial statements by management. The users of financial statements may include the company's owners, lending organizations, vendors, and investors. Fraudulent statements are used for a number of reasons; the most common is to increase the apparent prosperity of the organization in the eyes of potential and current investors. This not only may induce new investment, but it can help keep current investors satisfied. Fraudulent financial statements can be used to dispel negative perceptions of an organization in the open market. Company management often use financial statements to judge employee or manager performance. Employees are tempted to manipulate statements to ensure continued employment and additional compensation that may be tied to performance. Certain internal goals, such as meeting budgets, contribute added pressure to the manager responsible. Figure 14-1 displays the role of financial information and statements in the decision-making process of users.

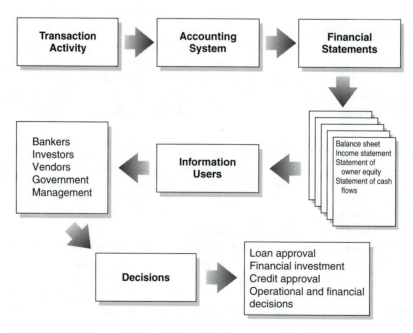

FIGURE 14-1 Users of Financial Statements

Types of Financial Statements

According to Statement on Auditing Standards (SAS) No. 62, published by the AICPA Auditing Standards Board, financial statements include presentations of financial data and accompanying notes prepared in conformity with generally accepted accounting principles or some other comprehensive basis of accounting. The following is a list of the financial statements:

- Balance sheet
- Statement of income or statement of operations
- Statement of retained earnings
- Statement of cash flows
- Statement of changes in owners' equity
- Statement of assets and liabilities that does not include owners' equity accounts
- Statement of revenue and expenses
- Summary of operations
- Statement of operations by product line
- Statement of cash receipts and disbursements

Although not specifically noted in SAS 62, financial statements also typically include other financial data presentations, such as

- Prospective financial information
- Pro forma financial statements
- Proxy statements
- Interim financial information
- Current-value financial representations
- Personal financial statements
- Bankruptcy financial statements
- Registration statement disclosures

Other comprehensive bases of accounting, according to SAS 62, include

- Government or regulatory agency accounting
- Tax basis accounting
- Cash receipts and disbursements, or modified cash receipts and disbursements
- Any other basis with a definite set of criteria applied to all material items, such as the price-level basis of accounting

As we see from the preceding lists, the term *financial statement* includes almost any financial data presentation prepared according to generally accepted accounting principles or another comprehensive basis of accounting. Throughout this chapter and the next, the term *financial statements* is assumed to include the above forms of reporting financial data, as well as the accompanying footnotes and management's discussion.

Types of Fraudulent Financial Statement Schemes Financial statement frauds can be broken down into five distinct categories: concealed liabilities and expenses, fictitious revenues, improper asset valuations, improper disclosures, and timing differences. The distribution of these scheme types has been shown to be fairly uniform in ACFE studies, with the first three categories being the most common. Timing differences were the least frequent scheme observed among the financial statement frauds in the ACFE research cases.

CASE STUDY: THAT WAY LIES MADNESS

"I'm Crazy Eddie!" a goggle-eyed man screams from the television set, pulling at his face with his hands. "My prices are *insane!*" Eddie Antar got into the electronics business in 1969, with a modest store called Sight and Sound. Less than twenty years later, he had become Crazy Eddie, a millionaire many times over and an international fugitive from justice. He was shrewd, daring, and self-serving; he was obsessive and greedy. But he was hardly *insane*. A U.S. Attorney said, "He was not Crazy Eddie. He was Crooked Eddie."

The man on the screen wasn't Eddie at all. The face so dutifully watched throughout New Jersey, New York, and Connecticut—that was an actor, hired to do a humiliating but effective characterization. The real Eddie Antar was not the kind of man to yell and rend his clothes. He was busy making money, and he was making a lot of it illegally. By the time his electronics empire folded, Antar and members of his family had distinguished themselves with a fraud of massive proportions, reaping more than $120 million. A senior official at the Securities and Exchange Commission (SEC) quipped, "This may not be the biggest stock fraud of all time, but for outrageousness it is going to be very hard to beat." The SEC was joined by the FBI, the Postal Inspection Service, and the U.S. Attorney in tracking Eddie down. They were able to show a multipronged fraud in which Antar:

1. Listed smuggled money from foreign banks as sales
2. Made false entries to accounts payable
3. Overstated Crazy Eddie, Inc.'s inventory by breaking into and altering audit records
4. Took credit for merchandise as "returned" while also counting it as inventory
5. "Shared inventory" from one store to boost other stores' audit counts
6. Arranged for vendors to ship merchandise and defer the billing, while also claiming discounts and advertising credits
7. Sold large lots of merchandise to wholesalers, then spread the money to individual stores as retail receipts

It was a long list and a profitable one for Eddie Antar and the inner circle of his family. The seven action items were designed to make Crazy Eddie's look like it was booming. In fact, it was. It was the single biggest retailer of stereos and televisions in the New York metropolitan area, with a dominant and seemingly impregnable share of the market. That wasn't enough for Eddie. He took the chain public, and then he made some real money. Shares that initially sold at $8 each would later peak at $80, thanks to the Antar team's masterful tweaking of company accounts.

Inflating Crazy Eddie's stock price wasn't the first scam that Antar had pulled. In the early days, as Sight and Sound grew into Crazy Eddie's and spawned multiple stores, Eddie was actually underreporting his earnings. Eddie's cousin, Sam Antar, remembered learning how the company did business by watching his father during the early days. "The store managers would drop off cash to the house after they closed at ten o'clock, and my father would make one bundle for deposit into the company account, and several bundles for others in the family," Sam Antar said. "Then he would drive over to their houses and drop off their bundles at two in the morning." For every few dollars to the company, the Antars took a dollar for themselves. The cash was secreted away into bank accounts at Bank Leumi of Israel. Eddie smuggled some of the money out of the country himself, by strapping stacks of large bills across his body. The Antars sneaked away with at least $7 million over several years. Skimming the cash meant tax-free profits and one gargantuan nest egg waiting across the sea.

But entering the stock market was another story. Eddie anticipated the initial public offering (IPO) of shares by quietly easing money from Bank Leumi back into the operation. The company really was growing, but injecting the pilfered funds as sales receipts made the growth look even more impressive. Now this looks sweet: skim the money and beat the tax man, then draw out funds as you need them to boost sales figures—keeps the ship running smoothly.

But Paul Hayes, a special agent who worked the case with the FBI, pointed out Crazy Eddie's problem. "After building up the books, they set a pattern of double-digit growth, which they had to sustain. When they couldn't sustain it, they started looking for new ways to fake it," Hayes said.

Eddie, his brothers, his cousins, and several family loyalists all owned large chunks of company stock. No matter what actually happened at the stores, they wanted that stock to rise. So the seven-point plan was born. There was the skimmed money waiting overseas, being brought back and disguised as sales. But there were limits to how much cash the family had available and could get back into the country, so they turned to other methods of inflating the company's financials. In a daring part of the expanded scam, Antar's people broke into auditors' records and boosted the inventory numbers. With the stroke of a pen, 13 microcassette players became 1,327.

Better than that, the Antars figured out how to make their inventory do double work. Debit memos were drawn up showing substantial lots of stereos or VCRs as "returned to manufacturer." Crazy Eddie's was given a credit for the wholesale cost due back from the manufacturer. But the machines were kept at the warehouse to be counted as inventory. In another variation of the inventory scam, at least one wholesaler agreed to ship Crazy Eddie's truckloads of merchandise, deferring the billing to a later date. That way Crazy Eddie's had plenty of inventory volume plus the return credits listed on the account book. And what if auditors got too close and began asking questions? Executives would throw the records away. A "lost" report was a safe report.

Eddie Antar didn't stop at simple bookkeeping and warehouse games; he "shared inventory" among his nearly 40 stores. After auditors had finished counting a warehouse's holdings and had gone for the day, workers tossed the merchandise into trucks. The inventory was hauled overnight to an early morning load-in at another store. When the auditors arrived at that store, they found a full stockroom waiting to be counted. Again, this ruse carried a double payoff. The audit looked strong because of the inventory items counted multiple times. And the bookkeeping looked good because only one set of invoices was entered as payable to Eddie's creditors. Also, the game could be repeated for as long as the audit route demanded.

Eddie's trump card was the supplier network. He had considerable leverage with area wholesalers because Crazy Eddie's was the biggest and baddest retail outlet in the region. Agent Paul Hayes remembers Eddie as "an aggressive businessman: He'd put the squeeze on a manufacturer and tell them he wasn't going to carry their product. Now, he was king of what is possibly the biggest consolidated retail market in the nation. Japanese manufacturers were fighting each other to get into this market. . . . So when Eddie made a threat, it was a threat with serious potential impact."

Suppliers gave Crazy Eddie's buyers extraordinary discounts and advertising rebates. If they didn't, the Antars had another method: they made up the discount. For example, Crazy Eddie's might owe George-Electronics $1 million; by claiming $500,000 in discounts or ad credits, the bill was cut in half. Sometimes there was a real discount, sometimes there wasn't. (It wasn't easy, after Eddie's fall, to tell what was a shrewd business deal and what was fraud. "They had legitimate discounts in there," says Hayes, "along with the criminal acts. That's why it was tough to know what was smoke and what was fire.")

Eddie had yet another arrangement with manufacturers. For certain high-demand items, high-end stereo systems, for example, a producing company would agree to sell only to Crazy Eddie's. Eddie placed an order big enough for what he needed, and then added a little more. The excess he sold to a distributor who had already agreed to send the merchandise outside Crazy Eddie's tri-state area. And then the really good part: By arrangement, the distributor paid for the merchandise in a series of small checks—$100,000 worth of portable stereos would be paid off with ten checks of $10,000 each. Eddie sprinkled this money into his stores as register sales. He knew that *Wall Street analysts used comparable store sales as a bedrock indicator*. New stores are compared with old stores, and any store open more than a year is compared with its performance during the previous term. The goal is to outperform the previous year. So the $10,000 injections made Eddie's "comps" look fantastic.

As the doctored numbers circulated in enthusiastic financial circles, CRZY stock doubled its earnings per share during its first year on the stock exchange. The stock split two-for-one in both of its first two fiscal terms as a publicly traded company. As chairman and chief executive, Eddie Antar used his newsletter to trumpet soaring profits, declining overhead costs, and a new 210,000-square-foot corporate headquarters. Plans were underway for a home-shopping arm of the business. Besides the electronics stores, there was now a subsidiary, Crazy Eddie Record and Tape Asylums, in the Antar fold. At its peak, the operation included 43 stores and reported sales of $350 million a year. This was a long way from the Sight and Sound storefront operation where it all began.

It was almost eerie how deliberately the Antar conspirators manipulated investors, and how directly their crimes impacted brokers' assessments. At the end of Crazy Eddie's second public year, a major brokerage firm issued a gushing recommendation to "buy." The recommendation was explicitly "based on 35 percent EPS [earnings per share] growth" and "comparable store sales growth in the low double-digit range." These double-digit expansions were from the "comps" that Eddie and his gang had cooked up

with wholesalers' money and by juggling inventories. CRZY stock, the report predicted, would double and then some during the next year. As if following an Antar script, the brokers declared, "Crazy Eddie is the only retailer in our universe that has not reported a disappointing quarter in the last two years. We do not believe that is an accident . . . . We believe Crazy Eddie is becoming the kind of company that can continually produce above-average comparable store sales growth." But what the analysts failed to do was ask a very basic but very pertinent question: what magic did Crazy Eddie's possess that was not available to its competitors?

The brokers could not have known what Herculean efforts were needed to yield just that impression. The report praised Eddie's management skills. "Mr. Antar has created a strong organization beneath him that is close-knit and directed . . . . Despite the boisterous (less charitable commentators would say obnoxious) quality of the commercials, Crazy Eddie management is quite conservative."

Well, yes, in a manner of speaking. They were certainly holding tightly to the money as it flowed through the market. According to federal indictments, the conspiracy inflated the company's value during the first year by about $2 million. By selling off shares of the overvalued stock, the partners pocketed over $28.2 million. The next year they illegally boosted income by $5.5 million and retail sales by $2.2 million. This time the group cashed in their stock for a cool $42.2 million windfall. In the last year before the boom went bust, Eddie and his partners inflated income by $37.5 million and retail by $18 million. They didn't have that much stock left, though, so despite the big blowup they cashed in for only about $8.3 million.

Maybe he knew the end was at hand, but with takeovers looming, Eddie kept fighting. He had started his business with one store in Brooklyn almost twenty years before, near the neighborhood where he grew up, populated mainly by Jewish immigrants from Syria. Despite these humble beginnings he would one day be called "the Darth Vader of capitalism" by a prosecuting attorney, referring not just to his professional inveigling but to his personal life as well. Eddie's affair with another woman broke up his marriage and precipitated a lifelong break with his father. Eventually he divorced his wife and married his lover. Rumors hinted that Eddie had been unhappy because he had five daughters and no sons from his first marriage. Neighbors said the rest of the family sided with the ex-wife. Eddie and his brothers continued in business together, but they had no contact outside the company. Allen Antar, a few years younger, should have been able to sympathize—he had also been estranged from the family when he filed for a divorce and married a woman who wasn't Jewish. (Allen eventually divorced that woman and remarried his first wife.) Later at trial, the brothers Antar were notably cold to one another. Even Eddie's own lawyer called him a "huckster."

But this Darth Vader had a compassionate side. Eddie was known as a quiet man, and modest. He was seldom photographed and almost never granted interviews. He was said to have waited hours at the bedside of a dying cousin, Mort Gindi, whose brother, also named Eddie, was named as a defendant in the Antars' federal trial. His cousin Sam remembers him as "a leader, someone I looked up to since I was a kid. Eddie was strong; he worked out with weights. When the Italian kids wanted to come into our neighborhood

and beat up on the Jewish kids, Eddie would stop them. That was when we were kids. Later, it turned out different."

Eddie had come a long way. He had realized millions of dollars by selling off company stock at inflated prices. This money was stashed in secret accounts around the world, held under various assumed identities. In fact, Eddie had done so well that he was left vulnerable as leader of the retail empire. When Elias Zinn, a Houston businessman, joined with the Oppenheimer-Palmieri Fund and waged a proxy battle for Crazy Eddie's, the Antars had too little shareholders power to stave off the bid. They lost. For the first time, Crazy Eddie's was out of Eddie's hands.

The new owners didn't have long to celebrate. They discovered that their ship was sinking fast. Stores were alarmingly understocked, shareholders were suing, and suppliers were shutting down credit lines because they were being paid either late or not at all. An initial review showed the company's inventory had been overstated by $65 million—a number later raised to over $80 million. In a desperate maneuver, the new management set up a computerized inventory system and established lines of credit. They made peace with the vendors and cut 150 jobs to reduce overhead. But it was too late. Less than a year after the takeover, Crazy Eddie's was dead.

Eddie Antar, on the other hand, was very much alive. But nobody knew where. He had disappeared when it became apparent that the takeover was forcing him out. He had set up dummy companies in Liberia, Gibraltar, and Panama, along with well-supplied bank accounts in Israel and Switzerland. Sensing his days as Crazy Eddie were numbered, he fled the United States, traveling the world with faked passports and calling himself, at different times, Harry Page Shalom and David Cohen. Shalom was a real person, a longtime friend of Eddie's, another in a string of chagrined and erstwhile companions.

It was as David Cohen that Eddie ended his flight from justice and reality. After 28 months on the run, he stalked into a police station in Bern, Switzerland, but not to turn himself in. "David Cohen" was demanding help from the police. He was mad because bank officials refused to let him at the $32 million he had on account there. The bank wouldn't tell Cohen anything, just that he couldn't access those funds. But officials discreetly informed police that the money had been frozen by the U.S. Department of Justice. Affidavits in the investigation had targeted the account as an Antar line. It didn't take long to realize that David Cohen, the irate millionaire in the Bern police station, was Eddie Antar. It was the last public part Crazy Eddie would play for a while. He eventually pled guilty to racketeering and conspiracy charges and was sentenced to 82 months in prison with credit for time served. This left him with about three and a half years of jail time. He was also ordered to repay $121 million to bilked investors. Almost $72 million was recovered from Eddie's personal accounts. "I don't ask for mercy," Eddie told the judge at his trial. "I ask for balance."

Eddie's brother, Mitchell, was first convicted and given four and a half years, with $3 million in restitution burdens, but his conviction was overturned because of a prejudicial remark by the judge in the first trial. Mitchell later pled guilty to two counts of securities fraud, and the rest of the charges were dropped. Allen Antar was acquitted at the first trial, but he and his father, Sam, were both later found guilty of insider trading and ordered to pay $11.9 million and $57.5 million, respectively, in disgorgement and interest.

What happened to the Crazy Eddie's stores? In 1998 Eddie's nephews attempted to revive the legacy and held a grand opening for a new electronics store in New Jersey. At the beginning of the new millennium, the store's doors closed and Crazy Eddie's shifted focus to become a dot-com retailer. But by 2004 the company had once again faltered and closed, this time amid allegations of reselling unauthorized products online.

FROM THE FRAUDSTER'S PERSPECTIVE

Adapted from the whitecollarfraud.com blog by Sam E. Antar, **Sunday, December 10, 2006**

Hiding Your Dirty Laundry in the Footnotes: Anatomy of the Crazy Eddie's Accounts Payable Fraud

Financial statements are often accompanied by footnotes that are seldom read and often not thoroughly analyzed by investors. One of the many frauds committed by me at Crazy Eddie's involved manipulating just two words in our footnotes.

Prior to 1987, Crazy Eddie's accounting policy for purchase discounts and allowances was: Purchase discounts and trade allowances are recognized *when received*. This accounting policy meant that even if Crazy Eddie's had "earned" a discount it could not be recognized as income until a credit was received from the vendor.

In fiscal year 1987, I changed Crazy Eddie's accounting policy (as reflected in the footnotes) to: Purchase discounts and trade allowances are recognized *when earned*. Now, in theory, Crazy Eddie could recognize a discount as income when it is earned (for example, when we reached the manufacturer's benchmark of buying 10,000 units to qualify for a volume rebate) and not have to wait for a credit from the vendor. I could simply write a debit memo (an offset to what I owed the vendor) to recognize the discount and increase our reported profits.

A change of accounting policy would normally give rise to a separate disclosure about its effect on earnings. However, in the Crazy Eddie's fraud we made no such disclosure and the auditors made no relevant computations despite the change in accounting principle. The auditors simply ignored the effects of the change in accounting for discounts.

By now being able to recognize discounts "when earned" instead of having to wait for credits to be received from vendors, I had the opportunity to add $20 million on phony debit memos (phony discounts and trade allowances) charged to vendors.

Crazy Eddie's accounts payable was reduced from about $70 million to $50 million through the use of phony debit memos, and this was facilitated by our change in accounting policies for purchase discounts and trade allowances from changing just two words in our footnotes.

How Did We Do It and How Could the Auditors Allow This to Happen?

The staff auditor primarily responsible for the accounts payable part of the audit had no retail accounts payable audit experience and only six months experience in auditing. He did not know what a debit memo was until he came to the Crazy Eddie's audit.

We engaged in a scheme of *obstruction by distraction*. Most staff accountants feel that audits are boring, and they really are. As soon as the young, relatively inexperienced staff members walked into our premises, my staff was instructed to be overly friendly so that they could be distracted from their work. We would constantly take the staff auditors out for long coffee breaks and lunches and engage in friendly conversations about mutual topics of interest unrelated to the audit in an effort to distract them from their work.

About two weeks before the audit was due to be completed and the accountants should have completed about 85 percent of their work, they would have only about 25 percent of their work done. During the remaining two weeks they would scramble to finish the audit on time.

When people "cram" or rush, they make mistakes and tend to skimp on their work. In addition, the auditors could not blame the overly friendly Crazy Eddie's staff for obstructing them. Therefore, in a mad scramble to "cover their asses" they covered ours. In the process they left out some very important audit procedures.

In fiscal year 1987, the staff auditor assigned to analyze accounts payable did not begin his work until the very day his firm had signed off on Crazy Eddie's "clean" audit opinion. The actual audit of the accounts payable was concluded weeks *after* the auditors signed off on our financial statements and gave our Board of Directors their approval for its release.

Lessons to Be Learned from the Crazy Eddie's Accounts Payable Fraud

1. Even sophisticated investors do not read footnotes. Had the auditors read the footnotes carefully, perhaps the proper critical questions would have been asked. All too often audits are used as training grounds for relatively inexperienced staff accountants who are not adequately supervised.

2. The audit was poorly planned, executed, and supervised. The auditors abandoned their requisite professional skepticism and objectivity by permitting Crazy Eddie's staff to distract them from their work by "bonding" with them. They did not follow basic audit procedures and permitted deadlines to guide the quality of their work.

3. Crazy Eddie's had weak internal controls over the issuance of debit memos. There was no documentation from external sources supporting any of the phony discounts. Sarbanes–Oxley would have required the auditors to evaluate our internal controls.

4. Finally, as Joseph T. Wells (retired founder and chairman of the Association of Certified Fraud Examiners) wrote in his award-winning article "So That's Why They Call it a Pyramid Scheme," published in the *Journal of Accountancy* in October 2000, "Were the auditors stupid? No, just too trusting. After all, no one wants to think the client is a crook. But it happens too often. That's why the profession requires the auditor to be skeptical."

Written by
Sam E. Antar *(former Crazy Eddie's CFO and convicted felon)*

In recent years, financial statement fraud has become a hot subject in the press, as scandals and criminal actions have challenged the corporate responsibility and integrity of major companies such as Lucent, Xerox, Rite Aid, U.S. Foodservice, Waste Management, MicroStrategy, Raytheon, Sunbeam, Enron, World-Com, Global Crossing, Adelphia, Qwest, and Tyco, all of whom have been alleged by the SEC to have committed fraud. Top management teams, including CEOs and CFOs of these companies and many more, are being accused of cooking the books. Occurrences of financial statement fraud by high-profile companies, coupled with the demise of Big Five accounting firm Arthur Andersen, have raised concerns about the integrity, transparency, and reliability of the financial reporting process and have challenged the role of corporate governance and audit functions in deterring and detecting financial statement fraud.

FRAUDULENT FINANCIAL STATEMENT SCHEMES

Defining Financial Statement Fraud

The definition of financial statement fraud can be found in a number of authoritative reports (e.g., The Treadway Commission 1987; SAS 99 2002). Financial statement fraud is defined as the use of deliberate misstatements or omissions of amounts or disclosures of financial statements to deceive financial statement users, particularly investors and creditors. Financial statement fraud may involve the following schemes:

1. Falsification, alteration, or manipulation of material financial records, supporting documents, or business transactions

2. Material intentional omissions or misrepresentations of events, transactions, accounts, or other significant information from which financial statements are prepared

3. Deliberate misapplication of accounting principles, policies, and procedures used to measure, recognize, report, and disclose economic events and business transactions

4. Intentional omissions of disclosures or presentation of inadequate disclosures regarding accounting principles and policies and related financial amounts[1]

Statement on Auditing Standards (SAS) No. 99, titled "Consideration of Fraud in a Financial Statement Audit" and issued by the Auditing Standards Board (ASB) of the AICPA in November 2002, defines two types of misstatements relevant to an audit of financial statements and subject to auditors' consideration of fraud.[2] The first type arises from fraudulent financial reporting and is defined as "intentional misstatements or omissions of amounts or disclosures in financial statements designed to deceive financial statement users".[3] The second type arises from misappropriation of assets and is commonly classified as theft or defalcation. (For reasons that are unclear, the definitions did not list corruption as a separate type of fraud.)

The primary focus of this chapter is on misstatements arising from fraudulent reporting that directly causes financial reports to be misleading and deceptive to investors and creditors. Fraudulent financial statements can be used to unjustifiably sell stock, obtain loans or trades credit, and/or improve managerial compensation and bonuses. The important issues addressed in this chapter are how to effectively and efficiently deter, detect, and counteract financial statement fraud.

Costs of Financial Statement Fraud

Published statistics on the possible costs of financial statement fraud are estimates at best. It is impossible to determine the actual total costs because not all fraud is detected, not all detected fraud is reported, and not all reported fraud is legally pursued. The reported statistics, however, are astonishing.

Albrecht and Searcy[4] state that more than 50 percent of U.S. corporations in 2000 were victims of fraud, with a loss of more than $500,000 on average for each company. The collapse of Enron's house of cards is estimated to have caused a loss of about $70 billion in market capitalization to investors, employees, and pensioners. Cotton[5] reports that shareholders have lost $460 billion in the Enron, WorldCom, Qwest, Global Crossing, and Tyco debacles.

These studies and their related statistics provide only estimated direct economic losses resulting from financial statement fraud. Other fraud costs are legal costs; increased insurance costs; loss of productivity; adverse impacts on employees' morale, customers' goodwill, and suppliers' trust; and negative stock market reactions. An important indirect cost of financial statement fraud is the loss of productivity due to dismissal of the fraudsters and hiring of their replacements. Although these indirect costs cannot possibly be estimated, they should be taken into consideration in assessing the consequences of financial statement fraud. Loss of public confidence in the quality and reliability of financial statements caused by alleged fraudulent activities is the most damaging and costly effect of fraud.

Financial statement fraud is harmful in many ways:

1. *It undermines the reliability, quality, transparency, and integrity of the financial reporting process.* An increasing number of required financial restatements and enforcement acts by the SEC against big corporations (e.g., Enron, WorldCom, Xerox, ImClone, Global Crossing, Qwest, Halliburton, Bristol-Myers, Tyco, Dynegy, Adelphia Communications, ComputerAssociates) for alleged financial statement fraud has severely undermined the public confidence in the veracity of financial reports.

2. *It jeopardizes the integrity and objectivity of the auditing profession, especially auditors and auditing firms.* Arthur Andersen, one of the Big Five CPA firms, dismantled its international network and allowed officers to join rival firms after it became embroiled in a scandal involving its shredding of documents related to its audit work for Enron. Although the Supreme Court ultimately overruled Andersen's conviction for obstruction of justice, it was too late; the accounting firm had irreparably crumbled in the wake of the document destruction debacle.

3. *It diminishes the confidence of the capital markets, as well as market participants, in the reliability of financial information.* The capital market and market participants, including investors, creditors, employees, and pensioners, are affected by the quality and transparency of the financial information they use in making investment decisions.

4. *It makes the capital markets less efficient.* Auditors reduce the information risk that is associated with the published financial statements and thus make them more transparent. Information risk is the likelihood that financial statements are inaccurate, false, misleading, biased, and deceptive. By applying the same financial standards to diverse businesses and by reducing the information risk, accountants contribute to the efficiency of our capital markets.

5. *It adversely affects the nation's economic growth and prosperity.* Accountants are expected to make financial statements among corporations more comparable by applying the same set of accounting standards to diverse businesses. This enhanced comparability makes business more transparent, the capital markets more efficient, the free enterprise system more attainable, and the economy more vibrant and prosperous. The efficiency of capital markets depends on our receiving objective, reliable, and transparent financial information. Thus, the accounting profession, especially practicing auditors, plays an important role in our free enterprise system and capital markets. However, the Enron, WorldCom, and Global Crossing debacles provide evidence that the role of accountants can be compromised.

6. *It results in huge litigation costs.* Corporations and their auditors are being sued for alleged financial statement fraud and related audit failures by a diverse group of litigants, including small investors bringing class action suits and the U.S. Justice Department. Investors are also given the right to sue and recover damages from those who aided and abetted securities fraud.

7. *It destroys the careers of the individuals involved.* For example, top executives are being barred from serving on the board of directors of any public company and auditors are being barred from the practice of public accounting.

8. *It leads to bankruptcy or substantial economic losses by the company.* WorldCom, with $107 billion in assets and $41 billion in debt, finally filed for Chapter 11 bankruptcy protection on July 21, 2002. WorldCom's is the largest U.S. bankruptcy ever, almost twice the size of Enron's.

9. *It encourages regulatory intervention.* Regulatory agencies (e.g., the SEC) have considerable influence over the financial reporting process and related audit functions. The recent undermining of confidence in the financial reporting process and audit functions ultimately encouraged lawmakers to establish accounting reform legislation (Sarbanes–Oxley Act of 2002). This Act is intended to drastically change the self-regulating environment of the accounting profession to a regulatory framework under the SEC oversight function.

10. *It is devastating to the normal operations and performance of companies.* Alleged financial statement frauds at Enron, WorldCom, Global Crossing, and Adelphia have caused these high-profile companies to file for bankruptcy; their top executives have been fined and, in some cases, indicted and even imprisoned for violation of securities laws.

11. *It raises serious doubts about the efficacy of financial statement audits.* The financial community is demanding higher-quality audits, and auditors need to effectively address this issue to bring about the desired assurance.

12. *It erodes public confidence and trust in the accounting and auditing profession.* One message that comes through loud and clear these days in response to the increasing number of financial restatements and alleged financial statement fraud is that the public's confidence in the financial reporting process and related audit functions has substantially eroded.

Fictitious Revenues

Fictitious or fabricated revenue schemes involve the recording of sales of goods or services that did not occur. Fictitious sales most often involve fake or phantom customers, but can also involve legitimate customers. For example, a fictitious invoice can be prepared (but not mailed) for a legitimate customer although the goods are not delivered or the services not rendered. At the beginning of the next accounting period, the sale might be reversed to help conceal the fraud, but this may lead to a revenue shortfall in the new period, creating the need for more fictitious sales. Another method is to use legitimate customers and artificially inflate or alter invoices to reflect higher amounts or quantities than were actually sold. Fictitious revenues are among the favorite schemes to inflate earnings.

Generally speaking, revenue is recognized when it is (1) realized or realizable and (2) earned. In December 2003 the Securities and Exchange Commission issued Staff Accounting Bulletin No. 104, "Revenue Recognition" (SAB 104), to update existing guidance on revenue recognition criteria. SAB 104

states that revenue is typically considered realized or realizable and earned when all of the following criteria are met:

- Persuasive evidence of an arrangement exists
- Delivery has occurred or services have been rendered
- The seller's price to the buyer is fixed or determinable
- Collectibility is reasonably assured

SAB 104 concedes that revenue may be recognized in some circumstances where delivery has not occurred, but sets out strict criteria limiting the ability to record such transactions as revenue.

At present, there are approximately 200 sources of standards and guidance on revenue recognition in U.S. GAAP, not all of which are based on consistent concepts. The current conceptual guidelines for revenue recognition are found in FASB Concepts Statement No. 5, "Recognition and Measurement in Financial Statements of Business Enterprises," and FASB Concepts Statement No. 6, "Elements of Financial Statements." Concepts Statement No. 6 defines revenue as "inflows or other enhancements of assets of an entity or settlements of its liabilities (or a combination of both) from delivering or producing goods, rendering services, or other activities that constitute the entity's ongoing major or central operations." However, because of possible conflicts in guidance between the two applicable Concepts Statements, the FASB is currently working to develop coherent conceptual guidance on revenue recognition to eliminate inconsistencies and to provide the basis for a comprehensive accounting standard on revenue recognition.

As part of this initiative, the FASB and the International Accounting Standards Board (IASB) have partnered on a project with the goal of promoting convergence of international accounting standards on revenue recognition. The boards' current perspective on this subject concentrates on "changes in assets and liabilities." The concept of realization or completion of the earnings process is not an integral part of their focus. This is consistent with FASB Concepts Statement No. 6. Although the boards have arrived at several tentative decisions as part of the project, these decisions will not change current accounting policy until they have gone through extensive due process and deliberations.

One example details a typical use of fictitious revenue. A publicly traded company engineered sham transactions for more than seven years to inflate their financial standing. The company's management utilized several shell companies supposedly making a number of favorable sales. The sales transactions were fictitious, as were the supposed customers. As the amounts of the sales grew, so did the suspicions of internal auditors. The sham transactions included the payment of funds for assets with the same funds being returned to the parent company as receipts on sales. The management scheme went undetected for so long that the company's books were eventually inflated by more than $80 million. The perpetrators were finally discovered and prosecuted in both civil and criminal courts.

A sample entry from this type of case is shown below. A fictional entry records a purported purchase of fixed assets. This entry debits fixed assets for the amount of the alleged purchase and the credit is to cash for the payment:

Date	Description	Ref.	Debit	Credit
12/01/09	Fixed assets	104	350,000	
	Cash	101		350,000

A fictitious sales entry is then made for the same amount as the false purchase, debiting accounts receivable and crediting the sales account. The cash outflow that supposedly paid for the fixed assets is "returned" as payment on the receivable account, though in practice the cash might never have moved if the fraudsters didn't bother to falsify that extra documentary support.

Date	Description	Ref.	Debit	Credit
12/01/09	Accounts receivable	120	350,000	
	Sales	400		350,000
12/15/09	Cash	101	350,000	
	Accounts receivable	120		350,000

The result of the completely fabricated sequence of events is an increase in both company assets and yearly revenue. The debit could alternatively be directed to other accounts, such as inventory or accounts payable, or it could simply be left in accounts receivable if the fraud were committed close to year-end and the receivable could be left outstanding without attracting undue attention.

Sales with Conditions Sales with conditions are a form of fictitious revenue scheme in which a sale is booked even though some terms have not been completed and the rights and risks of ownership have not passed to the purchaser. These transactions do not qualify for recording as revenue, but they may nevertheless be recorded in an effort to fraudulently boost a company's revenue. These types of sales are similar to schemes involving the recognition of revenue in improper periods, since the conditions for sale may become satisfied in the future, at which point revenue recognition would become appropriate. Premature recognition schemes will be discussed later in this chapter in the context of timing differences.

Pressures to Boost Revenues External pressures to succeed that are placed on business owners and managers by bankers, stockholders, families, and even communities often provide the motivation to commit fraud. In one example, a real estate investment company arranged for the sale of shares that it held in a nonrelated company. The sale occurred on the last day of the year and accounted for 45 percent of the company's income for that year.

A 30 percent down payment was recorded as received, with a corresponding receivable recorded for the balance. With the intent to show a financially healthier company, the details of the sale were made public in an announcement to the press, but the sale of the stock was completely fabricated. To cover the fraud, off-book loans were made in the amount of the down payment. Other supporting documents were also falsified. The $40 million misstatement was ultimately uncovered and the real estate company owner faced criminal prosecution.

In a similar instance, a publicly traded textile company engaged in a series of false transactions designed to improve its financial image. Receipts from the sale of stock were returned to the company in the form of revenues. The fraudulent management team even went so far as to record a bank loan on the company books as revenue. At the time that the scheme was uncovered, the company books were overstated by some $50,000, a material amount to this particular company.

Pressures to commit financial statement fraud may also come from within a company. Departmental budget requirements including income and profit goals can create situations in which financial statement fraud is considered as an option. In one case, the accounting manager of a small company misstated financial records to cover its financial shortcomings. The financial statements included a series of entries made by the accounting manager designed to meet budget projections and to cover up losses in the company's pension fund. Influenced by dismal financial performance in recent months, the accountant also consistently overstated period revenues. To cover his scheme, he debited liability accounts and credited the equity account. The perpetrator finally resigned, leaving a letter of confession. He was later prosecuted in criminal court.

Red Flags Associated with Fictitious Revenues Any of the following circumstances should sound the alarm for the potential of fraud.

- Rapid growth or unusual profitability, especially compared with other companies in the same industry
- Recurring negative cash flows from operations or an inability to generate cash flows from operations despite reported earnings and earnings growth
- Significant transactions with related parties or special-purpose entities not in the ordinary course of business or where those entities are not audited or are audited by another firm
- Significant, unusual, or highly complex transactions, especially those close to period end, that pose difficult "substance over form" questions
- Unusual growth in the number of days' sales in receivables
- A significant volume of sales to entities whose substance and ownership are not known

- An unusual surge in sales by a minority of units within a company, or in sales recorded by corporate headquarters

Timing Differences

As we mentioned earlier, financial statement fraud may also involve timing differences, that is, the recording of revenue and/or expenses in improper periods. This can be done to shift revenues or expenses between one period and the next, increasing or decreasing earnings as desired.

Matching Revenues with Expenses Remember, according to generally accepted accounting principles, revenues and corresponding expenses should be recorded or matched in the same accounting period; failing to do so violates GAAP's matching principle. For example, suppose a company accurately records sales that occurred in the month of December but fails to fully record expenses incurred as costs associated with those sales until January—in the next accounting period. The effect of this error would be to overstate the net income of the company in the period in which the sales were recorded, and also to understate net income in the subsequent period when the expenses are reported.

The following example depicts a sale transaction in which the cost of sales associated with the revenue is not recorded in the same period. A journal entry is made to record the billing of a project, which is not complete. Although a contract has been signed for this project, goods and services for the project have not been delivered and the project is not even scheduled to start until January. In an effort to boost revenues for the current year, the following sales transaction is recorded fraudulently before year-end:

Date	Description	Ref.	Debit	Credit
12/31/Y1	Accounts receivable	120	17,000	
	Sales—Project C	401		17,000
To record sale of product and services for Project C				
Fiscal Year-End—2009				

In January, the project is started and completed. The entries below show accurate recording of the $15,500 of costs associated with the sale:

Date	Description	Ref.	Debit	Credit
01/31/Y2	Cost of sales—Project C	702	13,500	
	Inventory	140		13,500
To record relief of inventory for Project C				
01/31/Y2	Labor costs—Project C	550	2,000	
	Cash	101		2,000
To record payroll expense for Project C				

If recorded correctly, the entries for the recognition of revenue and the costs associated with the sales would be recorded in the accounting period in which they actually occur: January. The effect on the income statement for the company is shown in the following table.

This example depicts exactly how nonadherence to GAAP's matching principle can cause material misstatement in yearly income statements. When the income and expenses were stated in error, year 1 yielded a net income of $17,000 while year 2 produced a loss ($13,400). Correctly stated, revenues and expenses are matched and recorded together within the same accounting period, showing moderate, yet accurate, net incomes of $0 and $3,600.

Income Statements	Incorrectly Stated		Correctly Stated	
	Year 1	Year 2	Year 1	Year 2
Sales Revenue				
Project B	25,000		25,000	
Project C	17,000			17,000
Project D		26,500		26,500
Total Sales	42,000	26,500	25,000	43,500
Cost of Sales				
Project B	22,500		22,500	
Project C		15,500		15,500
Project D		21,400		21,400
Total Cost of Sales	22,500	36,900	22,500	36,900
Gross Margin	19,500	(10,400)	2,500	6,600
G&A Expenses	2,500	3,000	2,500	3,000
Net Income	17,000	(13,400)	0	3,600

Premature Revenue Recognition   Generally, revenue should be recognized in the accounting records when a sale is complete, that is, when title is passed from the seller to the buyer. This transfer of ownership completes the sale and is usually not final until all obligations surrounding the sale are complete and the four criteria set out in SEC Staff Accounting Bulletin No. 104 have been satisfied. Again, those four criteria are

1. Persuasive evidence of an arrangement exists
2. Delivery has occurred or services have been rendered
3. The seller's price to the buyer is fixed or determinable
4. Collectibility is reasonably assured

The following case details how early recognition of revenue not only leads to financial statement misrepresentation but also can serve as a catalyst to further fraud. A retail drugstore chain's management got ahead of itself in recording income. In a scheme that was used repeatedly, management would enhance its earnings by recording unearned revenue prematurely, resulting in the impression that the drugstores were much more profitable than they actually were. When the situation came to light and was investigated, several embezzlement schemes, false expense reports, and instances of credit card fraud were also uncovered.

In another case, the president of a not-for-profit organization was able to illicitly squeeze out the maximum amount of private donations by cooking the company books. To enable the organization to receive additional funding, which was dependent on the amounts of already-received contributions, the organization's president recorded promised donations before they were actually received. By the time the organization's internal auditor discovered the scheme, the fraud had been perpetrated for more than four years.

When managers recognize revenues prematurely, one or more of the criteria set forth in SEC Staff Bulletin No. 104 are typically not met. Examples of common problems associated with premature revenue recognition are set out below.

Persuasive Evidence of an Arrangement Does Not Exist

- No written or verbal agreement exists
- A verbal agreement exists but a written agreement is customary
- A written order exists but is conditional upon sale to end users (such as a consignment sale)
- A written order exists but contains a right of return
- A written order exists, but a side letter alters the terms in ways that eliminate the required elements for an agreement
- The transaction is with a related party, which fact has not been disclosed

Delivery Has Not Occurred or Services Have Not Been Rendered

- Shipment has not been made and the criteria for recognizing revenue on "bill-and-hold" transactions set out in SEC Staff Accounting Bulletin No. 104 have not been met
- Shipment has been made not to the customer but to the seller's agent, to an installer, or to a public warehouse
- Some but not all of the components required for operation were shipped
- Items of the wrong specification were shipped
- Delivery is not complete until installation and customer testing and acceptance has occurred
- Services have not been provided at all
- Services are being performed over an extended period, and only a portion of the service revenues should have been recognized in the current period
- The mix of goods and services in a contract has been misstated in order to improperly accelerate revenue recognition

The Seller's Price to the Buyer Is Not Fixed or Determinable

- The price is contingent on some future event(s)
- A service or membership fee is subject to unpredictable cancellation during the contract period
- The transaction includes an option to exchange the product for others
- Payment terms are extended for a substantial period and additional discounts or upgrades may be required to induce continued use and payment as opposed to switching to alternative products

Collectibility Is Not Reasonably Assured

- Collection is contingent on some future event(s) (e.g., resale of the product, receipt of additional funding, or litigation)
- The customer does not have the ability to pay (e.g., it is financially troubled, it has purchased far more than it can afford, or it is a shell company with minimal assets)

Long-Term Contracts   Long-term contracts pose special problems for revenue recognition. Long-term construction contracts, for example, use either the completed-contract method or the percentage-of-completion method, depending partly on the circumstances. In the completed-contract method revenue is not recorded until the project is 100 percent complete. Construction costs are held in an inventory account until completion of the project. The percentage-of-completion method recognizes revenues and expenses as measurable progress on a project is made, but this method is particularly vulnerable to manipulation. Managers can often easily manipulate the percentage of completion and the estimated costs to complete a construction project in order to recognize revenues prematurely and conceal contract cost overruns.

Channel Stuffing   Another difficult area of revenue recognition is channel stuffing, which is also known as trade loading. This refers to the sale of an unusually large quantity of a product to distributors, who are encouraged to overbuy through the use of deep discounts and/or extended payment terms. This practice is especially attractive in industries with high gross margins (such as cigarettes, pharmaceuticals, perfume, soda concentrate, and branded consumer goods) because it can increase short-term earnings. The downside is that stealing from the next period's sales makes it harder to meet sales goals in the next period, and this sometimes leads to increasingly disruptive levels of channel stuffing and ultimately a restatement.

Although orders are received in a channel stuffing scheme, the terms of the order might raise some question about the collectibility of accounts receivable, and there may be side agreements that grant a right of return, effectively making the sales consignment sales. There may be a greater risk of returns for certain products if they cannot be sold before their shelf life expires. This is particularly a problem for pharmaceuticals because retailers will not accept drugs with a short shelf life remaining. As a result, channel stuffing should be viewed skeptically, as in certain circumstances it may constitute fraud.

Recording Expenses in the Wrong Period   The timely recording of expenses is often compromised due to pressures to meet budget projections and goals, or due to lack of proper accounting controls. As the expensing of certain costs is pushed into periods other than the ones in which they actually occur, they

are not properly matched against the income that they help produce. Consider a case in which supplies were purchased and applied to the current-year budget but were actually used in the following accounting period. A manager at a publicly traded company completed eleven months of operations remarkably under budget in comparison with total-year estimates. He therefore decided to get a head start on the next year's expenditures. In order to spend all current-year budgeted funds allocated to his department, the manager bought $50,000 in unneeded supplies. The supplies expense transactions were recorded against the current year's budget. Staff auditors noticed the huge leap in expenditures, however, and inquired about the situation. The manager came clean, explaining that he was under pressure to meet budget goals for the following year. Because the manager was not attempting to keep the funds for himself, no legal action was taken.

The correct recording of these transactions would be to debit supplies inventory for the original purchase and subsequently expense the items out of the account as they are used. The sample journal entries below reflect the correct method of expensing the supplies over time.

Date	Description	Ref.	Debit	Credit
01/31/09	Supplies inventory	109	50,000	
	Accounts payable	201		50,000
To record the purchase of supplies				
Record in	Supplies expense	851	2,000	
Period used	Supplies inventory	109		2,000
To record supplies consumed in current period				

Similar entries should be made monthly, as the supplies are used, until they are consumed and $50,000 in supplies expense is recorded.

Red Flags Associated with Timing Differences

Auditors and company monitors should be alert for any of the following signs of fraud relating to timing differences:

- Rapid growth or unusual profitability, especially compared with other companies in the same industry
- Recurring negative cash flows from operations or an inability to generate cash flows from operations while reporting earnings and earnings growth
- Significant, unusual, or highly complex transactions, especially those close to period end that pose difficult "substance over form" questions
- Unusual increase in gross margin or margin in excess of industry peers
- Unusual growth in the number of days' sales in receivables
- Unusual decline in the number of days' purchases in accounts payable

CASE STUDY: THE IMPORTANCE OF TIMING

What about a scheme in which nobody gets any money? One that was never intended to enrich its players or to defraud the company they worked for? It happened in Huntsville, Alabama, on-site at a major aluminum products plant with over $300 million in yearly sales. A few shrewd men cooked the company's books without taking a single dime for themselves. Several names may have been changed to preserve anonymity.

Terry Isbell was an internal auditor making a routine review of accounts payable. He was running a computer search to look at any transactions over $50,000 and found among the hits a bill for replacing two furnace liners. The payments went out toward the end of the year, to an approved vendor, with the proper signatures from Steven Leonyrd, a maintenance engineer, and Doggett Stine, the sector's purchasing manager. However, there was nothing else in the file. Maintenance and repair jobs of this sort were supposed to be done on a time-and-material basis. So there should have been work reports, vouchers, and inspection sheets in the file along with the paid invoices. But there was nothing.

Isbell talked with Steven Leonyrd, who showed him the furnaces, recently lined and working to perfection. So where was the paperwork? "It'll be in the regular work file for the first quarter," Leonyrd replied.

"The bill was for last year, November and December," Isbell pointed out. That was because the work was paid for in "advance payments," according to Leonyrd. There wasn't room in the work schedule to have the machines serviced in

November, so the work was billed to that year's nonrecurring maintenance budget. Later, sometime after the beginning of the year, the work was actually done.

Division management okayed Isbell to make an examination. He found $150,000 in repair invoices without proper documentation. The records for materials and supplies, which were paid for in one year and received in the next, totaled $250,000. A check of later records and an inspection showed that everything paid for had in fact been received, just later than promised.

So it was time to revisit Leonyrd, who said the whole thing was simple. "We had this money in the budget for maintenance and repair, supplies outside the usual scope of things. It was getting late in the year, looked like we were just going to lose those dollars, you know, they'd just revert back to the general fund. So we set up the work orders and made them on last year's budget. Then we got the actual stuff later." Who told Leonyrd to set it up that way? "Nobody. Just made sense, that's all."

Nobody, Isbell suspected, was the purchasing manager who handled Leonyrd's group, Doggett Stine. Stine was known as "a domineering-type guy" among the people who worked for him, a kind of storeroom bully. Isbell asked him about the arrangement with Leonyrd. "That's no big deal," Stine insisted. "Just spent the money while it was there. That's what it was put there for, to keep up the plant. That's what we did." It wasn't his idea, said Stine, but it wasn't really Leonyrd's either, just a discussion and an informal decision. The storeroom receiving supervisor agreed it was a grand idea, and made out the documents as he was told. Accounting personnel processed the invoices as they were told. A part-time bookkeeper said to Isbell she remembered some discussion about arranging to spend the money, but she didn't ask any questions.

Isbell was in a funny position, a little bit like Shakespeare's Malvolio, who spends his time in the play *Twelfth Night* scolding the other characters for having such a good time. Leonyrd hadn't pocketed anything, and neither had Stine; and being a bully was hardly a fraudulent offense. There was about $6,000 in interest lost, supposing the money had stayed in company bank accounts, but that wasn't exactly the point. More seriously, this effortless cash flow diversion represented a kink in the handling and dispersal of funds. Isbell's concern wasn't with rules for their own sake or standing on ceremony—money this easy to come by just meant the company had gotten a break. However, the next guys might not be so civic-minded and selfless; they might start juggling zeros and signatures instead of dates.

Under Isbell's recommendation, the receiving department started reporting directly to the plant's general accounting division, and its supervisor was assigned elsewhere. Doggett Stine, meanwhile, had retired. Steven Leonyrd was demoted and transferred to another sector; he was fired a year later in connection with an unrelated scheme. He had approached a contractor to replace the roof on his house, with the bill to be charged against "nonrecurring maintenance" at the plant. But the contractor alerted plant officials to their conniving employee, who was also known to be picking up extra money for "consulting work" with plant-related businesses. "Rats," Leonyrd must have thought, "foiled again."

Concealed Liabilities and Expenses

As previously discussed, understating liabilities and expenses is one of the ways financial statements can be manipulated to make a company appear more profitable. Because pretax income will increase by the full amount of the expense or liability not recorded, this financial statement fraud method can have a significant impact on reported earnings with relatively little effort by the fraudster. This method requires much less effort than falsifying many sales transactions. Missing transactions are generally harder for auditors to detect than improperly recorded ones because there is no audit trail.

There are three common methods for concealing liabilities and expenses:

1. Liability/expense omissions
2. Capitalized expenses
3. Failure to disclose warranty costs and liabilities

Liability/Expense Omissions The preferred and easiest method of concealing liabilities/expenses is simply to fail to record them. Multimillion-dollar judgments against the company from a recent court decision might be conveniently ignored. Rather than being posted into the accounts payable system, vendor invoices might be thrown away (they'll send another later) or stuffed into drawers, increasing reported earnings by the full amount of the invoices. In a retail environment, debit memos might be created for charge-backs to vendors, supposedly to claim permitted rebates or allowances, but sometimes just to create additional income. These items may or may not be properly recorded in a subsequent accounting period, but that does not change the fraudulent nature of the current financial statements.

One of the highest-profile liability omission cases of recent vintage involved Adelphia Communications. John Rigas, Adelphia's founder, purchased a small cable company in Coudersport, Pennsylvania, for the sum of $300 in 1952. By 2002 it had grown to become the nation's sixth-largest cable television company, with more than five million subscribers and $10 billion in assets.

Rigas, of Greek heritage, named his company Adelphia Communications Corporation, after the Greek word for "brothers." He and his brother Gus ran the company as their own. It was a style that came back to haunt him after the company went public. Later his three sons, Tim, Michael, and James—along with son-in-law Peter Venetis—became active in Adelphia's management. The family controlled the majority of the company's voting stock and constituted the majority on the board of directors. Accordingly, the family used Adelphia's money as their own. They also used company assets as their own. Three corporate jets took family members on exotic vacations, including African safaris. John Rigas was particularly egregious in his spending. At one time, he racked up personal debt of $66 million, forcing his son Timothy, who held the position of Adelphia CFO, to put his father on a "budget" of $1 million a month in personal draws.

As CFO, Timothy Rigas engineered the financial manipulations. He was in charge of manipulating the books to inflate the stock price to meet analysts' expectations. Investigators later discovered that the family members had looted the company to the tune of some $3 billion. The money transfers were made by journal entries that gave Adelphia debt that was not disclosed. Among other things, the Rigas family used the funds to

- Acquire other cable companies not owned by Adelphia
- Pay debt service on investments
- Purchase a controlling interest in the Buffalo Sabres hockey team
- Pay $700,000 in country club memberships
- Buy luxury vacation homes in Cancun, Beaver Creek (Colorado), and Hilton Head Island, and two apartments in Manhattan
- Purchase a $13 million golf course

The Rigas family's problems started with overexpansion in the late 1990s when they purchased Century Communications for the sum of $5.2 billion. By 2002 Adelphia's stock had fallen to historic lows and the company was unable to make payments on the debt it incurred from its acquisitions.

In July 2002 the SEC charged Adelphia with, among other crimes, fraudulently excluding over $2.3 billion in bank debt from its consolidated financial statements. According to the complaint filed by the SEC, Adelphia's founder and his three sons fraudulently excluded the liabilities from the company's annual and quarterly consolidated financial statements by deliberately shifting those liabilities onto the books of Adelphia's off-balance sheet unconsolidated affiliates. Failure to record this debt violated GAAP requirements and precipitated a series of misrepresentations about those liabilities by Adelphia and the defendants. These included (1) sham transactions backed by fictitious documents to give the false appearance that Adelphia had actually repaid debts when, in truth, it had simply shifted them to unconsolidated entities controlled by the founder; and (2) misleading financial statements that, in their footnotes, gave the false impression that liabilities listed in the company's financials included all outstanding bank debt. This led to a freefall of Adelphia's stock, and less than three months later the company filed for bankruptcy.

Perpetrators of liability and expense omissions commonly believe they can conceal their fraud in future periods. They often plan to compensate for their omitted liabilities with visions of other income sources such as profits from future price increases.

Because they are so easy to conceal, omitted liabilities are probably one of the most difficult types of financial statement frauds to uncover. A thorough review of all post-statement date transactions, such as accounts payable increases and decreases, can aid in the discovery of omitted liabilities in financial statements, as can a computerized analysis of expense records. Additionally, if the auditor requests and is granted unrestricted access to the client's files, a physical search could turn up concealed invoices and unposted liabilities. Probing interviews of accounts payable staff and other personnel can reveal unrecorded or delayed items too.

Capitalized Expenses Capital expenditures are costs that provide a benefit to a company over more than one accounting period. Manufacturing equipment is an example of this type of expenditure. Revenue expenditures or *expenses*, on the other hand, directly correspond to the generation of current revenue and provide benefits for only the current accounting period. An example of expenses is labor costs for one week of service. These costs correspond directly to revenues billed in the current accounting period.

Capitalizing revenue-based expenses is another way to increase income and assets since they are amortized over a period of years rather than taken immediately. If expenditures are capitalized as assets and not recognized during the current period, income will be overstated. As the assets are depreciated, income in subsequent periods will be understated.

Improper capitalization of expenses was one of the key methods of financial statement fraud allegedly used by WorldCom, Inc. in its high-profile fraud episode that came to light in early 2002. The saga of WorldCom, at one time the second-largest long-distance carrier in America (behind AT&T), began in 1983, when Bernie Ebbers drew a business plan on the back of a napkin at a coffee shop in Hattiesburg, Mississippi. Ebbers and his partners, attempting to benefit from the breakup of AT&T, decided to purchase long-distance time and sell it to local companies on a smaller scale. They named the fledgling business Long Distance Discount Service (LDDS).

Up until that time, Ebbers didn't know much about the telecommunications industry. He graduated from a small Mississippi college with a degree in physical education. He'd previously owned a small garment factory and several motels. LDDS turned out to be a success. The company was buying and selling a commodity—long-distance service—but it didn't have to invest in the costs of buying and installing expensive telephone lines. Along the way, LDDS acquired a half-dozen other communications companies.

In 1995 the business was renamed WorldCom, and the new company went on an acquisition rampage, purchasing over sixty companies. WorldCom's crown jewel was a $37 billion merger in 1997 with MCI, a much larger company. The following year, it bought Brooks Fiber Properties and CompuServe. In 1999 it attempted to acquire rival Sprint in a $115 billion merger, but the Federal Communications Commission blocked the deal because it would have breached antitrust laws.

Because of increasing competition in the telecommunications industry, WorldCom's once-spectacular growth started slowing dramatically in 1998 and came to a halt in 1999, resulting in a precipitous drop in its stock price. To reverse declining margins, the company began depleting the reserves it had established to cover the undisclosed liabilities of companies it had acquired. Between 1998 and 2000, this amounted to $2.8 billion.

However, in the opinion of management, the reduction in reserves was insufficient. Scott Sullivan, the CFO, directed certain WorldCom staffers to reclassify as assets $3.35 billion in fees paid to lease phone networks from other companies and $500 million in computer expenses, both operating costs. Rather than suffering a $2.5 billion loss in 2001, the company reported a $1.4 billion profit. Andersen LLP, WorldCom's external auditors, uncovered none of these machinations.

In 2002 Sullivan directed a WorldCom employee to classify another $400 million in expenses as assets. The employee complained to Cynthia Cooper, CFE, WorldCom's internal auditor, who directed her staff to conduct an investigation. Cooper's team first discovered that the $500 million in computer expenses reclassified as assets had no documentation to support the expenditures. Then they uncovered another $2 billion in questionable entries.

Internal auditors met with the audit committee in June 2002 to explain their findings. On June 25, WorldCom made a public announcement that it had inflated revenues by $3.8 billion over the previous five quarters. Within three weeks, the company had filed for bankruptcy. Subsequent investigations would show that WorldCom had overstated its profits and income by about $11 billion.

These improper accounting practices were designed to, and did, inflate income to conform with estimates by Wall Street analysts and to support the price of WorldCom's stock. As a result, several former WorldCom executives, including former CEO Bernie Ebbers, former CFO Scott Sullivan, former controller David F. Meyers, and former director of General Accounting Buford "Buddy" Yates, Jr., were charged with multiple criminal offenses and received prison sentences ranging from one to twenty-five years for their participation in the scheme.

Expensing Capital Expenditures Just as capitalizing expenses is improper, so is expensing costs that should be capitalized. An organization may want to minimize its net income due to tax considerations, or to increase earnings in future periods. Expensing an item that should be depreciated over a period of time would help accomplish just that—net income is lowered and so are taxes.

Returns and Allowances and Warranties Improper recording of sales returns and allowances occurs when a company fails to properly record or present the expense associated with sales returns and customer allowances stemming from customer dissatisfaction. It is inevitable that a certain percentage of products sold will, for one reason or another, be returned. When this happens, management should record the related expense as a contra-sales account, which reduces the amount of net sales presented on the company's income statement.

Likewise, when a company offers a warranty on product sales, it should estimate the amount of warranty expense it reasonably expects to incur over the warranty period and accrue a liability for that amount. In warranty liability fraud, the warranty liability is usually either omitted or substantially understated. Another similar area is the liability resulting from defective products (product liability).

Red Flags Associated with Concealed Liabilities and Expenses Any of the following conditions should raise a red flag with regard to the possibility of financial statement fraud:

- Recurring negative cash flows from operations or an inability to generate cash flows from operations while reporting earnings and earnings growth
- Assets, liabilities, revenues, or expenses based on significant estimates that involve subjective judgments or uncertainties that are difficult to corroborate
- Nonfinancial management's excessive participation in or preoccupation with the selection of accounting principles or the determination of significant estimates
- Unusual increase in gross margin or margin in excess of industry peers
- Allowances for sales returns, warranty claims, and so on that are shrinking in percentage terms or are otherwise out of line with industry peers' results
- Unusual reduction in the number of days' purchases in accounts payable
- Reducing accounts payable while competitors are stretching out payments to vendors

Improper Disclosures

As discussed earlier, accounting principles require that financial statements and notes include all the information necessary to prevent a reasonably discerning user of the statements from being misled. The notes should include narrative disclosures, supporting schedules, and any other information required to avoid misleading potential investors, creditors, or any other users of the financial statements.

Management has an obligation to disclose all significant information appropriately in the financial statements and in management's discussion and analysis. In addition, the disclosed information must not be misleading. Improper disclosures relating to financial statement fraud usually involve the following:

- Liability omissions
- Subsequent events
- Management fraud
- Related-party transactions
- Accounting changes

Liability Omissions Typical omissions include the failure to disclose loan covenants or contingent liabilities. Loan covenants are agreements—in addition to or part of a financing arrangement—that a borrower has promised to observe as long as the financing is in place. The agreements can contain various types of covenants, including certain financial ratio limits and restrictions on other major financing arrangements. Contingent liabilities are potential obligations that will materialize only if certain events occur in the future. A corporate guarantee of personal loans taken out by an officer or a private company

controlled by an officer is an example of a contingent liability. The company's potential liability, if material, must be disclosed.

Subsequent Events   Events occurring or becoming known after the close of the period may have a significant effect on the financial statements and should be disclosed. Fraudsters often avoid disclosing court judgments and regulatory decisions that undermine the reported values of assets, that indicate unrecorded liabilities, or that adversely reflect on management integrity. Public record searches can often reveal this information.

Management Fraud   Management has an obligation to disclose to the shareholders any acts of fraud committed by officers, executives, and others in positions of trust. Withholding such information from auditors would likely involve lying to them, an illegal act.

Related-Party Transactions   Related-party transactions occur when a company does business with another entity whose management or operating policies can be controlled or significantly influenced by the company or by some other party in common. There is nothing inherently wrong with related-party transactions as long as they are fully disclosed. If the transactions are not conducted on an arm's-length basis, the company may suffer economic harm, injuring stockholders.

The financial interest that a company official might have may not be readily apparent. Examples of related parties are common directors of two companies that do business with each other, any corporate general partner and the partnerships with which it does business, and any controlling shareholder of the corporation with which he/she/it does business. Family members can also be considered related parties. These relationships include all lineal descendants and ancestors, without regard to financial interests. Related-party transactions are sometimes referred to as "self-dealing." While these transactions are sometimes conducted at arm's length, they often are not.

In the highly publicized Tyco fraud case, which broke in 2002, the SEC charged former top executives of the company, including its former CEO, L. Dennis Kozlowski, with failing to disclose to shareholders hundreds of millions of dollars of low-interest and interest-free loans they took from the company. Moreover, Kozlowski forgave $50 million in loans to himself and another $56 million in loans for fifty-one favored Tyco employees. Tyco's board approved none of the charges.

Kozlowski also engaged in undisclosed nonarm's-length real estate transactions with Tyco or its subsidiaries and received undisclosed compensation and perks, including rent-free use of large New York City apartments and personal use of corporate aircraft at little or no cost. The SEC complaint alleged that three former executives, including Kozlowski, also sold restricted shares of Tyco stock valued at $430 million dollars while their self-dealing remained undisclosed.

In addition, Kozlowski participated in numerous improper transactions to fund an extravagant lifestyle. In January 2002 several empty boxes arrived at Tyco's headquarters in Exeter, New Hampshire. They were supposed to contain art worth at least $13 million to decorate the modest two-story facility. In fact, the art—consisting of original works by Renoir and Monet—was actually hanging on the walls of Kozlowski's lavish Fifth Avenue corporate apartment; the empty-box ruse was an effort to avoid New York state sales tax of 8.25 percent.

Less than six months later, Kozlowski resigned just before being accused of evading payment of taxes on the art. But the art, paid for by Tyco, was just the tip of the iceberg. A subsequent investigation would accuse Kozlowski and CFO Mark Schwartz of systematically looting their employer of more than $170 million. Both men were later found guilty of twenty-two charges and sentenced to up to twenty-five years in prison.

Most of the stolen money was simply charged to Tyco even though it personally benefited Kozlowski. For example, his compensation was reported at $400 million, but in addition Tyco paid for such outrageous charges as

- A $16.8 million apartment in New York City for Kozlowski
- $13 million in original art
- A $7 million apartment for Kozlowski's ex-wife

- An umbrella stand that cost $15,000
- A $17,000 traveling toilette box
- $5,960 for two sets of sheets
- A $6,300 sewing basket
- A $6,000 shower curtain
- Half sponsorship of a $2.1 million birthday party for his wife
- Up to $80,000 a month in personal credit card charges

Although Kozlowski's embezzlements were not material to the financial statements as a whole, they were nonetheless substantial and vividly portray the ultimate in corporate greed.

Accounting Changes Statement of Financial Accounting Standards No. 154 (SFAS 154), "Accounting Changes and Error Corrections," describes three types of accounting changes that must be disclosed to avoid misleading the user of financial statements: accounting principles, estimates, and reporting entities. Although the required treatment for each type of change is different, they are all susceptible to manipulation by the determined fraudster. For example, fraudsters may fail to properly retroactively restate the financial statements for a change in accounting principle if the change causes the company's financial statements to appear weaker. Likewise, they may fail to disclose significant changes in estimates such as the useful lives and estimated salvage values of depreciable assets on or the estimates underlying the determination of warranty or other liabilities. They may even secretly change the reporting entity, by adding entities owned privately by management or excluding certain company-owned units, in order to improve reported results.

Red Flags Associated with Improper Disclosures Any of the following should alert interested parties of potentially improper disclosures.

- Domination of management by a single person or small group (in a nonowner-managed business) with no compensating controls
- Ineffective board of directors or audit committee oversight of the financial reporting process and internal control
- Ineffective communication, implementation, support, or enforcement of the entity's values or ethical standards by management or the communication of inappropriate values or ethical standards
- Rapid growth or unusual profitability, especially compared to other companies in the same industry
- Significant, unusual, or highly complex transactions, especially those close to period end that pose difficult "substance over form" questions
- Significant related-party transactions not in the ordinary course of business or with related entities not audited or audited by another firm
- Significant bank accounts or subsidiary or branch operations in tax-haven jurisdictions for which there appears to be no clear business justification
- Overly complex organizational structure involving unusual legal entities or managerial lines of authority
- Known history of violations of securities laws or other laws and regulations, or claims against the entity, its senior management, or board members alleging fraud or violations of laws and regulations
- Recurring attempts by management to justify marginal or inappropriate accounting on the basis of materiality
- Formal or informal restrictions on the auditor that inappropriately limit access to people or information or the ability to communicate effectively with the board of directors or the audit committee

Improper Asset Valuation

Generally accepted accounting principles require that most assets be recorded at their historical (acquisition) cost. Under the "lower of cost or market value" rule, when an asset's cost exceeds its current market value (as happens often with obsolete technology), it must be written down to market value. With the exception of certain securities, asset values are not increased to reflect current market value.

It is often necessary to use estimates in accounting. For example, estimates are used in determining the residual value and the useful life of a depreciable asset, the uncollectible portion of accounts receivable, or the excess or obsolete portion of inventory. Whenever estimates are used, there is an additional opportunity for fraud through manipulation of those estimates.

Many schemes are used to inflate current assets at the expense of long-term assets. The net effect is seen in the current ratio. The misclassification of long-term assets as current assets can be of critical concern to lending institutions that require the maintenance of certain financial ratios. This is of particular consequence when the loan covenants are on unsecured or under-secured lines of credit and other short-term borrowings. Sometimes these misclassifications are referred to as "window dressing."

Most improper asset valuations involve the fraudulent overstatement of inventory or receivables. Other improper asset valuations include manipulation of the allocation of the purchase price of an acquired business in order to inflate future earnings, misclassification of fixed and other assets, and improper capitalization of inventory or startup costs. Improper asset valuations usually fall into one of the following categories.

- Inventory valuation
- Accounts receivable
- Business combinations
- Fixed assets

Inventory Valuation Since inventory must be valued at the acquisition cost, except when the cost is determined to be higher than the current market value, inventory should be written down to its current value, or written off altogether if it has no value. Failing to write down inventory will result in overstated assets and the mismatching of cost of goods sold with revenues. Inventory can also be improperly stated through the manipulation of the physical inventory count, by inflating the unit costs used to price out inventory, by failing to relieve inventory for costs of goods sold, or by other methods. Fictitious inventory schemes usually involve the creation of fake documents such as inventory count sheets and receiving reports. Companies have even programmed computers to produce special reports of inventory for auditors that incorrectly total the line item values to inflate the overall inventory balance. Computer-assisted audit techniques can significantly help auditors detect many of these inventory fraud techniques. One case involved an inventory valuation scheme in which the fraud was committed through tampering with the inventory count. During a routine audit of a publicly traded medical supply company, the audit team found a misstatement of the inventory value that could hardly be classified as routine. The client's inventory was measured in metric volumes, and apparently as the count was taken, an employee arbitrarily moved the decimal unit. This resulted in the inventory being grossly overstated. The discovery forced the company to restate its financial statements, resulting in a write-down of the inventory amount by more than $1.5 million.

One of the most popular methods of overstating inventory is through fictitious (phantom) inventory. In one example, a CFE conducting a systems control review at a large cannery and product wholesaler in the Southwest observed a forklift driver constructing a large façade of finished product in a remote location of the warehouse. The inventory was cordoned off and a sign indicated it was earmarked for a national food processor. The cannery was supposedly warehousing the inventory until requested by the customer. When the CFE investigated, he discovered that the inventory held for the food processor was later resold to a national fast-food supplier.

A review of the accounts receivable aging report indicated sales of approximately $1.2 million to this particular customer in prior months, and the aging also showed that cash receipts had been applied against those receivables. An analysis of ending inventory failed to reveal any improprieties because the

relief of inventory had been properly recorded with cost of sales. Copies of all sales documents to this particular customer were then requested. The product was repeatedly sold free on board (FOB) shipping point and title had passed. But bills of lading indicated that only $200,000 of inventory had been shipped to the original purchaser. There should have been a million dollars of finished product on hand for the food processor. However, there was nothing behind the façade of finished products. A comparison of bin numbers on the bill of lading with the sales documents revealed that the same product had been sold twice.

The corporate controller was notified and the plant manager questioned. He explained that "he was doing as he was told." The vice president of marketing and the vice president of operations both knew of the situation but felt there was "no impropriety." The CFO and president of the company felt differently and fired the vice presidents. The company eventually was forced into bankruptcy.

Accounts Receivable   Accounts receivable are subject to manipulation in the same manner as sales and inventory, and in many cases, the schemes are conducted together. The two most common schemes involving accounts receivable are fictitious receivables and failure to write off accounts receivable as bad debts (or failure to establish an adequate allowance for bad debts). Fictitious receivables commonly arise from fictitious revenues, which were discussed earlier. Accounts receivable should be reported at net realizable value, that is, the amount of the receivable less amounts expected not to be collected.

Fictitious Accounts Receivable   Fictitious accounts receivable are common among companies with financial problems, as well as among managers who receive a commission based on sales. The typical scheme for fictitious accounts receivable is to debit (increase) accounts receivable and credit (increase) sales. Of course, these schemes are more common around the end of the accounting period, since accounts receivable should be paid in cash within a reasonable time. Fraudsters commonly attempt to conceal fictitious accounts receivable by providing false confirmations of balances to auditors. They get the audit confirmations because the mailing address they provide for the phony customers is typically either a mailbox under their control, a home address, or the business address of a co-conspirator. Such schemes can be detected by checking business credit reports, public records, or even the telephone book to identify significant customers with no verifiable physical existence or no apparent business need for the product sold to them.

Failure to Write Down   Companies are required to accrue losses on uncollectible receivables when the criteria in Financial Accounting Standards Board Statement No. 5 are met, and to record impairment of long-lived assets under SFAS 144 and of goodwill under SFAS 142. Companies struggling for profits and income may be tempted to omit the recognition of such losses because of the negative impact on income.

Business Combinations   Companies are required to allocate the purchase price they have paid to acquire another business to the tangible and intangible assets of that business. Any excess of the purchase price over the value of the acquired assets is treated as goodwill. Changes in goodwill accounting have decreased the incentive for companies to allocate an excessive amount to purchased assets, to minimize the amount allocated to goodwill that previously should have been amortized and that reduced future earnings. However, companies may still be tempted to over-allocate the purchase price to in-process research and development assets, in order to write them off immediately. Or they may establish excessive reserves for various expenses at the time of acquisition, intending to quietly release those excess reserves into earnings at a future date.

Fixed Assets   Fixed assets are subject to manipulation through several different schemes. Some of the more common schemes are

- Booking fictitious assets
- Misrepresenting asset valuation
- Improperly capitalizing inventory and startup costs

Booking Fictitious Assets   One of the easiest methods of asset misrepresentation is the recording of fictitious assets. This false creation of assets affects account totals on a company's balance sheet. The corresponding account commonly used is the owners' equity account. Because company assets are often physically found in many different locations, this fraud can sometimes be easily overlooked. One of the most common fictitious asset schemes is simply to create fictitious documents. In one instance, a real estate development and mortgage financing company produced fraudulent statements that included fictitious and inflated asset amounts and illegitimate receivables. The company also recorded expenses that actually were for personal rather than business use. To cover the fraud, the company raised cash through various illegal securities offerings, guaranteeing over $110 million with real estate projects. They subsequently defaulted. The company declared bankruptcy shortly before the owner passed away.

In other cases, equipment is leased, not owned, and this fact is not disclosed during the audit of fixed assets. Bogus fixed assets can sometimes be detected because the fixed asset addition makes no business sense.

Misrepresenting Asset Value   Fixed assets should be recorded at cost. Although assets may appreciate in value, this increase in value generally should not be recognized on company financial statements. Many financial statement frauds have involved the reporting of fixed assets at market values instead of the lower acquisition costs, or at even higher inflated values with phony valuations to support them. Further, companies may falsely inflate the value of fixed assets by failing to record impairments of long-lived assets (as required by SFAS 144) and of goodwill (as required by SFAS 142). Misrepresentation of asset values frequently goes hand in hand with other schemes.

One of the highest-profile asset valuation fraud cases of recent years involved the collapse of Enron, the energy-trading company. Enron was created in 1985 as a merger between Houston Natural Gas and InterNorth, a Nebraska pipeline company. Although Enron began as a traditional natural gas supplier, under the lead of employee Jeffrey Skilling, it quickly developed a new and innovative strategy to make money: the creation of a "gas bank," where the company would buy gas from a network of suppliers and sell to a network of consumers. Its profits would be derived from contractually guaranteeing both the supply and the selling price, charging a fee for its services.

This new business segment required Enron to borrow enormous amounts of money, but by 1990 the company was the market leader. Kenneth Lay, Enron's CEO, created Enron Finance Corp. (EFC) to handle the new business and picked Skilling to run it. Based on the initial success of EFC and with the assistance of Skilling's new protégé, Andrew Fastow, the company's "gas bank" concept was expanded to include trading in electricity and in futures contracts for coal, paper, water, steel, and other commodities.

Since Enron was either a buyer or a seller in every transaction, the company's credit was crucial. Eventually, in 2000, Enron expanded into the telecommunications business by announcing plans to build a high-speed broadband network and to trade network capacity (bandwidth) in the same way it traded other commodities. Enron sunk hundreds of millions of dollars in borrowed money for this new venture, which quickly failed to produce the expected profits.

The money that Enron borrowed to finance its various ventures was kept off of its balance sheet by Fastow, using an accounting treatment called special-purpose entities (SPEs). Under accounting rules in place at the time, Enron could contribute up to 97 percent of an SPE's assets or equity. Then the SPE could borrow its own money, which would not show up on Enron's financial statements. But Enron could claim its profits (or losses).

In most of the SPEs established by Enron, the asset contributed was company stock. But since the stock contributions would have diluted earnings per share, Enron used another treatment, "mark-to-market accounting," to boost profits. Mark-to-market accounting required a company to book both realized and unrealized gains and losses on energy-related and other "derivative" contracts at the end of each quarter. Because there were no hard-and-fast rules on how to value such contracts, Enron consistently valued them to show gains, which would offset the effect of issuing more stock to fund the SPEs. Moreover, the accounting treatment that allowed Enron to keep the debt off of its balance sheet also allowed the company to claim the income from unrealized holding gains, which increased the return on assets. By 1999 Enron had derived more than half of its $1.4 billion pretax net income from unrealized holding gains.

Fastow became the master of the SPE, eventually creating thousands of them for various purposes. However, when the economic boom of the 1990s started to wane, Enron's unrealized holding gains on its "derivative" contracts started turning into losses. To keep these losses from showing up on Enron's

income statement, Fastow created SPEs to hide them. And in the process of creating SPEs, Fastow paid himself over $30 million in management fees. His wife was paid another $17 million.

One of the six transactions in the SEC's complaint against Fastow involved a special-purpose entity named Raptor I and a public company called Avici Systems Inc. According to the complaint, Enron and the Fastow-controlled partnership, LJM2, engaged in complex transactions with Raptor I to manipulate Enron's balance sheet and income statement, as well as to generate profits for LJM2 and Fastow, at Enron's expense. In September 2000, Fastow and others used Raptor I to effectuate a fraudulent hedging transaction and thus avoid a decrease in the value of Enron's investment in the stock of Avici Systems Inc. Specifically, Fastow and others back-dated documents to make it appear that Enron had locked in the value of its investment in Avici in August 2000, when Avici's stock was trading at its all-time high price.

The various deals that Enron cooked up should have been properly disclosed in the footnotes to its financial statements. But a number of analysts questioned the transparency of those disclosures. One said, "The notes just don't make any sense, and we read notes for a living."

Like other profits that are built on paper and risky deals, Enron was unable to continue without massive infusions of cash. When that didn't materialize, Enron in October 2001 was forced to disclose it was taking a $1 billion charge to earnings to account for poorly performing business segments. It also had to reverse $1.2 billion in assets and equities booked as a result of the failed SPEs. Later that month, it announced restatements that added $591 million in losses and $628 million in liabilities for the year ended in 2000.

The bubble had burst. On December 2, 2001, Enron filed for bankruptcy. Enron's auditor, Andersen & Co., closed its doors on August 30, 2002, for failing to discover the fraud. In the end, sixteen people pled guilty to crimes related to the scandal, and five others were convicted at trial. Many of the company's top executives were sentenced to jail time for their part in the fraud, including Fastow, Skilling, and former treasurer Ben Glisan, Jr. Ken Lay was also found guilty of six counts of fraud, but he died of a heart attack before his sentencing.

Understating Assets   In some cases, as with some government-related or regulated companies where additional funding is based on asset amounts, it may be advantageous to understate assets. This understatement can be done directly or through improper depreciation. In one example, the management of a company falsified its financial statements by manipulating the depreciation of the fixed assets. The depreciation reserve was accelerated by the amount of $2.9 million over a six-month period. The purpose of the scheme was to avoid cash contributions to a central government capital asset acquisition account.

Capitalizing Nonasset Cost   Excluded from the cost of a purchased asset are interest and finance charges incurred in the purchase. For example, as a company finances a capital equipment purchase, monthly payments include both principal liability reduction and interest payments. On initial purchase, only the original cost of the asset should be capitalized. The subsequent interest payments should be charged to interest expense—not to the asset. Without reason for intensive review, fraud of this type can go unchecked. In one case, a new investor in a closely held corporation sued for rescission of purchase of stock, alleging that the company compiled financial information that misrepresented the financial history of the business. A fraud examination uncovered assets that were overvalued because of capitalization of interest and other finance charges. Also discovered was the fact that one of the owners was understating revenue by $150,000 and embezzling the funds. In a civil fraud case, the parties subsequently settled out of court.

Misclassifying Assets   In order to meet budget requirements, and for various other reasons, assets are sometimes misclassified into general ledger accounts to which they don't belong. The manipulation can skew financial ratios and help in complying with loan covenants or other borrowing requirements. In a case where an employee from the purchasing department at a retail jewelry firm feared being called to the carpet for some bad jewelry purchases, rather than taking the blame for bad margins on many items, the employee arbitrarily redistributed costs of shipments to individual inventory accounts. The cover-up did not work, because the company's CFO detected the fraud after he initiated changes to control procedures.

When the CFO created a separation of duties between the buying function and the costing activities, the dishonest employee was discovered and terminated.

Red Flags Associated with Improper Asset Valuation   The following circumstances should raise suspicions regarding the propriety of asset valuation.

- Recurring negative cash flows from operations or an inability to generate cash flows from operations while reporting earnings and earnings growth
- Significant declines in customer demand and increasing business failures in either the industry or the overall economy
- Assets, liabilities, revenues, or expenses based on significant estimates that involve subjective judgments or uncertainties that are difficult to corroborate
- Nonfinancial management's excessive participation in or preoccupation with the selection of accounting principles or the determination of significant estimates
- Unusual increase in gross margin or margin in excess of industry peers
- Unusual growth in the number of days' sales in receivables
- Unusual growth in the number of days' purchases in inventory
- Allowances for bad debts, excess and obsolete inventory, and similar measures that are shrinking in percentage terms or are otherwise out of line with those of their industry peers
- Unusual change in the relationship between fixed assets and depreciation
- Adding to assets while competitors are reducing capital tied up in assets

Detection of Fraudulent Financial Statement Schemes

Financial Statement Analysis   Comparative financial statements provide information for current and past accounting periods. Accounts expressed in whole-dollar amounts yield a limited amount of information. The conversion of these numbers into ratios or percentages allows the reader of the statements to analyze them based on their relationship to each other, as well as to major changes in historical totals. In fraud detection and investigation, determination of the reasons for relationships and changes in amounts can be important. Such determinations are the red flags that point an examiner in the direction of possible fraud. If large enough, a fraudulent misstatement will affect the financial statements in such a way that relationships between the numbers become questionable. Many schemes are detected because the financial statements, when analyzed closely, do not make sense. Financial statement analysis includes

- Vertical analysis
- Horizontal analysis
- Ratio analysis

Percentage Analysis—Vertical and Horizontal   There are traditionally two methods of percentage analysis of financial statements. *Vertical analysis* is a technique for analyzing the relationships between the items on an income statement, balance sheet, or statement of cash flows by expressing components as percentages. This method is often referred to as "common sizing" of financial statements. In the vertical analysis of an income statement, net sales is assigned 100 percent; for a balance sheet, total assets is assigned 100 percent on the asset side, and total liabilities and equity is expressed as 100 percent. All other items in each of the sections are expressed as a percentage of these numbers.

Horizontal analysis is a technique for analyzing the percentage change in individual financial statement items from one year to the next. The first period in the analysis is considered the base, and the changes to subsequent periods are computed as a percentage of the base period. If more than two periods are presented, each period's changes are computed as a percentage of the preceding period. Like vertical analysis, this technique will not work for small, immaterial frauds.

Following are examples of financial statements that are analyzed using both vertical and horizontal analysis.

BALANCE SHEET	Vertical Analysis				Horizontal Analysis	
	Year 1		Year 2		Change	% Change
Assets						
Current assets	45,000		15,000		(30,000)	−67 %
Cash	14 %		4 %			
Accts. receivable	150,000	45 %	200,000	47 %	50,000	33 %
Inventory	75,000	23 %	150,000	35 %	75,000	100 %
Fixed assets (net)	60,000	18 %	60,000	14 %	–	0 %
Total	330,000	100 %	425,000	100 %	95,000	29 %
Accts. payable	95,000	29 %	215,000	51 %	120,000	126 %
Long-term debt	60,000	18 %	60,000	14 %	–	0 %
Stockholder's equity					–	
Common stock	25,000	8 %	25,000	6 %	–	0 %
Paid-in capital	75,000	23 %	75,000	18 %	–	0 %
Retained earnings	75,000	23 %	50,000	12 %	(25,000)	−33 %
Total	330,000	100 %	425,000	100 %	95,000	29 %

INCOME STATEMENT	Vertical Analysis				Horizontal Analysis	
	Year 1		Year 2		Change	% Change
Net sales	250,000	100 %	450,000	100 %	200,000	80 %
Cost of goods sold	125,000	50 %	300,000	67 %	175,000	140 %
Gross margin	125,000	50 %	150,000	33 %	25,000	20 %
Operating expenses						
Selling expenses	50,000	20 %	75,000	17 %	25,000	50 %
Administrative expenses	60,000	24 %	100,000	22 %	40,000	67 %
Net income	15,000	6 %	(25,000)	−6 %	(40,000)	−267 %
Additional Information						
Average net receivables	155,000		210,000			
Average inventory	65,000		130,000			
Average assets	330,000		425,000			

VERTICAL ANALYSIS DISCUSSION   Vertical analysis indicates the relationship or percentage of component part items with respect to a specific base item. In the vertical analysis of the income statement above, net sales is the base amount and all other items are analyzed as a percentage of that total. Vertical analysis emphasizes the relationships among statement items within each accounting period. These relationships can be used with historical averages to identify statement anomalies.

In the above example, we observe that accounts payable is 29 percent of total liabilities and stockholders' equity. We may find that historically this account averages slightly over 25 percent. In year 2, accounts payable rose to 51 percent. Although the change in the accounts payable total may be explainable as being correlated with a rise in sales, this significant increase might be a starting point in a fraud examination. Source documents should be examined to determine the basis for the rise in this percentage. With this type of examination, fraudulent activity can sometimes be detected. The same type of change can be seen in the decline of selling expenses as a part of sales in year 2 from 20 to 17 percent. Again, this change may be explainable by higher-volume sales or another legitimate influence. But close examination may point a fraud examiner to fictitious sales since accounts payable total rose significantly with no corresponding increase in selling expenses.

HORIZONTAL ANALYSIS DISCUSSION   Horizontal statement analysis uses percentage comparisons from one accounting period to the next. The percentage change is calculated by dividing the amount of increase or decrease for each item by the base period amount. It is important to consider the amount of change as well as the percentage in horizontal comparisons. A 5 percent change in an account with

a very large dollar amount may be much more significant than a 50 percent change in an account with much less activity.

In the above example, it is very obvious that the 80 percent increase in sales corresponds to a much greater increase in cost of goods sold, 140 percent. These accounts are often used to hide fraudulent expenses, withdrawals, or other illegal transactions.

Ratio Analysis   Ratio analysis is a means of measuring the relationship between two different financial statement amounts. Traditionally, financial statement ratios are used in comparison to an entity's industry average. They can be very useful in detecting red flags for a fraud examination. When the financial ratios highlight a significant change in key areas of an organization from one year to the next, or over a period of years, it becomes obvious that there may a problem. As in all other analyses, specific changes can often be explained by changes in the business operations. Changes in key ratios are not, in and of themselves, proof of any wrongdoing.

Whenever a change in specific ratios is detected, the appropriate source accounts should be researched and examined in detail to determine if fraud has occurred. For instance, a significant decrease in a company's current ratio may be the result of an increase in current liabilities or a reduction in assets, either of which could be used to conceal fraud.

Like vertical and horizontal analysis, ratio analysis is limited by its inability to detect fraud on a small, immaterial scale. Key financial ratios include

- Current ratio
- Quick ratio
- Receivables turnover
- Collection ratio
- Inventory turnover
- Average number of days inventory is in stock
- Debt to equity
- Profit margin
- Asset turnover

Many other kinds of financial ratios are analyzed in industry-specific situations, but the nine above are ratios that may lead to discovery of fraud. The following calculations are based on the sample financial statements presented earlier.

RATIO ANALYSIS

Ratio	Calculation	Year 1		Year 2	
Current ratio	$\dfrac{\text{Current assets}}{\text{Current liabilities}}$	$\dfrac{270{,}000}{95{,}000}$	2.84	$\dfrac{365{,}000}{215{,}000}$ =	1.70
Quick ratio	$\dfrac{\text{Cash + Securities + Receivables}}{\text{Current liabilities}}$	$\dfrac{195{,}000}{95{,}000}$	2.05	$\dfrac{215{,}000}{215{,}000}$ =	1.00
Receivables turnover	$\dfrac{\text{Net sales on account}}{\text{Average net receivables}}$	$\dfrac{250{,}000}{155{,}000}$	1.61	$\dfrac{450{,}000}{210{,}000}$ =	2.14
Collection ratio	$\dfrac{365}{\text{Receivables turnover}}$	$\dfrac{365}{1.61}$	226.30	$\dfrac{365}{2.14}$ =	170.56
Inventory turnover	$\dfrac{\text{Cost of goods sold}}{\text{Average inventory}}$	$\dfrac{125{,}000}{65{,}000}$	1.92	$\dfrac{300{,}000}{130{,}000}$ =	2.31
Average number of days inventory is in stock	$\dfrac{365}{\text{Inventory turnover}}$	$\dfrac{365}{1.92}$	190.10	$\dfrac{365}{2.31}$ =	158.01
Debt to equity	$\dfrac{\text{Total liabilities}}{\text{Total equity}}$	$\dfrac{155{,}000}{175{,}000}$	0.89	$\dfrac{275{,}000}{150{,}000}$ =	1.83
Profit margin	$\dfrac{\text{Net income}}{\text{Net sales}}$	$\dfrac{15{,}000}{250{,}000}$	0.06	$\dfrac{(25{,}000)}{450{,}000}$ =	(0.06)
Asset turnover	$\dfrac{\text{Net sales}}{\text{Average assets}}$	$\dfrac{250{,}000}{330{,}000}$	0.76	$\dfrac{450{,}000}{425{,}000}$ =	1.06

INTERPRETATION OF FINANCIAL RATIOS

$$\text{Current ratio} = \frac{\text{Current assets}}{\text{Current liabilities}}$$

The current ratio—current assets divided by current liabilities—is probably the most-used ratio in financial statement analysis. This comparison measures a company's ability to meet present obligations from its liquid assets. The number of times by which current assets exceed current liabilities has long been a convenient measure of financial strength.

In detecting fraud, this ratio can be a prime indicator of manipulation of accounts. Embezzlement will cause the ratio to decrease. Liability concealment will cause the ratio to appear more favorable.

In the present example, the drastic change in the current ratio from year 1 (2.84) to year 2 (1.70) should cause the examiner to look at these accounts in more detail. For instance, a billing scheme will usually result in a decrease in current assets—cash—which will in turn decrease the ratio.

$$\text{Quick ratio} = \frac{\text{Cash} + \text{Securities} + \text{Receivables}}{\text{Current liabilities}}$$

The quick ratio, often referred to as the acid-test ratio, compares assets that can be immediately liquidated. In this calculation the total of cash, securities, and receivables is divided by current liabilities. This ratio is a measure of a company's ability to meet sudden cash requirements. In turbulent economic times, it is used more extensively, giving the analyst a worst-case look at the company's working capital situation.

An examiner will analyze this ratio for fraud indicators. In year 1 of the example, the company balance sheet reflects a quick ratio of 2.05. This ratio drops in year 2 to 1.00. In this situation, a possible type of fraud is fictitious accounts receivable that have been added to inflate sales in one year. The ratio calculation will be abnormally high and there will not be an offsetting of current liability.

$$\text{Receivables turnover} = \frac{\text{Net sales on account}}{\text{Average net receivables}}$$

Receivables turnover is defined as net sales divided by average net receivables. It measures the number of times accounts receivable is turned over during the accounting period. In other words, it measures the time between credit sales and collection of funds. This ratio uses both income statement and balance sheet account information in its analysis. If the fraud involves fictitious sales, this is bogus income that will never be collected. As a result, the turnover of receivables will decrease.

$$\text{Collection ratio} = \frac{365}{\text{Receivables turnover}}$$

Accounts receivable aging is measured by the collection ratio. The ratio divides 365 days by the receivables turnover ratio to arrive at the average number of days used to collect receivables. In general, the lower the collection ratio, the faster receivables are collected. A fraud examiner may use this ratio as a first step in detecting fictitious receivables or larceny and skimming schemes. Normally, this ratio will stay fairly consistent from year to year, but changes in billing policies or collection efforts may cause a fluctuation. The example shows a favorable reduction in the collection ratio from 226.3 in year 1 to 170.56 in year 2. This means that the company is collecting its receivables more quickly in year 2 than in year 1.

$$\text{Inventory turnover} = \frac{\text{Cost of goods sold}}{\text{Average inventory}}$$

The relationship between a company's cost of goods sold and average inventory is shown through the inventory turnover ratio. This ratio measures the number of times inventory is sold during the period. This ratio is a good determinant of purchasing, production, and sales efficiency. In general, a higher inventory turnover ratio is considered more favorable. However, if cost of goods sold has increased due to theft of inventory (ending inventory has declined, but not through sales), for example, then this ratio will be abnormally high. In the present example, inventory turnover increases in year 2, signaling the possibility that an embezzlement is buried in the inventory account. An examiner should study the changes in the components of the ratio to determine where to look to uncover possible fraud.

$$\text{Average number of days inventory is in stock} = \frac{365}{\text{Inventory turnover}}$$

The average number of days inventory is in stock ratio is a restatement of the inventory turnover ratio expressed in days. This rate is important for several reasons. An increase in the number of days inventory

stays in stock causes additional expenses, including storage costs, risk of inventory obsolescence, and market price reductions, as well as interest and other expenses incurred from tying up funds in inventory stock. Inconsistency or significant variances in this ratio is a red flag for fraud investigators. Examiners may use this ratio to examine inventory accounts for possible larceny schemes. Purchasing and receiving inventory schemes can also affect the ratio, and false debits to cost of goods sold will result in an increase in the ratio. A significant change in the inventory turnover ratio is a good indicator of possible fraudulent inventory activity.

$$\text{Debt to equity} = \frac{\text{Total liabilities}}{\text{Total equity}}$$

The debt-to-equity ratio is computed by dividing total liabilities by total equity. This ratio is one that is heavily studied by lending institutions. It provides a clear picture of the comparison between the long-term and short-term debt of the company, and of the owner's financial injection plus earnings to date. This balance of the resources provided by creditors and what the owners provide is crucial for analyzing the financial status of a company. Debt-to-equity requirements are often included as borrowing covenants in corporate lending agreements. The example displays a year 1 ratio of 0.89 and a year 2 ratio of 1.83. The increase in the ratio corresponds with the rise in accounts payable. Sudden changes in this ratio may prompt an examiner to look for fraud.

$$\text{Profit margin} = \frac{\text{Net income}}{\text{Net sales}}$$

The profit margin ratio is defined as net income divided by net sales. This ratio is often referred to as the efficiency ratio, as it reveals profits earned per dollar of sales. The ratio of net income to sales relates not only to the effects of gross margin changes, but also to changes in sales and administrative expenses. Over time, this ratio should remain fairly consistent. As fraud is committed, artificially inflated sales will not have an accompanying increase in cost of goods sold, net income will be overstated, and the profit margin ratio will be abnormally high. False expenses and fraudulent disbursements will cause an increase in expenses and a decrease in the profit margin ratio.

$$\text{Asset turnover} = \frac{\text{Net sales}}{\text{Average assets}}$$

Net sales divided by average operating assets is the calculation used to determine the asset turnover ratio. This ratio determines the efficiency with which asset resources are utilized. The present example reflects a greater use of assets in year 2 than in year 1.

DETERRENCE OF FINANCIAL STATEMENT FRAUD

Deterring financial statement fraud is more complex than deterring asset misappropriation and similar frauds. Because of the breadth of the subject matter, this section cannot cover all possible deterrence measures. But it is clear that adding traditional internal controls is unlikely to be effective. As noted earlier, the 1999 COSO study indicated that either the CEO or the CFO was involved in 83 percent of the financial statement frauds studied. Although this study is ten years old, there are no current data to indicate that the trends have changed substantially. Those at the executive level can use their authority to override most internal controls, so those controls are often of limited value in preventing financial statement fraud. A different approach is needed.

Following the principles of the fraud triangle, introduced in the first chapter of this book, a general approach to reducing financial statement fraud is the following:

- Reduce pressures to commit financial statement fraud
- Reduce the opportunity to commit financial statement fraud
- Reduce grounds for rationalizing of financial statement fraud

Reduce Pressures to Commit Financial Statement Fraud

- Establish effective board oversight of the "tone at the top" created by management
- Avoid setting unachievable or unreasonable financial goals
- Avoid applying excessive pressure on employees to achieve goals

- Change goals if changed market conditions require it
- Ensure compensation systems are fair and do not create too much incentive to commit fraud
- Discourage excessive external expectations of future corporate performance
- Remove operational obstacles to effective performance

Reduce the Opportunity to Commit Financial Statement Fraud

- Maintain accurate and complete internal accounting records
- Carefully monitor the business transactions and interpersonal relationships of suppliers, buyers, purchasing agents, sales representatives, and others who participate in the transactions between financial units
- Establish a physical security system to secure company assets, including finished goods, cash, capital equipment, tools, and other valuable items
- Divide important functions among employees, sharing control of one area
- Maintain accurate personnel records, including background checks on new employees
- Encourage strong supervisory relationships and leadership within groups to promote enforcement of accounting procedures
- Establish clear and uniform accounting procedures with no exception clauses

Reduce Grounds for Rationalizing of Financial Statement Fraud

- Promote strong values, based on integrity, throughout the organization
- Have policies that clearly define prohibited behavior with respect to accounting and financial statement fraud
- Provide regular training to all employees, communicating prohibited behavior
- Establish confidential advice and reporting mechanisms for communicating inappropriate behavior
- Have senior executives communicate to employees that integrity takes priority and that goals must never be achieved through fraud
- Ensure that management practices what it preaches and sets an example by promoting honesty in the accounting area. Dishonest acts by management, even if they are directed at someone outside the organization, create an environment of corruption that can spread to other business activities and to other employees, internal and external
- Clearly define the consequences of violating the rules

CASE STUDY: ALL ON THE SURFACE

In this case example, several names may have been changed to preserve anonymity.

Michael Weinstein chuckled a lot. He smoked big cigars and laughed at the people who used to think he was just a chubby schmo. *Forbes* and *BusinessWeek* stoked the fire with adoring articles. *BusinessWeek* called Weinstein's Coated Sales, Inc. "the fourth fastest growing company in the country" and predicted greater returns to come. Of Coated Sales' 20 competitors, 11 were either defunct or absorbed. "The survivors," observed a writer in *Forbes*, "are more likely to cower than laugh when they see Weinstein." In a few years' time, revenues at Coated had jumped from $10 to $90 million per annum. The stock was peaking at eight times its opening price. "One of my goals," Weinstein stated dramatically, "is to see us be almost alone."

And that didn't take long.

Weinstein's auditors walked out on him. The Big Six firm resigned and announced publicly they had no trust in the management of Coated Sales. Senior management scrambled en masse to clear out. Weinstein was suspended. New people started looking at the books. Within two months, Coated Sales was filing for bankruptcy. The last laugh rang hollow down the empty hallways.

Michael Weinstein was once the All-American Businessman. At 19 he borrowed $1,000 from his father and bought into a drugstore. At 31 he had a chain of stores, which he sold, reaping several million dollars in take-home pay. Weinstein remembered thinking, "I have a problem." Just when all his contemporaries were reaching their 30-something years, starting careers, and raising families, he was retiring. What to do with all that time?

His buddy Dick Bober talked him into the coated fabrics business. Weinstein didn't know anything about coated fabrics. But neither was he a pharmacist, and that venture had proved fortuitous. Coating fabrics, he learned, was a crucial step in the manufacture of lots of products, from conveyer belts to bulletproof vests. Things like parachutes, helmet

liners, and camouflage suits all use coated fabrics. So there were some bulky government contracts waiting to be served. Uniforms and equipment have to be stain-proofed, fungus-proofed, waterproofed, and dyed. According to one estimate, coating adds from 10 to 50 percent to the base value of raw material, lending the luster of money to an otherwise workaday industry.

Weinstein threw himself into the business and eventually into the manufacturing process. As a pilot, he had hated the life vests stowed on commercial airliners. "They had always bugged me," he said. "They [are] heavy and expensive to make," he told Coated researchers. They designed a prototype using coated nylon, which was 60 percent lighter than the standard and 70 percent cheaper to make. Before his company's untimely demise, Weinstein could boast that every Western-based airline carried life vests manufactured with materials made by Coated Sales.

The Coated Sales laboratory helped develop a super-proofed denim to protect oil rig workers, firemen, and people handling hazardous materials. Coated Sales employees worked on aircraft emergency slides, radiator hoses, telephone earpieces, a sewage filtration fabric, marine diver suits, backpacks, and, just for flair, they made a portion of the sailcloth for the *Stars & Stripes*, the schooner Dennis Conner piloted to victory in the America's Cup. Weinstein must have had a charm wound up and running in his favor. Just two years before the crash, he became the first coated fabrics operator to own a large-scale finishing plant, a $27 million facility without rival in the industry.

At the same time, Weinstein's darling was digging its own grave. Expanding into new markets, developing cutting-edge product lines, herding new companies into the fold—all this takes money. Especially when the CEO and senior management like to live large and let people know about it. There's a constant cash crunch. Larger scale means larger crunch. Inside the workings of Coated Sales, shipments of fabric and equipment were being bought and sold quickly, often at a loss, just to get the short-term money.

For years Coated had used Main Hurdman for auditing, with no signs of trouble. But when Main Hurdman was acquired by Peat-Marwick (now KPMG), the new auditors came away with a very different picture. One associate called a luggage manufacturer to ask about 750,000 pieces of merchandise purchased from Coated. The luggage company said they never placed an order like that. No idea. When audit team members spoke about their concerns, Coated sent in its legal counsel to talk with the auditors. Philip Kagan tried to get them to make a deal, to forge ahead and let the financial statement slide; there were some problems, he admitted, but nothing beyond repair. The matter was being taken care of. No way, said the auditors, who then walked out.

Within a two month period, the company that once flew higher than the rest had fallen into bankruptcy. Early estimates put shareholder losses at more than $160 million. Coated's top twenty creditors claimed they were out at least $17 million. The bankruptcy court appointed Coopers & Lybrand's insolvency and litigation practice to work with the debtor in possession. Besides the usual assessments, the group was to determine what went wrong—and just how wrong, in dollar amounts, it had gone. CFE Harvey Creem says, "We knew there was something of concern with a loan and how the money was used. Once we started poking around, the iceberg got larger." Creem worked with the debtor's lawyers, who determined that the proceeds of a bank loan had been transferred to a brokerage account, one no longer carried in the ledgers. It was a supposedly dormant account from the company's first public offering, used for temporary investments until it was zeroed out. During the most recent fiscal year, there had been some activity in the account. Proceeds from a loan had been deposited into the brokerage account, transferred out to a cash account, and listed as if they were payments from customers against their accounts receivable. Coated Sales was due a lot of money, their receivables growing by $20 million a year. But a lot of the payments on those receivables were being made with Coated's own money, part of which originated from bank loans. The broad outline of the fraud was clear. "When you find a single check for, say $2 million, used to pay off several different accounts, you know something's up.... Usually each customer sends their own check to pay off their own debt. In this case, a check listed under one name was used to pay off debts for several different people. Now, a company that not only pays its own debts, but the debts of other companies, too—that's not impossible, but it's not likely. The basics of the operation took two or three hours to break," says Creem. "Then it was tracking the scope of what happened."

Creem describes how he and his colleagues started at the bankruptcy filing date and "went in and analyzed the receivables in-depth.... Large chunks of them were totally fallacious; they had nothing supporting them." The tracking effort was helped along by a number of lower-level employees: "Some of them didn't really know what was happening and they were willing to help. Some may have known, but they were repentant, so they were willing to talk." In about three years of scamming, Weinstein and his management had inflated their sales and profits, resulting in overstated equity of $55 million. They used these phony numbers to get loans from several banks, including a $52 million line of credit from BancBoston and a $15 million line from First Fidelity in Newark, New Jersey.

The rigged loans solved the cash flow problem, plus there were very pleasant side effects. Stock in Coated Sales—traded under the ticker symbol RAGS—had been headed through the roof. Huge leaps in revenue and a monstrous control of the market had propelled the stock to $12 a share, eight times more than what it opened for. The company's upper echelon, including Ernest Glantz (president) and Weinstein's long-time partner Dick Bober (vice president), were benefiting in a big way. Weinstein himself made more than $10 million in a short-term selling spree. What's more, one of the myriad lawsuits filed against him accused Weinstein of departing with $968,000 in company cash.

Creem followed the trail of rigged profits into several intriguing corners. "To float this past the auditors for as long as they did, they found several ways to create the fiction that customers were actually paying the fake receivables. They would create a fake receivable, say $10,000 due from a company. They'd hold it as long as they could, sometimes doctoring the dates on the aging, so it looked more recent than it was." Creem says the next step was "rigging a way to pay the account off: They'd transmit their own cash to a vendor. The vendor presumably was in on the scheme, too, since they had submitted a fake invoice for the $10,000. This vendor keeps 1 to 2 percent for their trouble, and sends the

rest back to Coated. That money would be reflected as a payment against the phony receivable."

Guys like Bernard Korostoff made the vendor trick work. Korostoff used his Kaye Mills International Corporation to create false invoices for several big Coated orders. Weinstein's team, having used their phony financials to get loans, sent out the money to Korostoff as if they were paying off a debt. Korostoff kept 1.5 percent for making the transaction possible, turning the rest back to Coated to pay off the falsified receivables. "I never really understood that," says Creem. "These guys are doing this for a measly little percentage. Why would they bother for no more than that? Maybe it was connected in other ways to the business."

The business, as it was being run, was a labyrinth of finagling and deception. Weinstein was faking how much he owed people in order to pay off receivables, which were also being faked. He was using receivables to get million-dollar loans and plowing chunks of the proceeds back into the system to keep suspicious eyes unaware. The false sales not only brought in loan dollars, they created portfolio dollars by driving RAGS stock higher and higher. To support the scam, Weinstein had three ways to keep his circle of money in motion: He could move loan money from the hidden brokerage account to wherever it was needed, he could use fake vendor invoices to launder funds back into the company, or he and his associates could sell off their own stock in the company and apply some of the proceeds to the delinquent receivables.

Four years of this action and Weinstein had demolished Coated Sales. The company exaggerated its accounts receivable by millions, fictionalizing half or more of its sales at any given point. At the time, it was the largest stock fraud ever perpetrated in the state of New Jersey. Weinstein and nine other senior managers were charged with planning, executing, and profiting from the scheme. Weinstein—called "a tall, plump man with a domineering personality" by *Forbes*—owned more than ten airplanes and several helicopters. He had two Rolls-Royces, one at each of his two residences, plus five other luxury automobiles scattered here and there. He and the other conspirators had used some of the proceeds to buy themselves smaller companies. As for flamboyance he had no better, and as for gall he was unrivaled. After Coated went belly up and federal charges joined the pile of lawsuits against him, Weinstein bought a 13,000-square-foot house in Boca Raton, Florida, valued at $2 million and sitting on a $1 million property. Three different yachts were docked along the Florida coast in case Weinstein needed to get away from all the hassle.

But Weinstein wouldn't slip past this one. He and his inner circle were presented with a 46-page indictment. Bruce Bloom, Coated's chief financial officer, pled guilty and pointed at his cohorts. Coated's lead counsel, Philip Kagan, first declared himself "totally innocent of any wrongdoing," but later decided to plead guilty to the racketeering and conspiracy charges against him. Kagan confessed to helping dupe company auditors, and described trying to entice them into ignoring the facts of their ledgers. He also admitted that he had once accepted $115,000 in legal fees from Coated Sales without reporting the money to the SEC as required. Kagan was sentenced to 18 months in prison. Jail terms for other low-level players ranged from a year to twenty-four months.

Coated President Ernest Glanz was given a year's sentence—part of a deal he made to cooperate with the government. Richard Bober, Weinstein's longtime friend, drew twenty months in prison and a $3 million fine, besides the $55.9 million civil judgment he shared with Weinstein. Creem remembers that when Bober testified in bankruptcy court, "The judge appeared shocked. He started asking Bober questions himself. I don't believe he had ever heard anything quite like this in his courtroom before."

Michael Weinstein struck a plea bargain, which nevertheless carried a pretty stout penalty. He forfeited virtually all of the properties, cars, and boats he had amassed, along with several businesses and numerous bank accounts worth several hundred thousand dollars each. He was given fifty-seven months in federal prison and charged to make restitution for any outstanding stockholder losses.

U.S. Attorney Michael Chertoff saw this as a decisive case, part of what he called "a new genre of corporate boardroom prosecutions." Fed up with the mega-scams of megalomaniac executives, legal agencies are using the tough Securities Law Enforcement Remedies Act to go after the big players. "Major financial fraud," Chertoff told a press conference after Weinstein's guilty plea, "not only harms banking institutions but also infects the securities market, victimizing the thousands of persons who invest in stock. When dishonesty roams the boardroom, it is the creditors and investors who suffer."

REVIEW QUESTIONS

14-1 Why might senior management overstate or understate business performance?

14-2 What are some of the ways in which financial statement fraud is committed?

14-3 What is the conceptual framework for financial reporting?

14-4 What are the five classifications of financial statement fraud?

14-5 How are fictitious revenue schemes committed?

14-6 What are the four criteria necessary for a sale to be complete?

14-7 How can understating liabilities and expenses make a company appear more profitable?

14-8 What issues are generally involved in improper disclosures?

14-9 How may improper asset valuation inflate the current ratio?

14-10 How can financial statement fraud be deterred?

ENDNOTES

1. Zabihollah Rezaee and Richard Riley, *Financial Statement Fraud: Precaution and Detection*, John Wiley & Sons, 2010, p. 7.

2. "Consideration of Fraud in a Financial Statement Audit," SAS No. 99, 2002.

3. Ibid.

4. W. Steve Albrecht and David J. Searcy, "Top 10 Reasons Why Fraud Is Increasing in the U.S." *Strategic Finance*, May 2001.

5. David L. Cotton, "Fixing CPA Ethics Can Be an Inside Job," *Washington Post*, October 20, 2002.

FINANCIAL LITIGATION ADVISORY SERVICES AND REMEDIATION

CONSULTING, LITIGATION SUPPORT, AND EXPERT WITNESSES: DAMAGES, VALUATIONS, AND OTHER ENGAGEMENTS

LEARNING OBJECTIVES

After completing this chapter, you should be able to do the following:

15-1 Discuss the purpose of practice aids in forensic and valuation services.

15-2 Identify the activities related to consulting and litigation support.

15-3 Describe what constitutes an expert's work product.

15-4 Explain the legal framework for damages.

15-5 List and explain the different types of commercial damages.

15-6 Identify the various categories and calculations used in ratio analysis.

15-7 Describe some of the decisions that need to be made with regard to quantifying lost revenues and increased expenses.

15-8 Identify typical benchmarks for calculating lost profits.

15-9 List the considerations related to forecasting income and cash flows.

15-10 Discuss the types of damages that may ensue as a result of personal injury, wrongful death, and survival actions.

CRITICAL THINKING EXERCISE

How many outs are there in an inning?

CONSULTING, LITIGATION SUPPORT, AND EXPERT WITNESSES

Professional Standards and Guidance

The American Institute of Certified Public Accountants (AICPA) created the "Forensic and Valuation Services Section." This section, in concert with the efforts of the greater AICPA organization, has created several practice aids, special reports, and other publications to support the certified public accountants' efforts with regard to litigation support and valuation engagements. However, the AICPA makes clear that a "practice aid" does not establish standards, preferred practices, methods, or approaches, nor is it to be used as a substitute for professional judgment. Other approaches, methodologies, procedures, and presentations may be appropriate in a particular matter because of the widely varying nature of the litigation services, as well as specific or unique facts about each client and engagement. Professionals involved in litigation support services are encouraged to consult with counsel about laws and local court requirements that may affect the general guidance contained in the practice aids.

As of this writing, the special reports, practice aids, and other publications that address the concerns, issues, methodologies, and other aspects of litigation support, forensic accounting services, and valuations include the following:

Special Reports

• Litigation Services and Applicable Professional Standards (03-1)

- Independence and Integrity and Objectivity in Performing Forensic and Valuation Services (08-1)
- Forensic Procedures and Specialists: Useful Tools and Techniques

Practice Aids

- Assets Acquired in a Business Combination to Be Used in Research and Development Activities: A Focus on Software, Electronic Devices, and Pharmaceutical Industries
- Valuation of Privately Held Company Equity Securities Issued as Compensation
- Engagement Letters for Litigation Services (04-1)
- A CPA's Guide to Family Law Services (05-1)
- Calculating Intellectual Property Infringement Damages (06-1)
- Preparing Financial Models (06-2)
- Analyzing Financial Ratios (06-3)
- Calculating Lost Profits (06-4)
- Forensic Accounting and Fraud Investigations (07-1)

Other Publications

- A CPA's Guide to Valuing a Closely Held Business
- CPAs Handbook of Fraud and Commercial Crime Prevention

Although these publications and their content are categorized as nonauthoritative, they provide useful information to practicing professionals. As fledgling fraud examiners and forensic accountants continue to develop their knowledge, skills, and abilities, these and other publications can be included in the professionals' libraries and maintained among their important resources.

Engagement Issues and Professional Responsibility

Fraud examination, forensic accounting, and litigation support activities can expose the traditional accountant to more risk than consulting engagements and, possibly, to more liability than traditional auditors. CPAs may be asked to evaluate business practices and transaction activities, and CPAs are normally engaged by one side or the other—looking for "defense" of their client's choices, decisions, and judgments while taking a critical view of the other side's similar actions.

CPAs and their firms' names may appear in the media, and CPAs may even be accused of using less than professional approaches, turning a "blind eye" to their clients' practices and activities; ignoring or not giving proper disclosure to important assumptions that constitute part of the engagement; as well as other professional shortcomings. Prior to entering into any litigation support, forensic accounting, or fraud examination activity, professionals are encouraged to consider the implications to their business reputation, professional stature, and possibly threats or personal harm or injury that may be attributable to their participation in the disputed issues. As with all engagements, CPAs need to ensure that they currently have or can obtain the necessary skills, training, experience, and other resources required to participate in the resolution of the issues at hand.

An engagement letter is recommended for such work. If a written engagement letter is not provided, the scope of the engagement and other relevant information may be obtained as part of an oral arrangement. If the engagement is agreed upon through verbal discussions, the practicing professional should clearly note the discussion in memo format, paying particular attention to the wording used by the client or the client's attorney.

The written engagement letter should describe the nature and extent of professional services to be provided. If the practicing professional is generating the engagement letter, the specialist should outline the degree of responsibility assumed and any limitations on liability. Importantly, any verbal or written understandings should not describe the expected outcomes of the work to be performed, make any guarantees regarding expected findings or results, and should not commit the practicing professional in any way to a particular position, opinion, or any aspect of the case that is grounded in judgment. That is the responsibility of the judge, jury, or other trier-of-fact.

Practicing professionals, because of the nature of their independence and objectivity, should not accept contingent fee arrangements. Instead, compensation should be based on hours worked and time spent on the engagements. The practicing professional may seek to obtain a retainer in advance. This

simply helps ensure that the client has the ability to pay for the services rendered. If not paid in a timely manner, he or she may seek to suspend the engagement until money has been collected. Further, the professional may withhold the sharing of work product until the fees have been paid. But unpaid fees provide an opportunity for the opposite side and its counsel to attack the professional's independence, judgment, and credibility. Opposing counsel may suggest that the arrangement is of a contingent fee engagement and that fees only be paid upon a favorable resolution for the client, even if this is untrue.

Fraud examination, litigation support, and forensic accounting activities can be staffed like any other engagement. Assistants and other professionals can be used to accomplish duties such as clerical tasks and sophisticated analyses; to conduct and document interviews; and to gather, compile, and analyze important books and records—financial, nonfinancial, and qualitative. However, the engaged professional is responsible for supervising the work performed by others, properly training assistants, and, ultimately, taking responsibility for all conclusions, judgments, decisions, and opinions.

Thus, although testifying professionals need not complete the work themselves, they are expected to be able to describe the nature, extent, and timing of all work performed. They must also be able to defend their conclusions, the outcomes, and their professional opinions. Given the adversarial nature of fraud examination, litigation support, and forensic accounting engagements, practicing professionals should expect their work product to be scrutinized closely, and they should be prepared to describe and defend all choices made.

Like the fraud examiner, the testifying expert should have no opinion concerning the ultimate outcome of the litigation. For practical reasons, the practicing professional is not an attorney, so he or she may not entirely understand or contemplate subtle nuances of the law. Similarly, forensic professionals may be working directly, indirectly, or tangentially with other experts whose areas of expertise may be unfamiliar to them. Thus, forensic accountants need to be wary of and appreciate their reliance on the work of others. From a more professional perspective, the ultimate decision maker is the trier-of-fact—the judge, jury, or other person or body, saddled with the responsibility for deciding the case based on its merits from the evidence offered. The fraud examiner can have no opinion about the guilt or innocence of alleged fraudsters. Similarly, the fraud examiner or forensic accountant should have no opinion concerning the ultimate outcome of the dispute. This position is consistent with practitioners remaining unbiased and performing their work with impartiality. Thus, they do not act as advocates for a client or their allegations, assertions, or positions in a dispute.

Professional standards for expert witnessing do not require independence, as described in the AICPA code of conduct. However, depending on the nature of potential conflicts of interest and other issues of independence, opposing counsel may raise concerns over this to question a practicing professional's credibility and objectivity. Further, although professional standards may not require independence, laws and regulations, such as the Sarbanes–Oxley Act of 2002, may preclude some CPAs from performing litigation support and other similar consulting services under certain circumstances. General standards require professional competence, due professional care, proper engagement planning and supervision, and the collection and analysis of sufficient relevant data to support (provide a reasonable basis for) the conclusions and opinions offered.

Types of Consulting and Litigation Support Activities

Fraud examiners and forensic accountants can be engaged as consultants and experts to provide a wide array of services. First, not every engagement is related to litigation. But fraud examination and forensic accounting professionals get involved in many different aspects of issues that may some day be the subject of litigation. First, fraud examination is a methodology for resolving fraud allegations—from inception to disposition, including obtaining evidence, interviewing, writing reports, and testifying. However, fraud examiners, as designated by the ACFE, also assist in fraud prevention, deterrence, detection, investigation, and remediation. Thus they may be engaged to consult regarding indications or allegations of fraud, but also in any number of other areas. Similarly, CPAs may provide consulting services that are concerned with fraud but are not necessarily fraud examination services, auditing, or litigation support services. These might include the following:[1]

- Assessing the risk of fraud and illegal acts
- Evaluating the adequacy of internal control systems
- Substantive testing of transactions during an attest or a general consulting engagement
- Designing and implementing internal control policies and procedures

- Proactive fraud auditing when fraud is not suspected
- Preparing company codes of business ethics and conduct
- Consulting about employee bonding
- Developing corporate compliance programs

In litigation advisory services, accountants use their knowledge, skills, abilities, experience, training, and education to support legal actions; such activities are normally carried out by forensic accountants and fraud examiners acting as consultants, expert witnesses, masters, and special masters. Even though forensic accountants may provide litigation support services in criminal cases, the majority of them are in the area of civil litigation.[2]

Experts and expert witnesses are professionals who have been offered as such by parties to the litigation. However, the ultimate decision to qualify a witness as an expert is at the judge's discretion. Experts in the litigation advisory services context are expected to provide testimony, before a trier-of-fact, that includes their findings, conclusions, and opinions. Testimony may be provided in any number of venues, including federal, state, or local courts, depositions, regulatory hearings, arbitration, and mediation. Generally, the entire work product of the designated expert is discoverable by the other party. Work product includes not only the expert's report and main analyses, but all notes, work papers, evidentiary materials collected as part of the case, supporting analyses, research, documents, and data reviewed or relied upon by the expert as part of their engagement. Drafts of reports, handwritten notes, and marginalia are all considered part of the expert witnesses' work product. Thus experts need to maintain careful vigilance over all aspects of their work and the impact that it can have on the parties to the litigation. That said, because the professional is not an advocate for one side or the other, the notes, marginalia, and draft reports should not typically be risky; however, they can give insight into how the professional developed conclusions and opinions, uncover any bias in performing the work and other procedures, and shed light on preliminary, but ultimately discarded, theories of the case that opposing counsel may find valuable to their side of the case.

Tools and Techniques: General Discussion

The term *forensic* is generally defined as used in or suitable to courts of law or public debate. When applied to fraud examination or forensic accounting, forensic has evolved to include procedures to gather evidence systematically, using investigative techniques such that the results derived from the procedures can be presented in a court of law or similar setting (arbitration, mediation, regulatory hearing, or other setting) where disputes are heard and resolved. Some of the various professional environments applicable to forensic engagements and fraud examination specifically associated with financial issues and disputes include accounting as well as the following:

- Auditing
- Fraud examination
- Law
- Sociology
- Psychology
- Criminal justice
- Intelligence
- Computer forensics
- Computer data extraction and analysis (data mining)
- Forensic sciences

In addition, most engagements are grounded in a specific industry, competitive environment, and/or business operational settings. Thus, the typical fraud examination, forensic accounting, or litigation support engagement usually requires the development of at least some knowledge of the business models, operational procedures, and other aspects unique to the organization under examination. The purpose of the engagement is to utilize the various methodologies appropriate to the issue at hand, combined with research and investigative skills, to collect, analyze, and evaluate evidence and then to interpret it and communicate the outcomes. Not all engagements in this area constitute litigation support, because, as a practical matter, most engagements do not result in courtroom testimony. Nevertheless, all engagements

require investigative tools and techniques to develop the most accurate and supportable conclusions and opinions. Therefore, the investigation needs to be organized and structured to assist in the evaluation and interpretation of the evidence.

AICPA Practice Aid 07-1 describes seven forensic investigative techniques and compares and contrasts them with similar evidence gathering activities of auditors:

Public Document Reviews and Background Investigations

Public records include information about individuals, businesses, and organizations concerning the entity itself, as well as its owners, executives, managers, employees, related parties, and competitors. They may include real and personal property records, corporate and partnership records, criminal and civil litigation records, stock trading activities for public companies by executives, officers, board members, and managers, inheritance information, birth records, press releases, news reports, and other matters. Records may be evaluated as evidence in a case in many areas, such as opportunity, pressure, or motivation and rationalization, as well as evidence of the elements of fraud: the act, the concealment, or the conversion.

Keep in mind that the elements of fraud and the fraud triangle are often as valuable in litigation support activity as they are in fraud examinations. Although directly applicable to fraud examination, in litigation support engagements, evidence of opportunity, pressure, and incentives and rationalizations are just as important in understanding the actions and motivations of the plaintiffs and defendants. Further, the act, concealment, and conversion provide a powerful investigative basis for evaluating the participation and intentions of a party to litigation.

Although most litigation stops short of fraud, the allegations made by one party against the other often mirror the issues associated with fraud allegations brought to fraud examination engagements. For example, a litigant involved in unethical and possibly fraudulent activities often attempts to conceal those nefarious aspects of their actions. Evidence of activities to hide the questionable transactions and the underlying motivations of the litigants can be used to help judges and juries understand the intent behind those actions. Similarly, showing how the litigants benefited from their actions (conversion), possibly at the expense of the other party, can help judges and juries understand the motives of litigants.

Although auditors rely heavily on documentation that supports transactions generated in the normal course of business, they typically do not often search public records. Auditors rely on documentation provided by clients, such as invoices, bank records, bank statements, etc. Some of those may be generated internally by the client; other documents may be solicited and obtained from third parties. The auditors tend to evaluate such records at face value. For example, an auditor often uses an invoice package to ensure that the transaction is properly reflected in the books and records of the client. The fraud examiner or forensic accountant often uses public records to verify the existence of the vendor business, the vendor's ownership, and the vendor's address and phone number—for investigation of similar phone numbers or addresses of employees. The fraud examiner or forensic accountant may go so far as to call the vendor to verify the contents and details of the invoice to ensure that the invoice is authentic and that the goods and services described therein agree with the books and records of the vendor and that no other terms (e.g., off-invoice side agreements) or conditions are involved. Fraud examiners and forensic accountants may even visit the vendor locations to authenticate the books and records of the transactions of the company under investigation.

Interviews of Knowledgeable Persons

The purpose of an interview is to gather testimonial evidence. Interviews are not normally conducted under oath, so they do not carry the same weight as testimony but are invaluable tools used by the fraud examiner and forensic accountant for gathering information. As discussed in a prior chapter, interviews have different goals, objectives, tools, and techniques than those of admission-seeking interrogations. Interviews are normally performed throughout the engagement to develop background information about the organization, the witnesses, and potential targets, as well as to help identify books, records, documentation, and other information that may be useful. In a litigation support context, the interview may be in the form of a deposition (under oath), and the counsel for whom the professional is working asks the questions.

In litigation-type engagements, forensic accountants and fraud examiners acting as consultants and experts generally do not conduct interrogations in order to obtain admissions of guilt. Such activities are better left to the attorneys involved in the case, because these involve specialized tools and techniques, and the admissibility of the outcomes often hinge upon following proper procedures to ensure that the rights of individuals have not been violated. For example, the person being interrogated may have the right to

have his or her attorney present—a legal issue. Thus, fraud examiners and forensic accountants simply gather information from interviews with witnesses and potential targets.

Auditors interact verbally with clients through inquiry; in fact, these are extensive and an integral part of the audit process. They gather information about procedures, policies, and processes, as well as explanations for red flags, anomalies, client positions, and other client decisions. Audit personnel may inquire about unexpected account balance fluctuations, unanticipated results of transaction testing, the general condition of the business, changes to the client's business model, internal control issues, standard operating procedures, and other matters deemed necessary by the audit team.

Further, all members of the audit team are expected to make inquiries of management, including the audit staff, senior accountants, managers, and partners. These outcomes may be documented as audit evidence or may be the launching point for further analytical procedures, substantive testing, or other work considered necessary. Traditionally, auditors have not been trained in interviewing and interrogation. In contrast, forensic accountants and fraud examiners, generally, have extensive training in assessing both verbal and nonverbal responses and interviewee reactions that may lead the interviewer to conclude the possibility of deceptive or dishonest responses to the questions.

Confidential Sources of Information and Evidence
In some situations, witnesses may be willing to share their knowledge only under the condition that their identities remain confidential. Optimally, each organization has an anonymous tip hotline where employees, vendors, managers, suppliers, customers, and other stakeholders can provide information without divulging who they are. The challenge is that allegations need to be detailed enough so that their reliability may be judged in an efficient and nonintrusionary manner. At least one organization dropped its use of the anonymous tip hotline for external stakeholders because the tips received were usually unsubstantiated personal vendettas rather than communication of important information. The "hidden motive" of the confidential source is a genuine risk to an investigation, and all tips received anonymously should be carefully evaluated before concluding that the allegations are justified. Hidden motives may be from former spouses, business partners, employees, neighbors, and friends. The key is to be able to gather enough information from the confidential source, so that claims can be checked for authenticity, without creating undue suspicion on a potentially innocent person. In some cases, even though the tip may have been made anonymously, the provider may be discovered via a variety of issues, such as the type of information provided or where it was derived. Thus, in some cases, the anonymity of the tip provider may not be able to be protected.

Rather than use confidential sources, auditors tend to complete their work out in the open. However, generally accepted audit standards require that auditors not only gather information from the company being audited but also collect evidence from third parties, usually in the form of confirmations. Auditors typically confirm transaction details, account balances, terms, and conditions of sales, as well as the existence of information not previously outlined in the documentation between the parties. A third party may be unwilling to sign a confirmation stating that "all terms and conditions are described in the confirmation" and that "no other terms and conditions exist" related to the transaction or account balance. Such a refusal should be a significant red flag.

In either case, the auditor, fraud examiner, or forensic accountant has a responsibility to assess the relevance and reliability of the information, whether received from third parties or confidential sources. The auditing or litigation support professional should look to other facts that either support or refute the information provided by individuals or outside entities. Such an approach allows the professional to either corroborate the claims made or disprove them because they do not appear to be supported by a preponderance of the evidence.

Laboratory Analysis of Physical and Electronic Evidence
Forensic accountants and fraud examiners tend to be suspicious about much of the information and data received. For example, in some cases, documents are not only subjected to confirmation with external transaction participants but also subjected to fingerprint analysis and procedures for forgery and/or fictitious or altered documents. Computer forensic specialists have the ability to image hard drives, search for hidden or deleted files and e-mail, as well as search the hard drive contents for various terms, conditions, numerical values, etc. Computer tools can also analyze multiple transactions to draw meaning, extract descriptive statistics, and examine manual and electronic (automatic) journal entries.

Observation is an integral part of all audits. Auditors observe the taking of physical inventories, recount inventories, recalculate account balances, and apply other procedures consistent with the objectives of observation and review of physical audit evidence. Although auditors generally consider that various

types of audit evidence may be created or altered to support transactions and account balances, they tend to react more to aberrations, anomalies, and other issues that come to their attention. Although auditors should rely on their professional skepticism to guide their judgments regarding the authenticity of documentary and other evidence, they typically do not have training and experience to evaluate intentionally altered and manufactured documents. Further, forensic accountants and fraud examiners tend to be more proactive in their search for evidence that corroborates or disputes the information and are more skeptical than auditors—almost always requiring some form of corroboration from multiple sources.

Forensic accountants and fraud examiners generally maintain a high degree of professional skepticism—a level that probably exceeds that of the traditional auditor—because the nature of their work is different. Forensic professionals understand that skilled fraudsters often manipulate the data provided by altering documents or limiting the amount and timing of data made available to the opposing side. Thus, forensic accountants and fraud examiners are more apt to rely on nonfinancial data as a corroboratory technique for evaluating data captured in the financial books and records. They also use data extraction and analysis techniques (e.g., data mining) to identify meaningful patterns, missing information, unusual items, and evidence of management override of the system of internal controls and procedures.

Physical and Electronic Surveillance

Law enforcement professionals engaged in white-collar crime investigations often conduct physical and electronic surveillance. Physical and video surveillance is permitted, but electronic audio evidence (capturing spoken words) requires court permission. The legal standard is the "reasonable expectation of privacy." When in a public place, persons do not have that expectation, but when engaging in telephone conversations, they do. Forensic accountants and fraud examiners do not usually conduct physical, video, or electronic surveillance unless they have the training and experience required to protect them from physical harm and to capture evidence in a competent manner so it is likely to be admissible in court. Although fraud examiners and forensic accountants may not conduct this type of work, it is common for them to receive results from law enforcement professionals or licensed private investigators. They then incorporate the results as evidence in their investigation into other aspects of the fraud examination, litigation support, or forensic accounting engagement.

Auditors seldom use physical, video, and electronic surveillance as a means of developing audit evidence. Generally, notwithstanding physical inventory and fixed assets observations, auditors rely on the books, records, and documents of the auditee, confirmations and other interactions with third parties, and inquiries of management and other personnel. If audit engagement evidence suggests that nefarious activities are taking place, the auditor normally assumes that the predication threshold has been met and calls in other professionals who are more qualified to use physical, video, and electronic surveillance to develop the appropriate evidence.

Undercover Operations

Undercover operations are another tool used primarily by law enforcement and sometimes by private investigators. The goal is that, by putting professionals in close proximity to alleged perpetrators, evidence that is not contained in documents and in other forms can be collected and preserved for use in the larger investigation. The outcomes may lead to the location of important books and records, the identification of previously unknown business partners, bank accounts, assets, and information that may be useful to further an investigation. Generally, neither the forensic accountant nor the fraud examiner has the knowledge, skills, or abilities to develop this type of evidence but may rely on the work of other professionals and incorporate their findings and results into the forensic or fraud investigation. This type of technique requires the trust of the alleged perpetrator, which requires time to develop. Thus, undercover operations generally take a lot of time and require a lot of patience, as well as financial resources. The physical safety of the undercover personnel is also an important consideration. Normally, auditors do not have procedures analogous to undercover operations.

Analysis of Financial Transactions

Forensic accountants and fraud examiners rely heavily on their analysis of financial transactions, the affect on related account balances, and the presentation of such in the financial statements and related notes. What typically separates fraud and forensic accounting professionals from auditors is their enhanced knowledge of fraud schemes and the red flags associated with them. Fraud and forensic professionals also need to have a greater understanding of the probability of any particular fraud scheme occurring and its relative magnitude, given the surrounding facts, circumstances, type of business, the business model, geographic locale, and types of customers, vendors, suppliers, and employees. Armed with the knowledge of the type of schemes that are likely, the red flags such a scheme would generate, the most common attempts at concealment, and the need for conversion (benefit) from

the activity, fraud examiners or forensic accountants can target their interviews and other procedures in a manner that is likely to yield the best information in the most efficient and effective manner. Thus, the fraud or forensic professional uses a targeted approach whether the engagement is centered on proactive fraud auditing or reactions to fraud allegations or suspicions.

Although litigation support activities may not have risen to the point where one side or the other is claiming fraud, the very nature of the adversarial action suggests that at least one side, if not both, have acted in bad faith. These individuals may be separated into two categories: predators or accidental fraudsters. Predators usually have little concern for ethical conduct and tend to be more interested in their own benefit. The accidental fraudster generally starts off with good intentions but, for various reasons, becomes less concerned about being ethical as time passes. Both types face fraud triangle-related issues: pressures (incentives), opportunity, and rationalization. Most investigations of bad acts are centered on the act, the concealment of that act, and the conversion or benefit arising therefrom. Fraud examiners and forensic accountants understand these issues from the outset and orient their work to answer the questions who, what, when, where, how, and why in the context of the fraud triangle and the elements of fraud centered on the issues associated with the bad act.

The analysis of financial transactions—vertical, horizontal, and ratio analysis—is central to the traditional audit. Auditors trace individual transactions through the books and records to their presentation and disclosure in the financial statements. They examine the accounts, transactions, and balances for management's financial statement assertions—existence, valuation, completeness, rights and obligations, and presentation and disclosure. Auditors also incorporate financial, nonfinancial, and qualitative data into their audit work.

The primary difference between fraud and forensic professionals and auditors is the relative degree of evidentiary support. Auditors are expected to maintain a degree of professional skepticism; however, they consider evidence at face value. Generally, fraud and forensic professionals require more corroboration.

Fraud examiners and forensic accountants are more aware of the issues associated with concealment and thus often require additional evidence to be convinced about the existence, timing, and nature of any transaction, account balance, or amount presented and disclosed in the financial records. Auditors also work within the confines of "fairly presented" and "not materially misstated." These characterizations limit the work of the auditor to those observed anomalies, red flags, and audit issues that are likely to have a material effect on the financial statements such that the financial statements may not be fairly presented.

Forensic accountants and fraud examiners are generally more concerned that an anomaly or two may actually just be the tip of the proverbial iceberg, and they are not likely to be satisfied until that anomaly has been considered from every angle and exhaustively examined. Auditors, on the other hand, are unlikely to pursue those issues, beyond putting specific anomalies to rest.

COMMERCIAL DAMAGES

Commercial damages provide a challenge to the forensic accountant because the cases vary considerably. The tools and techniques that work in one case may not work in another. More diverse than the tools and techniques are the fact patterns, circumstances, available evidence, and types of issues that require resolutions to the underlying dispute. In addition, the types of businesses and organizations and their related industries vary from one case to the next.

In each litigation support engagement, the forensic accountant must quickly get up to speed on key aspects of the business model, the industry, competition, operational performance, and financial profitability. Furthermore, the number of issues in dispute and the complexity of the case drive the amount of work required.

The ability to estimate damages is both an art and a science. The science comes from the understanding and appropriate use of proper accounting methods (i.e., generally accepted accounting procedures or "GAAP"). The art comes from knowing how the accounting information is used to create the required components of the damages estimate. The science is driven by the nature of the asserted damages, the complexity of the case, the underlying type of liability claimed, and other aspects. In some instances, the availability of data helps determine the types of analyses required. Critical thinking skills are important in litigation support engagements and to detect and investigate allegations of fraud.

At a basic level, the plaintiff and the defendant tell two different stories and have differing explanations for what happened and why, using similar facts that have been entered into evidence. As such, some of the damage calculations are, at least, partially affected by the diverse perspectives. The forensic

accountant as an independent, objective professional must examine those two storylines (who, what, when, where, how, and why) and compare those positions to the evidence. Often the evidence is in the form of deposition testimony of the fact witnesses and the professional expert's opinions. Important to the fraud or forensic professional's case are the various elements of financial evidence gathered, which is usually gathered by subpoenas traded by the opposing parties, but which also may be collected independently from publicly available sources, such as the Secretary of State's office.

In most damage and valuation litigation engagements, the forensic accountant is hired by one side or the other—the plaintiff or the defendant. The plaintiff usually seeks large damage awards, whereas the defendant generally tries to minimize the amount of the liability. Forensic professionals should be independent, objective, and unbiased and, as such, must prepare a defensible damage estimate. In most cases, attorneys prefer to know the estimated damages, even if that estimate is bad news for their client. Accurate, timely, and professional advice helps the attorney to formulate effective strategies for pursuing the case, including negotiated settlement, arbitration, mediation, or civil trial. Furthermore, recognizing that their reputation in the professional community is a valuable asset, no case is worth jeopardizing the professionals' integrity.

Legal Framework for Damages

Generally, in order to pursue a claim for legal damages successfully, the injured party must prove two points:

- **Liability:** That the other party was liable for all or part of the damages claimed
- **Damages:** That the injured party suffered damages as the result of the actions or lack of actions of the offending party

To prove that damages were sustained, the injured party also needs to prove three additional elements. First, that the accused party was the direct or proximate cause of the damages, by either causing or contributing to them as a result of their conduct. Second, the amount must be calculable to a reasonable degree of certainty. Third, the accused parties should have been reasonably able to foresee that damages were likely to accrue as a result of their conduct. Note that such conduct may include action or inaction; either may lead to large damage awards.

Generally, damages result from a tort or breach of contract. With a tort, the action itself leads to direct harm. In breach of contract, the relationship between the parties was previously defined in an agreement, and the courts are asked to interpret that contract. Some cases involve millions of dollars and may hinge on a single word or phrase found within a contract of hundreds of pages. Some clauses that seem clear at the inception of a contract are later interpreted differently by the parties. In those situations where the parties cannot reach agreement, the courts are asked to settle the matter. Further, no contract can anticipate every contingency. Those aspects of the relationship between the parties that are not specified in the contract are subject to negotiation; if the parties cannot negotiate a reasonable basis for moving forward, they may choose to litigate the matter and let the courts decide.

Torts, on the other hand, occur when a party has been injured, even though the parties to the suit do not have a contractual relationship. Torts may include theft, fraud, infringement of trademarks, copyrights, trade secrets or other intellectual property, professional malpractice, defamation, or negligence.

Causality is central to the issue of damages. Even if the damages sustained by a plaintiff are substantial but the impact of the defendant's actions cannot clearly and conclusively be associated with them, the plaintiff may not prevail in the action. The plaintiff's goal is to connect the plaintiff's conduct with the damages sustained. Plaintiffs may use graphics, such as timelines, or statistical methods to demonstrate the alleged causality between the defendant's conduct and their harm.

Types of Commercial Damages

Successful plaintiffs may be awarded different types of damages:

- Compensatory
- Economic loss or restitution
  - Lost wages
  - Incremental or incidental expenses

- Lost profits
- Lost value
- Reliance
- Punitive
- Special

Compensatory damages are those amounts designed to compensate the injured party for some specific loss. Economic loss or restitution damages compensate for a specific loss and recognize that the damages carry into future periods. Reliance damages put the injured parties back where they would have been if the cause of action had not happened. Punitive damages are monetary awards that have the intention of punishing the defendant sufficiently to act as a financial deterrent, to discourage similar actions in the future. Finally, courts may award special damages to plaintiff or defendants.

The Loss Period

One of the first steps in measuring commercial damages is determining the loss period. For a breach of contract claim, it is generally the remaining term of the contract. However, exceptions are sometimes warranted. In some cases, a period other than the contract term is more appropriate:

1. If the contract term is very long, courts may be reluctant to enforce it because of issues of uncertainty, especially in industries where contracts are altered prior to the completion of the full term
2. In other cases, the damages may extend beyond the contract term because the parties have a history of extending or renewing prior contracts

Thus, although the contract period may appear to be the logical choice, the facts and circumstances may indicate that a different measurement period is more appropriate.

The measurement period for commercial damages related to torts can be more difficult because, unlike breach of contract claims, a preliminary starting point is not available. With torts, the loss period starts when the tort begins and ends when business returns to normal—either when revenues rebound or expenses decline to appropriate levels. The damage period for a tort can be considered closed, open, or infinite. It can be infinite when the damaged company has effectively been put out of business. In such cases, business operations and performance obviously can never return to normal. A closed period, on the other hand, is when there is a loss in sales or additional expenses during a time frame that can be reasonably defined, which has ended prior to the calculation of damages. An open period of damages indicates that, at the time of the forensic work, the damage period still exists and is expected to continue into the future.

Economic Framework for Damages

Commercial damages do not occur in a vacuum. The amount of loss may be affected by the general economy, the conditions of the industry, the damaged entity's competitive environment, and other specific issues. In some cases, the damage assessment may be restricted to the organization without great formal evaluation given to the economy, industry, and competition because their impact is judged negligible. Therefore, even if not formally documented, this may be an inherent assumption behind the work of the anti-fraud professional or forensic accountant.

The impact of the overall economy on the entity under study and on the particular types and amounts of damages being sought is the first step in documenting losses as a result of commercial liability—tort or breach of contract. The global and national economies are cyclical, usually either expanding or contracting. For the United States, one of the most prominent indicators of the national economy is the gross domestic product (GDP). The more GDP generated, the better the economy is. Although very large firms are often affected by global or national economic trends, smaller firms can also be affected by regional economic conditions. If need be, economic performance can be further localized by evaluating a state, city, county, town, or even, in some cases, at the neighborhood level. Although data on the global, national, and, in some cases, the regional economy tend to be gathered with regularity and made available to the public, economic indicators by state, city, county, town, or neighborhood vary considerably by the amount of data available and how long it takes to have these data collected, summarized, analyzed, and released to the public. Nevertheless, the fraud examiner and forensic accountant should give consideration to the appropriate economic conditions as a starting point for any damage analysis.

Once the appropriate overall economic data have been identified and the impact, if any, on the damage claim has been assessed, the next level of consideration is the industry. It consists of the number of organizations that offer similar products or services and possibly compete with one another for customers and market share. An industry can be assessed based on the number of competitors, the degree of concentration, and the extent of vertical integration. Competition, combined with the overall economic conditions, often explains at least some portion of the organization's performance and thus may be an integral part of the damages analysis. It tends to follow the performance of the overall industry. When it is growing and performing well, the average organization tends to perform in a similar manner. The overall condition of the industry and its growth can be assessed on numerous levels, including sales and revenues, shipments to customers and around the world, employment levels, and other financial and nonfinancial dimensions.

The U.S. Department of Commerce tracks numerous statistics based on SIC (standard industrial classification) code. Further, companies such as Moody's, Value-Line, and others provide periodic industrial performance metrics. Like the overall economic data, the applicability of the industry data to a firm-specific damage claim cannot be arbitrarily assumed. The firm subject to damages analysis may be on the fringes of the industry and have very little in common with it. At the other end of the spectrum, the industry may have few participants, and the company under study may be the largest participant and overall driver of industry performance. Thus, even though the company and industry data are highly correlated, they have little meaning.

Notwithstanding the appropriate means by which industry data should be incorporated in damage analysis, the industry should be examined for the damage period or left out for appropriate reasons. Related to the overall industry, when appropriate, the performance of the entity under study to its key competitors may be an important part. The damaged organization can be compared along the dimensions of economies of scale—critical supplier and customer relations, technological advantages and shortcomings, life cycle of the company and its products—that help the fraud examiner or forensic accountant to understand the organization's situation.

Once the economic and industry data have been gathered and evaluated for applicability, and assessed for impact on firm performance, the next step is to compare them to those of the firm under consideration. As a starting point, financial statement data should be gathered, including balance sheets to assess financial condition; income statements to assess operational performance; and cash flow statements to determine the sources and uses of cash; and the ability of the company to generate cash flows from operations, invest in the future of the organization, and examine choices for financing (obtaining debt and equity capitals and paying returns on that capital in the form of dividends and principal repayments).

Optimally, the financial statements should be collected on a monthly basis, but, in many cases, quarterly and annual financial data will suffice. In addition to financial statements, another important source can be tax returns. They not only show the taxable income and other information provided to the Internal Revenue Service, but the return also has an annual balance sheet and a reconciliation of book to tax income. Another important source of data to assess commercial damage amounts is subsidiary, regional, divisional, and other financial statement data breakdowns. In many cases, the alleged liability (the cause of the damages) affects only a portion of the business, and such internal breakdowns allow for a more fine-tuned analysis and estimation of damages.

Finally, nonfinancial data are often very important for developing and evaluating the reasonableness of damage claims. Although it is not always available, the ability to break the financial statement numbers into prices and quantities can be valuable. Although it can be difficult to evaluate the numbers in financial statements, nonfinancial data (volumes or quantities) allow the data to be broken into prices and quantities (p's and q's). Then, each element can be considered independently and in concert with an effort to develop and evaluate damages.

Other important considerations can be the historical performance and financial conditions, rates of growth (historical and projected), sales data, and sales by product-line, key customers, regions, and divisions. Fraud and forensic accounting professionals understand that, for financial statements, the account balances and the accounting for specific transactions and groups of transactions—such as accounts receivable—are often affected by the numerous discretionary choices made by accountants. Executives and managers make choices about the applicability of specific, generally accepted accounting principles; the discretionary aspects of applying them; the necessity of using estimated and other judgments to determine the amounts reflected in the books and records; and the impact of unusual, one-time (nonrecurring) transactions.

These discretionary aspects are available so that financial managers and executives can make choices that best reflect the overall economic performance of the business. These can also be used for less than desirable goals, such as managing earnings and hitting one-time performance goals and objectives. Moreover,

they present the opportunity for management override of internal controls—in order to record fictitious journal entries; develop unsupportable accounting judgments and estimates; and record unusual, one-time events that do not reflect the economics of the underlying transactions. Such manipulations can also be systematic and embedded in the processes that have an impact on regularly recorded transaction amounts.

Using the financial and nonfinancial data collected, one of the most common firm-specific assessments is ratio analysis. Ratios are normally categorized as liquidity, profitability, efficiency, or capital structure ratios. The categories, specified in AICPA Practice Aid 06-3, *Analyzing Financial Ratios*, include the following:

Liquidity ratios

Current ratio

Quick ratio

Working capital

Inventory to working capital

Current assets turnover

Inventory to current liabilities

Profitability ratios

Gross profit percentages

Operating profit percentages

Net income before taxes (NIBT) percentage

Net income after taxes (NIAT) percentage

Return on equity
Return on assets

Efficiency ratios

Accounts receivable turnover

Accounts receivable collection period

Inventory turnover

Inventory to days in inventory

Operating cycle

Accounts payable turnover

Accounts payable days outstanding

Asset turnover

Net revenue to working capital turnover

Net fixed assets to stockholder's equity

Capital structure ratios

Debt to equity

Current debt to equity

Operating funds to current portion of long-term debt

Times interest earned

Long-term debt to equity

In addition, the growth in sales and revenues, accounts receivable, inventory, and accounts payable should approximately align with one another. If not, one should investigate the reasons.

Finally, an assessment of cash flows can also be useful. First, operating cash flows should be positive (i.e., meaning that the company is generating cash flows from operations). Maybe more importantly, cash flows from operations should generally be greater than operating income because of the add-back of depreciation and other noncash expenses to income (assuming that the indirect method is used to create the statement of cash flows). Normally, cash flows from investing transactions should be negative, indicating that the company is investing in its future. Whether these dollars have been targeted to the appropriate

long-term assets is a qualitative assessment that must be made. But it does not negate the expectation that investing cash flows be negative (for companies in growth and development stages).

Finally, financing cash flows can have either a positive or negative sign. Financing cash flows being positive suggests that equity and/or debt investors believe in the future of the company, and it also may indicate that the company will be expanding. Likewise, negative financing cash flows can be associated with dividend payments and debt principal payments. Qualitative assessments are required to determine whether the financing cash flows reflect preliminary signs of positive or deteriorating financial condition. Each of these assessments can be compared to industry norms, those of key competitors, and those of the company under study over time.

Quantifying Lost Revenues and Increased Expenses

The accepted concept for measuring lost revenues or excess expenses over a loss period is to project incremental lost sales or increased expenses. Essentially, the lost revenues are those that the damaged entity could have expected except for the actions of the adversarial party. Similarly, incremental expenses are those additional expenses incurred as a result of the actions of the adversarial party. A number of methods can be used to develop incremental lost sales or excess expenses; some of those are discussed in the following. Notwithstanding the choice of methodology, the anti-fraud professional or forensic accountant has two competing goals: a high degree of accuracy and simplicity.

The value of simplicity is that proving the foundations for the claim is relatively straightforward it is likely that the other side, the judge, and the jury understand the method and calculations. However, one risk with simplified methods is that they may be subject to attack, because they oversimplify the estimate of damages, and thus they may not meet the threshold of being provable with a reasonable degree of scientific certainty. More sophisticated methodologies may be more complete and accurate, but they risk the problem of being complicated and difficult to communicate.

Even if the trier-of-fact or other parties understand the methodologies and their inherent subtleties, they may not give the method the credibility it deserves, and that could affect the outcome of the court action. Thus, the anti-fraud professional or forensic accountant is left with the goal of trying to measure the damages in the most accurate, yet simple method, recognizing the threshold of a reasonable degree of scientific certainty.

Some of the decisions that need to be made include the following:

- The base amount of revenues or expenses, usually based on historical experience
- The choice of revenue or expense growth rates, recognizing that influences outside the control of the company (e.g., inflation, seasonality, prior forecasting accuracy for the industry, competition, or the organization under examination) have at least some impact on expected rates over time
- Whether historical rates of growth are applicable to the damage period
- Whether relatively straightforward calculations, using a tool such as Excel, are reasonable, or whether more sophisticated methods, such as regression, statistical, or econometric methods are better suited

Regardless of what choices are made, every method and calculation inherently incorporates certain assumptions and relies on the judgment of the professional. Ultimately, the decisions need to be described and outlined in oral or verbal reports and defended during a deposition or in court. As such, the professionals need to ask themselves: "Do the outcomes make sense?" Sometimes, damage estimates appear perfectly reasonable and defensible on the surface, but, when examined more closely, they are not. For example, consider the damage claim where a supplier—one of many, to a reseller—makes a damage claim that asserts they were not given credit for units supplied by them to the reseller, and the undercredited units total more than the company sold in its entirely. The damage claim makes no sense, because it claims more units than the company sold, not recognizing that the allegedly damaged supplier provided no more than 5 percent of the total units available for sale. When carefully examined, the damage claim looks ridiculous, but it has been made because professionals build up a damage claim but fail to take a step back and look at the damage amount from different angles and different perspectives. With revenues, the anti-fraud professional or forensic accountant must consider whether the organization has the infrastructure (operating capacity, fixed assets in place, intellectual horsepower, etc.) in order to meet the demands of the customers. If these are required, that cost needs to be deducted from projected lost sales.

Some of the methods that can be used to develop estimates of lost sales and incremental expenses include the following:

The Before and After Method. This compares sales and expenses before the actions or inactions of the adversarial party to those same financial statement line items after the action or inaction of the defendant. The method assumes that the actions or inactions of the opposing party had a direct impact on these line items and that, "but for" those, the results before would have been achievable. Because this method considers the historical amounts in the books and records as a basis for estimating lost sales or incremental expenses, it is not subject to as much dispute as some other methods. That said, fraud examiners or forensic accountants should consider other factors that could have effects on the "after" performance of the entity. At a minimum, professionals need to be able to defend their theory.

The Benchmark ("Yardstick") Method. This method assumes that some data exist that can be used to demonstrate how the revenues and expenses related to the liability claim for the loss period would have performed "but for" the actions or lack thereof by the adversarial party. According to AICPA Practice Aid 06-4, "Calculating Lost Profits," typical benchmarks may include the following:

- The performance of the plaintiff at different locations
- The plaintiff's actual experience, versus budgeted results from prior periods
- The actual experience of a similar business unaffected by the defendant's actions
- Comparable experience and projections by nonparties
- Industry averages
- Pre-litigation projections
- Profits realized by the defendant as a result of his or her actions related to the disputed revenues or incremental expenses. (An alternative way of looking at this is that the defendant, assuming a guilty verdict, may be required to disgorge wrongly obtained profits.)

Determining Lost Profits

Although the liability claim alleged by the plaintiff against the defendant is often centered on lost revenues and/or incremental expenses, the actual amount of damages is a function of lost profits. Thus, any incremental lost revenues or incurred expenses require additional evaluation that considers the impact on "bottom-line" net income or some appropriate derivation (e.g., cash flows) for at least a couple of reasons. First, from a practical perspective, in order to generate incremental revenues, most companies incur at least some increased expenses. In order for the best estimate to be developed, incremental costs, expenses, and infrastructure need to be subtracted from the incremental revenues. Second, the damaged party has a duty to mitigate its damages. As such, this obligation may result in incremental revenues from other sources. Conversely, the generation or reduction of some expenses might mitigate losses.

One example is related to a farmer. Assume that he loses a contract to provide corn to a distributor, and, as a result of market oversupply, no other distributors are willing to buy corn from the farmer. Assuming that the field is also in such a condition to grow a substitute crop—such as soybeans—the farmer is obligated to do so, even if the soybean contract is less profitable than that for corn. In this circumstance, the best estimate of damages not only assumes lost profits related to the loss of corn sales; it may also be reduced by the benefits of reasonable steps (e.g., the planting of soybeans) to mitigate its losses, whether or not such steps were actually taken.

One might assume that gross profit is a good starting point for determining incremental profits. However, the portion of gross profit attributed to the cost of goods sold may include some fixed costs, particularly if the damaged party is a manufacturer, and the assumption that all cost of goods sold is a variable (incremental) cost may be erroneous. Further, in addition to variable/incremental costs incorporated in gross profit, other expenses related to selling and distributing may also be incremental.

For example, many companies generate incremental sales through advertising and marketing campaigns. Likewise, salespersons often receive commissions based on actual sales and hitting various levels of sales volume. Other costs, such as incremental labor, shipping, administration, and miscellaneous expenses, may be incurred in order to expect reasonably to generate the incremental sales. There may also be cases where incremental revenues have zero associated incremental costs. An example of this is where the company was not given proper credit for sales by a distributor, but the company had, in fact, provided those

incremental goods and services and thus had incurred incremental costs. In such a case, the damage claim is the amount of sales that were not credited to the plaintiff and excludes associated variable costs.

The definition of lost profits needs to be explored as well. Most commercial damage claims assume lost profits—incremental revenues less incremental expenses—and other costs required to generate the lost sales. However, AICPA Practice Aid No. 7, "Litigation Services," indicates that losses can be characterized using a number of metrics, including lost profits, lost value, lost cash flows, net revenue, and incremental costs. The fraud examiner or forensic accountant needs to evaluate which of these metrics or some other is best suited to measure the damages applicable to the case, facts, and circumstances at hand.

Determining Incremental Costs

Although incremental revenues can be determined using the methodologies discussed previously, properly isolating incremental costs and expenses can be trickier. Incremental costs are defined as those incurred as a result of the plaintiff's action or inaction that would otherwise not be incurred (a type of damages) and those additional costs required in order to realize the projections of incremental lost revenues. First, as discussed previously, incremental costs associated with revenues may include infrastructure requirements, in order for the plaintiff to have the capacity necessary. Thus, some incremental costs are not those normally considered expenses associated with generally accepted accounting principles (GAAP). Second, as a starting point, in order to isolate incremental expenses, the anti-fraud professional or forensic accountant needs to be able to identify the type of cost.

At the most basic level, cost behavior can be described as fixed or variable. Fixed costs are those that do not change with the level of output (e.g., sales). In contrast, variable costs are those that move directly with output, such as sales. A few concepts need to be further discussed. First, when analyzing fixed costs, many make the mistake of assuming that fixed costs exist at zero output. The assumption is that, when the producing unit is completely inactive or shut down, fixed costs exist. Although that assessment of fixed costs is valid, most organizations cannot operate at zero output levels. More organizational output operates in some range of volume called the "relevant range."

Cost behavior should not be evaluated at zero production levels unless the levels are part of the relevant range. Zero production levels may be appropriate if one organization, the plaintiff, was put out of business by the defendant. In such a case, the relevant range may be zero units. However, assuming that the company produced 100,000 units but expected to produce (and sell) 110,000 units "but for" the actions of the defendant, the relevant range is between 100,000 and 110,000 units. It is the behavior of costs in this range, fixed and variable, that are appropriate for analysis purposes.

Further, some costs exhibit semi-fixed, semi-variable, or mixed. Take for example the output of one unit of labor (e.g., one incremental employee or one shift of workers). That unit has an ability or potential to produce some level of output, such as 20,000 tons of coal per day. If this unit is currently producing only 7,500 tons, the cost is fixed until the unit produces an incremental 12,500 tons per day. Once the incremental output reaches 20,000 tons of coal per day, in order to reach beyond those 20,000 units, incremental costs must be incurred. Those costs could include overtime, additional labor, or more shifts. Thus, if the relevant range included 5,000 to 30,000 incremental units, this cost behaves in a semi-variable manner. The cost is fixed for some time; once the output unit crosses the threshold of 20,000 units/day, the variable nature of the cost kicks in, and additional expense must be incurred.

A second example is related to computer servers. Each can house and process only so much data for any given period of time. Until the computer server reaches capacity, no incremental costs are required, and the cost is fixed. However, once it reaches capacity, another computer server must be added, and the costs become variable. In a similar manner, the computer server might require periodic software patches, maintenance, and updates. These aspects are variable. Unfortunately, in the world in which we operate, most costs tend to be mixed, semi-variable, or semi-fixed.

The fixed and variable nature of cost behavior may also change with time; a cost that is initially fixed may become variable, and vice versa. For example, an organization may own computer equipment for some time and then switch to a leasing arrangement where the costs are associated directly with volume of use. Thus, the anti-fraud professional or forensic accountant needs to analyze costs carefully in his or her effort to identify incremental increases.

Other concerns that must be considered include the following:

- **Allocated costs.** Not all costs can be directly associated with the activities that drive it. Other costs, such as administration and management, are indirectly associated with units of output. In many cases, in order to derive a sense of profitability by product, by product line, by segment, by division, etc.,

the organization allocates those costs not specifically identifiable with the units of output. These must be carefully analyzed to ensure that the basis is reasonable and defendable and that the true incremental costs have been isolated and allocated. Costs at the unit level can easily be evaluated as to their incremental nature, but those occurring at the batch level, production level, facility level, or back-office administrative level are far more difficult to isolate.

- **Accounting estimates.** A significant number of GAAP expenses require estimates. Examples include bad debts, warranty costs, returns and allowances, etc. In addition, at period end, in order to determine profitability, accountants attempt to get revenues in the appropriate period based on the revenue recognition principle, and they try to match expenses against revenues using the matching principle. Getting revenues and expenses in the right period also requires assumptions and estimates by the accountant. These judgments can have a significant impact on incremental revenue and expense calculation and should be carefully studied.

The methods for determining cost behavior include the following:

- Account analysis
- High to low method
- Graphics
- Statistical (regression, survey, and sampling)
- Engineering

When using the account analysis method, the anti-fraud professional or forensic accountant examines each general ledger account, each financial statement or tax return line item, or other identifiable category of costs from the books and records to understand the types included and the behavior exhibited by that account or cost category. This method is relatively inexpensive, requires interaction between the professional and entity representatives, and can only be defended with experience and good judgment.

The high to low method is a little more analytical in its approach, yet it is simple and easy to use and often serves as a starting point for more detailed analysis. The basic formula is $y = a + bx$, where

a is the fixed cost

b is the variable cost or slope of the cost

x is the independent variable or unit of output

y is the dependent or incremental cost

b is determined as follows

$$= \frac{\$ \text{ cost at the high level of output} - \$ \text{ cost at the low level of output}}{\text{Units of output at the high level} - \text{Units of output at the low level}}$$

$$= \frac{\text{Incremental \$ cost}}{\text{Incremental unit volume}}$$

$$= \text{Variable cost per unit of output}$$

For example, assume the following facts:

	Cost	Volume
High volume	$12,500	1,000
Low volume	$9,500	600
Incremental	$3,000	400

$$b = (\$12,500 - \$9,500 = \$3,000)/(1,000 - 600 = 400) = \$7.50$$

$$a = y - bx$$

$$= \$12,500 - (\$7.50 * 1,000)$$

$$= \$5,000$$

Proof:

High level: Total variable costs = $7.50 * 1,000 = $7,500

High level: Fixed costs = $12,500 − $7,500 = $5,000

Low level: Total variable costs = $7.50 * 750 = $4,500

Low level: Fixed costs = $9,500 − $4,500 = $5,000

A third methodology includes developing and examining graphs of the data that include costs and volumes. This analysis is useful when lots of data points and a clear association between costs and volume exist. For many real-world applications, one or both of those attributes is not available in enough quantity to discern a pattern.

A fourth methodology assumes some statistical approach. Like graphs, statistical methods require a large number of data points. Statistically, number, survey, experimental data can be evaluated. They require more sophistication in order to use them properly, and they require more skill in order to communicate and defend the results.

Finally, engineering studies can be conducted to isolate cost-volume relationships. The average fraud examiner or forensic accountant is generally not qualified to complete this type of work. However, such scientifically based engineering approaches can form the inputs for additional analysis by fraud examiners and forensic accountants. Engineering-type studies typically require a fair amount of time and are more expensive than other methods for isolating incremental costs.

The Time Value of Money

The use of money is not free. Similarly, money that is earned (e.g., profits or positive cash flows) may be used to earn additional money. When money could have been collected, the principles associated with the time value of money must be considered in the analysis. It may affect two different aspects of claims for damages. First, pre-judgment interest is used to denote lost profits that could or would have been earned prior to the date that the legal issue is resolved. The second aspect related to the time value of money is that associated with profits that will be earned with a reasonable degree of scientific certainty in the future—after the legal dispute is over. In both cases, the issue considers the risks involved in achieving the calculated results.

First, pre-judgment interest is associated with claims made for lost incremental profits before the matter can be resolved between the parties. It is therefore common for courts to award pre-judgment interest. The amount is often set by the courts or statutorily by legislation. For example, some states award pre-judgment interest of 10 percent annually, starting when the breach of contract or tortuous interference first occurred and ending when the dispute is resolved. In other cases, professionals are asked to offer testimony and evidence on an appropriate rate. Typically, the minimum is the risk-free rate on U.S. Treasury bills.

Some claim that what one could have earned on other types of debt instruments traded in the public domain do not fully compensate the plaintiff for the lost opportunity cost to invest in assets for which the risks are higher but the expected return is also higher. In such cases, it can be argued that the damaged organization should be awarded pre-judgment interest equal to its weighted average cost of capital (WACC). The methodology for calculating this is discussed in more detail later, and this topic is given extensive coverage in most finance textbooks.

The second aspect related to the time value of money are those amounts that would only be realized in future periods, after the dispute has been resolved between the parties. Essentially, the time value of money suggests that $1 dollar in my pocket today is worth more than $1 dollar that I do not receive until some future date. Conversely, if I must normally wait for that $1 dollar until some future period, but I can accept a cash payment today, I should be willing to accept less because I do not have to wait for that money and can put the cash to use immediately. Thus, $1 dollar to be received in the future is worth something less than $1 dollar if I can receive that lesser amount now.

In investment deals, venture capital as an example, discounted interest rates used to reduce future profits into today's dollars for valuation purposes can be significant. Observing venture capital interest rates in excess of 25 to 30 percent is not uncommon for some high-risk investments. Further, an organization's cost of equity capital can exceed 20 percent. Although courts have provided no overall guidance for estimating the appropriate discount rate, prior court rulings have indicated that they are most likely

(but not always) to assess discount (interest) rates that are far less than those required to complete venture capital deals or fund an organization's equity. The following list of cases was provided in AICPA Practice Aid 06-4, "Calculating Lost Profits."

Court Case	Interest Rate
American List Corp v. U.S. News and World Report, Inc. (1989)	18 % was rejected
Burger King Corp v. Barnes (1998)	9 %
Diesel Machinery, Inc. v. B. R. Lee Industries (2005)	Risk-free rate
Energy Capital v. United States (2002)	10 %
Fairmont Supply Company v. Hooks Industrial, Inc. (2005)	33–36 %
Knox v. Taylor (1999)	7 %
Kool, Mann, Coffee & Co. v. Coffee (2002)	18.5 %
Olson v. Neiman's (1998)	19.4 %
Schonfeld v. Hilliard (1999)	8 %

The cost of equity can be developed using a number of approaches. The build-up approach assumes that the starting point for the cost of equity capital is the risk-free rate. To that base, adjustments are made for systematic risk associated with an equity investment premium, size, and industry. The industry adjustment can be positive or negative. An adjustment for unsystematic risk, positive or negative, is also common using the build-up method. Unsystematic risk is usually associated with a number of company-specific factors, including the organization's financial condition, the quality and depth of management, the company's products and/or services and customer base, the competitive environment, and other factors affecting projected cash flows. Other methodologies that are beyond the scope of this text include the capital asset pricing model (CAPM), arbitrage pricing theory, the Fama-French three-factor model, and the weighted average cost of capital (WACC).

Communicating and Defending the Results of Commercial Damage Estimates

Regardless of the choices made and the underlying assumptions, the "tire hits the road" for anti-fraud professionals or forensic accountant when they communicate and defend their work. This process tends to be iterative, in the sense that issues may arise at various points as the court action proceeds, and these issues may require anti-fraud professionals or forensic accountants to revisit their work and evaluate it from new perspectives, based on data and testimony. Beyond completing the assignment at the highest levels of competence and quality, communicating and defending one's work are some of the most important aspects of consulting, litigation support, and being an expert witness. The venues where the fraud examiner or forensic accountant can expect to be evaluated, scrutinized, challenged, etc. include the following:

- Periodic meetings with attorneys for whom you have been engaged
- Pre-judgment testimony related to summary judgment
- Meetings with counsel where they determine how to proceed with the case
- The written report
- Deposition testimony
- Regulatory or administrative hearings
- Alternate dispute resolution forums such as mediation or arbitration
- Trial testimony
  - Direct examination
  - Cross examination
  - Re-direct examination
  - Re-cross

In addition to communicating and defending one's own work, the fraud examiner or forensic accountant is often asked to critique the expert engaged by the opposing side. At all times, the professional needs to maintain his or her independence and objectivity and be sure not to become emotionally involved in the process or its outcomes.

Communications—whether oral or written—that are related to work performed should reflect the professional's neutral and objective position. They should avoid conclusions concerning the ultimate resolution of the dispute or the likely appropriate findings of the judge or jury. The trier-of-fact has the ultimate decision, and the fraud examiner or forensic accountant should avoid usurping that responsibility. That said, the experts are expected to have opinions, conclusions, and findings and their interpretation. It's a fine line between having professional, defendable opinions, conclusions, and findings related to one's expertise and trampling on those that are better left to others because of their expertise, assignment, or responsibility under the law.

Reports created by fraud examiners and forensic accountants can take on many formats, including that of a letter, memorandum, affidavit, declaration, or summary, which usually provide an overall view of the main opinions, describe the bases for them, and include at least some charts, graphs, tables, or exhibits that summarize some of the important analyses. A reservation should be included similar to the following: "Should additional information become available, facts become known, or additional inquiry arises, I reserve the right to modify or supplement the analysis as necessary." Attached to the report may be detailed schedules, exhibits, copies of specific pieces of evidence, and other important work product necessary for the reader to understand its contents.

VALUATIONS

Valuation engagements are created to value a business, business ownership interest, security, or intangible asset. Similar to the estimates associated with commercial damages, in the case of these engagements, the work of the fraud examiner or forensic accountant requires professional competence and judgment. The AICPA provides guidance for CPAs in this area in the form of Statement on Standards for Valuation Services No. 1 (June 2007). This standard addresses overall engagement considerations, development of the valuation, the valuation report and appendices, with illustrative lists of assumptions, limiting conditions, and glossaries. Although the statement establishes standards only for AICPA members, the material can be useful to others performing valuation services, including those required in consulting, litigation support, and expert witness engagements.

A number of organizations have also developed certifications for professionals who work with valuation issues. The American Society of Appraisers (ASA) awards both an "Accredited Senior Appraiser" and an "Accredited Member" designation. The National Association of Certified Valuation Analysts (NACVA) awards the "Certified Valuation Analyst (CVA)" designation. The American Institute of Certified Public Accountants (AICPA) has an "Accredited in Business Valuation" (ABV). Finally, the Association for Investment Management and Research (AIMR) recognizes a "Chartered Financial Analyst" designation that includes significant coverage of valuation issues. Each of these groups provides members with training and education opportunities, including introductory and advance courses, continuing professional education, seminars, and periodic conferences.

Overall Engagement Considerations

Anti-fraud or forensic accounting professionals should undertake those examinations where they can reasonably expect to complete the work with professional competence, recognizing that valuations require specialized knowledge, skills, and abilities. In assessing what is necessary to complete a valuation engagement with professional competence, one should consider the ability to identify, gather, and analyze the relevant data; apply the appropriate valuation methodologies; and incorporate critical thinking, objectivity, and professional judgment in the decision-making process that will ultimately determine the amount of value.

Like a commercial damages case, the valuation engagement usually requires an assessment of economic and industry conditions and the competitive environment on the assets subject to valuation. All work that incorporates judgment inherently requires identifying assumptions on the part of the practicing professional. Further, those engaged to complete a valuation always face the trade-offs of simplified methodologies and ease of understanding versus theoretically more complex valuation methods. No matter how sophisticated the method, the outcomes are affected by assumptions and other conditions that limit the ability to develop the perfect valuation estimate. The professional should be aware of these inherent limitations and the impact of assumptions and limiting conditions on the value estimate.

The work of the fraud examiner or forensic accountant with regard to valuations should be impartial, intellectually honest, and free from conflicts of witness. Generally, notwithstanding the implications

of Sarbanes–Oxley related to public company engagements, the professional need not be independent; however, any issues that may result in challenges to his or her work related to independence should be disclosed. Although not a limiting factor, the expert needs to understand the nature of the client's expectations and planned use for the valuation services outcomes. If the client imposes any scope restrictions, those should be disclosed so that readers of the valuation report understand the context in which the valuation was developed. If the work of other specialists is incorporated into the services performed, that should be disclosed as well.

The Types of Valuation Engagements

AICPA Statement on Standards for Valuation Services No. 1 describes two types of engagements: valuation and calculation. The valuation engagement, even when considered beyond the scope of AICPA members, assumes that the fraud examiner or forensic accountant will analyze the value of the asset under examination, consider, choose, and apply the appropriate valuation tools, techniques, approaches, and methods and that the work will be appropriately documented. Valuation engagements are ongoing, iterative processes whereby data and information are continually gathered, updated, incorporated, and analyzed. Essentially, professionals are expected to utilize their experience, training, and expertise to select and apply the most appropriate methods and approaches.

With a calculation engagement, the client outlines the asset(s), valuation methods, and other aspects of the engagement. The service provider agrees in advance on the approaches, methods, tools, and techniques to be used and the extent of work to be performed. Given that understanding, the professional proceeds to apply the agreed-upon procedures. In either case, the amount of value can be expressed as a single amount or within a range. However, the nature of the engagement should be disclosed, so that readers can understand the context in which the amount or range was developed.

In some situations, the fraud examiner or forensic accountant may be asked to consider the impact of certain hypothetical conditions on the valuation of an asset. The request may be made, for example, as part of a commercial damages case where the plaintiff was put out of business or permanently impaired as a result of the alleged actions or inactions of the defendant. Such hypothetical scenarios should be disclosed as part of the report.

Valuations can be developed to address a number of issues. For example, they may help facilitate asset transfers by helping to determine value for the following:

Asset liquidations

Employee stock ownership plans

Management buyouts

Mergers and acquisitions

Minority shareholder transactions

Purchase and sale agreements

Purchase price allocations

Recapitalizations

Stock sales

Valuations may also be used to help resolve disputes among parties to a transaction and litigation:

Bankruptcy

Divorce

Lost profits and long-term value

Valuations are heavily utilized in tax situations:

Casualty losses

Charitable contributions

Estate and gift taxes

Gains and losses on sales of assets (e.g., home, business, stocks, bonds)

Purchase price allocations

By identifying the type of valuation and associated issues, the fraud examiner or forensic accountant better understands its specific purpose, the parties who make decisions based on the valuation work, and the types of assets involved. The date of valuation is a critical aspect of the engagement because, like a balance sheet, it represents a specific date in time.

Measures of Value

A number of measures of value have been developed over the years. Each has situations where they are reasonable measurement methodologies, and each has strengths and weaknesses. Some of those are as follows:

Book value represents an asset's balance sheet value, derived by subtracting accumulated depreciation from historical (acquisition) cost. For capital-intensive, slow, and moderate-growth organizations, book value may approximate market value. However, for fast-growing, high technology firms—those dependent on intellectual property and service firms—book value does not usually approximate market value.

Liquidation value represents the amount of cash likely to be received by owners of an asset, assuming that pressure exists that will require the sales transaction to be completed quickly. Liquidations can occur in an orderly fashion or are sometimes "forced." An orderly liquidation permits time to prepare the assets properly to derive a higher value and to locate buyers who can better utilize the available asset. Thus, an orderly liquidation tends to generate more cash than a forced one. However, because of time constraints, both liquidation values are likely to fall short of market amounts where the seller has time to find buyers. Book and liquidation values can often be used to determine the floor for the asset's worth.

Market value is used to describe the price of an asset, assuming that a willing buyer and willing seller can come to terms under normal market conditions. Fair market value is usually correlated with market value. It is used to describe the estimated purchase price at which a willing buyer and a willing seller would transfer the asset. Fair market value, like market value, assumes that each party is knowledgeable and can evaluate the risks and rewards associated with the transaction. Its determination often involves the expertise of a valuation professional and can be used as the starting point for negotiations from which a sale can be completed. Market value and fair market value place an amount on the entire asset(s), without regard to ownership and control rights and their marketability. Thus, the term *fair market value* or *fair value* assumes that one person has a 100-percent controlling interest in the asset. Other considerations include fair value when the asset holder has ownership and/or control rights of less than 50 percent (a minority interest). A minority interest, by definition, does not have a controlling interest in the asset and therefore may have limited marketability, which may reduce its market value.

Investment value assumes a specific buyer or class of buyers. This may dictate the type of use that the buyers have for the assets and thus may create a price that is something other than market value or fair market value. Other conditions attached to an asset may have an impact on its worth. For example, a minority interest may have selling rights only if the owner with controlling interest approves. Deed or zoning restrictions may come attached to a piece of real estate. In a divorce, state law is likely to affect the value of assets to be distributed. Any conditions that limit the flexibility and choices of the asset owner are likely to lower its overall value.

Determining Market, Fair Market, and Fair Value

Essentially, two considerations ultimately determine the market and fair market value of an asset: the future income stream that can be derived and the difference between that and the income stream from alternative investment options. Generally, a minimum income option for any investor is considered to be the risk-free interest rate on government bonds. This return is virtually guaranteed. As such, any risky investment or purchase of an asset requires an expected higher return. Ultimately, the value of an asset has to be associated with its income potential over the short and long term, recognizing that, over the life of an asset, income is correlated with its net cash flows.

Traditionally, three methods have been used to determine fair market values. Given fair market value, the impact of ownership and control rights, marketability considerations, and other issues related to use and alternative uses can be factored into the valuation estimate. The common method is discounted income or

cash flows.[3] In addition, market comparables valuation models and asset and liability market valuations can be used as substitutes, when appropriate, or as checks as to the reasonableness of the discounted method.

Discounted Earnings and Cash Flows

The discounted earnings or cash flows method (DCF) requires an estimate of future earnings or cash flows, a sense of the duration of those, and the derivation of an appropriate risk-adjusted discount rate. Assuming constant cash flows, value is a relatively straightforward formula:

$$\text{Value} = \sum_{t=1}^{n} \frac{CF^t}{(1+i)^t}$$

where CF is the constant periodic cash flow to be received in the future at time t, i is the risk-adjusted discount (interest) rate, and n is the number of years the cash flow stream is expected to be received. Because the cash flow stream will not be received with certainty, the risk-adjusted discount rate is used to incorporate the uncertainty into the calculation. Further, in this model, dividends can be substituted as long as they are equal to the firm's estimated free cash flow. Substituting earnings for cash flows is also functionally equivalent to assuming that those retained are reinvested and assumed to earn the risk-adjusted discount rate. Because cash flow projections are difficult to estimate, it is normally for some period, say five years, and then a terminal value must be estimated for the relatively uncertain amounts to be received in year six and beyond. The adjusted formula is as follows:

$$\text{Value} = \sum_{t=1}^{5} \frac{CF^t}{(1+i)^t} + \frac{V_5}{(1+i)^5}$$

V represents the terminal value at the end of year five, which can be estimated assuming constant growth after year five and incorporating a model such as the Gordon Growth Model (GGM). It assumes that the current value of a constantly growing income (dividend) stream is equal to the dividend divided by the growth adjusted net discount rate. Mathematically, the GGM is expresses as follows:

$$P_0 = \frac{D_1}{(k-g)}$$

where P is the price of the company's equity at time 0, D is the dividend in time period 1, k is the cost of equity capital, and g is the expected growth rate of future cash flows. Note that, if expected growth exceeds the cost of equity capital, this equation becomes nonsensical. As a practical matter, in some cases, the book value of equity using the projected balance at the end of year five is assumed to be the terminal value. In other cases, the year-five earnings are divided by the risk-adjusted discount rate.

The most important and challenging factor is the projection of cash flows, which are influenced by the company's historical performance and its prospects for performance in future periods.

Estimating the Risk-Adjusted Discount Rate

Risk and return are positively related. This means that, as risk increases for an investment, the return is expected to also rise. Mathematically, one can assume that the expected earnings are the sum of the risk-free return, plus an upward adjustment for inflation, plus the specific risks associated with the asset. Those can be derived from the overall economy or industry and the asset. Generally, at least four methodologies can be used to develop the risk-adjusted discount rate and its related cash flows (income): CAPM, the bond-equity additive method, the build-up method, and the weighted average cost of capital.

CAPM, the capital asset pricing model, is probably the most well-known methodology for estimating the expected risk-adjusted discount rate for equity. CAPM posits that the return required by an investor is the sum of the risk-free rate of return, plus an adjustment for the relative risk of the asset compared to the overall market rate. This model for estimating the risk-adjusted rate of return requires public market data for the company, the overall market, and the use of statistical estimation software. Although accounting-based data can be substituted for market-based data for privately held companies, those techniques add to the complexity of the overall estimation. The standard CAPM equation is as follows:

$$i = R_{risk\text{-}free} + B(R_M - R_{risk\text{-}free})$$

where R_M is the rate of return on the overall market. The estimate of i can be derived by using regression to estimate B (beta) over time and then applying the parameters for any estimation period. Historically, the rates of return of various market categories between 1926 and 1996 are as follows:[4]

Description	Geometric	Arithmetic
Large company stocks	10.7 %	12.7 %
Small company stocks	12.6 %	17.7 %
Long-term government bonds	5.1 %	6.0 %
T-bills total returns	3.7 %	3.8 %
Inflation	3.1 %	3.2 %
Equity risk premium	6.8 %	8.9 %
Small stock risk premium	1.8 %	5.0 %

The weighted average cost of capital (WACC) is another method traditionally used to estimate the risk-adjusted discount rate. The formula is as follows:

$$\text{WACC} = K_D (1 - \text{tax rate}) \left(\frac{MV_D}{MV_D + MV_E} \right) + K_E \left(\frac{MV_E}{MV_D + MV_E} \right)$$

where K_D is the expected return on debt financing, K_E is the expected return on equity financing, MV_D and MV_E are the market value of debt and equity financing, respectively. CAPM can be used to estimate K_E, whereas Copeland, Koller, and Murrin[5] provide detailed guidance on developing K_D and K_E. The WACC can be used as an estimate of i, the risk-adjusted discount rate.

The bond plus equity method is derived as follows:

$$i = R_b + \text{Equity Premium}$$

where R_b is the interest rate on firm bonds, and the equity premium is the rate of return on the market (R_M) less the risk-free rate of return $(R_{risk\,free})$; i is then used as the risk-adjusted discount rate.

The build-up method, described in the *Ibbotson Associates, Stocks, Bonds, Bills and Inflation Annual Yearbook*, is similar but more sophisticated than the bond plus equity method and can be derived as follows:

$$R_{risk\,free} - \text{the risk-free rate of return}$$
$$+ \text{Equity Premium (discussed previously)}$$
$$+ / - \text{Industry Adjustment}$$
$$+ / - \text{Capitalization (related to the size of the entity)}$$
$$+ / - \text{Other Special Adjustments affecting the risk}$$
$$= i \text{ (the risk-adjusted rate of return)}$$

One consideration that applies often to smaller organizations is leverage. Particularly with smaller, closely held enterprises, professionals are likely to encounter significant variations in the amount of debt (leverage) relative to equity. Some small businesses have no equity investment and have used creditors as essentially the only source of financing. In other cases, the venture was considered so risky that the balance sheet is financed almost exclusively with equity, with the exception of some short-term liabilities such as accounts payable and accruals. A methodology for dealing with differences in leverage is the Hamada adjustment. To incorporate this adjustment, the following data or their surrogates are required:

$$+ R_{risk-free}, \text{Beta, Debt/Equity Ratio, Tax Rate}$$

The Hamada adjustment can be used to modify the traditional CAPM model as follows:

$$i = R_{risk-free} + B (R_M - R_{risk-free}) + B (R_M - R_{risk-free}) * (1 - \text{Tax Rate}) \left(\frac{\text{Debt}}{\text{Equity}} \right)$$

Use i as the discount rate.

Forecasting Income and Cash Flows

One of the most challenging issues associated with the discounted income and cash flows model is projecting income and cash flows into the future. At a minimum, data should be considered in the following areas:[6]

1. The nature of the business
2. The general economic and industry outlook

3. The book value of equity (derived from the balance sheet)

4. The earnings (operating) capacity of the company

5. Dividend-paying capacity

6. Goodwill and other intangible assets

7. Previous sales of company securities

8. The market prices of comparable companies

Notice that these considerations are similar to those discussed when developing and critiquing estimates of damages. Various economic, industry, competitive, and company-specific factors are likely to have an impact on the projection of cash flows. These need to be considered either implicitly or explicitly in the analyses used to project future income, cash flows, and dividends. Other information that may affect the valuation includes the number, type, and age of organizational facilities; the management team; the classes of debt or equity and their associated rights, products, services; relative geographical reach (e.g., local, statewide, United States, North America, global, etc.), industry markets and conditions; key customers, suppliers, and competitors; business risks; strategic planning and planned changes in strategy or its operational execution; and the impact of government and regulators.

Most income and cash flow projections are grounded in historical financial performance. For an organization, it's difficult to know where it is going if it does not know where it's been. As such, a starting point for the projection of future cash flows is the historical financial statements: income statements, balance sheets, statements of cash flows, and the tax returns. Three to five years of historical financial statements are preferable. Even though tax returns are only available on an annual basis, public and internal balance sheets are usually available at least quarterly, and internal income statements are usually available monthly. The additional data points from monthly financial data often provide invaluable information and a solid basis for trend analysis.

Keep in mind that, if professionals are armed with beginning and ending period balance sheets and an income statement for the period, a reasonably good estimate of cash flows (operating, investing, and financing) can be developed. They may provide a significantly different picture than that suggested by the income statement, so the time used to create the statement of cash flows is usually justified. Texts and other authoritative guidance in this area often refer to free cash flows, but this definition often varies. At the most simplistic understanding, free cash flows are those that an owner could consume without injuring or reducing the value of the organization. When developing a valuation using this concept, the professional needs to ensure that free cash flows is defined so that users of the report can properly interpret valuation outcomes.

For smaller (nonpublic), closely held businesses, owners may combine personal financial transactions with those of the organization. Through inquiry, inspection, and analysis, the fraud examiner or forensic accountant needs to determine whether such transactions exist and consider appropriate adjustments, if any. In other cases, an owner may be providing sweat equity management services, meaning that the compensation for those services may be below market values or nonexistent. It may be proper therefore to add expenses to the projections. Another area of concern is with related parties. For example, suppliers or merchandise coming from a company owned or operated by a close family member may not be at "arm's length." Those transactions may be at, below, or above those that would be charged by an unrelated, independent third party.

Beyond the historical financial statements to be gathered, the fraud examiner or forensic accountant should attempt to gather the following:

- Forecasts of projected (future) financial results

- Articles on industry-related valuation issues

- Relevant client information from inquiries, interviews, and deposition transcripts, if available

From this historical information, the professional should calculate various ratios and interpret their meaning, particularly the impact of projected income and cash flows:

Common-size financial statements

Liquidity ratios

Profitability ratios

Efficiency ratios

Capital structure ratios

Long-term debt to equity

In addition, the professional should examine revenues for past trends, growth rates, variability in individual annual results, overall observed results, and the identification of appropriate questions for company management. Once a satisfactory understanding has been gained of revenues as a basis for projecting future revenues, gross profits and gross margins should be examined: both the components of goods sold and their calculations (and underlying inventory flow and valuation assumptions). Once satisfied, the valuation professional should turn to operating expenses, operating profits, other income and expense items, pretax profitability, EBITDA (earnings before interest, taxes, depreciation, and amortization), taxes, and net income. Particular attention should be paid to nonrecurring, one-time, and unusual transactions and their impact on operating performance. Because such items are nonrecurring, they generally should be excluded from projections of future operating performance. Once the analysis of the income statement has been completed, a similar one should be made of the balance sheet, the statement of cash flows, and the tax returns, where particular attention should be paid to the reconciliation of book to taxable income.

Beyond studying the organization's internal performance, the following should also be considered:

- Company's economics and business model
- Management's strengths and weaknesses and the impact on an investor's perception of risk
- Trends and what they say about the possible future
- Key elements of company strategy
- Industry forecasts, as a basis for comparing a company's performance to industry peers
- Key competitors
- Internal and external forces that affect the business
- Risk, future threats, and opportunities

Notice that much of this work entails an initial analysis, followed by applied judgment. Armed with these analyses and various judgments, the fraud examiner or forensic accountant can start to make projections of future periods, usually for approximately five years. Finally, using net present value methods discussed in the calculation of economic damages section, projected future earnings and cash flows (including an estimate of terminal value) can be discounted back to the present value.

Asset Valuation Models

The asset valuation model starts with the assumption that the organization's balance sheet does a reasonably good job of identifying the company's assets and liabilities. Using a detailed listing, the market value of each asset or liability can be estimated. Appraisers can be used to value the assets. Net present value techniques can be used to approximate the liabilities based on current interest rates and projected cash flows. Although this method makes a reasonable attempt to convert the traditional, historically cost-based balance sheet to one that incorporates market values, it has at least two shortcomings. First, it does not account for the sometimes significant benefits associated with asset synergy—where the value of the whole is greater, sometimes significantly greater, than the sum of the parts.

In addition, many companies have significant intangible assets, and the market-based balance sheet fails to account for those. Some include patents, trademarks, research, and development; they can be estimated by analyzing historical benefits. However, other intangibles, such as organizational know-how, knowledge, and a productive, efficient, and effective workforce do not lend themselves to analytical valuation with a reasonable level of confidence. Also, contingent and unknown liabilities may be significantly understated, which overvalues the actual market-based book value. Thus, if an attempt is made, the professional needs to consider adjustments that are not on the face of the balance sheet, but about which information is known. At least list those intangible assets and potential liabilities for cases in which no reasonable estimate of value is available, so that users of the valuation can determine for themselves what consideration, if any, they should be given.

Market and Accounting-Based Comparables Models

The use of comparable data from similar companies, the industry, and competitors are often referred to as methods involving benchmarks, guidelines, and rules of thumb. Such approaches are not valuation methods per se, in the sense that they do not make a detailed assessment of the underlying assets as a basis for current value. Inherently, these methods assume that the valuation associated with a comparable asset (sometimes

with adjustments) is applicable to the company. Generally, such approaches are useful as a reasonableness check on the results of other analyses but should not be used as a stand-alone method. If the comparables methodology is the only option, the significant shortcomings should be disclosed, as well as the reasons why a more theoretically sound analytical approach is not possible. Some of the comparables based on key competitors, the industry, or other attributes that suggest similarity include comparable revenue or income levels, the use of price-earnings (P/E) ratios, price-to-revenue models, and the use of market-to-book ratios for similar companies.

Valuation Discounts and Premiums

Many small businesses have majority and minority owners with various control rights. Finally, asset ownership interests have differing marketability or liquidity attributes. Some rights may have restrictions on sales; others may require that the ownership interest be sold in blocks. Each of these may have an impact on the valuation. Based on court cases, the following were observed with the value of various valuation discounts:[7]

Summary of Discounts: 1970–1994

	Type of Discount			
	Minority	**Liquidity**	**Restriction**	**Blockage**
	Percentage Reduction			
Range	5–50 %	5–30 %	22–100 %	5–35 %
Mean	24 %	22 %	45 %	21 %
Median	20 %	25 %	40 %	20 %

Mergerstat Review reports that median premiums for control purchases for the years 1986–1995 are in the range of 29–35 percent.

Other Ownership Interests Subject to Valuation

Other ownership-type interests that are subject to review include valuing debt, preferred stock, convertible debt, stock, warrants, options, and intangible assets. Each of these presents additional issues that require consideration.

Conclusion of Value

Once the valuation work is complete, the professional needs to set out a conclusion of value. It may be in the form of a number or specified range. In arriving at the conclusion, the expert should reconcile and correlate the results from more than one methodology or alternative assumption. Furthermore, the expert should consider the reliability of the valuation outcome as a result of deriving differing numbers using a variety of approaches and underlying assumptions. The valuation professional has a choice of relying primarily on one method, and using the others as reasonableness checks, or relying on multiple methods that incorporate a reconciling approach to determine the value or specified range.

The Valuation Report

Consensus among industry participants about what should be included in the valuation report differs. The Accredited Senior Appraiser's (ASA's) *Principles of Appraisal Practice* suggest the following items be included:

1. Description of the property that is the subject of the appraisal.
2. The objectives of the appraisal work.
3. The statement of contingent and limiting conditions to which the appraisal findings are subject.
4. A description and explanation of the appraisal method used.
5. A statement of the appraiser's disinterestedness.
6. The appraiser's responsibility to communicate each analysis, opinion, and conclusion in a manner that is not misleading.
7. A mandatory recertification statement.
8. Signatures and inclusion of dissenting opinions.

The Uniform Standards of the Professional Appraisal Practice (USPAP) requirements are similar:

1. Identify and describe the business enterprise, assets, or equity being appraised.

2. State the purpose and intended use of the appraisal.

3. Define the value to be estimated.

4. Set forth the effective date of the appraisal and the report.

5. Describe the extent of the appraisal process employed.

6. Describe all assumptions and limiting conditions that affect the analyses, opinions, and conclusions.

7. Describe the information considered, the appraisal procedures followed, and the reasoning that supports the analyses, opinions, and conclusions.

8. Include any additional information that may be appropriate to show compliance or clearly identify and explain permitted departures from requirement standard 9.[8]

9. State the rationale for the valuation methods and procedures used.

10. Provide a certification in accordance with Standards Rule 10-3, which states that the report is true and correct, the author is objective and has no financial interest in the entity, and the analyses and opinions are in conformity with USPAP valuation practices.

The reporting process and report contents outlined in the AICPA Statement on Standards for Valuation Services are specific. Given the decisions that need to be made during a valuation engagement and the judgment involved, the AICPA appears to want to be very clear about disclosing all items that may have an impact on decisions by the users. The AICPA valuation reports may be in a detailed or summary format, and the reporting requirements differ, depending on whether a valuation or calculation of value has been contracted. The objective is to provide sufficient information to permit intended users to understand the data, the reasoning, and the analyses underlying the conclusion of value.

Valuation Report	Valuation	Calculation
Detailed	**Summary**	**Summary**
Report Sections and Content		
Letter of Transmittal		
Table of Contents		
Introduction		
Identity of the client	Included	Included
Purpose and intended use of the valuation	Included	Included
Intended users of the valuation	Included	Included
Identity of the subject entity (asset)	Included	Included
Description of the subject entity	Included	Included
Whether the business interest has ownership control characteristics and its degree of marketability	Included	Included
Valuation date	Included	Calculation date
Report date	Included	Included
Type of report issues	Summary	Calculation
Applicable premise of value	Included	
Applicable standard to value	Included	
Assumptions and limiting conditions	Included	Included
Any restrictions or limitations in the scope of work or data availability for analysis	Included	Certain calculation procedures were performed
Any hypothetical conditions used in the valuation engagement, including the basis for use	Included	Included
If the work of a specialist was used in the valuation engagement, a description of how the specialist's work was relied upon	Included	Included
Disclosure of subsequent events in certain circumstances[9]	Included	Included

Valuation Report	Valuation	Calculation
Detailed	Summary	Summary
Any application of the jurisdictional exception[10] Any additional information the valuation analyst deems useful to enable the users of the report to understand the work performed	Included	Included
Source of Information: The extent to which the subject interest (asset) was visited For intangible assets, whether the legal registration, contractual documentation, or other tangible evidence of the asset was inspected Names, positions, and titles of persons interviewed and their relationship to the subject interest Financial information Tax information Industry data Market data Economic data Other empirical information Relevant documents and other sources	Included in summary format	
Analysis of the subject entity and related nonfinancial information		
Financial statement/information analysis, including the rationale for normalization or control adjustments, comparison of current with historical performance, and comparison to industry trends and norms		
Valuation approaches and methods considered		
Valuation approaches and methods used: For the income approach, include the composition of the benefits stream, the most relevant risk factors in developing the discount rate (capitalization rate), and other important factors. For the asset approach, include any adjustments made to the balance sheet data. For the cost approach, describe the type of cost used, how the cost was estimated, depreciation, and obsolescence, including how those amounts were estimated. For the market approach, where a guideline public company was used, describe how the guideline companies were selected, the pricing multiples used, how they were used and if adjusted, and the rationale for those adjustments. For the market approach, where a guideline transactions method was used, describe the sales transactions, the pricing multiples used, and the rationale for their selection. For the market approach, where a guideline sale of interest method was used, describe the sales transactions, how those sales were used, and the rationale for determining that they were arms-length transactions. Valuation adjustments, including all those considered and determined applicable, the rationale for the choices, and the pre-adjustment value	Included in summary format	Included in summary format: Describe the calculation procedures performed, that not all procedures of a valuation engagement were performed, and that, if a valuation engagement been conducted, results may differ

(Continued)

(Continued)

Valuation Report	Valuation	Calculation
Detailed	**Summary**	**Summary**
Nonoperating assets, liabilities, and excess or deficit operating assets (if any)		
Representation of the valuation analyst:	Included in summary format	Included in summary or detailed format
That the analyses, opinions, and conclusions of value included in the report are subject to assumptions and limiting conditions and that they are the personal analyses, opinions, and conclusions of value of the valuation analyst		
The economic and industry data were obtained from various printed or electronic reference sources that the analyst believes to be reliable, but no corroborating procedures have been performed.		
That the engagement was performed in accordance with AICPA Statement on Standards for Valuation Services		Included
The parties for which the information and use of the report is restricted, such parties have been identified, and the report is not intended to be and should not be used by anyone other than such parties		
The analyst's basis for compensation		
The reliance on the work of any specialists and the level of responsibility, if any, being assumed by the valuation analyst for such work	Included	Included
That the analyst has no obligation to update the report	Included	
The report should be signed by the professional assuming responsibility for the report.		
Reconciliation of estimates and conclusion of value That a valuation engagement was performed, including the subject interest and valuation date	Included in summary format	Included in summary format
That the analysis was performed solely for the purposes described in the report and that the resulting estimate should not be used for any other purpose	Included	Included
That the engagement was performed in accordance with AICPA Statement on Standards for Valuation Services		Included
The estimate is expressed as a conclusion of value.		Included
The scope of the work is explained, including any restrictions or limitations.		
A statement describing the conclusion of value, either a single amount or a range		Included
The conclusion of value is subject to the assumptions and limiting considerations and to the analyst's representation.		
The report is signed by the professional or in the name of the analyst's firm.	Included	Included
The date of the valuation report	Included	Included
That the analyst has no obligation to update the report	Included	Included
Qualifications of the valuation analyst		
Appendices and exhibits	Optional	Optional

PERSONAL INJURY, WRONGFUL DEATH, AND SURVIVAL ACTIONS

In this section, we consider litigation situations to which fraud examiners or forensic accountants may be engaged when a person has been injured, killed, or permanently disabled as a result of the actions of another. The three types of damages that may ensue are losses to the individual, losses to survivors, and losses to the estates of decedents. These types of engagements are more technical than analytical. As unfortunate as they are, these types of issues are relatively common, and a good deal of case and statutory law has been developed. Thus, the guidelines concerning how to develop the loss claims are relatively straightforward. That is not to suggest that the models do not require assumptions and judgment. However, the spectrum of choices is more well-defined in this area. Therefore, once the set of assumptions and types of losses have been identified, the numerical calculations follow those of previously developed models. The professional still needs to examine the results from the perspective of reasonableness. Does the resulting damage amount make sense? Will it make sense to a jury? Can I defend it, not just on technical grounds but also from a perspective of a trier-of-fact: judge or jury? Despite the developed nature of the calculations, the estimates are a rough approximation of the loss, especially when projected into the future—in some cases, for a lifetime.

One of the major challenges arises from inflation. It can have a significant negative impact on award calculation amounts over time. Inflation's magnitude and unpredictability create substantial risk for the damaged parties, who cannot work for some period, if at all, or for their families who were dependent on them. Another issue relates to career path. Some individuals may perform the same or similar tasks for their entire career; others may change career paths or advance to another level. In some industries and careers, the path from entry-level to the most likely position may be reasonably identifiable, but, in a world where technology is altering every aspect of our personal and professional lives, identifying a likely career path with reasonable confidence can be difficult at best.[11]

Losses: Personal Injury

The primary circumstance with court actions and related loss claims is that the injured person survived the incident and subsequently lost income. The expertise needed to investigate these types of cases and develop proof of losses includes that of the forensic financial specialist (accountant, financier, or economist). These experts estimate the reduced earnings and other forms of support as a result of the injury. In addition to earning losses, depending on the nature of the injury, the party may suffer some permanent injury and thus his or her earnings capacity may be reduced for indefinite periods. Moreover, the person's injury may be such that he or she needs to incur future costs for medicines, medical treatments, home health care, and other costs. If this is anticipated, the fraud examiner or forensic accountant may need to rely on the expertise of a specialist from the medical field, who can affirm the need for future medical care, outline the types of treatments that may be necessary, and help the financial professional locate data on the associated costs. If the person requires permanent health maintenance or special living arrangements, these concerns are probably beyond the medical expert and require someone who deals with after-care needs to estimate the costs of future living arrangements. The reports and testimony of the medical, life-care, and other experts should be incorporated into the work of the anti-fraud professional or forensic accountant.

Another form of expertise that may be needed could include human resources and labor relations professionals. They understand the vocational aspects of the injured party and his or her possible career paths. The human resources professional needs to consider the person's past work history and job opportunities and incorporate the information from the medical experts into the determination of potential career paths. They must also consider the possibility of permanent disability, which may be assessed from at least two perspectives. First, a permanently disabled person may never again be productively able to enter the workforce. A second possibility may involve a permanently diminished capacity to work at a level previously achieved, although gainful under-employment at reduced earnings is still possible.

An injured person may suffer up to five types of losses, both past and future, that need to be considered:

1. Loss of earnings
2. Loss of employment benefits associated with the earnings
3. Losses associated with the ability to perform "nonmarket services" (personal labor to the household that may need to be contracted to outsiders)

4. Medical costs

5. Life-care costs

Earnings losses include those associated with time off work and may also involve reductions in earnings capacity as a result of the nature of the injury. When a person loses his or her employment earnings, there are fringe benefits to consider: medical, dental, disability, unemployment, and life insurance; employer retirement plan contributions; Social Security and Medicare/Medicaid contributions; clothing allowances; and an employer-provided automobile for personal purposes. An injury to a person may also result in the need for incremental expenditures because of the inability of the person to complete usual household chores. For example, a person or the family may need to contract for home repairs, cooking, laundry, cleaning, child care, lawn maintenance, and other duties that had been performed by the injured party. For these types of nonmarket services, no money changed hands in the past; however, now workers must be hired for the household. Finally, there may be the need for redesigned living quarters, special tools and equipment, or special diets.

Losses: Wrongful Death and Survival Cases

The unfortunate death of a person where another party may be held accountable can result in two general types of cases: wrongful death and survival actions. The type of case depends on the laws of the state in which the "death with associated liability" occurred. In jurisdictions with wrongful death statutes, the primary right of recovery resides with the survivors. In a survival action (even though the person didn't survive), the estate of the deceased has the primary right of recovery. These actions proceed in a manner similar to those of a permanent disability. Once recovery has been awarded to the estate, the assets are transferred to the survivors through the settling of the estate. Thus, survival actions are akin to thinking "what if" the person survived the injury instead of dying. The resulting issue is important, because the losses are different when considered from the perspective of the "survivor" and those of the surviving family (as in wrongful death).

The decedent or his or her surviving family (in a wrongful death suit) may have suffered the following types of losses, both past and future, that need to be considered:

1. Loss of earnings

2. Loss of employment benefits associated with the earnings

3. Losses associated with the ability to perform "nonmarket services" (personal service contributions to the household that may need to be contracted to outsiders)

When his or her losses are compared to the list of losses to an injured person, the decedent has no need for medical or life-care costs; thus, categories 4 and 5, described in the previous section, do not apply to wrongful death and survival actions. However, much of the discussion with regard to earnings, both current and future, employment benefits, and costs associated with nonmarket services, which now must be contracted out or performed by a surviving member of the household, do apply. In the discussion that follows, generally, injuries (temporary or permanent) are considered first and then the changes, assuming wrongful death and survival actions are addressed.

Analysis of Earnings Losses

The estimate of earnings losses requires the evaluation of five investigative areas:

1. Determining the basis for earnings losses: expected earnings versus diminished earnings capacity

2. Analysis of employment history and related past earnings

3. Projection of probable career paths: before and after the loss

4. Determining the proper earnings for each projected career path

    a. Base earnings: before and after the earnings loss (injury or death)

    b. Earnings increases

    c. Application of present value

5. Consideration of other factors on earnings losses

    a. age and experience

b. probable duration in the workforce

c. probable periods of unemployment

First, the professional must determine whether to project either expected earnings or lost earnings capacity for the decedent. Expected earnings are an estimate of the amount an injured party would (could) have earned but for his or her wrongful death. Earnings capacity refers to the ability to produce future earnings. It assumes that some choices about earnings duration and type of work are made by the injured party and have an impact on the amount of likely earnings losses. Earnings capacity is a broader standard that considers the potential for the individual to generate earnings, notwithstanding the fact that the injured party may not have chosen to perform the work necessary in order to generate those earnings. These attributes may be reasonably understandable to some, yet confusing to others. An example may help clarify the differences.

Assume that an unmarried man, age fifty, with no children, has the necessary retirement funds accumulated such that he planned to retire and move to warmer climates at age fifty-five. However, prior to the planned retirement (age fifty-five), he is injured (died) at fifty years old. Given this scenario, his expected earnings period is five years, starting at age fifty and ending, as a result of the planned retirement, at age fifty-five. However, notwithstanding the impact of the injury, his profession might have allowed him to have earning capacity through age seventy or even longer. Generally, the legal standard for the jurisdiction determines either expected earnings or earnings capacity. In that regard, the professional needs to work closely with legal counsel in order to identify the proper basis for projections. In some cases, the expert needs to develop loss estimates for both expected earnings and earnings capacity.

Once the basis for projections has been determined, data should be collected on the injured party's employment and earnings history. If, for some reason, the records are incomplete or not available, the earnings history of a comparable uninjured person may be obtained. A further alternative is to identify and use descriptive statistical data (e.g., U.S. Department of Labor Statistics) that include averages for groups of persons who have similar duties and responsibilities. In order to develop lost earnings, the professional can rely on W-2 statements, pay stubs, tax returns, and data from the Social Security administration, as well as a résumé for the individual. Because many people do not maintain a current résumé, a professional may need to ask for assistance in preparing a listing of employers, positions, titles, duties, and responsibilities. The expert would also seek information on the injured person's educational history and any special training or on-the-job skills.

Generally, assuming that the information is available, the injured party's own experiences are given superior weight. However, recent employment changes—unrelated to the injury—may suggest that other comparables may be a better basis. For example, assume that a medical doctor recently completed his or her residency requirements and had moved into a chosen area of specialization. Under those conditions, past earnings may no longer serve as a reasonable basis for future projections. As another example, assume that the injured person had recently obtained a promotion to a new position with higher earnings. Under that scenario, the majority of the historical data would be at the lower pre-promotion levels and would no longer carry as much relevance for future projections.

The third consideration is that of the prior career path, the projected career path, and the possibility of multiple career paths. This is a particularly challenging area, because both expected earnings and earnings capacity may be affected, so there is a need to incorporate individual preferences into the analysis. The expert also needs to consider the market for the type of work and responsibilities associated with the decedent's chosen and desired career paths. For example, some professional services firms have mandatory retirement at age sixty. Thus, a principal in one of those firms would only have earnings capacity in that firm through that age. However, depending on the nature of the professional services, noncompete commitments, etc., and the individual's expertise, the injured person may have earning capacity in outside services firms after retirement.

The consideration of career path requires the incorporation of considerable judgment and uncertainty into the estimate of lost expected earnings or capacity. To develop a likely career path, the financial expert may need to rely on the work of others with human resources expertise. Another alternative is averages developed by economists related to the impact of age, education, region, sex, race, and other demographic characteristics on earnings history. To apply these criteria, the use of a human resources specialist is often warranted, an expert who may suggest several likely long-term professional career paths. In such cases, the fraud examiner or forensic accountant needs to develop multiple estimates based on the various assumptions suggested. The determination of earnings related to career path after injury is challenging and often entails using hypothetical input from human resource professionals or direction provided by the attorney.

The first three areas of consideration—expected earnings versus earning capacity, prior employment and related earnings, and projected career path(s)—serve as the foundation for projecting lost earnings into future periods. During this phase, the fraud examiner or forensic accountant projects earnings (expected or capacity) based on the probability of each potential career track. Notwithstanding recent changes in career path, the last full year of employment often serves as a defendable foundation or basis for projecting future earnings. In some cases, a range of years can be averaged to derive a starting place. If so, prior years' wages should most likely be adjusted for cost-of-living increases before averaging. For employees paid by the hour, for cases in which the hours tend to fluctuate, separate the total earnings into hours and wage rate. Each of these attributes can then be evaluated with the goal of developing a defendable basis.

From the data on historical employment and past earnings, determine their applicability to the facts and circumstances at the time of the injury and the period after the injury that requires projection. From a technical perspective, the fraud examiner or forensic accountant needs to develop two amounts: (a) one that assumes that the pre-injury earnings history would have continued into post-injury periods and (b) a projection of the probable (actual) employment income that would be earned in the post-injury period. The difference between the two amounts represents losses to the injured party. Incorporate recent actual events, such as promotions, education, or other changes that may have an impact on the projected earnings, either positively or negatively.

Notwithstanding these issues, the analysis of expected earnings and earnings capacity should incorporate judgment by the professional. For instance, mandatory retirement ages may be in place in the profession that have physical requirements, such as athletic skills or beauty. Assume a professional football player may say he plans to retire at age forty-five, but a quick review of historical statistics suggests that the probability is highly unlikely. Finally, the jurisdiction in which the case is being heard may determine whether expected earnings or earnings capacity is the proper basis. State laws and prior case law may make one or the other the chosen standard.

Given an assessment of past earnings and their impact on future earnings, the next consideration is increases in projecting earnings. A related issue is the discount rate to use for the projection, recognizing that most injury settlements are likely to be paid in lump sum in current dollars. In *Jones and Laughlin vs. Pfeifer*, the Supreme Court allowed three options for projecting earnings and the appropriate discount rate:

1. Case-by-case method
2. Below-market discount method
3. Total-offset method

When using the case-by-case method, wages and discount rates are projected in nominal terms (including estimated increases for inflation). Using this method, the "actual" dollars that would have been earned in the past or into the future are estimated. They are made on a year-by-year basis and include projections of earnings increases. Future earnings are then discounted back to the present, using discount rates based on projections for interest rates (recognizing that a portion of interest rates is for anticipated inflation). Incorporating earnings, earnings increases, and discount rates has the effect of compensating for the impact of inflation where purchasing power would otherwise decrease.

With the below-market discount method, earnings and discount rates are projected where the impact of inflation has been removed. By working in real dollars, the projections ensure that the purchasing power associated with the earnings remains approximately constant. Further, the earnings projections are more pure, in the sense that they reflect the benefits of experience, increased responsibility, etc. that are often recognized as a worker ages and becomes more productive. Further, because real discount rates have been adjusted downward for inflationary pressures, they tend to be lower than nominal discount rates. The term *below-market* refers explicitly to the fact that real discount (interest) rates will fall below those of nominal rates, recognizing that market rates of interest incorporate inflation and are more in line with nominal rates. Using real rates, there are two options: the real interest rate, which is the rate of return on borrowed money net of any premium for inflation, and net discount, which is calculated as the difference between the nominal rate of interest and the wage inflation rate.

To illustrate these two methods (case-by-case and below-market discount methods), assume that Pete is disabled on 1/1/2007 and that the disability is judged permanent. Further assume that Pete's salary indicated that he'd earn $40,000 in 2007. Earnings increases are expected to be approximately 3.5 percent, and a nominal discount rate of 6 percent per year is considered reasonable. Because Pete is near his fifty-sixth birthday, he is expected to lose ten years of earnings (for this illustration, assume that the hypothetical jurisdiction requires expected earnings to be the proper basis of consideration). Both the 3.5 percent

projected earnings increases and the 6 percent discount rate are nominal, in that they anticipate inflation. Assume further that, instead of using nominal rates for earnings and discount rate projections, the attorney prefers the use of real rates. Given Pete's chosen profession, age, and experience, it is further assumed that the only basis for his wage increase is inflation. Thus, the real wage rate increase is zero and his annual 3.5 percent projected earnings increase represents inflation. However, it is not only the projected increases in wages that are in nominal terms. The professional also needs to remove inflation from the discount rate, decreasing that estimate. For simplicity, assume that the real discount rate is 2.1453 percent. Thus, the real discount rate is 2.1453 percent, and the inflationary impact on the nominal discount rate is 3.8547 percent (the two amounts total 6 percent). The outcomes of those approaches appear in the following table.

		Nominal Approach			Net Discount Rate		
		3.5 %	6.0 %		0.0 %	2.4 %	
		Projected Earnings	Discount Rate	Present Value	Projected Earnings	Discount Rate	Present Value
2008	56	40,000	1.000	40,000	40,000	1.000	40,000
2009	57	41,400	0.943	39,057	40,000	0.976	39,057
2010	58	42,849	0.890	38,135	40,000	0.953	38,136
2011	59	44,349	0.840	37,236	40,000	0.931	37,236
2012	60	45,901	0.792	36,358	40,000	0.909	36,358
2013	61	47,507	0.747	35,500	40,000	0.888	35,501
2014	62	49,170	0.705	34,663	40,000	0.867	34,663
2015	63	50,891	0.665	33,846	40,000	0.846	33,846
2016	64	52,672	0.627	33,047	40,000	0.826	33,048
2017	65	54,516	0.592	32,268	40,000	0.807	32,268
Total		469,256		360,110	400,000		360,112

From these results, focusing on the nominal approach, we can see that the total loss using the nominal approach is $469,256, but, after discounting back to the present value, the actual projected loss is $360,110. Switching to the net discount rate in the right-most three columns, the real wage loss is $400,000 (ten years times $40,000 in real-dollar wages), but the discounted present value is $360,112. Note that the outcomes of the two approaches are almost equal. This stems from the fact that inflation adjustments were made to both the wage increase rate and the discount rate (or, in the case of the nominal approach, which inherently incorporates inflation in the wage increase rate and discount rate).

The third method for dealing with wage increases and inflationary pressures on the discount rate is the total-offset method. This simplifying assumption is that the wage increase rate is equal to (i.e., offset by) the discount rate. The same fact scenario previously discussed is recalculated in the following table.

		Total-Offset Approach #1			Total-Offset Approach #2		
		3.5 %	3.5 %		6.0 %	6.0 %	
		Projected Earnings	Discount Rate	Present Value	Projected Earnings	Discount Rate	Present Value
2008	56	40,000	1.000	40,000	40,000	1.000	40,000
2009	57	41,400	0.966	40,000	42,400	0.943	40,000
2010	58	42,849	0.934	40,000	44,944	0.890	40,000
2011	59	44,349	0.902	40,000	47,641	0.840	40,000
2012	60	45,901	0.871	40,000	50,499	0.792	40,000
2013	61	47,507	0.842	40,000	53,529	0.747	40,000
2014	62	49,170	0.814	40,000	56,741	0.705	40,000
2015	63	50,891	0.786	40,000	60,145	0.665	40,000
2016	64	52,672	0.759	40,000	63,754	0.627	40,000
2017	65	54,516	0.734	40,000	67,579	0.592	40,000
Total		469,256		400,000	527,232		400,000

In the left-side columns, total-offset approach #1, the projected wage increase is assumed to be offset by the discount rate. In the total-offset approach #2 example, the nominal discount rate previously discussed is assumed to be offset by the wage increase. In both cases, the net present value of the projected loss is $400,000. Thus, the simplest way to approach the total-offset method is to take current year wages and multiply that amount by the number of loss years. In the example given, $40,000 earnings times ten years of losses equals $400,000.

Related to projecting future wage rate increases and changes in the future discount rates, some argue that the past can be used to project the future. Others claim the future is too unpredictable for past rates to be a good indicator of future rates. The practical reality is that it is a matter of debate that never ends. However, at a minimum, the practicing professional should examine prior history to see what has happened to wages for the type of individual whose future earnings will be affected. In addition, to the extent that projections arise for future wages and related increases, those should be examined as well.

A further issue related to the appropriate discount rate requires discussion. As noted in the damages and valuation sections of this text, discount rates—when associated with business ventures and incorporated in court cases—can be relatively low compared to those observed for early-stage investment capital. In fact, in early-stage investment capital, discount rates can become quite high, such as in the market for angel-type investments and for venture capital. However, with loss wage engagements, the discount rates are generally low, lower than even those considered appropriate when a business has been damaged. The discount rates appropriate for wages and the ability to earn wages in the future should be analogous to those of relatively safe investments, not risky businesses or angel/venture capital investments. Generally, U.S. Government Securities is considered a high quality, safe investment, and the discount rates selected should reflect that standard. Alternatively stated, the discount rate should not incorporate premiums that are appropriate for investors who are willing to accept some risk that the return may be zero or that they may even lose their investment. Not to be confused, the risk-free rate does not eliminate the risk of inflation. It includes some adjustment for inflationary risk. However, the U.S. Treasury Inflation-Indexed Securities (TIIS bonds) are essentially risk-free, and they eliminate the risk of inflation as well.

The fifth area of consideration accounts for other factors that may have an impact on the analysis. Some of those may be age, experience, projected duration in the workforce, possible periods of unemployment, and life expectancy. As discussed previously, pressure for wages to increase is generated either from inflation or from productivity gains. The impact of inflation is generally unrelated to productivity gains, but some productivity gains may be associated with age and experience. The professional must keep these issues in mind as he or she develops projections. Although one may not always be able to disentangle the impact of inflation versus productivity, it is important to understand the foundation of the factors as a basis for wage rate increases.

If employment before the injured party enters the workforce on a full-time basis is ignored, the typical pattern for wage and experience for noncollege graduates starts around eighteen years of age, with relatively low-paying jobs. According to Ireland et al., the period of low pay continues until around age twenty-six, by which time the employee has gained some experience and confidence and has been able to establish a track record with the employer. With age, maturity, and experience, the employee's wages generally go through a period of rapid growth. Toward the end of the employee's work life, increases are usually lower than those of the average workers, and overall wages may even decline. The pattern for workers with college educations parallels that of the noncollege workers, with the exceptions of the age of entry into the workforce and of wage increases for older workers. For educated workers, wages for the fifty-five- to sixty-four-year-old age group tend to be lower than those of the forty-five- to fifty-four-year age group. Because, for the average worker, age and experience are very highly correlated, the practicing professional usually cannot disentangle the effects.

In cases where the individual cannot continue in the same field, his or her age or experience makes a difference in starting salaries and projected annual increases in a new field. The anti-fraud or forensic accounting professional can make assumptions with someone who has human resources experience; however, this does not provide the benefit of long-term statistical support, because such information is not captured in the U.S. census data.

Another complication is life expectancy. In order to earn income, the individual needs to be alive and employed. Thus, estimates of lost expected earnings and earnings capacity need to take into account the probability of being alive. At least two systems have been created to account for this. The first is the Statistical Work Life Expectancy (SWLE) method. Work life is defined as the period during a person's life when he or she participates in the workforce, either by being gainfully employed or by seeking employment. The U.S. Department of Labor provides work life estimates with the Effects of Race and Education tables.

The second system is the Life Probability, Participant Probability, and Employment Probability, or LPE system. Life probability is the likelihood that the person will survive through the year in question; participant probability is the chance that the individual will participate in the labor force in any particular year; finally, employment probability is the odds that the employee will be employed in any given year. The (department of) Vital Statistics of the United States maintains data on life probabilities; the U.S. Department of Labor has data related to the final two probabilities. The LPE system is the conditional probability that a person will be alive, a labor market participant, and employed in a future year.

Both the SWLE and LPE approaches have strengths and weaknesses the professional needs to be aware of those and, possibly, make adjustments when preliminary results appear misleading and when those issues can be associated with the shortcomings in the underlying statistical data. Some of the areas of concern for the probabilities include homemakers, single career women, consideration of periods of unemployment, and some issues concerning the timing of when a person is more likely to be in the workforce.

Considering that the professional needs to estimate two streams of expected earnings or earnings capacity—that of the worker pre-injury and that of the worker post-injury—a permanent disability is likely to have an impact on post-injury participation in the workforce. According to Ireland et al., from the Bureau of Census and Social Security administration data, workforce participation rates for disabled workers are lower than for those similar but nondisabled employees. Given the likely impact of disability on the injured person's ability to participate in the workforce and the challenge of determining how that may affect participation, the professional should consider input from a qualified expert.

Another area of concern for wages is associated with taxes. The objective is that the injured party comes out whole. As a result, a study of federal, state, and local taxes is necessary. Earnings, if received in the future, would be taxable when received. But, in some cases, lost earnings awards are not taxable. How the settlement is characterized may also have tax implications. Historical earnings had an amount associated with the tax liability. In cases where lost wages would not be subject to taxes, such as those covered by disability insurance where the premium was paid by the individual, taxes can be removed from the lost wages amount. In other cases, the lost wage award is taxable, because the award represents expected wages that would have been earned in future periods but for the injury. In those situations, the issue is the marginal tax rates. The tax on a single lump sum may be considerably higher than if the person earned those amounts in future years in lower tax brackets. The estimate of lost earnings needs to address this.

A related issue is the discount rate. Some government bonds generate interest tax free; others do not. So the expert should be careful when the discount rate explicitly considers the impact of taxable interest because of the type of investment. The simplest solution is to incorporate **Aaa-rated** municipal bonds as discount rates. Because earnings on these investments are tax free, the rate explicitly deals with the taxability of interest. If other investments are chosen to proxy for the risk-free rate of interest, an adjustment for taxes can be taken into account.

With regard to a survival action (where the decedent was assumed to have lived into the future), the standard of loss is that of the decedent. The calculation is generally the same as a total disability. Thus, the estimate of actual future earnings would be zero, and the total amount of expected future earnings or lost earnings capacity would be the amount of the loss. The lost earnings would be awarded to the estate, which would distribute the assets to the survivors based on wills and applicable state laws. With wrongful death, where the amount of loss is to the survivors, the total of lost earnings is normally too high. The argument is that the deceased person would have enjoyed at least some of those lost earnings him- or herself and that what the deceased individual enjoyed, the others could not. The challenge is determining how much of the total lost earnings would have been enjoyed by the deceased versus the amount enjoyed by the survivors. One clarification is necessary: Expected earnings are all that could be lost to the survivors. Only the deceased could have pursued any lost earnings capacity.

Analysis of Lost Employment Benefits Associated with Lost Earnings

Generally, not all employment benefits are lost when an injury or permanent disability occurs. The applicable standard is those benefits the injured party has lost. Discretionary employee benefits are those paid by that employer that are not government-mandated and include automobiles, bonuses, and other award plans (e.g., contest awards, trips, etc.), dental disability, medical, vision care, and life insurance; education; employee discounts, meals, employee uniforms, health and entertainment facilities; paid sick, vacation, and family leave; and prescription drug, retirement, and stock option purchase plans. The amount to include in the loss calculation is not the cost to the employer, but the value to the employee. It is the use of those benefits that determines the amount of the employee loss. A few complications arise.

For example, how should benefits be reflected that were available but not used? In some cases, such as a fitness facility, the person may have not used it before but now needs that benefit as a result of the injury and changes in lifestyle. Even if the injury does not necessitate the use of a previously unused benefit, it does not necessarily mean that the employee would never have elected to use it at some future date. For example, as people age, they often become more concerned about their overall fitness and may select the use of a facility when that option had not been used in prior years. The minimum seems to be that it would have been likely the employee might have elected that benefit in the future. In some cases, such as where disability insurance is utilized, the argument can be made that the particular benefit has been activated and that no future loss is possible.

Going back to the issue of loss to the employee versus the cost to the employer, it needs to be considered that an employer may have access to group discounts and other options that allow him or her to pay less than a worker seeking a benefit as an individual. For example, health insurance tends to be lower under employer group rates than for individual policies. Because it is the benefit to the employee that counts, the cost to the employee to obtain that benefit in the marketplace as an individual is the proper standard. Finally, given the need to project expected employment after injury, compared to what could (would) have been but for the injury, consider the types of benefits available with post-injury employment versus pre-injury employment and career path.

With regard to benefits mandated by government laws and regulations, additional analysis is required. Generally, mandated employment benefits are provided in four separate areas: Medicare, Social Security, unemployment, and workers compensation. Medicare payments are a type of tax, and a person's eligibility is not affected by amounts contributed or not contributed. The 1.45 percent mandated amount for Medicare is usually not counted as a lost job-related benefit. Social Security is 6.2 percent of earnings up to certain income levels. The U.S. Social Security administration maintains a record of earnings upon which the tax is paid by individuals. Social Security benefits are then paid based on the highest thirty-five years of wages. Thus, the elimination of employer payments into Social Security would likely have an impact on the employee's Social Security benefits later in life. However, determining the impact is challenging, because the amounts paid from Social Security are not analogous to amounts paid in.

A detailed analysis of the changes to Social Security contributions and resulting payouts is necessary to determine losses associated with Social Security benefits. Of the 6.2 percent, 5.35 percent is related to retirement income, and 0.85 percent is associated with disability insurance. If the injured party becomes eligible for disability, that person is likely to derive greater benefits from prior contributions than any loss of future benefits. Unemployment benefits can be estimated for workers who face joblessness with some regularity. Because workers compensation is designed to support workers during times of unemployment as a result of on-the-job injuries, the injured worker tends to lose no benefits when receiving lost earnings from other sources. As can be seen, employment benefits need to be carefully examined to ensure that the injured party is not made worse off as a result of the injury.

Assuming a survival action where the deceased is assumed to have lived, the analysis of lost benefits correlates highly with that of a permanent disability loss. However, in wrongful death cases, where the basis of evaluation is losses to the survivors, the analysis is more challenging. Each type of benefit—discretionary and mandated—needs to be examined to determine whether the survivors suffered losses because they would have received incremental benefits (because the deceased would have passed at least a portion of the benefit along to them). In a number of areas, the surviving spouse, children, and other beneficiaries would have received little or no benefits. For example, assuming that the deceased would not have drawn Social Security until age sixty-five, in all likelihood, the children would have grown by then and would have received little or no portion of those benefits. However, had the person been an older parent and the children not reached the age of eighteen, a portion of lost benefits would have been allocated to the underage children.

A similar case can be made for retirement plan contributions made by the employer. Assuming that the children had grown prior to distributions from the plan, they would have received little benefits. However, to the extent that the contributions would have created excess amounts in the retirement that would have been inherited by the children, a case can be made that the children suffered losses. Similarly, the surviving spouse often suffers from lower Social Security benefits because of the decedent's passing. Because the standard of loss is to that of the surviving spouse, an allocation needs to be made of lost benefits between the persons. However, if the major "bread winner" is lost in a wrongful death case, an argument might be made that the surviving spouse's quality of life and retirement income levels would be negatively affected. Life insurance that was previously paid by the employer, which was activated and paid off at the time of death, is arguably not a lost benefit because it had been received. The fundamental

premise in a wrongful death is that the loss must be sustained by the survivors. Each benefit must be carefully assessed to determine whether it was lost to the decedent or to the survivor, and if the loss is to the survivor, determine the amount involved.

Analysis of Lost Nonmarket Services

As discussed previously, persons not only generate earnings and related fringe benefits, but they also perform services—primarily around the living quarters and for parents, children, and others who may not reside with the injured person but who are dependent on the injured party for delivery of these services. Such services may include the following:

1. Auto maintenance and repair
2. Childcare
3. Cleaning
4. Cooking
5. Periodic home improvements
6. Home repairs and maintenance
7. Laundry
8. Lawn mowing, care, and maintenance
9. Painting
10. Plumbing
11. Sewing
12. Shopping
13. Teaching and other contributions to education
14. Transportation (to doctors, grocery stores, pharmacy, sporting events, etc.)

A number of approaches can be used to estimate these costs. First, the actual costs to develop and utilize substitute services in the marketplace can be used. Obtained on a piecemeal basis, such services may be expensive, but that may be the only option for some survivors when a provider is no longer able to deliver the service.

A second option is to accumulate the number of hours associated with these activities on a weekly basis and then multiply those hours by a reasonable rate to pay for those services in the marketplace. Some estimates suggest that the full-time male year-round worker contributes an average of seven hours of unskilled labor around the household and that the number of hours decreases as the need for skilled labor arises. For married full-time female workers, the estimate of household hours contributed can be two to three times the number for men. The wages applied to the different areas of household production can be based on the skills required and the availability of labor in the marketplace to perform those services. Further, the coordination and organization of household work are often considered skilled labor.

In the absence of actual hours worked each week, month, or year, an option is to develop a "per hour," "per week," or "per month" estimate and apply a reasonable wage rate. The amounts can serve as benchmarks for the trier-of-fact, and the judge or jury can decide how much time those services would have been provided into the future. For example, assume that a full-time working mother suffered an injury and that she worked approximately fifteen hours per week in the evenings and on weekends performing cooking, cleaning, and laundry for the family. Further assume that the going wage rate for these services is $8.00. Then, on average, the mother's weekly contribution was $120. This benchmark could be provided to the trier-of-fact. If it is determined that she would have provided these or similar services for the next twenty-five years, the value of her contribution, before discounting, is $156,000 ($120/week × 52 weeks × 25 years).

A couple of issues arise. First, the injured person may have provided these services well into retirement. Second, even if the injured person had not suffered the injury, he or she would not have provided these services for the remainder of life. These issues must be incorporated into the estimate of nonmarket services provided. For example, child care may only last until the children graduate from high school. Another issue arises when the injured party provides services to others outside his or her primary household. A couple of examples include services provided to older parents or to children who have left the household but still depend on the parents. Presume an injured father may have provided automobile repair and other household fix-it services to his children who reside locally. These are valuable to those receiving

explanations are sound and do not allow opposing counsel to reframe the analogy or metaphor to its advantage. Any examples that make the testimony more accessible and understandable for the jury and judge should be used. For example, if you state that the company spent $2.5 million for an airplane, hanger, fuel, and maintenance over a seven-year period, you could then explain that this breaks down to approximately $350,000 a year or almost $1,000 per day. Noting that a round-trip airline ticket from Pittsburgh to Atlanta costs about $250, this company with four executives, 200 employees, and one location would have had to send four people to and from Atlanta almost every day for seven years to justify this expense. It's easy now for the jury to understand what an expense of $2.5 million for an airplane may mean for a relatively small entity, their financial performance, and financial condition, and it's easy to see that the expense may be unnecessary for the few flights the company might require annually.

Other key points related to direct examination:

- Listen
- Watch the jury and judge to ensure that they seem to understand
- Use summaries of testimony and exhibits
- Enumerate points (1, 2, 3, etc.)
- Demonstrate "open-mindedness" without compromising the integrity of your conclusions and opinions
- Use visual aids to maintain attention

By the time the expert witness has finished testifying during direct examination, the jury should understand:

- Your conclusions and opinions
- The evidence upon which your conclusions and opinions are based
- How your work fits into the greater story: who, what, when, where, how, and possibly why
- How your work explains the act, concealment, and conversion
- How your work considered the fraud triangle: pressure, opportunity, and rationalization
- The motivation of the defendant to the extent possible: M.I.C.E.

Cross-Examination

Cross-examination is supposed to be a search for the truth. If testimony can withstand the onslaught of cross-examination by a skillful attorney, then the testimony must be credible. To a certain extent, that is true; however, skillful attorneys can lead unwary expert witnesses in directions they don't want to go and to conclusions the expert doesn't believe or intend to convey. Thus, in a perfect world, the truth may come out during cross-examination; but, it's far better to be prepared and understand how opposing counsel may twist your testimony to their advantage.

The first goal of the opposing attorney during cross examination is to destroy the expert's credibility, if possible. As noted above, credibility is earned and derives its power from a number of sources. Opposing counsel can attack credibility on any number of fronts. For example, the opposing attorney may ask if you are an industry expert; the answer is "no." If left at that, the expert's credibility in the eyes of the jury may be damaged. The better answer is "No, but I am a forensic accountant and the tools of my trade are examining books and records, income statements, balance sheets, cash flows, and the like. With those tools and techniques, I am an expert and I applied my expertise to my work in this case."

At the same time that opposing counsel is trying to destroy the other side's experts, they are trying to enhance their own theory of the case and minimize the impact of the expert's testimony. In contrast, the fraud examiner or forensic accountant should maintain a commitment to their objectives: keep teaching and using evidence-based conclusions and opinions while maintaining credibility and control of one's own testimony. For instance, in the example above, an answer of "no" would have been accurate and defensible. Nevertheless, in the eyes of the jury it could have been misleading; thus, the need to answer "no . . . but." That is an example of not surrendering control.

Opposing counsel may try to accomplish their goals by carefully controlling what they ask. Controlled confrontation occurs when opposing counsel continues to try to weave their own story by selectively asking questions of the expert. The opposing attorney may even go so far as to repeat his or her own story, using the expert to answer only selected inquiries where damage will be minimized. The question format for

Deposition Testimony

A deposition is a pre-trial process by which the parties to a civil litigation are allowed to examine the other side's fact witnesses and expert witnesses. Generally, depositions do not occur in criminal litigation; although many of the witnesses may have been interviewed, those interviews are typically not under oath. Essentially, based on discovery in civil litigation, (including depositions) each side knows the other side's theory of the case and what the witnesses are expected to say. As such, the civil trial becomes, to some extent, an act of presentation and choreography. The function of a deposition is to:

- Gather testimonial and documentary evidence from witnesses
- Limit the scope of what witnesses may say when the actual trial occurs
- Test or confirm theories and hypotheses
- Develop a record under oath and thereby "freeze" a witness's testimony
- Evaluate the credibility and persuasiveness of the witness as well as their work, conclusions, and opinions
- Move the case toward settlement or trial
- Compare the deposition testimony to prior statements and statements made by other witnesses
- Test the expert witness's report

In preparation for a deposition, expert witnesses should thoroughly review their report and the underlying data. Additionally, in a pre-deposition meeting, the fraud examiner or forensic accountant should meet with counsel to review the report and answer questions. Counsel will normally have one of two strategic goals for the expert with regard to the deposition: (1) show the strength of their hand and (2) limit the areas of inquiry to those examined by opposing counsel. Assuming that the attorney you are working with believes in the strength of the case and the opposing side understands the depth and import of your work, they will more than likely move to settle. Retained counsel will want their experts to be clear, be concise, and expound on their opinions. Of course, there is risk in this approach.

If the case does not settle, opposing counsel will have a thorough understanding of your conclusions and opinions and be in the best position to attempt to undermine your work. In other cases, counsel will recognize that the case is going to trial and will be heard by a jury and judge. In that situation, as an expert witness you must be clear and accurate in your testimony. Interestingly, opposing counsel may not explore every aspect of your work; your attorney may prefer that you only respond to those areas in which opposing counsel asks questions. Of course, if opposing counsel asks the blanket question, "Are those all of the conclusions and opinions that you plan to offer at trial?" the expert will need to cover areas not already explored.

The format of a deposition is more akin to cross-examination by opposing counsel. Though the attorney who retained you may ask some "clean up" questions near the end, it is common for only the opposing counsel to ask questions. Although the deposition typically takes place in an attorney's conference room or some other mutually agreed upon place, many aspects are similar to a trial. First, the testimony is recorded under oath by a stenographer. It will be prepared in transcript form and may be reviewed prior to finalization to ensure that the record is accurate. Further, opposing experts may observe the testimony of the fraud examiner or forensic accountant. When subpoenaed, the expert witness may receive a subpoena *duces tecum*, which requires that he or she arrive with his or her report and all documents that he or she reviewed, evaluated, and/or relied upon to develop his or her conclusions and opinions.

Direct Examination

Direct examination is the intersection of credibility and preparation.[3] It is the heart of the case for the attorney and a chance to frame the issues and the evidence from his or her perspective for the jury and judge. The presentation is that of question and answer; the attorney who retained the expert witness will frame the question and the expert witness must answer that specific question. Thus, the attorney must navigate through the goals and objectives of the direct testimony by carefully asking questions that elicit the topical information needed. The expert witness must be careful to listen to and then answer the questions presented. Even though the form is question and answer, the goal is to tell a story logically and dramatically.

The expert witness will often use analogies and metaphors to make difficult and technical testimony more understandable for the jury. Such tools should be thought through carefully in advance so that the

explanations are sound and do not allow opposing counsel to reframe the analogy or metaphor to its advantage. Any examples that make the testimony more accessible and understandable for the jury and judge should be used. For example, if you state that the company spent $2.5 million for an airplane, hanger, fuel, and maintenance over a seven-year period, you could then explain that this breaks down to approximately $350,000 a year or almost $1,000 per day. Noting that a round-trip airline ticket from Pittsburgh to Atlanta costs about $250, this company with four executives, 200 employees, and one location would have had to send four people to and from Atlanta almost every day for seven years to justify this expense. It's easy now for the jury to understand what an expense of $2.5 million for an airplane may mean for a relatively small entity, their financial performance, and financial condition, and it's easy to see that the expense may be unnecessary for the few flights the company might require annually.

Other key points related to direct examination:

- Listen
- Watch the jury and judge to ensure that they seem to understand
- Use summaries of testimony and exhibits
- Enumerate points (1, 2, 3, etc.)
- Demonstrate "open-mindedness" without compromising the integrity of your conclusions and opinions
- Use visual aids to maintain attention

By the time the expert witness has finished testifying during direct examination, the jury should understand:

- Your conclusions and opinions
- The evidence upon which your conclusions and opinions are based
- How your work fits into the greater story: who, what, when, where, how, and possibly why
- How your work explains the act, concealment, and conversion
- How your work considered the fraud triangle: pressure, opportunity, and rationalization
- The motivation of the defendant to the extent possible: M.I.C.E.

Cross-Examination

Cross-examination is supposed to be a search for the truth. If testimony can withstand the onslaught of cross-examination by a skillful attorney, then the testimony must be credible. To a certain extent, that is true; however, skillful attorneys can lead unwary expert witnesses in directions they don't want to go and to conclusions the expert doesn't believe or intend to convey. Thus, in a perfect world, the truth may come out during cross-examination; but, it's far better to be prepared and understand how opposing counsel may twist your testimony to their advantage.

The first goal of the opposing attorney during cross examination is to destroy the expert's credibility, if possible. As noted above, credibility is earned and derives its power from a number of sources. Opposing counsel can attack credibility on any number of fronts. For example, the opposing attorney may ask if you are an industry expert; the answer is "no." If left at that, the expert's credibility in the eyes of the jury may be damaged. The better answer is "No, but I am a forensic accountant and the tools of my trade are examining books and records, income statements, balance sheets, cash flows, and the like. With those tools and techniques, I am an expert and I applied my expertise to my work in this case."

At the same time that opposing counsel is trying to destroy the other side's experts, they are trying to enhance their own theory of the case and minimize the impact of the expert's testimony. In contrast, the fraud examiner or forensic accountant should maintain a commitment to their objectives: keep teaching and using evidence-based conclusions and opinions while maintaining credibility and control of one's own testimony. For instance, in the example above, an answer of "no" would have been accurate and defensible. Nevertheless, in the eyes of the jury it could have been misleading; thus, the need to answer "no . . . but." That is an example of not surrendering control.

Opposing counsel may try to accomplish their goals by carefully controlling what they ask. Controlled confrontation occurs when opposing counsel continues to try to weave their own story by selectively asking questions of the expert. The opposing attorney may even go so far as to repeat his or her own story, using the expert to answer only selected inquiries where damage will be minimized. The question format for

firing, personal injury, breach of contract, or tortuous interference): How did it occur? Where was the procedural or operational breakdown? How do we ensure that it does not occur in the future?

Finally, if the issue was financial statement fraud: Where was the deficiency in corporate governance? Was management override involved? How was the fraud hidden from the audit committee, auditors, and board of directors?

The investigative process from initial red flags through deposition and courtroom testimony provide an excellent foundation for developing a knowledge repository for sharing lessons learned.

RECOVERY OF MONEY AND OTHER ASSETS

Whereas some fraud victims undertake a thorough investigation from initial symptoms through litigation based on principle, others consider the cost-benefit aspect of the fraud examination. In other words, assuming that the auditors successfully identify the perpetrator and have evidence of the act, concealment, and conversion, is there likely to be any money in it for those injured? More simply stated, can the victim recover any money or other assets from the perpetrator? Why spend significant funds litigating a civil dispute if a successful verdict is likely to result in no recovery of funds for the victim(s)? In fact, the possibility of loss recovery might be the only aspect of a fraud investigation that is attractive to the victim.

Certainly, the investigative process requires significant resources and is both taxing and time consuming. Anti-fraud professionals would like their work product to be a resource that the client can use to obtain the largest recovery allowed by law. Of course, if the work was done to support a civil action, then recovery was the primary motive from inception. The plaintiff always has at least some focus on amounts to be recovered as a result of the perpetrator's action.

If the evidentiary support is significantly in favor of the prosecution (plaintiff), then the claimant approaches the recovery stage in a position of relative power. Certainly, upon winning a civil action, the plaintiff is in the strongest position to collect. But even pre-trial, civil attorneys for both the plaintiff and defense are constantly weighing the evidence and the relative positions of the parties to determine the optimal negotiating strategy. Keep in mind that a favorable verdict for the plaintiff in a civil case is only a necessary first step in the recovery process; it requires additional action to collect amounts awarded.

The types of monetary remuneration that may be available to victims and plaintiffs include:

Money stolen

Other assets stolen

Value lost

Interest

Fines and penalties

Punitive damages

Normally, some of the issues to consider when attempting to recover assets include:

1. Amounts stolen and amounts that may be recovered
2. The prospect of winning the case
3. The value of the assets held by the defendant and whether they are sufficient
4. The legal costs involved in pursuing the financial claim and subsequent collection

In addition, a multidisciplinary approach should be considered. For example, the fraud examiner or forensic accountant may need to obtain the assistance of individuals with international banking experience to trace money around the world, a private investigator to conduct surveillance, or an expert with knowledge of offshore banking techniques used to launder money and hide assets. Finally, claimants (victims and plaintiffs) should be proactive rather than reactive when it comes to the recovery of money and other assets.

Identification of Money and Assets for Recovery

The first step to successfully recover money and other assets is to identify them during the investigative process. To prove fraud, the investigator needs to provide evidence that the perpetrator was involved in the act (money or other assets are missing), the concealment (there was an attempt to hide the act and

possibly the assets), and the conversion (benefits accrued to the perpetrator). Inherently, the investigative process requires that the fraud examiner or forensic accountant is able to show that the perpetrator was the recipient of assets and what, if anything, the perpetrator did with those assets.

As noted in prior chapters, this requires access and evaluation of banking, public, business, and personal records—financial and nonfinancial. The identification of money, assets, and other items of value obtained directly or indirectly as a result of fraud is one of the important goals of the investigation. Such evidence not only facilitates the legal process, it also helps to ensure the maximum recoverable amounts for the victim or plaintiff. One aspect of a civil action is that the jury will often be required by the presiding judge to consider the defendant's ability to pay. If the defendant loses the civil issue in question, will they be able to pay the full amount of the award of damages or some lesser amount?

Generally, in order to be in a position to recover money from a civil suit, the injured party must prove two points:

1. Liability: the defendant was responsible for all or part of the damages claimed
2. Losses or damages: the claimant suffered damages as a result of the actions or inactions of the offending party

The types of losses available for recovery include (a) compensatory damages and restitution of losses such as value, cash, and other assets; (b) economic losses (e.g., wages, incremental expenses, or profits); (c) reliance, intended to restore the claimants back to where they would have been but for the actions of the defendant; and (d) punitive damages, to punish the defendant.

In a civil framework, the plaintiff must demonstrate three attributes:

1. That the defendant was the proximate cause of any damages, meaning that the plaintiff caused or contributed to the lost amounts as a direct result of the conduct at issue
2. Reasonable certainty as to the amounts (damages) claimed
3. That the defendant could reasonably foresee that his or her actions, or lack thereof, were likely to result in damages to the plaintiff

Following versus Tracing the Money

"Following the money" and "tracing the money" are slightly different activities and may have legal ramifications on amounts available for recovery. *Following* the money assumes an ability to directly track funds from the victim to the alleged perpetrator and involves specificity, whereby the investigator can track the exact assets in question from the plaintiff or victim to the defendant. When an investigator can follow the money with specificity, the ability of a victim or plaintiff to lay claim to the ill-gotten gains may determine the likelihood of asset recovery. Cash or other assets can only be *followed* if those assets remain in their original, identifiable form as they flow from place to place or person to person. *Following* provides for no exchanges or substitutions.

In many cases, defendants will convert their ill-gotten gains into another type of asset. The whole purpose behind money laundering, for example, is to take money derived from some illegal activity and clean it to make it appear to have come from a legitimate source. Once illegal money has been combined with money from legitimate sources, one can no longer *follow* the money; the money can only be *traced*.

In contrast to following the money, tracing the money is a process of identification: both its present location and form of value relevant to a claim brought by a plaintiff or victim. In such cases, the legal issues can be messy. For example, what if illegal money is combined in a bank account with the legitimate salary dollars of a spouse? To further complicate the matter, let's assume that the couple has children, and one of the items paid out of the bank account is the mortgage on their primary home where the children reside. Notwithstanding the legal issues involved, tracing is the process of determining what has happened to the money or property, who handled it, and where it is now. This helps to justify a claim against the property in its current form.

In theory, complex financial crimes, fraud, organized crime, drug trafficking, money laundering, and terrorism financing can be prosecuted by following the money. But to prevent investigators from following the money, perpetrators attempt to disguise its sources to make it difficult to connect them with their ill-gotten gains. Such efforts also act to limit the ability of investigators to lay claim to money that otherwise appears to be derived from legitimate sources.

A complicating factor is that "money" is no longer cash and coin; it can be anything of value that can be traded, transferred, or sold, such as cash, coin, certificates of deposit, stocks, bonds, money orders,

cashier's checks, cybercurrencies, airline tickets, gift certificates, gift cards, pre-paid credit and debit cards, diamonds, jewels, minerals, mineral rights, or deeds. Often times, money, such as Second Life's Linden dollars, is nothing more than a series of 0s and 1s, electronic off and on switches that another person or entity is willing to accept as value.

Once illegal money has been combined with money from legitimate sources, one can no longer *follow* the money; the money can only be *traced*. Even mixing money in a bank account creates the need to subsequently trace the money. Modern laws have addressed this issue to a certain extent by allowing claims to be made in situations in which illegal gains can only be traced. This requires additional work on the part of the investigator to identify the sources of assets that have been commingled and to make various assumptions to demonstrate how the conversion process was completed.

Other issues related to tracing involve what happens to the incremental value of assets for those assets that have increased in worth. For example, what if the perpetrator purchased a vacation home and the value increased by 20 percent annually? Generally, the courts have held that the perpetrator was acting to make an investment on behalf of the victim or plaintiff and any increases accrue to the victim or plaintiff; however, that may not always be the case in every jurisdiction. This "investment" approach means that, although rare, it may be possible for a plaintiff or victim to recover more than what was originally lost.

Legal Methods for Recovery of Assets

Depending on the jurisdiction, plaintiffs and victims have a number of possible legal mechanisms available to recover assets either through the civil or criminal justice system.

Freezing Orders Freezing orders, restraining orders, and judicial injunctions are used early in a legal action to secure funds so that they do not disappear prior to obtaining a favorable verdict or negotiated settlement. Assuming that the victim or plaintiff can establish the current whereabouts of money, a freezing order can be very effective, not only in protecting assets, but also in bringing the defendant to the negotiating table. Freezing orders, restraining orders, and judicial injunctions can protect the assets from dissipation while legal proceedings move forward.

In order to obtain a freezing order, the plaintiffs or victims will need to demonstrate that: they have a reasonably strong case, they have suffered significant damage or financial harm, there is a possibility that the assets will disappear if not protected by the courts, and any damage done to the defendant will be less than damages already suffered by the plaintiff or victim. Obtaining freezing orders can be risky because the courts may rule in favor of the defendants, thereby increasing their negotiating position and harming the negotiating power of the opposing side. On the other hand, a freezing order, once obtained, places pressure on the defendant to come to the negotiating table.

Plaintiffs and victims should attempt to get freezing orders in place at the earliest possible time to avoid losing track of assets or having them sold or disappear. Preferably, these orders are obtained *ex parte* so that they can surprise the defendant and prevent assets from disappearing before resolution of the case. The freezing order does not give the claimant the right to confiscate cash, assets, or property; it simply prevents the defendant from taking action to impair the value of those assets prior to resolving the issue via the judicial process. Freezing orders typically have time limits, so the claimant should attempt to get the longest period possible. The claimant should also try to get the order to cover as wide an array of property and other assets as possible. In some cases, specialists such as accountants or other experts may be needed to manage income-generating property pending the outcome of a civil or criminal trial.

Insurance and Bonds Companies, as part of their fraud protection activities, will often purchase insurance and bonds to cover losses caused by dishonest employees, vendors, or customers. Such loss-prevention efforts usually come in the form of fidelity bonds, or may be purchased with some property insurance policies as special riders. As with any insurance policy, this protection is subject to limits and exclusions.

To recover money from the policies, the claimant normally has to provide sworn proof of a loss claim within specified time frames. These claims require supporting evidence and a statement of the loss. The insurance company normally does not participate in the investigation but will reserve the right to satisfy itself as to the facts and circumstances as well as the amount of the loss. Some policies will pay for the cost of an investigation, but those costs may be specifically excluded by the insurance policy.

Once the insurance company pays a claim it normally, as a matter of the contract, obtains the rights against the defendants. This aspect can provide heartburn to the victim or plaintiff. Consider the example in which a company was defrauded in a significant manner by a large customer of the insured. If the

insurance company pays off the claimant and it obtains the rights against the customer, that positions the victim company as an adversary of their customer. Thus, in some cases, even if insurance is in place, companies may not want to jeopardize their relationship with important stakeholders, even when possible damage amounts are significant.

Judgments   A judgment is a formal and final decision made by a court of law. Once a civil or criminal trial is complete and damages are awarded, this can be taken to a separate court for the purposes of entering a judgment for the amounts owed. Because a judgment is a final order entered by the court, it leaves no further action available to the losing party, absent an appeal. Armed with a judgment, the plaintiff or victim is now in a more secure position to demand payments from the defendant. Further, the judgment will be entered on the defendant's credit report, effectively eliminating the ability to obtain credit until the judgment is satisfied. Judgments may cover not only amounts lost, but also interest and legal costs, depending on the jurisdiction.

Confiscation Orders, Compensation Orders, Forfeiture, and Seizure of Assets   When a defendant does not pay amounts owed to victims and plaintiffs as outlined in a judgment, the claimant may return to court to obtain various types of orders for the seizure and sale of specific property, usually at auction. In some jurisdictions, these court orders are referred to as confiscation orders, and in others they are called compensation orders or forfeiture orders. One of the primary differences is that forfeiture orders typically apply to specific assets, whereas confiscation and compensation orders refer to amounts that may be covered by available assets. Assuming that the value of assets included in a forfeiture order is sufficient to make a claimant whole, forfeiture is preferable in the sense that it effectively gives the claimant the right, and possibly title, to specific assets.

With a court order in hand, the sheriff or other officer of the court may enter the defendant's business, home, or property and take possession of goods and other assets. If those goods are later sold at auction "on the courthouse steps," the proceeds are paid to the victim or plaintiff. As noted above, assets that may be available for recovery need to be identified during the investigative stage and the claimant should proceed to court with a list of assets and their probable location. Normally, court orders are going to be limited in amount to the total assets held by the defendant or the amounts owed to the victim or plaintiff, whichever is lower.

Third Party Debt Orders   A third party debt order is similar to a garnishment and requires that the defendant's debtors pay the claimant (the victim or plaintiff) instead of remitting money to the defendant. For example, assume that the defendant has accounts receivable from five customers that arose from the sale of goods and services and that the amounts to be received will perfectly cover the judgment amount. The court may order those third party debtors to pay amounts owed to the defendant directly to the claimants. This has the effect of satisfying the third parties' obligations to the defendant and the defendant's obligation to the claimant all at the same time. It's as though the third party debtors made the payment to the defendant and the defendant turned around and immediately paid the victim or plaintiff.

Recovery against Third Party Defendants   In some cases, accountants, lawyers, executives, managers, directors, audit committee members, and officers may be held accountable for the actions of companies that they represent. The threshold for such legal action is normally negligence or gross negligence, although Sarbanes–Oxley has had the effect of making these parties more accountable in public companies for the quality of their work and the handling of their responsibilities. Direct claims can also be made against third parties who benefited from the fraud or financial crime even if the evidence isn't strong enough to demonstrate that they knowingly participated.

SUPPORT FOR CRIMINAL AND CIVIL COURT ACTIONS

The second major area of the remediation process involves supporting the plaintiff or prosecuting attorney through the legal process. This typically involves numerous consultations, periodic communication of findings and investigative issues, writing reports, attendance at opposing party depositions, being deposed, testifying in various hearings, being present during settlement negotiations, and testifying in court. In various types of fraud examination and forensic accounting investigations, the professional will do some

and possibly all of these activities at the direction of the attorneys and/or other officers of the court. The anti-fraud professional or forensic accountant may be hired as a consultant or an expert witness, or may be a court-appointed expert or master.

No matter what the engagement, you should remember that you are not an advocate for any side. In fact, at all times, you must remain the quintessential independent, objective professional. All facts and evidence are to be objectively evaluated using critical-thinking skills, analytical reasoning, and brainstorming. The anti-fraud professional is in search of the alternative explanation, an alternate hypothesis, and all the ways that one might characterize or mischaracterize the information, facts, and data to tell another side of the story.

The commitment to professionalism is the hallmark of the fraud examiner and forensic accountant. Although consultants are not expected to testify, it is common for the attorney to convert consultants into expert witnesses depending on the investigative outcomes and the strategic direction of the case. More importantly, most prosecutors and attorneys work a case with an eye toward pre-trial settlements: guilty or *nolo contendere* pleas, monetary settlements, and so forth. As such, they expect the forensic accountant and fraud examiner to provide them with all the information so that they can work toward a pre-trial resolution after assessing the likely outcomes with an objective view.

In addition to financial crimes, a forensic accountant may serve as an expert in a number of civil litigation matters: damage claims, personal injury, wrongful death, predatory pricing, antitrust, breach of contract, divorce, bankruptcy, torts and tortuous interference, valuations, and financial reconstruction.

Fact Witnesses versus Expert Witnesses

Most foundation testimony in a case is provided by fact or lay witnesses. These individuals testify to various facts that they put in perspective by talking about events, activities, and state of mind at the time the issues in question arose. Generally, fact witnesses must testify to firsthand facts and knowledge. They are not permitted to offer opinions unless those views are based on specialized knowledge required as part of their normal responsibilities. For example, mine supervisors with twenty years of experience can provide opinions on mining conditions because they make those same assessments as part of their jobs. Further, the lay opinion rule allows a fact witness to offer "everyday" opinions under three conditions:[1]

1. The opinion must be based on the witness's personal perceptions (as opposed to hearsay)
2. The opinion must be helpful to the trier-of-fact
3. The opinion must be the product of reasoning processes familiar to the average person in everyday life

In contrast to a fact or lay witness, an expert witness is one who, by virtue of education, profession, publication, or experience, is believed to have special knowledge of his or her subject beyond that of the average person, sufficient that others may officially (and legally) rely upon the opinion.

Generally, the role of the fraud examiner or forensic accountant when working with attorneys and other persons related to legal matters is to:

- Educate counsel
- Reconstruct cash flows and performance from records
- Guide additional investigation and discovery
- Make connections, draw conclusions, and offer observations
- Determine whether evidence supports theories of case
- Provide objective evaluations of the information, data, and evidence
- Draft report and exhibits
- Offer deposition and trial testimony

An expert's opinion is subject to two types of challenges:

1. With the Daubert Rule, the basis of foundation for the opinion may not be based on "junk science." Just because a person qualifies as an expert, that person cannot offer any opinion unless that opinion is reasonably grounded in scientific fact; and
2. The Frye Rule makes an opinion admissible only if that opinion has general acceptance in the scientific community.

In either case, the expert must provide the basis for his or her opinions as well as the facts, data, and other information relied upon. Not surprisingly, determining the amount of losses is both an art and a science. The science aspect requires the fraud examiner and forensic accountant to understand and use methods appropriate for their field such as generally accepted accounting principles and proper investigative tools and techniques. The artistic aspect is understanding the judgment inherent in accounting, accounting estimates, the ability to connect the dots, the need to use creative thinking, and the proper consideration of alternative theories of the case, to name a few.

Assuming that legal counsel initiated the investigation, the professional should complete the following steps:

1. Obtain a written engagement letter with the terms and conditions of the engagement clearly spelled out. The anti-fraud professional or forensic accountant should ensure that the terms are clear and ethical. For example, the engagement letter should not state what the professional is expected to find as a result of his or her investigation nor the topics on which the expert is expected to testify. Such language may suggest bias, may limit the investigation, and may provide grounds for opposing counsel to attack the professional's objectivity, integrity, and credibility.

2. Conduct an initial consultation to obtain an overview of the issues in question, determine the required areas in which expertise is required, and acquire initial direction and other information, facts, and data.

3. Complete the required investigative work. This requires fraud examiners and forensic accounting professionals to apply their judgment, develop insights, interpret the facts and data, draw conclusions, provide advice and counsel to the lawyers, and solicit additional data as needed. Typically, periodic consultations with the attorneys and others will be necessary to develop a complete picture of the issues in question, discuss preliminary findings and interpretations, and determine the next steps.

4. Wrap up the investigation, draw conclusions, and write the report.

5. Prepare for depositions, hearings, and courtroom testimony and appear in court as needed.

Naturally, the investigative process involves the evaluation and interpretation of information, facts, and data. Nonetheless, much of what attorneys rely on from experts is determining what data are needed and what appears to be missing. It's not so much what you see but what you don't see that needs to be identified. That requires the anti-fraud professional and forensic accountant to constantly apply their critical-thinking skills, analytical reasoning, and brainstorming techniques to challenge their interpretations and preliminary conclusions. Once the expert has identified the needed data, the prosecutor or civil attorney can pursue obtaining those data through the legal system.

One of the continuing challenges of fraud and forensic accounting professionals is "staying in their sandbox"—their area of expertise. As long as the professional remains within his or her field of expertise and develops conclusions grounded in the evidence, he or she has a safe haven. Determining what you can say as an expert is a challenge. For example, where are the boundaries of your expertise? When does accounting cross too far into finance, economics, marketing, management, and other business disciplines? Generally, when you have identified that you are relying on facts or another's expertise, you need to acknowledge that reliance. You need to evaluate the importance of that evidence and be cognizant that that evidence may not withstand the scrutiny of cross-examination. Thus, the fraud examiner or forensic accountant needs to continually evaluate what happens to his or her own opinions and conclusions when any piece of evidence is eliminated for any reason.

Further, fraud and forensic accounting professionals should not get into a position in which they are defending the opinions and conclusions of others. Such defense is beyond their expertise. At the same time, the fraud examiner is likely to be working in an industry or business with which they do not have complete familiarity. Although professionals need to develop comfort with their knowledge base in order to understand the attributes of a successful business model, fraud examiners or forensic accountants need to expect some level of discomfort with not being experts in all subject areas; their opinions, to some extent, usually rely on facts and opinions of others where their own understanding is limited. In those situations, tread lightly with opinions or risk being criticized for drawing conclusions and expressing opinions beyond your area of expertise.

Supporting the Investigation

The fraud examiner or forensic accountant needs to recognize that although what they do during an investigation may be second nature to them, others will not have the same knowledge or comfort level. For example, most law enforcement officers do not have training in following the money through checking

accounts, books and records. Many attorneys will miss basic accounting issues. This is not to suggest that the attorneys are not capable; in contrast, it is a result of their own training and specialization being directed toward other areas. That is why they rely on the expertise of the forensic accounting and fraud examination professional.

Thus, even though the forensic accountant and fraud examiner work easily through books and records and recognize issues quickly, attorneys and nonfinancial investigative individuals will need a specialist to take the time to educate them, explain the issues, and show them the books, records, and other evidence. Optimally, the forensic accountant and anti-fraud professional will explain the technical issues in such a manner that those orchestrating the broader legal activities can understand the underlying concepts and make the best strategic cases. As such, although attorneys will direct the work of the forensic accountant, the fraud examiner and accounting professional must take the initiative to look into issues that require further investigation beyond those flagged by counsel.

In a pure litigation support effort, the attorney will have the case first. At the inception of the engagement, the attorney should be giving the professional copies of court pleadings, interrogatories, whatever financial evidence has been accumulated thus far (e.g., selected depositions or portions of depositions that may impact the fraud or forensic accounting professional's work), and opposing expert testimony and reports. After an initial review of this material, the fraud examiner or forensic accountant will have more questions than answers, and it's time to communicate with the attorney. Let the attorney know what's missing, what is confusing, what doesn't seem to make sense, and what's still needed. The documentary evidence will usually be less than one would like to have; that is just a fact of the profession. Some evidence will be lost; some may be destroyed; some may go too far back in time. Nevertheless, the forensic accountant needs to keep digging, keep thinking, and keep asking questions of the attorneys and themselves.

At all times, the fraud examiner or forensic accountant is an independent, objective professional who works to evaluate evidence from every angle. This means that forensic accountants need to examine every piece of paper that comes across their desks and consider its implications to the case, if any. Data may need to be obtained independently; for example, industry data can be collected from the SEC's Edgar or other data sources. Consider a claim that unfair business practices forced a small enterprise to under-perform—at least that was the allegation. Yet after "Google-ing" information about the business's area of industry, a relatively unknown trade association was discovered. A brief phone call to the trade association found that it tracked key performance metrics for the United States and broke down those metrics into eight regions. The annual reports cost $40 per year, and they revealed that although the business climate where the plaintiff operated was challenging, the plaintiff operated at or above the industry averages for all periods except for the partial startup year. This type of information is greatly appreciated by attorneys and invaluable when developing conclusions and opinions.

As noted above, one of the major challenges is identifying any missing data. This challenge is ongoing. As long as the expert requested the data—even if it wasn't provided—he or she has minimized the risk of criticism for not being thorough. When the opposing attorney confronts the fraud and forensic accounting professional with insinuations that that he or she did not evaluate all the data needed, the response is twofold: (1) We asked for that data and it wasn't provided; and (2) If you will provide me with that data now, I'd be happy to reconsider my conclusions and opinions in light of any new information. This response provides an excellent safe haven. It communicates the professional's willingness to keep an open mind. Thus, the fraud examiner or forensic accountant's opinions and conclusions are based on the evidence provided to date and are subject to change based upon new evidence. One should always reserve the right to modify or supplement analyses and other work as necessary, should additional information become available, facts become known, or additional inquiry arise.

While working with law enforcement, attorneys, and other professionals, your critical-thinking, analytical reasoning, and brainstorming skills are some of your greatest strengths. The fraud examiner or forensic accountant should keep asking questions:

Where does the information lead?

Are things as they appear?

Has this scenario been seen before (experience has no substitute)?

Is data "mysteriously" missing?

How are various items or facts connected?

Keep asking who, what, where, when, why, and how.

Evaluation of the Evidence

When evaluating the evidence, the fraud examiner or forensic accountant is expected to be independent and honest. The professional should ensure that all conclusions and opinions are grounded in the evidence, supportable, and defensible. This leaves open the possibility that others may interpret the evidence differently; however, your conclusions and opinions are defensible because they are reasonable based on the entirety of the evidence evaluated.

The professional should identify key assumptions behind their conclusions and opinions. As noted in the earlier chapters of this book, the danger is not in dealing with identified assumptions, but in assumptions made subconsciously. A conclusion that may seem obvious to one person may not be as apparent to another; the major difference is in the basic assumptions that the two have made.

To the extent possible, the anti-fraud professional should identify any research literature, theories, or other resources used as a basis for the work performed and conclusions and opinions reached. Investigations may be challenged by the opposition based on missing data or other limitations. Anti-fraud and forensic professionals should be aware of potential weaknesses and vulnerabilities in the investigation. Once the evaluation is complete, the fraud examiner or forensic accountant needs to write a written report, if it is requested. After the report is written, the investigation is not necessarily complete. One should continue to follow up as necessary if additional information becomes available, facts become known, or other inquiries arise.

Report Writing

During the investigation, the anti-fraud professional or forensic accountant has likely developed a number of analyses and graphics. Some of these presentation tools include:

- Link charts
- Events and activities charts
- Timelines
- Commodity and other flow diagrams
- Direct and indirect financial analyses
- The Evidence/Hypothesis Matrix

These analyses will address the central issues of the investigation:

- The Elements of Fraud: the act, concealment, and conversion
- The Fraud Triangle: pressure, opportunity, and rationalization
- M.I.C.E. (money, ideology, coercion, and ego)

The analyses and central issues should be presented in a coherent storyline—clear, accurate, precise, and relevant to the issues under consideration; presented in reasonable depth to establish credibility; and logical. Most importantly, the storyline needs to be grounded in the evidence. The fraud examiner or forensic accountant could have vulnerability where the storyline is supported by weak evidence or the logical leap is rather large. All facts should be reported without bias or commentary and all relevant information should be included in the report, regardless of which side it favors or what it appears to prove or disprove.

Normally, the fraud examiner or forensic accountant will orally report preliminary findings prior to submitting a formal written report. This gives the entire investigative team a chance to learn what has been found and to put the findings in context, identify next steps, and develop a plan for moving forward.

Although each fraud examiner or forensic accountant has his or her own style, the report generally can be divided into several sections. First, the executive summary provides an overview of the case, the major issues considered, all opinions and conclusions, and the primary basis and reasons therefore. This can be challenging at first. As an examiner, accountant, or investigator, we have usually built the case from symptoms and red flags until we have conclusions and opinions that we feel are reasonable and grounded in the evidence. In contrast, rather than building the case in the report, the report starts with the ending: the conclusions and opinions. Then, the report dives into an introduction, an optional section that provides further information about the background of the case: where it came from, the major issues under consideration, and other investigative aspects that were considered. From there, the details of the case investigation and findings are presented in the case material section. This is the body of the report, develops an in-depth basis for all conclusions and opinions, and is where all of the presentation tools

are reviewed and discussed. At this point, key assumptions are noted. Finally, a concluding section will summarize the major points of the report.

Conclusions and opinions, though related, are distinct. Conclusions are positions grounded in the evidence, whereas opinions are based on the fraud examiner or forensic accountant's interpretation of the facts. Opinions require the professional to connect the dots. Normally, the conclusions are self-evident; but it is likely that opposing counsel will try to interpret the facts in such a way as to draw different opinions. Fraud examiners and forensic accountants should avoid opinions regarding the guilt or innocence of any person or party. This is the responsibility of the judge or the jury based on the entirety of the case in which the fraud or forensic accounting professional is only one player among many. As the writing progresses, you should remember that your report will be carefully scrutinized and that you will have to defend it. Some of the places where that defense occurs include:

- Deposition testimony
- Trial testimony
- Questioning by client's attorney
- Questioning by opposing attorney
- Preparation for trial testimony
- Rebuttal testimony (the other expert)

In addition, it is highly likely that the fraud examiner or forensic accountant will be asked to examine the expert report for the opposing side. Whether an alternative expert report is presented is dependent on the judgment of the opposing counsel. One thing is for certain, you can expect to be rigorously examined over your work. Thus, your ethics and professionalism will come into play in a big way. A professional should do the best job possible for the client, but the way to do that is by being independent, objective, maintaining confidentiality, avoiding conflicts of interest, and not accepting any contingency fees based on the outcome of the case. An open, honest assessment of the facts and circumstances is the best approach to high-quality client service.

Credibility

Throughout this chapter, the issue of credibility has been implicitly examined. For the fraud examiner or forensic accountant, credibility is essential—in substance and in appearance. It is earned as the professional performs his or her role as a teacher, investigatory guide, and advisor. It is a function of plain language—making complicated matters seem simple—and ensuring that the "audience," such as lawyers, opposing counsel, the judge, and jury, can follow the work through each step so that conclusions and opinions developed will seem reasonable and logical. The short of it is that credible information presented credibly is more likely to be believed and accepted. Furthermore, credibility is protected by being independent, honest, objective, and ethical.

If only one side's opinions were offered, credibility would be easier. But the essence of criminal and civil litigation is controlled confrontation: both sides get the opportunity to present the facts and circumstances from their opposing perspectives. Thus, the fraud examiner or forensic accountant, especially in civil litigation, is likely to face a situation of "dueling experts," in which each side takes roughly the same facts and circumstances and comes to different conclusions and opinions. How does one navigate through these troubled waters?

The answer lies in the professional's underlying theories and attention to detail. These two issues are paramount. Without a solid underlying theoretical approach to the investigation and theoretically based conclusions and opinions, the expert will lose not only the case, but his or her credibility. The weaker side usually has a weaker theoretical approach or ignores key facts and figures during their work to draw conclusions and opinions. It is only with attention to detail that the professional can identify the facts and information omitted.

Who ultimately decides on the issue of credibility? The judge and jury do. But importantly, as the counsel you are working for and the opposing counsel approach the negotiating table, one of the items that determines their position is your work and the outcomes of your investigation: your conclusions and opinions.

When considering credibility, it is important to understand how listeners evaluate your work.[2] First, they will set up a baseline by listening to the background information. This is the responsibility of both

attorneys during their opening arguments. Once the judge and jury have a basic storyline, they will add and incorporate new information into their pre-existing notions. The essence of this act is that people try to make decisions quickly based on their first impressions and subsequently are reluctant to revise prior beliefs.

It is also important to consider that this decision making occurs almost instantly after opinions are offered. Therefore, you should be clear and concise and get to the most important points first. Then, you, as the expert, can drill down into the details that further solidify your credibility in the eyes and minds of the judge and jury. As new facts and information are presented, the judge and jury will interpret that information for consistency within their pre-existing beliefs. Typically by the time the expert testifies, the jury may have already "made up their minds." If an expert is trying to change those pre-existing beliefs, he or she needs to clearly, concisely, and quickly explain the conclusions and the main reasons why the opposing expert's testimony is in error. Otherwise, the decision makers may reject your new information because it is inconsistent with their current beliefs.

Because most testimony has gaps, the jury and judge will likely fill in the gaps as needed and make their own connections, inherently drawing their own conclusions and opinions. How does the dueling expert deal with this issue of pre-existing beliefs? Story framing. One of the best techniques for getting a person to believe your version over an alternative account is to tell a better story, one grounded in the evidence and one that is complete with regard to attention to detail. Of course, the expert witness has a challenge: to provide enough detail to establish credibility without over complicating the issues and boring the listeners. The expert witness should work with counsel and pay attention to the jury's reaction to his or her testimony.

Rapport is another key attribute of the credible expert witness. The person needs to be likeable, interesting, interested, and lively. At the same time, each person has his or her own persona and personality; be natural but leverage your personal strengths and minimize your weaknesses to strike a chord with the jury.

Other attributes that help are to avoid bias in reporting, presentation, choice of theories, and use of facts. Fluency of communication also adds to your credibility. Professional accomplishments such as education, training, experience, familiarity with research in the field, professional organization affiliations, publications, and prior testimony experience all provide a foundation for credibility but are not sufficient by themselves.

Presenting a positive appearance can bolster credibility. Aspects of a positive appearance include:

- Body language, including attentiveness and sitting up straight
- Eye contact
- Business attire
- Concise organization
- Conversational language
- Varied formats throughout the presentation
- Illustrations and analogies
- Confidence
- Knowledge

In contrast, the expert witness can also present a negative impression through

- Abrupt or argumentative responses
- Rambling answers
- Hesitation when answering questions, especially from opposing counsel
- Constant self-references
- Anger or aggression
- Arrogance or condescension
- Shifting posture
- Folded arms
- Opinions without substance

that would determine his or her future. Although demographic characteristics of the parents may provide some statistical averages, they are no more than possibilities. The U.S. Census Bureau provides some statistics based on educational assumptions. And, in some cases, those can be documented. For example, the injured child's parents may have started an IRS-qualified 529 savings account for the child's education and may have made a number of contributions. Such evidence would lend credibility to the assertion that the child would have gone to college. Of course, the best laid plans of parents are not always borne out by the children. In addition, the lack of college savings and other planning activities does not indicate that the child would not have pursued higher education.

Homemakers have primary responsibility for the home and often child care as well. They may even be employed part-time or full-time and also provide necessary household and child care services. For those employed at some level, the projection of lost earnings is relatively straightforward. For those not in the labor force, the professional cannot project lost wages but needs to estimate the cost of the various home and child care services that now need to be contracted with outside parties.

With retired persons, the issue is not expected earnings—it is earnings capacity, combined with the probability that the retiree will ever enter the work force again. Like the part-time and full-time employed homemaker, assuming that the retiree is employed and has some proof of wages, the calculations for expected earnings and earnings capacity become more straightforward.

REVIEW QUESTIONS

15-1 What is the purpose of practice aids in forensic and valuation services?

15-2 What are the different types of consulting and litigation support activities for fraud and forensic professionals?

15-3 What is included as an expert's work product?

15-4 What must an injured party prove to be successful in a claim for damages?

15-5 What are the different types of commercial damages?

15-6 What are the various categories and calculations used in ratio analysis?

15-7 What are some of the decisions that need to be made with regard to quantifying lost revenues and increased expenses?

15-8 How may lost profits be calculated using typical benchmarks?

15-9 What are the considerations related to forecasting income and cash flows?

15-10 What types of damages may ensue as a result of personal injury, wrongful death, and survival actions?

ENDNOTES

1. AICPA Practice Aid 07-1, p. 2.
2. Adapted from D. Larry Crumbley, Lester E. Heitger, and G. Stevenson Smith, *Forensic and Investigative Accounting*, CCH, 2003.
3. Another methodology discussed is that of capitalized earnings or excess earnings. However, as noted in Thomas R. Ireland et al., *Expert Economic Testimony: Reference Guides for Judges and Attorneys*, Lawyers & Judges Publishing Co. Inc., 2007, discounting and capitalizing are functionally equivalent. For example, a discount rate of 20 percent is equivalent to a capitalization rate or earnings multiplier of five, assuming constant future cash flows.
4. Thomas R. Ireland et al., *Expert Economic Testimony: Reference Guides for Judges and Attorneys*, Lawyers & Judges Publishing Co. Inc., 2007, p. 183.
5. Thomas E. Copeland, Tim Koller, and Jack Murrin, *Valuation: Measuring and Managing the Value of Corporations*, 2nd ed., John Wiley & Sons, 1994.
6. Internal Revenue Service (IRS) Revenue Ruling 59–60 and subsequent rulings.
7. Thomas R. Ireland et al., *Expert Economic Testimony: Reference Guides for Judges and Attorneys*, Lawyers & Judges Publishing Co. Inc., 2007, p. 195.

8. Rules 9-1 through 9-5 provide guidelines for valuing a business or intangible asset, including requirements that the appraiser employ in recognized valuation methods.
9. Subsequent events are indicative of conditions that were not known or knowable at the valuation date. The valuation is not updated for those events, nor does the report normally include a discussion of those events or conditions. In situations where the valuation is meaningful to the intended user beyond the valuation date, subsequent events may warrant disclosure.
10. Jurisdictional exception occurs when AICPA Statement No. 1 differs from published government, judicial, or accounting authority. In such cases, the valuation professional should follow the applicable published authority or stated procedures.
11. The final three comments regarding the rough approximation of the estimates, the impact of inflation, and issues associated with identifiable and likely career paths were outlined by Supreme Court Justice Stevens in *Jones & Laughlin Steel Corp v. Pfeifer* (1983).

REMEDIATION AND LITIGATION ADVISORY SERVICES

LEARNING OBJECTIVES

After completing this chapter, you should be able to:

16-1 Explain the remediation process as it relates to fraud examination and forensic accounting.

16-2 Identify the two points that an injured party must prove to recover money in a civil lawsuit.

16-3 List the types of losses available for recovery.

16-4 Compare and contrast "following" versus "tracing" the money.

16-5 Describe the legal mechanisms used to recover assets through the civil and criminal justice systems.

16-6 Differentiate between fact witnesses and expert witnesses.

16-7 Explain the types of cases in which a forensic accountant may serve as an expert witness.

16-8 Discuss the implications of the Daubert rule and the Frye rule.

16-9 Describe a deposition and its function.

16-10 Explain the importance of corporate governance.

CRITICAL THINKING EXERCISE

This is an unusual paragraph. I'm curious how quickly you can find out what is so unusual about it. It looks so plain you would think nothing was wrong with it. In fact, nothing is wrong with it! It is unusual though. Study it, and think about it, but you still may not find anything odd. But if you work at it a bit, you might find out. Try to do so without any coaching!

What is unusual about this paragraph?

INTRODUCTION TO REMEDIATION

The fraud examiner or forensic accountant has finished the investigation. The investigator knows who did what to whom, when, where, how, and possibly why, and they have documented their findings; so their work is now done, correct? Not quite. The fraud and forensic accounting professional still has a few remaining obligations in the remediation process. Remediation is characterized as the steps necessary to "clean up the mess" after a fraud or financial crime has been discovered and investigated, and the results of the investigation have been reported.

First, and perhaps most important to the litigants or victims, the forensic accountant plays an integral role in the recovery of money and assets.

Second, the fraud examiner or forensic accountant should support the client through the litigation process. This includes preparing to testify, attending hearings and depositions, and completing other work on an as-needed basis.

Third, the forensic accountant or anti-fraud professional needs to return to the "scene of the crime" to determine how the offense was committed and how to prevent or deter its recurrence. If the issue was employee theft: Was there a breakdown of internal controls? How did the perpetrator misappropriate the assets? How were the acts concealed? If it was a civil litigation matter (such as discrimination, wrongful

cross-examination is normally yes or no. While on direct, the attorney wants the expert to tell the story and expound; on cross, opposing counsel does not want to give the opposing expert a chance to retell the opposition's story; thus, the strategy of asking yes or no questions. This technique limits the opportunity for explanation. The questions are usually safe. The expert needs to listen carefully and give a yes or a no answer when appropriate but be sure to explain when the answer may be misleading or misinterpreted. Although the expert might prefer to explain every answer, it will appear argumentative if he or she does not concede yes or no answers when, in the eyes of the judge or jury, they are appropriate.

During cross-examination, the fraud examiner or forensic accountant has several goals:

- Be cooperative. An uncooperative expert diminishes his or her own credibility.
- Maintain the credibility of his or her conclusions and opinions.
- Be alert for reasonable and proper opportunities to provide explanation and disagree.

The fraud examiner or forensic accountant should understand that the opposing lawyer will:

- Learn your field
- Know your report
- Know your resume
- Try to limit the scope of testimony
- Stress missing credentials
- Contrast your credentials with those of opposing experts
- Contrast your conclusions and opinions with those of opposing experts

Even if your work is completed to the highest quality levels and your conclusions and opinions are reasonable and are grounded in the evidence, opposing counsel will try nevertheless to score some points. For example, they may ask you to agree with an opposing expert's data or assumptions so that it appears you are agreeing with the opposing expert's conclusions and opinions. The fraud examiner or forensic accountant may be asked to criticize the conduct of his or her client or the shortcomings of issues in question.

In addition, opposing counsel may attempt to get the opposing expert to acknowledge a lack of knowledge about certain aspects of the case, even if the expert was not expected to be knowledgeable in that area. This creates the appearance of credibility problems where none exist. The opposing attorney may also challenge the professional's objectivity and the sources of information relied upon. It is also common for an opposing attorney in a position of weakness to offer "what if" scenarios that require facts and circumstances different from those of the examination you conducted. Such hypothetical questions must be answered, but it is also reasonable to point out where the facts and circumstances differ from those in the actual case.

Some of the techniques used in cross-examination include:

The Primrose Path: Using only selected and possibly hypothetical facts, the opposing attorney paints a picture differing from the one that existed in the real case. This is done by limiting testimony to "yes" and "no" questions and then offering a different conclusion: "Well, if that were true, you must agree that . . . . "

The Nodding Chicken: Similar to the primrose path, except the opposing attorney attempts to lull the expert into a false sense of security by asking a series of questions where the appropriate answer is "yes." Then, once the expert is nodding his or her head and saying "yes," a question that is better answered with a "no" or "yes, with explanation" is offered and the expert continues to answer "yes" before realizing what just happened.

Ask Until You Admit: Using this technique, opposing counsel keeps reframing the question until they have it in such a way that the "yes" or "no" answers are favorable to their client, at which time, they are done asking questions.

You've Got to be Kidding!: Opposing counsel takes particular aspects of your testimony or report out of context and acts indignant about the conclusion or opinion because, out of context or without additional evidence, it appears nonsensical or unsupported.

This Means Nothing: This is an attempt to get an admission that in the bigger picture, the findings are of minimal importance and have little bearing on the case or are applicable only to a small portion of it.

You Really Didn't Mean to Say . . . : Using this technique, opposing counsel attempts to minimize the impact of your testimony by suggesting that certain small aspects, taken out of context, seem to make little sense.

The fraud examiner or forensic accountant should remember to be alert for tricks such as these and to make sure to provide a response and an explanation when needed. For example, it may be okay to answer "yes" to two or three questions in a row, but after a few "yes" answers, the savvy expert tries to see where the opposing attorney is heading and limit his or her ability to score points that are form more than substance. At the same time, fraud and forensic accounting professionals need to understand that skillful attorneys have destroyed many a good expert witness's report—not because the work wasn't excellent or the conclusions and opinions weren't supportable and grounded in the evidence—but because the opposing attorney was able to wage a war of words and win. The fraud examiner or forensic accountant needs to understand that our world is fundamentally composed of numbers, and that understanding and interpreting them is second nature. Following the money through complex schemes that include skillful concealment is what we do, but when we walk into a deposition or courtroom, we move from an environment in which numbers are the primary focus to one in which words win the day. Expert witnesses need to develop knowledge, skills, and abilities in this world of words.

How the expert witness deals with the world of words:

- Draw reasonable conclusions and opinions that are grounded in the evidence
- Know your case and get the information that you need
- Exhibit self-confidence
- Maintain a steady focus and concentration
- Listen and think
- Stay in your sandbox!!!
- Periodically ask the attorney to clarify a question
- Cooperate within limits, but stand your ground
- Maintain your credibility
- Do not shoot from the hip
- Admit the unfavorable or unknown when it is reasonable to do so
- Be a teacher

RESTRUCTURE THE INTERNAL CONTROL ENVIRONMENT

"Once bitten, twice warned."

"Fool me once, shame on you; fool me twice, shame on me."

One of the attributes of the anti-fraud professional or forensic accountant is a willingness to prevent or deter future fraudulent activity. Even in civil litigation, an examination of policies and procedures should be carried out to determine what led to the dispute, how it evolved into litigation, and what could be done to prevent such action in the future. Once an issue, such as a civil dispute, gets into the context of the legal system, everyone loses something and spends more money.

Unfortunately, it is often only with the pain of civil or criminal litigation or a large financial loss that a company is willing to critically assess its anti-fraud program. As such, the time is right for consideration of anti-fraud tools and techniques.

Overview of an Anti-Fraud Environment

Creating an anti-fraud environment requires critical thinking and an ability to solve problems in an innovative way. If one can identify the risk, a system of internal control policies and procedures can be created to prevent it. The challenge is to find out how others, for example a potential perpetrator, might exploit the system for gain. To identify opportunities to exploit control weaknesses, the fraud examiner or forensic accountant must "think like a criminal." Further, they should understand the effective anti-fraud environment and its related processes and controls: "tone at the top," an ethical culture, strong control

environment, code of conduct, open communications with suppliers and customers, employee monitoring, hotlines, whistleblower protection, willingness to enforce penalties against perpetrators, and proactive fraud auditing.[4] The professional must then analyze potential frauds to identify systemic vulnerabilities and implement procedures to reduce the risk.

Internal Control Policies and Procedures

A company should develop a system of internal controls that provides reasonable assurance that assets are protected and financial statements are fairly presented. Of course, even the best system of internal controls may be at risk when employees collude to beat the system or management and executives override that system. Thus, despite efforts to install and maintain a reliable and effective system of internal control, it is impossible to prevent all frauds. That is not to suggest that anti-fraud procedures cannot be established to prevent most specific types of fraud; however, when considering the entire company the focus needs to shift from prevention to deterrence to create an anti-fraud environment.

A good system of internal controls has four separate areas of responsibility: one person is responsible for safeguarding the assets; another person has authority over transactions associated with the asset; a third person is responsible for recording transactions for assets; and a fourth person should orchestrate a system of audits, physical inventories, and reconciliations must be in place. A system with these attributes will not eliminate fraud but can alert the appropriate individuals to the occurrence of fraud at the earliest possible moment.

In addition to the above controls that are already in place, a system to constantly monitor the control environment is also necessary. The entity must undertake periodic risk assessment. What could go wrong? How could the system of internal controls be exploited? What new aspects of our business have arisen for which assets need identification and protection? A good control environment also generates information so that responsible persons can monitor it and facilitate communication. The control environment also includes:[5]

- Integrity and ethical values
- A commitment to competent employees
- An active board of directors and audit committee
- Clear signals from management about its philosophy and commitment to ethical operations
- An organizational structure that defines authority, responsibility, record keeping, and audit expectations
- Periodic assessment of the organizational structure
- Human resource policies and practices that facilitate a good control environment

Risk Assessment and Internal Control

At the inception of an investigation, the fraud examiner or forensic accountant needs to develop an understanding of the control environment. This can be accomplished by discussing internal controls with executives, management, and other employees. Such an understanding can be documented in narrative form that addresses the origination or source of the documents, the processing that takes place, the disposition of those documents, their recording in the system, and an assessment of the control risk. This kind of narrative supplemented with a graphic, such as a flowchart, can be very helpful in assessing risk. Each step in the process can be identified on the flowchart and an assessment done at each important point in the process. Internal questionnaires, pre-developed checklists, and policy and procedures manuals can also be used to develop an understanding of the system of internal controls.

Once this has been completed, the professional can then test the system by tracing documents through that system to determine whether it functions as designed. Operational breakdowns indicate that even though the system may be properly designed, it may not be functioning as planned. Such tests should address each aspect of the internal control environment: responsibility for physical safeguard, authority for transactions, record keeping, and the audit (reconciliation) process. Tests require the professional to scrutinize not only the flow of paper, but also to examine documents and records, observe activities as they occur, discuss policies and procedures with line personnel, and re-perform aspects of the procedures to ensure that the outcomes are accurate.

At this point, the fraud examiner or forensic accountant should also consider those key controls that should be in place but appear to be absent. Once vulnerabilities are identified, the professional needs to

communicate those findings and assist management in developing an appropriate cost-justified response. Ultimately, success requires a questioning mind, examining policies and procedures at the operational level, and looking for opportunities for management override.

The Importance of Corporate Governance

Corporate governance is the set of processes, customs, and policies that affect the way an organization is directed. It also considers the relationships among the stakeholders and the goals of the organization. The principal organizational leaders responsible for corporate governance include the board of directors, the audit committee, executives, management, and the shareholders. Other stakeholders with an interest in corporate governance include employees, suppliers, customers, banks and other creditors, regulators, and the community in which the organization operates. In general, corporate governance deals with issues of accountability and fiduciary duty, essentially those attributes advocating the implementation of guidelines and mechanisms to ensure good behavior by the organization and the protection of shareholder value.

The corporate governance fabric is critical for creating an environment in which the risk of fraud is minimized through a combination of fraud prevention, deterrence, and early detection and resolution tools and techniques. At a minimum, corporate governance should address three issues:[6]

1. Creating and maintaining a culture of honesty and high ethics
2. Evaluating fraud risks and implementing programs and controls to mitigate them
3. Developing an appropriate anti-fraud oversight process

Based on the concept that employees follow their leaders, management's and executives' first responsibility is to set an ethical "tone at the top," creating a culture that reinforces honesty and integrity. Beyond that, good corporate governance also fosters:

- Establishing a positive work environment by implementing programs and initiatives to enhance employee morale
- Hiring and promoting employees who meet the high ethical standards of the entity (including background checks, verifying employment and education, and contacting personal references)
- Training
- Supervising
- Confirming commitment to the code of conduct by educating personnel
- Disciplining those employees who fail to follow the code of conduct
- Identifying and measuring fraud risks
- Mitigating fraud risks within reasonable limits of cost constraints
- Monitoring fraud prevention programs and controls

The audit committee is an integral player in corporate governance, especially when it comes to financial reporting. The audit committee should manage the annual audit and also have internal audit report directly to them.

The Risk of Management Override

One of the most disturbing aspects of the audit process and corporate governance responsibility is that a certain cohort can do almost anything they want despite the systems of checks and balances designed to prevent asset misappropriation and financial statement fraud. This is referred to as management override. This issue is of such a concern that in 2005 the AICPA issued "Management Override of Internal Controls: The Achilles' Heel of Fraud Prevention." Essentially, the audit committee and the board of directors have the responsibility for addressing fraud risk. The document tasks audit committees as follows:

- Maintain skepticism
- Strengthen the audit committee's understanding of the business
- Brainstorm to identify fraud risks
- Use the code of conduct to assess the financial reporting culture
- Cultivate a vigorous whistleblower program
- Develop a broad information and feedback network including internal auditors, independent auditors, the compensation committee, and key employees

From a practical perspective, the audit committee should make sure that the auditors have examined journal entries and other adjustments for evidence of possible misstatement due to fraud, review accounting estimates for biases, and evaluate the business rationale for significant unusual transactions. Audit committees should be vigilant for the following:[7]

- Discrepancies in the accounting records
- Conflicting or missing evidential matter
- Problematic or unusual relationships between management and auditors
- Results from audit testing that indicate previously unidentified risks of fraud
- Responses to management inquiries that are vague or implausible

Early Reaction to Symptoms

Albrecht notes six types of symptoms that may indicate a fraud is occurring:[8]

- Accounting anomalies including irregular, unusual, or missing source documents, faulty journal entries, and inaccuracies in ledgers and sub-ledgers.
- Internal control weaknesses including the lack of segregation of duties, physical safeguards, independent checks, proper authorization of documents and records; override of existing controls by executives or management; and inadequate accounting and other (nonfinancial) information systems.
- Analytical anomalies including shortages of inventory and cash, deviations from design and quality specifications, excessive scrap, excessive voids, excessive purchasing levels, ratios that do not make sense, nonfinancial numbers that do not correlate with account balances and numbers presented in the financial statements, strange financial relationships, and excessive late charges.
- Extravagant lifestyles including new and expensive cars, expensive clothing, new or remodeled homes, and expensive recreational toys such as boats, cabins, and motor homes.
- Unusual behavior generated by stress including offering excuses for shortcomings, excessive frustration, being overly defensive, argumentative, irritable, suspicious or belligerent, complaints of sleeplessness, excessive drinking, or taking drugs.
- Tips and complaints from employees, customers, suppliers, family, and friends.

A good anti-fraud environment requires constant awareness of these types of symptoms and, once observed, quick reaction to ensure that any possible fraud is caught at the earliest possible moment. Eliminating fraud completely is impossible, but companies can be vigilant and react quickly by investigating the red flags that may indicate that fraud is taking place. The following is a five-step approach to fraud prevention, deterrence, and detection:

1. Know the exposures (brainstorming, risk assessment, audit planning)
2. Translate exposure into likely symptoms
3. Always be on the lookout for these symptoms
4. Build audit programs to look for symptoms
5. Follow up on these issues to their logical, evidence-based conclusions

AICPA Statement on Auditing Standard (SAS) No. 99, "Risk Factors Relating to Misstatements Arising from Fraudulent Financial Reporting"

The following are examples of risk factors relating to misstatements arising from fraudulent financial reporting.

Incentives/Pressures   A. Financial stability or profitability is threatened by economic, industry, or entity operating conditions such as (or as indicated by):

- High degree of competition or market saturation, accompanied by declining margins
- High vulnerability to rapid changes, such as changes in technology, product obsolescence, or interest rates
- Significant declines in customer demand and increasing business failures in either the industry or overall economy

- Operating losses making the threat of bankruptcy, foreclosure, or hostile takeover imminent
- Recurring negative cash flows from operations or an inability to generate cash flows from operations while reporting earnings and earnings growth
- Rapid growth or unusual profitability, especially compared to that of other companies in the same industry
- New accounting, statutory, or regulatory requirements

B. Excessive pressure exists for management to meet the requirements or expectations of third parties due to the following:

- Profitability or trend level expectations of investment analysts, institutional investors, significant creditors, or other external parties (particularly expectations that are unduly aggressive or unrealistic), including expectations created by management in, for example, overly optimistic press releases or annual report messages
- Need to obtain additional debt or equity financing to stay competitive, including financing of major research and development or capital expenditures
- Marginal ability to meet exchange listing requirements or debt repayment or other debt covenant requirements
- Perceived or real adverse effects of reporting poor financial results on significant pending transactions, such as business combinations or contract awards

C. Information available indicates that management's or the board of directors' personal financial situation is threatened by the entity's financial performance arising from the following:

- Significant financial interests in the entity
- Significant portions of their compensation (for example, bonuses, stock options, and earn-out arrangements) being contingent upon achieving aggressive targets for stock price, operating results, financial position, or cash flow
- Personal guarantees of debts of the entity

D. There is excessive pressure on management or operating personnel to meet financial targets set up by the board of directors or management, including sales or profitability incentive goals.

Opportunities A. The nature of the industry's or the entity's operations provides opportunities to engage in fraudulent financial reporting that can arise from the following:

- Significant related-party transactions not in the ordinary course of business or with related entities not audited or audited by another firm
- A strong financial presence or ability to dominate a certain industry sector that allows the entity to dictate terms or conditions to suppliers or customers that may result in inappropriate or nonarm's-length transactions
- Assets, liabilities, revenues, or expenses based on significant estimates that involve subjective judgments or uncertainties that are difficult to corroborate
- Significant, unusual, or highly complex transactions, especially those close to period end that pose difficult "substance over form" questions
- Significant operations located or conducted across international borders in jurisdictions where differing business environments and cultures exist
- Significant bank accounts or subsidiary or branch operations in tax-haven jurisdictions for which there appear to be no clear business justifications

B. There is ineffective monitoring of management as a result of the following:

- Domination of management by a single person or small group (in a nonowner-managed business) without compensating controls
- Ineffective board of directors or audit committee oversight over the financial reporting process and internal control

C. There is a complex or unstable organizational structure, as evidenced by the following:

- Difficulty in determining the organization or individuals that have controlling interest in the entity

- Overly complex organizational structure involving unusual legal entities or managerial lines of authority
- High turnover of senior management, counsel, or board members

D. Internal control components are deficient as a result of the following:

- Inadequate monitoring of controls, including automated controls and controls over interim financial reporting (where external reporting is required)
- High turnover rates or employment of ineffective accounting, internal audit, or information technology staff
- Ineffective accounting and information systems, including situations involving reportable conditions

Attitudes/Rationalizations Risk factors reflective of attitudes/rationalizations by board members, management, or employees that allow them to engage in and/or justify fraudulent financial reporting may not be susceptible to observation by the auditor. Nevertheless, the auditor who becomes aware of the existence of such information should consider it in identifying the risks of material misstatement arising from fraudulent financial reporting. For example, auditors may become aware of the following information that may indicate a risk factor:

- Ineffective communication, implementation, support, or enforcement of the entity's values or ethical standards by management, or the communication of inappropriate values or ethical standards
- Nonfinancial management's excessive participation in or preoccupation with the selection of accounting principles or the determination of significant estimates
- Known history of violations of securities laws or other laws and regulations, or claims against the entity, its senior management, or board members alleging fraud or violations of laws and regulations
- Excessive interest by management in maintaining or increasing the entity's stock price or earnings trend
- A practice by management of committing to analysts, creditors, and other third parties to achieve aggressive or unrealistic forecasts
- Management failing to correct known reportable conditions on a timely basis
- An interest by management in employing inappropriate means to minimize reported earnings for tax-motivated reasons
- Recurring attempts by management to justify marginal or inappropriate accounting on the basis of materiality
- The relationship between management and the current or predecessor auditor is strained, as exhibited by the following:
  - Frequent disputes with the current or predecessor auditor on accounting, auditing, or reporting matters
  - Unreasonable demands on the auditor, such as unreasonable time constraints regarding the completion of the audit or the issuance of the auditor's report
  - Formal or informal restrictions on the auditor that inappropriately limit access to people or information or the ability to communicate effectively with the board of directors or audit committee
  - Domineering management behavior in dealing with the auditor, especially involving attempts to influence the scope of the auditor's work or the selection or continuance of personnel assigned to or consulted on the audit engagement

AICPA Statement on Auditing Standard (SAS) No. 99, "Risk Factors Relating to Misstatements Arising from Misappropriation of Assets"

Risk factors that relate to misstatements arising from misappropriation of assets are also classified according to the three conditions generally present when fraud exists: incentives/pressures, opportunities, and attitudes/rationalizations. Some of the risk factors related to misstatements arising from fraudulent financial reporting may also be present when misstatements arising from misappropriation of assets occur. For

example, ineffective monitoring of management and weaknesses in internal control may be present when misstatements due to either fraudulent financial reporting or misappropriation of assets exist. The following are examples of risk factors related to misstatements arising from misappropriation of assets.

Incentives/Pressures A. Personal financial obligations may create pressure on management or employees with access to cash or other assets susceptible to theft to misappropriate those assets.

B. Adverse relationships between the entity and employees with access to cash or other assets susceptible to theft may motivate those employees to misappropriate those assets. For example, adverse relationships may be created by the following:

- Known or anticipated future employee layoffs
- Recent or anticipated changes to employee compensation or benefit plans
- Promotions, compensation, or other rewards inconsistent with expectations

Opportunities A. Certain characteristics or circumstances may increase the susceptibility of assets to misappropriation. For example, opportunities to misappropriate assets increase when there are the following:

- Large amounts of cash on hand or processed
- Inventory items that are small in size, of high value, or in high demand
- Easily convertible assets, such as bearer bonds, diamonds, or computer chips
- Fixed assets that are small in size, marketable, or lacking observable identification of ownership

B. Inadequate internal control over assets may increase the susceptibility of misappropriation of those assets. For example, misappropriation of assets may occur because there is the following:

- Inadequate segregation of duties or independent checks
- Inadequate management oversight of employees responsible for assets, for example, inadequate supervision or monitoring of remote locations
- Inadequate job applicant screening of employees with access to assets
- Inadequate record keeping with respect to assets
- Inadequate system of authorization and approval of transactions (for example, in purchasing)
- Inadequate physical safeguards over cash, investments, inventory, or fixed assets
- Lack of complete and timely reconciliations of assets
- Lack of timely and appropriate documentation of transactions, for example, credits for merchandise returns
- Lack of mandatory vacations for employees performing key control functions
- Inadequate management understanding of information technology, which enables information technology employees to perpetrate a misappropriation
- Inadequate access controls over automated records, including controls over and reviews of computer systems event logs

Attitudes/Rationalizations Risk factors reflective of employee attitudes/rationalizations that allow them to justify misappropriations of assets are generally not susceptible to observation by the auditor. Nevertheless, the auditor who becomes aware of the existence of such information should consider it in identifying the risks of material misstatement arising from misappropriation of assets. For example, auditors may become aware of the following attitudes or behavior of employees who have access to assets susceptible to misappropriation:

- Disregard for the need for monitoring or reducing risks related to misappropriations of assets
- Disregard for internal control over misappropriation of assets by overriding existing controls or by failing to correct known internal control deficiencies
- Behavior indicating displeasure or dissatisfaction with the company or its treatment of the employee
- Changes in behavior or lifestyle that may indicate assets have been misappropriated

FROM THE FRAUDSTER'S PERSPECTIVE

(Adapted from http://whitecollarfraud.blogspot.com)
Monday, December 29, 2008

A New Year's Message from a Convicted Felon:
While You Hope, Criminals Prey

My cousin, "Crazy Eddie" Antar, taught me that "people live on hope." As white collar criminals, we preyed on your hopes and dreams by feeding you our spin and lies.

Investors demand confident leadership and strong financial performance from company managements. They want to hear management exuding confidence about their company's future business prospects. Eddie and I built an image of strong and confident leadership by promising investors a prosperous future backed up by our phony financial reports.

As criminals, we considered the humanity of investors as a weakness to be exploited in the cold-blooded execution of our crimes. We measured our effectiveness by the comfort level of our victims.

Eddie and I built walls of false integrity around us to gain the trust of our victims. We claimed that Crazy Eddie's accounting policies were "conservative." In addition, we gave huge sums of money to charity and were involved in many popular social causes in an effort to make investors comfortable with us. While we were in effect, "helping old ladies cross the street," we were heartlessly executing a massive fraud that wiped out the life savings of thousands of investors and ultimately caused a few thousand people to lose their jobs.

My cousin, Eddie, and I never had a single conversation about morality or right and wrong. We simply did not care about the victims of our crimes. Our conversations only focused on the successful execution of our cold-blooded schemes to defraud investors.

At Crazy Eddie, we committed our crimes simply because we believed we could execute them successfully. We took advantage of investors' hopes, dreams, and aspirations for a better future. More importantly, we fully exploited investors' lack of skepticism that resulted from the wall of false integrity we built around ourselves.

Hope is a fine human quality that motivates us to build a better future. Unfortunately, criminals consider your hope as an exploitable weakness to aid them in the successful execution of their crimes.

Do not get mesmerized by neatly packaged story lines and well researched sound bites written by highly-paid, professional media consultants. Criminals know how to "talk the talk and walk the walk" as they inspire you with false promises of a prosperous future.

In the New Year, please do not let criminals exploit your hopes and dreams. Furthermore, you are cautioned to apply the same advice to our elected officials from all sides of the political spectrum who exploit your hopes with inspiring rhetoric to sell you flawed solutions to major problems facing our nation.

Have a skeptical New Year.

Sam E. Antar (former Crazy Eddie CFO and a convicted felon)

LESSONS LEARNED

Finally, the investigative process, including deposition and courtroom testimony, provides an excellent foundation for developing a knowledge repository for sharing lessons learned. This concept was developed at the Financial Investigative Services Division of the Bureau of Alcohol, Tobacco, Firearms and Explosives (ATF) under the direction of its chief, Franco Frande. This repository can be used as a basis for new employee training, periodic staff training and education, and as a place for investigative ideas. The tools and techniques of the fraudster and others who steal, conceal their efforts, and benefit from those efforts (the conversion) are only limited by the human imagination, and a knowledge repository is a perfect mechanism for gathering and storing lessons learned so that future fraud examiners and financial forensic professionals can be brought up to speed quickly and generate ideas as effectively and efficiently as possible.

Forensic accounting, as defined in this book, is the use of accounting for possible courtroom purposes. The reader has been exposed to a wide variety of concepts, including the core foundation related to fraud examination and forensic accounting; careers in this field; who commits fraud and why; various complex frauds and financial crimes; cybercrime; the legal, regulatory, and professional environment; fraud's red flags and targeted risk assessment; detection and investigations; effective interviewing and interrogation techniques; how to use information technology for fraud examination and financial forensics; various schemes used to perpetrate fraud; deterrence strategies; consulting, litigation support, and expert witness engagements; and fraud remediation.

But a major aspect is fraud; it may even be the largest single segment of forensic accounting, and that is why the topic is covered so extensively in these pages. Fraud is frequently investigated by those with little or no accounting knowledge. Except for fraudulent financial statements, not much accounting brainpower is needed to trace ill-gotten gains, examine bank accounts, or inspect phony documents. The

fraud examiner is part accountant, part detective, part legal scholar, and part criminologist. In short, all fraud examiners are not forensic accountants and vice versa, which is why the authors have made the distinction.

Both fraud examination and forensic accounting are growing fields with much career potential for the right individuals. They are both adversarial in nature—you are trying to prove something while your opponent is attempting to disprove it—and many people are uncomfortable with confrontation. In a civilized world, the courtroom is the ultimate venue for controlled confrontation.

Ultimately, the keys to advancement in any career are knowledge *and* experience. This book, which is a beginning, will add to your knowledge, but experience must be gained the old-fashioned way—by working in the field.

The authors close with this advice: By being thorough, detailed, knowledgeable, and scrupulously honest, you will win even if your case does not.

REVIEW QUESTIONS

16-1   What is meant by remediation?

16-2   What two points must an injured party prove to recover money in a civil lawsuit?

16-3   What are the types of losses available for recovery?

16-4   How does the legal system differentiate between "following" versus "tracing" the money?

16-5   What legal mechanisms may be used to recover assets in the civil and criminal justice systems?

16-6   What is the difference between fact witnesses and expert witnesses?

16-7   In what types of cases may a forensic accountant serve as an expert witness?

16-8   When may an expert's opinion be subject to challenge?

16-9   What is a deposition and why is it used?

16-10 What is meant by corporate governance and why is it important?

ENDNOTES

1. See *United States v. Garcia*, No. 03–1407 (2d Cir. June 21, 2005) (Calabresi, B.D. Parker, and Raggi, JJ.).

2. Steven Lubet, *Expert Testimony: A Guide for Expert Witnesses and the Lawyers Who Examine Them*, National Institute for Trial Advocacy, Notre Dame, Indiana, 1998.

3. Ibid.

4. Adapted from W. Steve Albrecht, Conan C. Albrecht, and Chad O. Albrecht, *Fraud Examination*, South-Western, 2006.

5. Alvin A. Arens, Randal J. Elder, and Mark S. Beasley, *Auditing and Assurance Services*, Pearson-Prentice Hall, 2005.

6. AICPA, "Management Antifraud Programs and Controls: Guidance to Help Prevent, Deter and Detect Fraud."

7. Alvin A. Arens, Randal J. Elder, and Mark S. Beasley, *Auditing and Assurance Services*, Pearson-Prentice Hall, 2005.

8. Adapted from W. Steve Albrecht, Conan C. Albrecht, and Chad O. Albrecht, *Fraud Examination*, South-Western, 2006.

REFERENCES AND RESOURCES

The authors do not endorse or make any specific recommendations regarding these references and resources. This is not intended to be a complete list of all resources available but lists the primary sources identified and utilized by the authors in the creation of this text.

CURRICULUM DEVELOPMENT

"*Education and Training in Fraud and Forensic Accounting: A Guide for Educational Institutions, Stakeholder Organizations, Faculty, and Students.*" National Institute of Justice: Document No.: 217589 (March 2007). Located at http://www.ncjrs.gov/pdffiles1/nij/grants/217589.pdf

SELECTED TEXT AND PROFESSIONAL BOOKS

Albanese, Jay S., *White Collar Crime in America*, Prentice Hall (1995)

Albrecht, W. Steve, Conan C. Albrecht, Chad O. Albrecht, and Mark F. Zimbelman, *Fraud Examination*, Thomson South-Western (2009)

Anastasi, Joe, *The New Forensics: Investigating Corporate Fraud and the Theft of Intellectual Property*, Wiley (2003)

Association of Certified Fraud Examiners, *Fraud Examiners Manual* (2010)

Arquilla, John, and David Ronfeldt, *The Advent of Netwar*, RAND National Defense Research Institute (1996)

Cheffers, Mark, and Michael Pakaluk, *Understanding Accounting Ethics*, Allen David Press (2005)

Crumbley, D. Larry, Lester E. Heitger, and G. Stevenson Smith, *Forensic and Investigative Accounting* (4th Edition), CCH (2009)

Dalal, Chetan, *Novel and Conventional Methods of Audit, Investigation and Fraud Detection*, CCH (2008)

DiGabriel, James (ed.), *Forensic Accounting in Matrimonial Divorce*, R.T. Edwards, Inc. (2005)

Ernst & Young, *The Guide to Investigating Business Fraud*, AICPA (2009)

Financial Investigations: A Forensic Approach to Detecting and Resolving Crimes, Internal Revenue Service Publication 1714 (Rev.1-2002)

Fox, Christopher, and Paul Zonneveld, Issued by the IT Governance Institute, IT *Control Objectives for Sarbanes–Oxley* (2006)

Friedman, Jack P., *Litigation Services Handbook Case Studies: Accounting, Economic, and Financial Issues in Litigation Support Research*, John Wiley & Sons (2003)

Geis, Gilbert, Robert F. Meier, and Lawrence M. Salinger, *White-Collar Crime: Classic and Contemporary Views* (3rd Edition), Free Press (1995)

Hopwood, William S., Jay J. Leiner, and George R. Young, *Forensic Accounting*, McGraw-Hill Irwin (2008)

Ireland, Thomas R., Stephen M. Homer, James D. Rodgers, Patrick A. Gaughan, Robert R. Trout, and Michael J. Piette, *Expert Economic Testimony: Reference Guides for Judges and Attorneys*, Lawyers & Judges Publishing Co., Inc. (1999)

Lanza, Richard B., *Proactively Detecting Occupational Fraud Using Computer Audit Reports*, The Institute of Internal Auditors (2003)

Lubet, Steven, and Elizabeth Boals, *Expert Testimony: A Guide for Expert Witnesses and the Lawyers Who Examine Them*, NITA (2009)

Lundelius, Charles R., *Financial Reporting Fraud: A Practical Guide to Detection and Internal Control*, AICPA (2003)

Rezaee, Zabihollah, and Richard Riley, *Financial Statement Fraud: Prevention and Detection* (2nd Edition), John Wiley & Sons (2010)

Schilit, Howard, *Financial Shenanigans: How to Detect Accounting Gimmicks & Fraud in Financial Reports* (2nd Edition), McGraw-Hill (2002)

Singleton, Tommie, Aaron J. Singleton, G. Jack Bologna, and Robert J. Lindquist, *Fraud Auditing and Forensic Accounting*, John Wiley & Sons (2006)

Singleton, Tommie, and James A. Hall, *Information Technology Auditing and Assurance* (2nd edition), Thomson South-Western (2004)

Wells, Joseph T., *Principles of Fraud Examination* (2nd Edition), John Wiley & Sons (2008)

Wells, Joseph T., *Occupational Fraud and Abuse*, Obsidian Publishing Co. (1997)

Zulawski, David E. and Douglas E. Wicklander, *Practical Aspects of Interview and Interrogation* (2nd Edition), CRC Press (2002)

SELECTED DATA EXTRACTION AND ANALYSIS SOFTWARE

IDEA Workbook (2009) Educators may purchase the IDEA Workbook at cost for student/classroom use. Student copies include the Education Version of IDEA, User Guides, Case Study for IDEA, and all applicable data files.

Arens, Alvin A., Randal J. Elder, and Armond Dalton, "Computerized Auditing Using ACL, 2/e" (2008) (Bundled with ACL 9 Education edition software)

Conan C. Albrecht, *Picalo Cookbook*, December 17, 2009, available free online at http://www.picalo.org/

SELECTED JOURNALS DEVOTED TO FORENSIC ACCOUNTING AND FRAUD EXAMINATION

Fraud Magazine

Journal of Forensic Accounting

Journal of Forensic Economics

The Journal of Forensic Studies in Accounting and Business

SELECTED CASE STUDIES

AICPA.org, *Case Studies and Fraud Schemes*

Association of Certified Fraud Examiners, ACFE Anti-Fraud Education Partnership

Beasley, Mark S., Frank A. Buckless, Steven M. Glover, and Douglas F. Prawitt, *Auditing Cases: An Active Learning Approach* (2nd Edition), Prentice Hall (2002)

Cullinan, Charles P., and Gail B. Wright, *Cases from the SEC Files: Topics in Auditing*, Prentice Hall (2002)

Cooper, Cynthia, *Extraordinary Circumstance: The Journey of a Corporate Whistleblower*, John Wiley & Sons (2008)

Fusaro, Peter C., and Ross M. Miller, *What Went Wrong at Enron: Everyone's Guide to the Largest Bankruptcy in U.S. History*, John Wiley & Sons (2002)

Pavlo, Walter, Jr., and Neil Weinberg, *Stolen Without A Gun: Confessions from Inside History's Biggest Accounting Fraud* (Worldcom), Etika (2007)

Thibodeau, Jay, and Deborah Freier, *Auditing after Sarbanes–Oxley: Illustrative Cases*, McGraw-Hill (2007)

Wells, Joseph (ed.), *Computer Fraud Casebook*, John Wiley & Sons (2009)

Wells, Joseph (ed.), *Fraud Casebook: Lesson from the Bad Side of Business*, John Wiley & Sons (2007)

SELECTED VIDEOS

Association of Certified Fraud Examiners:
- *Beyond the Numbers: Professional Interviewing Techniques*
- *Cooking the Books: What Every Accountant Should Know about Fraud*
- *The Corporate Con: Internal Fraud and the Auditor*
- *Finding the Truth: Effective Techniques for Interview and Communication*
- *The Fraud Trial*
- *Fundamentals of Computer Fraud*
- *How to Detect and Prevent Financial Statement Fraud*
- *Introduction to Fraud Examination*
- *Investment Swindles and Con Schemes*
- *Making Crime Pay: How to Locate Hidden Assets*
- *Other People's Money: The Basics of Asset Misappropriation*

How to Steal $500 Million (Pharmor), PBS Frontline

Illicit: The Dark Trade (Counterfeit Goods), National Geographic

The Madoff Affair, PBS Frontline

SELECTED ORGANIZATIONS

American College of Forensic Examiners Institute (ACFEI)

American Institute of Certified Public Accountants
    AICPA Consulting Standards in Litigation Engagements
    Antifraud and Corporate Responsibility Resource Center
    Business Valuation and Forensic and Litigation Services

Association of Certified Fraud Examiners

Association of Certified Fraud Specialists (ACFS)

Association of Government Accountants

Committee of Sponsoring Organizations (COSO)
    Report of the National Commission of Fraudulent Financial Reporting (1987)
    Internal Control—Integrated Framework (1992)
    Fraudulent Financial Reporting: 1987–1997, An Analysis of U.S. Public Companies (1999)
    Enterprise Risk Management—Integrated Framework (2004)

Federal Bureau of Investigation (FBI)

Financial Crimes Enforcement Network (FinCEN)

Forensic CPA Society (FCPAS)

Institute of Internal Auditors

Internal Revenue Service (IRS)

International Association for Asset Recovery (IAAR)

IT Governance Institute

Information Systems Audit and Control Association (ISACA)

National Association of Certified Valuation Analysts

National Association of Corporate Directors

National Litigation Support Services Association

Network of Independent Forensic Accountants (England)

Professional Liability Underwriting Society (PLUS)

Risk and Insurance Management Society (RIMS)

Society of Financial Examiners (SOFE)

U.S. Bureau of Alcohol, Tobacco, Firearms and Explosives (ATF)

U.S. Department of the Treasury

U.S. Drug Enforcement Agency (DEA)

U.S. Central Intelligence Agency (CIA)

U.S. Office of the Inspector General (OIG)

U.S. Postal Inspection Service

U.S. Secret Service

SELECTED INTERNATIONAL FORENSIC ACCOUNTING AND FRAUD EXAMINATION ORGANIZATIONS

- AAFM: American Academy of Financial Management (offers 16 separate financial certifications recognized worldwide)
- MFP: Master Financial Professional
- CWM: Chartered Wealth Manager
- CTEP: Chartered Trust and Estate Planner
- CAM: Chartered Asset Manager
- RFS: Registered Financial Specialist in Financial Planning
- CPM: Chartered Portfolio Manager
- RBA: Registered Business Analyst
- MFM: Master Financial Manager
- CMA: Chartered Market Analyst and FAD - Financial Analyst Designate
- CRA: Certified Risk Analyst and CRM - Certified in Risk Management
- CVM: Certified Valuation Manager
- CCC: Certified Cost Controller offered in the Middle East, Europe, Asia, and Africa
- CCA: Certified Credit Analyst offered in Asia, the Middle East, and Africa
- CCA: Chartered Compliance Analyst
- CITA: Certified International Tax Analyst (for lawyers or LLM holders)
- CAMC: Certified Anti-Money Laundering Consultant (for lawyers or LLM holders)
- Ch.E.: Chartered Economist (for PhDs and double master's degree holders)
- CAPA: Certified Asset Protection Analyst

FRAUD ACTS

In general, students should be familiar with the typical fraudulent acts listed below. Based on student employment opportunities, instructors may want to explore some of the fraud acts listed below in detail as examples of how to prevent, deter, detect, investigate, and remediate fraudulent activity.

Fraud Acts

Asset Misappropriation
    Cash
        Larceny (theft)
        Skimming (removal of cash before it hits books): Sales, A/R, Refunds, and Other
        Fraudulent Disbursement
            Billing Schemes (including shell companies, fictitious vendors, personal purchases)
            Payroll Schemes (ghost employees, commission schemes, workers compensation, and false hours and wages)
            Expense Reimbursement Schemes (including overstated expenses, fictitious expenses, and multiple reimbursements)
            Check Tampering
            Register Disbursements (including false voids and refunds)
    Inventory and Other Assets
        Inappropriate Use
        Larceny (theft)

Corruption
        Conflicts of Interest (unreported or undisclosed)
        Bribery
        Illegal Gratuities
        Economic Extortion

False Statements
        Fraudulent Financial Statements
        False Representations (e.g., employment credentials, contracts, identification)

Specific Fraud Contexts
        Bankruptcy Fraud
        Contract and Procurement Fraud
        Money Laundering
        Tax Fraud
        Investment Scams
        Terrorist Financing
        Consumer Fraud
            Identity Theft
            Check and Credit Card Fraud
            Computer and Internet Fraud
        Divorce Fraud (including hidden assets)
        Intellectual Property
        Business Valuation Fraud

(Continued)

(Continued)

Fraud Acts

Noteworthy Industry-Specific Fraud

    Financial Institutions

    Insurance Fraud

    Health Care Fraud

    Securities Fraud

    Public Sector Fraud

Source: "Education and Training in Fraud and Forensic Accounting: A Guide for Educational Institutions, Stakeholder Organizations, Faculty, and Students." National Institute of Justice: Document No.: 217589 (March 2007).

GLOSSARY

Abuse Petty crimes committed against organizations, such as excessive lunch hours or breaks, coming to work late or leaving early, using sick time when not sick, and pilfering supplies or products.

Abusive conduct Counterproductive, fraudulent, or other activities of employees that are detrimental to the organization.

Accidental fraudster An otherwise "good citizen" who succumbs to a perceived pressure, takes advantage of an opportunity, and is able to rationalize his or her behavior.

Altered payee scheme A check tampering scheme in which an employee intercepts a company check intended for a third party and alters the payee designation so the check can be converted by the employee or an accomplice.

Anatomical physical responses Involuntary reactions by the body to stress. They include increased heart rate, shallow or labored breathing, and excessive perspiration. These reactions are typical clues associated with deception.

Attorney–client privilege A right that precludes disclosure of communications between an attorney and client, but only if the client (1) retained the attorney, (2) did so to obtain legal advice, (3) thereafter communicated with the attorney on a confidential basis, and (4) has not waived the privilege.

Authorized maker scheme A check tampering scheme in which an employee with signature authority on a company account writes fraudulent checks for his own benefit and signs his own name as the maker.

Benchmark admission A small admission made to wrongdoing that signals a subject's willingness to confess. It is made as a result to an alternative question posed by the interviewer that gives the subject two ways to answer, either of which is an admission of culpability. Example: "Did you just want extra money, or did you do this because you had financial problems?"

Bid pooling A process by which several bidders conspire to split contracts, thereby ensuring that each gets a certain amount of work.

Bid rigging A process by which an employee assists a vendor to fraudulently win a contract through the competitive bidding process.

Bid splitting A fraudulent scheme in which a large project is split into several component projects so that each sectional contract falls below the mandatory bidding level, thereby avoiding the competitive bidding process.

Billing schemes A scheme in which a fraudster causes the victim organization to issue a fraudulent payment by submitting invoices for fictitious goods or services, inflated invoices, or invoices for personal purchases.

Bribery The offering, giving, receiving, or soliciting of something of value for the purpose of influencing an official act.

Business diversions A scheme that typically involves a favor done for a friendly client. Business diversions can include situations in which an employee starts his own company, and while still employed by the victim, steers existing or potential clients away from the victim and toward the employee's new company.

Capitalized expenses When expenditures are capitalized as assets and not expensed off during the current period, income will be overstated. As the assets are depreciated, income in subsequent periods will be understated.

Cash larceny The theft of an organization's cash after it has been recorded in the accounting system.

Cash receipts schemes Frauds that target incoming sales or receivables. Typically, the perpetrators in these schemes physically abscond with the victim organization's cash instead of relying on phony documents to justify the disbursement of the funds. Cash receipts frauds generally fall into two categories: skimming and cash larceny.

Certified fraud examiner (CFE) A professional who is trained to conduct complex fraud examinations from inception to conclusion. A CFE has training in all aspects of fraud examination, including identifying fraudulent transactions, obtaining evidence, and interviewing witnesses.

Chain of custody A record of who has had possession of an item of evidence and what they've done with it. The chain of custody must be preserved or else the item cannot be used at trial.

Character testimony A verbal clue to deception whereby an untruthful witness may attempt to add credibility to his lie by suggesting that the interviewer "check with my minister" or "ask my wife."

Check-for-currency substitution A skimming method whereby the fraudster steals an unrecorded check and substitutes it for recorded currency in the same amount.

Check tampering A type of fraudulent disbursement that occurs when an employee converts an organization's funds by either (1) fraudulently preparing a check drawn on the organization's account for his own benefit, or (2) intercepting a check drawn on the organization's account that is intended for a third party and converting that check to his own benefit.

Collusion A secret agreement between two or more people for a fraudulent, illegal, or deceitful purpose, such as overcoming the internal controls of their employer.

Commercial bribery The offering, giving, receiving, or soliciting of something of value for the purpose of influencing a business decision without the knowledge or consent of the principal.

Commission A form of compensation calculated as a percentage of the amount of sales an employee generates. A commissioned employee's wages are based on two factors, the amount of sales generated and the percentage of those sales he or she is paid.

Comparability and consistency Secondary qualitative characteristics that state that a company's information must be presented with the same consistent method from year to

year, in order for it to be useful for analytical purposes in decision making.

Concealed check scheme   A check tampering scheme in which an employee prepares a fraudulent check and submits it, usually along with legitimate checks, to an authorized maker who signs it without a proper review.

Conflict of interest   An undisclosed economic or personal interest in a transaction by an employee, manager, or executive that adversely affects the company.

Conversion   The unauthorized assumption of a right of ownership over the goods of another to the exclusion of the owner's rights. When an employee steals company assets, he or she also converts the use of them.

Corporate Sentencing Guidelines   A U.S. federal law passed in 1991 that provides sanctions for organizations that have engaged in criminal conduct. The sanctions can be mitigated if the organization can prove that it complied with one or more of seven steps designed to prevent or deter fraud.

Covert operations   An investigatory procedure in which the investigator assumes a fictitious identity in order to gather evidence.

Deposit lapping   A method of concealing deposit theft that occurs when an employee steals part or all of the deposit from one day and then replaces it with receipts from subsequent days.

Duty of loyalty   The requirement that an employee/agent must act solely in the best interest of the employer/principal, free of any self-dealing, conflicts of interest, or other abuse of the principal for personal advantage.

Duty of reasonable care   The expectation that a corporate officer, director, or high-level employee, as well as other people in a fiduciary relationship, will conduct business affairs prudently with the skill and attention normally exercised by people in similar positions.

Economic extortion   Obtaining property from another with the other party's "consent" having been induced by using threats of economic reprisal.

Employee deviance   Conduct by employees that is detrimental to both employer and employee, such as goldbricking, work slowdowns, and industrial sabotage.

Evidence   Anything perceivable by the five senses, and any proof such as testimony of witnesses, records, documents, facts, data, or tangible objects legally presented at trial to prove a contention and induce a belief in the minds of a jury.

Excuse clause   A clause inserted in a signed statement that encourages the confessor to sign the statement. It offers a moral, not legal, excuse for the wrongdoing. Example: "I wouldn't have done this if it had not been for pressing financial problems. I didn't mean to hurt anyone."

False (fictitious) refund scheme   One of two main categories of register disbursements. A scheme in which a fraudulent refund is processed at the cash register to account for stolen cash.

False void scheme   One of two main categories of register disbursements. A scheme in which an employee accounts for stolen cash by voiding a previously recorded sale.

Fictitious expense reimbursement schemes   A scheme in which an employee seeks reimbursement for wholly nonexistent items or expenses.

Fictitious revenue   The recording of sales of goods or services that never occurred.

Fiduciary relationship   In business, it is the trusting relationship that the employee is expected to hold toward the employer, requiring the employee's scrupulous good faith to act in the employer's best interests.

Financial statement fraud   A type of fraud where an individual or individuals purposefully misreport financial information about an organization in order to mislead those who read it.

Fleeing position   A posture adopted by an individual under stress during an interview. The head is facing the interviewer, while the feet and legs are pointed toward the door in an unconscious effort to flee the interview.

Force balancing   A method of concealing receivables skimming whereby the fraudster falsifies account totals to conceal the theft of funds. This is also sometimes known as "plugging." Typically, the fraudster will steal a customer's payment but nevertheless post it to the customer's account so that the account does not age past due. This causes an imbalance in the cash account.

Forced reconciliation   A method of concealing fraud by manually altering entries in an organization's books and records or by intentionally miscomputing totals. In the case of noncash misappropriations, inventory records are typically altered to create a false balance between physical and perpetual inventory.

Forged endorsement scheme   A check tampering scheme in which an employee intercepts a company check intended for a third party and converts the check by signing the third party's name on the endorsement line of the check.

Forged maker scheme   A check tampering scheme in which an employee misappropriates a check and fraudulently affixes the signature of an authorized maker thereon.

Forgery   The signing of another person's name to a document (such as a check) with a fraudulent intent, or the fraudulent alteration of a genuine instrument.

Fraud   Any crime for gain that uses deception as its principal modus operandi. There are four legal elements that must be present: (1) a material false statement, (2) knowledge that the statement was false when it was uttered, (3) reliance on the false statement by the victim, and (4) damages as a result.

Fraud deterrence   Discouraging fraudulent activities through the threat of negative sanctions.

Fraud examination   A process of resolving allegations of fraud from inception to disposition. It involves not only financial analysis, but also taking statements, interviewing witnesses, writing reports, testifying to findings, and assisting in the detection and prevention of fraud.

Fraud prevention   Removal of the root causes of fraudulent behavior, such as economic deprivation and social injustices.

Fraud risk   Risk of material misstatements in financial statements arising from fraudulent financial reporting and misappropriations of assets.

Fraud theory approach   The methodology used to investigate allegations of fraud. It involves developing a theory based on a worst-case scenario of what fraud scheme could have occurred, then testing the theory to see whether it is correct.

Fraud triangle   A model developed to explain the research of Cressey, who noted that most occupational frauds were caused by a combination of three elements: non-shareable

financial problems, perceived opportunity, and the ability to rationalize conduct.

Fraudulent disbursements Schemes in which an employee illegally or improperly causes the distribution of funds in a way that appears to be legitimate. Funds can be obtained by forging checks, submission of false invoices, or falsifying time records.

Fraudulent write-offs A method used to conceal the theft of noncash assets by justifying their absence on the books. Stolen items are removed from the accounting system by being classified as scrap, lost or destroyed, damaged, being bad debt, scrap shrinkage, discount and allowances, returns, etc.

Full disclosure A standard for financial reporting that states that any material deviation from generally accepted accounting principles must be explained to the reader of the financial information. Any potential adverse event must be disclosed in the financial statements.

Generally accepted accounting principles Recognition and measurement concepts that have evolved over time and have been codified by the Financial Accounting Standards Board and its predecessor organizations. The standards serve to guide regular business practices and deter financial statement fraud.

Ghost employee An individual on the payroll of a company who does not actually work for the company. This individual can be real or fictitious.

Horizontal analysis A technique for analyzing the percentage change in individual financial statement items from one year to the next.

Illegal gratuities The offering, giving, receiving, or soliciting of something of value for, or because of, an official act.

Illustrators Motions made primarily by the hands to demonstrate points when talking. The use of illustrators usually changes during deception.

Imperative ethical principle The school of ethical thought advocating concrete ethical principles that cannot be violated (e.g., the end does not justify the means).

Improper asset valuation Generally accepted accounting principles require that most assets be recorded at their historical (acquisition) cost with some exceptions. This type of fraud usually involves the fraudulent overstatement of inventory or receivables or the misclassification of fixed assets.

Kickbacks Schemes in which a vendor pays back a portion of the purchase price to an employee of the buyer in order to influence the buyer's decision.

Lapping A method of concealing the theft of cash designated for accounts receivable by crediting one account while abstracting money from a different account. This process must be continuously repeated to avoid detection.

Larceny The unlawful taking and carrying away of the property belonging to another with the intent to convert it to one's own use.

Liability/expense omissions Deliberate attempts to conceal liabilities and expenses already incurred.

Maker The person who signs a check.

Manipulators Motions made by individuals such as picking lint from clothing, playing with objects such as pencils, or holding one's hands while talking. Manipulators are displacement activities, done to reduce nervousness.

Mischaracterized expense scheme An attempt to obtain so that the perpetrator is reimbursed for an amount greater than the actual expense.

Multiple reimbursement schemes An attempt to obtain more than one reimbursement for the same business-related expense.

Need recognition scheme A pre-solicitation-phase bid-rigging conspiracy between the buyer and contractor where an employee of the buyer receives something of value to convince his company that they have a "need" for a particular product or service.

Non-shareable problems Financial difficulties that would be hard for a potential occupational offender to disclose to outsiders, such as excessive debt, gambling, drug use, business reversals, or extramarital affairs.

Norming or calibrating The process of observing behavior before critical questions are asked. The purpose is to help assess the subject's verbal and nonverbal reactions to threatening questions.

Oaths Certain phrases used frequently by liars to add weight to their false testimony. Examples include "honestly," "frankly," "to tell the truth," and "I swear to God."

Occupational fraud and abuse The use of one's occupation for personal enrichment through the deliberate misuse or misapplication of the employing organization's resources or assets.

Off-book fraud A fraud that occurs outside the financial system and therefore has no direct audit trail. Several kinds of off-book frauds are discussed in this book. Skimming is the most common off-book fraud.

Official act The decisions or actions of government agents or employees. Traditionally, bribery statutes proscribed only payments made to influence public officials.

Organizational controls Deterrence mechanisms used by organizations to discourage employee deviance and fraud, which include company policy, selection of personnel, inventory control, security, and punishment.

Overpurchasing A method of overstating business expenses in which a fraudster buys two or more business expense items at different prices (such as airline tickets). The perpetrator returns the more expensive item for a refund but he claims reimbursement for this item. As a result, he is reimbursed for more than his actual expenses.

Overstated expense reimbursements Schemes in which reimbursement for personal expenses by claiming they are business-related expenses are inflated on an expense report.

Overstated refund scheme A false refund scheme in which an employee overstates the amount of a legitimate customer refund, gives the customer the actual amount of the refund, and steals the excess.

Overstatements Type of financial statement fraud in which an individual exaggerates a company's assets or revenues to meet certain objectives.

Pass-through scheme A subcategory of a shell company scheme in which actual goods or services are sold to the victim company, with the fraudster acting as middleman and inflating the prices of the goods or services.

Pay-and-return scheme A fraud in which an employee intentionally mishandles payments that are owed to legitimate companies, then steals the excess payments when they are returned by the vendor.

Perception of detection The thought in the employee's mind that his or her fraudulent conduct will be discovered.

Periodicity A "time period" assumption, which deems that economic activity be divided into specific time intervals, such as monthly, quarterly, and annually.

Perpetual inventory A method of accounting for inventory in the records by continually updating the amount of inventory on hand as purchases and sales occur.

Personal purchases scheme A category of billing scheme in which an employee simply buys personal items with his company's funds or credit card.

Physical inventory A detailed count and listing of merchandise on hand.

Physical padding A fraud concealment scheme in which the fraudsters try to create the appearance that there are more assets on hand in a warehouse or stockroom than there actually are (e.g., by stacking empty boxes to create the illusion of extra inventory).

Predator A fraudster who continuously seeks out victims to defraud.

Purchasing scheme Conflict of interest scheme in which a victim company unwittingly buys something at a high price from a company in which one of its employees has a hidden interest.

Ratio analysis A means of measuring the relationship between two different financial statement amounts.

Rationalization The process by which an occupational fraudster explains and justifies his or her illegal conduct. Examples include: "I was only borrowing the money," "The company doesn't treat me fairly," "I must commit financial statement fraud because otherwise, employees will lose their jobs."

Receivables skimming A type of skimming scheme that involves the theft of incoming payments on accounts receivable. This form of skimming is more difficult to detect than sales skimming because the receivables are already recorded on the victim organization's books. In other words, the incoming payments are expected by the victim organization. The key to a receivables skimming scheme is to conceal either the fact that the payment was stolen or the fact that the payment was due.

Related-party transactions Occur when a company does business with another entity whose management or operating policies can be controlled or significantly influenced by the company or by some other party in common. There is nothing inherently wrong with related-party transactions, as long as they are fully disclosed.

Relevance and reliability Primary qualitative characteristics of financial reports as they relate to usefulness for decision making. Relevance implies that certain information will make a difference in arriving at a decision. Reliability means that the user can depend on the factual accuracy of the information.

Resource diversions Unlike business diversions, resource diversions consist of diverting assets from the victim company.

Reversing transactions A method used to conceal cash larceny. The perpetrator processes false transactions to void a sale or refund cash, which cause sales records to reconcile to the amount of cash on hand after the theft.

Rubber stamp supervisor A supervisor who neglects to review documents, such as timecards, prior to signing or approving them for payment.

Salaried employees Employees who are paid a set amount of money per period (weekly, two-week period, monthly, etc.). Unlike hourly employees, salaried employees are paid the same regardless of the actual number of hours they work.

Sales scheme Conflict of interest scheme in which a victim company unwittingly sells something at a low price to a company in which one of its employees has a hidden interest.

Sales skimming A type of skimming scheme that involves the theft of sales receipts, as opposed to payments on accounts receivable. Sales skimming schemes do not cause an imbalance in the victim organization's books because the sales transaction is not recorded.

Search warrant A legal order issued by a judge upon presentation of probable cause to believe the items being sought have been used in the commission of a crime.

Shell company A fictitious entity created for the sole purpose of committing fraud.

Shrinkage The unaccounted-for reduction in an organization's inventory that results from theft and is a common red flag of fraud.

Skimming The theft of cash prior to its entry into the accounting system.

Slush fund A noncompany account into which company money has been fraudulently diverted and from which bribes may be paid.

Social controls Informal deterrence mechanisms that help discourage employee deviance and fraud, such as loss of prestige and embarrassment to friends and family.

Specifications scheme A pre-solicitation-phase bid-rigging conspiracy between the buyer and vendor where an employee of the buyer receives something of value to set the specifications of the contract to accommodate that vendor's capabilities.

Subpoena duces tecum A legal order requiring the production of documents.

Surveillance An evidence gathering technique involving the secretive and continuous observance of a suspect's activities.

Turnaround sales A purchasing scheme where an employee knows his company plans to purchase a certain asset, takes advantage of the situation by purchasing the asset himself, and then sells the asset to his employer at an inflated price.

Unconcealed larceny Schemes in which an employee steals an asset without attempting to conceal the theft in the organization's books and records.

Underbilling A sales scheme that occurs when an employee underbills a vendor in which she has a hidden interest. As a result, the company ends up selling its goods or services at less than fair market value, which creates a diminished profit margin or loss on the sale.

Understated sales Variation of a sales skimming scheme in which only a portion of the cash received in a sales

transaction is stolen. This type of fraud is not off-book because the transaction is posted to the victim organization's books, but for a lower amount than what the perpetrator collected from the customer.

Understatements Type of financial statement fraud in which an individual minimizes a company's liabilities or expenses to meet certain objectives.

Utilitarian ethical principle The school of ethical thought that advocates situational ethics—each behavior should be evaluated on its own merits (e.g., the end justifies the means).

Vertical analysis The relationship or percentage of component part items to a specific base item.

Vicarious or imputed liability A legal theory that holds the organization liable for the criminal conduct of its employees.

Wages-in-kind A concept that deals with the motivations of employees to correct what they perceive as workplace "wrongs" by means of counterproductive behavior, including fraud and abuse.

White-collar crime Term coined by Edwin Sutherland. Originally, the definition included criminal acts only of corporations and individuals acting in their corporate capacity (e.g., management fraud or crime). However, it is now used to define almost any financial or economic crime.

INDEX

A

Aberration of conduct, 249
Absconders, 67–68
Abuse, 5, 60
  definition, 7
  versus fraud, 6–8
Abusive conduct, 6
ABV. *See* Accredited in Business Valuation (ABV)
Accidental fraudster, predators versus, 86–88
Accounting anomalies, 187–189
  irregularities in documentation, 187
  journal entry techniques for 'cooking the books', 187–189
Accounting changes, 433
Accounting principles, 151–156
  accounting flow through books and records, 151
  accrual accounting, 156
    expenses matched to revenue, conditions, 156
  backlog, 152
  balance sheet, 153–154
  cash general ledger account, 152
  'cash' transaction, 154
    cash flow from operating activities, 154
    financing activities, 154
    investing activities, 154
  company and its stakeholders, activities between, 151
  critical aspects of, 153
  electronic funds transfer (EFT), 152
  and fraud, 408–419. *See also* Financial statement fraud
  income statement, 154
  nonfinancial information flow, 152–153
  reconciliation process, 151
  statement of cash flows, 154
  transactions, 151
Accounting Research Bulletins (AICPA), 411
Accounting standards, 160
Accounts payable, 274
Accounts receivable, 273, 321
  improper asset valuation, 435
Accredited in Business Valuation (ABV), 48, 466
Accredited Valuation Analyst (AVA), 50
Accrual accounting, 156
  matching principles, 156
  revenue recognition, 156

Accusations, 248
ACFE. *See* Association of Certified Fraud Examiners (ACFE)
ACL Services Ltd., 279–282
Act, element of fraud, 25–26, 205
Adelphia Communications, 420, 429
Admission-seeking interview questions, 247–255. *See also* Judging deception
  benchmark admission, 251
  defuse alibis, 250
    discuss deceptions, 250
    discuss witnesses, 250
    display physical evidence, 250
    present the alternative, 250
  Miranda warnings, 247
  presence of outsiders, 247
  rationalization, establishing, 248–250
    aberration of conduct, 249
    accuser's actions, 249
    altruism, 250
    depersonalizing the victim, 250
    family problems, 249
    financial problems, 249
    genuine need, 250
    inadequate recognition, 249
    minor moral infraction, 250
    revenge, 249
    stress, drugs, alcohol, 249
    unfair treatment, 249
  signed statement, obtaining, 253–255
    approximate amounts of losses, 253
    approximate dates of offense, 253
    approximate number of instances, 253
    confessor reading the statement, 254
    excuse clause, 254
    intent, 253
    preparing a signed statement, 254
    truthfulness of statement, 254
    voluntary confessions, 253
    willingness to cooperate, 253
  steps in, 248
    accuse the subject of committing the offense, 248
    interrupt denials, 248
    observe reaction, 248
    repeat accusation, 248
  theme development, 247
  verbal confession, transition to, 251–253
    accused knew the conduct was wrong, 251
    disposition of proceeds, 252

estimate of number of instances/amounts, 252
    facts known only to perpetrator, 252
    location of assets, 252
    motive for offense, 252
    others involved, 252
    physical evidence, 252
    specifics of each offense, 253
    when offense commenced, 252
    when/if offense was terminated, 252
Admission-seeking stage of interrogation, 239
Affirmative Acts, 103
African organized crime, 91
After-hours sales, sales skimming, 297
Age and theft, 73
Age effect on median loss, 16–17
Aging of accounts, 279
AICPA. *See* American Institute of Certified Public Accountants (AICPA)
AIMR. *See* Association for Investment Management and Research (AIMR)
Albrecht, W. Steve, 12, 55, 69–71, 81, 84n45, 85n79
  Deterring Fraud: The Internal Auditor's Perspective, 69
  fraud scale, 70
  occupational fraud red flags, 170
Alibis, diffusing, 250
Allegations, in interviews, 241
Allocated costs, 462–463
Alteration
  of documents, 214–215
  of inventory records, 321
  of purchase orders, 335
  of receipts, 373
  of sales, 366–367
  of signatures, 373
  of transaction records, 303
Altered payee schemes, 347–349
  altering checks prepared by fraudster, 348–349
    blank checks, 349
    erasable ink, 348–349
  altering checks prepared by others, 347
    inserting a new payee, 347
    'tacking on', 347–348
  converting altered checks, 349
  detecting, 349
  preventing, 349
Alternatives, presenting, 250